GEORGE GROTE

HISTORY OF GREECE

VOLUME I

Elibron Classics
www.elibron.com

GEORGE GROTE.

HISTORY OF GREECE.

I. Legendary Greece.

II. Grecian History to the Reign of Peisistratus at Athens.

BY

GEORGE GROTE, Esq.

VOL. I.

REPRINTED FROM THE SECOND LONDON EDITION

NEW YORK:
HARPER & BROTHERS, PUBLISHERS,
329 AND 331 PEARL STREET.
1865.

PART I.— LEGENDARY GREECE

'Ανδρῶν ἡρώων θεῖον γένος, οἳ καλέονται
Ἡμίθεοι προτέρῃ γενέῃ. — HESIOD

PART II.— HISTORICAL GREECE.

... ...Πολιες μερόπων ἀνθρώπων. — HOMER

PREFACE.

THE first idea of this History was conceived many years ago, at a time when ancient Hellas was known to the English public chiefly through the pages of Mitford; and my purpose in writing it was to rectify the erroneous statements as to matter of fact which that History contained, as well as to present the general phenomena of the Grecian world under what I thought a juster and more comprehensive point of view. My leisure, however, was not at that time equal to the execution of any large literary undertaking; nor is it until within the last three or four years that I have been able to devote to the work that continuous and exclusive labor, without which, though much may be done to illustrate detached points, no entire or complicated subject can ever be set forth in a man ner worthy to meet the public eye.

Meanwhile the state of the English literary world, in reference to ancient Hellas, has been materially changed in more ways than one. If my early friend Dr. Thirlwall's History of Greece had appeared a few years sooner, I should probably never have conceived the design of the present work at all; I should certainly not have been prompted to the task by any deficiencies, such as those which I felt and regretted in Mitford. The comparison of the two authors affords, indeed, a striking proof of the progress of sound and enlarged

views respecting the ancient world during the present generation. Having studied of course the same evidences as Dr.
Thirwall, I am better enabled than others to bear testimony
to the learning, the sagacity, and the candor which pervade
his excellent work : and it is the more incumbent on me to
give expression to this sentiment, since the particular points
on which I shall have occasion to advert to it will, unavoidably,
be points of dissent oftener than of coincidence.

The liberal spirit of criticism, in which Dr. Thirwall stands
so much distinguished from Mitford, is his own : there are
other features of superiority which belong to him conjointly
with his age. For during the generation since Mitford's work,
philological studies have been prosecuted in Germany with
remarkable success : the stock of facts and documents, comparatively scanty, handed down from the ancient world,
has been combined and illustrated in a thousand different
ways : and if our witnesses cannot be multiplied, we at least
have numerous interpreters to catch, repeat, amplify, and explain their broken and half-inaudible depositions. Some of
the best writers in this department — Boeckh, Niebuhr,
O. Müller — have been translated into our language ; so that
the English public has been enabled to form some idea of the
new lights thrown upon many subjects of antiquity by the inestimable aid of German erudition. The poets, historians,
orators, and philosophers of Greece, have thus been all rendered both more intelligible and more instructive than they
were to a student in the last century; and the general picture of the Grecian world may now be conceived with a degree of fidelity, which, considering our imperfect materials, it
is curious to contemplate.

It is that general picture which an historian of Greece is
required first to embody in his own mind, and next to lay out
before his readers ; — a picture not merely such as to delight
the imagination by brilliancy of coloring and depth of sentiment, but also suggestive and improving to the reason   Not

omitting the points of resemblance as well as of contrast with the better-known forms of modern society, he will especially study to exhibit the spontaneous movement of Grecian intellect, sometimes aided but never borrowed from without, and lighting up a small portion of a world otherwise clouded and stationary. He will develop the action of that social system, which, while insuring to the mass of freemen a degree of protection elsewhere unknown, acted as a stimulus to the creative impulses of genius, and left the superior minds sufficiently unshackled to soar above religious and political routine, to overshoot their own age, and to become the teachers of posterity.

To set forth the history of a people by whom the first spark was set to the dormant intellectual capacities of our nature,— Hellenic phenomena, as illustrative of the Hellenic mind and character,— is the task which I propose to myself in the present work; not without a painful consciousness how much the deed falls short of the will, and a yet more painful conviction, that full success is rendered impossible by an obstacle which no human ability can now remedy,— the insufficiency of original evidence. For, in spite of the valuable expositions of so many able commentators, our stock of information respecting the ancient world still remains lamentably inadequate to the demands of an enlightened curiosity. We possess only what has drifted ashore from the wreck of a stranded vessel; and though this includes some of the most precious articles amongst its once abundant cargo, yet if any man will cast his eyes over the citations in Diogenes Laërtius, Athenæus, or Plutarch, or the list of names in Vossius de Historicis Græcis, he will see with grief and surprise how much larger is the proportion which, through the enslavement of the Greeks themselves, the decline of the Roman Empire, the change of religion, and the irruption of barbarian conquerors, has been irrecoverably submerged. We are thus reduced to judge of the whole Hellenic world, eminently multiform as it was

from a few compositions ; excellent, indeed, in themselves, but
bearing too exclusively the stamp of Athens. Of Thucydides
and Aristotle, indeed, both as inquirers into matter of fact,
and as free from narrow local feeling, it is impossible to speak
too highly ; but, unfortunately, that work of the latter which
would have given us the most copious information regarding
Grecian political life — his collection and comparison of one
hundred and fifty distinct town constitutions — has not been
preserved : and the brevity of Thucydides often gives us but a
single word where a sentence would not have been too much,
and sentences which we should be glad to see expanded into
paragraphs.

Such insufficiency of original and trustworthy materials, as
compared with those resources which are thought hardly sufficient for the historian of any modern kingdom, is neither to
be concealed nor extenuated, however much we may lament
it. I advert to the point here on more grounds than one.
For it not only limits the amount of information which an
historian of Greece can give to his readers,— compelling him
to leave much of his picture an absolute blank — but it also
greatly spoils the execution of the remainder. The question
of credibility is perpetually obtruding itself, and requiring a
decision, which, whether favorable or unfavorable, always introduces more or less of controversy ; and gives to those out
lines, which the interest of the picture requires to be straight
and vigorous, a faint and faltering character. Expressions
of qualified and hesitating affirmation are repeated until the
reader is sickened ; while the writer himself, to whom this
restraint is more painful still, is frequently tempted to break
loose from the unseen spell by which a conscientious criticism
binds him down, — to screw up the possible and probable
into certainty, to suppress counterbalancing considerations,
and to substitute a pleasing romance in place of half-
known and perplexing realities. Desiring, in the present
work, to set forth all which can be ascertained, together with

such conjectures and inferences as can be reasonably deduced
from it, but nothing more,—I notice, at the outset, that faulty
state of the original evidence which renders discussions of
credibility, and hesitation in the language of the judge, unavoidable. Such discussions, though the reader may be assured that they will become less frequent as we advance into
times better known, are tiresome enough, even with the comparatively late period which I adopt as the historical beginning; much more intolerable would they have proved, had I
thought it my duty to start from the primitive terminus of
Deukalion or Inachus, or from the unburied Pelasgi and
Leleges, and to subject the heroic ages to a similar scrutiny.
I really know nothing so disheartening or unrequited as the
elaborate balancing of what is called evidence,— the comparison of infinitesimal probabilities and conjectures all uncertified,—in regard to these shadowy times and persons.

The law respecting sufficiency of evidence ought to be the
same for ancient times as for modern ; and the reader will
find in this History an application, to the former, of criteria
analogous to those which have been long recognized in the
latter. Approaching, though with a certain measure of
indulgence, to this standard, I begin the real history of
Greece with the first recorded Olympiad, or 776 B. C. To
such as are accustomed to the habits once universal, and still
not uncommon, in investigating the ancient world, I may appear to be striking off one thousand years from the scroll of
history ; but to those whose canon of evidence is derived
from Mr. Hallam, M. Sismondi, or any other eminent historian of modern events, I am well assured that I shall appear
lax and credulous rather than exigent or sceptical. For
the truth is, that historical records, properly so called, do not
begin until long after this date : nor will any man, who can-
didly considers the extreme paucity of attested facts for two
centuries after 776 B. C., be astonished to learn that the state
of Greece in 900, 1000, 1100, 1200, 1300, 1400 B. C., etc.,

—or any earlier century which it may please chronologists to include in their computed genealogies,— cannot be described to him upon anything like decent evidence. I shall hope, when I come to the lives of Socrates and Plato, to illustrate one of the most valuable of their principles,— that conscious and confessed ignorance is a better state of mind, than the fancy, without the reality, of knowledge. Meanwhile, I begin by making that confession, in reference to the real world of Greece anterior to the Olympiads; meaning the disclaimer to apply to anything like a general history,— not to exclude rigorously every individual event.

The times which I thus set apart from the region of history are discernible only through a different atmosphere, — that of epic poetry and legend. To confound together these disparate matters is, in my judgment, essentially unphilosophical. I describe the earlier times by themselves, as conceived by the faith and feeling of the first Greeks, and known only through their legends, —without presuming to measure how much or how little of historical matter these legends may contain. If the reader blame me for not assisting him to determine this, — if he ask me why I do not undraw the curtain and disclose the picture, — I reply in the words of the painter Zeuxis, when the same question was addressed to him on exhibiting his master-piece of imitative art: " The curtain *is* the picture." What we now read as poetry and legend was once accredited history, and the only genuine history which the first Greeks could conceive or relish of their past time : the curtain conceals nothing behind, and cannot, by any ingenuity, be withdrawn. I undertake only to show it as it stands, — not to efface, still less to repaint it.

Three-fourths of the two volumes now presented to the public are destined to elucidate this age of historical faith, as distinguished from the later age of historical reason : to exhibit its basis in the human mind,— an omnipresent religious and personal interpretation of nature ; to illustrate it by com parison with the like mental habit in early modern Europe; to show its immense abundance and variety of narrative matter, with little care for consistency between one story and another; lastly, to set forth the causes which overgrew and partially supplanted the old epical sentiment, and introduced, in the room of literal faith, a variety of compromises and interpretations.

The legendary age of the Greeks receives its principal charm and dignity from the Homeric poems: to these, therefore, and to the other poems included in the ancient epic, an entire chapter is devoted, the length of which must be justified by the names of the Iliad and Odyssey. I have thought it my duty to take some notice of the Wolfian controversy as it now stands in Germany, and have even hazarded some speculations respecting the structure of the Iliad. The society and manners of the heroic age, considered as known in a general way from Homer's descriptions and allusions, are also described and criticized.

I next pass to the historical age, beginning at 776 B. C.; prefixing some remarks upon the geographical features of Greece. I try to make out, amidst obscure and scanty indications, what the state of Greece was at this period; and I indulge some cautious conjectures, founded upon the earliest verifiable facts, respecting the steps immediately antecedent by which that condition was brought about. In the present volumes, I have only been able to include the history of Sparta and the Peloponnesian Dorians, down to the age of Peisistratus and Crœsus. I had hoped to have comprised in them the entire history of Greece down to this last-mentioned period, but I find the space insufficient.

The history of Greece falls most naturally into six compartments, of which the first may be looked at as a period of preparation for the five following, which exhaust the free life of collective Hellas.

I. Period from 776 B. C. to 560 B. C., the accession of Peisistratus at Athens and of Crœsus in Lydia

A*

II. From the accession of Peisistratus and Crœsus to the repulse of Xerxes from Greece.

III. From the repulse of Xerxes to the close of the Pelo ponnesian war and overthrow of Athens.

IV. From the close of the Peloponnesian war to the battle of Leuktra.

V. From the battle of Leuktra to that of Chæroneia.

VI. From the battle of Chæroneia to the end of the generation of Alexander.

The five periods, from Peisistratus down to the death of Alexander and of his generation, present the acts of an historical drama capable of being recounted in perspicuous succession, and connected by a sensible thread of unity. I shall interweave in their proper places the important but outlying adventures of the Sicilian and Italian Greeks, — introducing such occasional notices of Grecian political constitutions, philosophy, poetry, and oratory, as are requisite to exhibit the many-sided activity of this people during their short but brilliant career.

After the generation of Alexander, the political action of Greece becomes cramped and degraded, — no longer interesting to the reader, or operative on the destinies of the future world. We may, indeed, name one or two incidents, especially the revolutions of Agis and Kleomenês at Sparta, which are both instructive and affecting; but as a whole, the period, between 300 B. C. and the absorption of Greece by the Romans, is of no interest in itself, and is only so far of value as it helps us to understand the preceding centuries. The dignity and value of the Greeks from that time forward belong to them only as individual philosophers, preceptors, astronomers, and mathematicians, literary men and critics, medical practioners, etc. In all these respective capacities, especially in the great schools of philosophical speculation, they still constitute the light of the Roman world; though, as communities, they have lost their own orbit, and have became satellites of more powerful neighbors.

I propose to bring down the history of the Grecian communities to the year 300 B. C., or the close of the generation which takes its name from Alexander the Great, and I hope to accomplish this in eight volumes altogether. For the next two or three volumes I have already large preparations made, and I shall publish my third (perhaps my fourth) in the course of the ensuing winter.

There are great disadvantages in the publication of one portion of a history apart from the remainder; for neither the earlier nor the later phenomena can be fully comprehended without the light which each mutually casts upon the other. But the practice has become habitual, and is indeed more than justified by the well-known inadmissibility of " long hopes" into the short span of human life. Yet I cannot but fear that my first two volumes will suffer in the estimation of many readers by coming out alone, — and that men who value the Greeks for their philosophy, their politics, and their oratory, may treat the early legends as not worth attention. And it must be confessed that the sentimental attributes of the Greek mind — its religious and poetical vein — here appear in disproportionate relief, as compared with its more vigorous and masculine capacities, — with those powers of acting, organizing, judging, and speculating, which will be revealed in the forthcoming volumes. I venture, however, to forewarn the reader, that there will occur numerous circumstances in the after political life of the Greeks, which he will not comprehend unless he be initiated into the course of their legendary associations. He will not understand the frantic terror of the Athenian public during the Peloponnesian war, on the occasion of the mutilation of the statues called Hermæ, unless he enters into the way in which they connected their stability and security with the domiciliation of the gods in the soil : nor will he adequately appreciate the habit of the Spartan king on military expeditions, — when he offered his daily public sacrifices on behalf of his army and his country, — "always to perform this morning service immediately before sunrise, in order that he might be beforehand in obtaining the favor of the gods,"[1] if he be not familiar with the Homeric conception of Zeus going to rest at night and awaking to rise at early dawn from the side of the "white-armed Hêrê." The occasion will, indeed, often occur for remarking how these legends illustrate and vivify the political phenomena of the succeeding times, and I have only now to urge the necessity of considering them as the beginning of a series, — not as an entire work.

---

[1] Xenophon, Repub. Lacedæmon. cap. xiii. 3. Ἀεὶ δὲ, ὅταν θύηται, ἄρχε-
ται μὲν τούτου τοῦ ἔργου ἔτι κνεφαῖος, πϳολαμβάνειν βουλόμενος τὴν τοῦ θεοῦ
εὔνοιαν.

LONDON, March 5 1846.

PREFACE TO THE SECOND EDITION OF VOLUMES I. AND II.

In preparing a Second Edition of the first two volumes of my History, I have profited by the remarks and corrections of various critics, contained in Reviews, both English and foreign. I have suppressed, or rectified, some positions which had been pointed out as erroneous, or as advanced upon inadequate evidence. I have strengthened my argument in some cases where it appeared to have been imperfectly understood, — adding some new notes, partly for the purpose of enlarged illustration, partly to defend certain opinions which had been called in question. The greater number of these alterations have been made in Chapters XVI. and XXI. of Part I., and in Chapter VI. of Part II.

I trust that these three Chapters, more full of speculation, and therefore more open to criticism than any of the others, will thus appear in a more complete and satisfactory form. But I must at the same time add that they remain for the most part unchanged in substance, and that I have seen no sufficient reason to modify my main conclusions even respecting the structure of the Iliad, controverted though they have been by some of my most esteemed critics.

In regard to the character and peculiarity of Grecian legend, as broadly distinguished throughout these volumes from Grecian history, I desire to notice two valuable publications

with which I have only become acquainted since the date of
my first edition.   One of these is, A Short Essay on Primæval History, by John Kenrick, M. A. (London, 1846, published just at the same time as these volumes,) which illustrates
with much acute reflection the general features of legend,
not only in Greece but throughout the ancient world, — see
especially pages 65, 84, 92, *et seq.*   The other work is,
Rambles and Recollections of an Indian Official, by Colonel
Sleeman, — first made known to me through an excellent notice of my History in the Edinburgh Review for October 1846.
The description given by Colonel Sleeman, of the state of
mind now actually prevalent among the native population of
Hindostan, presents a vivid comparison, helping the modern
reader to understand and appreciate the legendary era of
Greece.   I have embodied in the notes of this Second Edition two or three passages from Colonel Sleeman's instructive work: but the whole of it richly deserves perusal.

Having now finished six volumes of this History, without
attaining a lower point than the peace of Nikias, in the tenth
year of the Peloponnesian war, — I find myself compelled to
retract the expectation held out in the preface to my First
Edition, that the entire work might be completed in eight
volumes.   Experience proves to me how impossible it is to
measure beforehand the space which historical subjects will
require.   All I can now promise is, that the remainder of the
work shall be executed with as much regard to brevity as is
consistent with the paramount duty of rendering it fit for
public acceptance.

London, April 3, 1849

NAMES OF GODS, GODDESSES, AND HEROES.

FOLLOWING the example of Dr. Thirlwall and other excellent scholars, I call the Greek deities by their real Greek names, and not by the Latin equivalents used among the Romans. For the assistance of those readers to whom the Greek names may be less familiar, I here annex a table of the one and the other.

Greek.	Latin.
Zeus,	Jupiter.
Poseidôn,	Neptune.
Arês,	Mars.
Dionysus,	Bacchus.
Hermês,	Mercury.
Hêlios,	Sol.
Hêphæstus,	Vulcan.
Hadês,	Pluto.
Hêrê,	Juno.
Athênê,	Minerva.
Artemis,	Diana.
Aphroditê,	Venus.
Eôs,	Aurora.
Hestia,	Vesta.
Lêtô,	Latona.
Dêmêtêr,	Ceres.
Hêraklês,	Hercules.
Asklêpius,	Æsculapius.

A few words are here necessary respecting the orthography ot Greek names adopted in the above table and generally throughout this history. I have approximated as nearly as I dared to the Greek letters in preference to the Latin ; and on this point I venture upon an innovation which I should have little doubt of vindicating before the reason of any candid English student. For the ordinary practice of substituting, in a Greek name, the English C in place of the Greek K, is, indeed, so obviously incorrect, that

it admits of no rational justification. Our own K, precisely and
in every point, coincides with the Greek K: we have thus the
means of reproducing the Greek name to the eye as well as to
the ear, yet we gratuitously take the wrong letter in preference
to the right. And the precedent of the Latins is here against us
rather than in our favor, for their C really coincided in sound
with the Greek K, whereas our C entirely departs from it, and
becomes an S, before *e, i, æ, œ,* and *y.* Though our C has so far
deviated in sound from the Latin C, yet there is some warrant
for our continuing to use it in writing Latin names, — because we
thus reproduce the name to the eye, though not to the ear. But
this is not the case when we employ our C to designate the Greek
K, for we depart here not less from the visible than from the audi-
ble original; while we mar the unrivalled euphony of the Greek
language by that multiplied sibilation which constitutes the least
inviting feature in our own. Among German philologists, the K
is now universally employed in writing Greek names, and I have
adopted it pretty largely in this work, making exception for such
names as the English reader has been so accustomed to hear with
the C, that they may be considered as being almost Anglicised.
I have, farther, marked the long *e* and the long *o* (η, ω,) by a
circumflex (Hêrê) when they occur in the last syllable or in the
penultimate of a name.

CONTENTS.

VOL. I.

PART I.

LEGENDARY GREECE.

CHAPTER I.

LEGENDS RESPECTING THE GODS.

CHAPTER II.

LEGENDS RELATING TO HEROES AND MEN.

CHAPTER III.

LEGEND OF THE IAPETIDS.

CHAPTER IV.

HEROIC LEGENDS. — GENEALOGY OF ARGUS.

CHAPTER V.

DEUKALION, HELLEN, AND SONS OF HELLEN.

CHAPTER VI.

THE ÆOLIDS, OR SONS AND DAUGHTERS OF ÆOLUS.

CHAPTER VII.

THE PELOPIDS.

CHAPTER VIII.

LACONIAN AND MESSENIAN GENEALOGIES.

CHAPTER IX.

ARCADIAN GENEALOGY.

CHAPTER X

ÆAKUS AND HIS DESCENDANTS. — ÆGINA, SALAMIS, AND PHTHIA.

CHAPTER XI.

ATTIC LEGENDS AND GENEALOGIES.

CHAPTER XII.

KRETAN LEGENDS. — MINÔS AND HIS FAMILY.

CHAPTER XIII.

ARGONAUTIC EXPEDITION.

CHAPTER XIV.

LEGENDS OF THEBES.

CHAPTER XV.

LEGEND OF TROY.

CHAPTER XVI.

GRECIAN MYTHES, AS UNDERSTOOD, FELT, AND INTERPRETED BY THE GREEKS THEMSELVES

CHAPTER XVII.

THE GRECIAN MYTHICAL VEIN COMPARED WITH THAT OF MODERN EUROPE.

HISTORY OF GREECE.

PART I.

LEGENDARY GREECE.

CHAPTER I.

LEGENDS RESPECTING THE GODS.

THE mythical world of the Greeks opens with the gods,
anterior as well as superior to man : it gradually descends, first
to heroes, and next to the human race. Along with the gods are
found various monstrous natures, ultra-human and extra-human,
who cannot with propriety be called gods, but who partake with
gods and men in the attributes of freewill, conscious agency, and
susceptibility of pleasure and pain,— such as the Harpies, the
Gorgons, the Grææ, the Sirens, Scylla and Charybdis, Echidna,
Sphinx, Chimæra, Chrysaor, Pegasus, the Cyclôpes, the Centaurs,
etc. The first acts of what may be termed the great mythical
cycle describe the proceedings of these gigantic agents — the
crash and collision of certain terrific and overboiling forces,
which are ultimately reduced to obedience, or chained up, or
extinguished, under the more orderly government of Zeus, who
supplants his less capable predecessors, and acquires precedence
and supremacy over gods and men — subject however to certain
social restraints from the chief gods and goddesses around

him, as well as to the custom of occasionally convoking and consulting the divine agora.

I recount these events briefly, but literally, treating them simply as mythes springing from the same creative imagination, addressing themselves to analogous tastes and feelings, and depending upon the same authority, as the legends of Thebes and Troy. It is the inspired voice of the Muse which reveals and authenticates both, and from which Homer and Hesiod alike derive their knowledge — the one, of the heroic, the other, of the divine, foretime. I maintain, moreover, fully, the character of these great divine agents as Persons, which is the light in which they presented themselves to the Homeric or Hesiodic audience. Uranos, Nyx, Hypnos and Oneiros (Heaven, Night, Sleep and Dream), are Persons, just as much as Zeus and Apollo. To resolve them into mere allegories, is unsafe and unprofitable: we then depart from the point of view of the original hearers, without acquiring any consistent or philosophical point of view of our own.[1] For although some of the attributes and actions ascribed to these persons are often explicable by allegory the whole series and system of them never are so: the theorist who adopts this course of explanation finds that, after one or two simple and obvious steps, the path is no longer open, and he is forced to clear a way for himself by gratuitous refinements and conjectures. The allegorical persons and attributes are always found mingled with other persons and attributes not allegorical; but the two classes cannot be severed without breaking up the whole march of the mythical events, nor can any explanation which drives us to such a necessity be considered as admissible. To suppose indeed that these legends could be all traced by means of allegory into a coherent body of physical doctrine, would be inconsistent with all reasonable presumptions respecting the age or society in which they arose. Where the allegorical mark is clearly set upon any particular character, or attribute, or event, to that extent we may recognize it; but we can rarely venture to divine further, still less to alter the legends themselves on the faith of any such surmises. The theogony of the Greeks contains

---

[1] It is sufficient, here, to state this position briefly: more will be said respecting the allegorizing interpretation in a future chapter.

some cosmogonic ideas; but it cannot be considered as a system of cosmogony, or translated into a string of elementary, planetary, or physical changes.

In the order of legendary chronology, Zeus comes after Kronos and Uranos; but in the order of Grecian conception, Zeus is the prominent person, and Kronos and Uranos are inferior and introductory precursors, set up in order to be overthrown and to serve as mementos of the prowess of their conqueror. To Homer and Hesiod, as well as to the Greeks universally, Zeus is the great and predominant god, "the father of gods and men," whose power none of the other gods can hope to resist, or even deliberately think of questioning. All the other gods have their specific potency and peculiar sphere of action and duty, with which Zeus does not usually interfere; but it is he who maintains the lineaments of a providential superintendence, as well over the phænomena of Olympus as over those of earth. Zeus and his brothers Poseidôn and Hadês have made a division of power: he has reserved the æther and the atmosphere to himself — Poseidôn has obtained the sea — and Hadês the under-world or infernal regions; while earth, and the events which pass upon earth, are common to all of them, together with free access to Olympus.[1]

Zeus, then, with his brethren and colleagues, constitute the present gods, whom Homer and Hesiod recognize as in full dignity and efficiency. The inmates of this divine world are conceived upon the model, but not upon the scale, of the human. They are actuated by the full play and variety of those appetites, sympathies, passions and affections, which divide the soul of man; invested with a far larger and indeterminate measure of power, and an exemption as well from death as (with some rare exceptions) from suffering and infirmity. The rich and diverse types thus conceived, full of energetic movement and contrast, each in his own province, and soaring confessedly above the limits of

---

[1] See Iliad, viii. 405, 463; xv. 20, 130, 185. Hesiod, Theog. 885.

This unquestioned supremacy is the general representation of Zeus: at the same time the conspiracy of Hêrê, Poseidôn, and Athênê against him, suppressed by the unexpected apparition of Briareus as his ally, is among the exceptions. (Iliad, i. 400.) Zeus is at one time vanquished by Titan, but rescued by Hermês. (Apollodôr. i. 6, 3)

experience, were of all themes the most suitable for adventure
and narrative, and operated with irresistible force upon the
Grecian fancy. All nature was then conceived as moving and
working through a number of personal agents, amongst whom
the gods of Olympus were the most conspicuous; the reverential
belief in Zeus and Apollo being only one branch of this omnipresent personifying faith. The attributes of all these agents
had a tendency to expand themselves into illustrative legends —
especially those of the gods, who were constantly invoked in the
public worship. Out of this same mental source sprang both
the divine and heroic mythes — the former being often the more
extravagant and abnormous in their incidents, in proportion as
the general type of the gods was more vast and awful than that
of the heroes.

As the gods have houses and wives like men, so the present
dynasty of gods must have a past to repose upon;[1] and the
curious and imaginative Greek, whenever he does not find a
recorded past ready to his hand, is uneasy until he has created
one. Thus the Hesiodic theogony explains, with a certain degree
of system and coherence, first the antecedent circumstances under
which Zeus acquired the divine empire, next the number of his
colleagues and descendants.

First in order of time (we are told by Hesiod) came Chaos;
next Gæa, the broad, firm, and flat Earth, with deep and dark
Tartarus at her base. Erôs (Love), the subduer of gods as well
as men, came immediately afterwards.[2]

From Chaos sprung Erebos and Nyx; from these latter
Æthêr and Hêmera. Gæa also gave birth to Uranos, equal in
breadth to herself, in order to serve both as an overarching vault
to her, and as a residence for the immortal gods; she further
produced the mountains, habitations of the divine nymphs, and
Pontus, the barren and billowy sea.

Then Gæa intermarried with Uranos, and from this union
came a numerous offspring — twelve Titans and Titanides, three
Cyclôpes, and three Hekatoncheires or beings with a hundred

---

[1] Arist. Polit. i. l. ὥσπερ δὲ καὶ τὰ εἴδη ἑαυτοῖς ἀφομοιοῦσιν ἄνθρωποι, οὕτως καὶ τοὺς βίους, τῶν θεῶν.

[2] Hesiod, Theog. 116. Apollodôrus begins with Uranos and Gæa (i. l.);
ae does not recognize Erôs, Nyx, or Erebos.

hands each. The Titans were Oceanus, Kœos, Krios, Hyperiôn, Iapetos, and Kronos: the Titanides, Theia, Rhea, Themis, Mnêmosynê, Phœbê, and Têthys. The Cyclôpes were Brontês, Steropês, and Argês, — formidable persons, equally distinguished for strength and for manual craft, so that they made the thunder which afterwards formed the irresistible artillery of Zeus.[1] The Hekatoncheires were Kottos, Briareus, and Gygês, of prodigious bodily force.

Uranos contemplated this powerful brood with fear and horror; as fast as any of them were born, he concealed them in cavities of the earth, and would not permit them to come out. Gæa could find no room for them, and groaned under the pressure : she produced iron, made a sickle, and implored her sons to avenge both her and themselves against the oppressive treatment of their father. But none of them, except Kronos, had courage to undertake the deed : he, the youngest and the most daring, was armed with the sickle and placed in suitable ambush by the contrivance of Gæa. Presently night arrived, and Uranos descended to the embraces of Gæa : Kronos then emerged from his concealment, cut off the genitals of his father, and cast the bleeding member behind him far away into the sea.[2] Much of the blood was spilt upon the earth, and Gæa in consequence gave birth to the irresistible Erinnys, the vast and muscular Gigantes, and the Melian nymphs. Out of the genitals themselves, as they swam and foamed upon the sea, emerged the goddess Aphroditê, deriving her name from the foam out of which she had sprung. She first landed at Kythêra, and then went to Cyprus : the island felt her benign influence, and the green herb started up under her soft and delicate tread. Erôs immediately joined her, and partook with her the function of suggesting and directing the amorous impulses both of gods and men.[3]

---

[1] Hesiod, Theog. 140, 156. Apollod. *ut sup.*

[2] Hesiod, Theog. 160, 182. Apollod. i. 1, 4.

[3] Hesiod, Theog. 192. This legend respecting the birth of Aphroditê seems to have been derived partly from her name (ἀφρὸς, *foam*), partly from the surname Urania, 'Αφροδίτη Οὐρανία, under which she was so very extensively worshipped, especially both in Cyprus and Cythêra, seemingly originated in both islands by the Phœnicians. Herodot. i. 105. Compare the instructive section in Boeckh's Metrologie, c. iv. § 4.

Uranos being thus dethroned and disabled, Kronos and the Titans acquired their liberty and became predominant : the Cyclôpes and the Hekatoncheires had been cast by Uranos into Tartarus, and were still allowed to remain there.

Each of the Titans had a numerous offspring: Oceanus, especially, marrying his sister Têthys, begat three thousand daughters, the Oceanic nymphs, and as many sons: the rivers and springs passed for his offspring. Hyperiôn and his sister Theia had for their children Hêlios, Selênê, and Eôs; Kœos with Phœbê begat Lêtô and Asteria; the children of Krios were Astræos, Pallas, and Persês, — from Astræos and Eôs sprang the winds Zephyrus, Boreas, and Notus. Iapetos, marrying the Oceanic nymph Clymenê, counted as his progeny the celebrated Promêtheus, Epimêtheus, Menœtius, and Atlas. But the off spring of Kronos were the most powerful and transcendent of all. He married his sister Rhea, and had by her three daughters — Hestia, Dêmêtêr, and Hêrê — and three sons, Hadês, Poseidôn, and Zeus, the latter at once the youngest and the greatest.

But Kronos foreboded to himself destruction from one of his own children, and accordingly, as soon as any of them were born, he immediately swallowed them and retained them in his own belly. In this manner had the first five been treated, and Rhea was on the point of being delivered of Zeus. Grieved and indignant at the loss of her children, she applied for counsel to her father and mother, Uranos and Gæa, who aided her to conceal the birth of Zeus. They conveyed her by night to Lyktus in Crête, hid the new-born child in a woody cavern on Mount Ida, and gave to Kronos, in place of it, a stone wrapped in swaddling clothes, which he greedily swallowed, believing it to be his child. Thus was the safety of Zeus ensured.[1] As he grew up his vast powers fully developed themselves : at the suggestion of Gæa, he induced Kronos by stratagem to vomit up, first the stone which had been given to him, — next, the five children whom he had previously devoured. Hestia, Dêmêtêr, Hêrê, Poseidôn and Hadês, were thus allowed to grow up along with Zeus; and the stone to which the latter owed his preservation was placed near

---

[1] Hesiod, Theog. 452, 487. Apollod. i. 1, 6.

the temple of Delphi, where it ever afterwards stood, as a conspicuous and venerable memorial to the religious Greek.[1]

We have not yet exhausted the catalogue of beings generated during this early period, anterior to the birth of Zeus. Nyx, alone and without any partner, gave birth to a numerous progeny: Thanatos, Hypnos and Oneiros; Mômus and Oïzys (Grief); Klôthô, Lachesis and Atropos, the three Fates; the retributive and equalizing Nemesis; Apatê and Philotês (Deceit and amorous Propensity), Gêras (Old Age) and Eris (Contention). From Eris proceeded an abundant offspring, all mischievous and maleficent: Ponos (Suffering), Lêthê, Limos (Famine), Phonos and Machê (Slaughter and Battle), Dysnomia and Atê (Lawlessness and reckless Impulse), and Horkos, the everwatchful sanctioner of oaths, as well as the inexorable punisher of voluntary perjury.[2]

Gæa, too, intermarrying with Pontus, gave birth to Nereus, the just and righteous old man of the sea; to Thaumas, Phorkys and Kêtô. From Nereus, and Doris daughter of Oceanus, proceeded the fifty Nereids or Sea-nymphs. Thaumus also married Elektra daughter of Oceanus, and had by her Iris and the two Harpies, Allô and Okypetê, — winged and swift as the winds. From Phorkys and Kêtô sprung the Dragon of the Hesperides, and the monstrous Grææ and Gorgons: the blood of Medusa, one of the Gorgons, when killed by Perseus, produced Chrysaor and the horse Pegasus: Chrysaor and Kallirrhoê gave birth to Geryôn as well as to Echidna, — a creature half-nymph and half-serpent, unlike both to gods and to men. Other monsters arose from the union of Echidna with Typhaôn, — Orthros, the two-headed dog of Geryôn; Cerberus, the dog of Hadês, with fifty heads, and the Lernæan Hydra. From the latter proceeded the Chimæra, the Sphinx of Thêbes, and the Nemean lion.[3]

A powerful and important progeny, also, was that of Styx,

---

[1] Hesiod, Theog. 498. —

Τὸν μὲν Ζεὺς στήριξε κατὰ χθονὸς εὐρυοδείης
Πυθοῖ ἐν ἡγαθέῃ, γυάλοις ὑπὸ Παρνήσοιο,
Σῆμ' ἐμεν ἐξοπίσω, θαῦμα θνητοῖσι βροτοῖσι.

[2] Hesiod, Theog. 212–232.
[3] Hesiod, Theog. 240–320. Apollodôr. i. 2, 6, 7.

daughter of Oceanus, by Pallas; she had Zêlos and Nikê (Impe-
riousness and Victory), and Kratos and Bia (Strength and Force).
The hearty and early coöperation of Styx and her four sons with
Zeus was one of the main causes which enabled him to achieve
his victory over the Titans.

Zeus had grown up not less distinguished for mental capacity
than for bodily force. He and his brothers now determined to
wrest the power from the hands of Kronos and the Titans, and a
long and desperate struggle commenced, in which all the gods
and all the goddesses took part. Zeus convoked them to Olympus, and promised to all who would aid him against Kronos, that
their functions and privileges should remain undisturbed. The
first who responded to the call, came with her four sons, and
embraced his cause, was Styx. Zeus took them all four as his
constant attendants, and conferred upon Styx the majestic distinction of being the Horkos, or oath-sanctioner of the Gods,— what
Horkos was to men, Styx was to the Gods.[1]

Still further to strengthen himself, Zeus released the other
Uranids who had been imprisoned in Tartarus by their father,—
the Cyclôpes and the Centimanes,— and prevailed upon them to
take part with him against the Titans. The former supplied him
with thunder and lightning, and the latter brought into the fight
their boundless muscular strength.[2] Ten full years did the combat continue; Zeus and the Kronids occupying Olympus, and the
Titans being established on the more southerly mountain-chain
of Othrys. All nature was convulsed, and the distant Oceanus,
though he took no part in the struggle, felt the boiling, the noise,
and the shock, not less than Gæa and Pontus. The thunder of
Zeus, combined with the crags and mountains torn up and hurled
by the Centimanes, at length prevailed, and the Titans were defeated and thurst down into Tartarus. Iapetos, Kronos, and the
remaining Titans (Oceanus excepted) were imprisoned, perpetually and irrevocably, in that subterranean dungeon, a wall of brass
being built around them by Poseidôn, and the three Centimanes
being planted as guards. Of the two sons of Iapetos, Menœtius
was made to share this prison, while Atlas was condemned to

---

[1] Hesiod, Theog. 385–403.
[2] Hesiod, Theog. 140, 624, 657. Apollodôr. i. 2, 4.

stand for ever at the extreme west, and to bear upon his shoul
ders the solid vault of heaven.[1] Thus were the Titans subdued, and the Kronids with Zeus at
their head placed in possession of power. They were not, how-
ever, yet quite secure; for Gæa, intermarrying with Tartarus,
gave birth to a new and still more formidable monster called Typhôeus, of such tremendous properties and promise, that, had he
been allowed to grow into full development, nothing could have
prevented him from vanquishing all rivals and becoming supreme.
But Zeus foresaw the danger, smote him at once with a thunderbolt from Olympus, and burnt him up: he was cast along with
the rest into Tartarus, and no further enemy remained to question
the sovereignty of the Kronids.[2]

With Zeus begins a new dynasty and a different order of
beings. Zeus, Poseidôn, and Hadês agree upon the distribution
before noticed, of functions and localities: Zeus retaining the
Æthêr and the atmosphere, together with the general presiding
function; Poseidôn obtaining the sea, and administering subterranean forces generally; and Hadês ruling the under-world or region in which the half-animated shadows of departed men reside.

It has been already stated, that in Zeus, his brothers and his
sisters, and his and their divine progeny, we find the *present*
Gods; that is, those, for the most part, whom the Homeric and
Hesiodic Greeks recognized and worshipped. The wives of Zeus
were numerous as well as his offspring. First he married Mêtis,
the wisest and most sagacious of the goddesses; but Gæa and
Uranos forewarned him that if he permitted himself to have
children by her, they would be stronger than himself and dethrone
him. Accordingly when Mêtis was on the point of being deliv-

---

[1] The battle with the Titans, Hesiod, Theog. 627–735. Hesiod mentions
nothing about the Gigantes and the Gigantomachia: Apollodôrus, on the
other hand, gives this latter in some detail, but despatches the Titans in a
few words (i. 2, 4; i. 6, 1). The Gigantes seem to be only a second edition
of the Titans,— a sort of duplication to which the legendary poets were often
inclined.

[2] Hesiod, Theog. 820–869. Apollod. i. 6, 3. He makes Typhôn very
nearly victorious over Zeus. Typhôeus, according to Hesiod, is father of
the irregular, violent, and mischievous winds: Notus, Boreas, Argestês and
Zephyrus, are of divine origin (870).

ered of Athênê, he swallowed her up, and her wisdom and sagacity thus became permanently identified with his own being.[1] His
head was subsequently cut open, in order to make way for the
exit and birth of the goddess Athênê.[2] By Themis, Zeus begat
the Hôræ, by Eurynomê, the three Charities or Graces; by
Mnêmosynê, the Muses; by Lêtô (Latona), Apollo and Artemis;
and by Dêmêtêr, Persephonê. Last of all he took for his wife
Hêrê, who maintained permanently the dignity of queen of the
Gods; by her he had Hêbê, Arês, and Eileithyia. Hermês also
was born to him by Maia, the daughter of Atlas: Hêphæstos
was born to Hêrê, according to some accounts, by Zeus; according to others, by her own unaided generative force.[3] He was
born lame, and Hêrê was ashamed of him: she wished to secrete
him away, but he made his escape into the sea, and found shelter
under the maternal care of the Nereids Thetis and Eurynome.[4]
Our enumeration of the divine race, under the presidency of Zeus,
will thus give us,[5] —

1. The twelve great gods and goddesses of Olympus, — Zeus,
Poseidôn, Appollo, Arês, Hêphæstos, Hermês, Hêrê, Athênê,
Artemis, Aphroditê, Hestia, Dêmêtêr.

2. An indefinite number of other deities, not included among
the Olympic, seemingly because the number *twelve* was complete
without them, but some of them not inferior in power and dignity
to many of the twelve: — Hadês, Hêlios, Hekatê, Dionysos, Lêtô,
Diônê, Persephonê, Selênê, Themis, Eôs, Harmonia, the Charities, the Muses, the Eilaithyiæ, the Mœræ, the Oceanids and the
Nereids, Proteus, Eidothea, the Nymphs, Leukothea, Phorkys,
Æolus, Nemesis, etc.

3. Deities who perform special services to the greater gods: —
Iris, Hêbê, the Horæ, etc.

4. Deities whose personality is more faintly and unsteadily
conceived: — Atê, the Litæ, Eris, Thanatos, Hypnos, Kratos, Bia,
Ossa, etc.[6] The same name is here employed sometimes to designate the person, sometimes the attribute or event not personi-·

---

[1] Hesiod, Theog. 885-900.   [2] Apollod. i. 3, 6.
[3] Hesiod, Theog. 900-944.   [4] Homer, Iliad, xviii. 397.
[5] See Burckhardt, Homer, und Hesiod. Mythologie, sect. 102. (Leipz.
844).
[6] Λιμὸς — *Hunger* — is a person, in Hesiod, Opp. Di. 299.

fied,—an unconscious transition of ideas, which, when consciously performed, is called Allegory.

5. Monsters, offspring of the Gods:—the Harpies, the Gorgons, the Grææ, Pegasus, Chrysaor, Echidna, Chimæra, the Dragon of the Hesperides, Cerberus, Orthros, Geryôn, the Lernæan Hydra, the Nemean lion, Scylla and Charybdis, the Centaurs, the Sphinx, Xanthos and Balios the immortal horses, etc.

From the gods we slide down insensibly, first to heroes, and then to men; but before we proceed to this new mixture, it is necessary to say a few words on the theogony generally. I have given it briefly as it stands in the Hesiodic Theogonia, because that poem — in spite of great incoherence and confusion, arising seemingly from diversity of authorship as well as diversity of age — presents an ancient and genuine attempt to cast the divine foretime into a systematic sequence. Homer and Hesiod were the grand authorities in the pagan world respecting theogony; but in the Iliad and Odyssey nothing is found except passing allusions and implications, and even in the Hymns (which were commonly believed in antiquity to be the productions of the same author as the Iliad and the Odyssey) there are only isolated, unconnected narratives. Accordingly men habitually took their information respecting their theogonic antiquities from the Hesiodic poem, where it was ready laid out before them; and the legends consecrated in that work acquired both an extent of circulation and a firm hold on the national faith, such as independent legends could seldom or never rival. Moreover the scrupulous and sceptical Pagans, as well as the open assailants of Paganism in later times, derived their subjects of attack from the same source; so that it has been absolutely necessary to recount in their naked simplicity the Hesiodic stories, in order to know what it was that Plato deprecated and Xenophanês denounced. The strange proceedings ascribed to Uranos, Kronos and Zeus, have been more frequently alluded to, in the way of ridicule or condemnation, than any other portion of the mythical world.

But though the Hesiodic theogony passed as orthodox among the later Pagans,[1] because it stood before them as the only system anciently set forth and easily accessible, it was evidently not the

---

[1] See Göttling, Præfat. ad Hesiod. p. 23.

only system received at the date of the poem itself. Homer
knows nothing of Uranos, in the sense of an arch-God anterior
to Kronos. Uranos and Gæa, like Oceanus, Têthys and Nyx,
are with him great and venerable Gods, but neither the one nor
the other present the character of predecessors of Kronos and
Zeus.[1] The Cyclôpes, whom Hesiod ranks as sons of Uranos
and fabricators of thunder, are in Homer neither one nor the
other; they are not noticed in the Iliad at all, and in the Odyssey
they are gross gigantic shepherds and cannibals, having nothing
in common with the Hesiodic Cyclops except the one round central eye.[2] Of the three Centimanes enumerated by Hesiod, Briareus only is mentioned in Homer, and to all appearance, not as
the son of Uranos, but as the son of Poseidôn; not as aiding
Zeus in his combat against the Titans, but as rescuing him at a
critical moment from a conspiracy formed against him by Hêrê,
Poseidôn and Athênê.[3] Not only is the Hesiodic Uranos (with
the Uranids) omitted in Homer, but the relations between Zeus
and Kronos are also presented in a very different light. No
mention is made of Kronos swallowing his young children: on
the contrary, Zeus is the eldest of the three brothers instead of
the youngest, and the children of Kronos live with him and Rhea:
there the stolen intercourse between Zeus and Hêrê first takes
place without the knowledge of their parents.[4] When Zeus puts
Kronos down into Tartarus, Rhea consigns her daughter Hêrê
to the care of Oceanus: no notice do we find of any terrific battle
with the Titans as accompanying that event. Kronos, Iapetos,
and the remaining Titans are down in Tartarus, in the lowest
depths under the earth, far removed from the genial rays of
Hêlios; but they are still powerful and venerable, and Hypnos
makes Hêrê swear an oath in their name, as the most inviolable
that he can think of.[5]

---

[1] Iliad, xiv. 249; xix. 259. Odyss. v. 184. Oceanus and Têthys seem to be
presented in the Iliad as the primitive Father and Mother of the Gods:—

$$\text{'}Ωκεανόν \ τε \ θεῶν \ γένεσιν, \ καὶ \ μητέρα \ Τηθύν. \text{ (xiv. 201).}$$

[2] Odyss. ix. 87.   [3] Iliad, i. 401.   [4] Iliad, xiv. 203–295; xv. 204.
[5] Iliad, viii. 482; xiv. 274–279. In the Hesiodic Opp. et Di., Kronos is
represented as ruling in the Islands of the Blest in the neighborhood of
Oceanus (v. 168).

In Homer, then, we find nothing beyond the simple fact that Zeus thrust his father Kronos together with the remaining Titans into Tartarus; an event to which he affords us a tolerable parallel in certain occurrences even under the presidency of Zeus himself. For the other gods make more than one rebellious attempt against Zeus, and are only put down, partly by his unparalleled strength, partly by the presence of his ally the Centimane Briareus. Kronos, like Laërtes or Pêleus, has become old, and has been supplanted by a force vastly superior to his own. The Homeric epic treats Zeus as present, and, like all the interesting heroic characters, a father must be assigned to him: that father has once been the chief of the Titans, but has been superseded and put down into Tartarus along with the latter, so soon as Zeus and the superior breed of the Olympic gods acquired their full development.

That antithesis between Zeus and Kronos — between the Olympic gods and the Titans — which Homer has thus briefly brought to view, Hesiod has amplified into a theogony, with many things new, and some things contradictory to his predecessor; while Eumêlus or Arktinus in the poem called Titanomachia (now lost) also adopted it as their special subject.[1] As Stasinus, Arktinus, Lêsches, and others, enlarged the Legend of Troy by composing poems relating to a supposed time anterior to the commencement, or subsequent to the termination of the Iliad, — as other poets recounted adventures of Odysseus subsequent to his landing in Ithaka, — so Hesiod enlarged and systematized, at the same time that he corrupted, the skeleton theogony which we find briefly indicated in Homer. There is violence and rudeness in the Homeric gods, but the great genius of Grecian epic is no way accountable for the stories of Uranos and Kronos, — the standing reproach against Pagan legendary narrative.

---

[1] See the few fragments of the Titanomachia, in Düntzer, Epic. Græc. Fragm. p. 2; and Hyne, ad Apollodor. I. 2. Perhaps there was more than one poem on the subject, though it seems that Athenæus had only read one (viii. p. 277).

In the Titanomachia, the generations anterior to Zeus were still further lengthened by making Uranos the son of Æthêr (Fr. 4. Düntzer). Ægæon was also represented as son of Pontus and Gæa, and as having fought in the ranks of the Titans: in the Iliad he (the same who is called Briareus) is the fast ally of Zeus.

A *Titanographia* was ascribed to Musæus (Schol. Apollon. Rhod. iii. 1178 compare Lactant. de Fals. Rel. i. 21).

How far these stories are the invention of Hesiod himself is
impossible to determine.[1] They bring us down to a cast of fancy

---

[1] That the Hesiodic Theogony is referable to an age considerably later
than the Homeric poems, appears now to be the generally admitted opinion;
and the reasons for believing so are, in my opinion, satisfactory. Whether
the Theogony is composed by the same author as the Works and Days is a
disputed point. The Bœotian literati in the days of Pausanias decidedly
denied the identity, and ascribed to their Hesiod only the Works and Days:
Pausanias himself concurs with them (ix. 31. 4; ix. 35. 1), and Völcker
(Mithologie des Japetisch. Geschlechts, p. 14) maintains the same opinion,
as well as Göttling (Præf. ad Hesiod. xxi.): K. O. Müller (History of Grecian
Literature, ch. 8. § 4) thinks that there is not sufficient evidence to form a
decisive opinion.

Under the name of Hesiod (in that vague language which is usual in antiquity respecting authorship, but which modern critics have not much mend-
ed by speaking of the Hesiodic school, sect, or family) passed many different poems, belonging to three classes quite distinct from each other, but all
disparate from the Homeric epic:—1. The poems of legend cast into historical and genealogical series, such as the Eoiai, the Catalogue of Women,
etc. 2. The poems of a didactic or ethical tendency, such as the Works and
Days, the Precepts of Cheirôn, the Art of Augural Prophecy, etc. 3. Separate and short mythical compositions, such as the Shield of Hêraklês, the
Marriage of Keyx (which, however, was of disputed authenticity, Athenæ.
ii. p. 49), the Epithalamium of Pêleus and Thetis, etc. (See Marktscheffel,
Præfat. ad Fragment. Hesiod. p. 89).

The Theogony belongs chiefly to the first of these classes, but it has also
a dash of the second in the legend of Promêtheus, etc.: moreover in the portion which respects Hekatê, it has both a mystic character and a distinct
bearing upon present life and customs, which we may also trace in the allusions to Krête and Delphi. There seems reason to place it in the same age
with the Works and Days, perhaps in the half century preceding 700 B. C.,
and little, if at all, anterior to Archilochus. The poem is evidently conceived upon one scheme, yet the parts are so disorderly and incoherent, that it
is difficult to say how much is interpolation. Hermann has well dissected
the exordium ; see the preface to Gaisford's Hesiod (Poetæ Minor. p. 63).

K. O. Müller tells us (ut sup. p. 90), " The Titans, according to the notions
of Hesiod, represent a system of things in which elementary beings, natural
powers, and notions of order and regularity are united to form a whole. The
Cyclôpes denote the transient disturbances of this order of nature by storms,
and the Hekatoncheires, or hundred-handed Giants, signify the fearful power of the greater revolutions of nature." The poem affords little presumption that any such ideas were present to the mind of its author, as, I
think, will be seen if we read 140–155, 630–745.

The Titans, the Cyclôpes, and the Hekatoncheires, can no more be construed into physical phænomena than Chrysaor, Pegasus, Echidna, the Græææ,
or the Gorgons. Zeus, like Hêraklês, or Jasôn, or Perseus, if his adven-

more coarse and indelicate than the Homeric, and more nearly resembling some of the Holy Chapters (ἱεροὶ λόγοι) of the more recent mysteries, such (for example) as the tale of Dionysos Zagreus. There is evidence in the Theogony itself that the author was acquainted with local legends current both at Krête and at Delphi; for he mentions both the mountain-cave in Krête wherein the new-born Zeus was hidden, and the stone near the Delphian temple — the identical stone which Kronos had swallowed — "placed by Zeus himself as a sign and wonder to mortal men." Both these two monuments, which the poet expressly refers to, and had probably seen, imply a whole train of accessory and explanatory local legends — current probably among the priests of Krête and Delphi, between which places, in ancient times, there was an intimate religious connection. And we may trace further in the poem,— that which would be the natural feeling of Krêtan worshippers of Zeus, — an effort to make out that Zeus was justified in his aggression on Kronos, by the conduct of Kronos himself both towards his father and towards his children: the treatment of Kronos by Zeus appears in Hesiod as the retribution foretold and threatened by the mutilated Uranos against the son who had outraged him. In fact the relations of Uranos and Gæa are in almost all their particulars a mere copy and duplication of those between Kronos and Rhea, differing only in the mode whereby the final catastrophe is brought about. Now castration was a practice thoroughly abhorrent both to the feelings and to the customs of Greece;[1] but it was seen with melancholy fre-

---

tures are to be described, must have enemies, worthy of himself and his vast type, and whom it is some credit for him to overthrow. Those who contend with him or assist him must be conceived on a scale fit to be drawn on the same imposing canvas : the dwarfish proportions of man will not satisfy the sentiment of the poet or his audience respecting the grandeur and glory of the gods. To obtain creations of adequate sublimity for such an object, the poet may occasionally borrow analogies from the striking accidents of physical nature, and when such an allusion manifests itself clearly, the critic does well to point it out. But it seems to me a mistake to treat these approximations to physical phænomena as forming the *main scheme* of the poet,— to look for them everywhere, and to presume them where there is little or no indication.

[1] The strongest evidences of this feeling are exhibited in Herodotus, iii 48; viii 105. See an example of this mutilation inflicted upon a youth

quency in the domestic life as well as in the religious worship of
Phrygia and other parts of Asia, and it even became the special
qualification of a priest of the Great. Mother Cybelê,[1] as well as
of the Ephesian Artemis. The employment of the sickle ascribed to Kronos seems to be the product of an imagination familiar
with the Asiatic worship and legends, which were connected with
and partially resembled the Krêtan.[2] And this deduction becomes the more probable when we connect it with the first genesis of iron, which Hesiod mentions to have been produced for
the express purpose of fabricating the fatal sickle ; for metallurgy
finds a place in the early legends both of the Trojan and of the
Krêtan Ida, and the three Idæan Dactyls, the legendary inventors of it, are assigned sometimes to one and sometimes to the
other.[3]

As Hesiod had extended the Homeric series of gods by prefixing the dynasty of Uranos to that of Kronos, so the Orphic theog-

---

named Adamas by the Thracian king Kotys, in Aristot. Polit. v. 8, 12, and
the tale about the Corinthian Periander, Herod. iii. 48.

It is an instance of the habit, so frequent among the Attic tragedians, of
ascribing Asiatic or Phrygian manners to the Trojans, when Sophoclês in
his lost play Troilus (ap. Jul. Poll. x. 165) introduced one of the characters
of his drama as having been castrated by order of Hecuba, Σκαλμῇ γὰρ
ὄρχεις βασιλὶς ἐκτέμνουσ' ἐμούς,—probably the Παιδαγωγὸς, or guardian and
companion of the youthful Troilus. See Welcker, Griechisch. Tragöd. vol.
i. p. 125.

[1] Herodot. viii. 105, εὐνοῦχοι. Lucian, De Deâ Syriâ, c. 50. Strabo, xiv.
pp. 640–641.

[2] Diodôr. v. 64. Strabo, x. p. 460. Hoeckh, in his learned work Krêta
(vol. i. books 1 and 2), has collected all the information attainable respecting
the early influences of Phrygia and Asia Minor upon Krête : nothing seems
ascertainable except the general fact ; all the particular evidences are lamentably vague.

The worship of the Diktæan Zeus seemed to have originally belonged to
the Eteokrêtes, who were not Hellens, and were more akin to the Asiatic
population than to the Hellenic. Strabo, x. p. 478. Hoeckh, Krêta, vol. i.
p. 139.

[3] Hesiod, Theogon. 161,

Αἶψα δὲ ποιήσασα γένος πολιοῦ ἀδάμαντος,
Τεῦξε μέγα δρέπανον, etc.

See the extract from the old poem *Phorônis* ap. Schol. Apoll. Rhod. 1129 ;
and Strabo, x. p. 472.

ony lengthened it still further.[1] First came Chronos, or Time, as a person, after him Æthêr and Chaos, out of whom Chronos produced the vast mundane egg. Hence emerged in process of time the first-born god Phanês, or Mêtis, or Hêrikapæos, a person of double sex, who first generated the Kosmos, or mundane system, and who carried within him the seed of the gods. He gave birth to Nyx, by whom he begat Uranos and Gæa; as well as to Hêlios and Selênê.[2]

From Uranos and Gæa sprang the three Mœræ, or Fates, the three Centimanes and the three Cyclôpes: these latter were cast by Uranos into Tartarus, under the foreboding that they would rob him of his dominion. In revenge for this maltreatment of her sons, Gæa produced of herself the fourteen Titans, seven male and seven female: the former were Kœos, Krios, Phorkys, Kronos, Oceanus, Hyperiôn and Iapetos; the latter were Themis, Têthys, Mnêmosynê, Theia, Diônê, Phœbê and Rhea.[3] They received the name of Titans because they avenged upon Uranos the expulsion of their elder brothers. Six of the Titans, headed by Kronos the most powerful of them all, conspiring against Uranos, castrated and dethroned him: Oceanus alone stood aloof and took no part in the aggression. Kronos assumed the government and fixed his seat on Olympos; while Oceanus remained apart, master of his own divine stream.[4] The reign

---

[1] See the scanty fragments of the Orphic theogony in Hermann's edition of the Orphica, pp. 448, 504, which it is difficult to understand and piece together, even with the aid of Lobeck's elaborate examination (Aglaophamus, p. 470, etc.). The passages are chiefly preserved by Proclus and the later Platonists, who seem to entangle them almost inextricably with their own philosophical ideas.

The first few lines of the Orphic Argonautica contain a brief summary of the chief points of the theogony.

[2] See Lobeck, Aglaoph. p. 472-476, 490-500, Μῆτιν σπέρμα φέροντα θεῶν κλυτὸν 'Ηρικεπαῖον; again, Θῆλυς καὶ γενέτωρ κρατερὸς θεὸς 'Ηρικέπαιος. Compare Lactant. iv. 8, 4: Suidas, v. Φάνης: Athenagoras, xx. 296: Diodôr. i. 27.

This egg figures, as might be expected, in the cosmogony set forth by the Birds, Aristophan. Av. 695. Nyx gives birth to an egg, out of which steps the golden Erôs; from Erôs and Chaos spring the race of birds.

[3] Lobeck, Ag. p. 504. Athenagor. xv. p. 64.

[4] Lobeck, Ag. p. 507. Plato, Timæus, p. 41. In the Διονύσου τρόφοι of Æschylus, the old attendants of the god Dionysos were said to have been

of Kronos was a period of tranquillity and happiness, as well as of extraordinary longevity and vigor.

Kronos and Rhea gave birth to Zeus and his brothers and sisters. The concealment and escape of the infant Zeus, and the swallowing of the stone by Kronos, are given in the Orphic Theogony substantially in the same manner as by Hesiod, only in a style less simple and more mysticized. Zeus is concealed in the cave of Nyx, the seat of Phanês himself, along with Eidê and Adrasteia, who nurse and preserve him, while the armed dance and sonorous instruments of the Kurêtes prevent his infant cries from reaching the ears of Kronos. When grown up, he lays a snare for his father, intoxicates him with honey, and having surprised him in the depth of sleep, enchains and castrates him.[1] Thus exalted to the supreme mastery, he swallowed and absorbed into himself Mêtis, or Phanês, with all the preëxisting elements of things, and then generated all things anew out of his own being and conformably to his own divine ideas.[2] So scanty are the remains of this system, that we find it difficult to trace individually the gods and goddesses sprung from Zeus

cut up and boiled in a caldron, and rendered again young, by Medeia. Pherecydês and Simonidês said that Jasôn himself had been so dealt with. Schol. Aristoph. Equit. 1321.

[1] Lobeck, p. 514.   Porphyry, de Antro Nympharum, c. 16. φησὶ γὰρ παρ
'Ορφεῖ ἡ Νὺξ, τῷ Διὶ ὑποτιθεμένη τὸν διὰ τοῦ μέλιτος δόλον,

> Εὖτ' ἂν δή μιν ἴδηαι ὑπὸ δρυσὶν ὑψικόμοισι
> 'Εργοισιν μεθύοντα μελισσάων ἐριβόμβων,
> Αὐτικά μιν δῆσον.

Ο καὶ πάσχει ὁ Κρόνος καὶ δεθεὶς ἐκτέμνεται, ὡς Οὐρανός.

Compare Timæus ap. Schol. Apoll. Rhod. iv. 983.

[2] The Cataposis of Phanês by Zeus one of the most memorable points of the ·Orphic Theogony. Lobeck, p. 519.; also Fragm. vi. p. 456 of Hermann's Orphica.

From this absorption and subsequent reproduction of all things by Zeus, flowed the magnificent string of Orphic predicates about him, —

> Ζεὺς ἀρχὴ, Ζεὺς μέσσα, Διὸς δ' ἐκ πάντα τέτυκται, —

an allusion to which is traceable even in Plato, de Legg. iv. p. 715. Plutarch, de Defectu Oracul. T. ix. p. 379. c. 48. Diodôrus (i. 11) is the most ancient writer remaining to us who mentions the name of Phanês, in a line cited as proceeding from Orpheus; wherein, however, Phanês is identified with Dionysos. Compare Macrobius, Saturnal i. 18.

beyond Apollo, Dionysos, and Persephonê, — the latter being confounded with Artemis and Hekatê.

But there is one new personage, begotten by Zéus, who stands preëminently marked in the Orphic Theogony, and whose adventures constitute one of its peculiar features. Zagreus, "the horned child," is the son of Zeus by his own daughter Persephonê: he is the favorite of his father, a child of magnificent promise, and predestined, if he grow up, to succeed to supreme dominion as well as to the handling of the thunderbolt. He is seated, whilst an infant, on the throne beside Zeus, guarded by Apollo and the Kurêtes. But the jealous Hêrê intercepts his career and incites the Titans against him, who, having first smeared their faces with plaster, approach him on the throne, tempt his childish fancy with playthings, and kill him with a sword while he is contemplating his face in a mirror. They then cut up his body and boil it in a caldron, leaving only the heart, which is picked up by Athênê and carried to Zeus, who in his wrath strikes down the Titans with thunder into Tartarus ; whilst Apollo is directed to collect the remains of Zagreus and bury them at the foot of Mount Parnassus. The heart is given to Semelê, and Zagreus is born again from her under the form of Dionysos.[1]

---

[1] About the tale of Zagreus, see Lobeck, p. 552, *sqq.* Nonnus in his Dionysiaca has given many details about it : —

   Ζαγρέα γειναμένη κέρυεν βρέφος, etc..(vi. 264).

Clemens Alexandrin. Admonit. ad Gent. p. 11, 12, Sylb. The story was treated both by Callimachus and by Euphoriôn, Etymolog. Magu. v. Ζαγρεὺς, Schol. Lycophr. 208. In the old epic poem Alkmæônis or Epigoni, Zagreus is a surname of Hadês. See Fragm. 4, p. 7, ed. Düntzer. Respecting the Orphic Theogony generally, Brandis (Handbuch der Geschichte der Griechisch-Römisch. Philosophie, c. xvii., xviii.), K. O. Müller (Prolegg. Mythol. pp. 379-396), and Zoega (Abhandlungen, v. pp. 211-263) may be consulted with much advantage. Brandis regards this Theogony as *considerably older* than the first Ionic philosophy, which is a higher antiquity than appears probable: some of the ideas which it contains, such, for example, as that of the Orphic egg, indicate a departure from the string of purely personal generations which both Homer and Hesiod exclusively recount, and a resort to something like physical analogies. On the whole. we cannot reasonably claim for it more than half a century above the age of Onomakritus. The Theogony of Pherekydês of Syros seems to have

Such is the tissue of violent fancies comprehended under the title of the Orphic Theogony, and read as such, it appears, by Plato, Isokratês and Aristotle. It will be seen that it is based upon the Hesiodic Theogony, but according to the general expansive tendency of Grecian legend, much new matter is added: Zeus has in Homer one predecessor, in Hesiod two, and in Orpheus four.

The Hesiodic Theogony, though later in date than the Iliad and Odyssey, was coeval with the earliest period of what may be called Grecian history, and certainly of an age earlier than 700 B. C. It appears to have been widely circulated in Greece, and being at once ancient and short, the general public consulted it as their principal source of information respecting divine antiquity. The Orphic Theogony belongs to a later date, and contains the Hesiodic ideas and persons, enlarged and mystically disguised: its vein of invention was less popular, adapted more to the contemplation of a sect specially prepared than to the taste of a casual audience, and it appears accordingly to have obtained currency chiefly among purely speculative men.[1] Among the major-

---

borne some analogy to the Orphic. See Diogen. Laërt. i. 119, Sturz. Fragment. Pherekyd. § 5–6, Brandis, Handbuch, *ut sup.* c. xxii. Pherekydês partially deviated from the mythical track or personal successions set forth by Hesiod. ἐπεὶ οἵ γε μεμιγμένοι αὐτῶν καὶ τῷ μὴ μυϑικῶς ἅπαντα λέγειν, οἷον Φερεκύδης καὶ ἑτεροί τινες, etc. (Aristot. Metaphys. N. p. 301, ed. Brandis). Porphyrius, de Antro Nymphar. c. 31, καὶ τοῦ Συρίου Φερεκύδου μυχοὺς καὶ βόϑρους καὶ ἄντρα καὶ ϑύρας καὶ πύλας λέγοντος, καὶ διὰ τούτων αἰνιττομένου τὰς τῶν ψυχῶν γενέσεις καὶ ἀπογενέσεις, etc. Eudêmus the Peripatetic, pupil of Aristotle, had drawn up an account of the Orphic Theogony as well as of the doctrines of Pherekydês, Akusilaus and others, which was still in the hands of the Platonists of the fourth century, though it is now lost. The extracts which we find seem all to countenance the belief that the Hesiodic Theogony formed the basis upon which they worked. See about Akusilaus, Plato, Sympos. p. 178. Clem. Alex. Strom. p. 629.

[1] The Orphic Theogony is never cited in the ample Scholia on Homer, though Hesiod is often alluded to. (See Lobeck, Aglaoph. p. 540). Nor can it have been present to the minds of Xenophanês and Herakleitus, as representing any widely diffused Grecian belief: the former, who so severely condemned Homer and Hesiod, would have found Orpheus much more deserving of his censure : and the latter could hardly have omitted Orpheus from his memorable denunciation: — Πολυμαϑίη νόον οὐ διδάσκει· Ἡσίοδον γάρ ἂν ἐδίδαξε καὶ Πυϑαγόρην, αὖτις δὲ Ξενοφάνεά τε καὶ Ἑκαταῖον. Diog. Laër. ix. 1. Isokratês treats Orpheus as the most censurable of all the poets.

ity of these latter, however, it acquired greater veneration, and above all was supposed to be of greater antiquity, than the Hesiodic. The belief in its superior antiquity (disallowed by Herodotus, and seemingly also by Aristotle[1]), as well as the respect for its contents, increased during the Alexandrine age and through the declining centuries of Paganism, reaching its maximum among the New-Platonists of the third and fourth century after Christ: both the Christian assailants, as well as the defenders, of paganism, treated it as the most ancient and venerable summary of the Grecian faith. Orpheus is celebrated by Pindar as the harper and companion of the Argonautic maritime heroes: Orpheus and Musæus, as well as Pamphôs and Olên, the great supposed authors of theogonic, mystical, oracular, and prophetic verses and hymns, were generally considered by literary Greeks as older than either Hesiod or Homer:[2] and such was also the common opinion of modern scholars until a period comparatively recent. It has now been shown, on sufficient ground, that the

See Busiris, p. 229; ii. p. 309, Bekk. The Theogony of Orpheus, as conceived by Apollonius Rhodius (i. 504) in the third century B. C., and by Nigidius in the first century B. C. (Servius ad Virgil. Eclog. iv. 10), seems to have been on a more contracted scale than that which is given in the text. But neither of them notice the tale of Zagreus, which we know to be as old as Onomakritus.

[1] This opinion of Herodotus is implied in the remarkable passage about Homer and Hesiod, ii. 53, though he never once names Orpheus — only alluding once to " Orphic ceremonies," ii. 81. He speaks more than once of the prophecies of Musæus. Aristotle denied the past existence and reality of Orpheus. See Cicero de Nat. Deor. i. 38.

[2] Pindar Pyth. iv. 177. Plato seems to consider Orpheus as more ancient than Homer. Compare Theætêt. p. 179; Cratylus, p. 402; De Bepubl. ii. p. 364. The order in which Aristophanês (and Hippias of Elis, ap. Clem. Alex. Str. vi. p. 624) mentions them indicates the same view, Ranæ, 1030. It is unnecessary to cite the later chronologers, among whom the belief in the antiquity of Orpheus was universal; he was commonly described as son of the Muse Calliopê. Androtiôn seems to have denied that he was a Thracian, regarding the Thracians as incurably stupid and illiterate. Androtiôn, Fragm. 36, ed. Didot. Ephorus treated him as having been a pupil of the Idæan Dactyls of Phrygia (see Diodôr. v. 64), and as having learnt from them his τελετὰς and μυστήρια, which he was the first to introduce into Greece. The earliest mention which we find of Orpheus, is that of the poet Ibycus (about B. C. 530), ὀνομάκλυτον Ὀρφῆν. Ibyci Fragm. 9, p. 341, ed. Schneidewin.

compositions which passed under these names emanate for the most part from poets of the Alexandrine age, and subsequent to the Christian æra; and that even the earliest among them, which served as the stock on which the later additions were engrafted, belong to a period far more recent than Hesiod; probably to the century preceding Onomakritus (B. C. 610–510).

It seems, however, certain, that both Orpheus and Musæus were names of established reputation at the time when Onomakritus flourished; and it is distinctly stated by Pausanias that the latter was himself the author of the most remarkable and characteristic mythe of the Orphic Theogony — the discerption of Zagreus by the Titans, and his resurrection as Dionysos.[1]

The names of Orpheus and Musæus (as well as that of Pythagoras,[2] looking at one side of his character) represent facts of importance in the history of the Grecian mind — the gradual influx of Thracian, Phrygian, and Egyptian, religious ceremonies and feelings, and the increasing diffusion of special mysteries,[3]

---

[1] Pausan. viii. 37, 3. Τιτᾶνας δὲ πρῶτον ἐς ποίησιν ἐσήγαγεν Ὅμηρος, θεοὺς εἶναι σφᾶς ὑπὸ τῷ καλουμένῳ Ταρτάρῳ· καὶ ἐστιν ἐν Ἥρας ὅρκῳ τὰ ἐπη· παρὰ δὲ Ὁμήρου Ὀνομάκριτος, παραλαβὼν τῶν Τιτάνων τὸ ὄνομα, Διονύσῳ τε συνέθηκεν ὄργια, καὶ εἶναι τοὺς Τιτᾶνας τῷ Διονύσῳ τῶν παθημάτων ἐποίησεν αὐτουργούς. Both the date, the character and the function of Onomakritus are distinctly marked by Herodotus, vii. 6.

[2] Herodotus believed in the derivation both of the Orphic and Pythagorean regulations from Egypt — ὁμολογέουσι δὲ ταῦτα τοῖσι Ὀρφικοῖσι καλεομένοισι καὶ Βακχικοῖσι, ἐοῦσι δὲ Αἰγυπτίοισι (ii. 81). He knows the names of those Greeks who have borrowed from Egypt the doctrine of the metempsychosis, but he will not mention them (ii. 123): he can hardly allude to any one but the Pythagoreans, many of whom he probably knew in Italy. See the curious extract from Xenophanês respecting the doctrine of Pythagoras, Diogen. Laërt. viii. 37; and the quotation from the Silli of Timôn, Πυθαγόραν δὲ γόητος ἀποκλίναντ' ἐπὶ δόξαν, etc. Compare Porphyr. in Vit. Pythag. c. 41.

[3] Aristophan. Ran. 1030. —

Ὀρφεὺς μὲν γὰρ τελετάς θ' ἡμῖν κατέδειξε, φόνων τ' ἀπέχεσθαι·
Μουσαῖος τ', ἐξακέσεις τε νόσων καὶ χρησμούς· Ἡσίοδος δὲ,
Γῆς ἐργασίας, καρπῶν ὥρας, ἀρότους· ὁ δὲ θεῖος Ὅμηρος
Ἀπὸ τοῦ τίμην καὶ κλέος ἔσχεν, πλὴν τοῦθ', ὅτι χρήστ' ἐδίδασκεν,
Ἀρετὰς, τάξεις, ὁπλίσεις ἀνδρῶν· etc.

The same general contrast is to be found in Plato, Protagoras, p. 316; the opinion of Pausanias, ix. 30, 4. The poems of Musæus seem to have borne

schemes for religious purification, and orgies (I venture to angli-cize the Greek word, which contains in its original meaning no implication of the ideas of. excess to which it was afterwards diverted) in honor of some particular god — distinct both from the public solemnities and from the gentile solemnities of primi-tive Greece, — celebrated apart from the citizens generally, and approachable only through a certain course of preparation and initiation — sometimes even forbidden to be talked of in the presence of the uninitiated, under the severest threats of divine judgment. Occasionally such voluntary combinations assumed the form of permanent brotherhoods, bound together by periodical solemnities as well as by vows of an ascetic character: thus the Orphic life (as it was called) or regulation of the Orphic brother-hood, among other injunctions partly arbitrary and partly absti-nent, forbade animal food universally, and on certain occasions, the use of woollen clothing.[1] The great religious and political fraternity of the Pythagoreans, which acted so powerfully on the condition of the Italian cities, was one of the many manifestations of this general tendency, which stands in striking contrast with the simple, open-hearted, and demonstrative worship of the Homeric Greeks.

Festivals at seed-time and harvest — at the vintage and at the opening of the new wine — were doubtless coeval with the earli-est habits of the Greeks; the latter being a period of unusual joviality. Yet in the Homeric poems, Dionysos and Dêmêtêr, the patrons of the vineyard and the cornfield, are seldom men-tioned, and decidedly occupy little place in the imagination of the poet as compared with the other gods: nor are they of any con-spicuous importance even in the Hesiodic Theogony. But during the interval between Hesiod and Onomakritus, the revolution in the religious mind of Greece was such as to place both these deities in the front rank. According to the Orphic doctrine, Zagreus, son of Persephonê, is destined to be the successor of Zeus, and although the violence of the Titans intercepts this lot,

---

considerable analogy to the Melampodia ascribed to Hesiod (see Clemen. Alex. Str. vi. p. 628); and healing charms are ascribed to Orpheus as well as to Musæus. See Eurip. Alcestis, 986.

[1] Herod. ii. 81; Euripid. Hippol. 957, and the curious fragment of the lost Κρῆτες of Euripides. Ὀρφικοὶ βίοι, Plato, Legg. vii. 782.

yet even when he rises again from his discerption under the
name of Dionysos, he is the colleague and coëqual of his divine
father.

This remarkable change, occurring as it did during the sixth
and a part of the seventh century before the Christian æra, may
be traced to the influence of communication with Egypt (which
only became fully open to the Greeks about B. C. 660), as well
as with Thrace, Phrygia, and Lydia. From hence new religious
ideas and feelings were introduced, which chiefly attached themselves to the characters of Dionysos and Dêmêtêr. The Greeks
identified these two deities with the great Egyptian Osiris and
Isis, so that what was borrowed from the Egyptian worship of
the two latter naturally fell to their equivalents in the Grecian
system.[1] Moreover the worship of Dionysos (under what name
cannot be certainly made out) was indigenous in Thrace,[2]
as that of the Great Mother was in Phyrgia, and in Lydia —
together with those violent ecstasies and manifestations of temporary frenzy, and that clashing of noisy instruments, which we
find afterwards characterizing it in Greece. The great masters
of the pipe — as well as the dythyramb,[3] and indeed the whole
musical system appropriated to the worship of Dionysos, which

---

[1] Herodot. ii. 42, 59, 144.

[2] Herodot. v. 7, vii. 111; Euripid. Hecub. 1249, and Rhêsus, 969. and the
Prologue to the Bacchæ; Strabo, x. p. 470; Schol. ad Aristophan. Aves,
874; Eustath. ad Dionys. Perieg. 1069; Harpocrat. v. Σάβοι; Photius,
Εἰοῖ Σαβοῖ. The "Lydiaca" of Th. Menke (Berlin, 1843) traces the
early connection between the religion of Dionysos and that of Cybelê, c. 6,
7. Hoeckh's Krêta (vol. i. p. 128–134) is instructive respecting the Phrygian
religion.

[3] Aristotle, Polit. viii. 7, 9. Πᾶσα γὰρ Βάκχεια καὶ πᾶσα ἡ τοιαύτη κίνησις
μάλιστα τῶν ὀργάνων ἐστὶν ἐν τοῖς αὐλοῖς· τῶν δ' ἁρμονίων ἐν τοῖς Φρυγιστὶ
μέλεσι λαμβάνει ταυτα τὸ πρέπον, οἷον ὁ διθύραμβος δοκεῖ ὁμολογουμένως
εἶναι Φρύγιον. Eurip. Bacch. 58.—

Αἱρεσθε τἀπιχώρι' ἐν πόλει Φρυγῶν
Τύμπανα, 'Ρέας τε μητρὸς ἐμὰ ϑ' εὑρήματα, etc.

Plutarch, Εἰ. in Delph. c. 9; Philochor. Fr. 21, ed. Didot, p. 389. The complete and intimate manner in which Euripidês identifies the Bacchic rites of
Dionysos with the Phrygian ceremonies in honor of the Great Mother, is very
remarkable. The fine description given by Lucretius (ii. 600–640) of the
Phrygian worship is much enfeebled by his unsatisfactory allegorizing

contrasted so pointedly with the quiet solemnity of the Pæan addressed to Apollo — were all originally Phrygian.

From all these various countries, novelties, unknown to the Homeric men, found their way into the Grecian worship : and there is one amongst them which deserves to be specially noticed, because it marks the generation of the new class of ideas in their theology. Homer mentions many persons guilty of private or involuntary homicide, and compelled either to go into exile or to make pecuniary satisfaction; but he never once describes any of them to have either received or required purification for the crime.[1] Now in the time subsequent to Homer, purification for homicide comes to be considered as indispensable: the guilty person is regarded as unfit for the society of man or the worship of the gods until he has received it, and special ceremonies are prescribed whereby it is to be administered. Herodotus tells us that the ceremony of purification was the same among the Lydians and among the Greeks :[2] we know that it formed no part of the early religion of the latter, and we may perhaps reasonably suspect that they borrowed it from the former. The oldest instance known to us of expiation for homicide was contained in the epic poem of the Milesian Arktinus,[3] wherein Achillês is

---

[1] Schol. ad Iliad, xi. 690 — οὐ διὰ τὰ καθάρσια Ἱρίτου πορθεῖται ἡ Πύλος, ἐπεί τοι Ὀδυσσεὺς μείζων Νέστορος, καὶ παρ' Ὁμήρῳ οὐκ οἴδαμεν φονέα καθαιρόμενον, ἀλλ' ἀντιτίνοντα ἢ φυγαδευόμενον. The examples are numerous, and are found both in the Iliad and the Odyssey. Iliad, ii. 665 (Tlépolemos); xiii. 697 (Medón); xiii. 574 (Epeigeus); xxiii. 89 (Patroclos); Odyss. xv. 224 (Theoclymenos); xiv. 380 (an Ætolian). Nor does the interesting mythe respecting the functions of Atê and the Litæ harmonize with the subsequent doctrine about the necessity of purification. (Iliad, ix. 498).

[2] Herodot. i. 35 — ἔστι δὲ παραπλησίη ἡ κάθαρσις τοῖσι Λυδοῖσι καὶ τοῖσι Ἕλλησι. One remarkable proof, amongst many, of the deep hold which this idea took of the greatest minds in Greece, that serious mischief would fall upon the community if family quarrels or homicide remained without religious expiation, is to be found in the objections which Aristotle urges against the community of women proposed in the Platonic Republic. It could not be known what individuals stood in the relation of father, son or brother: if, therefore, wrong or murder of kindred should take place, the appropriate religious atonements (αἱ νομιζόμεναι λύσεις) could not be applied, and the crime would go unexpiated. (Aristot. Polit. ii. 1, 14. Compare Thucyd. i. 125–128).

[3] See the Fragm. of the Æthiopis of Arktinus, in Düntzer's Collection, p. 16.

purified by Odysseus for the murder of Thersitês : seveial others
occurred in the later or Hesiodic epic — Hêraklês, Pêleus, Bellerophôn, Alkmæôn, Amphiktyôn, Pœmander, Triopas, — from
whence they probably passed through the hands of the logographers to Apollodôrus, Diodôrus, and others.[1] The purification
of the murderer was originally operated, not by the hands of any
priest or specially sanctified man, but by those of a chief or king,
who goes through the appropriate ceremonies in the manner
recounted by Herodotus in his pathetic narrative respecting
Crœsus and Adrastus.

The idea of a special taint of crime, and of the necessity as
well as the sufficiency of prescribed religious ceremonies as a
means of removing it, appears thus to have got footing in Grecian
practice subsequent to the time of Homer. The peculiar rites
or orgies, composed or put together by Onomakritus, Methapus,[2]
and other men of more than the ordinary piety, were founded
upon a similar mode of thinking, and adapted to the same mental
exigencies. They were voluntary religious manifestations, superinduced upon the old public sacrifices of the king or chiefs on
behalf of the whole society, and of the father on his own family
hearth — they marked out the details of divine service proper to
appease or gratify the god to whom they were addressed, and to
procure for the believers who went through them his blessings
and protection here or hereafter — the exact performance of the
divine service in all its specialty was held necessary, and thus the
priests or Hierophants, who alone were familiar with the ritual,
acquired a commanding position.[3]   Generally speaking, these

---

[1] The references for this are collected in Lobeck's Aglaophamos. Epi-
metr. ii. ad Orphica, p. 968.

[2] Pausanias (iv. 1, 5) — μετεκόσμησε γὰρ καὶ Μέθαπος τῆς τελετῆς (the
Eleusinian Orgies, carried by Kaukon from Eleusis into Messênia), ἔστιν ἅ.
Ὁ δὲ Μέθαπος γένος μὲν ἦν Ἀθηναῖος, τελετῆς τε καὶ ὀργίων παντοίων
συνϑέτης.   Again, viii. 37, 3, Onomakritus Διονύσῳ συνέϑηκεν ὄργια,
etc.   This is another expression designating the same idea as the Rhêsus of
Euripidês, 944. —

> Μυστηρίων τε τῶν ἀπορρήτων φάνας
> Ἔδειξεν Ὀρφεύς.

[3] Têlinês, the ancestor of the Syracusan despot Gelô, acquired great
political power as possessing τὰ ἱρὰ τῶν χθονίων θεῶν (Herodot. vii. 153);

peculiar orgies obtained their admission and their influence at periods of distress, disease, public calamity and danger, or religious terror and despondency, which appear to have been but too frequent in their occurrence.

The minds of men were prone to the belief that what they were suffering arose from the displeasure of some of the gods, and as they found that the ordinary sacrifices and worship were insufficient for their protection, so they grasped at new suggestions proposed to them with the view of regaining the divine favor.[1] Such suggestions were more usually copied, either in whole or in part, from the religious rites of some foreign locality, or from some other portion of the Hellenic world; and in this manner many new sects or voluntary religious fraternities, promising to relieve the troubled conscience and to reconcile the sick or suffering with the offended gods, acquired permanent establishment as well as considerable influence. They were generally under the superintendence of hereditary families of priests, who imparted the rites of confirmation and purification to communicants generally; no one who went through the prescribed ceremonies being excluded. In many cases, such ceremonies fell into the hands of jugglers, who volunteered their services to wealthy men, and degraded their profession as well by obtrusive venality as by extravagant promises:[2] sometimes the price was lowered

---

he and his family became hereditary Hierophants of these ceremonies. How Télinês acquired the ἱρὰ Herodotus cannot say — ὅϑεν δὲ αὐτὰ ἔλαβε, ἢ αὐτὸς ἐκτήσατο, τοῦτο οὐκ ἔχω εἶπαι. Probably there was a traditional legend, not inferior in sanctity to that of Eleusis, tracing them to the gift of Dêmêtêr herself.

[1] See Josephus cont. Apiôn. ii. c. 35.; Hesych. Θεοὶ ξένιοι; Strabo, x. p 471; Plutarch, Περὶ Δεισιδαιμον. c. iii. p. 166; c. vii. p. 167.

[2] Plato, Republ. ii. p. 364; Demosthen. de Coronâ, c. 79, p. 313. The δεισιδαίμων of Theophrastus cannot be comfortable without receiving the Orphic communion monthly from the Orpheotelestæ (Theophr. Char. xvi.). Compare Plutarch, Περὶ τοῦ μὴ χρᾶν ἔμμετρα, etc., c. 25, p. 400. The comic writer Phrynichus indicates the existence of these rites of religious excitement, at Athens, during the Peloponnesian war. See the short fragment of his Κρόνος, ap. Schol. Aristoph. Aves, 989 –

'Ανὴρ χορεύει, καὶ τὰ τοῦ ϑεοῦ καλῶς·
Βούλει Διοπείϑη μεταδράμω καὶ τύμπανα ;

Diopeithês was a χρησμόλογος, or collecter and deliverer of prophecies,

to bring them within reach of the poor and even of slaves. But the wide diffusion, and the number of voluntary communicants of these solemnities, proves how much they fell in with the feeling of the time and how much respect they enjoyed — a respect, which the more conspicuous establishments, such as Eleusis and Samothrace, maintained for several centuries. And the visit of the Kretan Epimenidês to Athens — in the time of Solôn, and at a season of the most serious disquietude and dread of having offended the gods — illustrates the tranquillizing effect of new orgies[1] and rites of absolution, when enjoined by a man standing high in the favor of the gods and reputed to be the son of a nymph. The supposed Erythræan Sibyl, and the earliest collection of Sibylline prophecies,[2] afterwards so much multiplied and interpolated, and referred (according to Grecian custom) to an age even earlier than Homer, appear to belong to a date not long posterior to Epimenidês. Other oracular verses, such as those of Bakis, were treasured up in Athens and other cities : the sixth century before the Christian æra was fertile in these kinds of religious manifestations.

Amongst the special rites and orgies of the character just described, those which enjoyed the greatest Pan-Hellenic reputation were attached to the Idæan Zeus in Krête, to Dêmêtêr at Eleusis, to the Kabeiri in Samothrace, and to Dionysos at Delphi

---

which he sung (or rather, perhaps, recited) with solemnity and emphasis, in public. ὥστε ποιοῦντες χρησμοὺς αὐτοὶ Διόδασ' ᾄδειν Διοπείθει τῷ παραμαινομένῳ. (Ameipsias ap. Schol. Aristophan. ut sup., which illustrates Thucyd. ii. 21).

[1] Plutarch, Solôn, c. 12 ; Diogen. Laërt. i. 110.

[2] See Klausen, " Æneas und die Penaten:" his chapter on the connection between the Grecian and Roman Sibylline collections is among the most ingenious of his learned book. Book ii. pp. 210–240 ; see Steph. Byz. v. Γέργις.

To the same age belong the χρησμοὶ and καθαρμοὶ of Abaris and his marvellous journey through the air upon an arrow (Herodot. iv. 36).

Epimenidês also composed καθαρμοὶ in epic verse ; his Κουρήτων and Κορυβάντων γένεσις, and his four thousand verses respecting Minôs and Rhadamanthys, if they had been preserved, would let us fully into the ideas of a religious mystic of that age respecting the antiquities of Greece. (Strabo, x. p. 474 ; Diogen. Laërt. i. 10). Among the poems ascribed to Hesiod were comprised not only the Melampodia, but also ἔπη μαντικὰ and ἐξηγήσεις ἐπὶ τέρασιν. Pausan. ix. 31. 4.

and Thebes.[1] That they were all to a great degree analogous, is shown by the way in which they unconsciously run together and become confused in the minds of various authors: the ancient inquirers themselves were unable to distinguish one from the other, and we must be content to submit to the like ignorance. But we see enough to satisfy us of the general fact, that during the century and a half which elapsed between the opening of Egypt to the Greeks and the commencement of their struggle with the Persian kings, the old religion was largely adulterated by importations from Egypt, Asia Minor,[2] and Thrace. The rites grew to be more furious and ecstatic, exhibiting the utmost excitement, bodily as well as mental: the legends became at once more coarse, more tragical, and less pathetic. The manifestations of this frenzy were strongest among the women, whose religious susceptibilities were often found extremely unmanageable,[3] and who had everywhere congregative occasional ceremonies of their own, part from the men — indeed, in the case of the colonists, especially of the Asiatic colonists, the women had been originally women of the country, and as such retained to a great degree their non-Hellenic manners and feelings.[4] The god Diony-

---

[1] Among other illustrations of this general resemblance, may be counted an epitaph of Kallimachus upon an aged priestess, who passed from the service of Dêmêtêr to that of the Kabeiri, then to that of Cybelê, having the superintendence of many young women. Kallimachus, Epigram. 42. p. 308, ed. Ernest.

[2] Plutarch, (Defect. Oracul. c. 10, p. 415) treats these countries as the original seat of the worship of Dæmons (wholly or partially bad, and intermediate between gods and men), and their religious ceremonies as of a corresponding character: the Greeks were borrowers from them, according to him, both of the doctrine and of the ceremonies.

[3] Strabo, vii. p. 297. Ἅπαντες γὰρ τῆς δεισιδαιμονίας ἀρχηγοὺς οἴονται τὰς γυναῖκας· αὐταὶ δὲ καὶ τοὺς ἄνδρας προκαλοῦνται ἐς τὰς ἐπὶ πλέον θεραπείας τῶν θεῶν, καὶ ἑορτὰς, καὶ ποτνιασμούς. Plato (De Legg. x. pp. 909, 910) takes great pains to restrain this tendency on the part of sick or suffering persons, especially women, to introduce new sacred rites into his city.

[4] Herodot. i. 146. The wives of the Ionic original settlers at Miletos were Karian women, whose husbands they slew.

The violences of the Karian worship are attested by what Herodotus says of the Karian residents in Egypt, at the festival of Isis at Busiris. The Egyptians at this festival manifested their feeling by beating themselves, the Karians by cutting their faces with knives (ii. 61). The Καρικὴ μοῦσα became proverbial for funeral wailings (Plato, Legg. vii. p. 800): the un-

sos,[1] whom the legends described as clothed in feminine attire, and
leading a troop of frenzied women, inspired a temporary ecstasy,
and those who resisted the inspiration, being supposed to disobey
his will, were punished either by particular judgments or by
mental terrors; while those who gave full loose to the feeling, in
the appropriate season and with the received solemnities, satisfied
his exigencies, and believed themselves to have procured immunity from such disquietudes for the future.[2] Crowds of women,
clothed with fawn-skins and bearing the sanctified thyrsus, flocked
to the solitudes of Parnassus, or Kithærôn, or Taygetus, during
the consecrated triennial period, passed the night there with
torches, and abandoned themselves to demonstrations of frantic
excitement, with dancing and clamorous invocation of the god:
they were said to tear animals limb from limb, to devour the raw

measured effusions and demonstrations of sorrow for the departed, some
times accompanied by cutting and mutilation self-inflicted by the mourner
was a distinguishing feature in Asiatics and Egyptians as compared with
Greeks. Plutarch, Consolat. ad Apollon. c. 22, p. 123. Mournful feeling
was, in fact, a sort of desecration of the genuine and primitive Grecian festival, which was a season of cheerful harmony and social enjoyment, wherein the god was believed to sympathize (εὐφροσύνη). See Xenophanês ap.
Aristot. Rhetor. ii. 25; Xenophan. Fragm. l. ed. Schneidewin; Theognis,
776; Plutarch; De Superstit. p. 169. The unfavorable comments of Diony
sius of Halicarnassus, in so far as they refer to the festivals of Greece, apply
to the foreign corruptions, not to the native character, of Grecian worship.

[1] The Lydian Hêraklês was conceived and worshipped as a man in
female attire: this idea occurs often in the Asiatic religions. Mencke,
Lydiaca, c. 8, p. 22. Διόνυσος ἄῤῥην καὶ θῆλυς. Aristid. Or. iv. p. 28;
Æschyl. Fragm. Edoni, ap. Aristoph. Thesmoph. 135. Ποδαπὸς ὁ γύννις;
τίς πάτρα; τίς ἡ στολή;

[2] Melampos cures the women (whom Dionysos has struck mad for their
resistance to his rites), παραλαβὼν τοὺς δυνατωτάτους τῶν νεανίων μετ᾽ ἀλα-
λαγμοῦ καί τινος ἐνθέου χορείας. Apollodôr. ii. 2, 7. Compare Eurip.
Bacch. 861.

Plato (Legg. vii. p. 790) gives a similar theory of the healing effect of the
Korybantic rites, which cured vague and inexplicable terrors of the mind by
means of dancing and music conjoined with religious ceremonies — αἱ τὰ
τῶν Κορυβάντων ἰάματα τελοῦσαι (the practitioners were women), αἱ τῶν
ἐκφρόνων Βακχείων ἰάσεις — ἡ τῶν ἔξωθεν κρατεῖ κίνησις προσφερομένη τὴν
ἐντὸς φοβερὰν οὖσαν καὶ μανικὴν κίνησιν — ὀρχουμένους δὲ καὶ αὐλουμένους
μετὰ θεῶν, οἷς ἂν καλλιερήσαντες ἕκαστοι θύωσιν, κατειργάσατο ἀντὶ μανικῶν
ἡμῖν διαθέσεων ἕξεις ἔμφρονας ἔχειν.

flesh, and to cut themselves without feeling the wound.[1] The men yielded to a similar impulse by noisy revels in the streets, sounding the cymbals and tambourine, and carrying the image of the god in procession.[2] It deserves to be remarked, that the Athenian women never practised these periodical mountain excursions, so common among the rest of the Greeks : they had their feminine solemnities of the Thesmophoria,[3] mournful in their character and accompanied with fasting, and their separate congregations at the temples of Aphroditê, but without any extreme or unseemly demonstrations. The state festival of the Dyonysia, in the city of Athens, was celebrated with dramatic entertain· ments, and the once rich harvest of Athenian tragedy and comedy was thrown up under its auspices. The ceremonies of the Kurêtes in Krête, originally armed dances in honor of the Idæan Zeus, seem also to have borrowed from Asia so much of fury, of self-infliction, and of mysticism, that they became at last inextricably confounded with the Phrygian Korybantes or worshippers of the Great Mother; though it appears that Grecian reserve always stopped short of the irreparable self-mutilation of Atys.

The influence of the Thracian religion upon that of the Greeks cannot be traced in detail, but the ceremonies contained in it were of a violent and fierce character, like the Phrygian, and acted upon Hellas in the same general direction as the latter. And the like may be said of the Egyptian religion, which was in this case the more operative, inasmuch as all the intellectual Greeks were naturally attracted to go and visit the wonders on the banks of the

---

[1] Described in the Bacchæ of Euripidês (140, 735, 1135, etc.). Ovid, Trist. iv. i. 41. "Utque suum Bacchis non sentit saucia vulnus, Cum furit Edonis exululata jugis." In a fragment of the poet Alkman, a Lydian by birth, the Bacchanal nymphs are represented as milking the lioness, and making cheese of the milk, during their mountain excursions and festivals. (Alkman. Fragm. 14. Schn. Compare Aristid. Orat. iv. p. 29). Clemens Alexand. Admonit. ad Gent. p. 9, Sylb.; Lucian, Dionysos, c. 3, T. iii. p. 77, Hemsterh.

[2] See the tale of Skylês in Herod. iv. 79, and Athenæus, x. p. 445. Hero· dotus mentions that the Scythians abhorred the Bacchic ceremonies, accounting the frenzy which belonged to them to be disgraceful and monstrous.

[3] Plutarch, De Isid. et Osir. c. 69, p. 378; Schol. ad Aristoph. Thesmoph There were however Bacchic ceremonies practised to a certain extent by the Athenian women. (Aristoph. Lysist. 388).

Nile ; the powerful effect produced upon them is attested by many
evidences, but especially by the interesting narrative of Herodotus. Now the Egyptian ceremonies were at once more licentious,
and more profuse in the outpouring both of joy and sorrow, than
the Greek:[1] but a still greater difference sprang from the extraordinary power, separate mode of life, minute observances, and
elaborate organization, of the priesthood. The ceremonies of
Egypt were multitudinous, but the legends concerning them were
framed by the priests, and as a general rule, seemingly, known to
the priests alone : at least they were not intended to be publicly
talked of, even by pious men. They were "holy stories," which
it was sacrilege publicly to mention, and which from this very
prohibition only took firmer hold of the minds of the Greek visitors who heard them. And thus the element of secrecy and
mystic silence — foreign to Homer, and only faintly glanced at in
Hesiod — if it was not originally derived from Egypt, at least
received from thence its greatest stimulus and diffusion. The
character of the legends themselves was naturally affected by
this change from publicity to secrecy : the secrets when revealed
would be such as to justify by their own tenor the interdict on
public divulgation: instead of being adapted, like the Homeric
mythe, to the universal sympathies and hearty interest of a
crowd of hearers, they would derive their impressiveness from
the tragical, mournful, extravagant, or terror-striking character
of the incidents.[2] Such a tendency, which appears explicable
and probable even on general grounds, was in this particular case
rendered still more certain by the coarse taste of the Egyptian
priests. That any recondite doctrine, religious or philosophical,
was attached to the mysteries or contained in the holy stories,

---

[1] " Ægyptiaca numina fere plangoribus gaudent, Græca plerumque chor
eis, barbara autem strepitu cymbalistarum et tympanistarum et choraula-
rum." (Apuleius, De Genio Socratis, v. ii. p. 149, Oudend).

[2] The legend of Dionysos and Prosymnos, as it stands in Clemens, could
never have found place in an epic poem (Admonit. ad Gent. p. 22, Sylb.).
Compare page 11 of the same work, where however he so confounds together
Phrygian, Bacchic, and Eleusinian mysteries, that one cannot distinguish
them apart.

Demetrius Phalereus says about the legends belonging to these ceremonies
— Διὸ καὶ τὰ μυστήρια λέγεται ἐν ἀλληγορίαις π ρ ὸ ς ἔ κ π λ η ξ ι ν κ α ὶ φ ρ ί
κ η ν, ὥσπερ ἐν σκότω καὶ νυκτί. (De Interpretatione, c. 101).

has never been shown, and is to the last degree improbable though the affirmative has been asserted by many learned men.

Herodotus seems to have believed that the worship and ceremonies of Dionysos generally were derived by the Greeks from Egypt, brought over by Kadmus and taught by him to Melampus: and the latter appears in the Hesiodic Catalogue as having cured the daughters of Prœtus of the mental distemper with which they had been smitten by Dionysos for rejecting his ritual. He cured them by introducing the Bacchic dance and fanatical excitement: this mythical incident is the most ancient mention of the Dionysiac solemnities presented in the same character as they bear in Euripidês. It is the general tendency of Herodotus to apply the theory of derivation from Egypt far too extensively to Grecian institutions: the orgies of Dionysos were not originally borrowed from thence, though they may have been much modified by connection with Egypt as well as with Asia. The remarkable mythe composed by Onomakritus respecting the dismemberment of Zagreus was founded upon an Egyptian tale very similar respecting the body of Osiris, who was supposed to be identical with Dionysos :[1] nor was it unsuitable to the reckless fury of the Bacchanals during their state of temporary excitement, which found a still more awful expression in the mythe of Pentheus, — torn in pieces by his own mother Agavê at the head of her companions in the ceremony, as an intruder upon the feminine rites as well as a scoffer at the god.[2] A passage in the Iliad (the authenticity of which has been contested, but even as an interpolation it must be old)[3] also recounts how Lykurgus was struck blind by Zeus for having chased away with a whip " the nurses of the mad Dionysos," and frightened the god himself into the sea to take

---

[1] See the curious treatise of Plutarch, De Isid. et Osirid. c. 11-14, p. 356, and his elaborate attempt to allegorize the legend. He seems to have conceived that the Thracian Orpheus had first introduced into Greece the mysteries both of Dêmêtêr and Dionysos, copying them from those of Isis and Osiris in Egypt. See Fragm. 84, from one of his lost works, tom, v. p 891, ed. Wyttenb.

[2] Æschylus had dramatized the story of Pentheus as well as that of Lykurgus: one of his tetralogies was the Lykurgeia (Dindorf, Æsch. Fragm. 115). A short allusion to the story of Pentheus appears in Eumenid. 25. Compare Sophocl. Antigon. 985, and the Scholia.

[3] Iliad, vi. 130. See the remarks of Mr. Payne Knight ad loc.

refuge in the arms of Thetis : and the fact, that Dionysos is so frequently represented in his mythes as encountering opposition and punishing the refractory, seems to indicate that his worship under its ecstatic form was a late phænomenon and introduced not without difficulty. The mythical Thracian Orpheus was attached as Eponymos to a new sect, who seem to have celebrated the ceremonies of Dionysos with peculiar care, minuteness and fervor, besides observing various rules in respect to food and clothing. it was the opinion of Herodotus, that these rules, as well as the Pythagorean, were borrowed from Egypt. But whether this be the fact or not, the Orphic brotherhood is itself both an evidence, and a cause, of the increased importance of the worship of Dionysos, which indeed is attested by the great dramatic poets of Athens.

The Homeric Hymns present to us, however, the religious ideas and legends of the Greeks at an earlier period, when the enthusiastic and mystic tendencies had not yet acquired their full development. Though not referable to the same age or to the same author as either the Iliad or the Odyssey, they do to a certain extent continue the same stream of feeling, and the same mythical tone and coloring, as these poems — manifesting but little evidence of Egyptian, Asiatic, or Thracian adulterations. The difference is striking between the god Dionysos as he appears in the Homeric hymn and in the Bacchæ of Euripidês. The hymnographer describes him as standing on the sea-shore, in the guise of a beautiful and richly-clothed youth, when Tyrrhenian pirates suddenly approach: they seize and bind him and drag him on board their vessel. But the bonds which they employ burst spontaneously, and leave the god free. The steersman, perceiving this with affright, points out to his companions that they have unwittingly laid hands on a god, — perhaps Zeus himself, or Apollo, or Poseidôn. He conjures them to desist, and to replace Dionysos respectfully on the shore, lest in his wrath he should visit the ship with wind and hurricane : but the crew deride his scruples, and Dionysos is carried prisoner out to sea with the ship under full sail. Miraculous circumstances soon attest both his presence and his power. Sweet-scented wine is seen to flow spontaneously about the ship, the sail and mast appear adorned with vine and ivy-leaves, and the oar-pegs with garlands.

The terrified crew now too late entreat the helmsman to steer his course for the shore, and crowd round him for protection on the poop. But their destruction is at hand: Dionysos assumes the form of a lion — a bear is seen standing near him — this bear rushes with a loud roar upon the captain, while the crew leap overboard in their agony of fright, and are changed into dolphins. There remains none but the discreet and pious steersman, to whom Dionysos addresses words of affectionate encouragement, revealing his name, parentage and dignity.[1]

This hymn, perhaps produced at the Naxian festival of Dionysos, and earlier than the time when the dithyrambic chorus became the established mode of singing the praise and glory of that god, is conceived in a spirit totally different from that of the Bacchic Telatæ, or special rites which the Bacchæ of Euripidês so abundantly extol,— rites introduced from Asia by Dionysos himself at the head of a thiasus or troop of enthusiastic women,— inflaming with temporary frenzy the minds of the women of Thebes, —not communicable except to those who approach as pious communicants,— and followed by the most tragical results to all those who fight against the god.[2] The Bacchic Teletæ, and the Bacchic feminine frenzy, were importations from abroad, as Euripides represents them, engrafted upon the joviality of the primitive Greek Dionysia; they were borrowed, in all probability, from more than one source and introduced through more than one

---

[1] See Homer, Hymn 5, Διόνυσος ἢ Λῆσται. — The satirical drama of Euripidês, the Cyclôps, extends and alters this old legend. Dionysos is carried away by the Tyrrhenian pirates, and Silênus at the head of the Bacchanals goes everywhere in search of him (Eur. Cyc. 112). The pirates are instigated against him by the hatred of Hêrê, which appears frequently as a cause of mischief to Dionysos (Bacchæ, 286). Hêrê in her anger had driven him mad when a child, and he had wandered in this state over Egypt and Syria; at length he came to Cybela in Phrygia, was purified (καθαρθείς) by Rhea, and received from her female attire (Apollodôr. iii. 5, 1, with Heyne's note). This seems to have been the legend adopted to explain the old verse of the Iliad, as well as the maddening attributes of the god generally.

There was a standing antipathy between the priestesses and the religious establishments of Hêrê and Dionysos (Plutarch, Περὶ τῶν ἐν Πλαταίαις Δαιδάλων, c. 2, tom. v. p. 755, ed. Wytt.). Plutarch ridicules the legendary reason commonly assigned for this, and provides a symbolical explanation which he thinks very satisfactory.

[2] Eurip. Bacch. 325, 464, etc.

channel, the Orphic life or brotherhood being one of the varieties. Strabo ascribes to this latter a Thracian original, considering Orpheus, Musæus, and Eumolpus as having been all Thracians.[1] It is curious to observe how, in the Bacchæ of Euripidês, the two distinct and even conflicting ideas of Dionysos come alternately forward; sometimes the old Grecian idea of the jolly and exhilarating god of wine—but more frequently the recent and imported idea of the terrific and irresistible god who unseats the reason, and whose *æstrus* can only be appeased by a willing, though temporary obedience. In the fanatical impulse which inspired the votaries of the Asiatic Rhea or Cybelê, or of the Thracian Kotys, there was nothing of spontaneous joy; it was a sacred madness, during which the soul appeared to be surrendered to a stimulus from without, and accompanied by preternatural strength and temporary sense of power,[2] — altogether distinct from the unrestrained hilarity of the original Dionysia, as we see them in the rural demes of Attica, or in the gay city of Tarentum. There was indeed a side on which the two bore some analogy, inasmuch as,

---

[1] Strabo, x. p. 471. Compare Aristid. Or. iv. p. 28.

[2] In the lost *Xantrìæ* of Æschylus, in which seems to have been included the tale of Pentheus, the goddess Λύσσα was introduced, stimulating the Bacchæ, and creating in them spasmodic excitement from head to foot: ἐκ ποδῶν δ' ἄνω Ὑπέρχεται σπαραγμὸς εἰς ἄκρον κάρα, etc. (Fragm. 155, Dindorf). His tragedy called *Edoni* also gave a terrific representation of the Bacchanals and their fury, exaggerated by the maddening music: Πίμπλησι μέλος, Μανίας ἐπαγωγὸν ὁμοκλάν (Fr. 54).

Such also is the reigning sentiment throughout the greater part of the Bacchæ of Euripidês; it is brought out still more impressively in the mournful Atys of Catullus:—

> " Dea magna, Dea Cybele, Dindymi Dea, Domina,
> Procul a meâ tuus sit furor omnis, hera, domo :
> Alios age incitatos : alios age rabidos ! "

We have only to compare this fearful influence with the description of Dikæopolis and his exuberant joviality in the festival of the rural Dionysia (Aristoph. Acharn. 1051 *seq.*; see also Plato. Legg. i. p. 637), to see how completely the foreign innovations recolored the old Grecian Dionysos, — Διόνυσος πολυγηθὴς,— who appears also in the scene of Dionysos and Ariadnê in the Symposion of Xenophôn, c. 9. The simplicity of the ancient Dionysiac processions is dwelt upon by Plutarch, De Cupidine Divitiarum, p. 527 ; and the original dithyramb addressed by Archilochus to Dionysos is an effusion of drunken hilarity (Archiloch. Frag. 69, Schneid.).

according to the religious point of view of the Greeks, even the spontaneous joy of the vintage feast was conferred by the favor and enlivened by the companionship of Dionysos. It was upon this analogy that the framers of the Bacchic orgies proceeded but they did not the less disfigure the genuine character of the old Grecian Dionysia.

Dionysos is in the conception of Pindar the Paredros or companion in worship of Dêmêtêr:[1] the worship and religious estimate of the latter has by that time undergone as great a change as that of the former, if we take our comparison with the brief description of Homer and Hesiod: she has acquired[2] much of the awful and soul-disturbing attributes of the Phrygian Cybelê. In Homer, Dêmêtêr is the goddess of the corn-field, who becomes attached to the mortal man Jasiôn; an unhappy passion, since Zeus, jealous of the connection between goddesses and men, puts him to death. In the Hesiodic Theogony, Dêmêtêr is the mother of Persephonê by Zeus, who permits Hadês to carry off the latter as his wife: moreover Dêmêtêr has, besides, by Jasiôn a son called Plutos, born in Krête. Even from Homer to Hesiod, the legend of Dêmêtêr, has been expanded and her dignity exalted; according to the usual tendency of Greek legend, the expansion goes on still further. Through Jasiôn, Dêmêtêr becomes connected with the mysteries of Samothrace; through Persephonê, with those of Eleusis. The former connection it is difficult to follow out in detail, but the latter is explained and traced to its origin in the Homeric Hymn to Dêmêtêr.

---

[1] Pindar, Isthm. vi. 3. χαλκοκρότου πάρεδρον Δημήτερος, — the epithet marks the approximation of Dêmêtêr to the Mother of the Gods. ᾗ κροτάλων τυπάνων τ᾽ ἰαχὴ, σύν τε βρόμος αὐλῶν Εὔαδεν (Homer. Hymn. xiii.), — the Mother of the Gods was worshipped by Pindar himself along with Pan; she had in his time her temple and ceremonies at Thêbes (Pyth. iii. 78; Fragm. Dithyr. 5, and the Scholia ad l.) as well as, probably, at Athens (Pausan. i. 3, 3).

Dionysos and Dêmêtêr are also brought together in the chorus of Sophoklês, Antigonê, 1072. μέδεις δὲ παγκοίνοις Ἐλευσινίας Δηοῦς ἐν κόλποις; and in Kallimachus, Hymn. Cerer. 70. Bacchus or Dionysos are in the Attic tragedians constantly confounded with the Dêmêtrian Iacchos, originally so different, — a personification of the mystic word shouted by the Eleusinian communicants. See Strabo, x. p. 468.

[2] Euripidês in his Chorus in the Helena (1320 seq.) assigns to Dêmêtêr all the attributes of Rhea, and blends the two completely into one.

Though we find different statements respecting the date as well as the origin of the Eleusinian mysteries, yet the popular belief of the Athenians, and the story which found favor at Eleusis, ascribed them to the presence and dictation of the goddess Dêmêtêr herself; just as the Bacchic rites are, according to the Bacchæ of Euripidês, first communicated and enforced on the Greeks by the personal visit of Dionysos to Thêbes, the metropolis of the Bacchic ceremonies.[1] In the Eleusinian legend, preserved by the author of the Homeric Hymn, she comes voluntarily and identifies herself with Eleusis; her past abode in Krête being briefly indicated.[2] Her visit to Eleusis is connected with the deep sorrow caused by the loss of her daughter Persephonê, who had been seized by Hadês, while gathering flowers in a meadow along with the Oceanic Nymphs, and carried off to become his wife in the under-world. In vain did the reluctant Persephonê shriek and invoke the aid of her father Zeus: he had consented to give her to Hadês, and her cries were heard only by Hekatê and Hêlios. Dêmêtêr was inconsolable at the disappearance of her daughter, but knew not where to look for her: she wandered for nine days and nights with torches in search of the lost maiden without success. At length Hêlios, the "spy of gods and men," revealed to her, in reply to her urgent prayer, the rape of Persephonê, and the permission given to Hadês by Zeus. Dêmêtêr was smitten with anger and despair: she renounced Zeus and the society of Olympus, abstained from nectar and ambrosia, and wandered on earth in grief and fasting until her form could no longer be known. In this condition she came to Eleusis, then governed by the prince Keleos. Sitting down by a well at the wayside in the guise of an old woman, she was found by the daughters of Keleos, who came hither with their pails of brass for water. In reply to their questions, she told them that she had been brought by pirates from Krête to Thorikos, and had made her escape; she then solicited from them succor and employment as a servant or as a nurse. The damsels prevailed upon their mother Metaneira to receive her, and to entrust her with the

---

[1] Sophocl. Antigon. Βακχᾶν μητρόπολιν Θήβαν.

[2] Homer, Hymn. Cerer. 123. The Hymn to Dêmêtêr has been translated, accompanied with valuable illustrative notes, by J. H. Voss (Heidelb. 1826).

nursing of the young Dêmophoôn, their late-born brother, the only son of Keleos. Dêmêtêr was received into the house of Metaneira, her dignified form still borne down by grief: she sat long silent and could not be induced either to smile or to taste food, until the maid-servant Iambê, by jests and playfulness, succeeded in amusing and rendering her cheerful. She would not taste wine, but requested a peculiar mixture of barley-meal with. water and the herb mint.[1] The child Dêmophoôn, nursed by Dêmêtêr, throve and grew up like a god, to the delight and astonishment of his parents: she gave him no food, but anointed him daily with ambrosia, and plunged him at night in the fire like a torch, where he remained unburnt. She would have rendered him immortal, had she not been prevented by the indiscreet curiosity and alarm of Metaneira, who secretly looked in at night, and shrieked with horror at the sight of her child in the fire.[2] The indignant goddess, setting the infant on the ground, now revealed her true character to Metaneira: her wan and aged look disappeared, and she stood confest in the genuine majesty of her divine shape, diffusing a dazzling brightness which illuminated the whole house. " Foolish mother," she said, "thy. want of faith has robbed thy son of immortal life. I am the exalted Dêmêtêr, the charm and comfort both of gods and men: I was preparing for thy son exemption from death and old age; now it cannot be but he must taste of both. Yet shall he be ever honored, since he has sat upon my knee and slept in my arms. Let the people of Eleusis erect for me a temple and altar on yonder hill above the fountain; I will myself prescribe to them the orgies which they must religiously perform in order to propitiate my favor."[3]

---

[1] Homer, Hymn. Cerer. 202–210.

[2] This story was also told with reference to the Egyptian goddess Isis in her wanderings. See Plutarch, De Isid. et Osirid. c. 16, p. 357.

[3] Homer, Hymn. Cerer. 274.—

'Οργια δ' αὐτὴ ἐγὼν ὑποθήσομαι, ὡς ἀν ἔπειτα
Εὐαγέως ἔρδοντες ἐμὸν νόον ἱλάσκησθε.

The same story is told in regard to the infant Achilles. His mother Thetis was taking similar measures to render him immortal, when his father Peleus interfered and prevented the consummation. Thetis immediately left him in great wrath (Apollon. Rhod. iv. 866).

The terrified Metaneira was incapable even of lifting up her child from the ground; her daughters entered at her cries, and began to embrace and tend their infant brother, but he sorrowed and could not be pacified for the loss of his divine nurse. All night they strove to appease the goddess.[1]

Strictly executing the injunctions of Dêmêtêr, Keleos convoked the people of Eleusis and erected the temple on the spot which she had pointed out. It was speedily completed, and Dêmêtêr took up her abode in it,— apart from the remaining gods, still pining with grief for the loss of her daughter, and withholding her beneficent aid from mortals. And thus she remained a whole year, — a desperate and terrible year:[2] in vain did the oxen draw the plough, and in vain was the barley-seed cast into the furrow, — Dêmêtêr suffered it not to emerge from the earth. The human race would have been starved, and the gods would have been deprived of their honors and sacrifice, had not Zeus found means to conciliate her. But this was a hard task; for Dêmêtêr resisted the entreaties of Iris and of all the other goddesses and gods whom Zeus successively sent to her. She would be satisfied with nothing less than the recovery of her daughter. At length Zeus sent Hermês to Hadês, to bring Persephonê away: Persephonê joyfully obeyed, but Hadês prevailed upon her before she departed to swallow a grain of pomegranate, which rendered it impossible for her to remain the whole year away from him.[3]

With transport did Dêmêtêr receive back her lost daughter, and the faithful Hekatê sympathized in the delight felt by both at the reunion.[4] It was now an easier undertaking to reconcile her with the gods. Her mother Rhea, sent down expressly by Zeus, descended from Olympus on the fertile Rharan plain, then smitten with barrenness like the rest of the earth: she succeeded in appeasing the indignation of Dêmêtêr, who consented again to

---

[1] Homer, Hymn. 290. —

τοῦ δ' οὐ μειλίσσετο θυμὸς,
Χειρότεραι γὰρ δή μιν ἔχον τρόφοι ἠδὲ τιθῆναι.

[2] Homer, H. Cer. 305.—

Αἰνότατον δ' ἐνιαυτὸν ἐπὶ χθόνα πουλυβότειραν
Ποίησ' ἀνθρώποις. ἰδὲ κύντατον.

[3] Hymn, v. 375.   [4] Hymn, v. 442.

put forth her relieving hand. The buried seed came up in abundance, and the earth was covered with fruit and flowers. She would have wished to retain Persephonê constantly with her, but this was impossible; and she was obliged to consent that her daughter should go down for one-third of each year to the house of Hadês, departing from her every spring at the time when the seed is sown. She then revisited Olympus, again to dwell with the gods; but before her departure, she communicated to the daughters of Keleos, and to Keleos himself, together with Triptolemus, Dioklês and Eumolpus, the divine service and the solemnities which she required to be observed in her honor.[1] And thus began the venerable mysteries of Eleusis, at her special command: the lesser mysteries, celebrated in February, in honor of Persephonê; the greater, in August, to the honor óf Dêmêtêr herself. Both are jointly patronesses of the holy city and temple.

Such is a brief sketch of the temple legend of Eleusis, set forth at length in the Homeric Hymn to Dêmêtêr. It is interesting not less as a picture of the Mater Dolorosa (in the mouth of an Athenian, Dêmêtêr and Persephonê were always the Mother and Daughter, by excellence), first an agonized sufferer, and then finally glorified, — the weal and woe of man being dependent upon her kindly feeling, — than as an illustration of the nature and grouth of Grecian legend generally. Though we now read this Hymn as pleasing poetry, to the Eleusinians, for whom it was composed, it was genuine and sacred history. They believed in the visit of Dêmêtêr to Eleusis, and in the mysteries as a revelation from her, as implicitly as they believed in her existence and power as a goddess. The Eleusinian psalmist shares this belief in common with his countrymen, and embodies it in a continuous narrative, in which the great goddesses of the place, as well as the great heroic families, figure in inseparable conjunction

---

[1] Hymn, v. 475. —

Ἡ δὲ κίουσα θεμιστοπόλοις βασιλεῦσι
Δεῖξεν, Τριπτολέμῳ τε, Διοκλέϊ τε πληξίππῳ,
Εὐμόλπου τε βίῃ, Κελέῳ θ' ἡγήτορι λαῶν
Δρησμοσύνην ἱερῶν· καὶ ἐπέφραδεν ὄργια παισὶν
Πρεσβυτέρῃς Κελέοιο, etc.

Keleos is the son of the Eponymous hero Eleusis, and his daughters, with the old epic simplicity, carry their basins to the well for water. Eumolpus, Triptolemus, Dioklês, heroic ancestors of the privileged families who continued throughout the historical times of Athens to fulfil their special hereditary functions in the Eleusinian solemnities, are among the immediate recipients of inspiration from the goddess; but chiefly does she favor Metaneira and her infant son Dêmophoôn, for the latter of whom her greatest boon is destined, and intercepted only by the weak faith of the mother. Moreover, every incident in the Hymn has a local coloring and a special reference. The well, overshadowed by an olive-tree near which Dêmêtêr had rested, the stream Kallichorus and the temple-hill, were familiar and interesting places in the eyes of every Eleusinian; the peculiar posset prepared from barley-meal with mint was always tasted by the Mysts (or communicants) after a prescribed fast, as an article in the ceremony, — while it was also the custom, at a particular spot in the processional march, to permit the free interchange of personal jokes and taunts upon individuals for the general amusement. And these two customs are connected in the Hymn with the incidents, that Dêmêtêr herself had chosen the posset as the first interruption of her long and melancholy fast, and that her sorrowful thoughts had been partially diverted by the coarse playfulness of the servant-maid Iambê. In the enlarged representation of the Eleusinian ceremonies, which became established after the incorporation of Eleusis with Athens, the part of Iambê herself was enacted by a woman, or man in woman's attire, of suitable wit and imagination, who was posted on the bridge over the Kephissos, and addressed to the passers-by in the procession, [1] especially the great men of Athens, saucy jeers, probably not less piercing than those of Aristophanês on the stage. The torchbearing Hekatê received a portion of the worship in the nocturnal ceremonies of the Eleusinia: this too is traced, in the Hymn, to her kind and affectionate sympathy with the great goddesses.

---

[1] Aristophanês, Vesp. 1363. Hesych. v. Γεφυρίς. Suidas, v. Γεφυρίζων Compare about the details of the ceremony, Clemens Alexandr. Admon. ad Gent. p. 13. A similar license of unrestrained jocularity appears in the rites of Dêmêtêr in Sicily (Diodôr. v. 4; see also Pausan. vii. 27, 4), and in the worship of Damia and Auxesia at Ægina (Herodot. v. 83).

Though all these incidents were sincerely believed by the Eleusinians as a true history of the past, and as having been the real initiatory cause of their own solemnities, it is not the less certain that they are simply mythes or legends, and not to be treated as history, either actual or exaggerated. They do not take their start from realities of the past, but from realities of the present, combined with retrospective feeling and fancy, which fills up the blank of the aforetime in a manner at once plausible and impressive. What proportion of fact there may be in the legend, or whether there be any at all, it is impossible to ascertain and useless to inquire ; for the story did not acquire belief from its approximation to real fact, but from its perfect harmony with Eleusinian faith and feeling, and from the absence of any standard of historical credibility. The little town of Eleusis derived all its importance from the solemnity of the Dêmêtria, and the Hymn which we have been considering (probably at least as old as 600 B. C.) represents the town as it stood before its absorption into the larger unity of Athens, which seems to have produced an alteration of its legends and an increase of dignity in its great festival. In the faith of an Eleusinian, the religious as well as the patriotic antiquities of his native town were connected with this capital solemnity. The divine legend of the sufferings of Dêmêtêr and her visit to Eleusis was to him that which the heroic legend of Adrastus and the Siege of Thêbes was to a Sikyonian, or that of Erechtheus and Athênê to an Athenian grouping together in the same scene and story the goddess and the heroic fathers of the town. If our information were fuller, we should probably find abundance of other legends respecting the Dêmêtria : the Gephyræi of Athens, to whom belonged the celebrated Harmodios and Aristogeitôn, and who possessed special Orgies of Dêmêtêr the Sorrowful, to which no man foreign to their Gens was ever admitted,[1] would doubtless have told stories not only different but contradictory; and even in other Eleusinian mythes we discover Eumolpus as king of Eleusis, son of Poseidôn, and a Thracian, completely different from the character which he bears in the Hymn before us.[2] Neither discrepancies nor want of

---

[1] Herodot, v, 61.
[2] Pausan. i. 38, 3; Apollodôr. iii. 15, 4. Heyne in his Note admits seve-

evidence, in reference to alleged antiquities, shocked the faith of a non-historical public. What they wanted was a picture of the past, impressive to their feelings and plausible to their imagination; and it is important to the reader to remember, while he reads either the divine legends which we are now illustrating or the heroic legends to which we shall soon approach, that he is dealing with a past which never was present, — a region essentially mythical, neither approachable by the critic nor mensurable by the chronologer.

The tale respecting the visit of Dêmêtêr, which was told by the ancient Gens, called the Phytalids,[1] in reference to another temple of Dêmêtêr between Athens and Eleusis, and also by the Megarians in reference to a Dêmêtrion near their city, acquired under the auspices of Athens still further extension. The goddess was reported to have first communicated to Triptolemus at Eleusis the art of sowing corn, which by his intervention was disseminated all over the earth. And thus the Athenians took credit to themselves for having been the medium of communication from the gods to man of all the inestimable blessings of agriculture, which they affirmed to have been first exhibited on the fertile Rharian plain near Eleusis. Such pretensions are not to be found in the old Homeric hymn. The festival of the Thesmophoria, celebrated in honor of Dêmêtêr Thesmophoros at Athens, was altogether different from the Eleusinia, in this material respect, as well as others, that all males were excluded, and women only were allowed to partake in it: the surname Thesmophorus gave occasion to new legends in which the goddess was glorified as the first authoress of laws and legal sanctions to mankind.[2] This festival, for women apart and alone, was also

ral persons named Eumolpus. Compare Isokratês, Panegyr. p. 55. Philochorus the Attic antiquary could not have received the legend of the Eleusinian Hymn, from the different account which he gave respecting the rape of Persephonê (Philoch. Fragm. 46, ed. Didot), and also respecting Keleos (Fr. 28, ibid.).

[1] Phytalus, the Eponym or godfather of this gens, had received Dêmêtêr as a guest in his house, when she first presented mankind with the fruit of the fig-tree. (Pausan. i. 37, 2.)

[2] Kallimach. Hymn. Cerer. 19. Sophoklês, Triptolemos, Frag 1. Cicero, Legg. ii. 14, and the note of Servius ad Virgil. Æn. iv. 58.

celebrated at Paros, at Ephesus, and in many other parts of Greece.[1] Altogether, Dêmêtêr and Dionysos, as the Grecian counterparts of the Egyptian Isis and Osiris, seem to have been the great recipients of the new sacred rites borrowed from Egypt, before the worship of Isis in her own name was introduced into Greece: their solemnities became more frequently recluse and mysterious than those of the other deities. The importance of Dêmêtêr to the collective nationality of Greece may be gathered from the fact that her temple was erected at Thermopylæ, the spot where the Amphiktyonic assemblies were held, close by the temple of the Eponymous hero Amphiktyôn himself, and under the surname of the Amphiktyonic Dêmêtêr.[2]

We now pass to another and not less important celestial personage — Apollo.

The legends of Dêlos and Delphi, embodied in the Homeric Hymn to Apollo, indicate, if not a greater dignity, at least a more widely diffused worship of that god than even of Dêmêtêr. The Hymn is, in point of fact, an aggregate of two separate compositions, one emanating from an Ionic bard at Dêlos, the other from Delphi. The first details the birth, the second the mature divine efficiency, of Apollo; but both alike present the unaffected charm as well as the characteristic peculiarities of Grecian mythical narrative. The hymnographer sings, and his hearers accept in perfect good faith, a history of the past; but it is a past, imagined partly as an introductory explanation to the present, partly as a means of glorifying the god. The island of Dêlos was the accredited birth-place of Apollo, and is also the place in which he chiefly delights, where the great and brilliant Ionic festival is periodically convened in his honor. Yet it is a rock narrow, barren, and uninviting: how came so glorious a privilege to be awarded to it? This the poet takes upon himself to explain. Lêtô, pregnant with Apollo, and persecuted by the jealous Hêrê, could find no spot wherein to give birth to her offspring. In vain did she address herself to numerous places in Greece, the Asiatic coast and the intermediate islands; all were

---

[1] Herodot. vi. 16, 134. ἑρκος Θεσμοφόρου Δήμητρος — τὰ ἐς ἔρσενα γόνον ἄῥῤητα ἱερά.

[2] Herodot. vii. 200.

terrified at the wrath of Hêrê, and refused to harbor her. As a last resort, she approached the rejected and repulsive island of Dêlos, and promised that, if shelter were granted to her in her forlorn condition, the island should become the chosen resort of Apollo as well as the site of his temple with its rich accompanying solemnities.[1] Dêlos joyfully consented, but not without many apprehensions that the potent Apollo would despise her unworthiness, and not without exacting a formal oath from Lêtô,—who was then admitted to the desired protection, and duly accomplished her long and painful labor. Though Diônê, Rhea, Themis and Amphitritê came to soothe and succor her, yet Hêrê kept away the goddess presiding over childbirth, Eileithyia, and thus cruelly prolonged her pangs. At length Eileithyia came, and Apollo was born. Hardly had Apollo tasted, from the hands of Themis, the immortal food, nectar and ambrosia, when he burst at once his infant bands, and displayed himself in full divine form and strength, claiming his characteristic attributes of the bow and the harp, and his privileged function of announcing beforehand to mankind the designs of Zeus. The promise made by Lêtô to Dêlos was faithfully performed : amidst the numberless other temples and groves which men provided for him, he ever preferred that island as his permanent residence, and there the Ionians with their wives and children, and all their "bravery," congregated periodically from their different cities to glorify him. Dance and song and athletic contests adorned the solemnity, and the countless ships, wealth, and grace of the multitudinous Ionians had the air of an assembly of gods. The Delian maidens, servants of Apollo, sang hymns to the glory of the god, as well as of Artemis and Lêtô, intermingled with adventures of foregone men and women, to the delight of the listening crowd. The blind itinerant bard of Chios (composer of this the Homeric hymn, and confounded in antiquity with the author of the Iliad) had found honor and acceptance at this festival, and commends himself, in a

---

[1] According to another legend, Lêtô was said to have been conveyed from the Hyperboreans to Dêlos in twelve days, in the form of a she-wolf, to escape the jealous eye of Hêrê. In connection with this legend, it was affirmed that the she-wolves always brought forth their young only during these twelve days in the year (Aristot. Hist. Animal. vii. 35).

touching farewell strain, to the remembrance and sympathy of the Delian maidens.[1]

But Dêlos was not an oracular spot: Apollo did not manifest himself there as revealer of the futurities of Zeus. A place must be found where this beneficent function, without which mankind would perish under the innumerable doubts and perplexities of life, may be exercised and rendered available. Apollo himself descends from Olympus to make choice of a suitable site: the hymnographer knows a thousand other adventures of the god which he might sing, but he prefers this memorable incident, the charter and patent of consecration for the Delphian temple. Many different places did Apollo inspect; he surveyed the country of the Magnêtes and the Perrhæbians, came to Iôlkos, and passed over from thence to Eubœa and the plain of Lelanton. But even this fertile spot did not please him: he crossed the Euripus to Bœotia, passed by Teumêssus and Mykalêssus, and the then inaccessible and unoccupied forest on which the city of Thêbes afterwards stood. He next proceeded to Onchêstos, but the grove of Poseidôn was already established there; next across the Kêphissus to Okalea, Haliartus, and the agreeable plain and much-frequented fountain of Delphusa, or Tilphusa. Pleased with the place, Apollo prepared to establish his oracle there, but Tilphusa was proud of the beauty of her own site, and did not choose that her glory should be eclipsed by that of the god.[2] She alarmed him with the apprehension that the chariots which contended in her plain, and the horses and mules which watered at her fountain would disturb the solemnity of his oracle; and she thus induced him to proceed onward to the southern side of Parnassus, overhanging the harbor of Krissa. Here he established his oracle, in the mountainous site not frequented by chariots and horses, and near to a fountain, which however was guarded by a vast and terrific serpent, once the nurse of the monster Typhaôn. This serpent Apollo slew with an arrow, and suffered its body to rot in the sun: hence the name of the place, Pythô,[3] and the surname of the Pythian Apollo. The plan of his temple being marked out, it was built by Trophônios and Agamédês,

---

[1] Hom. Hymn. Apoll. i. 179.   [2] Hom. Hymn. Apoll. 262.

[3] Hom. Hymn. 363 — πύθεσθαι, to rot.

aided by a crowd of forward auxiliaries from the neighborhood.
He now discovered with indignation, however, that Tilphusa had
cheated him, and went back with swift step to resent it. "Thou
shalt not thus," he said, "succeed in thy fraud and retain thy
beautiful water; the glory of the place shall be mine, and not
thine alone." Thus saying, he tumbled down a crag upon the
fountain, and obstructed her limped current: establishing an altar
for himself in a grove hard by near another spring, where men
still worship him as Apollo Tilphusios, because of his severe
vengeance upon the once beautiful Tilphusa.[1]

Apollo next stood in need of chosen ministers to take care of
his temple and sacrifice, and to pronounce his responses at Pythô.
Descrying a ship, "containing many and good men," bound on
traffic from the Minoian Knossus in Krête, to Pylus in Peloponnêsus, he resolved to make use of the ship and her crew for his
purpose. Assuming the shape of a vast dolphin, he splashed
about and shook the vessel so as to strike the mariners with terror, while he sent a strong wind, which impelled her along the
coast of Peloponnêsus into the Corinthian Gulf, and finally to the
harbor of Krissa, where she ran aground. The affrighted crew
did not dare to disembark: but Apollo was seen standing on the
shore in the guise of a vigorous youth, and inquired who they
were, and what was their business. The leader of the Krêtans
recounted in reply their miraculous and compulsory voyage, when
Apollo revealed himself as the author and contriver of it, announcing to them the honorable function and the dignified post to which
he destined them.[2] They followed him by his orders to the rocky
Pytho on Parnassus, singing the solemn Io-Paian such as it is sung
in Krête, while the god himself marched at their head, with his
fine form and lofty step, playing on the harp. He showed them
the temple and site of the oracle, and directed them to worship
him as Apollo Delphinios, because they had first seen him in the
shape of a dolphin. "But how," they inquired, "are we to live in
a spot where there is neither corn, nor vine, nor pasturage?"
"Ye silly mortals," answered the god, "who look only for toil and
privation, know that an easier lot is yours. Ye shall live by the
cattle whom crowds of pious visitors will bring to the temple: ye

---

[1] Hom. Hymn. Apoll. 381.   [2] Hom. Hymn. Apoll 475 *sqq*

shall need only the knife to be constantly ready for sacrifice.[1] Your duty will be to guard my temple, and to officiate as ministers at my feasts : but if ye be guilty of wrong or insolence, either by word or deed, ye shall become the slaves of other men, and shall remain so forever. Take heed of the word and the warning."

Such are the legends of Dêlos and Delphi, according to the Homeric Hymn to Apollo. The specific functions of the god, and the chief localities of his worship, together with the surnames attached to them, are thus historically explained, being connected with his past acts and adventures. Though these are to us only interesting poetry, yet to those who heard them sung they possessed all the requisites of history, and were fully believed as such; not because they were partially founded in reality, but because they ran in complete harmony with the feelings; and, so long as that condition was fulfilled, it was not the fashion of the time to canvass truth or falsehood. The narrative is purely personal, without any discernible symbolized doctrine or allegory, to serve as a supposed ulterior purpose : the particular deeds ascribed to Apollo grow out of the general preconceptions as to his attributes, combined with the present realities of his worship. It is neither history nor allegory, but simple mythe or legend.

The worship of Apollo is among the most ancient, capital, and strongly marked facts of the Grecian world, and widely diffused over every branch of the race. It is older than the Iliad or Odyssey, in the latter of which both Pytho and Dêlos are noted, though Dêlos is not named in the former. But the ancient Apollo is different in more respects than one from the Apollo of later times. He is in an especial manner the god of the Trojans, unfriendly to the Greeks, and especially to Achilles; he has, moreover, only two primary attributes, his bow and his prophetic powers, without any distinct connection either with the harp, or with medicine, or with the sun, all which in later times he came to comprehend. He is not only, as Apollo Karneius, the chief

---

[1] Homer. Hymn. Apoll. 535.—

Δεξιτέρῃ μάλ' ἕκαστος ἔχων ἐν χειρὶ μάχαιραν
Σφάζειν αἰεὶ μῆλα · τὰ δ' ἄφθονα πάντα πάρεσται,
Ὅσσα ἐμοίγ' ἀγάγωσι περίκλυτα φῦλ' ἀνθρώπων.

god of the Doric race, but also (under the surname of Patrôus)
the great protecting divinity of the gentile tie among the Ionians:[1]
he is moreover the guide and stimulus to Grecian colonization,
scarcely any colony being ever sent out without encouragement
and direction from the oracle at Delphi: Apollo Archêgetês is
one of his great surnames.[2] His temple lends sanctity to the
meetings of the Amphiktyonic assembly, and he is always in
filial subordination and harmony with his father Zeus: Delphi
and Olympia are never found in conflict. In the Iliad, the warm
and earnest patrons of the Greeks are Hêrê, Athênê, and Poseidôn: here too Zeus and Apollo are seen in harmony, for Zeus is
decidedly well-inclined to the Trojans, and reluctantly sacrifices
them to the importunity of the two great goddesses.[3] The worship of the Sminthian Apollo, in various parts of the Troad and
the neighboring territory, dates before the earliest periods of
Æolic colonization:[4] hence the zealous patronage of Troy ascribed to him in the Iliad. Altogether, however, the distribution
and partialities of the gods in that poem are different from what
they become in later times, — a difference which our means of
information do not enable us satisfactorily to explain. Besides
the Delphian temple, Apollo had numerous temples throughout
Greece, and oracles at Abæ in Phôkis, on the Mount Ptôon, and
at Tegyra in Bœotia, where he was said to have been born,[5] at
Branchidæ near Milêtus, at Klarus in Asia Minor, and at Patara
in Lykia. He was not the only oracular god: Zeus at Dodona
and at Olympia gave responses also: the gods or heroes Trophônius, Amphiaraus, Amphilochus, Mopsus, etc., each at his own

---

[1] Harpocration v. Ἀπόλλων πατρῷος and Ἑρκεῖος Ζεύς. Apollo Delphinios also belongs to the Ionic Greeks generally. Strabo, iv. 179.

[2] Thucydid. vi. 3; Kallimach. Hymn. Apoll. 56.—

Φοῖβος γὰρ ἀεὶ πολίεσσι φιληδεῖ
Κτιζομέναις, αὐτὸς δὲ θεμείλια Φοῖβος ὑφαίνει.

[3] Iliad, iv. 30–46.

[4] Iliad, i. 38, 451; Stephan. Byz. Ἴλιον, Τένεδος. See also Klausen. Æneas
und die Penaten, b. i. p. 69. The worship of Apollo Sminthios and the festival of the Sminthia at Alexandria Troas lasted down to the time of Menander the rhetor, at the close of the third century after Christ.

[5] Plutarch. Defect. Oracul. c. 5, p. 412; c. 8, p. 414; Steph. Byz. v. Τεγύρα
The temple of the Ptôan Apollo had acquired celebrity before the days of
the poet Asius. Pausan. ix. 23, 3.

sanctuary and in his own prescribed manner, rendered the same service.

The two legends of Delphi and Dêlos, above noticed, form of course a very insignificant fraction of the narratives which once existed respecting the great and venerated Apollo. They serve only as specimens, and as very early specimens,[1] to illustrate what these divine mythes were, and what was the turn of Grecian faith and imagination. The constantly recurring festivals of the gods caused an incessant demand for new mythes respecting them, or at least for varieties and reproductions of the old mythes. Even during the third century of the Christian æra, in the time of the rhêtôr Menander, when the old forms of Paganism were waning and when the stock of mythes in existence was extremely abundant, we see this demand in great force; but it was incomparably more operative in those earlier times when the creative vein of the Grecian mind yet retained its pristine and unfaded richness. Each god had many different surnames, temples, groves, and solemnities; with each of which was connected more or less of mythical narrative, originally hatched in the prolific and spontaneous fancy of a believing neighborhood, to be afterwards expanded, adorned and diffused by the song of the poet. The earliest subject of competition[2] at the great Pythian festival was the singing of a hymn in honor of Apollo : other *agones* were subsequently added, but the ode or hymn constitu-

---

[1] The legend which Ephorus followed about the establishment of the Delphian temple was something radically different from the Homeric Hymn (Ephori Fragm. 70, ed. Didot) : his narrative went far to politicize and rationalize the story. The progeny of Apollo was very numerous, and of the most diverse attributes; he was father of the Korybantes (Pherekydes, Fragm. 6, ed. Didot), as well as of Asklêpios and Aristæus (Schol. Apollon. Rhod. ii. 500; Apollodôr. iii. 10, 3).

[2] Strabo, ix. p. 421. Menander the Rhetor (Ap. Walz. Coll. Rhett. t. ix. p. 136) gives an elaborate classification of hymns to the gods, distinguishing them into nine classes, — κλητικοί, ἀποπεμπτικοί, φυσικοί, μυϑικοί, γενεαλογικοί, πεπλασμένοι, εὐκτικοί, ἀπευκτικοί, μικτοί : — the second class had reference to the temporary absences or departure of a god to some distant place, which were often admitted in the ancient religion. Sappho and Alkman in their *kletic* hymns invoked the gods from many different places, — τὴν μὲν γὰρ 'Αρτέμιν ἐκ μυρίων μὲν ὀρεων, μυρίων δὲ πόλεων, ἔτι δὲ ποτάμων, ἀνακαλεῖ, — also Aphroditê and Apollo, etc. All these songs were full of adventures and details respecting the gods, — in other words of legendary matter.

ted the fundamental attribute of the solemnity: the Pythia at Sikyon and elsewhere were probably framed on a similar footing. So too at the ancient and celebrated Charitêsia, or festival of the Charites, at Orchomenos, the rivalry of the poets in their various modes of composition both began and continued as the predominant feature : [1] and the inestimable treasures yet remaining to us of Attic tragedy and comedy, are gleanings from the once numerous dramas exhibited at the solemnity of the Dionysia. The Ephesians gave considerable rewards for the best hymns in honor of Artemis, to be sung at her temple.[2] And the early lyric poets of Greece, though their works have not descended to us, devoted their genius largely to similar productions, as may be seen by the titles and fragments yet remaining.

Both the Christian and the Mahomedan religions have begun during the historical age, have been propagated from one common centre, and have been erected upon the ruins of a different pre-existing faith. With none of these particulars did Grecian Paganism correspond. It took rise in an age of imagination and feeling simply, without the restraints, as well as without the aid, of writing or records, of history or philosophy: it was, as a general rule, the spontaneous product of many separate tribes and localities, imitation and propagation operating as subordinate causes ; it was moreover a primordial faith, as far as our means of information enable us to discover. These considerations explain to us two facts in the history of the early Pagan mind: first, the divine mythes, the matter of their religion, constituted also the matter of their earliest history ; next, these mythes harmonized with each other only in their general types, but differed incurably in respect of particular incidents. The poet who sung a new adventure of Apollo, the trace of which he might have heard in some remote locality, would take care that it should be agreeable to the general conceptions which his hearers entertained respecting the god. He would not ascribe the cestus or amorous influences to Athênê, nor armed interference and the ægis to Aphroditê ; but, provided he maintained this general keeping, he might indulge his fancy without restraint in the particular

---

[1] Pindar, Olymp. xiv.; Boeckh, Staatshaushaltung der Athener, Appendix, § xx. p. 357.

[2] Alexander Ætolus, apud Macrobium, Saturn. v. 22.

events of the story.[1] The feelings and faith of his hearers went along with him, and there were no critical scruples to hold them back: to scrutinize the alleged proceedings of the gods was repulsive, and to disbelieve them impious. And thus these divine mythes, though they had their root simply in religious feelings, and though they presented great discrepancies of fact, served nevertheless as primitive matter of history to an early Greek: they were the only narratives, at once publicly accredited and interesting, which he possessed. To them were aggregated the heroic mythes (to which we shall proceed presently), — indeed the two are inseparably blended, gods, heroes and men almost always appearing in the same picture, — analogous both in their structure and their genesis, and differing chiefly in the circumstance that they sprang from the type of a hero instead of from that of a god.

We are not to be astonished if we find Aphroditê, in the Iliad, born from Zeus and Dionê, — and in the Theogony of Hesiod, generated from the foam on the sea after the mutilation of Uranos; nor if in the Odyssey she appears as the wife of Hêphæstos, while in the Theogony the latter is married to Aglaia, and Aphroditê is described as mother of three children by Arês.[2] The Homeric hymn to Aphroditê details the legend of Aphroditê and Anchisês, which is presupposed in the Iliad as the parentage of Æneas: but the author of the hymn, probably sung at one of the festivals of Aphroditê in Cyprus, represents the goddess as ashamed of her passion for a mortal, and as enjoining Anchisês under severe menaces not to reveal who the mother of Æneas was;[3] while in the Iliad she has no scruple in publicly

---

[1] The birth of Apollo and Artemis from Zeus and Lêtô is among the oldest and most generally admitted facts in the Grecian divine legends. Yet Æschylus did not scruple to describe Artemis publicly as daughter of Dêmêtêr (Herodot. ii. 156; Pausan. viii. 37, 3). Herodotus thinks that he copied this innovation from the Egyptians, who affirmed that Apollo and Artemis were the sons of Dionysos and Isis.

The number and discrepancies of the mythes respecting each god are attested by the fruitless attempts of learned Greeks to escape the necessity of rejecting any of them by multiplying homonymous personages, — three persons named Zeus; five named Athênê; six named Apollo, etc. (Cicero, de Natur. Deor. iii. 21: Clemen. Alexand. Admon. ad Gent. p. 17).

[2] Hesiod, Theogon. 188, 934, 945; Homer, Iliad, v. 371; Odyss. viii. 268

[3] Homer, Hymn. Vener. 248, 286; Homer, Iliad, v. 320, 386.

owning him, and he passes everywhere as her acknowledged son. Aphroditê is described in the hymn as herself cold and unimpress ible, but ever active and irresistible in inspiring amorous feelings to gods, to men, and to animals. Three goddesses are record- ed as memorable exceptions to her universal empire, — Athênê, Artemis, and Hestia or Vesta. Aphroditê was one of the most important of all the goddesses in the mythical world; for the number of interesting, pathetic and tragical adventures deducible from misplaced or unhappy passion was of course very great; and in most of these cases the intervention of Aphroditê was usually prefixed, with some legend to explain why she manifested herself. Her range of action grows wider in the later epic and lyric and tragic poets than in Homer.[1]

Athênê, the man-goddess,[2] born from the head of Zeus, with- out a mother and without feminine sympathies, is the antithesis partly of Aphroditê, partly of the effeminate or womanized god Dionysos — the latter is an importation from Asia, but Athênê is a Greek conception — the type of composed, majestic and unre- lenting force. It appears however as if this goddess had been conceived in a different manner in different parts of Greece. For we find ascribed to her, in some of the legends, attributes of in- dustry and home-keeping; she is represented as the companion

---

[1] A large proportion of the Hesiodic epic related to the exploits and adven- tures of the heroic women, — the Catalogue of Women and the Eoiai em bodied a string of such narratives. Hesiod and Stesichorus explained the conduct of Helen and Klytæmnestra by the anger of Aphroditê, caused by the neglect of their father Tyndareus to sacrifice to her (Hesiod, Fragm. 59, ed. Duntzer; Stesichor. Fragm. 9, ed. Schneidewin): the irresistible ascen- dency of Aphroditê is set forth in the Hippolytus of Euripidês not less for- cibly than that of Dionysos in the Bacchæ. The character of Daphnis the herdsman, well-known from the first Idyll of Theocritus, and illustrating the destroying force of Aphroditê, appears to have been first introduced into Greek poetry by Stesichorus (see Klausen, Æneas, und die Penaten, vol. i. pp. 526–529). Compare a striking piece among the Fragmenta Incerta of Sophoklês (Fr. 63, Brunck) and Euripid. Troad. 946, 995, 1048. Even in the Opp. et Di. of Hesiod, Aphroditê is conceived rather as a disturbing and injurious influence (v. 65).

Adonis owes his renown to the Alexandrine poets and their contemporary sovereigns (see Bion's Idyll and the Adoniazusæ of Theocritus). The favor- ites of Aphroditê, even as counted up by the diligence of Clemens Alexan- drinus, are however very few in number. (Admonitio ad Gent. p. 12, Sylb.)

[2] Ἀνδροθέᾳ δῶρον . . . . Ἀθάνᾳ Simmias Rhodius; Πέλεκυς, ap. He- phæstion. c. 9. p. 54, Gaisford.

of Hêphæstos, patronizing handicraft, and expert at the loom and
the spindle: the Athenian potters worshipped her along with
Promêtheus. Such traits of character do not square with the
formidable ægis and the massive and crushing spear which Homer
and most of the mythes assign to her. There probably were at first
at least two different types of Athênê, and their coalescence has
partially obliterated the less marked of the two.[1] Athênê is the
constant and watchful protectress of Hêraklês: she is also locally
identified with the soil and people of Athens, even in the Iliad:
Erechtheus, the Athenian, is born of the earth, but Athênê brings
him up, nourishes him, and lodges him in her own temple, where
the Athenians annually worship him with sacrifice and solemnities.[2] It was altogether impossible to make Erechtheus son of
Athênê,—the type of the goddess forbade it; but the Athenian
mythe-creators, though they found this barrier impassable, strove
to approach to it as near as they could, and the description which
they give of the birth of Erichthonios, at once un-Homeric and
unseemly, presents something like the phantom of maternity.[3]

The huntress Artemis, in Arcadia and in Greece proper generally, exhibits a well-defined type with which the legends
respecting her are tolerably consistent. But the Ephesian as
well as the Tauric Artemis partakes more of the Asiatic character, and has borrowed the attributes of the Lydian Great Mother
as well as of an indigenous Tauric Virgin :[4] this Ephesian Arte-

---

[1] Apollodôr. ap. Schol. ad Sophokl. Œdip. vol. 57; Pausan. i. 24, 3; ix. 26,
3; Diodôr. v. 73; Plato, Legg. xi. p. 920. In the Opp. et Di. of Hesiod,
the carpenter is the servant of Athênê (429): see also Phereklos the τέκτων
in the Iliad, v. 61: compare viii. 385; Odyss. viii. 493; and the Homeric
Hymn, to Aphroditê, v. 12. The learned article of O. Müller (in the Ency-
clopædia of Ersch and Gruber, since republished among his Kleine Deutsche
Schriften, p 134 seq.), *Pallas Athênê*, brings together all that can be known
about this goddess.

[2] Iliad, ii. 546; viii. 362.

[3] Apollodôr. iii. 4, 6. Compare the vague language of Plato, Kritias, c.
iv., and Ovid, Metamorph. ii. 757.

[4] Herodot. iv. 103; Strabo, xii. p. 534; xiii. p. 650. About the Ephesian
Artemis, see Guhl, Ephesiaca (Berlin, 1843), p. 79 sqq.; Aristoph. Nub. 590;
Autokrates in Tympanistis apud Ælian. Hist. Animal. xii. 9; and Spanheim
ad Kallimach. Hymn. Dian. 36. The dances in honor of Artemis sometimes appear to have approached to the frenzied style of Bacchanal movement. See the words of Timotheus ap. Plutarch. de Audiend. Poet. p. 22,
c 4, and περὶ Δεισιδ. c. 10, p. 170, also Aristoph. Lysist. 1314. They seem

mis passed to the colonies of Phokæa and Milêtus.[1] The
Homeric Artemis shares with her brother Apollo in the dexterous
use of the far-striking bow, and sudden death is described by the
poet as inflicted by her gentle arrow. The jealousy of the gods
at the withholding of honors and sacrifices, or at the presumption
of mortals in contending with them, — a point of character so
frequently recurring in the types of the Grecian gods, — manifests itself in the legends of Artemis : the memorable Kalydônian boar is sent by her as a visitation upon Œneus, because he
had omitted to sacrifice to her, while he did honor to other gods.[2]
The Arcadian heroine Atalanta is however a reproduction of
Artemis, with little or no difference, and the goddess is sometimes
confounded even with her attendant nymphs.

The mighty Poseidôn, the earth-shaker and the ruler of the
sea, is second only to Zeus in power, but has no share in those
imperial and superintending capacities which the Father of gods
and men exhibits. He numbers a numerous heroic progeny,
usually men of great corporeal strength, and many of them
belonging to the Æolic race: the great Neleid family of Pylus
trace their origin up to him; and he is also the father of Polyphêmus the Cyclôps, whose well-earned suffering he cruelly
revenges upon Odysseus. The island of Kalaureia is his Dêlos,[3]
and there was held in it an old local Amphiktyony, for the purpose of rendering to him joint honor and sacrifice : the isthmus
of Corinth, Helikê in Achaia, and Onchêstos in Bœotia, are also
residences which he much affects, and where he is solemnly worshipped. But the abode which he originally and specially selected for himself was the Acropolis of Athens, where by a blow
of his trident he produced a well of water in the rock : Athênê
came afterwards and claimed the spot for herself, planting in
token of possession the olive-tree which stood in the sacred grove
of Pandrosos : and the decision either of the autochthonous

---

to have been often celebrated in the solitudes of the mountains, which were
the favorite resort of Artemis (Kallimach. Hymn. Dian. 19), and these
ὀρειβάσιαι were always causes predisposing to fanatical excitement.

[1] Strabo, iv. p. 179.   [2] Iliad, ix. 529.

[3] Strabo, viii. p. 374. According to the old poem called Eumolpia, ascribed to Musæus, the oracle of Delphi originally belonged to Poseidôn and
Gæa, jointly: from Gæa it passed to Themis, and from her to Apollo, to
whom Poseidôn also made over his share as a compensation for the surrender of Kalaureia to him. (Pausan. x. 5, 3).

Cecrops, or of Erechtheus, awarded to her the preference, much to the displeasure of Poseidôn. Either on this account, or on account of the death of his son Eumolpus, slain in assisting the Eleusinians against Erechtheus, the Attic mythes ascribed to Poseidôn great enmity against the Erechtheid family, which he is asserted to have ultimately overthrown : Theseus, whose glorious reign and deeds succeeded to that family, is said to have been really his son.[1] In several other places, — in Ægina, Argos and Naxos, — Poseidôn had disputed the privileges of patron-god with Zeus, Hêrê and Dionysos : he was worsted in all, but bore his defeat patiently.[2] Poseidôn endured a long slavery, in common with Apollo, gods as they were,[3] under Laomedôn, king of Troy, at the command and condemnation of Zeus : the two gods rebuilt the walls of the city, which had been destroyed by Hêraklês. When their time was expired, the insolent Laomedôn withheld from them the stipulated reward, and even accompanied its refusal with appalling threats; and the subsequent animosity of the god against Troy was greatly determined by the sentiment of this injustice.[4] Such periods of servitude, inflicted upon individual gods, are among the most remarkable of all the incidents in the divine legends. We find Apollo on another occasion condemned to serve Admêtus, king of Pheræ, as a punishment for having killed the Cyclôpes, and Hêraklês also is sold as a slave to Omphalê. Even the fierce Arês, overpowered and imprisoned for a long time by the two Alôids,[5] is ultimately liberated only by extraneous aid. Such narratives attest the discursive range of Grecian fancy in reference to the gods, as well as the perfect commingling of things and persons, divine and human, in their conceptions of the past. The god who serves is for the time degraded: but the supreme god who commands the servitude is in the like proportion exalted, whilst the idea of some sort of order and government among these superhuman beings was never lost sight of. Nevertheless the mythes respecting the servitude of the gods became obnoxious afterwards, along with many others, to severe criticism on the part of philosophers.

---

[1] Apollodôr. iii. 14, 1; iii. 15, 3, 5.   [2] Plutarch, Sympos. viii. 6, p. 741.
[3] Iliad, ii. 716, 766 ; Euripid. Alkestis, 2.   See Panyasis, Fragm. 12, p. 24, ed. Düntzer.
[4] Iliad, vii. 452; xxi. 459.   [5] Iliad, v. 386.

The proud, jealous, and bitter Hêrê,—the goddess of the once-wealthy Mykênæ, the *fax et focus* of the Trojan war, and the ever-present protectress of Jasôn in the Argonautic expedition, [1] — occupies an indispensable station in the mythical world. As the daughter of Kronos and wife of Zeus, she fills a throne from whence he cannot dislodge her, and which gives her a right perpetually to grumble and to thwart him.[2] Her unmeasured jealousy of the female favorites of Zeus, and her antipathy against his sons, especially against Hêraklês, has been the suggesting cause of innumerable mythes: the general type of her character stands here clearly marked, as furnishing both stimulus and guide to the mythopœic fancy. The "Sacred Wedding," or marriage of Zeus and Hêrê, was familiar to epithalamic poets long before it became a theme for the spiritualizing ingenuity of critics.

Hêphæstos is the son of Hêrê without a father, and stands to her in the same relation as Athênê to Zeus : her pride and want of sympathy are manifested by her casting him out at once in consequence of his deformity.[3] He is the god of fire, and especially of fire in its practical applications to handicraft, and is indispensable as the right-hand and instrument of the gods. His skill and his deformity appear alternately as the source of mythical stories : wherever exquisite and effective fabrication is intended to be designated, Hêphæstos is announced as the maker, although in this function the type of his character is reproduced in Dædalos. In the Attic legends he appears intimately united both with Promêtheus and with Athênê, in conjunction with whom he was worshipped at Kolônus near Athens. Lemnos was the favorite residence of Hêphæstos; and if we possessed more knowledge of this island and its town Hêphæstias, we should doubtless find abundant legends detailing his adventures and interventions.

The chaste, still, and home-keeping Hestia, goddess of the family hearth, is far less fruitful in mythical narratives, in spite of her very superior dignity, than the knavish, smooth-tongued, keen, and acquisitive Hermês. His function of messenger of the

---

[1] Iliad, iv. 51 ; Odyss. xii. 72.
[2] Iliad, i. 544 ; iv. 29–38 : viii. 408.   [3] Iliad, xviii. 306.

gods brings him perpetually on the stage, and affords ample scope for portraying the features of his character. The Homeric hymn to Hermês describes the scene and circumstances of his birth, and the almost instantaneous manifestation, even in infancy, of his peculiar attributes; it explains the friendly footing on which he stood with Apollo, — the interchange of gifts and functions between them, — and lastly, the inviolate security of all the wealth and offerings in the Delphian temple, exposed as they were to thieves without any visible protection. Such was the innate cleverness and talent of Hermês, that on the day he was born he invented the lyre, stringing the seven chords on the shell of a tortoise :[1] and he also stole the cattle of Apollo in Pieria, dragging them backwards to his cave in Arcadia, so that their track could not be detected. To the remonstrances of his mother Maia, who points out to him the danger of offending Apollo, Hermês replies, that he aspires to rival the dignity and functions of Apollo among the immortals, and that if his father Zeus refuses to grant them to him, he will employ his powers of thieving in breaking open the sanctuary at Delphi, and in carrying away the gold and the vestments, the precious tripods and vessels.[2] Presently Apollo discovers the loss of his cattle, and after some trouble finds his way to the Kyllênian cavern, where he sees Hermês asleep in his cradle. The child denies the theft with effrontery, and even treats the surmise as a ridiculous impossibility : he persists in such denial even before Zeus, who however detects him at once, and compels him to reveal the place where the cattle are concealed. But the lyre was as yet unknown to Apollo, who has heard nothing except the voice of the Muses and the sound of the pipe. So powerfully is he fascinated by hearing the tones of the lyre from Hermês, and so eager to become possessed of it, that he is willing at once to pardon the past

---

[1] Homer. Hymn. Mercur. 18.—

Ἦῳος γεγονὼς, μέσῳ ἤματι ἐγκιϑάριζεν,
Ἑσπέριος βοῦς κλέψεν ἐκηβόλου Ἀπόλλωνος, etc.

[2] Homer. Hymn. Merc. 177. —

Εἰμὶ γὰρ ἐς Πύϑωνα, μέγαν δόμον ἀντιτορήσων,
Ἔνϑεν ἅλις τρίποδας περικαλλέας, ἠδὲ λέβητας
Πορϑήσω καὶ χρυσὸν, etc.

theft, and even to conciliate besides the friendship of Hermês.[1]
Accordingly a bargain is struck between the two gods and sanc-
tioned by Zeus. Hermês surrenders to Apollo the lyre, inventing for his own use the syrinx or panspipe, and receiving from
Apollo in exchange the golden rod of wealth, with empire over
flocks and herds as well as over horses and oxen and the wild
animals of the woods. He presses to obtain the gift of prophecy,
but Apollo is under a special vow not to impart that privilege to
any god whatever: he instructs Hermês however how to draw
information, to a certain extent, from the Mœræ or Fates themselves ; and assigns to him, over and above, the function of messenger of the gods to Hadês.

Although Apollo has acquired the lyre, the particular object
of his wishes, he is still under apprehension that Hermês will
steal it away from him again, together with his bow, and he
exacts a formal oath by Styx as security. Hermês promises
solemnly that he will steal none of the acquisitions, nor ever
invade the sanctuary of Apollo ; while the latter on his part
pledges himself to recognize Hermês as his chosen friend and
companion, amongst all the other sons of Zeus, human or divine.[2]

So came to pass, under the sanction of Zeus, the marked favor
shown by Apollo to Hermês. But Hermês (concludes the
hymnographer, with frankness unusual in speaking of a god)
" does very little good: he avails himself of the darkness of night
to cheat without measure the tribes of mortal men."[3]

---

[1] Homer. Hymn. Merc. 442–454.
[2] Homer. Hymn. Merc. 504–520. —

Καὶ τὸ μὲν Ἑρμῆς
Λητοίδην ἐφίλησε διαμπερὲς, ὡς ἔτι καὶ νῦν, etc.

*   *   *   *   *

Καὶ τότε Μαίαδος υἱὸς ὑποσχόμενος κατένευσε
Μή ποτ' ἀποκλέψειν, ὅσ' Ἑκήβολος ἐκτεάτισται,
Μηδέ ποτ' ἐμπελάσειν πυκίνῳ δόμῳ· αὐτὰρ Ἀπόλλων
Λητοίδης κατένευσεν ἐπ' ἀρθμῷ καὶ φιλότητι
Μή τινα φίλτερ:ν ἄλλον ἐν ἀθανάτοισιν ἔσεσθαι
Μήτε θεὸν, μήτ' ἄνδρα Διὸς γόνον, etc.

[3] Homer. Hymn. Merc. 574. —

Παῦρα μὲν οὖν ὀνίῃ σι, τὸ δ' ἄκριτον ἠπεροπεύει
Νύκτα δι' ὀρφναίην φῦλα θνητῶν ἀνθρώπων.

Here the general types of Hermês and Apollo, coupled with the present fact that no thief ever approached the rich and seemingly accessible treasures of Delphi, engender a string of expository incidents cast into a quasi-historical form and detailing how it happened that Hermês had bound himself by especial convention to respect the Delphian temple. The types of Apollo seem to have been different in different times and parts of Greece : in some places he was worshipped as Apollo Nomios,[1] or the patron of pasture and cattle ; and this attribute, which elsewhere passed over to his son Aristæus, is by our hymnographer voluntarily surrendered to Hermês, combined with the golden rod of fruitfulness. On the other hand, the lyre did not originally belong to the Far-striking King, nor is he at all an inventor : the hymn explains both its first invention and how it came into his possession. And the value of the incidents is thus partly expository, partly illustrative, as expanding in detail the general preconceived character of the Kyllênian god.

To Zeus more amours are ascribed than to any of the other gods, — probably because the Grecian kings and chieftains were especially anxious to trace their lineage to the highest and most glorious of all, — each of these amours having its representative progeny on earth.[2] Such subjects were among the most promising and agreeable for the interest of mythical narrative, and Zeus as a lover thus became the father of a great many legends, branching out into innumerable interferences, for which his sons, all of them distinguished individuals, and many of them persecuted by Hêrê, furnished the occasion. But besides this, the commanding functions of the supreme god, judicial and administrative, extending both over gods and men, was a potent stimulus to the mythopœic activity. Zeus has to watch over his own dignity, — the first of all considerations with a god : moreover as Horkios, Xenios, Ktêsios, Meilichios, (a small proportion of his thousand surnames,) he guaranteed oaths and punished perjurers, he enforced the observance of hospitality, he guarded the family hoard and the crop realized for the year, and he granted expia

---

[1] Kallimach. Hymn. Apoll. 47
[2] Kallimach. Hymn. Jov. 79. ’Εκ δὲ Διὸς βασιλῆες, etc.

tion to the repentant criminal.[1] All these different functions created a demand for mythes, as the means of translating a dim, but serious, presentiment into distinct form, both self-explaining and communicable to others. In enforcing the sanctity of the oath or of the tie of hospitality, the most powerful of all arguments would be a collection of legends respecting the judgments of Zeus Horkios or Xenios; the more impressive and terrific such legends were, the greater would be their interest, and the less would any one dare to disbelieve them. They constituted the natural outpourings of a strong and common sentiment, probably without any deliberate ethical intention : the preconceptions of the divine agency, expanded into legend, form a product analogous to the idea of the divine features and symmetry em· bodied in the bronze or the marble statue.

But it was not alone the general type and attributes of the gods which contributed to put in action the mythopœic propensities. The rites and solemnities forming the worship of each god, as well as the details of his temple and its locality, were a fertile source of mythes, respecting his exploits and sufferings, which to the people who heard them served the purpose of past history. The exegetes, or local guide and interpreter, belonging to each temple, preserved and recounted to curious strangers these traditional narratives, which lent a certain dignity even to the minutiæ of divine service. Out of a stock of materials thus ample, the poets extracted individual collections, such as the " Causes " (Αἴτια) of Kallimachus, now lost, and such as the Fasti of Ovid are for the Roman religious antiquities.[2]

It was the practice to offer to the gods in sacrifice the bones of the victim only, inclosed in fat : how did this practice arise ?

---

[1] See Herodot. i. 44. Xenoph. Anabas. vii. 8, 4. Plutarch, Thêseus, c. 12.

[2] Ovid, Fasti, iv. 211, about the festivals of Apollo : —

" Priscique imitamina facti
Æra Deæ comites raucaque terga movent."

And Lactantius, v. 19, 15. "Ipsos ritus ex rebus gestis (deorum) vel ex casibus vel etiam ex mortibus, natos :" to the same purpose Augustin. De Civ. D. vii. 18; Diodôr. iii. 56. Plutarch's Quæstiones Græcæ et Romaicæ are full of similar tales, professing to account for existing customs, many of them religious and liturgic. See Lobeck, Orphica, p. 675.

The author of the Hesiodic Theogony has a story which explains it: Promêtheus tricked Zeus into an imprudent choice, at the period when the gods and mortal men first came to an arrangement about privileges and duties (in Mekônê). Promêtheus, the tutelary representative of man, divided a large steer into two portions: on the one side he placed the flesh and guts, folded up in the omentum and covered over with the skin: on the other, he put the bones enveloped in fat. He then invited Zeus to determine which of the two portions the gods would prefer to receive from mankind. Zeus "with both hands" decided for and took the white fat, but was highly incensed on finding that he had got nothing at the bottom except the bones.[1] Nevertheless the choice of the gods was now irrevocably made: they were not entitled to any portion of the sacrificed animal beyond the bones and the white fat; and the standing practice is thus plausibly explained.[2] I select this as one amongst a thousand instances to illustrate the genesis of legend out of religious practices. In the belief of the people, the event narrated in the legend was the real producing cause of the practice: but when we come to apply a sound criticism, we are compelled to treat the event as existing only in its narrative legend, and the legend itself as having been, in the greater number of cases, engendered by the practice, — thus reversing the supposed order of production.

[1] Hesiod, Theog. 550.—

Φῆ ῥα δολοφρονέων · Ζεὺς δ' ἄφθιτα μήδεα εἰδὼς
Γνῶ ῥ' οὐδ' ἠγνοίησε δόλον · κακὰ δ' ὄσσετο θυμῷ
Θνητοῖς ἀνθρώποισι, τὰ καὶ τελέεσθαι ἔμελλεν.
Χερσὶ δ' ὅγ' ἀμφοτέρῃσιν ἀνείλετο λευκὸν ἄλειφαρ.
Χώσατο δὲ φρένας, ἀμφὶ χόλος δέ μιν ἵκετο θυμὸν,
Ὡς ἴδεν ὀστέα λευκὰ βοὸς δολίῃ ἐπὶ τέχνῃ.

In the second line of this citation, the poet tells us that Zeus saw through the trick, and was imposed upon by his own consent, foreknowing that after all the mischievous consequences of the proceeding would be visited on man. But the last lines, and indeed the whole drift of the legend, imply the contrary of this: Zeus was really taken in, and was in consequence very angry. It is curious to observe how the religious feelings of the poet drive him to save in words the prescience of Zeus, though in doing so he contradicts and nullifies the whole point of the story.

[2] Hesiod, Theog. 557.—

Ἐκ τοῦ δ' ἀθανάτοισιν ἐπὶ χθονὶ φῦλ' ἀνθρώπων
Καίουσ' ὀστέα λευκὰ θυηέντων ἐπὶ βωμῶν.

In dealing with Grecian mythes generally, it is convenient to
distribute them into such as belong to the Gods and such as
belong to the Heroes, according as the one or the other are the
prominent personages. The former class manifests, more palpably than the latter, their real origin, as growing out of the faith
and the feelings, without any necessary basis, either of matter
of fact or allegory : moreover, they elucidate more directly the
religion of the Greeks, so important an item in their character as
a people. But in point of fact, most of the mythes present to
us Gods, Heroes and Men, in juxtaposition one with the other,
and the richness of Grecian mythical literature arises from the
infinite diversity of combinations thus opened out ; first by the
three class-types, God, Hero, and Man ; next by the strict keeping with which each separate class and character is handled. We
shall now follow downward the stream of mythical time, which
begins with the Gods, to the Heroic legends, or those which
principally concern the Heroes and Heroines ; for the latter were
to the full as important in legend as the former.

CHAPTER II.

LEGENDS RELATING TO HEROES AND MEN.

THE Hesiodic theogony gives no account of anything like a
creation of man, nor does it seem that such an idea was much
entertained in the legendary vein of Grecian imagination ; which
commonly carried back the present men by successive generations
to some·primitive ancestor, himself sprung from the soil, or from
a neighboring river or mountain, or from a god, a nymph, etc.
But the poet of the Hesiodic "Works and Days" has given us a
narrative conceived in a very different spirit respecting the origin
of the human race, more in harmony with the sober and melancholy ethical tone which reigns through that poem.[1]

---

[1] Hesiod, as cited in the Etymologicon Magnum (probably the Hesiodic

First (he tells us) the Olympic gods made the golden race, — good, perfect, and happy men, who lived from the spontaneous abundance of the earth, in ease and tranquillity like the gods themselves: they suffered neither disease nor old age, and their death was like a gentle sleep. After death they became, by the award of Zeus, guardian terrestrial dæmons, who watch unseen over the proceedings of mankind — with the regal privilege of dispensing to them wealth, and taking account of good and bad deeds.[1]

Next, the gods made the silver race, — unlike and greatly inferior, both in mind and body, to the golden. The men of this race were reckless and mischievous towards each other, and disdainful of the immortal gods, to whom they refused to offer either worship or sacrifice. Zeus in his wrath buried them in the earth: but there they still enjoy a secondary honor, as the Blest of the under-world.[2]

Thirdly, Zeus made the brazen race, quite different from the silver. They were made of hard ash-wood, pugnacious and terrible; they were of immense strength and adamantine soul, nor did they raise or touch bread. Their arms, their houses, and their implements were all of brass: there was then no iron. This race, eternally fighting, perished by each other's hands, died out, and descended without name or privilege to Hadês.[3]

Catalogue of Women, as Marktscheffel considers it, placing it Fragm. 133), gives the parentage of a certain *Brotos*, who must probably be intended as the first of men: Βρότος, ὡς μὲν Εὐήμερος ὁ Μεσσήνιος, ἀπὸ Βρότου τινος αὐτόχθονος· ὁ δὲ Ἡσίοδος, ἀπὸ Βρότου τοῦ Αἰθέρος καὶ Ἡμέρας.

[1] Opp. Di. 120. —
Αὐτὰρ ἐπειδὴ τοῦτο γένος κατὰ γαῖα κάλυψεν
Τοὶ μὲν δαίμονές εἰσι Διὸς μεγάλου διὰ βουλὰς
Εσθλοὶ, ἐπιχθόνιοι, φύλακες θνητῶν ἀνθρώπων·
Οἱ ῥα φυλάσσουσίν τε δίκας καὶ σχέτλια ἔργα,
Ἡέρα ἐσσάμενοι, πάντη φοιτῶντες ἐπ' αἶαν
Πλουτόδοται· καὶ τοῦτο γέρας βασιληϊον ἔσχον.

[2] Opp. Di. 140. —
Αὐτὰρ ἐπεὶ καὶ τοῦτο γένος.κατὰ γαῖα κάλυψε,
Τοὶ μὲν ὑποχθόνιοι μάκαρες θνητοὶ καλέονται
Δεύτεροι, ἀλλ' ἔμπης τιμὴ καὶ τοῖσιν ὀπηδεῖ.

[3] The ash was the wood out of which spear-handles were made (Iliad, xvi 142): the Νύμφαι Μέλιαι are born along with the Gigantes and the Erin

Next, Zeus made a fourth race, far juster and better than the last preceding. These were the Heroes or demigods, who fought at the sieges of Troy and Thêbes. But this splendid stock also became extinct: some perished in war, others were removed by Zeus to a happier state in the islands of the Blest. There they dwell in peace and comfort, under the government of Kronos, reaping thrice in the year the spontaneous produce of the earth.[1]

The fifth race, which succeeds to the Heroes, is of iron: it is the race to which the poet himself belongs, and bitterly does he regret it. He finds his contemporaries mischievous, dishonest, unjust, ungrateful, given to perjury, careless both of the ties of consanguinity and of the behests of the gods: Nemesis and Ædôs (Ethical Self-reproach) have left earth and gone back to Olympus. How keenly does he wish that his lot had been cast either earlier or later![2] This iron race is doomed to continual guilt, care, and suffering, with a small infusion of good; but the time will come when Zeus will put an end to it. The poet does not venture to predict what sort of race will succeed.

Such is the series of distinct races of men, which Hesiod, or the author of the "Works and Days," enumerates as having existed down to his own time. I give it as it stands, without placing much confidence in the various explanations which critics have offered. It stands out in more than one respect from the general tone and sentiment of Grecian legend: moreover the sequence of races is neither natural nor homogeneous,—the heroic race not having any metallic denomination, and not occupying any legitimate place in immediate succession to the brazen. Nor is the conception of the dæmons in harmony either with Homer or with the Hesiodic theogony. In Homer, there is scarcely any distinction between gods and dæmons, while the gods

---

nyes (Theogon. 187),—"gensque virûm truncis et duro robore nata" (Virgil, Æneid, viii. 315),—hearts of oak.

[1] Opp. Di. 157.—

Ανδρῶν Ἡρώων θεῖον γένος, οἱ καλέονται
Ἡμίθεο: προτέρη γενέη κατ᾽ ἀπείρονα γαῖαν.

[2] Opp. Di. 173.—

Μήκετ᾽ ἔπειτ᾽ ὤφειλον ἐγὼ πέμπτοισι μετεῖναι
᾽Ανδράσιν, ἀλλ᾽ ἢ πρόσθε θανεῖν, ἢ ἔπειτα γενέσθαι.
Νῦν γὰρ δὴ γένος ἐστὶ σιδήρεον......

are stated to go about and visit the cities of men in various disguises for the purpose of inspecting good and evil proceedings.[1] But in the poem now before us, the distinction between gods and dæmons is generic. The latter are invisible tenants of earth, remnants of the once happy golden race whom the Olympic gods first made: the remnants of the second or silver race are not dæmons, nor are they tenants of earth, but they still enjoy an honorable posthumous existence as the Blest of the under-world. Nevertheless the Hesiodic dæmons are in no way authors or abettors of evil: on the contrary, they form the unseen police of the gods, for the purpose of repressing wicked behavior in the world.

We may trace, I think, in this quintuple succession of earthly races, set forth by the author of the " Works and Days," the confluence of two veins of sentiment, not consistent one with the other, yet both coëxisting in the author's mind. The drift of his poem is thoroughly didactic and ethical: though deeply penetrated with the injustice and suffering which darken the face of human life, he nevertheless strives to maintain, both in himself and in others, a conviction that on the whole the just and laborious man will come off well,[2] and he enforces in considerable detail the lessons of practical prudence and virtue. This ethical sentiment, which dictates his appreciation of the present, also guides his imagination as to the past. It is pleasing to him to bridge over the chasm between the gods and degenerate man, by

---

[1] Odyss. xvii. 486.

[2] There are some lines, in which he appears to believe that, under the present wicked and treacherous rulers, it is not the interest of any man to be just (Opp. Di. 270): —

Νῦν δὴ ἐγὼ μήτ' αὐτὸς ἐν ἀνθρώποισι δίκαιος
Εἴην, μήτ' ἐμὸς υἱός· ἐπεὶ κακόν ἐστι δίκαιον
Ἔμμεναι, εἰ μείζω γε δίκην ἀδικώτερος ἕξει·
'Αλλὰ τόδ' οὔπω ἔολπα τελεῖν Δία τερπικέραυνον.

On the whole, however, his conviction is to the contrary.

Plutarch rejects the above four lines, seemingly on no other ground than gecause he thought them immoral and unworthy of Hesiod (see Proclus ad loc.). But they fall in perfectly with the temper of the poem: and the rule of Plutarch is inadmissible, in determining the critical question of what is ber uine or spurious.

the supposition of previous races, — the first altogether pure, the
second worse than the first, and the third still worse than the
second; and to show further how the first race passed by gentle
death-sleep into glorious immortality; how the second race was
sufficiently wicked to drive Zeus to bury them in the under-world,
yet s'ill leaving them a certain measure of honor; while the
third was so desperately violent as to perish by its own animosi-
ties, without either name or honor of any kind.   The conception
of the golden race passing after death into good guardian dæmons,
which some suppose to have been derived from a comparison
with oriental angels, presents itself to the poet partly as approx-
imating this race to the gods, partly as a means of constituting a
triple gradation of post-obituary existence, proportioned to the
character of each race whilst alive.   The denominations of gold
and silver, given to the first two races, justify themselves, like
those given by Simonidês of Amorgos and by Phokylidês to the
different characters of women, derived from the dog, the bee, the
mare, the ass, and other animals; and the epithet of brazen is
specially explained by reference to the material which the pugnacious third race so plentifully employed for their arms and other
implements.

So far we trace intelligibly enough the moralizing vein: we
find the revolutions of the past so arranged as to serve partly as
an ethical lesson, partly as a suitable preface to the present.[1] But
fourth in the list comes "the divine race of Heroes:" and here
a new vein of thought is opened by the poet. The symmetry
of his ethical past is broken up, in order to make way for these
cherished beings of the national faith. For though the author of
the "Works and Days" was himself of a didactic cast of thought,

---

[1] Aratus (Phænomen. 107) gives only three successive races, — the golden,
silver, and brazen; Ovid superadds to these the iron race (Metamorph. i.
89–144): neither of them notice the heroic race.

The observations both of Buttmann (Mythos der ältesten Menschengesch-
lechter, t. ii. p. 12 of the Mythologus) and of Völcker (Mythologie des
Japetischen Geschlechts, § 6, pp. 250–279) on this series of distinct races,
are ingenious, and may be read with profit. Both recognize the disparate
character of the fourth link in the series, and each accounts for it in a different manner. My own view comes nearer to that of Völcker, with some considerable differences; amongst which one is, that he rejects the verses respecting the dæmons, which seem to me capital parts of the whole scheme.

like Phokylidês, or Solôn, or Theognis, yet he had present to his
feelings, in common with his countrymen, the picture of Grecian
foretime, as it was set forth in the current mythes, and still more
in Homer and those other epical productions which were then the
only existing literature and history. It was impossible for him
to exclude, from his sketch of the past, either the great persons
or the glorious exploits which these poems ennobled; and even
if he himself could have consented to such an exclusion, the
sketch would have become repulsive to his hearers. But the
chiefs who figured before Thêbes and Troy could not be well
identified either with the golden, the silver, or the brazen race:
morover it was essential that they should be placed in immediate
contiguity with the present race, because their descendants, real
or supposed, were the most prominent and conspicuous of existing men. Hence the poet is obliged to assign to them the fourth
place in the series, and to interrupt the descending ethical movement in order to interpolate them between the brazen and the
iron race, with neither of which they present any analogy. The
iron race, to which the poet himself unhappily belongs, is the
legitimate successor, not of the heroic, but of the brazen. Instead
of the fierce and self-annihilating pugnacity which characterizes
the latter, the iron race manifests an aggregate of smaller and
meaner vices and mischiefs. It will not perish by suicidal
extinction — but it is growing worse and worse, and is gradually
losing its vigor, so that Zeus will not vouchsafe to preserve much
longer such a race upon the earth.

We thus see that the series of races imagined by the poet of
the "Works and Days" is the product of two distinct and
incongruous veins of imagination, — the didactic or ethical
blending with the primitive mythical or epical. His poem is
remarkable as the most ancient didactic production of the Greeks,
and as one of the first symptoms of a new tone of sentiment
finding its way into their literature, never afterwards to become
extinct. The tendency of the "Works and Days" is anti-
heroic: far from seeking to inspire admiration for adventurous enterprise, the author inculcates the strictest justice, the
most unremitting labor and frugality, and a sober, not to say
anxious, estimate of all the minute specialties of the future.
Prudence and probity are his means,— practical comfort and

happiness his end. But he deeply feels, and keenly exposes, the manifold wickedness and short-comings of his contemporaries, in reference to this capital standard. He turns with displeasure from the present men, not because they are too feeble to hurl either the spear of Achilles or some vast boundary-stone, but because they are rapacious, knavish, and unprincipled.

The dæmons first introduced into the religious atmosphere of the Grecian world by the author of the " Works and Days," as generically different from the gods, but as essentially good, and as forming the intermediate agents and police between gods and men, — are deserving of attention as the seed of a doctrine which afterwards underwent many changes, and became of great importance, first as one of the constituent elements of pagan faith, then as one of the helps to its subversion. It will be recollected that the buried remnants of the half-wicked silver race, though they are not recognized as dæmons, are still considered as having a substantive existence, a name, and dignity, in the under-world. The step was easy, to treat them as dæmons also, but as dæmons of a defective and malignant character : this step was made by Empedoclês and Xenocratês, and to a certain extent countenanced by Plato.[1] There came thus to be admitted among the pagan philosophers dæmons both good and bad, in every degree : and these dæmons were found available as a means of explaining many phænomena for which it was not convenient to admit the agency of the gods. They served to relieve the gods from the odium of physical and moral evils, as well as from the necessity of constantly meddling in small affairs ; and the objectionable ceremonies of the pagan world were defended upon the ground that in no other way could the exigencies of such malignant beings be appeased. They were most frequently noticed as causes of evil, and thus the name (dæmon) came insensibly to convey with it a bad sense, — the idea of an evil being as contrasted with the goodness of a god. So it was found by the Christian writers when they commenced their controversy with paganism. One branch of their argument led them to identify the pagan gods with dæmons in the evil sense, and the insensible change in the received meaning of the word lent them a specious assistance. For they could easily

---

[1] See this subject further mentioned — *infra*, chap. xvi. p. 565.

show that not only in Homer, but in the general language of early pagans, all the gods generally were spoken of as dæmons — and therefore, verbally speaking, Clemens and Tatian seemed to affirm nothing more against Zeus or Apollo than was employed in the language of paganism itself. Yet the audience of Homer or Sophoklês would have strenuously repudiated the proposition, if it had been put to them in the sense which the word *dæmon* bore in the age and among the circle of these Christian writers.

In the imagination of the author of the "Works and Days," the dæmons occupy an important place, and are regarded as being of serious practical efficiency. When he is remonstrating with the rulers around him upon their gross injustice and corruption, he reminds them of the vast number of these immortal servants of Zeus who are perpetually on guard amidst mankind, and through whom the visitations of the gods will descend even upon the most potent evil doers.[1] His supposition that the dæmons were not gods, but departed men of the golden race, allowed him to multiply their number indefinitely, without too much cheapening the divine dignity.

As this poet has been so much enslaved by the current legends as to introduce the Heroic race into a series to which it does not legitimately belong, so he has under the same influence inserted in another part of his poem the mythe of Pandora and Promêtheus,[2] as a means of explaining the primary diffusion, and actual abundance, of evil among mankind. Yet this mythe can in no way consist with his quintuple scale of distinct races, and is in fact a totally distinct theory to explain the same problem, — the transition of mankind from a supposed state of antecedent happiness to one of present toil and suffering. Such an inconsistency is not a sufficient reason for questioning the genuineness of either passage; for the two stories, though one contradicts the other, both harmonize with that central purpose which governs the author's mind, — a querulous and didactic appreciation of the present. That such was his purpose appears not only from the whole tenor of his poem, but also from the remarkable fact that his own personality, his own adventures and kindred, and his own sufferings, figure in it conspicuously. And this introduction of self

---

[1] Opp. Di. 252. Τρὶς γὰρ μύριοί εἰσιν ἐπὶ χθονὶ πουλυβοτείρῃ, etc.
[2] Opp. Di. 50–105.

imparts to it a peculiar interest. The father of Hesiod came over from the Æolic Kymê, with the view of bettering his condition, and settled at Askra in Bœotia, at the foot of Mount Helicon. After his death his two sons divided the family inheritance: but Hesiod bitterly complains that his brother Persês cheated and went to law with him, and obtained through corrupt judges an unjust decision. He farther reproaches his brother with a preference for the suits and unprofitable bustle of the agora, at a time when he ought to be laboring for his subsistence in the field. Askra indeed was a miserable place, repulsive both in summer and winter. Hesiod had never crossed the sea, except once from Aulis to Eubœa, whither he went to attend the funeral games of Amphidamas, the chief of Chalkis: he sung a hymn, and gained as prize a tripod, which he consecrated to the muses in Helicon.[1]

These particulars, scanty as they are, possess a peculiar value, as the earliest authentic memorandum respecting the doing or suffering of any actual Greek person. There is no external testimony at all worthy of trust respecting the age of the "Works and Days." Herodotus treats Hesiod and Homer as belonging to the same age, four hundred years before his own time; and there are other statements besides, some placing Hesiod at an earlier date than Homer, some at a later. Looking at the internal evidences, we may observe that the pervading sentiment, tone and purpose of the poem is widely different from that of the Iliad and Odyssey, and analogous to what we read respecting the compositions of Archilochus and the Amorgian Simonidês. The author of the "Works and Days" is indeed a preacher and not a satirist: but with this distinction, we find in him the same predominance of the present and the positive, the same disposition to turn the muse into an exponent of his own personal wrongs, the same employment of Æsopic fable by way of illustration, and the same unfavorable estimate of the female sex,[2] all of which

---

[1] Opp. Di. 630–650, 27–45.

[2] Compare the fable ($a\tilde{i}\nu o\varsigma$) in the "Works and Days," v. 200, with those in Archilochus, Fr. xxxviii. and xxxix., Gaisford, respecting the fox and the ape; and the legend of Pandôra (v. 95 and v. 705) with the fragment of Simonidês of Amorgos respecting women (Fr. viii. ed. Welcker, v. 95–115); also Phokylidês ap. Stobæum Florileg. lxxi.

Isokratês assimilates the character of the "Works and Days" to that of Theognis and Phokylidês (ad Nikokl. Or. ii. p. 23).

may be traced in the two poets above mentioned, placing both of them in contrast with the Homeric epic. Such an internal analogy, in the absence of good testimony, is the best guide which we can follow in determining the date of the "Works and Days," which we should accordingly place shortly after the year 700 B. C. The style of the poem might indeed afford a proof that the ancient and uniform hexameter, though well adapted to continuous legendary narrative or to solemn hymns, was somewhat monotonous when called upon either to serve a polemical purpose or to impress a striking moral lesson. When poets, then the only existing composers, first began to apply their thoughts to the cut and thrust of actual life, aggressive or didactic, the verse would be seen to require a new, livelier and smarter metre; and out of this want grew the elegiac and the iambic verse, both seemingly contemporaneous, and both intended to supplant the primitive hexameter for the short effusions then coming into vogue.

CHAPTER III.

LEGEND OF THE IAPETIDS.

THE sons of the Titan god Iapetus, as described in the Hesiodic theogony, are Atlas, Menœtius, Promêtheus and Epimêtheus.[1] Of these, Atlas alone is mentioned by Homer in the Odyssey, and even he not as the son of Iapetus: the latter himself is named in the Iliad as existing in Tartarus along with Kronos. The Homeric Atlas "knows the depths of the whole sea, and keeps by himself those tall pillars which hold the heaven apart from the earth."[2]

---

[1] Hesiod, Theog. 510.
[2] Hom. Odyss. i. 120.—

᾽Ατλαντος θυγατὴρ ὀλοόφρονος, ὅστε θαλάσσης
Πάσης βένθεα οἶδε, ἔχει δέ τε κίονας αὐτὸς
Μακρὰς, αἳ γαῖάν τε καὶ οὐρανὸν ἀμφὶς ἔχουσιν.

As the Homeric theogony generally appears much expanded in Hesiod, so also does the family of Iapetus, with their varied adventures. Atlas is here described, not as the keeper of the intermediate pillars between heaven and earth, but as himself condemned by Zeus to support the heaven on his head and hands;[1] while the fierce Menœtius is thrust down to Erebus as a punishment for his ungovernable insolence. But the remaining two brothers, Promêtheus and Epimêtheus, are among the most interesting creations of Grecian legend, and distinguished in more than one respect from all the remainder.

First, the main battle between Zeus and the Titan gods is a contest of force purely and simply — mountains are hurled and thunder is launched, and the victory remains to the strongest. But the competition between Zeus and Promêtheus is one of craft and stratagem : the victory does indeed remain to the former, but the honors of the fight belong to the latter. Secondly, Promêtheus and Epimêtheus (the fore-thinker and the after-thinker [2]) are characters stamped at the same mint and by the same effort, the express contrast and antithesis of each other. Thirdly, mankind are here expressly brought forward, not indeed as active partners in the struggle, but as the grand and capital subjects interested, — as gainers or sufferers by the result. Promêtheus appears in the exalted character of champion of the human race, even against the formidable superiority of Zeus.

In the primitive or Hesiodic legend, Promêtheus is not the creator or moulder of man; it is only the later additions which invest him with this character.[3] The race are supposed as exist-

---

[1] Hesiod, Theog. 516.—

'Ατλας δ' οὐρανὸν εὐρὺν ἔχει κρατερῆς ὑπ' ἀνάγκης
'Εστηὼς, κεφαλῇ τε καὶ ἀκαμάτοισι χέρεσσι.

Hesiod stretches far beyond the simplicity of the Homeric conception.

[2] Pindar extends the family of Epimêtheus and gives him a daughter, Πρόφασις (Pyth. v. 25), Excuse, the offspring of After-thought.

[3] Apollodôr. i. 7. 1. Nor is he such either in Æschylus, or in the Platonic fable (Protag. c. 30), though this version became at last the most popular. Some hardened lumps of clay, remnants of that which had been employed by Promêtheus in moulding man, were shown to Pausanias at Panopeus in Phokis (Paus. x. 4, 3).

The first Epigram of Erinna (Anthol. i. p. 58, ed. Brunck) seems to allude

ing, and Prométheus, a member of the dispossessed body of Titan gods, comes forward as their representative and defender. The advantageous bargain which he made with Zeus on their behalf, in respect to the partition of the sacrificial animals, has been recounted in the preceding chapter. Zeus felt that he had been outwitted, and was exceeding wroth. In his displeasure he withheld from mankind the inestimable comfort of fire, so that the race would have perished, had not Prométheus stolen fire, in defiance of the command of the Supreme Ruler, and brought it to men in the hollow of a ferule.[1]

Zeus was now doubly indignant, and determined to play off a still more ruinous stratagem. Héphæstos, by his direction, moulded the form of a beautiful virgin; Athéné dressed her, Aphrodité and the Charities bestowed upon her both ornament and fascination, while Hermés infused into her the mind of a dog, a deceitful spirit, and treacherous words.[2] The messenger of the gods conducted this "fascinating mischief" to mankind, at a time when Prométheus was not present. Now Epimétheus had received from his brother peremptory injunctions not to accept from the hands of Zeus any present whatever; but the beauty of Pandóra (so the newly-formed female was called) was not to be resisted. She was received and admitted among men, and from that moment their comfort and tranquillity was exchanged for suffering of every kind.[3] The evils to which mankind are liable had been before enclosed in a cask in their own keeping: Pandóra in her malice removed the lid of the cask, and out flew these thousand evils and calamities, to exercise forever their destroying force. Hope alone remained imprisoned, and therefore without efficacy, as before — the inviolable lid being replaced before she could escape. Before this incident (says the legend) men had lived without disease or suffering; but now both earth and sea are full of mischiefs, while maladies of every description stalk abroad by day as well as by night,[4] without any hope for man of relief to come.

---

to Prométheus as moulder of man. The expression of Aristophanés (Aves, 689) — πλάσματα πηλοῦ — does not necessarily refer to Prométheus.

[1] Hesiod, Theog. 566; Opp. Di. 52.　　[2] Theog. 580; Opp. Di. 50–85.

[3] Opp. Di. 81–90.

[4] Opp. Di. 93. Pandóra does not *bring with her* the cask, as the common

The Theogony gives the legend here recounted, with some variations—leaving out the part of Epimêtheus altogether, as well as the cask of evils. Pandôra is the ruin of man, simply as the mother and representative of the female sex.[1] And the variations are thus useful, as they enable us to distinguish the essential from the accessory circumstances of the story.

"Thus (says the poet, at the conclusion of his narrative) it is not possible to escape from the purposes of Zeus."[2] His mythe, connecting the calamitous condition of man with the malevolence of the supreme god, shows, first, by what cause such an unfriendly feeling was raised; next, by what instrumentality its deadly results were brought about. The human race are not indeed the creation, but the protected flock of Promêtheus, one of the elder or dispossessed Titan gods: when Zeus acquires supremacy, mankind along with the rest become subject to him, and are to make the best bargain they can respecting worship and service to be yielded. By the stratagem of their advocate Promêtheus, Zeus

version of this story would have us suppose : the cask exists fast closed in the custody of Epimêtheus, or of man himself, and Pandôra commits the fatal treachery of removing the lid. The case is analogous to that of the closed bag of unfavorable winds which Æolus gives into the hands of Odysseus, and which the guilty companions of the latter force open, to the entire ruin of his hopes (Odyss. x. 19–50). The idea of the two casks on the threshhold of Zeus, lying ready for dispensation—one full of evils the other of benefits—is Homeric (Iliad, xxiv. 527) :—

Δοιοὶ γάρ τε πίθοι κατακείαται ἐν Διὸς οὔδει, etc.

Plutarch assimilates to this the πίθος opened by Pandôra, Consolat. ad Apollon. c. 7. p. 105. The explanation here given of the Hesiodic passage relating to Hope, is drawn from an able article in the Wiener Jahrbucher, vol. 109 (1845), p. 220, Ritter; a review of Schömmann's translation of the Promêtheus of Æschylus. The diseases and evils are inoperative so long as they remain shut up in the cask: the same mischief-making influence which lets them out to their calamitous work, takes care that Hope shall still continue a powerless prisoner in the inside.

[1] Theog. 590.—

Ἐκ τῆς γὰρ γένος ἐστὶ γυναικῶν θηλυτεράων, ,
Τῆς γὰρ ὀλώϊόν ἐστι γένος· καὶ φῦλα γυναικῶν
Πῆμα μέγα θνητοῖσι μετ᾽ ἀνδράσι ναιετάουσι, etc.

[2] Opp Di 105.—

Οὕτως οὔτι πῇ ἐστὶ Διὸς νόον ἐξαλέασθαι.

is cheated into such a partition of the victims as is eminently un-profitable to him; whereby his wrath is so provoked, that he tries to subtract from man the use of fire. Here however his scheme is frustrated by the theft of Prométheus: but his second attempt is more successful, and he in his turn cheats the unthinking Epimé-theus into the acceptance of a present (in spite of the peremptory interdict of Prométheus) by which the whole of man's happiness is wrecked. This legend grows out of two feelings; partly as to the relations of the gods with man, partly as to the relation of the female sex with the male. The present gods are unkind to-wards man, but the old gods, with whom man's lot was originally cast, were much kinder — and the ablest among them stands for-ward as the indefatigable protector of the race. Nevertheless, the mere excess of his craft proves the ultimate ruin of the cause which he espouses. He cheats Zeus out of a fair share of the sacrificial victim, so as both to provoke and justify a retaliation which he cannot be always at hand to ward off: the retaliation is, in his absence, consummated by a snare laid for Epimétheus and voluntarily accepted. And thus, though Hesiod ascribes the calamitous condition of man to the malevolence of Zeus, his piety suggests two exculpatory pleas for the latter: mankind have been the first to defraud Zeus of his legitimate share of the sacrifice — and they have moreover been consenting parties to their own ruin. Such are the feelings, as to the relation between the gods and man, which have been one of the generating elements of this legend. The other element, a conviction of the vast mischief arising to man from women, whom yet they cannot dispense with, is frequently and strongly set forth in several of the Greek poets — by Simonidés of Amorgos and Phokylidês, not less than by the notorious misogynist Euripidês.

But the miseries arising from woman, however great they might be, did not reach Prométheus himself. For him, the rash champion who had ventured "to compete in sagacity"[1] with Zeus, a different punishment was in store. Bound by heavy chains to a pillar, he remained fast imprisoned for several gene-rations: every day did an eagle prey upon his liver, and every night did the liver grow afresh for the next day's suffering. At

---

[1] Theog. 534. Οὕνεκ' ἐρίζετο βουλὰς ὑπερμενέϊ Κρονίωνι.

length Zeus, eager to enhance the glory of his favorite son Hêraclês, permitted the latter to kill the eagle and rescue the captive.[1] Such is the Promêthean mythe as it stands in the Hesiodic poems; its earliest form, as far as we can trace. Upon it was founded the sublime tragedy of Æschylus, "The Enchained Promêtheus," together with at least one more tragedy, now lost, by the same author.[2] Æschylus has made several important alterations; describing the human race, not as having once enjoyed and subsequently lost a state of tranquillity and enjoyment, but as originally feeble and wretched. He suppresses both the first trick played off by Promêtheus upon Zeus respecting the partition of the victim — and the final formation and sending of Pandôra — which are the two most marked portions of the Hesiodic story; while on the other hand he brings out prominently and enlarges upon the theft of fire,[3] which in Hesiod is but slightly touched. If he has thus relinquished the antique simplicity of the story, he has rendered more than ample compensation by imparting to it a grandeur of *idéal*, a large reach of thought combined with appeals to our earnest and admiring sympathy, and a pregnancy of suggestion in regard to the relations between the gods and man, which soar far above the Hesiodic level — and which render his tragedy the most impressive, though not the most artistically composed, of all Grecian dramatic productions. Promêtheus there appears not only as the heroic champion and sufferer in the cause and for the protection of the human race, but also as the gifted teacher of all the arts, helps, and ornaments of life, amongst which fire is only one:[4] all this against the will and in defiance of the purpose of Zeus, who, on acquiring his empire, wished to destroy the human race and to

---

[1] Theog. 521–532.

[2] Of the tragedy called Προμηθεὺς Λυόμενος some few fragments yet remain: Προμηθεὺς Πύρφορος was a satyric drama, according to Dindorf Welcker recognizes a third tragedy, Προμηθεὺς Πύρφορος, and a satyric drama, Προμηθεὺς Πυρκαεύς (Die Griechisch. Tragödien, vol. i. p. 30). The story of Promêtheus had also been handled by Sapphô in one of her lost songs (Servius ad Virgil. Eclog. vi. 42).

[3] Apollodôrus too mentions only the theft of fire (i. 7. 1).

[4] Æsch. Prom. 442–506.—

Πᾶσαι τέχναι βροτοῖσιν ἐκ Προμηθέως.

beget some new breed.[1] Moreover, new relations between Promêtheus and Zeus are superadded by Æschylus. At the commencement of the struggle between Zeus and the Titan gods, Promêtheus had vainly attempted to prevail upon the latter to conduct it with prudence; but when he found that they obstinately declined all wise counsel, and that their ruin was inevitable, he abandoned their cause and joined Zeus. To him and to his advice Zeus owed the victory : yet the monstrous ingratitude and tyranny of the latter is now manifested by nailing him to a rock, for no other crime than because he frustrated the purpose of extinguishing the human race, and furnished to them the means of living with tolerable comfort.[2] The new ruler Zeus, insolent with his victory over the old gods, tramples down all right, and sets at naught sympathy and obligation, as well towards gods as towards man. Yet the prophetic Promêtheus, in the midst of intense suffering, is consoled by the foreknowledge that the time will come when Zeus must again send for him, release him, and invoke his aid, as the sole means of averting from himself dangers otherwise insurmountable. The security and means of continuance for mankind have now been placed beyond the reach of Zeus — whom Promêtheus proudly defies, glorying in his generous and successful championship,[3] despite the terrible price which he is doomed to pay for it.

As the Æschylean Promêtheus, though retaining the old lineaments, has acquired a new coloring, soul and character, so he has also become identified with a special locality. In Hesiod, there is no indication of the place in which he is imprisoned; but Æschylus places it in Scythia,[4] and the general belief of the Greeks supposed it to be on Mount Caucasus. So long and so firmly did

---

[1] Æsch. Prom. 231.—

βροτῶν δὲ τῶν ταλαιπώρων λόγον
Οὐκ ἔσχεν οὐδέν', ἀλλ' ἀϊστώσας γένος
Τὸ πᾶν, ἔχρῃζεν ἄλλο φιτῦσαι νέον.

[2] Æsch. Prom. 198–222. 123.—

διὰ τὴν λίαν φιλότητα βροτῶν.

[3] Æsch. Prom. 169–770.

[4] Prometh. 2. See also the Fragments of the Promêtheus Solutus, 177–179, ed. Dindorf, where Caucasus is specially named; but v. 719 of the Promêtheus Vinctus seems to imply that Mount Caucasus is a place different from that to which the suffering prisoner is chained.

this belief continue, that the Roman general Pompey, when in command of an army in Kolchis, made with his companion, the literary Greek Theophanês, a special march to view the spot in Caucasus where Promêtheus had been transfixed.[1]

CHAPTER IV.

HEROIC LEGENDS.—GENEALOGY OF ARGOS.

HAVING briefly enumerated the gods of Greece, with their chief attributes as described in legend, we come to those genealogies which connected them with historical men.

In the retrospective faith of a Greek, the ideas of worship and ancestry coalesced. Every association of men, large or small, in whom there existed a feeling of present union, traced back that union to some common initial progenitor; that progenitor being either the common god whom they worshipped, or some semi-divine person closely allied to him. What the feelings of the community require is, a continuous pedigree to connect them with this respected source of existence, beyond which they do not think of looking back. A series of names, placed in filiation or fraternity, together with a certain number of family or personal adventures ascribed to some of the individuals among them, constitute the ante-historical past through which the Greek looks back to his gods. The names of this genealogy are, to a great degree, gentile or local names familiar to the people,— rivers, mountains, springs, lakes, villages, demes, etc.,— embodied as persons, and introduced as acting or suffering. They are moreover called kings or chiefs, but the existence of a body of subjects surrounding them is tacitly implied rather than distinctly set forth; for their own personal exploits or family proceedings constitute for the most part the whole matter of narrative. And thus the gene-

---

[1] Appian, Bell. Mithridat. c. 103.

alogy was made to satisfy at once the appetite of the Greeks for romantic adventure, and their demand for an unbroken line of filiation between themselves and the gods. The eponymous personage, from whom the community derive their name, is sometimes the begotten son of the local god, sometimes an indigenous man sprung from the earth, which is indeed itself divinized.

It will be seen from the mere description of these genealogies that they included elements human and historical, as well as elements divine and extra-historical. And if we could determine the time at which any genealogy was first framed, we should be able to assure ourselves that the men then represented as present, together with their fathers and grandfathers, were real persons of flesh and blood. But this is a point which can seldom be ascertained; moreover, even if it could be ascertained, we must at once set it aside, if we wish to look at the genealogy in the point of view of the Greeks. For to them, not only all the members were alike real, but the gods and heroes at the commencement were in a certain sense the most real; at least, they were the most esteemed and indispensable of all. The value of the genealogy consisted, not in its length, but in its continuity; not (according to the feeling of modern aristocracy) in the power of setting out a prolonged series of human fathers and grandfathers, but in the sense of ancestral union with the primitive god. And the length of the series is traceable rather to humility, inasmuch as the same person who was gratified with the belief that he was descended from a god in the fifteenth generation, would have accounted it criminal insolence to affirm that a god was his father or grandfather. In presenting to the reader those genealogies which constitute the supposed primitive history of Hellas, I make no pretence to distinguish names real and historical from fictitious creations; partly because I have no evidence upon which to draw the line, and partly because by attempting it I should altogether depart from the genuine Grecian point of view.

Nor is it possible to do more than exhibit a certain selection of such as were most current and interesting; for the total number of them which found place in Grecian faith exceeds computation. As a general rule, every deme, every gens, every aggregate of men accustomed to combined action, religious or political, had its own. The small and unimportant demes into which Attica was divided had each its ancestral god and heroes, just as much as the great Athens herself. Even among the villages of Phokis, which Pausanias will hardly permit himself to call towns, deductions of legendary antiquity were not wanting. And it is important to bear in mind, when we are reading the legendary genealogies of Argos, or Sparta, or Thêbes, that these are merely samples amidst an extensive class, all perfectly analogous, and all exhibiting the religious and patriotic retrospect of some fraction of the Hellenic world. They are no more matter of historical tradition than any of the thousand other legendary genealogies which men delighted to recall to memory at the periodical festivals of their gens, their deme, or their village.

With these few prefatory remarks, I proceed to notice the most conspicuous of the Grecian heroic pedigrees, and first, that of Argos.

The earliest name in Argeian antiquity is that of Inachus, the son of Oceanus and Têthys, who gave his name to the river flowing under the walls of the town. According to the chronological computations of those who regarded the mythical genealogies as substantive history, and who allotted a given number of years to each generation, the reign of Inachus was placed 1986 B. C., or about 1100 years prior to the commencement of the recorded Olympiads.[1]

The sons of Inachus were Phorôneus and Ægialeus; both of whom however were sometimes represented as autochthonous men, the one in the territory of Argos, the other in that of Sikyôn. Ægialeus gave his name to the north-western region of the Peloponnêsus, on the southern coast of the Corinthian Gulf.[2] The name of Phorôneus was of great celebrity in the Argeian mythical genealogies, and furnished both the title and the subject of the ancient poem called Phorônis, in which he is styled "the father of mortal men."[3] He is said to have imparted to

---

[1] Apollodôr. ii. 1. Mr. Fynes Clinton does not admit the historical reality of Inachus; but he places Phorôneus seventeen generations, or 570 years prior to the Trojan war, 978 years earlier than the first recorded Olympiad. See Fasti Hellenici, vol. iii. c. 1. p. 19.

[2] Pausan. ii. 5, 4.

[3] See Düntzer, Fragm. Epic. Græc. p. 57. The Argeian author Akusilaus, treated Phorôneus as the first of men, Fragm. 14. Didot ap. Clem. Alex.

mankind, who had before him lived altogether isolated, the first
notion and habits of social existence, and even the first knowledge of fire : his dominion extended over the whole Peloponnêsus. His tomb at Argos, and seemingly also the place called the
Phorônic city, in which he formed the first settlement of mankind, were still shown in the days of Pausanias.[1] The offspring
of Phorôneus, by the nymph Teledikê, were Apis and Niobê.
Apis, a harsh ruler, was put to death by Thelxiôn and Telchin,
having given to Peloponnêsus the name of Apia:[2] he was succeeded by Argos, the son of his sister Niobê by the god Zeus.
From this sovereign Peloponnêsus was denominated Argos. By
his wife Evadnê, daughter of Strymôn,[3] he had four sons, Ekbasus, Peiras, Epidaurus, and Kriasus. Ekbasus was succeeded by
his son Agênôr, and he again by his son Argos Panoptês, — a

Stromat. i. p. 321. Φορωνῆες, a synonym for Argeians; Theocrit. Idyll.
xxv. 200.

[1] Apollodôr. ii. 1, 1 ; Pausan. ii. 15, 5 ; 19, 5 ; 20, 3.

[2] Apis in Æschylus is totally different: ἰατρόμαντις or medical charmer,
son of Apollo, who comes across the gulf from Naupactus, purifies the territory of Argos from noxious monsters, and gives to it the name of Apia
(Æschyl. Suppl. 265). Compare Steph. Byz. v. Ἀπίη ; Soph. Œdip.
Colon. 1303. The name Ἀπία for Peloponnêsus remains still a mystery,
even after the attempt of Buttmann (Lexilogus, s. 19) to throw light upon
it.
     Eusebius asserts that Niobê was the wife of Inachus and mother of Pho-
rôneus, and pointedly contradicts those who call her daughter of Phorôneus
— φασὶ δέ τινες Νιόβην Φορωνέως εἶναι θυγατέρα, ὅπερ οὐκ ἀληθές (Chronic.
p. 23, ed. Scalig.) : his positive tone is curious, upon such a matter.
     Hellanicus in his Argolica stated that Phorôneus had three sons, Pelasgus,
Iasus and Agênôr, who at the death of their father divided his possessions
by lot. Pelasgus acquired the country near the river Erasinus, and built the
citadel of Larissa : Iasus obtained the portion near to Elis. After their
decease, the younger brother Agênôr invaded and conquered the country, at
the head of a large body of horse. It was from these three persons that
Argos derived three epithets which are attached to it in the Homeric
poems —Ἄργος Πελασγικὸν, Ἴασον, Ἱππόβοτον (Hellanik. Fr. 38, ed. Didot;
Phavorin. v. Ἄργος). This is a specimen of the way in which legendary
persons as well as legendary events were got up to furnish an explanation
of Homeric epithets : we may remark as singular, that Hellanicus seems to
apply Πελασγικὸν Ἄργος to a portion of Peloponnêsus, while the Homeric
Catalogue applies it to Thessaly.

[3] Apollod. l. c. The mention of Strymôn seems connected with Æschylus,
Suppl. 255.

very powerful prince who is said to have had eyes distributed over all his body, and to have liberated Peloponnêsus from several monsters and wild animals which infested it :[1] Akusilaus and Æschylus make this Argos an earth-born person, while Pherekydês reports him as son of Arestôr. Iasus was the son of Argos Panoptês by Ismênê, daughter of Asôpus. According to the authors whom Apollodôrus and Pausanias prefer, the celebrated Iô was his daughter: but the Hesiodic epic (as well as Akusilaus) represented her as daughter of Peiras, while Æschylus and Kastor the chronologist affirmed. the primitive king Inachus to have been her father.[2] A favorite theme, as well for the ancient genealogical poets as for the Attic tragedians, were the adventures of Iô, of whom, while priestess of Hêrê, at the ancient and renowned Hêræon between Mykênæ and Argos, Zeus became amorous. When Hêrê discovered the intrigue and taxed him with it, he denied the charge, and metamorphosed Iô into a white cow. Hêrê, requiring that the cow should be surrendered to her, placed her under the keeping of Argos Panoptês; but this guardian was slain by Hermês, at the command of Zeus: and Hêrê then drove the cow Iô away from her native land by means of the incessant stinging of a gad-fly, which compelled her to wander without repose or sustenance over an immeasurable extent of foreign regions. The wandering Iô gave her name to the Ionian Gulf, traversed Epirus and Illyria, passed the chain of Mount Hæmus and the lofty summits of Caucasus. and swam across the Thracian or Cimmerian Bosporus (which also from her derived its appellation) into Asia. She then went through Scythia, Cimmeria, and many Asiatic regions, until she arrived in Egypt, where Zeus at length bestowed upon her rest, restored her to her original form, and enabled her to give birth to his black son Epaphos.[3]

---

[1] Akusil. Fragm. 17, ed. Didot; Æsch. Prometh. 568; Pherekyd. Fragm. 22, ed. Didot; Hesiod. Ægimius. Fr. 2, p. 56, ed. Düntzer: among the varieties of the story, one was that Argos was changed into a peacock (Schol. Aristoph. Aves, 102). Macrobius (i. 19) considers Argos as an allegorical expression of the starry heaven; an idea which Panofska also upholds in one of the recent Abhandlungen of the Berlin Academy, 1837, p. 121 seq.

[2] Apollod. ii. 1, 1; Pausan. ii. 16, 1; Æsch. Prom. v. 590–663.

[3] Æschyl. Prom. v. 790–850; Apollod. ii. 1. Æschylus in the Supplices

Such is a general sketch of the adventures which the ancient poets, epic, lyric, and tragic, and the logographers after them, connect with the name of the Argeian Iô, — one of the numerous tales which the fancy of the Greeks deduced from the amorous dispositions of Zeus and the jealousy of Hêrê. That the scene should be laid in the Argeian territory appears natural, when we recollect that both Argos and Mykênæ were under the special guardianship of Hêrê, and that the Hêræon between the two was one of the oldest and most celebrated temples in which she was worshipped. It is useful to compare this amusing fiction with the representation reported to us by Herodotus, and derived by him as well from Phœnician as from Persian antiquarians, of the circumstances which occasioned the transit of Iô from Argos to Egypt, — an event recognized by all of them as historical matter of fact. According to the Persians, a Phœnician vessel had arrived at the port near Argos, freighted with goods intended for sale to the inhabitants of the country. After the vessel had remained a few days, and disposed of most of her cargo, several

gives a different version of the wanderings of Iô from that which appears in the Promêtheus: in the former drama he carries her through Phrygia, Mysia, Lydia, Pamphylia and Cilicia into Egypt (Supplic. 544–566) : nothing is there said about Promêtheus, or Caucasus or Scythia, etc.

The track set forth in the Supplices is thus geographically intelligible: that in the Promêtheus (though the most noticed of the two) defies all comprehension, even as a consistent fiction; nor has the erudition of the commentators been successful in clearing it up. See Schutz, Excurs. iv. ad Prometh. Vinct. pp. 144–149; Welcker, Æschylische Trilogie, pp. 127–146, and especially Völcker, Mythische Geographie der Griech. und Römer, part i. pp. 3–13.

The Greek inhabitants at Tarsus in Cilicia traced their origin to Argos: their story was, that Triptolemus had been sent forth from that town in quest of the wandering Iô, that he had followed her to Tyre, and then renounced the search in despair. He and his companions then settled partly at Tarsus, partly at Antioch (Strabo, xiv. 673; xv. 750). This is the story of Kadmos and Eurôpê inverted, as happens so often with the Grecian mythes.

Homer calls Hermês Ἀργειφόντης; but this epithet hardly affords suffi cient proof that he was acquainted with the mythe of Iô, as Völcker sup poses: it cannot be traced higher than Hesiod. According to some authors, whom Cicero copies, it was on account of the murder of Argos that Hermês was obliged to leave Greece and go into Egypt: then it was that he taught the Egyptians laws and letters (De Natur. Deor. iii. 22).

Argeian women, and among them Iô the king's daughter, coming on board to purchase, were seized and carried off by the crew, who sold Iô in Egypt.[1] The Phœnician antiquarians, however, while they admitted the circumstance that Iô had left her own country in one of their vessels, gave a different color to the whole by affirming that she emigrated voluntarily, having been engaged in an amour with the captain of the vessel, and fearing that her parents might come to the knowledge of her pregnancy. Both Persians and Phœnicians described the abduction of Iô as the first of a series of similar acts between Greeks and Asiatics, committed each in revenge for the preceding. First came the rape of Eurôpê from Phœnicia by Grecian adventurers, — perhaps, as Herodotus supposed, by Krêtans: next, the abduction of Mêdeia from Kolchis by Jasôn, which occasioned the retaliatory act of Paris, when he stole away Helena from Menelaos. Up to this point the seizures of women by Greeks from Asiatics, and by Asiatics from Greeks, had been equivalents both in number and in wrong. But the Greeks now thought fit to equip a vast conjoint expedition to recover Helen, in the course of which they took and sacked Troy. The invasions of Greece by Darius and Xerxes were intended, according to the Persian antiquarians, as a long-delayed retribution for the injury inflicted on the Asiatics by Agamemnôn and his followers.[2]

The account thus given of the adventures of Iô, when contrasted with the genuine legend, is interesting, as it tends to illus-

---

[1] The story in Parthênius (Narrat. 1) is built upon this version of Iô's adventures.

[2] Herodot. i. 1–6. Pausanias (ii. 15, 1) will not undertake to determine whether the account given by Herodotus, or that of the old legend, respecting the cause which carried Iô from Argos to Egypt, is the true one: Ephorus (ap. Schol. Apoll. Rhod. ii. 168) repeats the abduction of Iô to Egypt, by the Phœnicians, subjoining a strange account of the Etymology of the name Bosporus. The remarks of Plutarch on the narrative of Herodotus are curious : he adduces as one proof of the κακοήθεια (bad feeling) of Herodotus, that the latter inserts so discreditable a narrative respecting Iô, daughter of Inachus, " whom all Greeks believe to have been divinized by foreigners, to have given name to seas and straits, and to be the source of the most illustrious regal families." He also blames Herodotus for rejecting Epaphus, Iô, Iasus and Argos, as highest members of the Perseid genealogy. He calls Herodotus φιλοβάρβαρος (Plutarch, De Malign. Herodoti, c. xi. xii. xiv. pp. 856, 857).

trate the phænomenon which early Grecian history is constantly presenting to us, — the way in which the epical furniture of an unknown past is recast and newly colored so as to meet those changes which take place in the retrospective feelings of the present. The religious and poetical character of the old legend disappears : nothing remains except the names of persons and places, and the voyage from Argos to Egypt : we have in exchange a sober, quasi-historical narrative, the value of which consists in its bearing on the grand contemporary conflicts between Persia and Greece, which filled the imagination of Herodotus and his readers.

To proceed with the genealogy of the kings of Argos, Iasus was succeeded by Krotôpus, son of his brother Agênôr ; Krotôpus by Sthenelas, and he again by Gelanôr.[1] In the reign of the latter, Danaos came with his fifty daughters from Egypt to Argos ; and here we find another of those romantic adventures which so agreeably decorate the barrenness of the mythical genealogies. Danaos and Ægyptos were two brothers descending from Epaphos, son of Iô : Ægyptos had fifty sons, who were eager to marry the fifty daughters of Danaos, in spite of the strongest repugnance of the latter. To escape such a necessity, Danaos placed his fifty daughters on board of a penteconter (or vessel with fifty oars) and sought refuge at Argos ; touching in his voyage at the island of Rhodes, where he erected a statue of Athênê at Lindos, which was long exhibited as a memorial of his

---

[1] It would be an unprofitable fatigue to enumerate the multiplied and irreconcilable discrepancies in regard to every step of this old Argeian genealogy. Whoever desires to see them brought together, may consult Schubart, Quæstiones in Antiquitatem Heroicam, Marpurg, 1832, capp. 1 and 2.

The remarks which Schubart makes (p. 35) upon Petit-Radel's Chronological Tables will be assented to by those who follow the unceasing string of contradictions, without any sufficient reason to believe that any one of them is more worthy of trust than the remainder, which he has cited : — "Videant alii, quomodo genealogias heroicas, et chronologiæ rationes, in concordiam redigant. Ipse abstineo, probe persuasus, stemmata vera, historiæ fide comprobata, in systema chronologiæ redigi posse : at cre per sæcula tradita, a poetis reficta, sæpe mutata, prout fabula postulare videba tur, ab historiarum deinde conditoribus restituta, scilicet, brevi, qualia prostant stemmata — chronologiæ secundum annos distributæ vincula semper recusatura esse."

passage. Ægyptos and his sons followed them to Argos and still
pressed their suit, to which Danaos found himself compelled to
assent; but on the wedding night he furnished each of his daughters with a dagger, and enjoined them to murder their husbands
during the hour of sleep. His orders were obeyed by all, with
the single exception of Hypermnêstra, who preserved her husband Lynkeus, incurring displeasure and punishment from her
father. He afterwards, however, pardoned her; and when, by
the voluntary abdication of Gelanôr, he became king of Argos,
Lynkeus was recognized as his son-in-law and ultimately succeeded him. The remaining daughters, having been purified by
Athênê and Hermês, were given in marriage to the victors in a
gymnic contest publicly proclaimed. From Danaos was derived
the name of Danai, applied to the inhabitants of the Argeian
territory,[1] and to the Homeric Greeks generally.

From the legend of the Danaïdes we pass to two barren names
of kings, Lynkeus and his son Abas. The two sons of Abas
were Akrisios and Prœtos, who, after much dissension, divided
between them the Argeian territory; Akrisios ruling at Argos,
and Prœtos at Tiryns. The families of both formed the theme
of romantic stories. To pass over for the present the legend of
Bellerophôn, and the unrequited passion which the wife of Prœtos
conceived for him, we are told that the daughters of Prœtos,
beautiful, and solicited in marriage by suitors from all Greece-
were smitten with leprosy and driven mad, wandering in unseemly
guise throughout Peloponnêsus. The visitation had overtaken
them, according to Hesiod, because they refused to take part in
the Bacchic rites; according to Pherekydês and the Argeian
Akusilaus,[2] because they had treated scornfully the wooden statue

---

[1] Apollod. ii. 1. The Supplices of Æschylus is the commencing drama
of a trilogy on this subject of the Danaïdes, — Ἱκετίδες, Αἰγύπτιοι, Δαναΐ-
δες. Welcker, Griechisch. Tragödien, vol. i. p. 48: the two latter are lost.
The old epic poem called Danaïs or Danaïdes, which is mentioned in the
Tabula Iliaca as containing 5000 verses, has perished, and is unfortunately
very little alluded to: see Düntzer, Epic. Græc. Fragm. p. 3; Welcker, Der
Episch. Kyklus, p. 35.

[2] Apollod. 1. c.; Pherekyd. ap. Schol. Hom. Odyss. xv. 225; Hesiod,
Fragm. Marktsch. Fr. 36, 37, 38. These Fragments belong to the Hesiodic
Catalogue of Women: Apollodôrus seems to refer to some other of the
numerous Hesiodic poems. Diodôrus (iv. 68) assigns the anger of Dionysos as the cause.

and simple equipments of Hêrê: the religious character of the old legend here displays itself in a remarkable manner. Unable to cure his daughters, Prœtos invoked the aid of the renowned Pylian prophet and leech, Melampus son of Amythaôn, who undertook to remove the malady on condition of being rewarded with the third part of the kingdom. Prœtos indignantly refused these conditions: but the state of his daughters becoming aggravated and intolerable, he was compelled again to apply to Melampus; who, on the second request, raised his demands still higher, and required another third of the kingdom for his brother Bias. These terms being acceded to, he performed his part of the covenant. He appeased the wrath of Hêrê by prayer and sacrifice; or, according to another account, he approached the deranged women at the head of a troop of young men, with shouting and ecstatic dance, — the ceremonies appropriate to the Bacchic worship of Dionysos, — and in this manner effected their cure. Melampus, a name celebrated in many different Grecian mythes, is the legendary founder and progenitor of a great and long-continued family of prophets. He and his brother Bias became kings of separate portions of the Argeian territory: he is recognized as ruler there even in the Odyssey, and the prophet Theoklymenos, his grandson, is protected and carried to Ithaca by Telemachus.[1] Herodotus also alludes to the cure of the women, and to the double kingdom of Melampus and Bias in the Argeian land: he recognizes Melampus as the first person who introduced to the knowledge of the Greeks the name and worship of Dionysos, with its appropriate sacrifices and phallic processions. Here again he historicizes various features of the old legend in a manner not unworthy of notice.[2]

But Danaê, the daughter of Akrisios, with her son Perseus

---

[1] Odyss. xv. 240–256.

[2] Herod. ix. 34; ii. 49: compare Pausan. ii. 18, 4. Instead of the Prœtides, or daughters of Prœtos, it is the Argeian women generally whom he represents Melampus as having cured, and the Argeians generally who send to Pylus to invoke his aid: the heroic personality which pervades the primitive story has disappeared.

Kallimachus notices the Prœtid virgins as the parties suffering from madness, but he treats Artemis as the healing influence (Hymn. ad Dianam 235).

acquired still greater celebrity than her cousins the Prœtides An oracle had apprized Akrisios that his daughter would give birth to a son by whose hand he would himself be slain. To guard against this danger, he imprisoned Danaê in a chamber of brass under ground. But the god Zeus had become amorous of her, and found means to descend through the roof in the form of a shower of gold: the consequence of his visits was the birth of Perseus. When Akrisios discovered that his daughter had given existence to a son, he enclosed both the mother and the child in a coffer, which he cast into the sea.[1] The coffer was carried to the isle of Seriphos, where Diktys, brother of the king Polydektês, fished it up, and rescued both Danaê and Perseus. The exploits of Perseus, when he grew up, against the three Phorkides or daughters of Phorkys, and the three Gorgons, are among the most marvellous and imaginative in all Grecian legend: they bear a stamp almost Oriental. I shall not here repeat the details of those unparalleled hazards which the special favor of Athênê enabled him to overcome, and which ended in his bringing back from Libya the terrific head of the Gorgon Medusa, endued with the property of turning every one who looked upon it into stone. In his return, he rescued Andromeda, daughter of Kêpheus, who had been exposed to be devoured by a sea-monster, and brought her back as his wife. Akrisios trembled to see him after this victorious expedition, and retired into Thessaly to avoid him; but Perseus followed him thither, and having succeeded in calming his apprehensions, became competitor in a gymnic contest where his grandfather was among the spectators. By an incautious swing of his quoit, he unintentionally struck Akrisios, and caused his death: the predictions of the oracle were thus at last fulfilled. Stung with remorse at the catastrophe, and unwilling to return to Argos, which had been the principality of Akrisios, Perseus made an exchange with Megapenthês, son of Prœtos king of Tiryns. Megapenthês became king of Argos, and Perseus of Tiryns: moreover, the latter founded, within ten miles of Argos, the far-famed city of Mykênæ. The massive walls of this city,

---

[1] The beautiful fragment of Simonidês (Fragm. vii. ed. Gaisford. Poet. Min.), describing Danaê and the child thus exposed, is familiar to every classical reader.

like those of Tiryns, of which remains are yet to be seen, were built for him by the Lykian Cyclôpes.[1]

We here reach the commencement of the Perseid dynasty of Mykênæ. It should be noticed, however, that there were among the ancient legends contradictory accounts of the foundation of this city. Both the Odyssey and the Great Eoiai enumerated, among the heroines, Mykênê, the Eponyma of the city; the former poem classifying her with Tyrô and Alkmênê, the latter describing her as the daughter of Inachus and wife of Arestôr. And Akusilaus mentioned an Eponymus Mykêneus, the son of Spartôn and grandson of Phorôneus.[2]

The prophetic family of Melampus maintained itself in one of the three parts of the divided Argeian kingdom for five generations, down to Amphiaraos and his sons Alkmæôn and Amphi lochos. The dynasty of his brother Bias, and that of Megapenthês, son of Prœtos, continued each for four generations: a list of barren names fills up the interval.[3] The Perseids of Mykênæ boasted a descent long and glorious, heroic as well as historical, continuing down to the last sovereigns of Sparta.[4] The issue of Perseus was numerous: his son Alkæos was father of Amphitryôn; another of his sons, Elektryôn, was father of Alkmênê;[5] a third, Sthenelos, father of Eurystheus.

After the death of Perseus, Alkæos and Amphitryôn dwelt at Tiryns. The latter became engaged in a quarrel with Elektryôn

---

[1] Paus. ii. 15, 4; ii. 16, 5. Apollod. ii. 2. Pherekyd. Fragm. 26, Dind.

[2] Odyss. ii. 120. Hesiod. Fragment. 154. Marktscheff. — Akusil. Fragm. 16. Pausan. ii. 16, 4. Hekatæus derived the name of the town from the μύκης of the sword of Perseus (Fragm. 360, Dind.). The Schol. ad Eurip. Orest. 1247, mentions Mykêneus as son of Spartôn, but grandson of Phêgeus the brother of Phorôneus.

[3] Pausan. ii. 18, 4.   [4] Herodot. vi. 53.

[5] In the Hesiodic Shield of Hêraklês, Alkmênê is distinctly mentioned as daughter of Elektryôn; the genealogical poet, Asios, called her the daughter of Amphiaraos and Eriphyle (Asii Fragm. 4, ed. Markt. p. 412). The date of Asios cannot be precisely fixed; but he may be probably assigned to an epoch between the 30th and 40th Olympiad.

Asios must have adopted a totally different legend respecting the birth of Hêraklês and the circumstances preceding it, among which the deaths of her father and brothers are highly influential. Nor could he have accepted the received chronology of the sieges of Thêbes and Troy.

respecting cattle, and in a fit of passion killed him :[1] moreover the piratical Taphians from the west coast of Akarnania invaded the country, and slew the sons of Elektryôn, so that Alkmênê alone was left of that family. She was engaged to wed Amphitryôn ; but she bound him by oath not to consummate the marriage until he had avenged upon the Têleboæ the death of her brothers. Amphitryôn, compelled to flee the country as the murderer of his uncle, took refuge in Thêbes, whither Alkmênê accompanied him: Sthenelos was left in possession of Tiryns. The Kadmeians of Thêbes, together with the Locrians and Phocians, supplied Amphitryôn with troops, which he conducted against the Têleboæ and the Taphians :[2] yet he could not have subdued them without the aid of Komæthô, daughter of the Taphian king Pterelaus, who conceived a passion for him, and cut off from her father's head the golden lock to which Poseidôn had attached the gift of immortality.[3] Having conquered and expelled his enemies, Amphitryôn returned to Thêbes, impatient to consummate his marriage: but Zeus on the wedding-night assumed his form and visited Alkmênê before him: he had deter-mined to produce from her a son superior to all his prior offspring, — "a specimen of invincible force both to gods and men."[4] At the proper time, Alkmênê was delivered of twin sons: Hêraklês the offspring of Zeus, — the inferior and unhonored Iphiklês, offspring of Amphitryôn.[5]

When Alkmênê was on the point of being delivered at Thêbes, Zeus publicly boasted among the assembled gods, at the instigation of the mischief-making Atê, that there was on that day about

---

[1] So runs the old legend in the Hesiodic Shield of Hêraklês (12–82). Apollodôrus (or Pherekydês, whom he follows) softens it down, and repre-sents the death of Elektryôn as accidentally caused by Amphitryôn. (Apollod. ii. 4, 6. Pherekydês, Fragm. 27, Dind.)

[2] Hesiod, Scut. Herc. 24. Theocrit. Idyll. xxiv. 4. Teleboas, the Epo-nym of these marauding people, was son of Poseidôn (Anaximander ap. Athenæ. xi. p. 498).

[3] Apollod. ii. 4, 7. Compare the fable of Nisus at Megara, *infra*, chap xii. p. 302.

[4] Hesiod, Scut. Herc. 29. ὄφρα θεοῖσιν 'Ανδράσι τ' ἀλφηστῇσιν ἀρῆς ἑλκτῆρα φυτεύσῃ.

[5] Hesiod. Sc. H. 50–56.

to be born on earth, from his breed, a son who should rule over all his neighbors. Hêrê treated this as an empty boast, calling upon him to bind himself by an irremissible oath that the prediction should be realized. Zeus incautiously pledged his solemn word; upon which Hêrê darted swiftly down from Olympus to the Achaic Argos, where the wife of Sthenelos (son of Perseus, and therefore grandson of Zeus) was already seven months gone with child. By the aid of the Eileithyiæ, the special goddesses of parturition, she caused Eurystheus, the son of Sthenelos, to be born before his time on that very day, while she retarded the delivery of Alkmênê. Then returning to Olympus, she announced the fact to Zeus: "The good man Eurystheus, son of the Perseid Sthenelos, is this day born of thy loins: the sceptre of the Argeians worthily belongs to him." Zeus was thunderstruck at the consummation which he had improvidently bound himself to accomplish. He seized Atê his evil counsellor by the hair, and hurled her forever away from Olympus: but he had no power to avert the ascendency of Eurystheus and the servitude of Hêraklês. "Many a pang did he suffer, when he saw his favorite son going through his degrading toil in the tasks imposed upon him by Eurystheus."[1]

The legend, of unquestionable antiquity, here transcribed from the Iliad, is one of the most pregnant and characteristic in the Grecian mythology. It explains, according to the religious ideas familiar to the old epic poets, both the distinguishing attributes and the endless toil and endurances of Hêraklês, — the most renowned and most ubiquitous of all the semi-divine personages worshipped by the Hellênes, — a being of irresistible force, and especially beloved by Zeus, yet condemned constantly to labor for others and to obey the commands of a worthless and cowardly persecutor. His recompense is reserved to the close of his career, when his afflicting trials are brought to a close: he is then admitted to the godhead and receives in marriage Hêbê.[2] The

---

Homer, Iliad, xix. 90–133; also viii. 361. —

Τὴν ἀεὶ στενάχεσχ', ὅθ' ἑὸν φίλον υἱὸν ὁρῷτο
Ἔργον ἀεικὲς ἔχοντα, ὑπ' Εὐρυσθῆος ἀέθλων.

[2] Hesiod, Theogon. 951, τελέσας στονόεντας ἀέθλους. Hom. Odyss. xi. 620; Hesiod, Eœæ, Fragm. 24, Düntzer, p. 36, πονηρότατον καὶ ἄριστον

twelve labors, as they are called, too notorious to be here detailed, form a very small fraction of the exploits of this mighty being, which filled the Hêrakleian epics of the ancient poets. He is found not only in most parts of Hellas, but throughout all the :ther regions then known to the Greeks, from Gadês to the river Thermôdôn in the Euxine and to Scythia, overcoming all difficulties and vanquishing all opponents. Distinguished families are everywhere to be traced who bear his patronymic, and glory in the belief that they are his descendants. Among Achæans, Kadmeians, and Dôrians, Hêraklês is venerated: the latter especially reat him as their principal hero, — the Patron Hero-God of the race: the Hêrakleids form among all Dôrians a privileged gens, in which at Sparta the special lineage of the two kings was included.

His character lends itself to mythes countless in number as well as disparate in their character. The irresistible force remains constant, but it is sometimes applied with reckless violence against friends as well as enemies, sometimes devoted to the relief of the oppressed. The comic writers often brought him out as a coarse and stupid glutton, while the Athênian philosopher Prodikos, without at all distorting the type, extracted from it the simple, impressive, and imperishable apologue still known as the Choice of Hercules.

After the death and apotheosis of Hêraklês, his son Hyllos and his other children were expelled and persecuted by Eurystheus: the fear of his vengeance deterred both the Trachinian king Kêyx and the Thêbans from harboring them, and the Athênians alone were generous enough to brave the risk of offering them shelter. Eurystheus invaded Attica, but perished in the attempt by the hand of Hyllos, or by that of Iolaos, the old companion and nephew of Hêraklês.[1] The chivalrous courage which the Athênians had on this occasion displayed in behalf of oppressed innocence, was a favorite theme for subsequent eulogy by Attic poets and orators.

All the sons of Eurystheus lost their lives in the battle along with him, so that the Perseid family was now represented only by the Hêrakleids, who collected an army and endeavored to

---

[1] Apollod. ii. 8, 1 ; Hecatæ. ap. Longin. c. 27; Diodôr. iv. 57.

recover the possessions from which they had been expelled. The united forces of Iônians, Achæans, and Arcadians, then inhabiting Peloponnêsus, met the invaders at the isthmus, when Hyllos, the eldest of the sons of Hêraklês, proposed that the contest should be determined by a single combat between himself and any champion of the opposing army. It was agreed, that if Hyllos were victorious, the Hêrakleids should be restored to their possessions — if he were vanquished, that they should forego all claim for the space of a hundred years, or fifty years, or three generations, — for in the specification of the time, accounts differ. Echemos, the hero of Tegea in Arcadia, accepted the challenge, and Hyllos was slain in the encounter ; in consequence of which the Hêrakleids retired, and resided along with the Dôrians under the protection of Ægimios, son of Dôrus.[1] As soon as the stipulated period of truce had expired, they renewed their attempt upon Peloponnêsus conjointly with the Dôrians, and with complete success: the great Dôrian establishments of Argos, Sparta, and Messênia were the result. The details of this victorious invasion will be hereafter recounted.

Sikyôn, Phlios, Epidauros, and Trœzen[2] all boasted of respected eponyms and a genealogy of dignified length, not exempt from the usual discrepancies — but all just as much entitled to a place on the tablet of history as the more renowned Æolids or Hêrakleids. I omit them here because I wish to impress upon the reader's mind the salient features and character of the legendary world, — not to load his memory with a full list of legendary names.

---

[1] Herodot. ix. 26 ; Diodôr. iv. 58.

[2] Pausan. ii. 5, 5 ; 12, 5; 26, 3. His statements indicate how much the predominance of a powerful neighbor like Argos tended to alter the genealogies of these inferior towns.

CHAPTER V.

DEUKALION, HELLEN, AND SONS OF HELLEN.

In the Hesiodic Theogony, as well as in the "Works and Days," the legend of Promêtheus and Epimêtheus presents an import religious, ethical, and social, and in this sense it is carried forward by Æschylus; but to neither of the characters is any genealogical function assigned. The Hesiodic Catalogue of Women brought both of them into the stream of Grecian legendary lineage, representing Deukaliôn as the son of Promêtheus and Pandôra, and seemingly his wife Pyrrha as daughter of Epimêtheus.[1]

Deukaliôn is important in Grecian mythical narrative under two points of view. First, he is the person specially saved at the time of the general deluge: next, he is the father of Hellên, the great eponym of the Hellenic race; at least this was the more current story, though there were other statements which made Hellên the son of Zeus.

The name of Deukaliôn is originally connected with the Lokrian towns of Kynos and Opus, and with the race of the Leleges, but he appears finally as settled in Thessaly, and ruling in the portion of that country called Phthiôtis.[2] According to what seems to have been the old legendary account, it is the

---

[1] Schol. ad Apollôn. Rhod. iii. 1085. Other accounts of the genealogy of Deukaliôn are given in the Schol. ad Homer. Odyss. x. 2, on the authority both of Hesiod and Akusilaus.

[2] Hesiodic Catalog. Fragm. xi.; Gaisf. lxx. Dûntzer—

> Ἤτοι γὰρ Λοκρὸς Δελέγων ἡγήσατο λαῶν,
> Τούς ῥά ποτε Κρονίδης Ζεὺς, ἄφθιτα μήδεα εἰδὼς,
> Λεκτοὺς ἐκ γαίης λάας πόρε Δευκαλίωνι.

The reputed lineage of Deukaliôn continued in Phthia down to the time of Dikæarchus, if we may judge from the old Phthiot Pherekratês, whom he introduced in one of his dialogues as a disputant, and whom he expressly announced as a descendant of Deukaliôn (Cicero, Tuscul. Disp. i. 10).

deluge which transferred him from the one to the other; but according to another statement, framed in more historicizing times, he conducted a body of Kurêtes and Leleges into Thessaly, and expelled the prior Pelasgian occupants.[1]

The enormous iniquity with which earth was contaminated — as Apollodorus says, by the then existing brazen race, or as others say, by the fifty monstrous sons of Lykaôn — provoked Zeus to send a general deluge.[2] An unremitting and terrible rain laid the whole of Greece under water, except the highest mountain-tops, whereon a few stragglers found refuge. Deukalion was saved in a chest or ark, which he had been forewarned by his father Promêtheus to construct. After floating for nine days on the water, he at length landed on the summit of Mount Parnassus. Zeus having sent Hermês to him, promising to grant whatever he asked, he prayed that men and companions might be sent to him in his solitude: accordingly Zeus directed both him and Pyrrha to cast stones over their heads: those cast by Pyrrha became women, those by Deukaliôn men. And thus the "stony race of men" (if we may be allowed to translate an etymology which the Greek language presents exactly, and which has not been disdained by Hesiod, by Pindar, by Epicharmus, and by Virgil) came to tenant the soil of Greece.[3] Deukaliôn

---

[1] The latter account is given by Dionys. Halic. i. 17; the former seems to have been given by Hellanikus, who affirmed that the ark after the deluge stopped upon Mount Othrys, and not upon Mount Parnassus (Schol. Pind. *ut. sup.*) the former being suitable for a settlement in Thessaly.

Pyrrha is the eponymous heroine of Pyrrhæa or Pyrrha, the ancient name of a portion of Thessaly (Rhianus, Fragm. 18. p. 71, ed, Düntzer).

Hellanikus had written a work, now lost, entitled Δευκαλιώνεια: all the fragments of it which are cited have reference to places in Thessaly, Lokris and Phokis. See Preller, ad Hellanitum, p. 12 (Dörpt. 1840). Probably Hellanikus is the main source of the important position occupied by Deukaliôn in Grecian legend. Thrasybulus and Akestodôrus represented Deukaliôn as having founded the oracle of Dôdôna, immediately after the deluge (Etm. Mag. v. Δωδωναῖος).

[2] Apollodôrus connects this deluge with the wickedness of the brazen race in Hesiod, according to the practice general with the logographers of stringing together a sequence out of legends totally unconnected with each other (i. 7, 2).

[3] Hesiod, Fragm. 135. ed. Markts. ap. Strabo. vii. p. 322, where the word λάας, proposed by Heyne as the reading of the unintelligible text, appears to

on landing from the ark sacrificed a grateful offering to Zeus
Phyxios, or the God of escape; he also erected altars in Thessaly
to the twelve great gods of Olympus.[1]

The reality of this deluge was firmly believed throughout the
historical ages of Greece: the chronologers, reckoning up by genealogies, assigned the exact date of it, and placed it at the same
time as the conflagration of the world by the rashness of Phaë-
tôn, during the reign of Krotôpas king of Argus, the seventh
from Inachus.[2] The meteorological work of Aristotle admits and
reasons upon this deluge as an unquestionable fact, though he
alters the locality by placing it west of Mount Pindus, near Dôdôna and the river Achelôus.[3] He at the same time treats it as
a physical phænomenon, the result of periodical cycles in the
atmosphere, thus departing from the religious character of the
old legend, which described it as a judgment inflicted by Zeus
upon a wicked race. Statements founded upon this event were
in circulation throughout Greece even to a very late date. The
Megarians affirmed that Megaros, their hero, son of Zeus by a
local nymph, had found safety from the waters on the lofty sum-

---

me preferable to any of the other suggestions. Pindar, Olymp. ix. 47.
Ἀτερ δ' Εὐνᾶς ὁμόδαμον Κτησάσθαν λίθινον γόνον· Λαοὶ δ' ὠνόμασθεν.
Virgil, Georgic i. 63. "Unde homines nati, durum genus." Epicharmus ap.
Schol. Pindar. Olymp. ix. 56. Hygin. f. 153. Philochorus retained the ety-
mology, though he gave a totally different fable, nowise connected with
Deukaliôn, to account for it; a curious proof how pleasing it was to the
fancy of the Greek (see Schol. ad Pind. l. c. 68).

  [1] Apollod. i. 7, 2. Hellanic. Fragm. 15. Didot. Hellanikus affirmed that
the ark rested on Mount Othrys, not on Mount Parnassus (Fragm. 16. Didot).
Servius (ad Virgil. Eclog. vi. 41) placed it on Mount Athôs — Hyginus (f.
153) on Mount Ætna.

  [2] Tatian adv. Græc. c. 60, adopted both by Clemens and Eusebius. The
Parian marble placed this deluge in the reign of Kranaos at Athens, 752
years before the first recorded Olympiad, and 1528 years before the Christian
æra; Apollodôrus also places it in the reign of Kranaos, and in that of
Nyctimus in Arcadia (iii. 8, 2; 14, 5).

  The deluge and the ekpyrosis or conflagration are connected together also
in Servius ad Virgil. Bucol. vi. 41: he refines both of them into a "muta-
tionem temporum."

  [3] Aristot. Meteorol. i. 14. Justin rationalizes the fable by telling us that
Deukaliôn was king of Thessaly, who provided shelter and protection to
the fugitives from the deluge (ii. 6, 11)

mit of their mountain Geraneia, which had not been completely submerged. And in the magnificent temple of the Olympian Zeus at Athens, a cavity in the earth was shown, through which it was affirmed that the waters of the deluge had retired. Even in the time of Pausanias, the priests poured into this cavity holy offerings of meal and honey.[1] In this, as in other parts of Greece, the idea of the Deukalionian deluge was blended with the religious impressions of the people and commemorated by their sacred ceremonies.

The offspring of Deukaliôn and Pyrrha were two sons, Hellên and Amphiktyôn, and a daughter, Prôtogeneia, whose son by Zeus was Aëthlius: it was however maintained by many, that Hellên was the son of Zeus and not of Deukaliôn. Hellên had by a nymph three sons, Dôrus, Xuthus, and Æolus. He gave to those who had been before called Greeks,[2] the name of Hellênes, and partitioned his terrritory among his three children. Æolus reigned in Thessaly; Xuthus received Peloponnêsus, and had by Creüsa as his sons, Achæus and Iôn; while Dôrus occupied the country lying opposite to the Peloponnêsus, on the northern side of the Corinthian Gulf. These three gave to the inhabitants of their respective countries the names of Æolians, Achæans and Iônians, and Dôrians.[3]

Such is the genealogy as we find it in Apollodôrus. In so far as the names and filiation are concerned, many points in it are given differently, or implicitly contradicted, by Euripidês and other writers. Though as literal and personal history it deserves

---

[1] Pausan. i. 18, 7; 40, 1. According to the Parian marble (s. 5), Deukaliôn had come to Athens after the deluge, and had there himself founded the temple of the Olympian Zeus. The etymology and allegorization of the names of Deukaliôn and Pyrrha, given by Völcker in his ingenious Mythologie des Iapetischen Geschlechts (Giessen, 1824), p. 343, appears to me not at all convincing.

[2] Such is the statement of Apollodôrus (i. 7, 3); but I cannot bring myself to believe that the name (Γραϊκοὶ) Greeks is at all old in the legend, or that the passage of Hesiod, in which Græcus and Latinus purport to be mentioned, is genuine.

See Hesiod, Theogon. 1013. and Catalog. Fragm. xxix. ed. Göttling. with the note of Göttling; also Wachsmuth, Hellen. Alterth. i. 1. p. 311, and Bernhardy, Griech, Literat. vol. i. p. 167.

[3] Apollod. i. 7, 4.

ᴏꝑ notice, its import is both intelligible and comprehensive. It expounds and symbolizes the first fraternal aggregation of Hellênic men, together with their territorial distribution and the institutions which they collectively venerated. There were two great holding-points in common for every section of Greeks. One was the Amphiktyonic assembly, which met half-yearly, alternately at Delphi and at Thermopylæ; originally and chiefly for common religious purposes, but indirectly and occasionally embracing political and social objects along with them. The other was, the public festivals or games, of which the Olympic came first in importance; next, the Pythian, Nemean and Isthmian, — institutions which combined religious solemnities with recreative effusion and hearty sympathies, in a manner so imposing and so unparalleled. Amphiktyôn represents the first of these institutions, and Aëthlius the second. As the Amphiktyonic assembly was always especially connected with Thermopylæ and Thessally, Amphiktyôn is made the son of the Thessalian Deukaliôn; but as the Olympic festival was nowise locally connected with Deukaliôn, Aëthlius is represented as having Zeus for his father, and as touching Deukaliôn only through the maternal line. It will be seen presently, that the only matter predicated respecting Aëthlius is, that he settled in the territory of Elis, and begat Endymiên: this brings him into local contact with the Olympic games, and his function is then ended.

Having thus got Hellas as an aggregate with its main cementing forces, we march on to its subdivision into parts, through Æolus, Dôrus and Xuthus, the three sons of Hellen;[1] a distribution which is far from being exhaustive: nevertheless, the genealogists whom Apollodôrus follows recognize no more than three sons.

The genealogy is essentially post-Homeric; for Homer knows Hellas and the Hellênes only in connection with a portion of

---

[1] How literally and implicitly even the ablest Greeks believed in eponymous persons, such as Hellên and Iôn, as the real progenitors of the races called after him, may be seen by this, that Aristotle gives this common descent as the definition of γένος (Metaphysic. iv. p. 118, Brandis):—

Γένος λέγεται, τὸ μὲν ...... τὸ δὲ, ἀφ' οὗ ἂν ὦσι πρώτου κινήσαντος εἰς τὸ εἶναι. Οὕτω γὰρ λέγονται οἱ μὲν, Ἕλληνες τὸ γένος, οἱ δὲ, Ἴωνες· τῷ, οἱ ᴍὲν ἀπὸ Ἕλληνος, οἱ δὲ ἀπὸ Ἴωνος, εἶναι πρώτου γεννήσαντος.

Achaia Phthiôtis. But as it is recognized in the Hesiodic Catalogue [1] — composed probably within the first century after the commencement of recorded Olympiads, or before 676 B. C. — the peculiarities of it, dating from so early a period, deserve much attention. We may remark, first, that it seems to exhibit to us Dôrus and Æolus as the only pure and genuine offspring of Hellên. For their brother Xuthus is not enrolled as an eponymus; he neither founds nor names any people; it is only his sons Achæus and Iôn, after his blood has been mingled with that of the Erechtheid Kreüsa, who become eponyms and founders, each of his own separate people. Next, as to the territorial distribution, Xuthus receives Peloponnêsus from his father, and unites himself with Attica (which the author of this genealogy seems to have conceived as originally unconnected with Hellên) by his marriage with the daughter of the indigenous hero, Erechtheus. The issue of this marriage, Achæus and Iôn, present to us the population of Peloponnêsus and Attica conjointly as related among themselves by the tie of brotherhood, but as one degree more distant both from Dôrians and Æolians. Æolus reigns over the regions about Thessaly, and called the people in those parts Æolians ; while Dôrus occupies " the country over against Peloponnêsus on the opposite side of the Corinthian Gulf," and calls the inhabitants after himself, Dôrians.[2] It is at once evident that

---

[1] Hesiod, Fragm. 8. p. 278, ed. Marktsch.—

'Έλληνος δ' ἐγένοντο θεμιστόπολοι βασιλῆες
Δῶρός τε, Ξοῦθός τε, καὶ Αἴολος ἱππιοχάρμης
Αἰολίδαι δ' ἐγένοντο θεμιστόπολοι βασιλῆες
Κρηθεὺς ἠδ' Ἀθάμας καὶ Σίσυφος αἰολομήτης
Σαλμωνεύς τ' ἄδικος καὶ ὑπέρθυμος Περιήρης.

[2] Apollod. i. 7, 3. Ἕλληνος δὲ καὶ Νύμφης Ὀρσηΐδος (?), Δῶρος, Ξοῦθος, Αἴολος. Αὐτὸς μὲν οὖν ἀφ' αὑτοῦ τοὺς καλουμένους Γραικοὺς προσηγόρευσεν Ἕλληνας, τοῖς δὲ παῖσιν ἐμέρισε τὴν χώραν. Καὶ Ξοῦθος μὲν λαβὼν τὴν Πελοπόννησον, ἐκ Κρεούσης τῆς Ἐρεχθέως Ἀχαιὸν ἐγέννησε καὶ Ἴωνα, ἀφ' ὧν Ἀχαιοὶ καὶ Ἴωνες καλοῦνται. Δῶρος δὲ, τ ὴ ν π έ ρ α ν χ ώ ρ α ν Π ε λ ο - π ο ν ν ή σ ο υ λ α β ὼ ν, τ ο ὺ ς κ α τ ο ί κ ο υ ς ἀ φ' ἑ α υ τ ο ῦ Δ ω ρ ι ε ῖ ς ἐ κ ά - λ ε σ ε ν. Αἴολος δὲ, βασιλεύων τῶν περὶ Θετταλίαν τόπων, τοὺς ἐνοικοῦντας Αἰολεῖς προσηγόρευσε.
Strabo (viii. p. 383) and Conôn (Narr. 27), who evidently copy from the same source, represent Dôrus as going to settle in the territory properly known as Dôris.

this designation is in no way applicable to the confined district
between Parnassus and Œta, which alone is known by the name
of Dôris, and its inhabitants by that of Dôrians, in the historical
ages. In the view of the author of this genealogy, the Dôrians
are the original occupants of the large range of territory north
of the Corinthian Gulf, comprising Ætôlia, Phôkis, and the
territory of the Ozolian Lokrians. And this farther harmonizes
with the other legend noticed by Apollodôrus, when he states
that Ætolus, son of Endymiôn, having been forced to expatriate
from Peloponnêsus, crossed into the Kurêtid territory,[1] and was
there hospitably received by Dôrus, Laodokus and Polypœtês,
sons of Apollo and Phthia. He slew his hosts, acquired the territory, and gave to it the name of Ætôlia: his son Pleurôn married Xanthippê, daughter of Dôrus; while his other son, Kalydôn,
marries Æolia, daughter of Amythaôn. Here again we have the
name of Dôrus, or the Dôrians, connected with the tract subsequently termed Ætôlia. That Dôrus should in one place be
called the son of Apollo and Phthia, and in another place the son
of Hellên by a nymph, will surprise no one accustomed to the
fluctuating personal nomenclature of these old legends: moreover
the name of Phthia is easy to reconcile with that of Hellên, as
both are identified with the same portion of Thessaly, even from
the days of the Iliad.

This story, that the Dôrians were at one time the occupants, or
the chief occupants, of the range of territory between the river
Achelôus and the northern shore of the Corinthian Gulf, is at
least more suitable to the facts attested by historical evidence
than the legends given in Herodotus, who represents the Dôrians
as originally in the Phthiôtid; then as passing under Dôrus, the
son of Hellên, into the Histiæôtid, under the mountains of Ossa and
Olympus; next, as driven by the Kadmeians into the regions of
Pindus; from thence passing into the Dryopid territory, on Mount
Œta; lastly, from thence into Peloponnêsus.[2] The received

---

[1] Apollod. i. 7, 6. Αἰτωλὸς . . . . φυγὼν εἰς τὴν Κουρητίδα χώραν,
κτείνας τοὺς ὑποδεξαμένους Φθίας καὶ Ἀπόλλωνος υἱοὺς, Δῶρον καὶ Λαόδοκον
καὶ Πολυποίτην, ἀφ' ἑαυτοῦ τὴν χώραν Αἰτωλίαν ἐκάλεσε. Again, i. 8, 1.
Πλευρὼν (son of Ætolus) γήμας Ξανθίππην τὴν Δώρου, παῖδα ἐγέννησεν
Αγήνορα.
[2] Herod. i. 56.

story was, that the great Dôrian establishments in Peloponnêsus were formed by invasion from the north, and that the invaders crossed the gulf from Naupaktus, — a statement which, however disputable with respect to Argos, seems highly probable in regard both to Sparta and Messênia. That the name of Dôrians comprehended far more than the inhabitants of the insignificant tetrapolis of Dôris Proper, must be assumed, if we believe that they conquered Sparta and Messênia : both the magnitude of the conquest itself, and the passage of a large portion of them from Naupaktus, harmonize with the legend as given by Apollodôrus, in which the Dorians are represented as the principal inhabitants of the northern shore of the gulf. The statements which we find in Herodotus, respecting the early migrations of the Dôrians, have been considered as possessing greater historical value than those of the fabulist Apollodôrus. But both are equally matter of legend, while the brief indications of the latter seem to be most in harmony with the facts which we afterwards find attested by history.

It has already been mentioned that the genealogy which makes Æolus, Xuthus and Dôrus sons of Hellên, is as old as the Hesiodic Catalogue ; probably also that which makes Hellên son of Deukaliôn. Aëthlius also is an Hesiodic personage : whether Amphiktyôn be so or not, we have no proof.[1] They could not have been introduced into the legendary genealogy until after the Olympic games and the Amphiktyonic council had acquired an

[1] Schol. Apollon. Rhod. iv. 57.   Τὸν δὲ Ἐνδυμίωνα Ἡσίοδος μὲν Ἀεθλίου τοῦ Διὸς καὶ Καλύκης παῖδα λέγει . . . .   Καὶ Πείσανδρος δὲ τὰ αὐτά φησι, καὶ Ἀκουσίλαος, καὶ Φερεκύδης, καὶ Νίκανδρος ἐν δευτέρῳ Αἰτωλικῶν, καὶ Θεόπομπος ἐν Ἐποποιίαις.

Respecting the parentage of Hellên, the references to Hesiod are very confused. Compare Schol. Homer. Odyss. x. 2, and Schol. Apollon. Rhod. iii. 1086. See also Hellanic. Frag. 10. Didot.

Apollodôrus, and Pherekydês before him (Frag. 51. Didot), called Protôgeneia daughter of Deukaliôn ; Pindar (Olymp. ix. 64) designated her as daughter of Opus. One of the stratagems mentioned by the Scholiast to get rid of this genealogical discrepancy was, the supposition that Deukaliôn had two names (διώνυμος) ; that he was also named Opus. (Schol. Pind. Olymp. ix. 85).

That the Deukalidæ or posterity of Deukaliôn reigned in Thessaly, was mentioned both by Hesiod and Hekatæus, ap. Schol. Apollon. Rhod. iv. 265.

established ascendancy and universal reverence throughout Greece.

Respecting Dôrus the son of Hellên, we find neither legends nor legendary genealogy; respecting Xuthus, very little beyond the tale of Kreüsa and Iôn, which has its place more naturally among the Attic fables. Achæus however, who is here represented as the son of Xuthus, appears in other stories with very different parentage and accompaniments. According to the statement which we find in Dionysius of Halicarnassus, Achæus, Phthius and Pelasgus are sons of Poseidôn and Larissa. They migrate from Peloponnêsus into Thessaly, and distribute the Thessalian territory between them, giving their names to its principal divisions : their descendants in the sixth generation were driven out of that country by the invasion of Deukaliôn at the head of the Kurêtes and the Leleges.[1] This was the story of those who wanted to provide an eponymus for the Achæans in the southern districts of Thessaly : Pausanias accomplishes the same object by different means, representing Achæus, the son of Xuthus as having gone back to Thessaly and occupied the portion of it to which his father was entitled. Then, by way of explaining how it was that there were Achæans at Sparta and at Argos, he tells us that Archander and Architelês, the sons of Archæus, came back from Thessaly to Peloponnêsus, and married two daughters of Danaus : they acquired great influence at Argos and Sparta, and gave to the people the name of Achæans after their father Achæus.[2]

Euripidês also deviates very materially from the Hesiodic

---

[1] Dionys. H. A. R. i. 17.

[2] Pausan. vii. 1, 1–3. Herodotus also mentions (ii. 97) Archander, son of Phthius and grandson of Achæus, who married the daughter of Danaus. Larcher (Essai sur la Chronologie d'Herodote, ch. x. p. 321) tells us that this cannot be the Danaus who came from Egypt, the father of the fifty daughters, who must have lived two centuries earlier, as may be proved by chronological arguments : this must be another Danaus, according to him.

Strabo seems to give a different story respecting the Achæans in Peleponnêsus : he says that they were the original population of the peninsula, that they came in from Phthia with Pelops, and inhabited Laconia, which was from them called Argos Achaicum, and that on the conquest of the Dôrians, they moved into Achaia properly so called, expelling the Iônians therefrom (Strabo, viii. p. 365). This narrative is, I presume, borrowed from Ephorus.

genealogy in respect to these eponymous persons. In the drama called Iôn, he describes Iôn as son of Kreüsa by Apollo, but adopted by Xuthus: according to him, the real sons of Xuthus and Kreüsa are Dôrus and Achæus,[1] — eponyms of the Dôrians and Achæans in the interior of Peloponnêsus. And it is a still more capital point of difference, that he omits Hellên altogether — making Xuthus an Achæan by race, the son of Æolus, who is the son of Zeus.[2] This is the more remarkable, as in the fragments of two other dramas of Euripidês, the Melanippê and the Æolus, we find Hellên mentioned both as father of Æolus and son of Zeus.[3] To the general public even of the most instructed city of Greece, fluctuations and discrepancies in these mythical genealogies seem to have been neither surprising nor offensive.

CHAPTER VI.

THE ÆOLIDS, OR SONS AND DAUGHTERS OF ÆOLUS.

IF two of the sons of Hellên, Dôrus and Xuthus, present to us families comparatively unnoticed in mythical narrative, the third son, Æolus, richly makes up for the deficiency. From him we pass to his seven sons and five daughters, amidst a great abundance of heroic and poetical incident.

In dealing however with these extensive mythical families, it is necessary to observe, that the legendary world of Greece, in the manner in which it is presented to us, appears invested with a degree of symmetry and coherence which did not originally belong to it. For the old ballads and stories which were sung or

---

[1] Eurip. Ion, 1590. [2] Eurip. Ion, 64.

[3] See the Fragments of these two plays in Matthiae's edition; compare Welcker, Griechisch. Tragöd. v. ii. p. 842. If we may judge from the Fragments of the Latin Melanippê of Ennius (see Fragm. 2, ed. Bothe), Hellên was introduced as one of the characters of the piece.

recounted at the multiplied festivals of Greece, each on its own
special theme, have been lost : the religious narratives, which the
Exegêtês of every temple had present to his memory, explanatory of the peculiar religious ceremonies and local customs in his
own town or Dême, have passed away : all these primitive elements, originally distinct and unconnected, are removed out of
our sight, and we possess only an aggregate result, formed by
many confluent streams of fable, and connected together by the
agency of subsequent poets and logographers.   Even the earliest
agents in this work of connecting and systematizing — the Hesiodic poets — have been hardly at all preserved.   Our information
respecting Grecian mythology is derived chiefly from the prose
logographers who followed them, and in whose works, since a
continuous narrative was above all things essential to them, the
fabulous personages are woven into still more comprehensive
pedigrees, and the original isolation of the legends still better
disguised.   Hekatæus, Pherekydês, Hellanikus, and Akusilaus
lived at a time when the idea of Hellas as one great whole, composed of fraternal sections, was deeply rooted in the mind of
every Greek; and when the fancy of one or a few great families,
branching out widely from one common stem, was more popular
and acceptable than that of a distinct indigenous origin in each of
the separate districts.   These logographers, indeed, have themselves been lost; but Apollodôrus and the various scholiasts, our
great immediate sources of information respecting Grecian mythology, chiefly borrowed from them : so that the legendary world of
Greece is in fact known to us through them, combined with the
dramatic and Alexandrine poets, their Latin imitators, and the
still later class of scholiasts — except indeed such occasional
glimpses as we obtain from the Iliad and the Odyssey, and the
remaining Hesiodic fragments, which exhibit but too frequently a
hopeless diversity when confronted with the narratives of the
logographers.

Though Æolus (as has been already stated) is himself called
the son of Hellên along with Dôrus and Xuthus, yet the legends
concerning the Æolids, far from being dependent upon this
genealogy, are not all even coherent with it : moreover the name
of Æolus in the legend is older than that of Hellên, inasmuch as

It occurs both in the Iliad and Odyssey.[1] Odysseus sees in the under-world the beautiful Tyrô, daughter of Salmôneus, and wife of Krêtheus, son of Æolus.

Æolus is represented as having reigned in Thessaly: his seven sons were Krêtheus, Sisyphus, Athamas, Salmôneus, Deiôn, Magnês and Periêrês: his five daughters, Canacê, Alcyonê, Peisidikê, Calycê and Perimêdê. The fables of this race seem to be distinguished by a constant introduction of the god Poseidôn, as well as by an unusual prevalence of haughty and presumptuous attributes among the Æolid heroes, leading them to affront the gods by pretences of equality, and sometimes even by defiance. The worship of Poseidôn must probably have been diffused and preëminent among a people with whom these legends originated.

SECTION I.—SONS OF ÆOLUS.

Salmôneus is not described in the Odyssey as son of Æolus, but he is so denominated both in the Hesiodic Catalogue, and by the subsequent logographers. His daughter Tyrô became enamoured of the river Enipeus, the most beautiful of all streams that traverse the earth: she frequented the banks assiduously, and there the god Poseidôn found means to indulge his passion for her, assuming the character of the river god himself. The fruit of this alliance were the twin brothers, Pelias and Nêleus: Tyrô afterwards was given in marriage to her uncle Krêtheus, another son of Æolus, by whom she had Æsôn, Pherês and Amythaôn — all names of celebrity in the heroic legends.[2] The adventures of Tyro formed the subject of an affecting drama of Sophoklês, now lost. Her father had married a second wife, named Sidêrô, whose cruel counsels induced him to punish and torture his daughter on account of her intercourse with Poseidôn. She was shorn of her magnificent hair, beaten and ill-used in

---

[1] Iliad, vi. 154. Σίσυφος Αἰολίδης, etc.
Again Odyss. xi. 234.—
   Ἐνθ' ἤτοι πρώτην Τυρὼ ἴδον εὐπατέρειαν,
   Ἡ φάτο Σαλμωνῆος ἀμύμονος ἔκγονος εἶναι,
   Φῆ δὲ Κρηθῆος γυνὴ ἔμμεναι Αἰολίδαο.
[2] Homer, Odyss. xi. 234–257; xv. 226.

various ways, and confined in a loathsome dungeon. Unable to take care of her two children, she had been compelled to expose them immediately on their birth in a little boat on the river Enipeus; they were preserved by the kindness of a herdsman, and when grown up to manhood, rescued their mother, and revenged her wrongs by putting to death the iron-hearted Sidêrô.[1] This pathetic tale respecting the long imprisonment of Tyrô is substituted by Sophoklês in place of the Homeric legend, which represented her to have become the wife of Krêtheus and mother of a numerous offspring.[2]

Her father, the unjust Salmôneus, exhibited in his conduct the most insolent impiety towards the gods. He assumed the name and title even of Zeus, and caused to be offered to himself the sacrifices destined for that god: he also imitated the thunder and lightning, by driving about with brazen caldrons attached to his chariot and casting lighted torches towards heaven. Such wickedness finally drew upon him the wrath of Zeus, who smote him with a thunderbolt, and effaced from the earth the city which he had founded, with all its inhabitants.[3]

Pelias and Nêleus, "both stout vassals of the great Zeus," became engaged in dissension respecting the kingdom of Iôlkos in

---

[1] Diodôrus, iv. 68. Sophoklês, Fragm. 1. Τυρώ. Σαφῶς Σίδηρὼ καὶ φέρουσα τοὔνομα. The genius of Sophoklês is occasionally seduced by this play upon the etymology of a name, even in the most impressive scenes of his tragedies. See Ajax, 425. Compare Hellanik, Fragm. p. 9, ed. Preller There was a first and second edition of the Tyrô — τῆς δευτέρας Τυροῦς. Schol. ad Aristoph. Av. 276. See the few fragments of the lost drama in Dindorf's Collection, p. 53. The plot was in many respects analogous to the Antiopê of Euripidês.

[2] A third story, different both from Homer and from Sophoklês, respecting Tyrô, is found in Hyginus (Fab. lx.): it is of a tragical cast, and borrowed, like so many other tales in that collection, from one of the lost Greek dramas.

[3]. Apollod. i. 9, 7. Σαλμωνεύς τ' ἄδικος καὶ ὑπέρθυμος Περιήρης. Hesiod, Fragm. Catal. 8. Marktscheffel.

Where the city of Salmôneus was situated, the ancient investigators were not agreed; whether in the Pisatid, or in Elis, or in Thessaly (see Strabo, viii. p. 356). Euripidês in his Æolus placed him on the banks of the Alpheius (Eurip. Fragm. Æol. 1). A village and fountain in the Pisatid bore the name of Salmônê; but the mention of the river Enipeus seems to mark Thessaly as the original seat of the legend. But the naïveté of the tale preserved by Apollodôrus (Virgil in the Æneid, vi. 586, has retouched it)

Thessaly. Pelias got possession of it, and dwelt there in plenty and prosperity; but he had offended the goddess Hêrê by killing Sidêrô upon her altar, and the effects of her wrath were manifested in his relations with his nephew Jason.[1] Nêleus quitted Thessaly, went into Peloponnêsus, and there founded the kingdom of Pylos. He purchased by immense marriage presents, the privilege of wedding the beautiful Chlôris, daughter of Amphiôn, king of Orchomenos, by whom he had twelve sons and but one daughter[2]—the fair and captivating Pêrô, whom suitors from all the neighborhood courted in marriage. But Nêleus, "the haughtiest of living men,"[3] refused to entertain the pretensions of any of them: he would grant his daughter only to that man who should bring to him the oxen of Iphiklos, from Phylakê in Thessaly. These precious animals were carefully guarded, as well by herdsmen as by a dog whom neither man nor animal could approach. Nevertheless, Bias, the son of Amythaôn, nephew of Nêleus, being desperately enamored of Pêrô, prevailed upon his brother Melampus to undertake for his sake the perilous adventure, in spite of the prophetic knowledge of the latter, which forewarned him that though he would ultimately succeed, the prize must be purchased by severe captivity and suffering. Melampus, in attempting to steal the oxen, was seized and put in prison; from whence nothing but his prophetic powers rescued him. Being acquainted with the language of worms, he heard these animals communicating to each other, in the roof over his head, that the beams were nearly eaten through and about to fall in. He communicated this intelligence to his guards, and demanded to be conveyed to another place of confinement, announcing that the roof would presently fall in and bury them. The prediction was fulfilled, and Phylakos, father of

marks its ancient date: the final circumstance of that tale was, that the city and its inhabitants were annihilated.

Ephorus makes Salmôneus king of the Epeians and of the Pisatæ (Fragm. 15, ed. Didot).

The lost drama of Sophoklês, called Σαλμωνεὺς, was a δρᾶμα σατυρικόν See Dindorf's Fragm. 483.

[1] Hom. Od. xi. 280. Apollod. i. 9, 9. κρατέρω θεραπόντε Διὸς, etc.
[2] Diodôr. iv. 68.
[3] Νηλέα τε μεγάθυμον, ἀγανότατον ζωόντων (Hom. Odyss. xv. 228).

Iphiklos, full of wonder at this specimen of prophetic power, immediately caused him to be released. He further consulted him respecting the condition of his son Iphiklos, who was childless; and promised him the possession of the oxen on condition of his suggesting the means whereby offspring might be ensured. A vulture having communicated to Melampus the requisite information, Podarkês, the son of Iphiklos, was born shortly afterwards. In this manner Melampus obtained possession of the oxen, and conveyed them to Pylos, obtaining for his brother Bias the hand of Pêrô.[1] How this great legendary character, by miraculously healing the deranged daughters of Prœtos, procured both for himself and for Bias dominion in Argos, has been recounted in a preceding chapter.

Of the twelve sons of Nêleus, one at least, Periklymenos, — besides the ever-memorable Nestôr, — was distinguished for his ex ploits as well as for his miraculous gifts. Poseidôn, the divine father of the race, had bestowed upon him the privilege of changing his form at pleasure into that of any bird, beast, reptile, or insect.[2] He had occasion for all these resources, and he employed them for a time with success in defending his family against the terrible indignation of Hêraklês, who, provoked by the refusal of Nêleus to perform for him the ceremony of purification after his murder of Iphitus, attacked the Nêleids at Pylos. Periklymenos by his extraordinary powers prolonged the resistance, but the hour of his fate was at length brought upon him by the intervention of Athênê, who pointed him out to Hêraklês while he was perched as a bee upon the hero's chariot. He was killed, and Hêraklês became completely victorious, overpowering Poseidôn, Hêrê, Arês, and Hadês, and even wounding the three latter, who assisted in the

---

[1] Hom. Od. xi. 278; xv. 234. Apollod. i. 9, 12. The basis of this curious romance is in the Odyssey, amplified by subsequent poets. There are points however in the old Homeric legend, as it is briefly sketched in the fifteenth book of the Cdyssey, which seem to have been subsequently left out or varied. Nêleus seizes the property of Melampus during his absence; the latter, returning with the oxen from Phylakê, revenges himself upon Nêleus for the injury. Odyss. xv. 233.

[2] Hesiod, Catalog. ap Schol. Apollôn. Rhod. i. 156; Ovid, Metam. xii. p. 556; Eustath. ad Odyss. xi. p. 284. Poseidôn carefully protects Antilochus son of Nestôr, in the Iliad, xiii. 554–563.

defence. Eleven of the sons of Nêleus perished by his hand, while Nestôr, then a youth, was preserved only by his accidental absence at Gerêna, away from his father's residence.[1] The proud house of the Nêleids was now reduced to Nestôr; but Nestôr singly sufficed to sustain its eminence. He appears not only as the defender and avenger of Pylos against the insolence and rapacity of his Epeian neighbors in Elis, but also as aiding the Lapithæ in their terrible combat against the Centaurs, and as companion of Thêseus, Peirithöus, and the other great legendary heroes who preceded the Trojan war. In extreme old age his once marvellous power of handling his weapons has indeed passed away, but his activity remains unimpaired, and his sagacity as well as his influence in counsel is greater than ever. He not only assembles the various Grecian chiefs for the armament against Troy, perambulating the districts of Hellas along with Odysseus, but takes a vigorous part in the siege itself, and is of preëminent service to Agamemnôn. And after the conclusion of the siege, he is one of the few Grecian princes who returns to his original dominions, and is found, in a strenuous and honored old age, in the midst of his children and subjects, — sitting with the sceptre of authority on the stone bench before his house at Pylos, — offering sacrifice to Poseidôn, as his father Nêleus had done before him, — and mourning only over the death

---

[1] Hesiod, Catalog. ap. Schol. Ven. ad Iliad. ii. 336; and Steph. Byz. v. Γερηνία; Homer, Il. v. 392; xi. 693; Apollodôr. ii. 7, 3; Hesiod, Scut. Herc. 360; Pindar, Ol. ix. 32.

According to the Homeric legend, Nêleus himself was not killed by Hêraklês: subsequent poets or logographers, whom Apollodôrus follows, seem to have thought it an injustice, that the offence given by Nêleus himself should have been avenged upon his sons and not upon himself; they therefore altered the legend upon this point, and rejected the passage in the Iliad as spurious (see Schol. Ven. ad Iliad. xi. 682).

The refusal of purification by Nêleus to Hêraklês is a genuine legendary cause: the commentators, who were disposed to spread a coating of history over these transactions, introduced another cause, — Nêleus, as king of Pylos, had aided the Orchomenians in their war against Hêraklês and the Thêbans (see Sch. Ven. ad Iliad. xi. 689).

The neighborhood of Pylos was distinguished for its ancient worship both of Poseidôn and of Hadês: there were abundant local legends respecting them (see Strabo, viii. pp. 344, 345).

of his favorite son Antilochus, who had fallen, along with so many brave companions in arms, in the Trojan war.[1]

After Nestôr the line of the Nêleids numbers undistinguished names, — Bôrus, Penthilus, and Andropompus, — three successive generations down to Melanthus, who on the invasion of Peloponnêsus by the Herakleids, quitted Pylos and retired to Athens, where he became king, in a manner which I shall hereafter recount. His son Kodrus was the last Athênian king; and Nêleus, one of the sons of Kodrus, is mentioned as the principal conductor of what is called the Ionic emigration from Athens to Asia Minor.[2] It is certain that during the historical age, not merely the princely family of the Kodrids in Milêtus, Ephesus, and other Ionic cities, but some of the greatest families even in Athens itself, traced their heroic lineage through the Nêleids up to Poseidon: and the legends respecting Nestôr and Periklymenos would find especial favor amidst Greeks with such feelings and belief. The Kodrids at Ephesus, and probably some other Ionic towns, long retained the title and honorary precedence of kings, even after they had lost the substantial power belonging to the office. They stood in the same relation, embodying both religious worship and supposed ancestry, to the Nêleids and Poseidôn, as the chiefs of the Æolic colonies to Agamemnôn and Orestês. The Athenian despot Peisistratus was named after the son of Nestôr in the Odyssey; and we may safely presume that the heroic worship of the Nêleids was as carefully cherished at the Ionic Milêtus as at the Italian Metapontum.[3]

Having pursued the line of Salmôneus and Nêleus to the end of its legendary career, we may now turn back to that of another son of Æolus, Krêtheus, — a line hardly less celebrated in respect of the heroic names which it presents. Alkêstis, the most beautiful of the daughters of Pelias,[4] was promised by her father in

---

[1] About Nestôr, Iliad, i. 260–275; ii. 370; xi. 670–770; Odyss. iii. 5, 110, 409.

[2] Hellanik. Fragm. 10, ed. Didot; Pausan. vii. 2, 3; Herodot. v. 65; Strabo, xiv. p. 633. Hellanikus, in giving the genealogy from Nêleus to Melanthus, traces it through Periklymenos and not through Nestôr: the words of Herodotus imply that *he* must have included Nestôr.

[3] Herodot. v. 67; Strabo, vi. p. 264; Mimnermus, Fragm. 9, Schneidewin.

[4] Iliad, ii. 715.

marriage to the man that could bring him a lion and a boar tamed to the yoke and drawing together. Admêtus, son of Pherês, the eponymus of Pheræ in Thessaly, and thus grandson of Krêtheus, was enabled by the aid of Apollo to fulfil this condition, and to win her;[1] for Apollo happened at that time to be in his service as a slave (condemned to this penalty by Zeus for having put to death the Cyclôpes), in which capacity he tended the herds and horses with such success, as to equip Eumêlus (the son of Admêtus) to the Trojan war with the finest horses in the Grecian army. Though menial duties were imposed upon him, even to the drudgery of grinding in the mill,[2] he yet carried away with him a grateful and friendly sentiment towards his mortal master, whom he interfered to rescue from the wrath of the goddess Artemis, when she was indignant at the omission of her name in his wedding sacrifices. Admêtus was about to perish by a premature death, when Apollo, by earnest solicitation to the Fates, obtained for him the privilege that his life should be prolonged, if he could find any person to die a voluntary death in his place. His father and his mother both refused to make this sacrifice for him, but the devoted attachment of his wife Alkêstis disposed her to embrace with cheerfulness the condition of dying to preserve her

---

[1] Apollodôr. i. 9, 15; Eustath. ad Iliad. ii. 711.

[2] Euripid. Alkêst. init. Welcker; Griechisch. Tragœd. (p. 344) on the lost play of Sophoklês called Admêtus or Alkêstis; Hom. Iliad. ii. 766; Hygin. Fab. 50-51 (Sophoklês, Fr. Inc. 730; Dind. ap. Plutarch. Defect. Orac. p. 417). This tale of the temporary servitude of particular gods, by order of Zeus as a punishment for misbehavior, recurs not unfrequently among the incidents of the mythical world. The poet Panyasis (ap. Clem. Alexand. Adm. ad Gent. p. 23) —

Τλῆ μὲν Δημήτηρ, τλῆ δὲ κλυτὸς Ἀμφιγυήεις,
Τλῆ δὲ Ποσειδάων, τλῆ δ' ἀργυρότοξος Ἀπολλὼν
Ἀνδρὶ παρὰ θνητῷ θητεύσεμεν εἰς ἐνιαυτόν·
Τλῆ δὲ καὶ ὀβριμόθυμος Ἄρης ὑπὸ πατρὸς ἀνάγκης.

The old legend followed out the fundamental idea with remarkable consistency: Laômedôn, as the temporary master of Poseidôn and Apollo, threatens to bind them hand and foot, to sell them in the distant islands, and to cut off the ears of both, when they come to ask for their stipulated wages (Iliad, xxi. 455). It was a new turn given to the story by the Alexandrine poets, when they introduced the motive of love, and made the servitude voluntary on the part of Apollo (Kallimachus, Hymn. Apoll. 49; Tibullus, Eleg. ii. 3, 11-30).

husband. She had already perished, when Hêraklês, the ancient
guest and friend of Admêtus, arrived during the first hour of
lamentation; his strength and daring enabled him to rescue the
deceased Alkêstis even from the grasp of Thanatos (Death), and
to restore her alive to her disconsolate husband.[1]

The son of Pelias, Akastus, had received and sheltered Pêleus
when obliged to fly his country in consequence of the involuntary
murder of Eurytiôn. Krêthêis, the wife of Akastus, becoming
enamored of Pêleus, made to him advances which he repudiated. Exasperated at his refusal, and determined to procure his
destruction, she persuaded her husband that Pêleus had attempted her chastity : upon which Akastus conducted Pêleus out upon
a hunting excursion among the woody regions of Mount Pêlion,
contrived to steal from him the sword fabricated and given by
Hêphæstos, and then left him, alone and unarmed, to perish
by the hands of the Centaurs or by the wild beasts. By the
friendly aid of the Centaur Cheirôn, however, Pêleus was preserved, and his sword restored to him : returning to the city, he
avenged himself by putting to death both Akastus and his perfidious wife.[2]

But amongst all the legends with which the name of Pelias
is connected, by far the most memorable is that of Jasôn and the
Argonautic expedition. Jasôn was son of Æson, grandson of
Krêtheus, and thus great-grandson of Æolus. Pelias, having
consulted the oracle respecting the security of his dominion at
Iôlkos, had received in answer a warning to beware of the man
who should appear before him with only one sandal. He was
celebrating a festival in honor of Poseidôn, when it so happened
that Jasôn appeared before him with one of his feet unsandaled :
he had lost one sandal in wading through the swollen current of
the river Anauros. Pelias immediately understood that this was

---

[1] Eurip. Alkêstis, Arg.; Apollod. i. 9, 15. To bring this beautiful legend
more into the color of history, a new version of it was subsequently framed :
Hêraklês was eminently skilled in medicine, and saved the life of Alkêstis
when she was about to perish from a desperate malady (Plutarch. Amator
c. 17. vol. iv. p. 53, Wytt.).

[2] The legend of Akastus and Pêleus was given in great detail in the Catalogue of Hesiod (Catalog. Fragm. 20–21, Marktscheff.); Schol. Pindar
Nem. iv. 95. Schol. Apoll. Rhod. i. 224; Apollod. iii. 13, 2.

the enemy against whom the oracle had forewarned him. As a means of averting the danger, he imposed upon Jasôn the desperate task of bringing back to Iôlkos the Golden Fleece, — the fleece of that ram which had carried Phryxos from Achaia to Kolchis, and which Phryxos had dedicated in the latter country as an offering to the god Arês. The result of this injunction was the memorable expedition — of the ship Argô and her crew called the Argonauts, composed of the bravest and noblest youths of Greece — which cannot be conveniently included among the legends of the Æolids, and is reserved for a separate chapter.

The voyage of the Argô was long protracted, and Pelias, persuaded that neither the ship nor her crew would ever return, put to death both the father and mother of Jasôn, together with their infant son. Æsôn, the father, being permitted to choose the manner of his own death, drank bull's blood while performing a sacrifice to the gods. At length, however, Jasôn did return, bringing with him not only the golden fleece, but also Mêdea, daughter of Æêtês, king of Kolchis, as his wife, — a woman distinguished for magical skill and cunning, by whose assistance alone the Argonauts had succeeded in their project. Though determined to avenge himself upon Pelias, Jasôn knew he could only succeed by stratagem: he remained with his companions at a short distance from Iôlkos, while Mêdea, feigning herself a fugitive from his ill-usage, entered the town alone, and procured access to the daughters of Pelias. By exhibitions of her magical powers she soon obtained unqualified ascendency over their minds. For example, she selected from the flocks of Pelias a ram in the extremity of old age, cut him up and boiled him in a caldron with herbs, and brought him out in the shape of a young and vigorous lamb:[1] the daughters of Pelias were made to believe that their old father could in like manner be restored to youth. In this persuasion they cut him up with their own hands and cast his limbs into the

---

[1] This incident was contained in one of the earliest dramas of Euripidès, the Πελιάδες, now lost. Moses of Chorênê (Progymnasm. ap. Maii ad Euseb. p. 43), who gives an extract from the argument, says that the poet " extremos mentiendi fines attingit."

The 'Ριζότομοι of Sophoklês seems also to have turned upon the same catastrophe (see Fragm. 479, Dindorf.).

caldron, trusting that Mêdea would produce upon him the same magical effect. Mêdea pretended that an invocation to the moon was a necessary part of the ceremony: she went up to the top of the house as if to pronounce it, and there lighting the fire-signal concerted with the Argonauts, Jasôn and his companions burst in and possessed themselves of the town. Satisfied with having thus revenged himself, Jasôn yielded the principality of Iôlkos to Akastus, son of Pelias, and retired with Mêdea to Corinth. Thus did the goddess Hêrê gratify her ancient wrath against Pelias: she had constantly watched over Jasôn, and had carried the "all-notorious" Argo through its innumerable perils, in order that Jasôn might bring home Mêdea to accomplish the ruin of his uncle.[1]   The misguided daughters of Pelias departed

---

[1] The kindness of Hêrê towards Jasôn seems to be older in the legend than her displeasure against Pelias; at least it is specially noticed in the Odyssey, as the great cause of the escape of the ship Argô : Ἀλλ' Ἥρη παρέπεμψεν, ἐπεὶ φίλος ἦεν Ἰήσων (xii. 70). In the Hesiodic Theogony Pelias stands to Jasôn in the same relation as Eurystheus to Hêraklês, — a severe taskmaster as well as a wicked and insolent man, — ὑβριστὴς Πελίης καὶ ἀτάσθαλος, ὀβριμόεργος (Theog. 995). Apollônius Rhodius keeps the wrath of Hêrê against Pelias in the foreground, i. 14; iii. 1134; iv. 242; see also Hygin, f. 13.

There is great diversity in the stories given of the proximate circumstances connected with the death of Pelias : Eurip. Mêd. 491 ; Apollodôr. i. 9, 27; Diodôr. iv, 50–52; Ovid, Metam. vii. 162, 203, 297, 347 ; Pausan. viii 11, 2; Schol. ad Lycoph. 175.

In the . legend of Akastus and Pêleus as recounted above, Akastus was made to perish by the hand of Pêleus. I do not take upon me to reconcile these contradictions.

Pausanias mentions that he could not find in any of the poets, so far as he had read, the names of the daughters of Pelias, and that the painter Mikôn had given to them names (ὀνόματα δ' αὐταῖς ποιητὴς μὲν ἔθετο οὐδείς, ὅσα γ' ἐπιλεξάμεθα ἡμεῖς, etc., Pausan. viii. 11, 1). Yet their names are given in the authors whom Diodôrus copied; and Alkêstis, at any rate, was most memorable. Mikôn gave the names Asteropeia and Antinoê, altogether different from those in Diodôrus. Both Diodôrus and Hyginus exonerate Al kêstis from all share in the death of her father (Hygin. f. 24).

The old poem called the Νόστοι (see Argum. ad Eurip. Mêd., and Schol. Aristophan. Equit. 1321) recounted, that Mêdea had boiled in a caldron the old Æsôn, father of Jasôn, with herbs and incantations, and that she had brought him out young and strong. Ovid copies this (Metam. vii. 162–203) It is singular that Pherêkydês and Simonidês said that she had performed

as voluntary exiles to Arcadia: Akastus his son celebrated splendid funeral games in honor of his deceased father.[1]

Jasôn and Mêdea retired from Iôlkos to Corinth, where they resided ten years: their children were — Medeius, whom the Centaur Cheirôn educated in the regions of Mount Pêlion,[2] — and Mermerus and Pherôs, born at Corinth. After they had resided there ten years in prosperity, Jasôn set his affections on Glaukê, daughter of Kreôn[3] king of Corinth; and as her father was willing to give her to him in marriage, he determined to repudiate Mêdea, who received orders forthwith to leave Corinth. Stung with this insult and bent upon revenge, Mêdea prepared a poisoned robe, and sent it as a marriage present to Glaukê: it was unthinkingly accepted and put on, and the body of the unfortunate bride was burnt up and consumed. Kreôn, her father, who tried to tear from her the burning garment, shared her fate and perished. The exulting Mêdea escaped by means of a chariot with winged serpents furnished to her by her grandfather Hêlios: she placed herself under the protection of Ægêus at Athens, by whom she had a son named Mêdus. She left her young children in the sacred enclosure of the Arkræan Hêrê, relying on the protection of the altar to ensure their safety; but the Corinthians were so exasperated against her for the murder

---

this process upon Jasôn himself (Schol. Aristoph, *l. c.*). Diogenes (ap. Stobæ. Florileg. t. xxix. 92) rationalizes the story, and converts Mêdea from an enchantress into an improving and regenerating preceptress. The death of Æsôn, as described in the text, is given from Diodôrus and Apollodôrus. Mêdea seems to have been worshipped as a goddess in other places besides Corinth (see Athenagor. Legat. pro Christ. 12; Macrobius, i. 12, p. 247, Gronov.).

[1] These funeral games in honor of Pelias were among the most renowned of the mythical incidents: they were celebrated in a special poem by Stesichorus, and represented on the chest of Kypselus at Olympia. Kastôr, Meleager, Amphiaraos, Jasôn, Pêleus, Mopsos, etc. contended in them (Pausan. v. 17. 4; Stesichori Fragm. 1. p. 54, ed. Klewe; Athên. iv. 172). How familiar the details of them were to the mind of a literary Greek is indirectly attested by Plutarch, Sympos. v. 2, vol. iii. p. 762, Wytt.

[2] Hesiod, Theogon. 998.

[3] According to the Schol. ad Eurip. Mêd. 20, Jason marries the daughter of Hippotês the son of Kreôn, who is the son of Lykæthos. Lykæthos, after the departure of Bellerophôn from Corinth, reigned twenty-seven years; then Kreôn reigned thirty-five years; then came Hippotês.

of Kreôn and Glaukê, that they dragged the children away from
the altar and put them to death. The miserable Jasôn perished
by a fragment of his own ship Argô, which fell upon him while
he was asleep under it,[1] being hauled on shore, according to the
habitual practice of the ancients.

The first establishment at Ephyrê, or Corinth, had been founded by Sisyphus, another of the sons of Æolus, brother of Salmô-

---

[1] Apollodôr. i. 9, 27; Diodôr. iv. 54. The Mêdea of Eurypidês, which has
fortunately been preserved to us, is too well known to need express reference.
He makes Mêdea the destroyer of her own children, and borrows from this
circumstance the most pathetic touches of his exquisite drama. Parmenis-
kôs accused him of having been bribed by the Corinthians to give this turn to
the legend ; and we may regard the accusation as a proof that the older and
more current tale imputed the murder of the children to the Corinthians
(Schol. Eurip. Med. 275, where Didymos gives the story out of the old poem
of Kreophylos). See also Ælian, V. H. v. 21 ; Pausan. ii. 3, 6.

The most significant fact in respect to the fable is, that the Corinthians
celebrated periodically a propitiatory sacrifice to Hêrê Akræa and to Mermerus and Pherês, as an atonement for the sin of having violated the sanctuary
of the altar. The legend grew out of this religious ceremony, and was so
arranged as to explain and account for it (see Eurip. Mêd. 1376, with the
Schol. Diodôr. iv. 55).

Mermerus and Pherês were the names given to the children of Mêdea and
Jasôn in the old Naupaktian Verses ; in which, however, the legend must
have been recounted quite differently, since they said that Jasôn and Mêdea
had gone from Iôlkos, not to Corinth, but to Corcyra ; and that Mermerus
had perished in hunting on the opposite continent of Epirus. Kinæthôn
again, another ancient genealogical poet, called the children of Mêdea and
Jasôn Eriôpis and Mêdos (Pausan. ii. 3, 7). Diodôrus gives them different
names (iv. 34). Hesiod, in the Theogony, speaks only of Medeius as the son
of Jasôn.

Mêdea does not appear either in the Iliad or Odyssey : in the former, we
find Agamêdê, daughter of Augeas, " who knows all the poisons (or medi-
cines) which the earth nourishes" (Iliad, xi. 740) ; in the latter, we have
Circê, sister of Æêtês, father of Mêdea, and living in the Ææan island (Odyss.
x. 70). Circê is daughter of the god Hêlios, as Mêdea is his granddaughter,
— she is herself a goddess. She is in many points the parallel of Mêdea ;
she forewarns and preserves Odysseus throughout his dangers, as Mêdea aids
Jasôn : according to the Hesiodic story, she has two children by Odysseus,
Agrius and Latinus (Theogon. 1001).

Odysseus goes to Ephyrê to Ilos the son of Mermerus, to procure poison
for his arrows : Eustathius treats this Mermerus as the son of Mêdea (see
Odyss. i. 270, and Eust.). As Ephyrê is the legendary name of Corinth, we
may presume this to be a thread of the same mythical tissue.

neus and Krêtheus.[1] The Æolid Sisyphus was distinguished as
an unexampled master of cunning and deceit. He blocked up
the road along the isthmus, and killed the strangers who came
along it by rolling down upon them great stones from the mountains above. He was more than a match even for the arch thief
Autolycus, the son of Hermês, who derived from his father the
gift of changing the color and shape of stolen goods, so that they
could no longer be recognized : Sisyphus, by marking his sheep
under the foot, detected Autolycus when he stole them, and
obliged him to restore the plunder. His penetration discovered
the amour of Zeus with the nymph Ægina, daughter of the river-
god Asôpus. Zeus had carried her off to the island of Œnônê
(which subsequently bore the name of Ægina) ; upon which
Asôpus, eager to recover her, inquired of Sisyphus whither she
was gone : the latter told him what had happened, on condition
that he should provide a spring of water on the summit of the
Acro-Corinthus. Zeus, indignant with Sisyphus for this revelation, inflicted upon him in Hadês the punishment of perpetually
heaving up a hill a great and heavy stone, which, so soon as it
attained the summit, rolled back again in spite of all his efforts,
with irresistible force into the plain.[2]

In the application of the Æolid genealogy to Corinth, Sisyphus,
the son of Æolus, appears as the first name : but the old Corin-

---

[1] See Euripid. Æol. — Fragm. 1, Dindorf; Dikæarch. Vit. Græc. p. 22.

[2] Respecting Sisyphus, see Apollodôr. i. 9, 3 ; iii. 12, 6. Pausan. ii. 5, 1. Schol
ad Iliad. i. 180. Another legend about the amour of Sisyphus with Tyrô, is
in Hygin. fab. 60, and about the manner in which he overreached even Hadês
(Pherekydês ap. Schol. Iliad. vi. 153). The stone rolled by Sisyphus in the
under-world appears in Odyss. xi. 592. The name of Sisyphus was given
during the historical age to men of craft and stratagem, such as Derkyllidês
(Xenoph. Hellenic. iii. 1, 8). He passed for the real father of Odysseus,
though Heyne (ad Apollodôr. i. 9, 3) treats this as another Sisyphus, whereby he destroys the suitableness of the predicate as regards Odysseus. The
duplication and triplication of synonymous personages is an ordinary
resource for the purpose of reducing the legends into a seeming chronological
sequence.

Even in the days of Eumêlus a religious mystery was observed respecting
the tombs of Sisyphus and Nêleus, — the latter had also died at Corinth, —
no one could say where they were buried (Pausan. ii. 2, 2).

Sisyphus even overreached Persephonê, and made his escape from the
under-world (Theognis, 702).

thian poet Eumêlus either found or framed an heroic genealogy
for his native city independent both of Æolus and Sisyphus.
According to this genealogy, Ephyrê, daughter of Oceanus and
Têthys, was the primitive tenant of the Corinthian territory,
Asôpus of the Sikyônian: both were assigned to the god Hêlios,
in adjusting a dispute between him and Poseidôn, by Briareus.
Hêlios divided the territory between his two sons Æêtês and
Alôeus: to the former he assigned Corinth; to the latter Sikyôn.
Æêtês, obeying the admonition of an oracle, emigrated to Kolchis,
leaving his territory under the rule of Bunos, the son of Hermês,
with the stipulation that it should be restored whenever either he
or any of his descendants returned. After the death of Bunos,
both Corinth and Sikyôn were possessed by Epôpeus, son of
Alôeus, a wicked man. His son Marathôn left him in disgust
and retired into Attica, but returned after his death and succeeded
to his territory, which he in turn divided between his two sons
Corinthos and Sikyôn, from whom the names of the two districts
were first derived. Corinthos died without issue, and the Corinthians then invited Mêdea from Iôlkos as the representative of
Æêtês: she with her husband Jasôn thus obtained the sovereignty
of Corinth.[1] This legend of Eumêlus, one of the earliest of the
genealogical poets, so different from the story adopted by Neo-
phrôn or Euripidês, was followed certainly by Simonidês and
seemingly by Theopompus.[2] The incidents in it are imagined
and arranged with a view to the supremacy of Mêdea; the
emigration of Æêtês and the conditions under which he transferred his sceptre, being so laid out as to confer upon Mêdea an
hereditary title to the throne. The Corinthians paid to Mêdea
and to her children solemn worship, either divine or heroic, in
conjunction with Hêrê Akræa,[3] and this was sufficient to give to

---

[1] Pausan. ii. 1, 1; 3, 10. Schol. ad Pindar. Olymp. xiii. 74. Schol.
Lycoph. 174–1024. Schol. Apoll. Rhod. iv. 1212.

[2] Simonid. ap. Schol. ad Eurip. Mêd. 10–20; Theopompus, Fragm. 340,
Didot; though Welcker (Der Episch. Cycl. p. 29) thinks that this does not
belong to the historian Theopompus. Epimenidês also followed the story of
Eumêlus in making Æêtês a Corinthian (Schol. ad Apoll. Rhod. iii. 242).

[3] Περὶ δὲ τῆς εἰς Κόρινθον μετοικήσεως, Ἵππυς ἐκτίθεται καὶ Ἑλλάνικος·
ὅτι κὲ βεβασίλευκε τῆς Κορίνθου ἡ Μήδεια, Εὔμηλος ἱστορεῖ καὶ Σιμωνίδης·
Ὅτι δὲ καὶ ἀθάνατος ἦν ἡ Μήδεια, Μουσαῖος ἐν τῷ περὶ Ἰσθμίων ἱστορεῖ, ἅμα
καὶ περὶ τῶν τῆς Ἀκραίας Ἥρας ἑορτῶν ἐκτιθείς. (Schol. Eurip. Mêd, 10)

Mêdea a prominent place in the genealogy composed by a Corinthian poet, accustomed to blend together gods, heroes and men in the antiquities of his native city. According to the legend of Eumêlus, Jasôn became (through Mêdea) king of Corinth; but she concealed the children of their marriage in the temple of Hêrê, trusting that the goddess would render them immortal. Jasôn, discovering her proceedings, left her and retired in disgust to Iôlkos; Mêdea also, being disappointed in her scheme, quitted the place, leaving the throne in the hands of Sisyphus, to whom, according to the story of Theopompus, she had become attached.[1] Other legends recounted, that Zeus had contracted a passion for Mêdea, but that she had rejected his suit from fear of the displeasure of Hêrê; who, as a recompense for such fidelity, rendered her children immortal :[2] moreover Mêdea had erected, by special command of Hêrê, the celebrated temple of Aphroditê at Corinth. The tenor of these fables manifests their connection with the temple of Hêrê: and we may consider the legend of Mêdea as having been originally quite independent of that of Sisyphus, but fitted on to it, in seeming chronological sequence, so as to satisfy the feelings of those Æolids of Corinth who passed for his descendants.

Sisyphus had for his sons Glaukos and Ornytiôn. From Glaukos sprang Bellerophôn, whose romantic adventures commence with the Iliad, and are further expanded by subsequent poets: according to some accounts he was really the son of Poseidôn, the prominent deity of the Æolid family.[3] The youth

---

Compare also v. 1376 of the play itself, with the Scholia and Pausan. ii. 3, 6. Both Alkman and Hesiod represented Mêdea as a goddess (Athenogoras, Legatia pro Christianis, p. 54, ed. Oxon.).

[1] Pausan. ii. 3, 10; Schol. Pindar. Olymp. xiii. 74.

[2] Schol. Pindar. Olymp. xiii. 32-74; Plutarch. De Herodot. Malign. p. 871.

[3] Pindar. Olymp. xiii. 98. and Schol. ad 1; Schol. ad Iliad. vi. 155; this seems to be the sense of Iliad, vi. 191.

The lost drama called *Iobatés* of Sophoklês, and the two by Euripidês called *Stheneboea* and *Bellerophôn*, handled the adventures of this hero. See the collection of the few fragments remaining in Dindorf, Fragm. Sophok. 280; Fragm. Eurip. p. 87–108; and Hygin. fab. 67.

Welcker (Griechische Tragöd. ii. p. 777–800) has ingeniously put together all that can be divined respecting the two plays of Euripidês.

Völcker seeks to make out that Bellerophôn is identical with Poseidôn

and beauty of Bellerophôn rendered him the object of a strong passion on the part of the Anteia, wife of Prœtos king of Argos. Finding her advances rejected, she contracted a violent hatred towards him, and endeavored by false accusations to prevail upon her husband to kill him. Prœtos refused to commit the deed under his own roof, but despatched him to his son-in-law the king of Lykia in Asia Minor, putting into his hands a folded tablet full of destructive symbols. Conformably to these suggestions, the most perilous undertakings were imposed upon Bellerophôn. He was directed to attack the monster Chimæra and to conquer the warlike Solymi as well as the Amazons : as he returned victorious from these enterprises, an ambuscade was laid for him by the bravest Lykian warriors, all of whom he slew. At length the Lykian king recognized him "as the genuine son of a god," and gave him his daughter in marriage together with half of his kingdom. The grand-children of Bellerophôn, Glaukos and Sarpêdôn, — the latter a son of his daughter Laodameia by Zeus, — combat as allies of Troy against the host of Agamemnon.[1] Respecting the winged Pegasus, Homer says nothing; but later poets assigned to Bellerophôn this miraculous steed, whose parentage is given in the Hesiodic Theogony, as the instrument both of his voyage and of his success.[2] Heroic worship was paid at Corinth to Bellerophôn, and he seems to have been a favorite theme of recollection not only among the Corinthians themselves, but also among the numerous colonists whom they sent out to other regions.[3]

From Ornytiôn, the son of Sisyphus, we are conducted through a series of three undistinguished family names, — Thoas, Damophôn, and the brothers Propodas and Hyanthidas, — to the time

---

Hippios, — a separate personification of one of the attributes of the god Poseidôn. For this conjecture he gives some plausible grounds (Mythologie des Japetisch. Geschlechts, p. 129 seq.).

[1] Iliad. vi. 155–210.   [2] Hesiod, Theogon. 283.

[3] Pausan. ii. 2, 4. See Pindar, Olymp. xiii. 90, addressed to Xenophôn the Corinthian, and the Adoniazusæ of the Syracusan Theocritus, a poem in which common Syracusan life and feeling are so graphically depicted, Idyll xv. 91. —

Συρακοσίαις ἐπιτάσσεις;
'Ως δ' εἰδῇς καὶ τοῦτο, Κορίνθιαι εἰμες ἄνωθεν
'Ως καὶ ὁ Βελλερόφων· Πελοποννασιστὶ λαλεῦμες.

of the Dôrian occupation of Corinth[1], which will be hereafter recounted.

We now pass from Sisyphus and the Corinthian fables to another son of Æolus, Athames, whose family history is not less replete with mournful and tragical incidents, abundantly diversified by the poets. Athamas, we are told, was king of Orchomenos; his wife Nephelê was a goddess, and he had by her two children, Phryxus and Hellê. After a certain time he neglected Nephelê, and took to himself as a new wife Inô, the daughter of Kadmus, by whom he had two sons, Learchus and Melikertês. Inô, looking upon Phryxus with the hatred of a step-mother, laid a snare for his life. She persuaded the women to roast the seed-wheat, which, when sown in this condition, yielded no crop, so that famine overspread the land. Athamas sent to Delphi to implore counsel and a remedy: he received for answer, through the machinations of Inô with the oracle, that the barrenness of the fields could not be alleviated except by offering Phryxus as a sacrifice to Zeus. The distress of the people compelled him to execute this injunction, and Phryxus was led as a victim to the altar. But the power of his mother Nephelê snatched him from destruction, and procured for him from Hermês a ram with a fleece of gold, upon which he and his sister Hellê mounted and were carried across the sea. The ram took the direction of the Euxine sea and Kolchis: when they were crossing the Hellespont, Hellê fell off into the narrow strait, which took its name from that incident. Upon this, the ram, who was endued with speech, consoled the terrified Phryxus, and ultimately carried him safe to Kolchis: Æêtês, king of Kolchis son of the god Hêlios and brother of Circê, received Phryxus kindly, and gave him his daughter Chalciopê in marriage. Phryxus sacrificed the ram to Zeus Phyxios, and suspended the golden fleece in the sacred grove of Arês.

Athamas — according to some both Athamas and Inô — were afterwards driven mad by the anger of the goddess Hêrê; insomuch that the father shot his own son Learchus, and would also have put to death his other son Melikertês, if Inô had not snatched him away. She fled with the boy, across the Megarian

---

[1] Pausan. ii. 4, 3.

territory and Mount Geraneia, to the rock Moluris, overhanging
the Sarônic Gulf: Athamas pursued her, and in order to escape
him she leaped into the sea. She became a sea-goddess under
the title of Leukothea; while the body of Melikertês was cast
ashore on the neighboring territory of Schœnus, and buried by
his uncle Sisyphus, who was directed by the Nereïds to pay to
him heroic honors under the name of Palæmôn. The Isthmian
games, one of the great periodical festivals of Greece, were celebrated in honor of the god Poseidôn, in conjunction with Palæmôn as a hero. Athamas abandoned his territory, and became
the first settler of a neighboring region called from him Athman-
tia, or the Athamantian plain.[1]

---

[1] Eurip. Mèd. 1250, with the Scholia, according to which story Inô killed
both her children:—

Ἴνω μανεῖσαν ἐκ θεῶν, ὅθ' ἡ Διὸς
Δάμαρ νιν ἐξέπεμψε δώματων ἄλη.

Compare Valckenaer, Diatribe in Eurip.; Apollodôr. i. 9, 1-2; Schol. ad
Pindar. Argum. ad Isthm. p. 180. The many varieties of the fable of Athamas and his family may be seen in Hygin. fab. 1-5; Philostephanus ap.
Schol. Iliad. vii. 86: it was a favorite subject with the tragedians, and was
handled by Æschylus, Sophoklês and Euripidês in more than one drama
(see Welcker, Griechische Tragöd. vol. i. p. 312-332; vol. ii. p. 612). Heyne
says that the proper reading of the name is *Phrixus*, not *Phryxus*,—incor-
rectly, I think: Φρύξος connects the name both with the story of roasting the
wheat (φρύγειν), and also with the country Φρυγία, of which it was pretended
that Phryxus was the Eponymus. Inô, or Leukothea, was worshipped as a
heroine at Megara as well as at Corinth (Pausan. i. 42, 3): the celebrity of
the Isthmian games carried her worship, as well as that of Palæmôn,
throughout most parts of Greece (Cicero, De Nat. Deor. iii. 16). She is the
only personage of this family noticed either in the Iliad or Odyssey: in the
latter poem she is a sea-goddess, who has once been a mortal, daughter of
Kadmus; she saves Odysseus from imminent danger at sea by presenting
to him her κρήδεμνον (Odyss. v. 433; see the refinements of Aristidês, Orat.
iii. p. 27). The voyage of Phryxus and Hellê to Kolchis was related in the
Hesiodic Eoiai: we find the names of the children of Phryxus by the
daughter of Æêtês quoted from that poem (Schol. ad Apollon. Rhod. ii.
1123): both Hesiod and Pherekydês mentioned the golden fleece of the ram
(Eratosthen. Catasterism. 19; Pherekyd. Fragm. 53, Didot).

Hekatæus preserved the romance of the speaking ram (Schol. Apoll. Rhod.
ι. 256)· but Hellanikus dropped the story of Hellê having fallen into the

The legend of Athamas connects itself with some sanguinary religious rites and very peculiar family customs, which prevailed at Alos, in Achaia Phthiôtis, down to a time[1] later than the historian Herodotus, and of which some remnant existed at Orchomenos even in the days of Plutarch. Athamas was worshipped at Alos as a hero, having both a chapel and a consecrated grove, attached to the temple of Zeus Laphystios. On the family of which he was the heroic progenitor, a special curse and disability stood affixed. The eldest of the race was forbidden to enter the prytaneion or government-house; and if he was found within the doors of the building, the other citizens laid hold of him on his going out, surrounded him with garlands, and led him in solemn procession to be sacrificed as a victim at the altar of Zeus Laphystios. The prohibition carried with it an exclusion from all the public meetings and ceremonies, political as well as religious, and from the sacred fire of the state: many of the individuals marked out had therefore been bold enough to transgress it. Some had been seized on quitting the building and actually sacrificed; others had fled the country for a long time to avoid a similar fate.

The guides who conducted Xerxês and his army through southern Thessaly detailed to him this existing practice, coupled with the local legend, that Athamas, together with Inô, had sought to compass the death of Phryxus, who however had escaped to Kolchis; that the Achæans had been enjoined by an oracle to offer up Athamas himself as an expiatory sacrifice to release the country from the anger of the gods; but that Kytissoros, son of Phryxus, coming back from Kolchis, had intercepted the sacrifice of Athamas,[2] whereby the anger of the gods re-

---

sea: according to him she died at Pactyê in the Chersonesus (Schol. Apoll. Rhod. ii. 1144).

The poet Asius seems to have given the genealogy of Athamas by Themistô much in the same manner as we find it in Apollodôrus (Pausan. ix. 23, 3).

According to the ingenious refinements of Dionysius and Palæphatus (Schol. ad Apoll. Rhod. ii. 1144; Palæphat. de Incred. c. 31) the ram of Phryxus was after all a man named Krios, a faithful attendant who aided in his escape; others imagined a ship with a ram's head at the bow.

: Plutarch, Quæst. Græc. c. 38. p. 299. Schol. Apoll. Rhod. ii. 655.

² Of the Athamas of Sophoklês, turning upon this intended, but not con-

mained still unappeased, and an undying curse rested upon the
family.[1]

That such human sacrifices continued to a greater or less
extent, even down to a period later than Herodotus, among the
family who worshipped Athamas as their heroic ancestor, appears
certain : mention is also made of similar customs in parts of
Arcadia, and of Thessaly, in honor of Pêleus and Cheirôn.[2]
But we may reasonably presume, that in the period of greater
humanity which Herodotus witnessed, actual sacrifice had become
very rare. The curse and the legend still remained, but were

---

summated sacrifice, little is known, except from a passage of Aristophanês
and the Scholia upon it (Nubes, 258).—

ἐπὶ τί στέφανον ; οἴμοι, Σώκρατες,
ὥσπερ με τὸν 'Αθάμανθ' ὅπως μὴ θύσετε.

Athamas was introduced in this drama with a garland on his head, on the
point of being sacrificed as an expiation for the death of his son Phryxus,
when Hêraklês interposes and rescues him.

[1] Herodot. vii. 197.   Plato, Minôs, p. 315.

[2] Plato, Minôs, c. 5.   Καὶ οἱ τοῦ 'Αθάμαντος ἔκγονοι, οἵας θυσίας θύουσιν,
Ελληνες ὄντες.   As a testimony to the fact still existing or believed to exist,
this dialogue is quite sufficient, though not the work of Plato.

Μόνιμος δ' ἱστορεῖ, ἐν τῇ τῶν θαυμασίων συναγωγῇ, ἐν Πέλλῃ τῆς Θεττα-
λίας 'Αχαιὸν ἄνθρωπον Πηλεῖ καὶ Χείρωνι καταθύεσθαι.   (Clemens Alexand.
Admon. ad Gent. p. 27, Sylb.)   Respecting the sacrifices at the temple of
Zeus Lykœns in Arcadia, see Plato, Republ. viii. p. 565.   Pausanias (viii. p.
38, 5) seems to have shrunk, when he was upon the spot, even from inquiring what they were — a striking proof of the fearful idea which he had conceived of them.   Plutarch (De Defectu Oracul. c. 14) speaks of τὰς πάλαι
ποιουμένας ἀνθρωποθυσίας.   The Schol. ad Lycophron. 229, gives a story
of children being sacrificed to Melikertês at Tenedos ; and Apollodôrus
(ad Porphyr. de Abstinentiâ, ii. 55, see Apollod. Fragm. 20, ed. Didot) said
that the Lacedæmonians had sacrificed a man to Arês — καὶ Λακεδαιμονίους
φησὶν ὁ 'Απολλόδωρος τῷ 'Αρει θύειν ἄνθρωπον.   About Salamis in Cyprus,
see Lactantius, De Falsâ Religione, i. c. 21.   "Apud Cypri Salaminem,
humanam hostiam Jovi Teucrus immolavit, idque sacrificium posteris tradi-
dit : quod est nuper Hadriano imperante sublatum."

Respecting human sacrifices in historical Greece, consult a good section in
K. F. Hermann's Gottesdienstliche Alterthümer der Griechen (sect. 27).
Such sacrifices had been a portion of primitive Grecian religion, but had
gradually become obsolete everywhere — except in one or two solitary cases,
which were spoken of with horror.   Even in these cases, too, the reality of
the fact, in later times, is not beyond suspicion.

not called into practical working, except during periods of intense national suffering or apprehension, during which the religious sensibilities were always greatly aggravated. We cannot at all doubt, that during the alarm created by the presence of the Persian king with his immense and ill-disciplined host, the minds of the Thessalians must have been keenly alive to all that was terrific in their national stories, and all that was expiatory in their religious solemnities. Moreover, the mind of Xerxês himself was so awe-struck by the tale, that he reverenced the dwelling-place consecrated to Athamas. The guides who recounted to him the romantic legend, gave it as the historical and generating cause of the existing rule and practice: a critical inquirer is forced (as has been remarked before) to reverse the order of precedence, and to treat the practice as having been the suggesting cause of its own explanatory legend.

The family history of Athamas, and the worship of Zeus Laphystios, are expressly connected by Herodotus with Alos in Achæa Phthiôtis — one of the towns enumerated in the Iliad as under the command of Achilles. But there was also a mountain called Laphystion, and a temple and worship of Zeus Laphystios between Orchomenos and Korôneia, in the northern portion of the territory known in the historical ages as Bœotia. Here also the family story of Athamas is localized, and Athamas is presented to us as king of the districts of Korôneia, Haliartus and Mount Laphystion: he is thus interwoven with the Orchomenian genealogy.[1] Andreas (we are told), son of the river Pênefos, was the first person who settled in the region: from him it received the name Andrêis. Athamas, coming subsequently to Andreus, received from him the territory of Korôneia and Haliartus with Mount Laphystion: he gave in marriage to Andreus, Euippê, daughter of his son Leucôn, and the issue of this marriage was Eteoklês, said to be the son of the river Kêphisos. Korônos and Haliartus, grandsons of the Corinthian Sisyphus, were adopted by Athamas, as he had lost all his children: but when his grandson Presbôn, son of Phryxus, returned to him from Kolchis, he divided his territory in such manner that Korônos and Haliartus became the founders of the towns which

---

[1] Pausan. ix. 34, 4.

bore their names. Almôn, the son of Sisyphus, also received from Eteoklês a portion of territory, where he established the village Almônes.[1]

With Eteoklês began, according to a statement in one of the Hesiodic poems, the worship of the Charites or Graces, so long and so solemnly continued at Orchomenos in the periodical festival of the Charitêsia, to which many neighboring towns and districts seem to have contributed.[2] He also distributed the inhabitants into two tribes—Eteokleia and Kêphisias. He died childless, and was succeeded by Almos, who had only two daughters, Chrysê and Chrysogeneia. The son of Chrysê by the god Arês was Phlegyas, the father and founder of the warlike and predatory Phlegyæ, who despoiled every one within their reach, and assaulted not only the pilgrims on their road to Delphi, but even the treasures of the temple itself. The offended god punished them by continued thunder, by earthquakes, and by pestilence, which extinguished all this impious race, except a scanty remnant who fled into Phokis.

Chrysogeneia, the other daughter of Almos, had for issue, by the god Poseidôn, Minyas: the son of Minyas was Orchomenos. From these two was derived the name both of Minyæ for the people, and of Orchomenos for the town.[3] During the reign of Orchomenos, Hyêttus came to him from Argos, having become an exile in consequence of the death of Molyros: Orchomenos assigned to him a portion of land, where he founded the village called Hyêttus.[4] Orchomenos, having no issue, was succeeded by Klymenos, son of Presbôn, of the house of Athamas: Klymenos was slain by some Thêbans during the festival of Poseidôn at Onchêstos; and his eldest son, Erginus, to avenge his death, attacked the Thêbans with his utmost force;—an attack, in which he was so successful, that the latter were forced to submit, and to pay him an annual tribute.

---

[1] Pausan. ix. 34, 5.   [2] Ephorus, Fragm. 68, Marx.

[3] Pausan. ix. 36, 1–3. See also a legend, about the three daughters of Minyas, which was treated by the Tanagræan poetess Korinna, the contempo rary of Pindar (Antonin. Liberalis, Narr. x.).

[4] This exile of Hyêttus was recounted in the Eoiai. Hesiod, Fragm. 148, Markt.

The Orchomenian power was now at its height: both Minyas and Orchomenos had been princes of surpassing wealth, and the former had built a spacious and durable edifice which he had filled with gold and silver. But the success of Erginus against Thêbes was soon terminated and reversed by the hand of the irresistible Hêraklês, who rejected with disdain the claim of tribute, and even mutilated the envoys sent to demand it: he not only emancipated Thêbes, but broke down and impoverished Orchomenos.[1] Erginus in his old age married a young wife, from which match sprang the illustrious heroes, or gods, Trophônius and Agamêdês; though many (amongst whom is Pausanius himself) believed Trophônius to be the son of Apollo.[2] Trophônius, one of the most memorable persons in Grecian mythology, was worshipped as a god in various places, but with especial sanctity as Zeus Trophônius at Lebadeia: in his temple at this town, the prophetic manifestations outlasted those of Delphi itself.[3] Trophônius and Agamêdês, enjoying matchless renown as architects, built[4] the temple of Delphi, the thalamus of Amphitryôn at Thêbes, as well as the inaccessible vault of Hyrieus at Hyria, in which they are said to have left one stone removable at pleasure, so as to reserve for themselves a secret entrance. They entered so frequently, and stole so much gold and silver, that Hyrieus, astonished at his losses, at length spread a fine net, in which Agamêdês was inextricably caught: Trophônius cut off his brother's head and carried it away, so that the

---

[1] Pausan. ix. 37, 2. Apollod. ii. 4, 11. Diodôr. iv. 10. The two latter tell us that Erginus was slain. Klymenê is among the wives and daughters of the heroes seen by Odysseus in Hadés: she is termed by the Schol. daughter of Minyas (Odyss. xi. 325).

[2] Pausan. ix. 37, 1–3. Λέγεται δὲ ὁ Τροφώνιος 'Απόλλωνος εἶναι, καὶ οὐκ 'Εργίνου · καὶ ἐγώ τε πείθομαι, καὶ ὅστις παρὰ Τροφώνιου ἦλθε δὴ μαντευσόμενος.

[3] Plutarch, De Defectu Oracul. c. 5, p. 411. Strabo, ix. p. 414. The mention of the honeyed cakes, both in Aristophanês (Nub. 508) and Pausanias (ix. 39, 5), indicates that the curious preliminary ceremonies, for those who consulted the oracle of Trophônius, remained the same after a lapse of 550 years. Pausanias consulted it himself. There had been at one time an oracle of Teiresias at Orchomenos: but it had become silent at an early period (Plutarch. Defect. Oracul. c. 44, p. 434).

[4] Homer. Hymn. Apoll. 296. Pausan. ix. 11, 1.

body, which alone remained, was insufficient to identify the thief. Like Amphiaraos, whom he resembles in more than one respect, Trophônius was swallowed up by the earth near Lebadeia.[1]

From Trophônius and Agamêdês the Orchomenian genealogy passes to Ascalaphos and Ialmenos, the sons of Arês by Astyochê, who are named in the Catalogue of the Iliad as leaders of the thirty ships from Orchomenos against Troy. Azeus, the grandfather of Astyochê in the Iliad, is introduced as the brother of Erginus[2] by Pausanias, who does not carry the pedigree lower.

The genealogy here given out of Pausanias is deserving of the more attention, because it seems to have been copied from the special history of Orchomenos by the Corinthian Kallippus, who again borrowed from the native Orchomenian poet, Chersias : the works of the latter had never come into the hands of Pausanias. It illustrates forcibly the principle upon which these mythical genealogies were framed, for almost every personage in the series is an Eponymus. Andreus gave his name to the country, Athamas to the Athamantian plain ; Minyas, Orchomenos, Korônus, Haliartus, Almos and Hyêttos, are each in like manner connected with some name of people, tribe, town or village ; while Chrysê and Chrysogeneia have their origin in the reputed ancient wealth of Orchomenos. Abundant discrepancies are found, however, in respect to this old genealogy, if we look to other accounts. According to one statement, Orchomenos was the son of Zeus by Isionê, daughter of Danaus ; Minyas was the son of Orchomenos (or rather of Poseidôn) by Hermippê, daughter of Bœôtos ; the sons of Minyas were Presbôn, Orchomenos, Athamas and Diochthôndas.[3] Others represented Minyas as son of Poseidôn

---

[1] Pausan. ix. 37, 3. A similar story, but far more romantic and amplified, is told by Herodotus (ii. 121), respecting the treasury vault of Rhampsinitus, king of Egypt. Charax (ap. Schol. Aristoph. Nub. 508) gives the same tale, but places the scene in the treasury-vault of Augeas, king of Elis, which he says was built by Trophônius, to whom he assigns a totally different genealogy. The romantic adventures of the tale rendered it eminently fit to be interwoven at some point or another of legendary history, in any country.

[2] Pausan. ix. 38, 6 ; 29, 1.

[3] Schol. Apollôn. Rhod. i. 230. Compare Schol. ad Lycophron. 873.

by Kallirrhoê, an Oceanic nymph,[1] while Dionysius called him son of Arês, and Aristodêmus, son of Aleas: lastly, there were not wanting authors who termed both Minyas and Orchomenos sons of Eteoklês.[2] Nor do we find in any one of these genealogies the name of Amphiôn, the son of Iasus, who figures so prominently in the Odyssey as king of Orchomenos, and whose beautiful daughter Chlôris is married to Nêleus. Pausanias mentions him, but not as king, which is the denomination given to him in Homer.[3]

The discrepancies here cited are hardly necessary in order to prove that these Orchomenian genealogies possess no historical value. Yet some probable inferences appear deducible from the general tenor of the legends, whether the facts and persons of which they are composed be real or fictitious.

Throughout all the historical age, Orchomenos is a member of the Bœôtian confederation. But the Bœôtians are said to have been immigrants into the territory which bore their name from Thessaly ; and prior to the time of their immigration, Orchomenos and the surrounding territory appear as possessed by the Minyæ, who are recognized in that locality both in the Iliad and in the Odyssey,[4] and from whom the constantly recurring Eponymus, King Minyas, is borrowed by the genealogists. Poetical legend connects the Orchomenian Minyæ on the one side, with Pylos and Tryphylia in Peloponnêsus ; on the other side, with Phthiôtis and the town of Iôlkos in Thessaly ; also with Corinth,[5]

---

[1] Schol. Pindar, Olymp. xiv. 5.

[2] Schol. Pindar, Isthm. i. 79. Other discrepancies in Schol. Vett. ad Iliad. ii. Catalog. 18.

[3] Odyss. xi. 283. Pausan. ix. 36, 3.

[4] Iliad, ii. 5, 11. Odyss. xi. 283. Hesiod, Fragm. Eoiai, 27, Düntz. Ἵξεν δ᾽ Ὀρχόμενον Μινυήϊον. Pindar, Olymp. xiv. 4. Παλαιγόνων Μινυᾶν ἐπίσκοποι. Herodot. i. 146. Pausanias calls them Minyæ even in their dealings with Sylla (ix. 30, 1). Buttmann, in his Dissertation (über die Minyæ der Altesten- Zeit, in the Mythologus, Diss. xxi. p. 218), doubts whether the name Minyæ was ever a real name ; but all the passages make against his opinion.

[5] Schol. Apoll. Rhod. ii. 1186. i. 230. Σκήψιος δὲ Δημήτριος φησι τοὺς περὶ τὴν Ἰωλκὸν οἰκοῦντας Μινύας καλεῖσθαι ; and i. 763. Τὴν γὰρ Ἰωλκὸν οἱ Μίνναι ᾤκουν, ὥς φησι Σιμωνίδης ἐν Συμμικτοῖς : also Eustath. ad Iliad. ii. 512. Steph. Byz. v. Μινύα. Orchomenos and Pylos run together in the mind of the poet of the Odyssey, xi. 458.

through Sisyphus and his sons. Pherekydês represented Nêleus, king of Pylos, as having also been king of Orchomenos.[1] In the region of Triphylia, near to or coincident with Pylos, a Minyeian river is mentioned by Homer; and we find traces of residents called Minyæ even in the historical times, though the account given by Herodotus of the way in which they came thither is strange and unsatisfactory.[2]

Before the great changes which took place in the inhabitants of Greece from the immigration of the Thesprôtians into Thessaly, of the Bœôtians into Bœôtia, and of the Dôrians and Ætôlians into Peloponnêsus, at a date which we have no means of determining, the Minyæ and tribes fraternally connected with them seem to have occupied a large portion of the surface of Greece, from Iôlkos in Thessaly to Pylos in the Peloponnêsus. The wealth of Orchomenos is renowned even in the Iliad;[3] and when we study its topography in detail, we are furnished with a probable explanation both of its prosperity and its decay. Orchomenos was situated on the northern bank of the lake Kôpaïs, which receives not only the river Kêphisos from the valleys of Phôkis, but also other rivers from Parnassus and Helicôn. The waters of the lake find more than one subterranean egress — partly through natural rifts and cavities in the limestone mountains, partly through a tunnel pierced artificially more than a mile in length — into the plain on the north-eastern side, from whence they flow into the Eubœan sea near Larymna :[4] and it appears

---

[1] Pherekyd. Fragm. 56, Didot. We see by the 55th Fragment of the same author, that he extended the genealogy of Phryxos to Pheræ in Thessaly.

[2] Herodot. iv. 145. Strabo, viii. 337–347. Hom. Iliad, xi. 721. Pausan. v. 1, 7. ποταμὸν Μιννήϊον, near Elis.

[3] Iliad, ix. 381.

[4] See the description of these channels or Katabothra in Colonel Leake's Travels in Northern Greece, vol. ii. c. 15, p. 281–293, and still more elaborately in Fiedler, Reise durch alle Theile des Königreichs Griechenlands, Leipzig, 1840. He traced fifteen perpendicular shafts sunk for the purpose of admitting air into the tunnel, the first separated from the last by about 5900 feet: they are now of course overgrown and stopped up (vol. i. p. 115).

Forchhammer states the length of this tunnel as considerably greater than what is here stated. He also gives a plan of the Lake Kopaïs with the sur-

that, so long as these channels were diligently watched and kept clear, a large portion of the lake was in the condition of alluvial land, preëminently rich and fertile. But when the channels came to be either neglected, or designedly choked up by an enemy, the water accumulated to such a degree, as to occupy the soil of more than one ancient town, to endanger the position of Kôpæ, and to occasion the change of the site of Orchomenos itself from the plain to the declivity of Mount Hyphanteion. An engineer, Kratês, began the clearance of the obstructed water-courses in the reign of Alexander the Great, and by his commission — the destroyer of Thêbes being anxious to reëstablish the extinct prosperity of Orchomenos. He succeeded so far as partially to drain and diminish the lake, whereby the site of more than one ancient city was rendered visible: but the revival of Thêbes by Kassander, after the decease of Alexander, arrested the progress of the undertaking, and the lake soon regained its former dimensions, to contract which no farther attempt was made.[1]

According to the Thêban legend,[2] Hêraklês, after his defeat of Erginus had blocked up the exit of the waters, and converted the Orchomenian plain into a lake. The spreading of these waters is thus connected with the humiliation of the Minyæ; and there can be little hesitation in ascribing to these ancient tenants of Orchomenos, before it became bœotized, the enlargement and preservation of these protective channels. Nor could such an object have been accomplished, without combined action and acknowledged ascendency on the part of that city over its neighbors, extending even to the sea at Larymna, where the river Kôphisos discharges itself. Of its extended influence, as well as of its maritime activity, we find a remarkable evidence in the ancient and venerated Amphiktyony at Kalauria. The little is-

---

rounding region, which I have placed at the end of the second volume of this History. See also *infra*, vol. ii. ch. iii. p. 391.

[1] We owe this interesting fact to Strabo, who is however both concise and unsatisfactory, viii. p. 406–407. It was affirmed that there had been two ancient towns, named Eleusis 'and Athênæ, originally founded by Cecrôps, situated on the lake, and thus overflowed (Steph. Byz. v. Ἀθῆναι. Diogen. Laërt. iv. 23. Pausan. ix. 24, 2). For the plain or marsh near Orchomenos, see Plutarch, Sylla, c. 20-22.

[2] Diodôr. iv. 18. Pausan. ix. 38, 5

land so named, near the harbor of Trœzên, in Peloponnêsus, was sacred to Poseidôn, and an asylum of inviolable sanctity. At the temple of Poseidôn, in Kalauria, there had existed, from unknown date, a periodical sacrifice, celebrated by seven cities in common — Hermionê, Epidaurus, Ægina, Athens, Prasiæ, Nauplia, and the Minyeian Orchomenos. This ancient religious combination dates from the time when Nauplia was independent of Argos, and Prasiæ of Sparta: Argos and Sparta, according to the usual practice in Greece, continued to fulfil the obligation each on the part of its respective dependent.[1] Six out of the seven states are at once sea-towns, and near enough to Kalauria to account for their participation in this Amphiktyony. But the junction of Orchomenos, from its comparative remoteness, becomes inexplicable, except on the supposition that its territory reached the sea, and that it enjoyed a considerable maritime traffic — a fact which helps to elucidate both its legendary connection with Iôlkos, and its partnership in what is called the Iônic emigration.[2] The mythical genealogy, whereby Ptôos, Schœneus and Erythrios are enumerated among the sons of Athamas, goes farther to confirm the idea that the towns and localities on the south-east of the lake recognized a fraternal origin with the Orchomenian Minyæ, not less than Korôneia and Haliartus on the south-west.[3]

The great power of Orchomenos was broken down, and the city reduced to a secondary and half-dependent position by the Bœôtians of Thêbes; at what time, and under what circumstances, history has not preserved. The story, that the Thêban hero, Hêraklês, rescued his native city from servitude and tribute to Orchomenos, since it comes from a Kadmeian and not from an Orchomenian legend, and since the details of it were favorite subjects of commemoration in the Thêbian temples,[4] affords a presumption that Thêbes was really once dependent on Orcho-

---

[1] Strabo, viii. p. 374. Ἦν δὲ καὶ Ἀμφικτυονία τις περὶ τὸ ἱερὸν τοῦτο, ἑπτα πόλεων αἳ μετεῖχον τῆς θυσίας· ἦσαν δὲ Ἑρμιὼν, Ἐπίδαυρος, Αἴγινα, Ἀθῆναι, Πρασιεῖς, Ναυπλιεῖς, Ὀρχόμενος ὁ Μινύειος. Ὑπὲρ μὲν οὖν τῶν Ναυπλιέων Ἀργεῖοι, ὑπὲρ Πρασιέων δὲ Δακεδαιμόνιοι, ξυνετέλουν.

[2] Pausan. ix. 17, 1; 26, 1.

[3] See Müller, Orchomenos und die Minyer, p. 214. Pausan. ix. 23, 3 24, 3. The genealogy is as old as the poet Asios.

[4] Herod. i. 146. Pausan. vii. 2, 2.

menos. Moreover the savage mutilations inflicted by the hero on the tribute-seeking envoys, so faithfully portrayed in his surname Rhinokoloustês, infuse into the mythe a portion of that bitter feeling which so long prevailed between Thêbes and Orchomenos, and which led the Thêbans, as soon as the battle of Leuctra had placed supremacy in their hands, to destroy and depopulate their rival.[1] The ensuing generation saw the same fate retorted upon Thêbes, combined with the restoration of Orchomenos. The legendary grandeur of this city continued, long after it had ceased to be distinguished for wealth and power, imperishably recorded both in the minds of the nobler citizens and in the compositions of the poets ; the emphatic language of Pausanias shows how much he found concerning it in the old epic.[2]

SECTION II.—DAUGHTERS OF ÆOLUS.

With several of the daughters of Æolus memorable mythical pedigrees and narratives are connected. Alcyêne married Kêyx, the son of Eôsphoros, but both she and her husband displayed in a high degree the overweening insolence common in the Æolic race. The wife called her husband Zeus, while he addressed her as Hêrê, for which presumptuous act Zeus punished them by changing both into birds.[3]

Canacê had by the god Poseidôn several children, amongst

---

[1] Theocrit. xvi. 104.—

῾Ω ᾽Ετεόκλειοι θύγατρες θεαὶ, αἱ Μινύειον
᾽Ορχόμενον φιλέοισαι, ἀπεχθόμενόν ποκα Θήβαις.

The scholiast gives a sense to these words much narrower than they really bear. See Diodôr. xv. 79; Pausan. ix. 15. In the oration which Isokratês places in the mouth of a Platæan, complaining of the oppressions of Thêbes, the ancient servitude and tribute to Orchomenos is cast in the teeth of the Thêbans (Isokrat. Orat. Plataic. vol. iii. p. 32, Auger).

[2] Pausan. ix. 34, 5. See also the fourteenth Olympic Ode of Pindar, addressed to the Orchomenian Asopikus. The learned and instructive work of K. O. Müller, Orchomenos und die Minyer, embodies everything which can be known respecting this once-memorable city; indeed the contents of the work extends much farther than its title promises.

[3] Apollodôr. i. 7, 4. A. Kêyx,—king of Trachin,—the friend of Hêraklês and protector of the Hêrakleids to the extent of his power (Hesiod. Scut. Hercul. 355–473 : Apollodôr. ii. 7, 5 ; Hekatæ. Fragm. 353, Didot.).

whom were Epôpeus and Alôeus.[1] Alôeus married Imphimêdea,
who became enamored of the god Poseidôn, and boasted of her
intimacy with him. She had by him two sons, Otos and Ephialtês, the huge and formidable Alôids, — Titanic beings, nine
fathoms in height and nine cubits in breadth, even in their boy-
hood, before they had attained their full strength. These Alôids
defied and insulted the gods in Olympus; they paid their court
to Hêrê and Artemis, and they even seized and bound Arês,
confining him in a brazen chamber for thirteen months. No one
knew where he was, and the intolerable chain would have worn
him to death, had not Eribœa, the jealous stepmother of the
Alôids, revealed the place of his detention to Hermês, who carried
him surreptitiously away when at the last extremity; nor could
Arês obtain any atonement for such an indignity. Otus and
Ephialtês even prepared to assault the gods in heaven, piling up
Ossa on Olympus and Pelion on Ossa, in order to reach them.
And this they would have accomplished had they been allowed
to grow to their full maturity; but the arrows of Apollo put a
timely end to their short-lived career.[2]

---

[1] Canacê, daughter of Æolus, is a subject of deep tragical interest both in
Euripidês and Ovid. The eleventh Heroic Epistle of the latter, founded
mainly on the lost tragedy of the former called Æolus, purports to be from
Canacê to Macareus, and contains a pathetic description of the ill-fated passion between a brother and sister: see the fragments of the Æolus in Dindorf's collection. In the tale of Kaunos and Byblis, both children of Milêtos,
the results of an incestuous passion are different but hardly less melancholy
(Parthenios, Narr. xi.).

Makar, the son of Æolus, is the primitive settler of the island of Lesbos
(Hom, Hymn. Apoll. 37): moreover in the Odyssey, Æolus son of Hippotês,
the dispenser of the winds, has six sons and six daughters, and marries
the former to the latter (Odyss. x. 7). The two persons called Æolus are
brought into connection genealogically (see Schol. ad Odyss. l. c., and Diodôr. iv. 67), but it seems probable that Euripidês was the first to place the
names of Macareus and Canacê in that relation which confers upon them
their poetical celebrity. Sostratus (ap. Stobæum, t. 614, p. 404) can hardly
be considered to have borrowed from any older source than Euripidês.
Welcker (Griech. Tragöd. vol. ii. p. 860) puts together all that can be known
respecting the structure of the lost drama of Euripidês.

[2] Iliad, v. 386; Odyss. xi. 306; Apollodôr. i. 7. 4. So Typhôeus, in the
Hesiodic Theogony, the last enemy of the gods, is killed before he comes
to maturity (Theog. 837), For the different turns given to this ancient Ho

The genealogy assigned to Calycê, another daughter of Æolus, conducts us from Thessaly to Elis and Ætôlia. She married Aëthlius (the son of Zeus by Prôtogeneia, daughter of Deukaliôn and sister of Hellên), who conducted a colony out of Thessaly and settled in the territory of Elis. He had for his son Endymiôn, respecting whom the Hesiodic Catalogue and the Eoiai related several wonderful things. Zeus granted him the privilege of determining the hour of his own death, and even translated him into heaven, which he forfeited by daring to pay court to Hêrê: his vision in this criminal attempt was cheated by a cloud, and he was cast out into the under-world.[1] According to other

meric legend, see Heyne, ad Apollodôr. l. c., and Hyginus, f. 28. The Alôids were noticed in the Hesiodic poems (ap. Schol. Apoll. Rhod. i. 482). Odysseus does not see *them* in Hadès, as Heyne by mistake says; he sees their mother Iphimêdea. Virgil (Æn. vi. 582) assigns to them a place among the sufferers of punishment in Tartarus.

Eumêlus, the Corinthian poet, designated Alôeus as son of the god Hêlios and brother of Æêtês, the father of Mêdea (Eumêl. Fragm. 2, Marktscheffel). The scene of their death was subsequently laid in Naxos (Pindar, Pyth. iv. 88): their tombs were seen at Anthêdôn in Bœôtia (Pausan. ix. 22, 4). The very curious legend alluded to by Pausanias from Hegesinoos, the author of an Atthis, — to the effect that Otos and Ephialtês were the first to establish the worship of the Muses in Helicôn, and that they founded Ascra along with Œoklos, the son of Poseidôn, — is one which we have no means of tracing farther (Pausan. ix. 29, 1).

The story of the Alôids, as Diodôrus gives it (v. 51, 52), diverges on almost every point: it is evidently borrowed from some Naxian archæologist, and the only information which we collect from it is, that Otos and Ephialtês received heroic honors at Naxos. The views of O. Muller (Orchomenos, p. 387) appear to me unusually vague and fanciful.

Ephialtês takes part in the combat of the giants against the gods (Apollodôr. t. 6, 2), where Heyne remarks, as in so many other cases, "Ephialtês hic non confundendus cum altero Alôei filio;" an observation just indeed, if we are supposed to be dealing with personages and adventures historically real, but altogether misleading in regard to these legendary characters; for here the general conception of Ephialtês and his attributes is in both cases the same; but the particular adventures ascribed to him cannot be made to consist, as facts, one with the other.

[1] Hesiod, Akusilaus and Pherekydês, ap. Schol. Apollôn. Rhod. iv, 57. Ἴν δ' αὐτῷ θανάτου ταμίης. The Scholium is very full of matter, and exhibits many of the diversities in the tale of Endymiôn: see also Apollodôr. i. 7, 5; Pausan. v. 1, 2; Conôn. Narr. 14.

stories, his great beauty caused the goddess Sêlênê to become enamored of him, and to visit him by night during his sleep:—the
sleep of Endymiôn became a proverbial expression for enviable,
undisturbed, and deathless repose.[1] Endymiôn had for issue
(Pausanias gives us three different accounts, and Apollodôrus a
fourth, of the name of his wife) Epeios, Ætôlus, Pæôn, and a
daughter Eurykydê. He caused his three sons to run a race on
the stadium at Olympia, and Epeios, being victorious, was rewarded by becoming his successor in the kingdom: it was after
him that the people were denominated Epeians.

Both the story here mentioned, and still more, the etymological signification of the names Aëthlius and Endymiôn, seem
plainly to indicate (as has before been remarked) that this genealogy was not devised until after the Olympic games had become
celebrated and notorious throughout Greece.

Epeios had no male issue, and was succeeded by his nephew
Eleios, son of Euykydê by the god Poseidôn: the name of the
people was then changed from Epeians to Eleians. Ætôlus, the
brother of Epeios, having slain Apis, son of Phorôneus, was compelled to flee from the country: he crossed the Corinthian gulf
and settled in the territory then called Kurêtis, but to which he
gave the name of Ætôlia.[2]

The son of Eleios,—or, according to other accounts, of the
god Hêlios, of Poseidôn, or of Phorbas,[3]—is Augeas, whom we
find mentioned in the Iliad as king of the Epeians or Eleians.
Nestôr gives a long and circumstantial narrative of his own exploits at the head of his Pylian countrymen against his neighbors
the Epeians and their king Augeas, whom he defeated with great
loss, slaying Mulios, the king's son-in-law, and acquiring a vast

---

[1] Theocrit. iii. 49; xx. 35; where, however, Endymiôn is connected with
Latmos in Caria (see Schol. ad loc).

[2] Pausan. v. 1. 3–6; Apollodôr. i. 7, 6.

[3] Apollodôr. ii. 5, 5; Schol. Apoll. Rhod. i. 172. In all probability, the
old legend made Augeas the son of the god Hêlios: Hêlios, Augeas and Agamêdê are a triple series parallel to the Corinthian genealogy, Hêlios, Æêtês
and Mêdia; not to mention that the etymology of Augeas connects him
with Hêlios. Theocritus (xx. 55) designates him as the son of the god Hêlios, through whose favor his cattle are made to prosper and multiply with
such astonishing success (xx. 117).

booty.[1] Augeas was rich in all sorts of rural wealth, and possessed herds of cattle so numerous, that the dung of the animals accumulated in the stable or cattle enclosures beyond all power of endurance. Eurystheus, as an insult to Hêraklês, imposed upon him the obligation of cleansing this stable: the hero, disdaining to carry off the dung upon his shoulders, turned the course of the river Alpheios through the building, and thus swept the encumbrance away.[2] But Augeas, in spite of so signal a service, refused to Hêraklês the promised reward, though his son Phyleus protested against such treachery, and when he found that he could not induce his father to keep faith, retired in sorrow and wrath to the island of Dulichiôn.[3] To avenge the deceit practised upon him, Hêraklês invaded Elis; but Augeas had powerful auxiliaries, especially his nephews, the two Molionids (sons of Poseidôn by Molionê, the wife of Aktôr), Eurytos and Kteatos. These two miraculous brothers, of transcendent force, grew together, — having one body, but two heads and four arms.[4]

---

[1] Iliad, xi. 670–760; Pherekyd. Fragm. 57, Didot.

[2] Diodôr. iv. 13. Ὑβρεως ἕνεκεν Εὐρυσθεὺς προσέταξε καθᾶραι ὁ δὲ Ἡρακλῆς τὸ μὲν τοῖς ὤμοις ἐξενεγκεῖν αὐτὴν ἀπεδοκίμασιν, ἐκκλίνων τὴν ἐκ τῆς ὑβρεως αἰσχύνην, etc. (Pausan. v. 1. 7; Apollodôr. ii. 5, 5).

It may not be improper to remark that this fable indicates a purely pastoral condition, or at least a singularly rude state of agriculture; and the way in which Pausanias recounts it goes even beyond the genuine story: ὡς καὶ τὰ πολλὰ τῆς χώρας αὐτῷ ἤδη διατελεῖν ἀργὰ ὄντα ὑπὸ τῶν βοσκημάτων τῆς κόπρου. The slaves of Odysseus however know what use to make of the dung heaped before his outer fence (Odyss. xvii. 299); not so the purely carnivorous and pastoral Cyclôps (Odyss. ix. 329). The stabling into which the cattle go from their pasture, is called κόπρος in Homer, — Ἐλθοῦσας ἐς κόπρον, ἐπὴν βοτανῆς κορέσωνται (Odyss. x. 411): compare Iliad, xviii. 575 — Μυκηθμῷ δ' ἀπὸ κόπρου ἐπεσσεύοντο πέδονδε.

The Augeas of Theocritus has abundance of wheat-land and vineyard, as well as cattle: he ploughs his land three or four times, and digs his vineyard diligently (xx. 20–32).

[3] The wrath and retirement of Phyleus is mentioned in the Iliad (ii. 633), but not the cause of it.

[4] These singular properties were ascribed to them both in the Hesiodic poems and by Pherekydês (Schol. Ven. ad Il. xi. 715–750, et ad Il. xxiii. 638), but not in the Iliad. The poet Ibykus (Fragm. 11, Schneid. ap. Athenæ. ii. 57) calls them ἅλικας ἰσοκεφάλους, ἐνιγυίους, Ἀμφοτέρους γεγαῶτας ἐν ὠέῳ ἀργυρέῳ.

There were temples and divine honors to Zeus Moliôn (Lactantius. de Falsâ Religionc. i. 22)

Such was their irresistible might, that Hêraklês was defeated
and repelled from Elis: but presently the Eleians sent the two
Molionid brothers as *Theôri* (sacred envoys) to the Isthmian
games, and Hêraklês, placing himself in ambush at Kleônæ, surprised and killed them as they passed through. For this murder-
ous act the Eleians in vain endeavored to obtain redress both at
Corinth and at Argos; which is assigned as the reason for the
self-ordained exclusion, prevalent throughout all the historical
age, that no Eleian athlête would ever present himself as a competitor at the Isthmian games.[1] The Molionids being· thus removed, Hêraklês again invaded Elis, and killed Augeas along
with his children,— all except Phyleus, whom he brought over
from Dulichiôn, and put in possession of his father's kingdom. According to the more gentle narrative which Pausanias adopts, Augeas was not killed, but pardoned at the requêst of Phyleus.[2] He
was worshipped as a hero[3] even down to the time of that author.

It was on occasion of this conquest of Elis, according to the old
mythe which Pindar has ennobled in a magnificent ode, that
Hêraklês first consecrated the ground of Olympia, and established
the Olympic games. Such at least was one of the many fables
respecting the origin of that memorable institution.[4]

Phyleus, after having restored order in Elis, retired again to
Dulichiôn, and left the kingdom to his brother Agasthenês, which
again brings us into the Homeric series. For Polyxenos, son of
Agasthenês, is one of the four commanders of the Epeian forty
ships in the Iliad, in conjunction with the two sons of Eurytos

---

[1] Pausan. v. 2, 4. The inscription cited by Pausanias proves that this was
the reason assigned by the Eleian athlêtes themselves for the exclusion; but
there were several different stories.

[2] Apollodôr. ii. 7, 2. Diodôr. iv. 33. Pausan. v. 2, 2; 3, 2. It seems evident from these accounts that the genuine legend represented Hêraklês as
having been defeated by the Molionids: the unskilful evasions both of Apollodôrus and Diodôrus betray this. Pindar (Olymp. xi. 25–50) gives the story
without any flattery to Hêraklês.

[3] Pausan. v. 4, 1.

[4] The Amenian copy of Eusebius gives a different genealogy respecting
Elis and Pisa: Aëthlius, Epeius, Endymiôn, Alexinus; next Œnomaus and
Pêlops, then Hêraklês. Some counted *ten* generations, others *three*, between
Hêraklês and Iphitus, who renewed the discontinued Olympic games (see
Armem. Euseb. copy c. xxxii. p. 140).

and Kteatos, and with Diôrês son of Amarynceus. Megês, the
son of Phyleus, commands the contingent from Dulichiôn and the
Echinades.[1] Polyxenos returns safe from Troy, is succeeded by
his son Amphimachos, — named after the Epeian chief who had
fallen before Troy, — and he again by another Eleios, in whose
time the Dôrians and the Hêrakleids invade Peloponnêsus.[2]
These two names, barren of actions or attributes, are probably
introduced by the genealogists whom Pausanias followed, to fill
up the supposed interval between the Trojan war and the Dôrian
invasion. We find the ordinary discrepancies in respect to the series and
the members of this genealogy. Thus some called Epeios son of
Aëthlius, others son of Endymiôn :[3] a third pedigree, which carries the sanction of Aristotle and is followed by Cônon, designated
Eleios, the first settler of Elis, as son of Poseidôn and Eurypylê,
daughter of Endymiôn, and Epeios and Alexis as the two sons of
Eleios.[4] And Pindar himself, in his ode to Epharmostus the
Locrian, introduces with much emphasis another king of the
Epeians named Opus, whose daughter, pregnant by Zeus, was
conveyed by that god to the old and childless king Locrus : the
child when born, adopted by Locrus ànd named Opus, became the
eponymous hero of the city so called in Locris.[5] Moreover Hekatæus the Milesian not only affirmed (contrary both to the Iliad
and the Odyssey) that the Epeians and the Eleians were different
people, but also added that the Epeians had assisted Hêraklês in
his expedition against Augeas and Elis ; a narrative very different from that of Apollodôrus and Pausanias, and indicating besides
that he must have had before him a genealogy varying from
theirs.[6]

It has already been mentioned that Ætôlus, son of Endymiôn,

---

[1] Iliad, ii. 615–630.　　　　　　　　　　[2] Pausan. v. 3, 4.
[3] Schol. Pindar, Olymp. ix. 86.
[4] Schol. Ven. ad Il. xi. 687 ; Conôn, Narrat. xv. ap. Scriptt. Mythogr. West
p. 130.
[5] Pindar, Olymp. ix. 62: Schol. ibid. 86. 'Οποῦντος ἦν θυγάτηρ 'Ηλείων
βασιλέως, ἣν 'Αριστοτέλης Καμβύσην καλεῖ.
[6] 'Εκαταῖος δὲ ὁ Μιλήσιος ἑτέρους λέγει τῶν 'Ηλείων τοὺς 'Επείους· τῷ γοῦν
'Ηρακλεῖ συστρατεῦσαι τοὺς 'Επείους καὶ συνανελεῖν αὐτῷ τόν τε Αὐγέαν καὶ
τὴν Ἦλιν (Hekat. ap. Strab. viii. p. 341).

quitted Peloponnêsus in consequence of having slain Apis.[1] The country on the north of the Corinthian gulf, between the rivers Euênus and Achelôus, received from him the name of Ætôlia instead of that of Kurêtis : he acquired possession of it after having slain Dôrus, Laodokus and Polypœtes, sons of Apollo and Phthia, by whom he had been well received. He had by his wife Pronoê (the daughter of Phorbas) two sons, Pleurôn and Kalydôn, and from them the two chief towns in Ætôlia were named.[2] Pleurôn married Xanthippê, daughter of Dôrus, and had for his son Agênôr, from whom sprang Portheus, or Porthaôn, and Demonikê : Euênos and Thestius were children of the latter by the god Arês.[3]

Portheus had three sons, Agrius, Melas and Œneus : among the offspring of Thestius were Althæa and Lêda,[4] — names which bring us to a period of interest in the legendary history. Lêda marries Tyndareus and becomes mother of Helena and the Dioscuri : Althæa marries Œneus, and has, among other children, Meleager and Deianeira ; the latter being begotten by the god Dionysus, and the former by Arês.[5] Tydeus also is his son, the

---

[1] Ephorus said that Ætôlus had been expelled by Salmôneus king of the Epeians and Pisatæ (ap. Strabo. viii. p. 357) : he must have had before him a different story and different genealogy from that which is given in the text.

[2] Apollodôr. i. 7, 6. Dôrus, son of Apollo and Phthia, killed by Ætôlus, after having hospitably received him, is here mentioned. Nothing at all is known of this ; but the conjunction of names is such as to render it probable that there was some legend connected with them : possibly the assistance given by Apollo to the Kuretes against the Ætolians, and the death of Meleager by the hand of Apollo, related both in the Eoiai and the Minyas (Pausan. x. 31, 2), may have been grounded upon it. The story connects itself with what is stated by Apollodôrus about Dôrus son of Hellên (see *supra*, p. 136).

[3] According to the ancient genealogical poet Asius, Thestius was son of Agênôr the son of Pleurôn (Asii Fragm. 6, p. 413, ed. Marktsch.). Compare the genealogy of Ætôlia and the general remarks upon it, in Brandstäter, Geschichte des Ætol. Landes, etc., Berlin, 1844, p. 23 *seq.*

[4] Respecting Lêda, see the statements of Ibykus, Phcrekydês, Hellanikus, etc. (Schol. Apollôn. Rhod. i. 146). The reference to the Corinthiaca of Eümêlus is curious : it is a specimen of the matters upon which these old genealogical poems dwelt.

[5] Apollodôr. i. 8, 1 ; Euripidês, Meleager, Frag. 1. The three sons of Portheus are named in the Iliad (xiv. 116) as living at Pleurôn and Kalydôn The name Œneus doubtless brings Dionysus into the legend.

father of Diomêdês: warlike eminence goes hand in hand with tragic calamity among the members of this memorable family.

We are fortunate enough to find the legend of Althæa and Meleager set forth at considerable length in the Iliad, in the speech addressed by Phœnix to appease the wrath of Achilles. Œneus, king of Kalydôn, in the vintage sacrifices which he offered to the gods, omitted to include Artemis: the misguided man either forgot her or cared not for her;[1] and the goddess, provoked by such an insult, sent against the vineyards of Œneus a wild boar, of vast size and strength, who tore up the trees by the root and laid prostrate all their fruit. So terrible was this boar, that nothing less than a numerous body of men could venture to attack him: Meleager, the son of Œneus, however, having got together a considerable number of companions, partly from the Kurêtes of Pleurôn, at length slew him. But the anger of Artemis was not yet appeased, and she raised a dispute among the combatants respecting the possession of the boar's head and hide, — the trophies of victory. In this dispute, Meleager slew the brother of his mother Althæa, prince of the Kurêtes of Pleurôn: these Kurêtes attacked the Ætôlians of Kalydôn in order to avenge their chief. So long as Meleager contended in the field the Ætôlians had the superiority. But he presently refused to come forth, indignant at the curses imprecated upon him by his mother: for Althæa, wrung with sorrow for the death of her brother, flung herself upon the ground in tears, beat the earth violently with her hands, and implored Hades and Persephonê to inflict death upon Meleager, — a prayer which the unrelenting Erinnys in Erebus heard but too well. So keenly did the hero resent this behavior of his mother, that he kept aloof from the war; and the Kurêtes not only drove the Ætôlians from the field, but assailed the walls and gates of Kalydôn, and were on the point of overwhelming its dismayed inhabitants. There was no hope of safety except in the arm of Meleager; but Meleager lay in his chamber by the side of his beautiful wife Kleopatra, the daughter of Idas, and heeded not the necessity.

---

[1] Ἡ λάϑετ', ἢ οὐκ ἐνόησεν· ἀάσσατο δὲ μέγα θυμῷ (Iliad, ix. 533). The destructive influence of Atè is mentioned before, v. 502. The piety of Xenophôn reproduces this ancient circumstance, — Οἰνέως δ' ἐν γήρᾳ ἐπιλαϑομένον τῆς ϑεοῦ, etc. (De Venat. c. i.)

While the shouts of expected victory were heard from the assailants at the gates, the ancient men of Ætôlia and the priests of the
gods earnestly besought Meleager to come forth,[1] offering him his
choice of the fattest land in the plain of Kalydôn. His dearest
friends, his father Œneus, his sisters, and even his mother herself
added their supplications, but he remained inflexible. At length
the Kurêtes penetrated into the town and began to burn it: at
this last moment, Kleopatra his wife addressed to him her pathetic
appeal, to avert from her and from his family the desperate horrors impending over them all. Meleager could no longer resist
he put on his armor, went forth from his chamber, and repelled
the enemy. But when the danger was over, his countrymen withheld from him the splendid presents which they had promised,
because he had rejected their prayers, and had come forth only
when his own haughty caprice dictated.[2]

Such is the legend of Meleager in the Iliad: a verse in the
second book mentions simply the death of Meleager, without farther details, as a reason why Thoas appeared in command of the
Ætôlians before Troy.[3] Though the circumstance is indicated only
indirectly, there seems little doubt that Homer must have conceived the death of the hero as brought about by the maternal
curse: the unrelenting Erinnys executed to the letter the invoca-
tions of Althæa, though she herself must have been willing to retract them.

Later poets both enlarged and altered the fable. The Hesiodic Eoiai, as well as the old poem called the Minyas, represented
Meleager as having been slain by Apollo, who aided the Kurêtes
in the war; and the incident of the burning brand, though quite
at variance with Homer, is at least as old as the tragic poet Phrynichus, earlier than Æschylus.[4] The Mœræ, or Fates, presenting
themselves to Althæa shortly after the birth of Meleager, predicted that the child would die so soon as the brand then burning
on the fire near at hand should be consumed. Althæa snatched
it from the flames and extinguished it, preserving it with the
utmost care, until she became incensed against Meleager for the

---

[1] These priests formed the Chorus in the Meleager of Sophoklês(Schol.
d Iliad. ib. 575).

[2] Iliad, ix. 525–595.   [3] Iliad, ii. 642.

[4] Pausan. x. 31. 2. The Πλευρώνιαι, a lost tragedy of Phrynichus.

death of her brother. She then cast it into the fire, and as soon as it was consumed the life of Meleager was brought to a close.

We know, from the sharp censure of Pliny, that Sophoklês heightened the pathos of this subject by his account of the mournful death of Meleager's sisters, who perished from excess of grief. They were changed into the birds called Meleagrides, and their never-ceasing tears ran together into amber.[1] But in the hands of Euripidês — whether originally through him or not,[2] we cannot tell — Atalanta became the prominent figure and motive of the piece, while the party convened to hunt the Kalydônian boar was made to comprise all the distinguished heroes from every quarter of Greece. In fact, as Heyne justly remarks, this event is one of the four aggregate dramas of Grecian heroic life,[3] along with the Argonautic expedition, the siege of Thêbes, and the Trojan war. To accomplish the destruction of the terrific animal which Artemis in her wrath had sent forth, Meleager assembled not merely the choice youth among the Kurêtes and Ætôlians (as we fine in the Iliad), but an illustrious troop, including Kastôr and Pollux, Idas and Lynkeus, Pêleus and Telamôn, Thêseus and Peirithous, Ankæus and Kêpheus, Jasôn, Amphiaraus, Admêtus, Eurytiôn and others. Nestôr and Phœnix, who appear as old men before the walls of Troy, exhibited their early prowess as auxiliaries to the suffering Kalydônians.[4] Conspicuous amidst them all stood the virgin Atalanta, daughter of the Arcadian

---

[1] Plin. H. N. xxxvii. 2, 11.

[2] There was a tragedy of Æschylus called Ἀταλάντη, of which nothing remains (Bothe, Æschyli Fragm. ix. p. 18).

Of the more recent dramatic writers, several selected Atalanta as their subject (See Brandstäter, Geschichte Ætoliens, p. 65).

[3] There was a poem of Stesichorus, Σύοθηραι (Stesichor. Fragm. 15. p. 72).

[4] The catalogue of these heroes is in Apollodôr. i. 8, 2; Ovid, Metamor. viii. 300; Hygin. fab. 173. Euripidês, in his play of Meleager, gave an enumeration and description of the heroes (see Fragm. 6 of that play, ed. Matth.). Nestôr, in this picture of Ovid, however, does not appear quite so invincible as in his own speeches in the Iliad. The mythographers thought it necessary to assign a reason why Hêraklês was *not* present at the Kalydônian adventure: he was just at that time in servitude with Omphalê in Lydia (Apollod. ii. 6, 3). This seems to have been the idea of Ephorus, and it is much in his style of interpretation (see Ephor. Fragm. 9, ed. Didot.).

Schœneus ; beautiful and matchless for swiftness of foot, but living in the forest as a huntress and unacceptable to Aphroditê.[1] Several of the heroes were slain by the boar, others escaped by various stratagems : at length Atalanta first shot him in the back, next Amphiaraus in the eye, and, lastly, Meleager killed him. Enamoured of the beauty of Atalanta, Meleager made over to her the chief spoils of the animal, on the plea that she had inflicted the first wound. But his uncles, the brothers of Thestius, took them away from her, asserting their rights as next of kin,[2] if Meleager declined to keep the prize for himself : the latter, exasperated at this behavior, slew them. Althæa, in deep sorrow for her brothers and wrath against her son, is impelled to produce the fatal brand which she had so long treasured up, and consign it to the flames.[3]   The tragedy concludes with the voluntary death both of Althæa and Kleopatra.

Interesting as the Arcadian huntress, Atalanta, is in herself, she is an intrusion, and not a very convenient intrusion, into the Homeric story of the Kalydônian boar-hunt, wherein another female Kleopatra, already occupied the foreground.[4]   But the more recent version became accredited throughout Greece, and

---

[1] Euripid. Meleag. Fragm. vi. Matt. —

Κύπριδος δὲ μίσημ', Ἀρκὰς Ἀταλάντη, κύνας
Καὶ τόξ' ἔχουσα, etc.

There was a drama "Meleager " both of Sophoklês and Euripidês : of the former hardly any fragments remain, — a few more of the latter.

[2] Hyginus, fab. 229.

[3] Diodôr. iv. 34. Apollodôrus (i. 8 ; 2–4) gives first the usual narrative, including Atalanta ; next, the Homeric narrative with some additional circumstances, but not including either Atalanta or the fire-brand on which Meleager's life depended.   He prefaces the latter with the words οἱ δέ φασι, etc Antoninus Liberalis gives this second narrative only, without Atalanta, from Nicander (Narrat. 2).

The Latin scenic poet, Attius, had devoted one of his tragedies to this subject, taking the general story as given by Euripidês : " Remanet gloria apud me : exuvias dignavi Atalantæ dare," seems to be the speech of Meleager. (Attii Fragm. 8, ap. Poet. Scen. Lat. ed. Bothe, p. 215).   The readers of the Æneid will naturally think of the swift and warlike virgin Camilla, as the parallel of Atalanta.

[4] The narrative of Apollodôrus reads awkwardly — Μελέαγρος ἔχων γυναῖκα Κλεοπάτραν, βουλόμενος δὲ καὶ ἐξ Ἀταλάντης τεκνοποιήσασθαι, etc (i. 8, 2).

was sustained by evidence which few persons in those days felt any inclination to controvert. For Atalanta carried away with her the spoils and head of the boar into Arcadia; and there for successive centuries hung the identical hide and the gigantic tusks, of three feet in length, in the temple of Athênê Alea at Tegea. Kallimachus mentions them as being there preserved, in the third century before the Christian æra;[1] but the extraordinary value set upon them is best proved by the fact that the emperor Augustus took away the tusks from Tegea, along with the great statue of Athênê Alea, and conveyed them to Rome, to be there preserved among the public curiosities. Even a century and a half afterwards, when Pausanias visited Greece, the skin worn out with age was shown to him, while the robbery of the tusks had not been forgotten. Nor were these relics of the boar the only memento preserved at Tegea of the heroic enterprise. On the pediment of the temple of Athênê Alea, unparalleled in Peloponnêsus for beauty and grandeur, the illustrious statuary Skopas had executed one of his most finished reliefs, representing the Kalydônian hunt. Atalanta and Meleager were placed in the front rank of the assailants, and Ankæus, one of the Tegean heroes, to whom the tusks of the boar had proved fatal,[2] was represented as sinking under his death-wound into the arms of his brother Epochos. And Pausanias observes, that the Tegeans, while they had manifested the same honorable forwardness as other Arcadian communities in the conquest of Troy, the repulse of Xerxês, and the battle of Dipæ against Sparta — might fairly claim to themselves, through Ankæus and Atalanta, that they alone amongst all Arcadians had participated in the glory of the Kalydônian boar-hunt.[3] So entire and unsuspecting is the faith

---

[1] Kallimachus, Hymn. ad Dian. 217.—

Οὐ μιν ἐπίκλητοὶ Καλυδώνιοι ἀγρευτῆρες
Μέμφονται κάπροιο· τὰ γὰρ σημηΐα νίκης
'Αρκαδίην εἰσῆλθεν, ἔχει δ' ἔτι θηρὸς ὀδόντας.

[2] See Pherekyd. Frag. 81, ed. Didot.
[3] Pausan. viii. 45, 4; 46, 1-3; 47, 2. Lucian, adv. Indoctum, c. 14. t. iii. p. 111, Reiz.

The officers placed in charge of the public curiosities or wonders at Rome (οἱ ἐπὶ τοῖς θαύμασιν) affirmed that one of the tusks had been accidentally

both of the Tegeans and of Pausanias in the past historical reality of this romantic adventure. Strabo indeed tries to transform
the romance into something which has the outward semblance of
history, by remarking that the quarrel respecting the boar's head
and hide cannot have been the real cause of war between the
Kurêtes and the Ætôlians; the true ground of dispute (he contends) was probably the possession of a portion of territory.[1] His
remarks on this head are analogous to those of Thucydidês and
other critics, when they ascribe the Trojan war, not to the rape of
Helen, but to views of conquest or political apprehensions. But
he treats the general fact of the battle between the Kurêtes and
the Ætôlians, mentioned in the Iliad, as something unquestionably real and historical — recapitulating at the same time a variety of discrepancies on the part of different authors, but not
giving any decision of his own respecting their truth or falsehood.

In the same manner as Atalanta was intruded into the Kalydônian hunt, so also she seems to have been introduced into the
memorable funeral games celebrated after the decease of Pelias
at Iôlkos, in which she had no place at the time when the works
on the chest of Kypselus were executed.[2] But her native and
genuine locality is Arcadia; where her race-course, near to the
town of Methydrion, was shown even in the days of Pausanias.[3]
This race-course had been the scene of destruction for more than

broken in the voyage from Greece: the other was kept in the temple of Bacchus in the Imperial Gardens.

It is numbered among the memorable exploits of Thêseus that he van
quished and killed a formidable and gigantic sow, in the territory of Krom-
myôn near Corinth. According to some critics, this Krommyônian sow was
the mother of the Kalydônian boar (Strabo, viii. p. 380).

[1] Strabo, x. p. 466. Πολέμου δ' ἐμπεσόντος τοῖς Θεστιάδαις πρὸς (ἰνέα
καὶ Μελέαγρον, ὁ μὲν Ποιητῆς, ἀμφὶ συὸς κεφαλῇ καὶ δέρματι, κατὰ τὴν περὶ
τοῦ κάπρου μυθολογίαν· ὡς δὲ τὸ εἰκὸς, περὶ μέρους τῆς χώρας, etc. This
remark is also similar to Mr. Payne Knight's criticism on the true causes of the
Trojan war, which were (he tells us) of a political character, independent of
Helen and her abduction (Prolegom. ad Homer. c. 53).

[2] Compare Apollodôr. iii. 9, 2, and Pausan. v. 17, 4. She is made to
wrestle with Pêleus at these funeral games, which seems foreign to her character.

[3] Pausan. viii. 35, 8.

one unsuccessful suitor. For Atalanta, averse to marriage, had proclaimed that her hand should only be won by the competitor who could surpass her in running: all who tried and failed were condemned to die, and many were the persons to whom her beauty and swiftness, alike unparalleled, had proved fatal. At length Meilaniôn, who had vainly tried to win her affections by assiduous services in her hunting excursions, ventured to enter the perilous lists. Aware that he could not hope to outrun her except by stratagem, he had obtained by the kindness of Aphroditê, three golden apples from the garden of the Hesperides, which he successively let fall near to her while engaged in the race. The maiden could not resist the temptation of picking them up, and was thus overcome: she became the wife of Meilaniôn and the mother of the Arcadian Parthenopæus, one of the seven chiefs who perished in the siege of Thêbes.[1]

---

[1] Respecting the varieties in this interesting story, see Apollod. iii. 9, 2; Hygin. f. 185; Ovid, Metam. x. 560–700; Propert. i. 1, 20; Ælian, V. H xiii. i. Μειλανίωνος σωφρονέστερος. Aristophan. Lysistrat. 786 and Schol In the ancient representation on the chest of Kypselus (Paus. v. 19, 1), Meilaniôn was exhibited standing near Atalanta, who was holding a fawn: no match or competition in running was indicated.

There is great discrepancy in the naming and patronymic description of the parties in the story. Three different persons are announced as fathers of Atalanta, Schœneus, Jasus and Mænalos; the successful lover in Ovid (and seemingly in Euripidês also) is called Hippomenês, not Meilaniôn. In the Hesiodic poems Atalanta was daughter of Schœneus; Hellanikus called her daughter of Jasus. See Apollodôr. 1. c.; Kallimach. Hymn to Dian. 214, with the note of Spanheim; Schol. Eurip. Phœniss. 150; Schol. Theocr. Idyll. iii. 40; also the ample commentary of Bachet de Meziriac, Sur les Epîtres d'Ovide, vol. i. p. 366. Servius (ad Virg. Eclog. vi. 61; Æneid, iii 113) calls Atalanta a native of Scyros.

Both the ancient scholiasts (see Schol. Apoll. Rhod. i. 769) and the modern commentators, Spanheim and Heyne, seek to escape this difficulty by supposing two Atalantas, — an Arcadian and a Bœôtian: assuming the principle of their conjecture to be admissible, they ought to suppose at least three.

Certainly, if personages of the Grecian mythes are to be treated as historically real, and their adventures as so many exaggerated and miscolored facts, it will be necessary to repeat the process of multiplying entities to an infinite extent. And this is one among the many reasons for rejecting the fundamental supposition.

But when we consider these personages as purely legendary, so that an

We have yet another female in the family of Œneus, whose name the legend has immortalized. His daughter Deianeira was sought in marriage by the river Achelôus, who presented himself in various shapes, first as a serpent and afterwards as a bull. From the importunity of this hateful suitor she was rescued be the arrival of Hêraklês, who encountered Achelôus, vanquished him and broke off one of his horns, which Achelôus ransomed by surrendering to him the horn of Amaltheia, endued with the miraculous property of supplying the possessor with abundance of any food or drink which he desired. Hêraklês was rewarded for his prowess by the possession of Deianeira, and he made over the horn of Amaltheia as his marriage-present to Œneus.[1] Compelled to leave the residence of Œneus in consequence of having in a fit of anger struck the youthful attendant Eunomus, and involuntarily killed him,[2] Hêraklês retired to Trachin, crossing the river Euênus at the place where the Centaur Nessus was

---

historical basis can neither be affirmed nor denied respecting them, we escape the necessity of such inconvenient stratagems. The test of identity is then to be sought in the attributes, not in the legal description, — in the predicates, not in the subject. Atalanta, whether born of one father or another, whether belonging to one place or another, is beautiful, cold, repulsive, daring, swift of foot and skilful with the bow, — these attributes constitute her identity. The Scholiast on Theocritus (iii. 40), in vindicating his supposition that there were two Atalantas, draws a distinction founded upon this very principle: he says that the Bœôtian Atalanta was τοξοτὶς, and the Arcadian Atalanta δρομαία. But this seems an over-refinement: both the shooting and the running go to constitute an accomplished huntress.

In respect to Parthenopæus, called by Euripidês and by so many others the son of Atalanta, it is of some importance to add, that Apollodôrus, Aristarchus, and Antimachus, the author of the Thebaid, assigned to him a pedigree entirely different, — making him an Argeian, the son of Talaos and Lysimachê, and brother of Adrastus. (Apollodôr. i. 9, 13 ; Aristarch. ap. Schol. Soph. Œd. Col. 1320; Antimachus ap. Schol. Æschyl. Sep. Theb. 532; and Schol. Supplem. ad Eurip. Phœniss. t. viii. p. 461, ed. Matth Apollodôrus is in fact inconsistent with himself in another passage).

[1] Sophokl. Trachin. 7. The horn of Amaltheia was described by Pherekydès (Apollod. ii. 7, 5); see also Strabo, x. p. 458 and Diodôr. iv. 35, who cites an interpretation of the fables (οἱ εἰκάζοντες ἐξ αὐτῶν τἀληθές) to the effect that it was symbolical of an embankment of the unruly river by Hêraklês, and consequent recovery of very fertile land.

[2] Hellanikus (ap. Athen. ix. p. 410) mentioning this incident, in two different works, called the attendant by two different names.

accustomed to carry over passengers for hire. Nessus carried over Deianeira, but when he had arrived on the other side, began to treat her with rudeness, upon which Hêraklês slew him with an arrow tinged by the poison of the Lernæan hydra. The dying Centaur advised Deianeira to preserve the poisoned blood which flowed from his wound, telling her that it would operate as a philtre to regain for her the affections of Hêraklês, in case she should ever be threatened by a rival. Some time afterwards the hero saw and loved the beautiful Iolê, daughter of Eurytos, king of Œchalia: he stormed the town, killed Eurytos, and made Iolê his captive. The misguided Deianeira now had recourse to her supposed philtre: she sent as a present to Hêraklês a splendid tunic, imbued secretly with the poisoned blood of the Centaur. Hêraklês adorned himself with the tunic on the occasion of offering a solemn sacrifice to Zeus on the promontory of Kênæon in Eubœa: but the fatal garment, when once put on, clung to him indissolubly, burnt his skin and flesh, and occasioned an agony of pain from which he was only relieved by death. Deianeira slew herself in despair at this disastrous catastrophe.[1]

---

[1] The beautiful drama of the Trachiniæ has rendered this story familiar: compare Apollod. ii. 7, 7. Hygin. f. 36. Diodôr. iv. 36-37.

The capture of Œchalia (Οἰχαλίας ἅλωσις) was celebrated in a very ancient epic poem by Kreophylos, of the Homeric and not of the Hesiodic character: it passed with many as the work of Homer himself. (See Düntzer, Fragm. Epic. Græcor. p. 8. Welcker, Der Epische Cyclus, p. 229). The same subject was also treated in the Hesiodic Catalogue, or in the Eoiai (see Hesiod, Fragm. 129, ed. Marktsch.): the number of the children of Eurytos was there enumerated.

This exploit seems constantly mentioned as the last performed by Hêraklês, and as immediately preceding his death or apotheosis on Mount Œta: but whether the legend of Deianeira and the poisoned tunic be very old, we cannot tell.

The tale of the death of Iphitos, son of Eurytos, by Hêraklês, is as ancient as the Odyssey (xxi. 19-40): but it is there stated, that Eurytos dying left his memorable bow to his son Iphitos (the bow is given afterwards by Iphitos to Odysseus, and is the weapon so fatal to the suitors), — a statement not very consistent with the story that Œchalia was taken and Eurytos slain by Hêraklês. It is plain that these were distinct and contradictory legends. Compare Soph. Trachin. 260-285 (where Iphitos dies before Eurytos), not only with the passage just cited from the Odyssey, but also with Pherekydês, Fragm. 34, Didot.

Hyginus (f. 33) differs altogether in the parentage of Deianeira: he calls

We have not yet exhausted the eventful career of Œneus and
his family — ennobled among the Ætôlians especially, both by
religious worship and by poetical eulogy — and favorite themes
not merely in some of the Hesiodic poems, but also in other
ancient epic productions, the Alkmæênis and the Cyclic Thêbais.[1]
By another marriage, Œneus had for his son Tydeus, whose
poetical celebrity is attested by the many different accounts given
both of the name and condition of his mother. Tydeus, having
slain his cousins, the sons of Melas, who were conspiring against
Œneus, was forced to become an exile, and took refuge at Argos
with Adrastus, whose daughter Deipylê he married. The issue
of this marriage was Diomêdês, whose brilliant exploits in the
siege of Troy were not less celebrated than those of his father at
the siege of Thêbes. After the departure of Tydeus, Œneus
was deposed by the sons of Agrios, and fell into extreme poverty
and wretchedness, from which he was only rescued by his grandson Diomêdês, after the conquest of Troy.[2] The sufferings of
this ancient warrior, and the final restoration and revenge by
Diomêdês, were the subject of a lost tragedy of Euripidês, which
even the ridicule of Aristophanês demonstrates to have been
eminently pathetic.[3]

Though the genealogy just given of Œneus is in part Homeric, and seems to have been followed generally by the mythographers, yet we find another totally at variance with it in
Hekatæus, which he doubtless borrowed from some of the old
poets: the simplicity of the story annexed to it seems to attest
its antiquity. Orestheus, son of Deukaliôn, first passed into

---

her daughter of Dexamenos : his account of her marriage with Hêraklês is
in every respect at variance with Apollodôrus. In the latter, Mnêsimachê
is the daughter of Dexamenos ; Hêraklês rescues her from the importunities
of the Centaur Eurytiôn (ii. 5, 5).

[1] See the references in Apollod. i, 8, 4–5. Pindar, Isthm. iv. 32. Μελέταν
δὲ σοφισταῖς Διὸς ἕκατι πρόσβαλον σεβιζόμενοι Ἐν μὲν Αἰτωλῶν θυσίαισι
φαενναῖς Οἰνεῖδαι κρατεροί, etc.

[2] Hekat. Fragm. 341, Didot. In this story Œneus is connected with the
first discovery of the vine and the making of wine (οἶνος) : compare Hygin.
f. 129, and Servius ad Virgil. Georgic. i. 9.

[3] See Welcker (Griechisch. Tragöd. ii. p. 583) on the lost tragedy called
Œneus.

Ætôlia, and acquired the kingdom: he was father of Phytios, who was father of Œneus. Ætôlus was son of Œneus.[1] The original migration of Ætôlus from Elis to Œtôlia — and the subsequent establishment in Elis of Oxylus, his descendant in the tenth generation, along with the Dôrian invaders of Peloponnêsus — were commemorated by two inscriptions, one in the agora of Elis, the other in that of the Ætôlian chief town, Thermum, engraved upon the statues of Ætôlus and Oxylus,[2] respectively.

CHAPTER VII.

THE PELOPIDS.

AMONG the ancient legendary genealogies, there was none which figured with greater splendor, or which attracted to itself

---

[1] Timoklês, Comic. ap. Athenæ. vii. p. 223.—

Γέρων τις ἀτυχεῖ; κατέμαθεν τὸν Οἰνέα.

Ovid. Heroid. ix. 153.—

"Heu! devota domus! Solio sedet Agrios alto
Œnea desertum nuda senecta premit."

The account here given is in Hyginus (f. 175): but it is in many points different both from Apollodôrus (i. 8, 6; Pausan. ii. 25) and Pherekydês (Fragm. 83, Didot). It seems to be borrowed from the lost tragedy of Euripidês. Compare Schol. ad Aristoph. Acharn. 417. Antonin. Liberal. c. 37. In the Iliad, Œneus is dead before the Trojan war (ii. 641).

The account of Ephorus again is different (ap. Strabo. x. p. 462); he joins Alkmæòn with Diomêdês: but his narrative has the air of a tissue of quasi-historical conjectures, intended to explain the circumstance that the Ætôlian Diomêdês is king of Argos during the Trojan war.

Pausanias and Apollodôrus affirm that Œneus was buried at Œnoê between Argos and Mantineia, and they connect the name of this place with him. But it seems more reasonable to consider him as the eponymous hero of Œniadæ in Ætôlia.

[2] Ephor. Fragm. 29. Didot ap. Strab. x.

7*

a higher degree of poetical interest and pathos, than that of the
Pelopids — Tantalus, Pelops, Atreus and Thyestês, Agamemnôn
and Menelaus and Ægisthus, Helen and Klytæmnêstra, Orestês
and Elektra and Hermionê. Each of these characters is a star
of the first magnitude in the Grecian hemisphere: each name
suggests the idea of some interesting romance or some harrowing
tragedy: the curse which taints the family from the beginning
inflicts multiplied wounds at every successive generation. So, at
least, the story of the Pelopids presents itself, after it had been
successively expanded and decorated by epic, lyric and tragic
poets. It will be sufficient to touch briefly upon events with
which every reader of Grecian poetry is more or less familiar,
and to offer some remarks upon the way in which they were colored and modified by different Grecian authors.

Pelops is the eponym or name-giver of the Peloponnêsus: to
find an eponym for every conspicuous local name was the invariable turn of Grecian retrospective fancy. The name Peloponnêsus
is not to be found either in the Iliad or the Odyssey, nor any other
denomination which can be attached distinctly and specially to
the entire peninsula. But we meet with the name in one of the
most ancient post-Homeric poems of which any fragments have
been preserved — the Cyprian Verses — a poem which many
(seemingly most persons) even of the contemporaries of Herodotus ascribed to the author of the Iliad, though Herodotus contradicts the opinion.[1] The attributes by which the Pelopid Agamemnôn and his house are marked out and distinguished from
the other heroes of the Iliad, are precisely those which Grecian
imagination would naturally seek in an eponymus — superior
wealth, power, splendor and regality. Not only Agamemnôn

---

[1] Hesiod. ii. 117.   Fragment. Epicc. Græc. Düntzer, ix. Κύπρια, 8. —

Αἶψα τε Λυγκεὺς
Ταΰγετον προσέβαινε ποσὶν ταχέεσσι πεποιθὼς,
Ἀκρότατον δ' ἀναβὺς διεδέρκετο νῆσον ἅπασαν
Τανταλίδεω Πέλοπος.

Also the Homeric Hymn. Apoll. 419, 430, and Tyrtæus, Fragm. 1. —

(Εὐνομία) — Εὐρεῖαν Πέλοπος νῆσον ἀφικόμεθα.

The Schol. ad Iliad. ix. 246, intimates that the name Πελοπόννησος occurred
in one or more of the Hesiodic epics.

himself, but his brother Menelaus, is "more of a king" even than Nestôr or Diomêdês. The gods have not given to the king of the "much-golden" Mykênæ greater courage, or strength, or ability, than to various other chiefs; but they have conferred upon him a marked superiority in riches, power and dignity, and have thus singled him out as the appropriate leader of the forces.[1] He enjoys this preëminence as belonging to a privileged family and as inheriting the heaven-descended sceptre of Pelops, the transmission of which is described by Homer in a very remarkable way. The sceptre was made "by Hêphæstos, who presented it to Zeus; Zeus gave it to Hermês, Hermês to the charioteer Pelops; Pelops gave it to Atreus, the ruler of men; Atreus at his death left it to Thyestês, the rich cattle-owner; Thyestês in his turn left it to his nephew Agamemnôn to carry, that he might hold dominion over many islands and over all Argos."[2]

We have here the unrivalled wealth and power of the "king of men, Agamemnôn," traced up to his descent from Pelops, and accounted for, in harmony with the recognized epical agencies, by the present of the special sceptre of Zeus through the hands of Hermês; the latter being the wealth-giving god, whose bless-

---

[1] Iliad, ix. 37. Compare ii. 580. Diomêdês addresses Agamemnôn

Σοὶ δὲ διάνδιχα δῶκε Κρόνου παῖς ἀγκυλομήτεω
Σκῆπτρῳ μέν τοι δῶκε τετιμῆσθαι περὶ πάντων·
'Αλκὴν δ' οὔτοι δῶκεν, ὅ, τε κράτος ἐστὶ μέγιστον.

A similar contrast is drawn by Nestôr (Il. i. 280) between Agamemnôn and Achilles. Nestôr says to Agamemnôn (Il. ix. 60) —

'Ατρείδη, σὺ μὲν ἄρχε· σὺ γὰρ β α σ ι λ ε ύ τ α τ ό ς ἐσσι.

And this attribute attaches to Menelaus as well as to his brother. For when Diomêdês is about to choose his companion for the night expedition into the Trojan camp, Agamemnôn thus addresses him (x. 232):

Τὸν μὲν δὴ ἕταρόν γ' αἱρήσεαι, ὃν κ' ἐθέλησθα
Φαινομένων τὸν ἄριστον, ἐπεὶ μεμάασί γε πολλοί
Μηδὲ σύ γ' αἰδόμενος σῆσι φρεσί, τὸν μὲν ἀρείω
Καλλείπειν σὺ δὲ χείρον' ὀπάσσεαι αἰδοῖ εἴκων,
'Ες γενεὴν ὁρόων, εἰ καὶ βασιλεύτερός ἐστιν.
'Ως ἔφατ', ἔδδεισε δὲ περὶ ξανθῷ Μενελάῳ.

[2] Iliad, ii. 101.

ing is most efficacious in furthering the process of acquisition,
whether by theft or by accelerated multiplication of flocks and
herds.[1] The wealth and princely character of the Atreids were
proverbial among the ancient epic poets. Paris not only carries
away Hellen, but much property along with her:[2] the house of
Menelaus, when Têlemachus visits it in the Odyssey, is so re-
splendent with gold and silver and rare ornament,[3] as to strike
the beholder with astonishment and admiration. The attributes
assigned to Tantalus, the father of Pelops, are in conformity with
the general idea of the family — superhuman abundance and enjoyments, and intimate converse with the gods, to such a degree
that his head is turned, and he commits inexpiable sin. But
though Tantalus himself is mentioned, in one of the most suspi-
cious passages of the Odyssey (as suffering punishment in the
under-world), he is not announced, nor is any one else announced,
as father of Pelops, unless we are to construe the lines in the
Iliad as implying that the latter was son of Hermês. In the conception of the author of the Iliad, the Pelopids are, if not of divine origin, at least a mortal breed specially favored and ennobled by the gods — beginning with Pelops, and localized at Mykênæ. No allusion is made to any connection of Pelops either
with Pisa or with Lydia.

The legend which connected Tantalus and Pelops with Mount
Sipylus may probably have grown out of the Æolic settlements
at Magnêsia and Kymê. Both the Lydian origin and the Pisatic
sovereignty of Pelops are adapted to times later than the Iliad,
when the Olympic games had acquired to themselves the general
reverence of Greece, and had come to serve as the religious and
recreative centre of the Peloponnêsus — and when the Lydian

---

[1] Iliad, xiv. 491. Hesiod. Theog. 444. Homer, Hymn. Mercur. 526–568.
'Ολβου καὶ πλούτου δώσω περικάλλεα ῥάβδον. Compare Eustath. ad Iliad.
xvi. 182.

[2] Iliad, iii. 72 ; vii. 363. In the Hesiodic Eoiai was the following couplet
(Fragm. 55. p. 43, Düntzer) :—

    'Αλκὴν μὲν γὰρ ἔδωκεν 'Ολύμπιος Αἰακίδῃσιν,
    Νοῦν δ' 'Αμυθαονίδαις, πλοῦτον δ' ἔπορ' 'Ατρείδῃσι.

Again, Tyrtæus, Fragm. 9, 4. —

    Οὐδ' εἰ Τανταλίδεω Πέλοπος βασιλεύτερος εἴη, etc.

[3] Odyss. iv. 45–71.

and Phrygian heroic names, Midas and Gygês, were the types of wealth and luxury, as well as of chariot driving, in the imagination of a Greek. The inconsiderable villages of the Pisatid derived their whole importance from the vicinity of Olympia: they are not deemed worthy of notice in the Catalogue of Homer. Nor could the genealogy which connected the eponym of the entire peninsula with Pisa have obtained currency in Greece unless it had been sustained by preëstablished veneration for the locality of Olympia. But if the sovereign of the humble Pisa was to be recognized as forerunner of the thrice-wealthy princes of Mikênæ, it became necessary to assign some explanatory cause of his riches. Hence the supposition of his being an immigrant, son of a wealthy Lydian named Tantalus, who was the offspring of Zeus and Ploutô. Lydian wealth and Lydian chariot-driving rendered Pelops a fit person to occupy his place in the legend, both as ruler of Pisa and progenitor of the Mykenæan Atreids. Even with the admission of these two circumstances there is considerable difficulty, for those who wish to read the legends as consecutive history, in making the Pelopids pass smoothly and plausibly from Pisa to Mykênæ.

I shall briefly recount the legends of this great heroic family as they came to stand in their full and ultimate growth, after the localization of Pelops at Pisa had been tacked on as a preface to Homer's version of the Pelopid genealogy.

Tantalus, residing near Mount Sipylus in Lydia, had two children, Pelops and Niobê. He was a man of immense possessions and preëminent happiness, above the lot of humanity : the gods communicated with him freely, received him at their banquets, and accepted of his hospitality in return. Intoxicated with such prosperity, Tantalus became guilty of gross wickedness. He stole nectar and ambrosia from the table of the gods, and revealed their secrets to mankind : he killed and served up to them at a feast his own son Pelops. The gods were horror-struck when they discovered the meal prepared for them : Zeus restored the mangled youth to life, and as Dêmêtêr, then absorbed in grief for the loss of her daughter Persephonê, had eaten a portion of the shoulder, he supplied an ivory shoulder in place of it. Tantalus expiated his guilt by exemplary punishment. He was placed in the under-world, with fruit and water seemingly close

to him, yet eluding his touch as often as he tried to grasp them,
and leaving his hunger and thirst incessant and unappeased.[1]
Pindar, in a very remarkable passage, finds this old legend revolting to his feelings: he rejects the tale of the flesh of Pelops
having been served up and eaten, as altogether unworthy of the
gods.[2]

Niobê, the daughter of Tantalus, was married to Amphion,
and had a numerous and flourishing offspring of seven sons and
seven daughters. Though accepted as the intimate friend and
companion of Lêto, the mother of Apollo and Artemas,[3] she was
presumptuous enough to triumph over that goddess, and to place
herself on a footing of higher dignity, on account of the superior
number of her children. Apollo and Artemas avenged this insult by killing all the sons and all the daughters: Niobê, thus
left a childless and disconsolate mother, wept herself to death,
and was turned into a rock, which the later Greeks continued
always to identify on Mount Sipylus.[4]

Some authors represented Pelops as not being a Lydian, but a
king of Paphlagônia; by others it was said that Tantalus, having become detested from his impieties, had been expelled from
Asia by Ilus the king of Troy, — an incident which served the
double purpose of explaining the transit of Pelops to Greece,
and of imparting to the siege of Troy by Agamemnôn the character of retribution for wrongs done to his ancestor.[5]   When Pelops came over to Greece, he found Œnomaus, son of the god
Arês and Harpinna, in possession of the principality of Pisa,

---

[1] Diodôr. iv. 77. Hom. Odyss. xi. 582. Pindar gives a different version
of the punishment inflicted on Tantalus: a vast stone was perpetually impending over his head, and threatening to fall (Olymp. i. 56; Isthm. vii. 20).

[2] Pindar, Olymp. i. 45. Compare the sentiment of Iphigeneia in Euripidês, Iph. Taur. 387.

[3] Sapphô (Fragm. 82, Schneidewin)—

Λατὼ καὶ Νιόβα μάλα μὲν φίλαι ἦσαν ἑταῖραι.

Sapphô assigned to Niobê eighteen children (Aul. Gell. N. A. iv. Δ. xx. 7);
Hesiod gave twenty; Homer twelve (Apollod. iii. 5).

The Lydian historian Xanthus gave a totally different version both of the
genealogy and of the misfortunes of Niobê (Parthen. Narr. 33).

[4] Ovid, Metam. vi. 164-311. Pausan. i. 21, 5; viii. 2, 3.

[5] Apollôn. Rhod. ii. 358, and Schol.; Ister. Fragment. 59, Dindorf; Diodôr. iv. 74.

immediately bordering on the district of Olympia. Œnomaus, having been apprized by an oracle that death would overtake him if he permitted his daughter Hippodameia to marry, refused to give her in marriage except to some suitor who should beat him in a chariot-race from Olympia to the isthmus of Corinth;[1] the ground here selected for the legendary victory of Pelops deserves attention, inasmuch as it is a line drawn from the assumed centre of Peloponnêsus to its extremity, and thus comprises the whole territory with which Pelops is connected as eponym. Any suitor overmatched in the race was doomed to forfeit his life ; and the fleetness of the Pisan horses, combined with the skill of the charioteer Myrtilus, had already caused thirteen unsuccessful competitors to perish by the lance of Œnomaus.[2] Pelops entered the lists as a suitor : his prayers moved the god Poseidôn to supply him with a golden chariot and winged horses; or according to another story, he captivated the affections of Hippodameia herself, who persuaded the charioteer Myrtilus to loosen the wheels of Œnomaus before he started, so that the latter was overturned and perished in the race. Having thus won the hand of Hippodameia, Pelops became Prince of Pisa.[3] He put to death the charioteer Myrtilus, either from indignation at his treachery to Œnomaus,[4] or from jealousy on the score of Hippodameia : but Myrtilus was the son of Hermês, and though Pelops erected a temple in the vain attempt to propitiate that god, he left a curse upon his race which future calamities were destined painfully to work out.[5]

Pelops had a numerous issue by Hippodameia : Pittheus, Trœzen and Epidaurus, the eponyms of the two Argolic cities

---

[1] Diodôr. iv. 74.

[2] Pausanias (vi. 21, 7) had read their names in the Hesiodic Eoiai.

[3] Pindar, Olymp. i. 140. The chariot race of Pelops and Œnomaus was represented on the chest of Kypselus at Olympia : the horses of the former were given as having wings (Pausan, v. 17, 4). Pherekydês gave the same story (ap. Schol. ad Soph. Elect. 504).

[4] It is noted by Herodotus and others as a remarkable fact, that no mules were ever bred in the Eleian territory : an Eleian who wished to breed a mule sent his mare for the time out of the region. The Eleians themselves ascribed this phænomenon to a disability brought on the land by a curse from the lips of Œnomaus (Herod. iv. 30; Plutarch, Quæst. Græc. p. 303).

[5] Paus. v. 1, 1; Sophok. Elektr. 508; Eurip. Orest. 985, with Schol., Plato, Kratyl. p. 395

so called, are said to have been among them: Atreus and Thy-
estes were also his sons, and his daughtër Nikippê married Sthenelus of Mykênæ, and became the mother of Eurystheus.[1] We
hear nothing of the principality of Pisa afterwards: the Pisatid
villages became absorbed into the larger aggregate of Elis, after
a vain struggle to maintain their separate right of presidency
over the Olympic festival. But the legend ran that Pelops left
his name to the whole peninsula: according to Thucycidês, he
was enabled to do this because of the great wealth which he had
brought with him from Lydia into a poor territory. The histo
rian leaves out all the romantic interest of the genuine legends —
preserving only this one circumstance, which, without being better attested than the rest, carries with it, from its common-place
and prosaic character, a pretended historical plausibility.[2]

Besides his numerous issue by Hippodameia, Pelops had an
illegitimate son named Chrysippus, of singular grace and beauty,
towards whom he displayed so much affection as to rouse the
jealousy of Hippodameia and her sons. Atreus and Thyestês
conspired together to put Chrysippus to death, for which they
were banished by Pelops and retired to Mykênæ,[3] — an event
which brings us into the track of the Homeric legend. For
Thucydidês, having found in the death of Chrysippus a suitable
ground for the secession of Atreus from Pelops, conducts him at
once to Mykênæ, and shows a train of plausible circumstances
to account for his having mounted the throne. Eurystheus, king
of Mykênæ, was the maternal nephew of Atreus: when he
engaged in any foreign expeditioñ, he naturally entrusted the
regency to his uncle; the people of Mykênæ thus became accustomed to be governed by him, and he on his part made efforts to
conciliate them, so that when Eurystheus was defeated and slain
in Attica, the Mykênæan people, apprehensive of an invasion
from the Hêrakleids, chose Atreus as at once the most powerful

---

[1] Apollod. ii. 4, 5. Pausan. ii. 30, 8; 26, 3; v. 8, 1. Hesiod. ap. Schol
ad Iliad. xx. 116.

[2] Thucyd. i. 5.

[3] We find two distinct legends respecting Chrysippus : his abduction by
Laius king of Thêbes, on which the lost drama of Euripidês called Chrysippus turned (see Welcker, Griech. Tragödien, ii. p. 536), and his death by
he hands of his half-brothers. Hyginus (f. 85) blends the two together.

and most acceptable person for his successor.[1] Such was the tale which Thucydidês derived "from those who had learnt ancient Peloponnêsian matters most clearly from their forefathers." The introduction of so much sober and quasi-political history, unfortunately unauthenticated, contrasts strikingly with the highly poetical legends of Pelops and Atreus, which precede and follow it.

Atreus and Thyestês are known in the Iliad only as successive possessors of the sceptre of Zeus, which Thyestês at his death bequeathes to Agamemnôn. The family dissensions among this fated race commence, in the Odyssey, with Agamemnôn the son of Atreus, and Ægisthus the son of Thyestês. But subsequent poets dwelt upon an implacable quarrel between the two fathers. The cause of the bitterness was differently represented: some alleged that Thyestês had intrigued with the Krêtan Aeropê, the wife of his brother; other narratives mentioned that Thyestês procured for himself surreptitiously the possession of a lamb with a golden fleece, which had been designedly introduced among the flocks of Atreus by the anger of Hermês, as a cause of enmity and ruin to the whole family.[2] Atreus, after a violent

---

[1] Thucyd. i. 9. λέγουσι δὲ οἱ τὰ Πελοποννησίων σαφέστατα μνήμῃ παρὰ τῶν πρότερον δεδεγμένοι.. According to Hellanikus, Atreus the elder son returns to Pisa after the death of Pelops with a great army, and makes himself master of his father's principality (Hellanik. ap Schol. ad Iliad. ii. 105) Hellanikus does not seem to have been so solicitous as Thucydidês to bring the story into conformity with Homer. The circumstantial genealogy given in Schol. ad Eurip. Orest. 5. makes Atreus and Thyestês reside during their banishment at Makestus in Triphylia : it is given without any special authority, but may perhaps come from Hellanikus.

[2] Æschil. Agamem. 1204, 1253, 1608; Hygin. 86; Attii Fragm.19. This was the story of the old poem entitled Alkmæônis; seemingly also of Pherekydês, though the latter rejected the story that Hermês had produced the golden lamb with the special view of exciting discord between the two brothers, in order to avenge the death of Myrtilus by Pelops (see Schol. ad Eurip. Orest. 996).

A different legend, alluded to in Soph. Aj. 1295 (see Schol. ad loc.), recounted that Aeropê had been detected by her father Katreus in unchaste commerce with a low-born person; he entrusted her in his anger to Nauplius, with directions to throw her into the sea: Nauplius however not only spared her life, but betrothed her to Pleisthenês, father of Agamemnôn and son of Atreus.

The tragedy entitled Atreus of the Latin poet Attius, seems to have

burst of indignation, pretended to be reconciled, and invited Thyestês to a banquet, in which he served up to him the limbs of
his own son, and the father ignorantly partook of the fatal meal.
Even the all-seeing Hêlios is said to have turned back his chariot
to the east in order that he might escape the shocking spectacle
of this Thyestêan banquet: yet the tale of Thyestêan revenge
— the murder of Atreus perpetrated by Ægisthus, the incestuous
offspring of Thyestês by his daughter Pelopia — is no less replete
with horrors.[1]

Homeric legend is never thus revolting. Agamemnôn and
Menelaus are known to us chiefly with their Homeric attributes,
which have not been so darkly overlaid by subsequent poets as
those of Atreus and Thyestês. Agamemnôn and Menelaus are
affectionate brothers: they marry two sisters, the daughters of
Tyndareus king of Sparta, Klytæmnêstra and Helen; for Helen,
the real offspring of Zeus, passes as the daughter of Tyndarius.[2]
The "king of men" reigns at Mykênæ; Menelaus succeeds Tyndareus at Sparta. Of the rape of Helen, and the siege of Troy
consequent upon it, I shall speak elsewhere: I now touch only
upon the family legends of the Atreids. Menelaus, on his return
from Troy with the recovered Helen, is driven by storms far
away to the distant regions of Phœnicia and Egypt, and is exposed to a thousand dangers and hardships before he again sets
foot in Peloponnêsus. But at length he reaches Sparta, resumes
his kingdom, and passes the rest of his days in uninterrupted
happiness and splendor: being moreover husband of the godlike
Helen and son-in-law of Zeus, he is even spared the pangs of
death. When the fulness of his days is past he is transported
to the Elysian fields, there to dwell along with "the golden-haired
Rhadamanthus" in a delicious climate and in undisturbed re
pose.[3]

Far different is the fate of the king of men, Agamemnôn.

---

brought out, with painful fidelity, the harsh and savage features of this
family legend (see Aul. Gell. xiii. 2, and the fragments of Attius now remain
ing, together with the tragedy called Thyestês, of Seneca).

[1] Hygin. fab. 87–88.

[2] So we must say, in conformity to the ideas of antiquity: compare Ho
mer, Iliad, xvi. 176 and Herodot. vi. 53.

[3] Hom. Odyss. iii. 280–300; iv. 83–560.

During his absence, the unwarlike Ægisthus, son of Thyestês, had seduced his wife Klytæmnêstra, in spite of the special warning of the gods, who, watchful over this privileged family, had sent their messenger Hermês expressly to deter him from the attempt.[1] A venerable bard had been left by Agamemnôn as the companion and monitor of his wife, and so long as that guardian was at hand, Ægisthus pressed his suit in vain. But he got rid of the bard by sending him to perish in a desert island, and then won without difficulty the undefended Klytæmnêstra. Ignorant of what had passed, Agamemnôn returned from Troy victorious and full of hope to his native country; but he had scarcely landed when Ægisthus invited him to a banquet, and there with the aid of the treacherous Klytæmnêstra, in the very hall of festivity and congratulation, slaughtered him and his companions "like oxen tied to the manger." His concubine Kassandra, the prophetic daughter of Priam, perished along with him by the hand of Klytæmnêstra herself.[2] The boy Orestês, the only male offspring of Agamemnôn, was stolen away by his nurse, and placed in safety at the residence of the Phokian Strophius.

For seven years Ægisthus and Klytæmnêstra reigned in tranquillity at Mykênæ on the throne of the murdered Agamemnôn. But in the eighth year the retribution announced by the gods overtook them : Orestês, grown to manhood, returned and avenged his father by killing Ægisthus, according to Homer; subsequent poets add, his mother also. He recovered the kingdom of Mykênæ, and succeeded Menelaus in that of Sparta. Hermionê, the only daughter of Menelaus and Helen, was sent into the realm of the Myrmidons in Thessaly, as the bride of Neoptolemus, son of Achilles, according to the promise made by her father during the siege of Troy.[3]

Here ends the Homeric legend of the Pelopids, the final act of Orestês being cited as one of unexampled glory.[4] Later poets made many additions: they dwelt upon his remorse and hardly-

---

[1] Odyss. i. 38 ; iii. 310.—ἀνάλκιδος Αἰγίσθοιο.

[2] Odyss. iii. 260–275 ; iv. 512–537 ; xi. 408. Deinias in his Argolica, and other historians of that territory, fixed the precise day of the murder of Agamemnôn,—the thirteenth of the month Gamêliôn (Schol. ad Sophokl Elektr. 275).

[3] Odyss. iii. 306 ; iv. 9   [4] Odyss. i. 299.

earned pardon for the murder of his mother, and upon his devoted friendship for Pylades; they wove many interesting tales, too, respecting his sisters Iphigeneia and Elektra and his cousin Hermionê, — names which have become naturalized in every climate and incorporated with every form of poetry.

These poets did not at all scruple to depart from Homer, and to give other genealogies of their own, with respect to the chief persons of the Pelopid family. In the Iliad and Odyssey, Agamemnôn is son of Atreus: in the Hesiodic Eoiai and in Stesichorus, he is son of Pleisthenês the son of Atreus.[1] In Homer, he is specially marked as reigning at Mykênæ; but Stesichorus, Simonidês and Pindar[2] represented him as having both resided and perished at Sparta or at Amyklæ. According to the ancient Cyprian Verses, Helen was represented as the daughter of Zeus and Nemesis: in one of the Hesiodic poems she was introduced as an Oceanic nymph, daughter of Oceanus and Têthys.[3] The genealogical discrepancies, even as to the persons of the principal heroes and heroines, are far too numerous to be cited, nor is it necessary to advert to them, except as they bear upon the unavailing attempt to convert such legendary parentage into a basis of historical record or chronological calculation.

The Homeric poems probably represent that form of the legend, respecting Agamemnôn and Orestês, which was current and popular among the Æolic colonists. Orestês was the great heroic chief of the Æolic emigration; he, or his sons, or his descendants, are supposed to have conducted the Achæans to seek

---

[1] Hesiod. Fragm. 60. p. 44, ed. Düntzer; Stesichor. Fragm. 44, Kleine. The Scholiast ad Soph. Elektr. 539, in reference to another discrepancy between Homer and the Hesiodic poems about the children of Helen, remarks that we ought not to divert our attention from that which is moral and salutary to ourselves in the poets (τὰ ἠθικὰ καὶ χρήσιμα ἡμῖν τοῖς ἐντυγχάνουσι), in order to cavil at their genealogical contradictions.

Welcker in vain endeavors to show that Pleisthenês was originally introduced as the father of Atreus, not as his son (Griech. Tragöd. p. 678).

[2] Schol. ad Eurip. Orest. 46. Ὅμηρος ἐν Μυκήναις φησὶ τὰ βασιλεῖα τοῦ Ἀγαμέμνονος· Στησίχορος δὲ καὶ Σιμωνίδης, ἐν Λακεδαιμονίᾳ. Pindar, Pyth. xi. 31; Nem. viii. 21. Stêsichorus had composed an Ὀρέστεια, copied in many points from a still more ancient lyric Oresteia by Xanthus: compare Athen. xii. p. 513, and Ælian, V. H. iv. 26.

[3] Hesiod, ap. Schol. ad Pindar, Nem. x. 150.

a new home, when they were no longer able to make head against the invading Dôrians: the great families at Tenedos and other Æolic cities even during the historical æra, gloried in tracing back their pedigrees to this illustrious source.[1] The legends connected with the heroic worship of these mythical ancestors form the basis of the character and attributes of Agamemnôn and his family, as depicted in Homer, in which Mykênæ appears as the first place in Peloponnêsus, and Sparta only as the second: the former the special residence of "the king of men;" the latter that of his younger and inferior brother, yet still the seat of a member of the princely Pelopids, and moreover the birth-place of the divine Helen. Sparta, Argos and Mykênæ are all three designated in the Iliad by the goddess Hêrê as her favorite cities;[2] yet the connection of Mykênæ with Argos, though the two towns were only ten miles distant, is far less intimate than the connection of Mykênæ with Sparta. When we reflect upon the very peculiar manner in which Homer identifies Hêrê with the Grecian host and its leader, — for she watches over the Greeks with the active solicitude of a mother, and her antipathy against the Trojans is implacable to a degree which Zeus cannot comprehend,[3] — and when we combine this with the ancient and venerated Hêræon, or temple of Hêrê, near Mykênæ, we may partly explain to ourselves the preëminence conferred upon Mykênæ in the Iliad and Odyssey. The Hêræon was situated between Argos and Mykênæ; in later times its priestesses were named and its affairs administered by the Argeians: but as it was much nearer

---

[1] See the ode of Pindar addressed to Aristagoras of Tenedos (Nem. xi. 35; Strabo, xiii. p. 582). There were Penthilids at Mitylênê, from Penthilus, son of Orestês (Aristot. Polit. v. 8, 13, Schneid.).

[2] Iliad, iv. 52. Compare Euripid. Hêrakleid. 350

[3] Iliad, iv. 31. Zeus says to Hêrê,—

Δαιμονίη, τί νύ σε Πρίαμος, Πριάμοιό τε παῖδες
Τόσσα κακὰ ῥέζεσκον ὅτ' ἀσπερχὲς μενεαίνεις
Ἰλίου ἐξαλάπαξαι ἐϋκτίμενον πτολίεθρον;
Εἰ δὲ σύ γ', εἰσελθοῦσα πύλας καὶ τείχεα μακρὰ,
Ὠμὸν βεβρώθοις Πρίαμον Πριάμοιό τε παῖδας,
Ἄλλους τε Τρῶας, τότε κεν χόλον ἐξακέσαιο.

Again, xviii. 358,—

ἦ ῥά νυ σεῖο
Ἐξ αὐτῆς ἐγένοντο καρηκομόωντες Ἀχαιοί.

to Mykênæ than to Argos, we may with probability conclude that it originally belonged to the former, and that the increasing power of the latter enabled them to usurp to themselves a religious privilege which was always an object of envy and contention among the Grecian communities. The Æolic colonists doubtless took out with them in their emigration the divine and heroic legends, as well as the worship and ceremonial rites, of the Hê-ræon; and in those legends the most exalted rank would be as signed to the close-adjoining and administering city.

Mykênæ maintained its independence even down to the Persian invasion. Eighty of its heavy-armed citizens, in the ranks of Leonidas at Thermopylæ, and a number not inferior at Platæa, upheld the splendid heroic celebrity of their city during a season of peril, when the more powerful Argos disgraced itself by a treacherous neutrality. Very shortly afterwards Mykenæ was enslaved and its inhabitants expelled by the Argeians. Though this city so long maintained a separate existence, its importance had latterly sunk to nothing, while that of the Dôrian Argos was augmented very much, and that of the Dôrian Sparta still more.

The name of Mykênæ is imperishably enthroned in the Iliad and Odyssey; but all the subsequent fluctuations of the legend tend to exalt the glory of other cities at its expense. The recognition of the Olympic games as the grand religious festival of Peloponnêsus gave vogue to that genealogy which connected Pelops with Pisa or Elis and withdrew him from Mykênæ. Moreever, in the poems of the great Athenian tragedians, Mykênæ is constantly confounded and treated as one with Argos. If any one of the citizens of the former, expelled at the time of its final subjugation by the Argeians, had witnessed at Athens a drama of Æschylus, Sophoklês, or Euripidês, or the recital of an ode of Pindar, he would have heard with grief and indignation the city of his oppressors made a partner in the heroic glories of his own.[1] But the great political ascendency acquired by Sparta contributed still farther to degrade Mykênæ, by disposing subsequent poets to treat the chief of the Grecian armament against Troy as having been a Spartan. It has been already mentioned that Stêsichorus, Simonidês and Pindar adopted this version of

---

[1] See the preface of Dissen to the tenth Nem. of Pindar.

the legend: we know that Zeus Agamemnôn, as well as the hero Menelaus, was worshipped at the Dôrian Sparta,[1] and the feeling of intimate identity, as well as of patriotic pride, which had grown up in the minds of the Spartans connected with the name of Agamemnôn, is forcibly evinced by the reply of the Spartan Syagrus to Gelôn of Syracuse at the time of the Persian invasion of Greece. Gelôn was solicited to lend his aid in the imminent danger of Greece before the battle of Salamis: he offered to furnish an immense auxiliary force, on condition that the supreme command should be allotted to him. "Loudly indeed would the Pelopid Agamemnôn cry out (exclaimed Syagrus in rejecting this application), if he were to learn that the Spartans had been deprived of the headship by Gelôn and the Tyracusans."[2] Nearly a century before this event, in obedience to the injunctions of the Delphian oracle, the Spartans had brought back from Tegea to Sparta the bones of "the Lacônian Orestês," as Pindar denominates him:[3] the recovery of these bones was announced to them as the means of reversing a course of ill-fortune, and of procuring victory in their war against Tegea.[4] The value which they set upon this acquisition, and the decisive results ascribed to it, exhibit a precise analogy with the recovery of the bones of Theseus from Skyros by the Athenian Cimôn shortly after the Persian invasion.[5] The remains sought were those of a hero properly belonging to their own soil, but who had died in a foreign land, and of whose protection and assistance they were for that reason deprived. And the superhuman magnitude of the bones, which were contained in a coffin seven cubits long, is well suited to the legendary grandeur of the son of Agamemnôn.

---

[1] Clemens Alexandr. Admonit. ad Gent. p. 24. Ἀγαμέμνονα γοῦν τινα Δία ἐν Σπάρτῃ τιμᾶσθαι Στάφυλος ἱστορεῖ. See also Œnomaus ap. Euseb. Præparat. Evangel. v. 28.

[2] Herôdot. vii. 159. Ἦ κε μέγ' οἰμώξειεν ὁ Πελοπίδης Ἀγαμέμνων, πυθόμενος Σπαρτιήτας ἀπαραιρῆσθαι τὴν ἡγεμονίαν ὑπὸ Γέλωνός τε καὶ τῶν Συρακοσίων : compare Homer, Iliad, vii. 125. See what appears to be an imitation of the same passage in Josephus, De Bello Judaico, iii. 8, 4. Ἦ μέλαλά γ' ἂν στενάξειαν οἱ πάτριοι νόμοι, etc.

[3] Pindar, Pyth. xi. 16.   [4] Herodot. i 68.

[5] Plutarch. Thêseus, c. 36, Cimôn, c. 8; Pausan. iii. 3, 6.

CHAPTER VIII.

LACONIAN AND MESSENIAN GENEALOGIES.

THE earliest names in Lacônian genealogy are, an autochthonous Lelex and a Naiad nymph Kleochareia. From this pair
sprung a son Eurôtas, and from him a daughter Sparta, who became the wife of Lacedæmôn, son of Zeus and Taygetê, daughter
of Atlas. Amyklas, son of Lacedæmôn, had two sons, Kynortas
and Hyacinthus — the latter a beautiful youth, the favorite of
Apollo, by whose hand he was accidentally killed while playing
at quoits: the festival of the Hyacinthia, which the Lacedæmônians generally, and the Amyklæans with special solemnity, celebrated throughout the historical ages, was traced back to this
legend. Kynortas was succeeded by his son Periêrês, who married Gorgophonê, daughter of Perseus, and had a numerous issue
— Tyndareus, Ikarius, Aphareus, Leukippus, and Hippokoon.
Some authors gave the genealogy differently, making Periêrês,
son of Æolus, to be the father of Kynortas, and Œbalus son of
Kynortas, from whom sprung Tyndareus, Ikarius and Hippokoon.[1]

Both Tyndareus and Ikarius, expelled by their brother Hippokoon, were forced to seek shelter at the residence of Thestius,
king of Kalydôn, whose daughter, Lêda, Tyndareus espoused.
It is numbered among the exploits of the omnipresent Hêraklês,
that he slew Hippokoon and his sons, and restored Tyndareus to
his kingdom, thus creating for the subsequent Hêrakleidan kings
a mythical title to the throne. Tyndareus, as well as his brothers,
are persons of interest in legendary narrative: he is the father
of Kastôr, of Timandra, married to Echemus, the hero of Tegea,[2]
and of Klytæmnêstra, married to Agamemnôn. Pollux and the
ever-memorable Helen are the offspring of Lêda by Zeus. Ika-

---

[1] Compare Apollod. iii. 10, 4. Pausan. iii. 1, 4.
[2] Hesiod. ap Schol Pindar. Olymp. xi. 79.

nus is the father of Penelopê, wife of Odysseus: the contrast
between her behavior and that of Klytæmnêstra and Helen
became the more striking in consequence of their being so nearly
related. Aphareus is the father of Idas and Lynkeus, while
Leukippus has for his daughters, Phœbê and Ilaëira. According to one of the Hesiodic poems, Kastôr and Pollux were both
sons of Zeus by Lêda, while Helen was neither daughter of Zeus
nor of Tyndareus, but of Oceanus and Têthys.[1]

The brothers Kastôr and (Polydeukês, or) Pollux are no less
celebrated for their fraternal affection than for their great bodily
accomplishments: Kastôr, the great charioteer and horse-master;
Pollux, the first of pugilists. They are enrolled both among the
hunters of the Kalydônian boar and among the heroes of the
Argonautic expedition, in which Pollux represses the insolence
of Amykus, king of the Bebrykes, on the coast of Asiatic Thrace
—the latter, a gigantic pugilist, from whom no rival has ever
escaped, challenges Pollux, but is vanquished and killed in the
fight.[2]

The two brothers also undertook an expedition into Attica, for
the purpose of recovering their sister Helen, who had been
carried off by Thêseus in her early youth, and deposited by him
at Aphidna, while he accompanied Perithous to the under-world,
in order to assist his friend in carrying off Persephonê. The
force of Kastôr and Pollux was irresistible, and when they re-
demanded their sister, the people of Attica were anxious to restore
her: but no one knew where Thêseus had deposited his prize.
The invaders, not believing in the sincerity of this denial, proceeded to ravage the country, which would have been utterly
ruined, had not Dekelus, the eponymus of Dekeleia, been able to
indicate Aphidna as the place of concealment. The autochthonous Titakus betrayed Aphidna to Kastôr and Pollux, and Helen

---

[1] Hesiod. ap. Schol. Pindar. Nem. x. 150. Fragm. Hesiod. Düntzer, 58.
p. 44. Tyndareus was worshipped as a god at Lacedæmôn (Varro ap. Serv.
ad Virgil. Æneid. viii. 275).

[2] Apollôn. Rhod. ii. 1-96. Apollod. i. 9, 20. Theocrit. xxii. 26-133. In
the account of Apollônius and Apollodôrus, Amykus is slain in the contest;
in that of Theocritus he is only conquered and forced to give in, with a
promise to renounce for the future his brutal conduct; there were several
different narratives. See Schol. Apollon. Rhod. ii. 106.

was recovered: the brothers in evacuating Attica, carried away
into captivity Æthra, the mother of Thêseus. In after-days,
when Kastôr and Pollux, under the title of the Dioskuri, had
come to be worshipped as powerful gods, and when the Athenians
were greatly ashamed of this act of Thêseus — the revelation
made by Dekelus was considered as entitling him to the lasting
gratitude of his country, as well as to the favorable remembrance
of the Lacedæmônians, who maintained the Dekeleians in the
constant enjoyment of certain honorary privileges at Sparta,[1] and
even spared that dême in all their invasions of Attica. Nor is it
improbable that the existence of this legend had some weight in
determining the Lacedæmônians to select Dekelia as the place of
their occupation during the Peleponnêsian war.

The fatal combat between Kastôr and Polydeukês on the one
side, and Idas and Lynkeus on the other, for the possession of
the daughters of Leukippus, was celebrated by more than one
ancient poet, and forms the subject of one of the yet remaining
Idylls of Theocritus. Leukippus had formally betrothed his
daughters to Idas and Lynkeus; but the Tyndarids, becoming
enamored of them, outbid their rivals in the value of the customary nuptial gifts, persuaded the father to violate his promise,
and carried off Phœbê and Ilaëira as their brides. Idas and
Lynkeus pursued them and remonstrated against the injustice:
according to Theocritus, this was the cause of the combat. But
there was another tale, which seems the older, and which assigns
a different cause to the quarrel. The four had jointly made a
predatory incursion into Arcadia, and had driven off some cattle,
but did not agree about the partition of the booty — Idas carried
off into Messênia a portion of it which the Tyndarids claimed as

---

[1] Diodôr. iv. 63. Herod. iv. 73. Δεκελέων δὲ τῶν τότε ἐργασαμένων ἔργον χρήσιμον ἐς τὸν πάντα χρόνον, ὡς αὐτοὶ Ἀθηναῖοι λέγουσι. According
to other authors, it was Akadêmus who made the revelation, and the spot
called Akadêmia, near Athens, which the Lacedæmônians spared in consideration of this service (Plutarch, Thêseus, 31, 32, 33, where he gives
several different versions of this tale by Attic writers, framed with the view
of exonerating Thêseus). The recovery of Helen and the captivity of Æthra
were represented on the ancient chest of Kypselus, with the following curious
inscription:

Τυνδαρίδα ᾽Ελέναν φέρετον, Αἴθραν δ᾽ Ἀθέναθεν
᾽Ελκετον.   Pausan. v. 19, 1

their own. To revenge and reimburse themselves, the Tyndarids invaded Messênia, placing themselves in ambush in the hollow of an ancient oak. But Lynkeus, endued with preternatural powers of vision, mounted to the top of Taygetus, from whence, as he could see over the whole Peleponnêsus, he detected them in their chosen place of concealment. Such was the narrative of the ancient Cyprian Verses. Kastôr perished by the hand of Idas, Lynkeus by that of Pollux. Idas, seizing a stone pillar from the tomb of his father Aphareus, hurled it at Pollux, knocked him down and stunned him; but Zeus, interposing at the critical moment for the protection of his son, killed Idas with a thunderbolt. Zeus would have conferred upon Pollux the gift of immortality, but the latter could not endure existence without his brother: he entreated permission to share the gift with Kastôr, and both were accordingly permitted to live, but only on every other day.[1]

The Dioskuri, or sons of Zeus, — as the two Spartan heroes, Kastôr and Pollux, were denominated, — were recognized in the historical days of Greece as gods, and received divine honors. This is even noticed in a passage of the Odyssey,[2] which is at any rate a very old interpolation, as well as in one of the Homeric hymns. What is yet more remarkable is, that they were invoked during storms at sea, as the special and all-powerful protectors of the endangered mariner, although their attributes and their celebrity seem to be of a character so dissimilar. They were worshipped throughout most parts of Greece, but with preëminent sanctity at Sparta.

Kastôr and Pollux being removed, the Spartan genealogy passes from Tyndareus to Menelaus, and from him to Orestês.

Originally it appears that Messênê was a name for the western portion of Lacônia, bordering on what was called Pylos: it is so represented in the Odyssey, and Ephorus seems to have included it amongst the possessions of Orestês and his descendants.

---

[1] Cypria Carm. Fragm. 8. p. 13, Düntzer. Lycophrôn, 538–566 with Schol. Apollod. iii. 11, 1. Pindar, Nem. x. 55–90. ἑτερήμερον ἀθανασίαν· also Homer, Odyss. xi. 302, with the Commentary of Nitzsch, vol. iii. p. 245.

The combat thus ends more favorably to the Tyndarids; but probably the account least favorable to them is the oldest, since their dignity went on continually increasing, until at last they became great deities.

[2] **Odyss. xxi.** 15. Diodôr. xv. 66.

Throughout the whole duration of the Messênico-Dôrian kingdom, there never was any town called Messênê: the town was
first founded by Epameinondas, after the battle of Leuctra. The
heroic genealogy of Messenia starts from the same name as that
of Lacônia — from the autochthonous Lelex: his younger son,
Polykaôn, marries Messênê, daughter of the Argeian Triopas,
and settles the country. Pausanias tells us that the posterity of
this pair occupied the country for five generations; but he in
vain searched the ancient genealogical poems to find the names
of their descendants.[1] To them succeeded Periêrês, son of
Æolus; and Aphareus and Leukippus, according to Pausanias,
were sons of Periêrês. Idas and Lynkeus are the only heroes,
distinguished for personal exploits and memorable attributes,
belonging to Messênia proper. They are the counterpart of the
Dioskuri; and were interesting persons in the old legendary
poems. Marpêssa was the daughter of Euênus, and wooed by
Apollo: nevertheless Idas[2] carried her off by the aid of a winged
chariot which he had received from Poseidôn, Euênus pursued
them, and when he arrived at the river Lykormas, he found
himself unable to overtake them: his grief caused him to throw
himself into the river, which ever afterwards bore his name. Idas
brought Marpêssa safe to Messênia, and even when Apollo there
claimed her of him, he did not fear to risk a combat with the god.
But Zeus interfered as mediator, and permitted the maiden to
choose which of the two she preferred. She attached herself to
Idas, being apprehensive that Apollo would desert her in her old
age: on the death of her husband she slew herself. Both Idas
and Lynkeus took part in the Argonautic expedition and in
the Kalydônian boar-hunt.[3]

---

[1] Pausan. iv. 2, 1.

[2] Iliad, ix. 553. Simonidês had handled this story in detail (Schol. Ven.
Il. ix. p. 553). Bacchylidês (ap, Schol. Pindar. Isthm. iv. 92) celebrated in
one of his poems the competition among many eager suitors for the hand of
Marpêssa, under circumstances similar to the competition for Hippodameia,
daughter of Œnomaus. Many unsuccessful suitors perished by the hand of
Euênas: their skulls were affixed to the wall of the temple of Poseidôn.

[3] Apollod. i. 7, 9. Pausan. iv. 2, 5. Apollônius Rhodius describes Idas as
full of boast and self-confidence, heedless of the necessity of divine aid.
Probably this was the character of the brothers in the old legend, as the
enemies of the Dioskuri.

The wrath of the Dioskuri against Messênia was treated, even in the

Aphareus, after the death of his sons, founded the town of Arênê, and made over most part of his dominions to his kinsman Nêleus, with whom we pass into the Pylian genealogy.

CHAPTER IX.

ARCADIAN GENEALOGY.

THE Arcadian divine or heroic pedigree begins with Pelasgus, whom both Hesiod and Asius considered as an indigenous man, though Akusilaus the Argeian represented him as brother of Argos and son of Zeus by Niobê, daughter of Phorôneus: this logographer wished to establish a community of origin between the Argeians and the Arcadians.

Lykaên, son of Pelasgus and king of Arcadia, had, by different wives, fifty sons, the most savage, impious and wicked of mankind: Mænalus was the eldest of them. Zeus, in order that he might himself become a witness of their misdeeds, presented himself to them in disguise. They killed a child and served it up to him for a meal; but the god overturned the table and struck dead with thunder Lykaôn and all his fifty sons, with the single exception of Nyktimus, the youngest, whom he spared at the earnest intercession of the goddess Gæa (the Earth). The town near which the table was overturned received the name of Trapezus (Tabletown).

This singular legend (framed on the same etymological type as that of the ants in Ægina, recounted elsewhere) seems ancient, and may probably belong to the Hesiodic Catalogue. But Pausanias tells us a story in many respects different, which was represented to him in Arcadia as the primitive local account, and which becomes the more interesting, as he tells us that he himself fully believes it. Both tales indeed go to illustrate the same

historical times, as the grand cause of the subjection of the Messênians by the Spartans: that wrath had been appeased at the time when Epameinondas reconstituted Messênê (Pausan. iv. 27, 1).

point — the ferocity of Lykaôn's character, as well as the cruel rites which he practised. The latter was the first who established the worship and solemn games of Zeus Lykæus: he offered up a child to Zeus, and made libations with the blood upon the altar. Immediately after having perpetrated this act, he was changed into a wolf.[1]

"Of the truth of this narrative (observes Pausanias) I feel persuaded: it has been repeated by the Arcadians from old times, and it carries probability along with it. For the men of that day, from their justice and piety, were guests and companions at table with the gods, who manifested towards them approbation when they were good, and anger if they behaved ill, in a palpable manner: indeed at that time there were some, who having once been men, became gods, and who yet retain their privileges as such — Aristæus, the Krêtan Britomartis, Hêraklês son of Alkmêna, Amphiaraus the son of Oiklês, and Pollux and Kastôr besides. We may therefore believe that Lykaôn became a wild beast, and that Niobê, the daughter of Tantalus, became a stone. But in my time, wickedness having enormously increased, so as to overrun the whole earth and all the cities in it, there are no farther examples of men exalted into gods, except by mere title and from adulation towards the powerful: moreover the anger of the gods falls tardily upon the wicked, and is reserved for them after their departure from hence."

---

[1] Apollodôr. iii. 8, 1. Hygin. fab. 176. Eratosthen. Catasterism. 8. Pausan. viii. 2, 2-3. A different story respecting the immolation of the child is in Nikolaus Damask. Frag. p. 41, Orelli. Lykaôn is mentioned as the first founder of the temple of Zeus Lykæus in Schol. Eurip. Orest. 1662; but nothing is there said about the human sacrifice or its consequences. In the historical times, the festival and solemnities of the Lykæa do not seem to have been distinguished materially from the other agônes of Greece (Pindar, Olymp. xiii. 104; Nem. x. 46): Xenias the Arcadian, one of the generals in the army of Cyrus the younger, celebrated the solemnity with great magnificence in the march through Asia Minor (Xen. Anab. i. 2, 10). But the fable of the human sacrifice, and the subsequent transmutation of the person who had eaten human food into a wolf, continued to be told in connection with them (Plato, de Republic. viii. c. 15. p. 417). Compare Pliny, H. N. viii. 34. This passage of Plato seems to afford distinct indication that the practice of offering human victims at the altar of the Lykæan Zeus was neither prevalent nor recent, but at most only traditional and antiquated; and it therefore limits the sense or invalidates the authority of the Pseudo-Platonic dialogue, Minos, c. 5.

Pausanias then proceeds to censure those who, by multiplying false miracles in more recent times, tended to rob the old and genuine miracles of their legitimate credit and esteem. The passage illustrates forcibly the views which a religious and instructed pagan took of his past time — how inseparably he blended together in it gods and men, and how little he either recognized or expected to find in it the naked phænomena and historical laws of connection which belonged to the world before him. He treats the past as the province of legend, the present as that of history; and in doing this he is more sceptical than the persons with whom he conversed, who believed not only in the ancient, but even in the recent and falsely reported miracles. It is true that Pausanias does not always proceed consistently with this position : he often rationalizes the stories of the past, as if he expected to find historical threads of connection ; and sometimes, though more rarely, accepts the miracles of the present. But in the present instance he draws a broad line of distinction between present and past, or rather between what is recent and what is ancient : his criticism is, in the main, analogous to that of Arrian in regard to the Amazons — denying their existence during times of recorded history, but admitting it during the early and unrecorded ages.

In the narrative of Pausanias, the sons of Lykaôn, instead of perishing by thunder from Zeus, become the founders of the various towns in Arcadia. And as that region was subdivided into a great number of small and independent townships, each having its own eponym, so the Arcadian heroic genealogy appears broken up and subdivided. Pallas, Orestheus, Phigalus, Trapezeus, Mænalus, Mantinêus, and Tegeatês, are all numbered among the sons of Lykaôn, and are all eponyms of various Arcadian towns.[1]

The legend respecting Kallistô and Arkas, the eponym of Arcadia generally, seems to have been originally quite independent of and distinct from that of Lykaôn. Eumêlus, indeed, and some other poets made Kallistô daughter of Lykaôn ; but neither Hesiod, nor Asius, nor Pherekydês, acknowledged any relationship between them.[2] The beautiful Kallistô, companion of

---

[1] Paus. viii. 3. Hygin. fab. 177.   [2] Apollod. iii. 8, 2.

Artemis in the chase, had bound herself by a vow of chastity
Zeus, either by persuasion or by force, obtained a violation of the
vow, to the grievous displeasure both of Hêrê and Artemis. The
former changed Kallistô into a bear, the latter when she was in
that shape killed her with an arrow. Zeus gave to the unfortunate Kallistô a place among the stars, as the constellation of the
Bear: he also preserved the child Arkas, of which she was
pregnant by him, and gave it to the Atlantid nymph Maia to
bring up.[1]

Arkas, when he became king, obtained from Triptolemus and
communicated to his people the first rudiments of agriculture;
he also taught them to make bread, to spin, and to weave. He
had three sons — Azan, Apheidas, and Elatus : the first was the
eponym of Azania, the northern region of Arcadia ; the second
was one of the heroes of Tegea ; the third was father of Ischys
(rival of Apollo for the affections of Korônis), as well as of
Æpytus and Kyllên : the name of Æpytus among the heroes of
Arcadia is as old as the Catalogue in the Iliad.[2]

Aleus, son of Apheidas and king of Tegea, was the founder
of the celebrated temple and worship of Athênê Alea in that
town. Lykurgus and Kêpheus were his sons, Augê his daughter, who was seduced by Hêraklês, and secretly bore to him a
child : the father, discovering what had happened, sent Augê to
Nauplius to be sold into slavery : Teuthras, king of Mysia in
Asia Minor, purchased her and made her his wife : her tomb was
shown at Pergamus on the river Kaikus even in the time of
Pausanias.[3]

---

[1] Pausan. viii. 3, 2. Apollod. iii. 8, 2. Hesiod. apud Eratosthen. Catasterism. 1. Fragm. 182, Marktsch. Hygin. f. 177.

[2] Homer, Iliad, ii. 604. Pind. Olymp. vi. 44–63.

The tomb of Æpytus, mentioned in the Iliad, was shown to Pausanias
between Pheneus and Stymphalus (Pausan. viii. 16, 2). Æpytus was a cognomen of Hermês (Pausan. viii. 47, 3).

The hero Arkas was worshipped at Mantineia, under the special injunction of the Delphian oracle (Pausan. viii. 9, 2).

[3] Pausan. viii. 4, 6. Apollod. iii. 9, 1. Diodôr. iv. 33.

A separate legend respecting Augê and the birth of Têlephus was current
at Tegea, attached to the temple, statue, and cognomen of Eileithyia in the
Tegeatic agora (Pausan. viii. 48, 5).

Hekatæus seems to have narrated in detail the adventures of Augê (Pausan. viii. 4, 4 ; 47, 3. Hekatæ. Fragm. 345, Didot.).

Euripidês followed a different story about Augê and the birth of Têlephus

The child Têlephus, exposed on Mount Parthenius, was wonderfully sustained by the milk of a doe: the herdsmen of Korythus brought him up, and he was directed by the Delphian oracle to go and find his parents in Mysia. Teuthras adopted him, and he succeeded to the throne: in the first attempt of the army of Agamemnôn against Troy, on which occasion they mistook their point and landed in Mysia, his valor signally contributed to the repulse of the Greeks, though he was at last vanquished and desperately wounded by the spear of Achilles — by whom however he was afterwards healed, under the injunction of the oracle, and became the guide of the Greeks in their renewed attack upon the Trojans.[1]

From Lykurgus,[2] the son of Aleus and brother of Augê, we pass to his son Ankæus, numbered among the Argonauts, finally killed in the chase of the Kalydônian boar, and father of Agapenôr, who leads the Arcadian contingent against Troy, — (the adventurers of his niece, the Tegeatic huntress Atalanta, have already been touched upon), — then to Echemus, son of Aëropus and grandson of the brother of Lykurgus, Kêpheus. Echemus is the chief heroic ornament of Tegea. When Hyllus, the son of Hêraklês, conducted the Hêrakleids on their first expedition against Peloponnêsus, Echemus commanded the Tegean troops who assembled along with the other Peloponnêsians at the isthmus of Corinth to repel the invasion: it was agreed that the dispute should be determined by single combat, and Echemus, as the champion of Peloponnêsus, encountered and killed Hyllus.

---

in his lost tragedy called Augê (See Strabo, xiii. p. 615). Respecting the Μυσοὶ of Æschylus, and the two lost dramas, ᾽Αλεαδαὶ and Μυσοὶ of Sophoklês, little can be made out. (See Welcker, Griechisch. Tragöd. p. 53, 408–414).

[1] Têlephus and his exploits were much dwelt upon in the lost old epic poem, the Cyprian Verses. See argument of that poem ap. Düntzer, Ep. Fragm. p. 10. His exploits were also celebrated by Pindar (Olymp. ix. 70–79); he is enumerated along with Hectôr, Cycnus, Memnôn, the most distinguished opponents of Achilles (Isthm. iv. 46). His birth, as well as his adventures, became subjects with most of the great Attic tragedians.

[2] There were other local genealogies of Tegea deduced from Lykurgus: Bôtachus, eponym of the Dême Bôtachidæ at that place, was his grandson (Nicolaus ap. Steph. Byz. v. Βωταχίδαι).

Pursuant to the stipulation by which they had bound themselves, the Hêrakleids retired, and abstained for three generations from pressing their claim upon Peloponnêsus. This valorous exploit of their great martial hero was cited and appealed to by the Tegeates before the battle of Platæa, as the principal evidence of their claim to the second post in the combined army, next in point of honor to that of the Lacedæmônians, and superior to that of the Athenians : the latter replied to them by producing as counter-evidence the splendid heroic deeds of Athens, — the protection of the Hêrakleids against Eurystheus, the victory over the Kadmeians of Thêbes, and the complete defeat of the Amazons in Attica.[1] Nor can there be any doubt that these legendary glories were both recited by the speakers, and heard by the listeners, with profound and undoubting faith, as well as with heart-stirring admiration.

One other person there is — Ischys, son of Elatus and grand son of Arkas — in the fabulous genealogy of Arcadia whom it would be improper to pass over, inasmuch as his name and adventures are connected with the genesis of the memorable god or hero Æsculapius, or Asklêpius. Korônis, daughter of Phlegyas, and resident near the lake Bœbëis in Thessaly, was beloved by Apollo and became pregnant by him : unfaithful to the god, she listened to the propositions of Ischys son of Elatus, and consented to wed him : a raven brought to Apollo the fatal news, which so incensed him that he changed the color of the bird from white, as it previously had been, into black.[2] Artemis, to

---

[1] Herodot. ix. 27. Echemus is described by Pindar (Ol. xi. 69) as gaining the prize of wrestling in the fabulous Olympic games, on their first establishment by Hêraklês. He also found a place in the Hesiodic Catalogue as husband of Timandra, the sister of Helen and Klytæmnêstra (Hesiod, Fragm. 105, p. 318, Marktscheff.).

[2] Apollodôr. iii. 10, 3; Hesiod, Fragm. 141–142, Marktscheff.; Strab. is p. 442; Pherekydês, Fragm. 8; Akusilaus, Fragm. 25, Didot.

Τῷ μὲν ἄρ' ἄγγελος ἦλθε κόραξ, ἱερῆς ἀπὸ δαιτὸς
Πυθὼ ἐς ἠγαθέην, καὶ ῥ' ἔφρασεν ἔργ' ἀίδηλα
Φοίβῳ ἀκερσεκόμῃ, ὅτι Ἴσχυς γῆμε Κόρωνιν
Εἰλατίδης, Φλεγύαο διογνήτοιο θύγατρα. (Hesiod, Fr.)

The change of the color of the crow is noticed both in Ovid, Metamorph. ii. 632, in Antonin. Liberal. c. 20, and in Servius ad Virgil. Æneid. vii. 761.

avenge the wounded dignity of her brother, put Korônis to
death; but Apollo preserved the male child of which she was
about to be delivered, and consigned it to the Centaur Cheirôn to
be brought up. The child was named Asklêpius or Æsculapius,
and acquired, partly from the teaching of the beneficent leech
Cheirôn, partly from inborn and superhuman aptitude, a knowledge of the virtues of herbs and a mastery of medicine and sur-
gery, such as had never before been witnessed. He not only
cured the sick, the wounded, and the dying, but even restored the
dead to life. Kapaneus, Eriphylê, Hippolytus, Tyndareus and
Glaukus were all affirmed by different poets and logographers to
have been endued by him with a new life.[1] But Zeus now found
himself under the necessity of taking precautions lest mankind,
thus unexpectedly protected against sickness and death, should
no longer stand in need of the immortal gods : he smote Asklêpius with thunder and killed him. Apollo was so exasperated
by this slaughter of his highly-gifted son, that he killed the
Cyclôpes who had fabricated the thunder, and Zeus was about to
condemn him to Tartarus for doing so ; but on the intercession
of Latôna he relented, and was satisfied with imposing upon him
a temporary servitude in the house of Admêtus at Pheræ.

Asklêpius was worshipped with very great solemnity at Trikka,
at Kôs, at Knidus, and in many different parts of Greece, but especially at Epidaurus, so that more than one legend had grown up

---

though the name "*Corvo* custode ejus" is there printed with a capital letter,
as if it were a man named *Corvus*.

[1] Schol. Eurip. Alkêst. 1; Diodôr. iv. 71; Apollodôr. iii. 10, 3; Pindar,
Pyth. iii. 59; Sextus Empiric. adv. Grammatic. i. 12. p. 271. Stesichorus
named Eriphylê — the Naupaktian verses, Hippolytus — (compare Servius
ad Virgil. Æneid. vii. 761) ; Panyasis, Tyndareus; a proof of the popularity
of this tale among the poets. Pindar says that Æsculapius was "tempted by
gold" to raise a man from the dead, and Plato (Legg. iii. p. 408) copies
him : this seems intended to afford some color for the subsequent punishment. "Mercede id captum (observes Boeckh. ad Pindar. l. c.) Æscula-
pium fecisse recentior est fictio ; Pindari fortasse ipsius, quem tragici secuti
sunt : haud dubie a medicorum avaris moribus profecta, qui Græcorum
medicis nostrisque communes sunt." The rapacity of the physicians (granting it to be ever so well-founded, both then and now) appears to me less
likely to have operated upon the mind of Pindar, than the disposition to
extenuate the cruelty of Zeus, by imputing guilty and sordid views to Asklêpius. Compare the citation from Dikæarchus, *infrà* p. 249, note 1.

respecting the details of his birth and adventures: in particular, his mother was by some called Arsinoê. But a formal application had been made on this subject (so the Epidaurians told Pausanias) to the oracle of Delphi, and the god in reply acknowledged that Asklêpius was his son by Korônis.[1] The tale above recounted seems to have been both the oldest and the most current. It is adorned by Pindar in a noble ode, wherein however he omits all mention of the raven as messenger — not specifying who or what the spy was from whom Apollo learnt the infidelity of Korônis. By many this was considered as an improvement in respect of poetical effect, but it illustrates the mode in which the characteristic details and simplicity of the old fables[2] came to be exchanged for dignified generalities, adapted to the altered taste of society.

Machaôn and Podaleirius, the two sons of Asklêpius, command the contingent from Trikka, in the north-west region of Thessaly, at the siege of Troy by Agamemnôn.[3] They are the leeches of the Grecian army, highly prized and consulted by all the wounded chiefs. Their medical renown was further prolonged in the subsequent poem of Arktinus, the Iliu-Persis, wherein the one was represented as unrivalled in surgical óperations, the other as sagacious in detecting and appreciating morbid symptoms. It was Podaleirius who first noticed the glaring

---

[1] Pausan. ii. 26, where several distinct stories are mentioned, each springing up at some one or other of the sanctuaries of the god: quite enough to justify the idea of these Æsculapii (Cicero, N. D. iii. 22).

Homer, Hymn. ad Æsculap. 2. The tale briefly alluded to in the Homeric Hymn. ad Apollin. 209. is evidently different: Ischys is there the companion of Apollo, and Korônis is an Arcadian damsel.

Aristidês, the fervent worshipper of Asklêpius, adopted the story of Korônis, and composed hymns on the γάμον Κορωνίδος καὶ γένεσιν τοῦ θεοῦ (Orat. 23. p. 463, Dind.).

[2] See Pindar, Pyth. iii. The Scholiast puts a construction upon Pindar's words which is at any rate far-fetched, if indeed it be at all admissible: he supposes that Apollo knew the fact from his own omniscience, without any informant, and he praises Pindar for having thus transformed the old fable. But the words οὐδ' ἔλαϑε σκόπον seem certainly to imply some informant: to suppose that σκόπον means the god's own mind, is a strained interpretation.

[3] Iliad, ii. 730. The Messênians laid claim to the sons of Asklêpius as their heroes, and tried to justify the pretension by a forced construction of Homer (Pausan. iii. 4, 2 .

eyes and disturbed deportment which preceded the suicide of Ajax.[1]

Galen appears uncertain whether Asklêpius (as well as Dionysus) was originally a god, or wheth, r he was first a man and then became afterwards a god;[2] but Apollodôrus professed to fix the exact date of his apotheosis.[3] Throughout all the historical ages the descendants of Asklêpius were numerous and widely diffused. The many families or gentes called Asklêpiads, who devoted themselves to the study and practice of medicine, and who principally dwelt near the temples of Asklêpius, whither sick and suffering men came to obtain relief — all recognized the god not merely as the object of their common worship, but also as their actual progenitor. Like Solôn, who reckoned Nêleus and Poseidôn as his ancestors, or the Milêsian Hekatæus, who traced his origin through fifteen successive links to a god — like the privileged gens at Pêlion in Thessaly,[4] who considered the wise Centaur Cheirôn as their progenitor, and who inherited from him their precious secrets respecting the medicinal herbs of which

---

[1] Arktinus, Epicc. Græc. Fragm. 2. p. 22, Düntzer. The Ilias Minor mentioned the death of Machaôn by Eurypylus, son of Têlephus (Fragm. 5. p. 19, Düntzer).

[2] Ἀσκληπιός γέ τοι καὶ Διόνυσος, εἶτ' ἄνθρωποι πρότερον ἤστην εἴτε καὶ ἀρχῆθεν θεοί (Galen, Protreptic. 9. t. 1. p. 22, Kuhn.). Pausanias considers him as θεὸς ἐξ ἀρχῆς (ii. 26, 7). In the important temple at Smyrna he was worsnipped as Ζεὺς Ἀσκληπιός (Aristidês, Or. 6. p. 64 ; Or. 23. p. 456, Dind.).

[3] Apollodôr. ap. Clem. Alex, Strom. i. p. 381 ; see Heyne, Fragment. Apollodôr. p. 410. According to Apollodôrus, the apotheosis of Hêraklês and of Æsculapius took place at the same time, thirty-eight years after Hêraklês began to reign at Argos.

[4] About Hekatæus, Herodot. ii. 143 ; about Solôn, Diogen. Laërt, Vit. Platon. init.

A curious fragment, preserved from the lost works of Dikæarchus, tells us of the descendants of the Centaur Cheirôn at the town of Pêlion, or perhaps at the neighboring town of Dêmêtrias, — it is not quite certain which, perhaps at both (see Dikæarch Fragment. ed. Fuhr, p. 408). Ταύτην δὲ τὴν δύναμιν ἐν τῶν πολιτῶν οἶδε γένος, ὁ δὴ λέγεται Χείρωνος ἀπόγονον εἶναι παραδίδωσι δὲ καὶ δείκνυσι πατὴρ υἱῷ, καὶ οὕτως ἡ δύναμις φυλάσσεται, ὡς οὐδεὶς ἄλλος οἶδε τῶν πολιτῶν · οὐχ ὅσιον δὲ τοὺς ἐπισταμένους τὰ φάρμακα μισθοῦ τοῖς καμνοῖσι βοηθεῖν, ἀλλὰ προῖκα.

Plato, de Republ iii. 4 (p. 391). Ἀχιλλιὺς ὑπὸ τῷ σοφωτάτῳ Χείρωνι τεθράμμενος. Compare Xenophôn, De Venat. c. 1

their neighborhood was full,— Asklêpiads, even of the later
times, numbered and specified all the intermediate links which
separated them from their primitive divine parent. One of these
genealogies has been preserved to us, and we may be sure that
there were many such, as the Asklêpiads were found in many
different places.[1] Among them were enrolled highly instructed
and accomplished men, such as the great Hippocratês and the
historian Ktêsias, who prided themselves on the divine origin of
themselves and their gens[2] — so much did the legendary element
pervade even the most philosophical and positive minds of historical Greece. Nor can there be any doubt that their means of
medical observation must have been largely extended by their
vicinity to a temple so much frequented by the sick, who came in
confident hopes of divine relief, and who, whilst they offered up
sacrifice and prayer to Æsculapius, and slept in his temple in
order to be favored with healing suggestions in their dreams,
might, in case the god withheld his supernatural aid, consult his

---

[1] See the genealogy at length in Le Clerc, Historie de la Médecine, lib. ii.
c. 2. p. 78, also p. 287; also Littré, Introduction aux Œuvres Complètes
d'Hippocrate, t. i. p. 35. Hippocratês was the seventeenth from Æsculapius.

Theopompus the historian went at considerable length into the pedigree
of the Asklêpiads of Kôs and Knidus, tracing them up to Podaleirius and
his first settlement at Syrnus in Karia (see Theopomp. Fragm. 111, Didot) :
Polyanthus of Kyrênê composed a special treatise περὶ τῆς τῶν Ἀσκληπια-
δῶν γενέσεως (Sextus Empiric. adv. Grammat. i. 12. p. 271); see Stephan.
Byz. v. Κῶς, and especially Aristidês, Orat. vii. Asclêpiadæ. The Asklêpiads
were even reckoned among the Ἀρχηγέται of Rhodes, jointly with the Hêrakleids (Aristidês, Or. 44, ad Rhod. p. 839, Dind.).

In the extensive sacred enclosure at Epidaurus stood the statues of Asklêpius and his wife Epionê (Pausan. ii. 29, 1) : two daughters are coupled with
him by Aristophanês, and he was considered especially εὔπαις (Plutus, 654)
Jaso, Panakeia and Hygieia are named by Aristidês.

[2] Plato, Protagor. c. 6 (p. 311). Ἱπποκράτη τὸν Κῶον, τὸν τῶν Ἀσκλη-
πιαδῶν; also Phædr. c. 121. (p. 270). About Ktêsias, Galen, Opp. t. v. p.
652, Basil.; and Bahrt, Fragm. Ktêsiæ, p. 20. Aristotle (see Stahr. Aristotelia, i. p. 32) and Xenophôn, the physician of the emperor Claudius, were
both Asklêpiads (Tacit. Annal. xii. 61). Plato, de Republ. iii. 405, calls
them τοὺς κομψοὺς Ἀσκληπιάδας.

Pausanias, a distinguished physician at Ge'a in Sicily, and contemporary
of the philosopher Empedoklés, was also an Asklêpiad : see the verses of
Empedoklês upon him, Diogen. Laërt. viii. 61.

living descendants.[1] The sick visitors at Kôs, or Trikka, or
Epidaurus, were numerous and constant, and the tablets usually
hung up to record the particulars of their maladies, the remedies
resorted to, and the cures operated by the god, formed both an
interesting decoration of the sacred ground and an instructive
memorial to the Asklêpiads.[2]

The genealogical descent of Hippocratês and the other Asklêpiads from the god Asklêpius is not only analogous to that of
Hekatæus and Solôn from their respective ancestoral gods, but
also to that of the Lacedæmônian kings from Hêraklês, upon the
basis of which the whole supposed chronology of the ante-historical times has been built, from Eratosthenês and Apollodôrus
down to the chronologers of the present century.[3] I shall revert
to this hereafter.

---

[1] Strabo, viii. p. 374; Aristophan. Vesp. 122; Plutus, 635–750; where the
visit to the temple of Æsculapius is described in great detail, though with
a broad farcical coloring.

During the last illness of Alexander the Great, several of his principal
officers slept in the temple of Serapis, in the hope that remedies would be
suggested to them in their dreams (Arrian, vii. 26).

Pausanias, in describing the various temples of Asklêpius which he saw,
announces as a fact quite notorious and well-understood, "Here cures are
wrought by the god" (ii. 36, 1; iii. 26, 7; vii. 27, 4): see Suidas, v. Ἀρίσ-
ταρχος. The Orations of Aristidês, especially the 6th and 7th, Asklépius
and the Asklépiadœ, are the most striking manifestations of faith and thanks-
giving towards Æsculapius, as well as attestations of his extensive working
throughout the Grecian world; also Orat. 23 and 25, Ἱερῶν Λόγος, 1 and 3;
and Or. 45 (De Rhetoricâ, p. 22. Dind.), αἱ τ' ἐν Ἀσκληπιοῦ τῶν ἀεὶ διατρι-
βόντων ἀγελαὶ, etc.

[2] Pausan. ii. 27, 3; 36, 1. Ταύταις ἐγγεγράμμενά ἐστι καὶ ἀνδρῶν καὶ
γυναικῶν ὀνόματα ἀκεσθέντων ὑπὸ τοῦ Ἀσκληπιοῦ, πρόσετι δὲ καὶ νόσημα,
ὅ, τι ἕκαστος ἐνόησε, καὶ ὅπως ἰάθη, — the cures are wrought by the god
himself.

[3] "Apollodôrus ætatem Herculis pro cardine chronologiæ habuit" (Heyne,
ad Apollodôr. Fragm. p. 410).

CHAPTER X.

ÆAKUS AND HIS DESCENDANTS.—ÆGINA, SALAMIS, AND PHTHIA.

THE memorable heroic genealogy of the Æakids establishes a fabulous connection between Ægina, Salamis, and Phthia, which we can only recognize as a fact, without being able to trace its origin.

Æakus was the son of Zeus, born of Ægina, daughter of Asôpus, whom the god had carried off and brought into the island to which he gave her name: she was afterwards married to Aktôr, and had by him Menœtius, father of Patroclus. As there were two rivers named Asôpus, one between Phlius and Sikyôn, and another between Thêbes and Platæa—so the Æginêtan heroic genealogy was connected both with that of Thêbes and with that of Phlius: and this belief led to practical consequences in the minds of those who accepted the legends as genuine history. For when the Thêbans, in the 68th Olympiad, were hard-pressed in war by Athens, they were directed by the Delphian oracle to ask assistance of their next of kin: recollecting that Thêbê and Ægina had been sisters, common daughters of Asôpus, they were induced to apply to the Æginôtans as their next of kin, and the Æginêtans gave them aid, first by sending to them their common heroes, the Æakids, next by actual armed force.[1] Pindar dwells emphatically on the heroic brotherhood between Thêbes, his native city, and Ægina.[2]

Æakus was alone in Ægina: to relieve him from this solitude, Zeus changed all the ants in the island into men, and thus provided him with a numerous population, who, from their origin, were called Myrmidons.[3] By his wife Endêis, daughter of Chei-

---

[1] Herodot. v. 81.　　　[2] Nem. iv. 22. Isthm. vii. 16.

[3] This tale, respecting the transformation of the ants into men, is as old as the Hesiodic Catalogue of Women. See Düntzer, Fragm. Epicc. 21. p. 34 ; evidently an etymological tale from the name Myrmidones. Pausanias throws aside both the etymology and the details of the miracle : he says

κôn, Æakus had for his sons Pêleus and Telamôn: by the Nereid Psamathê, he had Phôkus. A monstrous crime had then recently been committed by Pelops, in killing the Arcadian prince, Stymphalus, under a simulation of friendship and hospitality: for this the gods had smitten all Greece with famine and barrenness. The oracles affirmed that nothing could relieve Greece from this intolerable misery except the prayers of Æakus, the most pious of mankind. Accordingly envoys from all quarters flocked to Ægina, to prevail upon Æakus to put up prayers for them: on his supplications the gods relented, and the suffering immediately ceased. The grateful Greeks established in Ægina the temple and worship of Zeus Pànhellênius, one of the lasting monuments and institutions of the island, on the spot where Æakus had offered up his prayer. The statues of the envoys who had come to solicit him were yet to be seen in the Æakeium, or sacred edifice of Æakus, in the time of Pausanias: and the Athenian Isokratês, in his eulogy of Evagoras, the despot of Salamis in Cyprus (who traced his descent through Teukrus to Æakus), enlarges upon this signal miracle, recounted and believed by other Greeks as well as by the Æginêtans, as a proof both of the great qualities and of the divine favor and patronage displayed in the career of the Æakids.[1] Æakus was also employed to aid Poseidôn and Apollo in building the walls of Troy.[2]

Pêleus and Telamôn, the sons of Æakus, contracting a jeal-

---

that Zeus raised men from the earth, at the prayer of Æakus (ii. 29, 2): other authors retained the etymology of Myrmidons from μύρμηκες, but gave a different explanation (Kallimachus, Fragm. 114, Düntzer). Μυρμιδόνων ἐσσῆνα (Strabo, viii. p. 375). Ἐσσῆν, ὁ οἰκιστής (Hygin. fab. 52).

According to the Thessalian legend, Myrmidôn was the son of Zeus by Eurymedusa, daughter of Kletor; Zeus having assumed the disguise of an ant (Clemens Alex. Admon. ad Gent. p. 25. Sylb.).

[1] Apollod. iii. 12, 6. Isokrat. Evagor. Encom. vol. ii. p. 278, Auger. Pausan. i. 45, 13; ii. 29, 6. Schol. Aristoph. Equit. 1253.

So in the 106th Psalm, respecting the Israelites and Phinees, v. 29, "They provoked the Lord to anger by their inventions, and the plague was great among them;" "Then stood up Phinees and prayed, and so the plague ceased;" "And that was counted unto him for righteousness, among all posterities for evermore."

[2] Pindar, Olymp. viii. 41, with the Scholia. Didymus did not find this story in any other poet older than Pindar.

ousy of their bastard brother, Phôkus, in consequence of his
eminent skill in gymnastic contests, conspired to put him to death.
Telamôn flung his quoit at him while they were playing together,
and Pêleus despatched him by a blow with his hatchet in the
back. They then concealed the dead body in a wood, but Æakus,
having discovered both the act and the agents, banished the
brothers from the island.[1] For both of them eminent destinies
were in store.

While we notice the indifference to the moral quality of actions implied in the old Hesiodic legend, when it imputes distinctly and nakedly this proceeding to two of the most admired
persons of the heroic world — it is not less instructive to witness
the change of feeling which had taken place in the age of Pindar.
That warm eulogist of the great Æakid race hangs down his
head with shame, and declines to recount, though he is obliged
darkly to glance at the cause which forced the pious Æakus to
banish his sons from Ægina. It appears that Kallimachus, if
we may judge by a short fragment, manifested the same repugnance to mention it.[2]

Telamôn retired to Salamis, then ruled by Kychreus, the son
of Poseidôn and Salamis, who had recently rescued the island
from the plague of a terrible serpent. This animal, expelled
from Salamis, retired to Eleusis in Attica, where it was received
and harbored by the goddess Dêmêtêr in her sacred domicile.[3]
Kychreus dying childless left his dominion to Telamôn, who, mar-

---

[1] Apollod. iii. 12, 6, who relates the tale somewhat differently; but the old
epic poem Alkmæônis gave the details (ap. Schol. Eurip. Andromach. 685) —

Ἔνθα μὲν ἀντίθεος Τελαμὼν τροχοειδέϊ δίσκῳ
Πλῆξε κάρη· Πηλεὺς δὲ θοῶς ἀνὰ χεῖρα τανύσσας
Ἀξίνην εὐχαλκον ἐπεπλήγει μετὰ νῶτα.

[2] Pindar, Nem. v. 15, with Scholia, and Kallimach. Frag. 136. Apollônius Rhodius represents the fratricide as inadvertent and unintentional (i. 92);
one instance amongst many of the tendency to soften down and moralize
the ancient tales.

Pindar, however, seems to forget this incident when he speaks in other
places of the general character of Pêleus (Olymp. ii. 75–86. Isthm. vii. 40).

[3] Apollod. iii. 12, 7. Euphoriòn, Fragm. 5, Düntzer, p. 43, Epicc. Græc.
There may have been a tutelary serpent in the temple at Eleusis, as there was
in that of Athênê Polias at Athens (Herodot. viii. 41. Photius, v. Οἰκοῦρον
ὄφιν. Aristophan. Lysistr. 759, with the Schol.).

rying Peribœa, daughter of Alkathoos, and grand-daughter of
Pelops, had for his son the celebrated Ajax. Telamôn took
part both in the chase of the Kalydônian boar and in the Argonautic expedition: he was also the intimate friend and companion
of Hêraklês, whom he accompanied in his enterprise against the
Amazons, and in the attack made with only six ships upon Laomedôn, king of Troy. This last enterprise having proved completely successful, Telamôn was rewarded by Hêraklês with the
possession of the daughter of Laomedôn, Hêsionê — who bore to
him Teukros, the most distinguished archer amidst the host of
Agamennôn, and the founder of Salamis in Cyprus.[1]

Pêleus went to Phthia, where he married the daughter of
Eurytiôn, son of Aktôr, and received from him the third part of
his dominions. Taking part in the Kalydônian boar-hunt, he
unintentionally killed his father-in-law Eurytiôn, and was obliged
to flee to Iôlkos, where he received purification from Akastus,
son of Pelias: the danger to which he became exposed by the
calumnious accusations of the enamoured wife of Akastus has
already been touched upon in a previous section. Pêleus also
was among the Argonauts; the most memorable event in his life
however was his marriage with the sea-goddess Thetis. Zeus
and Poseidôn had both conceived a violent passion for Thetis.
But the former, having been forewarned by Promêtheus that
Thetis was destined to give birth to a son more powerful than
his father, compelled her, much against her own will, to marry
Pêleus; who, instructed by the intimations of the wise Cheirôn,
was enabled to seize her on the coast called Sêpias in the southern region of Thessaly. She changed her form several times,
but Pêleus held her fast until she resumed her original appearance, and she was then no longer able to resist. All the gods
were present, and brought splendid gifts to these memorable nuptials: Apollo sang with his harp, Poseidôn gave to Pêleus the
immortal horses Xanthus and Balius, and Cheirôn presented a

---

[1] Appollod. iii. 12, 7. Hesiod. ap. Strab. ix. p. 393.
The libation and prayer of Hêraklês, prior to the birth of Ajax, and his
fixing the name of the yet unborn child, from an eagle (αἰετὸς) which appeared in response to his words, was detailed in the Hesiodic Eoia, and is
celebrated by Pindar (Isthm v. 30–54). See also the Scholia

formidable spear, cut from an ash-tree on Mount Pêlion. We shall have reason hereafter to recognize the value of both these gifts in the exploits of Achilles.[1]

The prominent part assigned to Thetis in the Iliad is well known, and the post-Homeric poets of the Legend of Troy introduced her as actively concurring first to promote the glory, finally to bewail the death of her distinguished son.[2] Pêleus, having survived both his son Achilles and his grandson Neoptolemus, is ultimately directed to place himself on the very spot where he had originally seized Thetis, and thither the goddess comes herself to fetch him away, in order that he may exchange the desertion and decrepitude of age for a life of immortality along with the Nêreids.[3] The spot was indicated to Xerxês when he marched into Greece by the Iônians who accompanied him, and his magi offered solemn sacrifices to her as well as to the other Nêreids, as the presiding goddesses and mistresses of the coast.[4]

Neoptolemus or Pyrrhus, the son of Achilles, too young to engage in the commencement of the siege of Troy, comes on the stage after the death of his father as the indispensable and prominent agent in the final capture of the city. He returns victor from Troy, not to Phthia, but to Epirus, bringing with him the captive Andromachê, widow of Hectôr, by whom Molossus is

---

[1] Appollodôr. iii. 13, 5. Homer, Iliad, xviii. 434 ; xxiv. 62. Pindar, Nem. iv. 50–68 ; Isthm. vii. 27–50. Herodot. vii. 192. Catullus, Carm. 64. Epithal. Pel. et Thetidos, with the prefatory remarks of Dœring.

The nuptials of Pêleus and Thetis were much celebrated in the Hesiodic Catalogue, or perhaps in the Eoiai (Düntzer, Epic. Græc. Frag. 36. p. 39), and Ægimius — see Schol. ad Apollon. Rhod. iv. 869 — where there is a curious attempt of Staphylus to rationalize the marriage of Pêleus and Thetis.

There was a town, seemingly near Pharsalus in Thessaly, called Thetide ium. Thetis is said to have been carried by Pêleus to both these places: probably it grew up round a temple and sanctuary of this goddess (Pherekyd. Frag. 16, Didot; Hellank. ap. Steph. Byz. Θεστίδειον).

[2] See the arguments of the lost poems, the Cypria and the Æthiopis, as given by Proclus, in Düntzer, Fragm. Epic. Gr. p. 11–16; also Schol. ad· Iliad. xvi. 140; and the extract from the lost Ψυχοστασία of Æschylus, ap. Plato. de Republic. ii. c. 21 (p. 382, St.).

[3] Eurip. Androm. 1242–1260; Pindar, Olymp. ii. 86.
Herodot. vii. 198.

born to him. He himself perishes in the full vigor of life at Delphi by the machinations of Orestês, son of Agamemnôn. But his son Molossus — like Fleance, the son of Banquo, in Macbeth — becomes the father of the powerful race of Molossian kings, who played so conspicuous a part during the declining vigor of the Grecian cities, and to whom the title and parentage of Æakids was a source of peculiar pride, identifying them by community of heroic origin with genuine and undisputed Hellênes.[1]

The glories of Ajax, the second grandson of Æakus, before Troy, are surpassed only by those of Achilles. He perishes by his own hand, the victim of an insupportable feeling of humiliation, because a less worthy claimant is allowed to carry off from him the arms of the departed Achilles. His son Philæus receives the citizenship of Athens, and the gens or dême called Philaidæ traced up to him its name and its origin: moreover the distinguished Athenians, Militiadês and Thucydidês, were regarded as members of this heroic progeny.[2]

Teukrus escaped from the perils of the siege of Troy as well as from those of the voyage homeward, and reached Salamis in safety. But his father Telamôn, indignant at his having returned without Ajax, refused to receive him, and compelled him to expatriate. He conducted his followers to Cyprus, where he founded the city of Salamis: his descendant Evagoras was recognized as a Teukrid and as an Æakid even in the time of Isokratês.[3]

---

[1] Plutarch, Pyrrh. 1; Justin, xi. 3; Eurip. Androm. 1253; Arrian, Exp. Alexand. i. 11.

[2] Pherekydês and Hellanikus ap. Marcelliu. Vit. Thucydid. init.; Pausan. ii. 29, 4; Plutarch, Solôn, 10. According to Apollodôrus, however, Phere kydês said that Telamôn was only the friend of Pêleus, not his brother, — not the son of Æakus (iii. 12, 7): this seems an inconsistency. There was however a warm dispute between the Athenians and the Megarians respecting the title to the hero Ajax, who was claimed by both (see Pausan. i. 42, 4; Plutarch, l. c.): the Megarians accused Peisistratus of having interpolated a line into the Catalogue in the Iliad (Strabo, ix. p. 394).

[3] Herodot. vii. 90; Isokrat. Enc. Evag. ut sup.; Sophokl. Ajax, 984–995; Vellei. Patercul. i. 1; Æschyl. Pers. 891, and Schol. The return from Troy of Teukrus, his banishment by Telamôn, and his settlement in Cyprus, formed the subject of the Τεῦκρος of Sophoklês, and of a tragedy under a similar

Such was the splendid heroic genealogy of the Æakids, — a family renowned for military excellence. The Æakeion at Ægina, in which prayer and sacrifice were offered to Æakus, remained in undiminished dignity down to the time of Pausanias.[1] This genealogy connects together various eminent gentes in Achaia Phthiôtis, in Ægina, in Salamis, in Cyprus, and amongst the Epirotic Molossians. Whether we are entitled to infer from it that the island of Ægina was originally peopled by Myrmidones from Achaia Phthiôtis, as O. Müller imagines,[2] I will not pretend to affirm. These mythical pedigrees seem to unite together special clans or gentes, rather than the bulk of any community — just as we know that the Athenians generally had no part in the Æakid genealogy, though certain particular Athenian families laid claim to it. The intimate friendship between Achilles and the Opuntian hero Patroclus — and the community of name and frequent conjunction between the Locrian Ajax, son of Oïleus, and Ajax, son of Telamôn — connect the Æakids with Opus and the Opuntian Locrians, in a manner which we have no farther means of explaining. Pindar too represents Menœtius, father of Patroclus, as son of Aktôr and Ægina, and therefore maternal brother of Æakus.[3]

---

title by Pacuvius (Cicero de Orat. i. 58; ii. 46); Sophokl. Ajax, 892; Pacuvii Fragm. Teucr. 15.—

" Te repudio, nec recipio, natum abdico,
    Facesse."

The legend of Teukros was connected in Attic archæology with the peculiar functions and formalities of the judicature, ἐν Φρεαττοῖ (Pausan. i. 28, 12; ii. 29, 7).

[1] Hesiod, Fragm. Düntz. Eoiai, 55, v. 43.—

Ἀλκὴν μὲν γὰρ ἔδωκεν Ὀλύμπιος Αἰακίδαισι,
Νοῦν δ᾿ Ἀμυθαονίδαις, πλοῦτον δ᾿ ἔπορ᾿ Ἀτρείδῃσι.

Polyb. v. 2.—

Αἰακίδας, πολέμῳ κεχαρηότας ἠΰτέ δαιτί.

[2] See his Æginetica, p. 14, his earliest work.

[3] Pindar, Olymp. ix. 74. The hero Ajax, son of Oïleus, was especially worshipped at Opus; solemn festivals and games were celebrated in his honor.

CHAPTER XI.

ATTIC LEGENDS AND GENEALOGIES.

THE most ancient name in Attic archæology, as far as our means of information reach, is that of Erechtheus, who is mentioned both in the Catalogue of the Iliad and in a brief allusion of the Odyssey. Born of the Earth, he is brought up by the goddess Athênê, adopted by her as her ward, and installed in her temple at Athens, where the Athenians offer to him annual sacrifices. The Athenians are styled in the Iliad, " the people of Erechtheus."[1] This is the most ancient testimony concerning Erechtheus, exhibiting him as a divine or heroic, certainly a superhuman person, and identifying him with the primitive germination (if I may use a term, the Grecian equivalent of which would have pleased an Athenian ear) of Attic man. And he was recognized in this same character, even at the close of the fourth century before the Christian æra, by the Butadæ, one of the most ancient and important Gentes at Athens, who boasted of him as their original ancestor: the genealogy of the great Athenian orator Lykurgus, a member of this family, drawn up by his son Abrôn, and painted on a public tablet in the Erechtheion, contained as its first and highest name, Erechtheus, son of Hêphæstos and the Earth. In the Erechtheion, Erechtheus was worshipped conjointly with Athênê: he was identified with the god Poseidôn, and bore the denomination of Poseidôn Erech-

---

[1] Iliad, ii. 546. Odyss. vii. 81.—

Οἳ δ' ἄρ' Ἀθήνας εἶχον.........
Δῆμον Ἐρεχθῆος μεγαλήτορος, ὃν ποτ' Ἀθήνη
Θρέψε, Διὸς θυγάτηρ, τέκε δὲ ζείδωρος Ἄρουρα,
Κὰδ δ' ἐν Ἀθήνῃσ' εἶσεν ἑῷ ἐνὶ πίονι νηῷ,
Ἐνθάδε μιν ταύροισι καὶ ἀρνειοῖς ἱλάονται
Κοῦροι Ἀθηναίων, περιτελλουένων ἐνιαυτῶν.

theus : one of the family of the Butadæ, chosen among themselves
by lot, enjoyed the privilege and performed the functions of his
hereditary priest.[1] Herodotus also assigns the same earth-born
origin to Erechtheus:[2] but Pindar, the old poem called the Da-
nais, Euripidês and Apollodôrus — all name Erichthonius, son of
Hêphæstos and the Earth, as the being who was thus adopted
and made the temple-companion of Athênê, while Apollodôrus in
another place identifies Erichthonius with Poseidôn.[3] The Homeric scholiast treated Erechtheus and Erichthonius as the same
person under two names :[4] and since, in regard to such mythical
persons, there exists no other test of identity of the subject except perfect similarity of the attributes, this seems the reasonable
conclusion.

We may presume, from the testimony of Homer, that the first
and oldest conception of Athens and its sacred acropolis places it
under the special protection, and represents it as the settlement
and favorite abode of Athênê, jointly with Poseidôn ; the latter
being the inferior, though the chosen companion of the former,
and therefore exchanging his divine appellation for the cognomen of Erechtheus. But the country called Attica, which,
during the historical ages, forms one social and political aggregate
with Athens, was originally distributed into many independent

---

[1] See the Life of Lykurgus, in Plutarch's (I call it by that name, as it is
always printed with his works) Lives of the Ten Orators, tom. iv. p. 382–
384, Wytt. Κατῆγον δὲ τὸ γένος ἀπὸ τούτων καὶ 'Ερεχθέως τοῦ Γῆς καὶ
'Ηφαίστου ....καὶ εστιν αὐτὴ ἡ καταγωγὴ τοῦ γένους τῶν ἱερασαμένων
τοῦ Ποσειδῶνος, etc. °Ος τὴν ἱερωσύνην Ποσειδῶνος 'Ερεχθέως εἶχε (pp.
382, 383). Erechtheus Πάρεδρος of Athênê—Aristidês, Panathenaic. p.
184, with the Scholia of Frommel.

Butês, the eponymus of the Butadæ, is the first priest of Poseidôn Erichthonius: Apollod. iii. 15, 1. So Kallais (Xenoph. Sympos. viii. 40), ἱερεὺς
θεῶν τῶν ἀπ' 'Ερεχθέως.

[2] Herodot. viii. 55.

[3] Harpokration, v. Αὐτοχθών. 'Ο δὲ Πίνδαρος καὶ ὁ τὴν Δαναίδα πεποιηκὼς
φασιν, 'Εριχθόνιον ἐξ 'Ηφαίστου καὶ Γῆς φανῆναι. Euripidês, Ion. 21.
Apollod. iii. 14, 6 ; 15, 1. Compare Plato, Timæus, c. 6.

[4] Schol. ad Iliad. ii. 546, where he cites also Kallimachus for the story of
Erichthonius. Etymologicon Magn. 'Ερεχθεύς. Plato (Kritias, c. 4) employs vague and general language to describe the agency of Hêphæstos and
Athênê, which the old fable in Apollodôrus (iii. 14, 6) details in coarser
terms. See Ovid, Metam. ii. 757.

dêmes or cantons, and included, besides, various religious clans or hereditary sects (if the expression may be permitted); that is, a multitude of persons not necessarily living together in the same locality, but bound together by an hereditary communion of sacred rites, and claiming privileges, as well as performing obligations, founded upon the traditional authority of divine persons for whom they had a common veneration. Even down to the beginning of the Peloponnêsian war, the demots of the various Attic dêmes, though long since embodied in the larger political union of Attica, and having no wish for separation, still retained the recollection of their original political autonomy. They lived in their own separate localities, resorted habitually to their own temples, and visited Athens only occasionally for private or political business, or for the great public festivals. Each of these aggregates, political as well as religious, had its own eponymous god or hero, with a genealogy more or less extended, and a train of mythical incidents more or less copious, attached to his name, according to the fancy of the local exegetes and poets. The eponymous heroes Marathôn, Dekelus, Kolônus, or Phlius, had each their own title to worship, and their own position as themes of legendary narrative, independent of Erechtheus, or Poseidôn, or Athênê, the patrons of the acropolis common to all of them.

But neither the archæology of Attica, nor that of its various component fractions, was much dwelt upon by the ancient epic poets of Greece. Thêseus is noticed both in the Iliad and Odyssey as having carried off from Krête Ariadnê, the daughter of Minos — thus commencing that connection between the Krêtan and Athenian legends which we afterwards find so largely amplified — and the sons of Thêseus take part in the Trojan war.[1] The chief collectors and narrators of the Attic mythes were, the prose logographers, authors of the many compositions called Atthides, or works on Attic archæology. These writers — Hellanikus, the contemporary of Herodotus, is the earliest composer of an Atthis expressly named, though Pherekydês also touched upon the Attic fables — these writers, I say, interwove into one chronological series the legends which either greatly occupied their own fancy, or commanded the most general reverence

---

[1] Æthra, mother of Thêseus, is also mentioned (Homer, Iliad, iii. 144).

among their countrymen. In this way the religious and politicai legends of Eleusis, a town originally independent of Athens, but incorporated with it before the historical age, were worked into one continuous sequence along with those of the Erechtheids. In this way, Kekrops, the eponymous hero of the portion of Attica called Kekropia, came to be placed in the mythical chronology at a higher point even than the primitive god or hero Erechtheus.

Ogygês is said to have reigned in Attica [1] 1020 years before the first Olympiad, or 1796 years B. C. In his time happened the deluge of Deukaliôn, which destroyed most of the inhabitants of the country: after a long interval, Kekrops, an indigenous person, half man and half serpent, is given to us by Apollodôrus as the first king of the country: he bestowed upon the land, which had before been called Actê, the name of Kekropia. In his day there ensued a dispute between Athênê and Poseidôn respecting the possession of the acropolis at Athens, which each of them coveted. First, Poseidôn struck the rock with his trident, and produced the well of salt water which existed in it, called the Erechthêis: next came Athênê, who planted the sacred olive-tree ever afterwards seen and venerated in the portion of Erechtheion called the cell of Pandrosus. The twelve gods decided the dispute; and Kekrops having testified before them that Athênê had rendered this inestimable service, they adjudged the spot to her in preference to Poseidôn. Both the ancient olive-tree and the well produced by Poseidôn were seen on the acropolis, in the temple consecrated jointly to Athênê and Erechtheus, throughout the historical ages. Poseidôn, as a mark of his wrath for the

---

[1] Hellanikus, Fragm. 62; Philochor. Fragm. 8, ap. Euseb. Præp. Evang. x. 10. p. 489. Larcher (Chronologie d'Hérodote, ch. ix. s. 1. p. 278) treats both the historical personality and the date of Ogygês as perfectly well authenticated.

It is not probable that Philochorus should have given any calculation of time having reference to Olympiads; and hardly conceivable that Hellanikus should have done so. Justin Martyr quotes Hellanikus and Philochorus as having mentioned Moses, — ὡς σφόδρα ἀρχαίου καὶ παλαιοῦ τῶν Ἰουδαίων ἄρχοντος Μωϋσέως μέμνηνται — which is still more incredible even than the assertion of Eusebius about their having fixed the date of Ogygês by Olympiads (see Philochor. Fragm. 9).

preference given to Athênê, inundated the Thriasian plain with water.[1]
During the reign of Kekrops, Attica was laid waste by Karian pirates on the coast, and by invasions of the Aônian inhabitants from Bœôtia. Kekrops distributed the inhabitants of Attica into twelve local sections — Kekropia, Tetrapolis, Epakria, Dekeleia, Eleusis, Aphidna, Thorikus, Braurôn, Kythêrus, Sphêttus, Kêphisius, Phalerus. Wishing to ascertain the number of inhabitants, he commanded each man to cast a single stone into a general heap: the number of stones was counted, and it was found that there were twenty thousand.[2]

Kekrops married the daughter of Aktæus, who (according to Pausanias's version) had been king of the country before him, and had called it by the name of Aktæa.[3] By her he had three daughters, Aglaurus, Ersê and Pandrosus, and a son, Erysichthôn. Kekrops is called by Pausanias contemporary of the Arcadian Lykaôn, and is favorably contrasted with that savage prince in respect of his piety and humanity.[4] Though he has been often designated in modern histories as an immigrant from Egypt into Attica,

---

[1] Apollod. iii. 14,1; Herodot. viii. 55; Ovid. Metam. vi. 72. The story current among the Athenians represented Kekrops as the judge of this controversy (Xenoph. Memor. iii. 5, 10).

The impressions of the trident of Poseidôn were still shown upon the rock in the time of Pausanias (Pausan. i. 26, 4). For the sanctity of the ancient olive-tree, see the narrative of Herodotus (l. c.), relating what happened to it when Xerxês occupied the acropolis. As this tale seems to have attached itself specially to the local peculiarities of the Erechtheium, the part which Poseidôn plays in it is somewhat mean: that god appears to greater advantage in the neighborhood of the Ἱπποτὴς Κολωνὸς, as described in the beautiful Chorus of Sophoklês (Œdip. Colon. 690–712).

A curious rationalization of the monstrous form ascribed to Kekrops (διφυὴς) in Plutarch (Sera Num. Vindict. p. 551).

[2] Philochor. ap. Strabo. ix. p. 397.

[3] The Parian chronological marble designates Aktæus as an autochthonous person. Marmor Parium, Epoch. 3. Pausan. i. 2, 5. Philochorus treated Aktæus as a fictitious name (Fragm. 8, ut sup.).

[4] Pausan. viii. 2. 2. The three daughters of Kekrops were not unnoticed in the mythes (Ovid, Metam. ii. 739): the tale of Kephalus, son of Hersê by Hermês, who was stolen away by the goddess Eôs or Hêmera in consequence of his surpassing beauty, was told in more than one of the Hesiodic poems (Pausan. i. 3, 1; Hesiod. Theog. 986). See also Eurip. Ion. 269.

yet the far greater number of ancient authorities represent him as indigenous or earth-born.[1]

Erysichthôn died without issue, and Kranaus succeeded him, — another autochthonous person and another eponymus, — for the name Kranai was an old denomination of the inhabitants of Attica.[2] Kranaus was dethroned by Amphiktyôn, by some called an autochthonous man; by others, a son of Deukaliôn: Amphiktyôn in his turn was expelled by Erichthonius, son of Hêphæstos and the Earth, — the same person apparently as Erechtheus, but inserted by Apollodôrus at this point of the series. Erichthonius, the pupil and favored companion of Athênê, placed in the acropolis the original Palladium or wooden statue of that goddess, said to have dropped from heaven : he was moreover the first to celebrate the festival of the Panathenæa. He married the nymph Pasithea, and had for his son and successor Pandiôn.[3] Erichthonius was the first person who taught the art of breaking in horses to the yoke, and who drove a chariot and four.[4]

In the time of Pandiôn, who succeeded to Erichthonius, Dionysus and Dêmêtêr both came into Attica : the latter was received by Keleos at Eleusis.[5] Pandiôn married the nymph Zeuxippê, and had twin sons, Erechtheus and Butês, and two daughters, Proknê and Philomêla. The two latter are the subjects of a memorable and well-known legend. Pandiôn having received aid in repelling the Thêbans from Têreus, king of Thrace, gave him his daughter Proknê in marriage, by whom he had a son, Itys. The beautiful Philomêla, going to visit her sister, inspired the barbarous Thracian with an irresistible passion : he violated her person, confined her in a distant pastoral hut, and pretended that she was dead, cutting out her tongue to prevent her from revealing the truth. After a long interval, Philomêla found means to acquaint her sister of the cruel deed which had been perpetrated ; she wove into a garment words describing her melancholy condition, and despatched it

---

[1] Jul. Africanus also (ap. Euseb. x. 9. p. 486–488) calls Kekrops γηγενὴς and αὐτοχϑών.

[2] Herod. viii. 44. Κρανααὶ 'Αϑῆναι, Pindar.

[3] Apollod. iii. 14. Pausan. i. 26, 7.　　　[4] Virgil, Georgic iii. 114.

[5] The mythe of the visit of Dêmêtêr to Eleusis, on which occasion she vouchsafed to teach her holy rites to the leading Eleusinians, is more fully touched upon in a previous chapter (see *ante*, p. 50).

by a trusty messenger. Proknê, overwhelmed with sorrow and anger, took advantage of thé free egress enjoyed by women during the Bacchanalian festival to go and release her sister: the two sisters then revenged themselves upon Têreus by killing the boy Itys, and serving him up for his father to eat: after the meal had been finished, the horrid truth was revealed to him. Têréus snatched a hatchet to put Proknê to death: she fled, along with Philomêla, and all the three were changed into birds—Proknê became a swallow, Philomêla a nightingale, and Têreus an hoopoe.[1] This tale, so popular with the poets, and so illustrative of the general character of Grecian legend, is not less remarkable in another point of view—that the great historian Thucydidês seems to allude to it as an historical fact,[2] not however directly mentioning the final metamorphosis.

After the death of Pandiôn, Erechtheus succeeded to the kingdom, and his brother, Butês, became priest of Poseidôn Erichthonius, a function which his descendants ever afterwards exercised, the Butadæ or Eteobutadæ. Erechtheus seems to appear in three characters in the fabulous history of Athens—as a god,

---

[1] Apollod. iii. 14, 8; Æsch. Supplic. 61; Soph. Elektr. 107; Ovid, Metamorph. vi. 425–670. Hyginus gives the fable with some additional circum stances, fab. 45. Antoninus Liberalis (Narr. 11), or Bœus, from whom he copies, has composed a new narrative by combining together the names of Pandareos and Aêdon, as given in the Odyssey, xix. 523, and the adventures of the old Attic fable. The hoopoe still continued the habit of chasing the nightingale; it was to the Athenians a present fact. See Schol. Aristoph. Aves, 212.

[2] Thucyd. ii. 29. He makes express mention of the nightingale in connection with the story, though not of the metamorphosis. See below, chap. xvi. p. 544, note 2. So also does Pausanias mention and reason upon it as a real incident: he founds upon it several moral reflections (i. 5, 4; x. 4, 5): the author of the Λόγος 'Επιτάφιος, ascribed to Demosthenês, treats it in the same manner, as a fact ennobling the tribe Pandionis, of which Pandiôn was the eponymus. The same author, in touching upon Kekrops, the eponymus of the Kekropis tribe, cannot believe literally the story of his being half man and half serpent: he rationalizes it by saying that Kekrops was so called because in wisdom he was like a man, in strength like a serpent (Demosth. p. 1397, 1398, Reiske). Hesiod glances at the fable (Opp. Di. 566), ὀρθρογόη Πανδιονὶς ὧρτο χελιδών; see also Ælian, V. H. xii. 20. The subject was handled by Sophoklês in his lost Têreus.

Poseidôn Erechtheus[1] — as a hero, Erechtheus, son of the Earth — and now, as a king, son of Pandiôn : so much did the ideas of divine and human rule become confounded and blended together in the imagination of the Greeks in reviewing their early times. The daughters of Erechtheus were not less celebrated in Athenian legend than those of Pandiôn. Prokris, one of them, is among the heroines seen by Odysseus in Hadês : she became the wife of Kephalus, son of Deionês, and lived in the Attic dême of Thorikus. Kephalus tried her fidelity by pretending that he was going away for a long period; but shortly returned, disguising his person and bringing with him a splendid necklace. He presented himself to Prokris without being recognized, and succeeded in triumphing over her chastity. Having accomplished this object, he revealed to her his true character : she earnestly besought his forgiveness, and prevailed upon him to grant it. Nevertheless he became shortly afterwards the unintentional author of her death : for he was fond of hunting, and staid out a long time on his excursions, so that Prokris suspected him of visiting some rival. She determined to watch him by concealing herself in a thicket near the place of his midday repose; and when Kephalus implored the presence of Nephelê (a cloud) to protect him from the sun's rays, she suddenly started from her hiding-place : Kephalus, thus disturbed, cast his hunting-spear unknowingly into the thicket and slew his wife. Erechtheus interred her with great magnificence, and Kephalus was tried for the act before the court of Areopagus, which condemned him to exile.[2]

Kreüsa, another daughter of Erechtheus, seduced by Apollo, becomes the mother of Iôn, whom she exposes immediately after his birth in the cave north of the acropolis, concealing the fact from every one. Apollo prevails upon Hermês to convey the new-born child to Delphi, where he is brought up as a servant of the temple, without knowing his parents. Kreüsa marries Xuthus, son of Æolus, but continuing childless, she goes with Xuthus to

---

[1] Poseidôn is sometimes spoken of under the name of Erechtheus simply (Lycophrôn, 158). See Hesychius, v. 'Ερεχθεύς.

[2] Pherekydês, Fragm. 77, Didot; ap. Schol. ad Odyss. xi. 320; Hellanikus Fr. 82; ap. Schol. Eurip. Orest. 1648: Apollodôrus (iii 15, 1) gives the story differently.

the Delphian oracle to inquire for a remedy. The god presents
to them Iôn, and desires them to adopt him as their son: their
son Achæus is afterwards born to them, and Iôn and Achæus
become the eponyms of the Iônians and Achæans.[1]

Oreithyia, the third daughter of Erechtheus, was stolen away
by the god Boreas while amusing herself on the banks of the
Ilissus, and carried to his residence in Thrace. The two sons of
this marriage, Zêtês and Kalais, were born with wings: they
took part in the Argonautic expedition, and engaged in the pursuit of the Harpies : they were slain at Tênos by Hêraklês.
Kleopatra, the daughter of Boreas and Oreithyia, was married to
Phineus, and had two sons, Plexippus and Pandiôn ; but Phineus
afterwards espoused a second wife, Idæa, the daughter of Dardanus, who, detesting the two sons of the former bed, accused them
falsely of attempting her chastity, and persuaded. Phineus in his
wrath to put out the eyes of both. For this cruel proceeding he
was punished by the Argonauts in the course of their voyage.[2]

On more than one occasion the Athenians derived, or at least
believed themselves to have derived, important benefits from this
marriage of Boreas with the daughter of their primæval hero:
one inestimable service, rendered at a juncture highly critical for

---

[1] Upon this story of Iôn is founded the tragedy of Euripidês which bears
that name. I conceive many of the points of that tragedy to be of the invention of Euripidês himself: but to represent Iôn as son of Apollo, not of
Xuthus, seems a genuine Attic legend. Respecting this drama, see O. Müller, Hist. of Dorians, ii. 2, 13–15. I doubt however the distinction which he
draws between the Ionians and the other population of Attica.

[2] Apollodôr. iii. 15, 2; Plato, Phædr. c. 3 ; Sophok. Antig. 984; also the
copious Scholion on Apollôn. Rhod. i. 212.

The tale of Phineus is told very differently in the Argonautic expedition
as given by Apollônius Rhodius, ii. 180. From Sophoklês we learn that
this·was the Attic version.

The two winged sons of Boreas and their chase of the Harpies were noticed in the Hesiodic Catalogue (see Schol. Apollôn. Rhod. ii. 296). But
whether the Attic legend of Oreithyia was recognized in the Hesiodic poems
seems not certain.

Both Æschylus and Sophoklês composed dramas on the subject of Oreithyia (Longin. de Sublimit. c. 3). " Orithyia Atheniensis, filia Terrigenæ,
et a Borea in Thraciam rapta." (Servius ad Virg. Æneid. xii. 83). Terrigenæ is the γηγενὴς Ἐρεχθεύς. Philochorus (Fragm. 30) rationalized the
story, and said that it alluded to the effects of a violent wind.

Grecian independence, deserves to be specified.¹ At the time of
the invasion of Greece by Xerxês, the Grecian fleet was assembled at Chalcis and Artemision in Eubœa, awaiting the approach
of the Persian force, so overwhelming in its numbers as well by
sea as on land. The Persian fleet had reached the coast of Magnêsia and the south-eastern corner of Thessaly without any material damage, when the Athenians were instructed by an oracle
" to invoke the aid of their son-in-law." Understanding the advice to point to Boreas, they supplicated his aid and that of Oreithyia, most earnestly, as well by prayer as by sacrifice,² and the
event corresponded to their wishes. A furious north-easterly wind
immediately arose, and continued for three days to afflict the Persian fleet as it lay on an unprotected coast: the number of ships
driven ashore, both vessels of war and of provision, was immense,
and the injury done to the armament was never thoroughly repaired. Such was the powerful succor which the Athenians derived, at a time of their utmost need, from their son-in-law Boreas;
and their gratitude was shown by consecrating to him a new temple on the banks of the Ilissus.

The three remaining daughters of Erechtheus — he had six in
all³ — were in Athenian legend yet more venerated than their
sisters, on account of having voluntarily devoted themselves to
death for the safety of their country. Eumolpus of Eleusis was
the son of Poseidôn and the eponymous hero of the sacred gens
called the Eumolpids, in whom the principal functions, appertain-
ing to the mysterious rites of Dêmêtêr at Eleusis, were vested
by hereditary privilege: he made war upon Erechtheus and the

---

¹ Herodot. vii. 189. Οἱ δ' ὦν Ἀθηναῖοί σφι λέγουσι βοηθήσαντα τὸν Βορῆν
πρότερον, καὶ τότε ἐκεῖνα κατεργάσασθαι· καὶ ἱρὸν ἀπελθόντες Βορέω ἱδρύσαντο παρὰ ποταμὸν Ἰλισσον

² Herodot. l. c. Ἀθηναῖοι τὸν Βορῆν ἐκ θεοπροπίου ἐπεκαλέσαντο, ἐλθόν-
τος σφι ἄλλου χρηστηρίου, τὸν γαμβρὸν ἐπίκουρον καλέσασθαι. Βορῆς δὲ,
κατὰ τὸν Ἑλλήνων λόγον ἔχει γυναῖκα Ἀττικὴν, Ὠρειθυίην τὴν Ἐρεχθῆος.
Κατὰ δὴ τὸ κῆδος τοῦτο, οἱ Ἀθηναῖοι, συμβαλλεόμενοί σφι τὸν Βορῆν γαμβρὸν·
εἶναι, etc.

³ Suidas and Photius, v. Πάρθενοι: Protogeneia and Pandôra are given
as the names of two of them. The sacrifice of Pandôra, in the Iambi of
Hippônax (Hippônact. Fragm. xxi. Welck. ap. Athen. ix. p. 370), seems to
allude to this daughter of Erechtheus.

Athenians, with the aid of a body of Thracian allies; indeed it appears that the legends of Athens, originally foreign and un- friendly to those of Eleusis, represented him as having been him- self a Thracian born and an immigrant into Attica.[1] Respecting Eumolpus however and his parentage, the discrepancies much exceed even the measure of license usual in the legendary ge nealogies, and some critics, both ancient and modern, have sough*t* to reconcile these contradictions by the usual stratagem of sup- posing two or three different persons of the same name. Even Pausanias, so familiar with this class of unsworn witnesses, com- plains of the want of native Eleusinian genealogists,[2] and of the extreme license of fiction in which other authors had indulged.

In the Homeric Hymn to Dêmêtêr, the most ancient testimony before us, — composed, to all appearance, earlier than the com- plete incorporation of Eleusis with Athens, — Eumolpus appears (to repeat briefly what has been stated in a previous chapter) as one of the native chiefs or princes of Eleusis, along with Tripto-

---

[1] Apollodôr. iii. 15, 3; Thucyd. ii. 15; Iskoratês (Panegyr, t. i. p. 206; Panathenaic. t. ii. p. 560, Auger), Lykurgus, cont. Leocrat. p. 201, Reiske; Pausan. i. 38, 3; Euripid. Erechth. Fragm. The Schol. ad. Soph. Œd. Col. 1048 gives valuable citations from Ister, Akestodorus and Androtiôn : we see that the inquirers of antiquity found it difficult to explain how the Eumol- pids could have acquired their ascendant privileges in the management of the Eleusinia, seeing that Eumolpus himself was a foreigner. — Ζητεῖται, τί δήποτε οἱ Εὐμολπίδαι τῶν τελετῶν ἐξάρχουσι, ξένοι ὄντες. Thucydidês does *not* call Eumolpus a Thracian: Strabo's language is very large and vague (vii. p. 321): Iskoratês says that he assailed Athens in order to vindicate the rights of his father Poseidôn to the sovereign patronage of the city. Hy- ginus copies this (fab. 46).

[2] Pausan. i. 38, 3. Ἐλευσίνιοί τε ἀρχαῖοι, ἅτε οὐ προσόντων σφίσι γενεα- λόγων, ἄλλα τε πλάσασθαι δεδώκασι καὶ μάλιστα ἐς τὰ γένη τῶν ἡρώων. See Heyne ad Apollodôr. iii. 15, 4. "Eumolpi nomen modo communicatum pluribus, modo plurium hominum res et facta cumulata in unum. Is ad quem Hercules venisse dicitur, senior ætate fuit: antiquior est is de quo hoc loco agitur .... antecessisse tamen hunc debet alius, qui cum Triptolemo vixit," etc. See the learned and valuable comments of Lobeck in his Aglao- phamus, tom. i. p. 206–213: in regard to the discrepancies of this narrative he observes, I think, with great justice (p. 211), " quo uno exemplo ex innu- merabilibus delecto, arguitur eorum temeritas, qui ex variis discordibusque poetarum et mythographorum narratiunculis, antiquæ famæ formam et quasi lineamenta recognosci posse sperant."

9*

lemus, Dioklês, Polyxeinus and Dolichus: Keleos is the king,
or principal among these chiefs, the son or lineal descendant of
the eponymous Eleusis himself. To these chiefs, and to the three
daughters of Keleos, the goddess Dêmêtêr comes in her sorrow
for the loss of her daughter Persephonê: being hospitably entertained by Keleos she reveals her true character, commands that
a temple shall be built to her at Eleusis, and prescribes to them
the rites according to which they are to worship her.[1] Such
seems to have been the ancient story of the Eleusinians respecting their own religious antiquities: Keleos, with Metaneira his
wife, and the other chiefs here mentioned, were worshipped at
Eleusis, and from thence transferred to Athens as local gods or
heroes.[2] Eleusis became incorporated with Athens, apparently
not very long before the time of Solôn; and the Eleusinian worship of Dêmêtêr was then received into the great religious
solemnities of the Athenian state, to which it owes its remarkable
subsequent extension and commanding influence. In the Atti-
cized worship of the Eleusinian Dêmêtêr, the Eumolpids and the
Kêrȳkes were the principal hereditary functionaries: Eumolpus,
the eponym of this great family, came thus to play the principal
part in the Athenian legendary version of the war between
Athens and Eleusis. An oracle had pronounced that Athens
could only be rescued from his attack by the death of the three
daughters of Erechtheus; their generous patriotism consented to
the sacrifice, and their father put them to death. He then went
forth confidently to the battle, totally vanquished the enemy, and

---

[1] Homer, Hymn. ad Cerer. 153–475. —

.........'Η δὲ κίουσα θεμιστοπόλοις βασιλεῦσι
Δεῖξεν Τριπτολέμῳ τε, Διόκλεί τε πληξίππῳ,
Εὐμόλπου τε βίῃ, Κελέῳ θ' ἡγήτορι λαῶν,
Δρησμοσύνην ἱερῶν.

Also v. 105.

Τὴν δὲ ἴδον Κελέοιο 'Ελευσινίδαο θύγατρες.

The hero Eleusis is mentioned in Pausanias, i. 38, 7: some said that he was
the son of Hermês, others that he was the son of Ogygus. Compare Hygin.
f. 147.

[2] Keleos and Metaneira were worshipped by the Athenians with divine
honors (Athenagoras, Legat. p. 53, ed. Oxon.): perhaps he confounds divine
and heroic honors, as the Christian controversialists against Paganism were
disposed to do. Triptolemus had a temple at Eleusis (Pausan. i. 38, 6).

killed Eumolpus with his own hand.¹ Erechtheus was worshipped as a god, and his daughters as goddesses, at Athens.² Their names and their exalted devotion were cited along with those of the warriors of Marathôn, in the public assembly of Athens, by orators who sought to arouse the languid patriot, or to denounce the cowardly deserter; and the people listened both to one and the other with analogous feelings of grateful veneration, as well as with equally unsuspecting faith in the matter of fact.³

---

¹ Apollodôr. iii. 15, 4. Some said that Immaradus, son of Eumolpus, had been killed by Erechtheus (Pausan. i. 5, 2); others, that both Eumolpus and his son had experienced this fate (Schol. ad Eurip. Phœniss. 854). But we learn from Pausanias himself what the story in the interior of the Erechtheion was, — that Erechtheus killed Eumolpus (i. 27, 3).

² Cicero, Nat. Deor. iii. 19; Philochor. ap. Schol. Œdip. Col. 100. Three daughters of Erechtheus perished, and three daughters were worshipped (Apollodôr. iii. 15, 4; Hesychius, Ζεύγος τριπάρϑενον; Eurip. Erechtheus. Fragm. 3, Dindorf); but both Euripidês and Apollodôrus said that Erechtheus was only required to sacrifice, and only did sacrifice, one, — the other two slew themselves voluntarily, from affection for their sister. I cannot but think (in spite of the opinion of Welcker to the contrary, Griechisch. Tragöd. ii. p. 722) that the genuine legend represented Erechtheus as having sacrificed all three, as appears in the Iôn of Euripidês (276) : —

> Ιôν.   Πατὴρ 'Ερεχϑεὺς σὰς ἔϑυσε συγγόνους;
> CREÜSA.   'Ετλη πρὸ γαίας σφάγια παρϑένους κτανεῖν.
> Ιôν.   Σὺ δ' ἐξεσώϑης πῶς κασιγνήτων μόνη;
> CREÜSA.   Βρέφος νέογνον μητρὸς ἦν ἐν ἀγκάλαις.

Compare with this passage, Demosthen. Λόγος 'Επιτάφ. p. 1397, Reisk. Just before, the death of the three daughters of Kekrops, for infringing the commands of Athênê, had been mentioned. Euripidês modified this in his Erechtheus, for he there introduced the mother Praxithea consenting to the immolation of one daughter, for the rescue of the country from a foreign invader: to propose to a mother the immolation of three daughters at once, would have been too revolting. In most instances we find the strongly marked features, the distinct and glaring incidents as well as the dark contrasts, belong to the Hesiodic or old Post-Homeric legend; the changes made afterwards go to soften, dilute, and to complicate, in proportion as the feelings of the public become milder and more humane; sometimes however the later poets add new horrors.

³ See the striking evidence contained in the oration of Lykurgus against Leocratês (p. 201-204. Reiske; Demosthen. Λόγ. 'Επιτάφ. l. c.; and Xenophon, Memor. iii. 5, 9): from the two latter passages we see that the Athenian story represented the invasion under Eumolpus as a combined assault from the western continent.

Though Erechtheus gained the victory over Eumolpus, yet the story represents Poseidôn as having put an end to the life and reign of Erechtheus, who was (it seems) slain in the battle. He was succeeded by his son Kekrops II., and the latter again by his son Pandiôn II.,[1] — two names unmarked by any incidents, and which appear to be mere duplication of the former Kekrops and Pandiôn, placed there by the genealogizers for the purpose of filling up what seemed to them a chronological chasm. The Attic legends were associated chiefly with a few names of respected eponymous personages; and if the persons called the children of Pandiôn were too numerous to admit of their being conveniently ascribed to one father, there was no difficulty in supposing a second prince of the same name.

Apollodôrus passes at once from Erechtheus to his son Kekrops II., then to Pandiôn II., next to the four sons of the latter, Ægeus, Pallas, Nisus and Lykus. But the tragedians here insert the story of Xuthus, Kreüsa and Iôn; the latter being the son of Kreüsa by Apollo, but given by the god to Xuthus, and adopted by the latter as his own. Iôn becomes the successor of Erechtheus, and his sons Teleon, Hoplês, Argadês and Aigikorês become the eponyms of the four ancient tribes of Athens, which subsisted until the revolution of Kleisthenês. Iôn himself is the eponym of the Iônic race both in Asia, in Europe, and in the Ægean islands: Dôrus and Achæus are the sons of Kreüsa by Xuthus, so that Iôn is distinguished from both of them by being of divine parentage.[2] According to the story given by Philochorus, Iôn rendered such essential service in rescuing the Athenians from the attack of the Thracians under Eumolpus, that he was afterwards made king of the country, and distributed all the inhabitants into four tribes or castes, corresponding to different modes of life, — soldiers, husbandmen, goatherds, and artisans.[3] And it seems that the legend explanatory of the origin of the festival Boëdromia, originally important enough to furnish a name

---

[1] Apollodôr. iii. 15, 5; Eurip. Iôn, 282; Erechth. Fragm. 20, Dindorf.

[2] Eurip. Iôn. 1570–1595   The Kreüsa of Sophoklês, a lost tragedy, seems to have related to the same subject.

Pausanias (vii. 1, 2) tells us that Xuthus was chosen to arbitrate between the contending claims of the sons of Erechtheus.

[3] Philochor. ap. Harpocrat. v. Βοηδρόμια; Strabo, viii. p. 383

to one of the Athenian months, was attached to the aid thus rendered by Iôn.[1]
We pass from Iôn to persons of far greater mythical dignity and interest, — Ægeus and his son Thêseus.

Pandiôn had four sons, Ægeus, Nisus, Lykus, and Pallas, between whom he divided his dominions. Nisus received the territory of Megaris, which had been under the sway of Pandiôn, and there founded the seaport of Nisæa. Lykus was made king of the eastern coast, but a dispute afterwards ensued, and he quitted the country altogether, to establish himself on the southern coast of Asia Minor among the Termilæ, to whom he gave the name of Lykians.[2] Ægeus, as the eldest of the four, became king of Athens; but Pallas received a portion both of the southwestern coast and the interior, and he as well as his children appear as frequent enemies both to Ægeus and to Thêseus. Pallas is the eponym of the dême Pallênê, and the stories respecting him and his sons seem to be connected with old and standing feuds among the different dêmes of Attica, originally independent communities. These feuds penetrated into the legend, and explain the story which we find that Ægeus and Thêseus were not genuine Erechtheids, the former being denominated a supposititious child to Pandiôn.[3]

Ægeus[4] has little importance in the mythical history except as the father of Thêseus : it may even be doubted whether his name is anything more than a mere cognomen of the god Poseidôn, who was (as we are told) the real father of this great Attic Hêraklês. As I pretend only to give a very brief outline of the general territory of Grecian legend, I cannot permit myself to recount in

---

[1] Philochor. ap. Harpocrat. v. Βοηδρόμια.

[2] Sophokl. ap. Strab. ix. p. 392; Herodot. i. 173; Strabo, xii. p. 573.

[3] Plutarch, Thêseus, c. 13. Αἰγεὺς θετὸς γενόμενος Πανδίονι, καὶ μηδὲν τοῖς Ἐρεχθείδαις προσήκων. Apollodôr. iii. 15, 6.

[4] Ægeus had by Mêdea (who took refuge at Athens after her flight from Corinth) a son named Mêdus, who passed into Asia, and was considered as the eponymus and progenitor of the Median people. Datis, the general who commanded the invading Persian army at the battle of Marathôn, sent a formal communication to the Athenians announcing himself as the descendant of Mêdus, and requiring to be admitted as king of Attica : such is the statement of Diodôrus (Exc. Vatic. vii.– x. 48 : see also Schol. Aristophan Pac. 289).

detail the chivalrous career of Thêseus, who is found both in the
Kalydônian boar-hunt and in the Argonautic expedition — his
personal and victorious encounters with the robbers Sinnis, Pro-
crustês, Periphêtês, Scirôn and others — his valuable service in
ridding his country of the Krommyonian sow and the Marathônian bull — his conquest of the Minotaur in Krête, and his escape
from the dangers of the labyrinth by the aid of Ariadnê, whom
he subsequently carries off and abandons — his many amorous
adventures, and his expeditions both against the Amazons and
into the under-world along with Peirithous.[1]

Thucydidês delineates the character of Thêseus as a man who
combined sagacity with political power, and who conferred upon
his country the inestimable benefit of uniting all the separate and
self-governing dêmes of Attica into one common political society.[2]
From the well-earned reverence attached to the assertion of
Thucydidês, it has been customary to reason upon this assertion
as if it were historically authentic, and to treat the romantic
attributes which we find in Plutarch and Diodôrus as if they were
fiction superinduced upon this basis of fact. Such a view of the
case is in my judgment erroneous. The athletic and amorous
knight-errant is the old version of the character — the profound

---

[1] Ovid, Metamorph. vii. 433.—

.................." Te, maxime Theseu,
Mirata est Marathon Cretæi sanguine Tauri :
Quodque Suis securus arat Cromyona colonus,
Munus opusque tuum est. Tellus Epidauria per te
Clavigeram vidit Vulcani occumbere prolem :
Vidit et immanem Cephisias ora Procrustem.
Cercyonis letum vidit Cerealis Eleusin.
Occidit ille Sinis," etc.

Respecting the amours of Thêseus, Ister especially seems to have entereo
into great details ; but some of them were noticed both in the Hesiodic
poems and by Kekrops, not to mention Pherekydês (Athen. xiii. p. 557).
Peirithous, the intimate friend and companion of Thêseus, is the epónymous
hero of the Attic dême or gens Perithoidæ (Ephorus ap. Photium, v. Πϵρι-
ϑοῖδαι).

[2] Thuc. ii. 15. ' Επειδὴ δὲ Θησεὺς ἐβασίλευσε, γενόμενος μετὰ τοῦ ξυνετοῦ
καὶ δυνατὸς, τά τε ἄλλα διεκόσμησε τὴν χώραν, καὶ κατάλυσας τῶν ἄλλων
πόλεων τά τε βουλευτήρια καὶ τὰς ἀρχὰς, ἐς τὴν νῦν πόλιν........ ξυνῴκισϵ
πάντας.

and long-sighted politician is a subsequent correction, introduced indeed by men of superior mind, but destitute of historical warranty, and arising out of their desire to find reasons of their own for concurring in the veneration which the general public paid more easily and heartily to their national hero. Thêseus, in the Iliad and Odyssey, fights with the Lapithæ against the Centaurs: Thêseus, in the Hesiodic poems, is misguided by his passion for the beautiful Ægle, daughter of Panopeus:[1] and the Thêseus described in Plutarch's biography is in great part a continuation and expansion of these same or similar attributes, mingled with many local legends, explaining, like the Fasti of Ovid, or the lost Aitia of Kallimachus, the original genesis of prevalent religious and social customs.[2] Plutarch has doubtless greatly softened down and modified the adventures which he found in the Attic logographers as well as in the poetical epics called Thêsêis. For in his preface to the life of Thêseus, after having emphatically declared that he is about to transcend the boundary both of the known and the knowable, but that the temptation of comparing the founder of Athens with the founder of Rome is irresistible, he concludes with the following remarkable words: " I pray that this fabulous matter may be so far obedient to my endeavors as to receive, when purified by reason, the aspect of history: in those cases where it haughtily scorns plausibility and will admit no alliance with what is probable, I shall beg for indulgent hearers, willing to receive antique narrative in a mild spirit."[3] We see here that Plutarch sat down, not to recount the old fables as he found them, but to purify them by reason and to impart to them the aspect of history. We have to thank him for having retained, after this purification, so much of what is romantic and marvellous ; but we may be sure that the sources from which he borrowed were more romantic and marvellous still. It was the

---

[1] Iliad, i. 265; Odyss. xi. 321. I do not notice the suspected line, Odyss. xi. 630.

[2] Diodôrus also, from his disposition to assimilate Thêseus to Hêraklês, has given us his chivalrous as well as his political attributes(iv. 61).

[3] Plutarch, Thêseus, i. Εἴη μὲν οὖν ἡμῖν, ἐκκαθαιρόμενον λόγῳ τὸ μυθῶδες ὑπακοῦσαι καὶ λαβεῖν ἱστορίας ὄψιν· ὅπου δ' ἂν αὐθαδῶς τοῦ πιθανοῦ περιφρονῇ, καὶ μὴ δέχηται τὴν πρὸς τὸ εἰκὸς μίξιν, εὐγνωμόνων ἀκροατῶν δεησόμεθα, καὶ πρᾴως τὴν ἀρχαιολογίαν προσδεχομένων.

tendency of the enlightened men of Athens, from the days of
Solôn downwards, to refine and politicize the character of Thêseus :[1] even Peisistratus expunged from one of the Hesiodic
poems the line which described the violent passion of the hero
for the fair Ægle :[2] and the tragic poets found it more congenial
to the feelings of their audience to exhibit him as a dignified
and liberal sovereign, rather than as an adventurous single-handed
fighter. But the logographers and the Alexandrine poets remained more faithful to the old fables. The story of Hekalê, the
hospitable old woman who received and blessed Thêseus when
he went against the Marathônian bull, and whom he found dead
when he came back to recount the news of his success, was
treated by Kallimachus :[3] and Virgil must have had his mind
full of the unrefined legends when he numbered this Attic Hêraklês among the unhappy sufferers condemned to endless penance
in the under-world.[4]

Two however among the Thêseian fables cannot be dismissed
without some special notice, — the war against the Amazons, and
the expedition against Krête. The former strikingly illustrates
the facility as well as the tenacity of Grecian legendary faith ;
the latter embraces the story of Dædalus and Minos, two of the
most eminent among Grecian ante-historical personages.

The Amazons, daughters of Arês and Harmonia,[5] are both

---

[1] See Isokratês, Panathenaic. (t. ii. p. 510–512, Auger) ; Xenoph. Memor.
iii. 5, 10. In the Helenæ Encomium, Isokratês enlarges more upon the personal exploits of Thêseus in conjunction with his great political merits (t. ii.
p. 342–350, Auger).

[2] Plutarch, Thêseus, 20.

[3] See the epigram of Krinagoras, Antholog. Pal. vol. ii. p. 144 ; ep. xv.
ed. Brunck. and Kallimach. Frag. 40.

'Αείδει δ' (Kallimachus) 'Εκάλης τε φιλοξείνοιο καλιήν,
Καὶ Θησεῖ Μαραθὼν οὓς ἐπέθηκε πόνους.

Some beautiful lines are preserved by Suidas, v. 'Επαύλια, περὶ 'Εκάλης
θανούσης (probably spoken by Thêseus himself, see Plutarch, Theseus, c.
14).

'Ιθι, πρηεῖα γυναικῶν,
Τὴν ὁδὸν, ἣν ἀνίαι θυμαλγέες οὐ περόωσιν ·
Πόλλακι σεῖ', ὦ μαῖα, φιλοξείνοιο καλιῆς
Μνησόμεθα· ξυνὸν γὰρ ἐπαύλιον ἔσκεν ἅπασι.

[4] Virgil, Æneid, vi. 617. "Sedet æternumque sedebit Infelix Thêseus."

[5] Pherekyd. Fragm. 25, Didot.

early creations and frequent reproductions of the ancient epic — which was indeed, we may generally remark, largely occupied both with the exploits and sufferings of women, or heroines, the wives and daughters of the Grecian heroes — and which recognized in Pallas Athênê the finished type of an irresistible female warrior. A nation of courageous, hardy and indefatigable women, dwelling apart from men, permitting only a short temporary intercourse for the purpose of renovating their numbers, and burning out their right breast with a view of enabling themselves to draw the bow freely, — this was at once a general type stimulating to the fancy of the poet and a theme eminently popular with his hearers. Nor was it at all repugnant to the faith of the latter — who had no recorded facts to guide them, and no other standard of credibility as to the past except such poetical narratives themselves — to conceive communities of Amazons as having actually existed in anterior time. Accordingly we find these warlike females constantly reappearing in the ancient poems, and universally accepted as past realities. In the Iliad, when Priam wishes to illustrate emphatically the most numerous host in which he ever found himself included, he tells us that it was assembled in Phyrgia, on the banks of the Sangarius, for the purpose of resisting the formidable Amazons. When Bellerophôn is to be employed on a deadly and perilous undertaking,[1] by those who indirectly wish to procure his death, he is despatched against the Amazons. In the Æthiopis of Arktinus, describing the post-Homeric war of Troy, Penthesileia, queen of the Amazons, appears as the most effective ally of the besieged city, and as the most formidable enemy of the Greeks, succumbing only to the invincible might of Achilles.[2] The Argonautic heroes find the Amazons on the river Thermôdon, in their expedition along

---

[1] Iliad, iii. 186 ; vi. 152.

[2] See Proclus's Argument of the lost Æthiopis (Fragm. Epicor. Græcor. ed. Düntzer, p. 16). We are reduced to the first book of Quintus Smyrnæus for some idea of the valor of Penthesileia ; it is supposed to be copied more or less closely from the Æthiopis. See Tychsen's Dissertation prefixed to his edition of Quintus, sections 5 and 12. Compare Dio. Chrysostom. Or. xi. p. 350, Reiske. Philostratus (Heroica, c. 19. p. 751) gives a strange transformation of this old epical narrative into a descent of Amazons upon the island sacred to Achilles.

the southern coast of the Euxine. To the same spot Hêraclês
goes to attack them, in the performance of the ninth labor imposed upon him by Eurystheus, for the purpose of procuring the
girdle of the Amazonian queen, Hippolytê;[1] and we are told
that they had not yet recovered from the losses sustained in this
severe aggression when Thêseus also assaulted and defeated them,
carrying off their queen, Antiopê.[2] This injury they avenged
by invading Attica,—an undertaking as Plutarch justly observes)
"neither trifling nor feminine," especially if according to the
statement of Hellanikus, they crossed the Cimmerian Bosporus
on the winter ice, beginning their march from the Asiatic side of
the Paulus Mæotis.[3] They overcame all the resistances and difficulties of this prodigious march, and penetrated even into Athens
itself, where the final battle, hard-fought and at one time doubtful, by which Thêseus crushed them, was fought—in the very

---

[1] Apollôn. Rhod. ii. 966, 1004; Apollod. ii. 5–9; Diodôr. ii. 46; iv. 16.
The Amazons were supposed to speak the Thracian language (Schol. Apoll
Rhod. ii. 953), though some authors asserted them to be natives of Libyia,
others of Æthiopia (*ib.* 965).

Hellanikus (Frag. 33, ap. Schol. Pindar. Nem. iii. 65) said that all the
Argonauts had assisted Hêraklês in this expedition: the fragmec t of the old
epic poem (perhaps the Ἀμαζόνια) there quoted mentions Telamôn specially.

[2] The many diversities in the story respecting Thêseus and the Amazon
Antiopê are well set forth in Bachet de Meziriac (Commentaires sur Ovide
t. i. p. 317).

Welcker (Der Epische Cyclus, p. 313) supposes that the ancient epic poem
called by Suidas Ἀμαζόνια, related to the invasion of Attica by the Amazons, and that this poem is the same, under another title, as the Ἀτθίς of
Hegesinous cited by Pausanias : I cannot say that he establishes this conjecture satisfactorily, but the chapter is well worth consulting. The epic
Thêsêis seems to have given a version of the Amazonian contest in many
respects different from that which Plutarch has put together out of the logographers (see Plut. Thês. 28): it contained a narrative of many unconnected exploits belonging to Thêseus, and Aristotle censures it on that account
as ill-constructed (Poetic. c. 17).

The Ἀμαζονίς or Ἀμαζονικὰ of Onasus can hardly have been (as Heyne
supposes, ad Apollod. ii. 5, 9) an epic poem : we may infer from the rationalizing tendency of the citation from it (Schol. ad Theocrit. xiii. 46, and
Schol. Apollôn. Rhod. i. 1207) that it was a work in prose. There was an
Ἀμαζονίς by Possis of Magnêsia (Athenæus, vii. p. 296).

[3] Plutarch, Thêseus, 27. Pindar (Olymp. xiii. 84) represents the Amazons
as having come from the extreme north, when Bellerophôn conquers them.

heart of the city. Attic antiquaries confidently pointed out the exact position of the two contending armies : the left wing of the Amazons rested upon the spot occupied by the commemorative monument called the Amazoneion; the right wing touched the Pnyx, the place in which the public assemblies of the Athenian democracy were afterwards held. The details and fluctuations of the combat, as well as the final triumph and consequent truce, were recounted by these authors with as complete faith and as much circumstantiality as those of the battle of Platæa by Herodotus. The sepulchral edifice called the Amazoneion, the tomb or pillar of Antiopê near the western gate of the city — the spot called the Horkomosion near the temple of Thêseus — even the hill of Areiopagus itself, and the sacrifices which it was customary to offer to the Amazons at the periodical festival of the Thêseia — were all so many religious mementos of this victory;[1] which was moreover a favorite subject of art both with the sculptor and the painter, at Athens as well as in other parts of Greece.

No portion of the ante-historical epic appears to have been more deeply worked into the national mind of Greece than this invasion and defeat of the Amazons. It was not only a constant theme of the logographers, but was also familiarly appealed to by the popular orators along with Marathôn and Salamis, among those antique exploits of which their fellow-citizens might justly be proud. It formed a part of the retrospective faith of Herodotus, Lysias, Plato and Isokratês,[2] and the exact date of the event was settled

---

[1] Plutarch, Thêseus, 27–28; Pausan. i. 2, 4; Plato, Axiochus, c. 2; Harpocratiôn, v. 'Αμαζονεῖον; Aristophan. Lysistrat. 678, with the Scholia. Æschyl. (Eumenid. 685) says that the Amazons assaulted the citadel from the Areiopagus : —

Πάγον τ' 'Άρειον τόνδ', 'Αμαζόνων ἕδραν
Σκηνάς τ', ὅτ' ἦλθον Θησέως κατὰ φθόνον
Στρατηλατοῦσαι, καὶ πόλιν νεόπτολιν
Τήνδ' ὑψίπυργον ἀντεπύργωσάν ποτε.

[2] Herodot. ix. 27, Lysias (Epitaph, c. 3) represents the Amazons as ἄρχουσαι πολλῶν ἐθνῶν: the whole race, according to him, was nearly extinguished in their unsuccessful and calamitous invasion of Attica. Isokratês (Panegyric. t. i. p. 206, Auger) says the same; also Panathênaic, t. iii. p. 560, Auger; Demosth. Epitaph. p. 1391. Reisk. Pausanias quotes Pindar's notice of the invasion, and with the fullest belief of its historical reality (vii. 2, 4)

by the chronologists.¹ Nor did the Athenians stand alone in such
a belief. Throughout many other regions of Greece, both European and Asiatic, traditions and memorials of the Amazons were
found. At Megara, at Trœzen, in Laconia near Cape Tænarus,
at Chæroneia in Bœôtia, and in more than one part of Thessaly,
sepulchres or monuments of the Amazons were preserved. The
warlike women (it was said), on their way to Attica, had not
traversed those countries, without leaving some evidences of their
passage.²

Amongst the Asiatic Greeks the supposed traces of the Amazons
were yet more numerous. Their proper territory was asserted to
be the town and plain of Themiskyra, near the Grecian colony of
Amisus, on the river Thermôdôn, a region called after their name
by Roman historians and geographers.³ But they were believed
to have conquered and occupied in early times a much wider range
of territory, extending even to the coast of Iônia and Æolis.
Ephesus, Smyrna, Kymê, Myrina, Paphos and Sinopê were affirmed to have been founded and denominated by them.⁴ Some

Plato mentions the invasion of Attica by the Amazons in the Menexenus
(c. 9), but the passage in the treatise De Legg. c. ii. p. 804, — ἀκούων γὰρ δὴ
μύθους παλαιοὺς πέπεισμαι, etc. — is even a stronger evidence of his own belief. And Xenophôn in the Anabasis, when he compares the quiver and the
hatchet of his barbarous enemies to " those which the Amazons carry," evidently believed himself to be speaking of real persons, though he could have
seen only the costumes and armature of those painted by Mikôn and others
(Anabas. iv. 4, 10 ; compare Æschl. Supplic. 293, and Aristophan. Lysistr.
678 ; Lucian. Anachars, c. 34. v. iii. p. 318).

How copiously the tale was enlarged upon by the authors of the Atthides,
we see in Plutarch, Thêseus, 27–28.

Hekatæus (ap. Steph. Byz. 'Αμαζονεῖον ; also Fragm. 350, 351, 352, Didot) and Xanthus (ap. Hesychium, v. Βουλεψίη) both treated of the Amazons : the latter passage ought to be added to the collection of the Fragments
of Xanthus by Didot.

¹ Clemens Alexandr. Stromat, i. p. 336 ; Marmor Parium, Epoch. 21.
² Plutarch, Thês. 27–28. Steph. Byz. v. 'Αμαζονεῖον. Pausan. ii. 32, 8 ;
iii. 25, 2.
³ Pherekydês ap. Schol. Apollon. Rh. ii. 373–992 ; Justin, ii. 4 ; Strabo,
xii. p. 547, Θεμίσκυραν, τὸ τῶν 'Αμαζόνων οἰκητήριον ; Diodôr. ii. 45–46;
Sallust ap. Serv. ad Virgil. Æneid. xi. 659 ; Pompon. Mela, i. 19 ; Plin. H.
N. vi. 4. The geography of Quintus Curtius (vi. 4) and of Philostratus (Heroic. c. 19) is on this point indefinite, and even inconsistent.

Ephor. Fragm. 87, Didot. Strabo, xi. p. 505 ; xiii p. 573 ; xiii. p. 622

authors placed them in Libya or Ethiopia; and when the Pontic
Greeks on the north-western shore of the Euxine had become
acquainted with the hardy and daring character of the Sarmatian
maidens, — who were obliged to have slain each an enemy in
battle as the condition of obtaining a husband, and who artificially
prevented the growth of the right breast during childhood, — they
could imagine no more satisfactory mode of accounting for such
attributes than by deducing the Sarmatians from a colony of va-
grant Amazons, expelled by the Grecian heroes from their territory on the Thermôdôn.[1] Pindar ascribed the first establishment
of the memorable temple of Artemis at Ephesus to the Amazons.
And Pausanias explains in part the preëminence which this temple enjoyed over every other in Greece by the widely diffused
renown of its female founders,[2] respecting whom he observes
(with perfect truth, if we admit the historical character of the old
epic), that women possess an unparalleled force of resolution in
resisting adverse events, since the Amazons, after having been
first roughly handled by Hêraklês and then completely defeated

Pausan. iv. 31, 6 ; vii. 2. 4. Tacit. Ann. iii. 61. Schol. Apollon. Rhod. ii.
965.
The derivation of the name Sinopê from an Amazon was given by Heka
tæus (Fragm. 352). Themiskyra also had one of the Amazons for its eponymus (Appian, Bell. Mithridat. 78).
Some of the most venerated religious legends at Sinopê were attached to
the expedition of Hêraklês against the Amazons : Autolykus, the oracle-
giving hero, worshipped with great solemnity even at the time when the town
was besieged by Lucullus, was the companion of Hêraclês (Appian, ib. c.83).
Even a small mountain village in the territory of Ephesus, called Latoreia,
derived its name from one of the Amazons (Athenæ. i. p. 31).
[1] Herodot. iv. 108-117, where he gives the long tale, imagined by the Pontic Greeks, of the origin of the Sarmatian nation. Compare Hippokratês, De
Aëre, Locis et Aquis, c. 17 ; Ephorus, Fragm. 103 ; Skymn. Chius, v. 102;
Plato, Legg. vii. p. 804; Diodôr. ii. 34.
The testimony of Hippokratês certifies the practice of the Sarmatian women to check the growth of the right breast : Τὸν δέξιον δὲ μαζὸν οὐκ ἔχουσιν.
Παιδίοισι γὰρ ἐοῦσιν ἔτι νηπίοισιν αἱ μητέρες χαλκεῖον τετεχνημένον ἐπ' αὐτέῳ
τούτῳ διάπυρον ποιέουσαι, πρὸς τὸν μαζὸν τιθέασι τὸν δέξιον · καὶ ἐπικαίεται,
ὥστε τὴν αὔξησιν φθείρεσθαι, ἐς δὲ τὸν δέξιον ὦμον καὶ βραχίονα πᾶσαν τὴν
ἰσχυν καὶ τὸ πλῆθος ἐκδιδόναι.
Ktêsias also compares a warl'ke Sakian woman to the Amazons (Fragm.
Persic. ii. pp. 221, 449, Bähr).
[2] Pausan. iv. 31, 6 ; vii. 2, 4. Dionys. Periêgêt. 828

by Thêseus, could yet find courage to play so conspicuous a part in the defence of Troy against the Grecian besiegers.[1]

It is thus that in what is called early Grecian history, as the Greeks themselves looked back upon it, the Amazons were among the most prominent and undisputed personages. Nor will the circumstance appear wonderful if we reflect, that the belief in them was first established at a time when the Grecian mind was fed with nothing else but religious legend and epic poetry, and that the incidents of the supposed past, as received from these sources, were addressed to their faith and feelings, without being required to adapt themselves to any canons of credibility drawn from present experience. But the time came when the historians of Alexander the Great audaciously abused this ancient credence. Amongst other tales calculated to exalt the dignity of that monarch, they affirmed that after his conquest and subjugation of the Persian empire, he had been visited in Hyrcania by Thalestris, queen of the Amazons, who admiring his warlike prowess, was anxious to be enabled to return into her own country in a condition to produce offspring of a breed so invincible.[2] But the Greeks had now been accustomed for a century and a half to historical and philosophical criticism — and that uninquiring faith, which was readily accorded to the wonders of the past, could no longer be invoked for them when tendered as present reality. For the fable of the Amazons was here reproduced in its naked simplicity, without being rationalized or painted over with historical colors.

Some literary men indeed, among whom were Dêmêtrius of Skepsis, and the Mitylenæan Theophanês, the companion of Pompey in his expeditions, still continued their belief both in Amazons present and Amazons past ; and when it becomes notorious that at least there were none such on the banks of the Thermôdôn, these authors supposed them to have migrated from their original locality, and to have settled in the unvisited regions north of Mount Caucasus.[3] Strabo, on the contrary, feeling that the grounds

---

[1] Pausan. i.15, 2.

[2] Arrian, Exped. Alex. vii. 13; compare iv. 15; Quint. Curt. vi. 4; Justin, xlii. 4. The note of Freinshemius on the above passage of Quintus Curtius is full of valuable references on the subject of the Amazons.

[3] Strabo, xi. p. 503-504; Appian, Bell. Mithridat. c. 103; Plutarch, Pom

of disbelief applied with equal force to the ancient stories and to
the modern, rejected both the one and the other. But he remarks
at the same time, not without some surprise, that it was usual
with most persons to adopt a middle course, — to retain the Amazons as historical phænomena of the remote past, but to disallow
them as realities of the present, and to maintain that the breed
had died out.¹ The accomplished intellect of Julius Cæsar did not
scruple to acknowledge them as having once conquered and held
in dominion a large portion of Asia;² and the compromise between early, traditional, and religious faith on the one hand, and

peius, c. 35. Plin. N. H. vi. 7.   Plutarch still retains the old description of
Amazons from the mountains near the Thermôdôn.   Appian keeps clear of
this geographical error, probably copying more exactly the language of Theophanês, who must have been well aware that when Lucullus besieged Themiskyra, he did not find it defended by the Amazons (see Appian, Bell. Mithridat. c. 78).   Ptolemy (v. 9) places the Amazons in the imperfectly known
regions of Asiatic Sarmatia, north of the Caspian and near the river Rha
(Volga).   " This fabulous community of women (observes Forbiger) Hand
buch der alten Geographie, ii. 77, p. 457) was a phænomenon much too interesting for the geographers easily to relinquish."
   ¹ Strabo, xi. p. 505. Ἴδιον δέ τι συμβέβηκε τῷ λόγῳ περὶ τῶν Ἀμαζόνων
Οἱ μὲν γὰρ ἄλλοι τὸ μυθῶδες καὶ τὸ ἱστορικὸν διωρίσμενον ἔχουσι· τὰ γὰρ παλαιὰ καὶ ψευδῆ καὶ τερατώδη, μῦθοι καλοῦνται· [Note. Strabo does not always
speak of the μῦθοι in this disrespectful tone; he is sometimes much displeased
with those who dispute the existence of an historical kernel in the inside,
especially with regard to Homer.] ἡ δ' ἱστορία βούλεται τἀληθές, ἄντε παλαιὸν, ἄντε νέον· καὶ τὸ τερατῶδες ἢ οὐκ ἔχει, ἢ σπάνιον. Περὶ δὲ τῶν Ἀμαζόνων
τὰ αὐτὰ λέγεται καὶ νῦν καὶ παλαὶ, τερατώδη τ' ὄντα, καὶ πίστεως πόρρω.
Τίς γὰρ ἂν πιστύσειεν, ὡς γυναικῶν στράτος, ἢ πόλις, ἢ ἔθνος, συσταίη ἂν πότε
χωρὶς ἀνδρῶν ; καὶ οὐ μόνον συσταίη, ἀλλὰ καὶ ἐφόδους ποιήσαιτο ἐπὶ τὴν ἀλ-
λοτρίαν, καὶ κρατήσειεν οὐ τῶν ἐγγὺς μόνον, ὥστε καὶ μέχρι τῆς νῦν Ἰωνίας
προελθεῖν, ἀλλὰ καὶ διαπόντιον στείλαιτο στρατίαν μέχρι τῆς Ἀττικῆς ; Ἀλλὰ
μὴν ταῦτά γε αὐτὰ καὶ νῦν λέγεται περὶ αὐτῶν· ἐπιτείνει δὲ τὴν
ἰδιότητα καὶ τὸ πιστεύεσθαι τὰ παλαιὰ μᾶλλον ἢ τὰ
νῦν. There are however, other passages in which he speaks of the Amazons as realities.
   Justin (ii. 4) recognizes the great power and extensive conquests of the
Amazons in very early times, but says that they gradually declined down to
the reign of Alexander, in whose time there were *just a few remaining;* the
queen with these few visited Alexander, but shortly afterwards the whole
breed became extinct.   This hypothesis has the merit of convenience, perhaps of ingenuity.
   ² Suetonius, Jul. Cæsar, c 22.   " In Syriâ quoque regnassé Semiramin

established habits of critical research on the other, adopted by
the historian Arrian, deserves to be transcribed in his own words,
as illustrating strikingly the powerful sway of the old legends
even over the most positive-minded Greeks: — " Neither Aris-
tobulus nor Ptolemy (he observes), nor any other competent witness, has recounted this (visit of the Amazons and their queen
to Alexander): nor does it seem to me that the race of the
Amazons was preserved down to that time, nor have they been
noticed either by any one before Alexander, or by Xenophôn,
though he mentions both the Phasians and the Kolchians, and
the other barbarous nations which the Greeks saw both before
and after their arrival at Trapezus, in which marches they must
have met with the Amazons, if the latter had been still in existence. Yet *it is incredible to me* that this race of women, celebrated as they have been by authors so many and so commanding,
should never have existed at all. The story tells of Hêraklês,
that he set out from Greece and brought back with him the
girdle of their queen Hippolytê; also of Thêseus and the Athenians, that they were the first who defeated in battle and repelled these women in their invasion of Europe; and the combat
of the Athenians with the Amazons has been painted by Mikôn,
not less than that between the Athenians and the Persians. Moreover Herodotus has spoken in many places of these women, and
those Athenian orators who have pronounced panegyrics on the
citizens slain in battle, have dwelt upon the victory over the
Amazons as among the most memorable of Athenian exploits.
If the satrap of Media sent any equestrian women at all to Alexander, I think that they must have come from some of the neighboring tribes, practised in riding and equipped in the costume
generally called Amazonian."[1]

There cannot be a more striking evidence of the indelible force

---

(Julius Cæsar said this), magnamque Asiæ partem Amazonas tenuisse quondam."

In the splendid triumph of the emperor Aurelian at Rome after the defeat
of Zenobia, a few Gothic women who had been taken in arms were exhibited
among the prisoners; the official placard carried along with them announced them as *Amazons* (Vopiscus Aurel. in Histor. August. Scrip. p. 260, ed.
Paris).

[1] Arrian, Expedit. Alexand. vii. 13.

with which these ancient legends were worked into the national faith and feelings of the Greeks, than these remarks of a judicious historian upon the fable of the Amazons. Probably if any plausible mode of rationalizing it, and of transforming it into a quasi-political event, had been offered to Arrian, he would have been better pleased to adopt such a middle term, and would have rested comfortably in the supposition that he believed the legend in its true meaning, while his less inquiring countrymen were imposed upon by the exaggerations of poets. But as the story was presented to him plain and unvarnished, either for acceptance or rejection, his feelings as a patriot and a religious man prevented him from applying to the past such tests of credibility as his untrammelled reason acknowledged to be paramount in regard to the present. When we see moreover how much his belief was strengthened, and all tendency to scepticism shut out by the familiarity of his eye and memory with sculptured or painted Amazons[1]—we may calculate the irresistible force of this sensible demonstration on the convictions of the unlettered public, at once more deeply retentive of passive impressions, and unaccustomed to the countervailing habit of rational investigation into evidence. Had the march of an army of warlike women, from the Thermôdôn or the Tanais into the heart of Attica, been recounted to Arrian as an incident belonging to the time of Alexander the Great, he would have rejected it no less emphatically than Strabo; but cast back as it was into an undefined past, it took rank among the hallowed traditions of divine or heroic antiquity, — gratifying to extol by rhetoric, but repulsive to scrutinize in argument.[2]

---

[1] Ktésias described as real animals, existing in wild and distant regions, the heterogeneous and fantastic combinations which he saw sculptured in the East (see this stated and illustrated in Bähr, Preface to the Fragm. of Ktésias, pp. 58, 59).

[2] Heyne observes (Apollodôr. ii. 5, 9) with respect to the fable of the Amazons, "In his historiarum fidem aut vestigia nemo quæsiverit." Admitting the wisdom of this counsel (and I think it indisputable), why are we required to presume, in the absence of all proof, an historical basis for each of those *other* narratives, such as the Kalydônian boar-hunt, the Argonautic expedition, or the siege of Troy, which go to make up, along with the story of the Amazons, the aggregate matter of Grecian legendary faith ? If the tale of

CHAPTER XII.

KRETAN LEGENDS.—MINOS AND HIS FAMILY.

To understand the adventures of Thêseus in Krête, it will be necessary to touch briefly upon Minôs and the Krêtan heroic genealogy.

Minôs and Rhadamanthus, according to Homer, are sons of Zeus, by Europê,[1] daughter of the widely-celebrated Phœnix,

---

the Amazons could gain currency without any such support, why not other portions of the ancient epic ?

An author of easy belief, Dr. F. Nagel, vindicates the historical reality of the Amazons (Geschichte der Amazonen, Stutgart, 1838). I subjoin here a different explanation of the Amazonian tale, proceeding from another author who rejects the historical basis, and contained in a work of learning and value' (*Guhl, Ephesiaca*, Berlin, 1843, p. 132) : —

" Id tantum monendum videtur, Amazonas nequaquam historice accipien das esse, sed e contrario totas ad mythologiam pertinere. Earum enim fabulas quum ex frequentium hierodularum gregibus in cultibus et sacris Asiaticis ortas esse ingeniose ostenderit Tolken, jam *inter omnes mythologiæ peritos constat*, Amazonibus nihil fere nisi peregrini cujusdam cultûs notionem expressum esse, ejusque cum Græcorum religione certamen frequentibus istis pugnis designatum esse, quas cum Amazonibus tot Græcorum heroes habuisse credebantur, Hercules, Bellerophon, Theseus, Achilles, et vel ipse, quem Ephesi cultum fuisse supra ostendimus, Dionysus. Quæ Amazonum notio primaria, quum paulatim Euemeristicâ (ut ita dicam) ratione ita transformaretur, ut Amazones pro vero feminarum populo haberentur, necesse quoque erat, ut omnibus fere locis, ubi ejusmodi religionum certamina locum habuerunt, Amazones habitasse, vel eo usque processisse, crederentur. Quod cum nusquam manifestius fuerit, quam in Asiâ minore, et potissimum in eâ parte quæ Græciam versus vergit, haud mirandum est omnes fere ejus oræ urbes ab Amazonibus conditas putari."

I do not know the evidence upon which this conjectural interpretation rests, but the statement of it, though it boasts so many supporters among mythological critics, carries no appearance of probability to my mind. Priam fights against the Amazons as well as the Grecian heroes.

[1] Europê was worshipped with very peculiar solemnity in the island of Krête (see Dictys Cretensis, De Bello Trojano, i. c. 2).

The venerable plane-tree, under which Zeus and Europê had reposed, was

born in Krête. Minôs is the father of Deukaliôn, whose son Idomeneus, in conjunction with Mêrionês, conducts the Krêtan troops to the host of Agamemnôn before Troy. Minôs is ruler of Knossus, and familiar companion of the great Zeus. He is spoken of as holding guardianship in Krête — not necessarily meaning the whole of the island : he is farther decorated with a golden sceptre, and constituted judge over the dead in the under-world to settle their disputes, in which function Odysseus finds him — this however by a passage of comparatively late interpolation into the Odyssey. He also had a daughter named Ariadnê, for whom the artist Dædalus fabricated in the town of Knossus the representation of a complicated dance, and who was ultimately carried off by Thêseus : she died in the island of Dia, deserted by Thêseus and betrayed by Dionysos to the fatal wrath of Artemis. Rhadamanthus seems to approach to Minôs both in judicial functions and posthumous dignity. He is conveyed expressly to Eubœ, by the semi-divine sea-carriers the Phæacians, to inspect the gigantic corpse of the earth-born Tityus — the longest voyage they ever undertook. He is moreover after death promoted to an abode of undisturbed bliss in the Elysian plain at the extremity of the earth.[1]

According to poets later than Homer, Europê is brought over by Zeus from Phœnicia to Krête, where she bears to him three sons, Minôs, Rhadamanthus and Sarpêdôn. The latter leaves Krête and settles in Lykia, the population of which, as well as that of many other portions of Asia Minor, is connected by va-

---

still shown, hard by a fountain at Goetyn in Krête, in the time of Theophrastus : it was said to be the only plane-tree in the neighborhood which never cast its leaves (Theophrast. Hist. Plant. i. 9).

[1] Homer, Iliad, xiii. 249, 450 ; xiv. 321. Odyss. xi. 322–568 ; xix. 179 ; iv. 564–vii. 321.

The Homeric Minôs in the under-world is not a judge of the previous lives of the dead, so as to determine whether they deserve reward or punishment for their conduct on earth : such functions are not assigned to him earlier than the time of Plato. He administers justice *among* the dead, who are conceived as a sort of society, requiring some presiding judge : θεμιστεύοντα νεκύεσσι, with regard to Minôs, is said very much like (Odyss. xi. 484) νῦν δ' αὖτε μέγα κρατέεις νεκύεσσι with regard to Achilles. See this matter partially illustrated in Heyne's Excursus xi. to the sixth book of the Æneid of Virgil.

rious mythical genealogies with Krête, though the Sarpêdôn of
the Iliad has no connection with Krête, and is not the son of
Europê. Sarpêdôn having become king of Lykia, was favored
by his father, Zeus, with permission to live for three generations.[1]
At the same time the youthful Milêtus, a favorite of Sarpêdôn,
quitted Krête, and established the city which bore his name on
the coast of Asia Minor. Rhadamanthus became sovereign of
and lawgiver among the islands in the Ægean: he subsequently
went to Bœôtia, where he married the widowed Alkmênô,
mother of Hêraklês.

Europê finds in Krête a king Asterius, who marries her and
adopts her children by Zeus: this Astêrius is the son of Krês,
the eponym of the island, or (according to another genealogy by
which it was attempted to be made out that Minôs was of Dôrian
race) he was a son of the daughter of Krês by Tektamus, the
son of Dôrus, who had migrated into the island from Greece.

Minôs married Pasiphaê, daughter of the god Hêlios and Per-
seïs, by whom he had Katreus, Deukaliôn, Glaukus, Androgeos,
names marked in the legendary narrative, — together with several daughters, among whom were Ariadnê and Phædra. He
offended Poseidôn by neglecting to fulfil a solemnly-made vow,
and the displeased god afflicted his wife Pasiphaê with a monstrous passion for a bull. The great artist Dœdalus, son of Eu-
palamus, a fugitive from Athens, became the confidant of this
amour, from which sprang the Minôtaur, a creature half man and
half bull.[2] This Minôtaur was imprisoned by Minôs in the labyrinth, an inextricable inclosure constructed by Dædalus for that
express purpose, by order of Minôs.

Minôs acquired great nautical power, and expelled the Karian
inhabitants from many of the islands of the Ægean, which he
placed under the government of his sons on the footing of tribu-

----

[1] Apollodôr. iii. 1, 2. Καὶ αὐτῷ δίδωσι Ζεὺς ἐπὶ τρεῖς γενεὰς ζῆν. This
circumstance is evidently imagined by the logographers to account for the
appearance of Sarpêdôn in the Trojan war, fighting against Idomeneus, the
grandson of Minôs. Nisus is the eponymus of Nisæa, the port of the town
of Megara: his tomb was shown at Athens (Pausan. i. 19, 5). Minôs is the
eponym of the island of Minoa (opposite the port of Nisæa), where it was
affirmed that the fleet of Minôs was stationed (Pausan. i. 44, 5).

[2] Apollodôr iii. 1. 2.

taries. He undertook several expeditions against various places on the coast—one against Nisos, the son of Pandiôn, king of Megara, who had amongst the hair of his head one peculiar lock of a purple color: an oracle had pronounced that his life and reign would never be in danger so long as he preserved this precious lock. The city would have remained inexpugnable, if Scylla, the daughter of Nisus, had not conceived a violent passion for Minôs. While her father was asleep, she cut off the lock on which his safety hung, so that the Krêtan king soon became victorious. Instead of performing his promise to carry Scylla away with him to Krête, he cast her from the stern of his vessel into the sea :[1] both Scylla and Nisus were changed into birds.

Androgeos, son of Minôs having displayed such rare qualities as to vanquish all his competitors at the Panathenaic festival in Athens, was sent by Ægeus the Athenian king to contend against the bull of Marathôn,—an enterprise in which he perished, and Minôs made war upon Athens to avenge his death. He was for a long time unable to take the city : at length he prayed to his father Zeus to aid him in obtaining redress from the Athenians, and Zeus sent upon them pestilence and famine. In vain did they endeavor to avert these calamities by offering up as propitiatory sacrifices the four daughters of Hyacinthus. Their sufferings still continued, and the oracle directed them to submit to any terms which Minôs might exact. He required that they should send to Krête a tribute of seven youths and seven maidens, periodically, to be devoured by the Minôtaur,[2]—offered to him in a labyrinth constructed by Dædalus, including countless different passages, out of which no person could escape. Every ninth year this offering was to be despatched. The more common story was, that the youths and maidens thus destined to destruction were selected by lot—but the logographer Hellaníkus said that Minôs came to Athens and chose them himself.[3] The third period for despatching the victims had arrived,

[1] Apollodôr. iii. 15, 8. See the Ciris of Virgil, a juvenile poem on the subject of this fable; also Hyginus, f. 198; Schol. Eurip. Hippol. 1200. Propertius (iii. 19, 21) gives the features of the story with tolerable fidel ity; Ovid takes considerable liberties with it (Metam. vii. 5–150).

[2] Apollodôr. iii. 15, 8.

[3] See, on the subject of Thêseus and the Minôtaur, Eckermann, Lehrbuch

and Athens was plunged in the deepest affliction, when Thêseus
determined to devote himself as one of them, and either to ter-
minate the sanguinary tribute or to perish. He prayed to Poseidôn for help, and the Delphian god assured him that Aphroditê
would sustain and extricate him. On arriving at Knossus he
was fortunate enough to captivate the affections of Ariadnê, the
daughter of Minôs, who supplied him with a sword and a clue of
thread. With the former he contrived to kill the Minôtaur, the
latter served to guide his footsteps in escaping from the labyrinth.
Having accomplished this triumph, he left Krête with his ship
and companions unhurt, carrying off Ariandê, whom however he
soon abandoned on the island of Naxos. On his way home to
Athens, he stopped at Dêlos, where he offered a grateful sacrifice
to Apollo for his escape, and danced along with the young men
and maidens whom he had rescued from the Minôtaur, a dance
called the Geranus, imitated from the twists and convolutions of
the Krêtan labyrinth. It had been concerted with his father
Ægeus, that if he succeeded in his enterprise against the Minôtaur, he should on his return hoist white sails in his ship in place
of the black canvas which she habitually carried when employed
on this mournful embassy. But Thêseus forgot to make the
change of sails; so that Ægeus, seeing the ship return with her
equipment of mourning unaltered, was impressed with the sorrowful conviction that his son had perished, and cast himself into the
sea. The ship which made this voyage was preserved by the
Athenians with careful solicitude, being constantly repaired with
new timbers, down to the time of the Phalerian Dêmêtrius: every
year she was sent from Athens to Dêlos with a solemn sacrifice
and specially-nominated envoys. The priest of Apollo decked
her stern with garlands before she quitted the port, and during
the time which elapsed until her return, the city was understood
to abstain from all acts carrying with them public impurity, so
that it was unlawful to put to death any person even under formal sentence by the dikastery. This accidental circumstance

---

der Religions Geschichte und Mythologie, vol. ii. ch. xiii. p. 133. He maintains that the tribute of these human victims paid by Athens to Minôs is an
historical fact. Upon what this belief is grounded, I confess I do not
see.

becomes especially memorable, from its having postponed for thirty days the death of the lamented Socratês.[1]

The legend respecting Thêseus, and his heroic rescue of the seven noble youths and maidens from the jaws of the Minôtaur, was thus both commemorated and certified to the Athenian public, by the annual holy ceremony and by the unquestioned identity of the vessel employed in it. There were indeed many varieties in the mode of narrating the incident; and some of the Attic logographers tried to rationalize the fable by transforming the Minôtaur into a general or a powerful athlete, named Taurus, whom Thêseus vanquished in Krête.[2] But this altered version never overbore the old fanciful character of the tale as maintained by the poets. A great number of other religious ceremonies and customs, as well as several chapels or sacred enclosures in honor of different heroes, were connected with different acts and special ordinances of Thêseus. To every Athenian who took

---

[1] Plato, Phædon, c. 2, 3; Xenoph. Memor. iv. 8. 2. Plato especially noticed τοὺς δὶς ἑπτα ἐκείνους, the seven youths and the seven maidens whom Thêseus conveyed to Krête and brought back safely: this number seems an old and constant feature in the legend, maintained by Sappho and Bacchylidês as well as by Euripidês (Herc. Fur. 1318). See Servius ad Virgil Æneid. vi. 21.

[2] For the general narrative and its discrepancies, see Plutarch, Thês c. 15–19; Diodôr, iv. 60–62; Pausan. i. 17, 3; Ovid, Epist. Ariadn. Thês 104. In that other portion of the work of Diodôrus which relates more especially to Krête, and is borrowed from Kretan logographers and historians (v. 64–80), he mentions nothing at all respecting the war of Minôs with Athens.

In the drama of Euripidês called Thêseus, the genuine story of the youths and maidens about to be offered as food to the Minôtaur was introduced (Schol. ad Aristoph. Vesp. 312).

Ariadnê figures in the Odyssey along with Thêseus: she is the daughter of Minôs, carried off by Thêseus from Krête, and killed by Artemis in the way home: there is no allusion to Minôtaur, or tribute, or self-devotion of Thêseus (Odyss. xi. 324). This is probably the oldest and simplest form of the legend — one of the many amorous (compare Theognis, 1232) adventures of Thêseus: the rest is added by post-Homeric poets.

The respect of Aristotle for Minôs induces him to adopt the hypothesis that the Athenian youths and maidens were not put to death in Krête, but grew old in servitude (Aristot. Fragm. Βοττιαίων Πολιτεία, p. 106. ed. Neumann. of the Fragments of the treatise Περὶ Πολιτειῶν. Plutarch, Quæst Græc. p. 298).

part in the festivals of the Oschophoria, the Pyanepsia, or the
Kybernêsia, the name of this great hero was familiar, and the
motives for offering to him solemn worship at his own special
festival of the Thêseia, became evident and impressive.

The same Athenian legends which ennobled and decorated the
character of Thêseus, painted in repulsive colors the attributes
of Minôs; and the traits of the old Homeric comrade of Zeus
were buried under those of the conqueror and oppressor of
Athens. His history like that of the other legendary personages
of Greece, consists almost entirely of a string of family romances
and tragedies. His son Katreus, father of Aëropê, wife of Atreus,
was apprized by an oracle that he would perish by the hand of
one of his own children: he accordingly sent them out of the
island, and Althæmenês, his son, established himself in Rhodes.
Katreus having become old, and fancying that he had outlived
the warning of the oracle, went over to Rhodes to see Althæmenês. In an accidental dispute which arose between his attendants and the islanders, Althæmenês inadvertently took part and
slew his father without knowing him. Glaukus, the youngest
son of Minôs, pursuing a mouse, fell into a reservoir of honey and
was drowned. No one knew what had become of him, and his
father was inconsolable; at length the Argeian Polyeidus, a
prophet wonderfully endowed by the gods, both discovered the
boy and restored him to life, to the exceeding joy of Minôs.[1]

The latter at last found his death in an eager attempt to overtake and punish Dædalus. This great artist, the eponymous
hero of the Attic gens or dême called the Dædalidæ, and the
descendant of Erechtheus through Mêtion, had been tried at the
tribunal of Areiopagus and banished for killing his nephew
Talos, whose rapidly improving skill excited his envy.[2] He took
refuge in Krête, where he acquired the confidence of Minôs, and
was employed (as has been already mentioned) in constructing
the labyrinth; subsequently however he fell under the displeasure
of Minôs, and was confined as a close prisoner in the inextricable
windings of his own edifice. His unrivalled skill and resource
however did not forsake him. He manufactured wings both for

---

[1] Apollodôr. iii. cap. 2–3.

[2] Pherekyd. Fragm. 105; Hellanik. Fragm. 82 (Didot); Pausan. vii. 4, 5

himself and for his son Ikarus, with which they flew over the sea: the father arrived safely in Sicily at Kamikus, the residence of the Sikanian king Kokalus, but the son, disdaining paternal example and admonition, flew so high that his wings were melted by the sun and he fell into the sea, which from him was called the Ikarian sea.[1]

Dædalus remained for some time in Sicily, leaving in various parts of the island many prodigious evidences of mechanical and architectural skill.[2] At length Minôs bent upon regaining possession of his person, undertook an expedition against Kokalus with a numerous fleet and army. Kokalus affecting readiness to deliver up the fugitive, and receiving Minôs with apparent friendship, ordered a bath to be prepared for him by his three daughters, who, eager to protect Dædalus at any price, drowned the Krêtan king in the bath with hot water.[3] Many of the Krêtans who had accompanied him remained in Sicily and founded the town of Minoa, which they denominated after him. But not long afterwards Zeus roused all the inhabitants of Krête (except the towns of Polichna and Præsus) to undertake with one accord an expedition against Kamikus for the purpose of avenging the death of Minôs. They besieged Kamikus in vain for five years, until at last famine compelled them to return. On their way along the coast of Italy, in the Gulf of Tarentum, a terrible storm destroyed their fleet and obliged them to settle permanently in the country: they founded Hyria with other cities, and became Messapian Iapygians. Other settlers, for the most part Greeks, immigrated into Krête to the spots which this movement

---

[1] Diodôr. iv. 79; Ovid, Metamorph. viii. 181. Both Ephorus and Philistus mentioned the coming of Dædalus to Kokalus in Sicily (Ephor. Fr. 99; Philist. Fragm. 1, Didot): probably Antiochus noticed it also (Diodôr. xii. 71). Kokalus was the point of commencement for the Sicilian historians.

[2] Diodôr. iv. 80.

[3] Pausan. vii. 4, 5; Schol. Pindar. Nem. iv. 95; Hygin. fab. 44; Conon, Narr. 25; Ovid, Ibis, 291.—

"Vel tua maturet, sicut Minoia fata,
Per caput infusæ fervidus humor aquæ."

This story formed the subject of a lost drama of Sophoklês, Καμίκιοι ος Μίνως; it was also told by Kallimachus, ἐν Αἰτίοις, as well as by Philostoραπιυς (Schol. Iliad, ii. 145).

VOL. I.   10*   ,   15oc.

had left vacant, and in the second generation after Minôs occurred the Trojan war. The departed Minôs was exceedingly offended with the Krêtans for coöperating in avenging the injury
to Menelaus, since the Greeks generally had lent no aid to the
Krêtans in their expedition against the town of Kamikus. He
sent upon Krête, after the return of Idomeneus from Troy, such
terrible visitations of famine and pestilence, that the population
again died out or expatriated, and was again renovated by fresh
immigrations. The intolerable suffering[1] thus brought upon the
Krêtans by the anger of Minôs, for having coöperated in the
general Grecian aid to Menelaus, was urged by them to the
Greeks as the reason why they could take no part in resisting
the invasion of Xerxês; and it is even pretended that they were
advised and encouraged to adopt this ground of excuse by the
Delphian oracle.[2]

Such is the Minôs of the poets and logographers, with his
legendary and romantic attributes: the familiar comrade of the
great Zeus, — the judge among the dead in Hadês, — the husband
of Pasiphaê, daughter of the god Hêlios, — the father of the goddess Ariadnê, as well as of Androgeos, who perishes and is worshipped at Athens,[3] and of the boy Glaukus, who is miraculously
restored to life by a prophet, — the person beloved by Scylla, and
the amorous pursuer of the nymph or goddess Britomartis,[4] —

---

[1] This curious and very characteristic narrative is given by Herodot. vii.
169–171.

[2] Heredot. vii. 169. The answer ascribed to the Delphian oracle, on the
question being put by the Krêtan envoys whether it would be better for them
to aid the Greeks against Xerxês or not, is highly emphatic and poetical:
Ὦ νήπιοι, ἐπιμέμφεσθε ὅσα ὑμῖν ἐκ τῶν Μενελέω τιμωρημάτων Μίνως ἔπεμψε
μηνίων δακρύματα, ὅτι οἱ μὲν οὐ ξυνεξεπρήξαντο αὐτῷ τὸν ἐν Καμίκῳ θάνατον
γενόμενον, ὑμεῖς δὲ κείνοισι τὴν ἐκ Σπάρτης ἁρπαχθεῖσαν ὑπ᾽ ἀνδρὸς βαρβά-
ρου γυναῖκα.

If such an answer was ever returned at all, I cannot but think that it
must have been from some oracle in Krête itself, not from Delphi. The
Delphian oracle could never have so far forgotten its obligations to the
general cause of Greece, at that critical moment, which involved moreover
the safety of all its own treasures, as to deter the Krêtans from giving assistance.

[3] Hesiod, Theogon. 949; Pausan. i. 1, 4.

[4] Kallimach. Hymn. ad Dian. 189. Strabo (x. p. 476) dwells also upon

the proprietor of the Labyrinth and of the Minôtaur, and the
exacter of a periodical tribute of youths and maidens from Athens
as food for this monster, — lastly, the follower of the fugitive
artist Dædalus to Kamikus, and the victim of the three ill-dis
posed daughters of Kokalus in a bath. With this strongly-
marked portrait, the Minôs of Thucydidês and Aristotle has
searcely anything in common except the name. He is the first
to acquire *Thalassokraty*, or command of the Ægæan sea: he ex-
pels the Karian inhabitants from the Cyclades islands, and sends
thither fresh colonists under his own sons ; he puts down piracy,
in order that he may receive his tribute regularly ; lastly, he attempts to conquer Sicily, but fails in the enterprise and perishes.[1]
Here we have conjectures, derived from the analogy of the
Athenian maritime empire in the historical times, substituted in
place of the fabulous incidents, and attached to the name of
Minôs.

In the fable, a tribute of seven youths and seven maidens is
paid to him periodically by the Athenians ; in the historicized
narrative this character of a tribute-collector is preserved, but
the tribute is money collected from dependent islands ;[2] and Aris-

---

the strange contradiction of the legends concerning Minôs : I agree with
Hoeckh (Kreta, ii. p. 93) that δασμόλογος in this passage refers to the tribute
exacted from Athens for the Minôtaur.

[1] Thuycd. i. 4. Μίνως γὰρ ʹωυλαίτατος ὧν ἀκοῇ ἴσμεν, ναυτικὸν ἐκτήσατο,
καὶ τῆς νῦν Ἑλληνικῆς θαλάσσης ἐπὶ πλεῖστον ἐκράτησε, καὶ τῶν Κυκλάδων
νήσων ἦρξέ τε καὶ οἰκιστὴς αὐτὸς τῶν πλείστων ἐγένετο, Κᾶρας ἐξελάσας καὶ
τοὺς ἑαυτοῦ παῖδας ἡγεμόνας ἐγκαταστήσας· τό τε ληστικὸν, ὡς εἰκὸς, καθῄ-
ρει ἐκ τῆς θαλάσσης, ἐφ' ὅσον ἠδύνατο, τοῦ τὰς προσόδους μᾶλλον ἰέναι αὐτῷ.
See also c. 8.

Aristot. Polit. ii. 7, 2, Δοκεῖ δ' ἡ νῆσος καὶ πρὸς τὴν ἀρχὴν τὴν Ἑλληνικὴν
πεφυκέναι καὶ κεῖσθαι καλῶς . . . . διὸ καὶ τὴν τῆς θαλάσσης ἀρχὴν κατε-
σχεν ὁ Μίνως, καὶ τὰς νήσους τὰς μὲν ἐχειρώσατο, τὰς δὲ ᾤκισε· τέλος δ' ἐπι
θέμενος τῇ Σικελίᾳ τὸν βίον ἐτελεύτησεν ἐκεῖ περὶ Κάμικον.

Ephorus (ap. Skymn. Chi. 542) repeated the same statement: he men
tioncd also the autochthonous king Krês.

[2] It is curious that Herodotus expressly denies this, and in language which
shows that he had made special inquiries about it: he says that the Karians
or Leleges in the islands (who were, according to Thucydidês, expelled by
Minôs) paid no tribute to Minôs, but manned his navy, i. e. they stood to
Minôs much in the same relation as Chios and Lesbos stood to Athens
(Herodot. i. 171). One may trace here the influence of those discussions

totle points out to us how conveniently Krête is situated to exercise empire over the Ægæan. The expedition against Kamikus, instead of being directed to the recovery of the fugitive
Dædalus, is an attempt on the part of the great thalassokrat to
conquer Sicily. Herodotus gives us generally the same view of
the character of Minôs as a great maritime king, but his notice
of the expedition against Kamicus includes the mention of Dædalus as the intended object of it.[1] Ephorus, while he described
Minôs as a commanding and comprehensive lawgiver imposing
his commands under the sanction of Zeus, represented him as
the imitator of an earlier lawgiver named Rhadamanthus, and
also as an immigrant into Krête from the Æolic Mount Ida, along
with the priests or sacred companions of Zeus called the Idæi
Dactyli. Aristotle too points him out as the author of the Sys-
sitia, or public meals common in Krête as well as at Sparta,—
other divergences in a new direction from the spirit of the old
fables.[2]

The contradictory attributes ascribed to Minôs, together with
the perplexities experienced by those who wished to introduce a
regular chronological arrangement into these legendary events,
has led both in ancient and in modern times to the supposition of
two kings named Minôs, one the grandson of the other, — Minôs
I., the son of Zeus, lawgiver and judge, — Minôs II., the thalassokrat, — a gratuitous conjecture, which, without solving the problem required, only adds one to the numerous artifices employed
for imparting the semblance of history to the disparate matter of
legend. The Krêtans were at all times, from Homer downward,
expert and practised seamen. But that they were ever united

---

which must have been prevalent at that time respecting the maritime empire
of Athens.

[1] Herodot. vii. 170. Λέγεται γὰρ Μίνω κατὰ ζήτησιν Δαιδάλου ἀπικόμενον
ἐς Σικανίην, τὴν νῦν Σικαλίην καλουμένην, ἀποθανεῖν βιαίῳ θανάτῳ. Ἀνὰ
δὲ χρόνον Κρῆτας, θεοῦ σφὶ ἐποτρ ύνοντος, etc.

[2] Aristot. Polit. ii. 7, 1; vii. 9, 2. Ephorus, Fragm. 63, 64, 65. He set
aside altogether the Homeric genealogy of Minôs, which makes him brother
of Rhadamanthus and born in Krête.

Strabo, in pointing out the many contradictions respecting Minôs, remarks, Ἐστι δὲ καὶ ἄλλος λόγος οὐχ ὁμολογούμενος, τῶν μὲν ξένον τῆς νήσου
τὸν Μίνω λεγόντων, τῶν δὲ ἐπιχώριον. By the former he doubtless means
Ephorus, though he has not here specified him (x. p. 477).

under one government, or ever exercised maritime dominion in the Ægæan is a fact which we are neither able to affirm nor to deny. The Odyssey, in so far as it justifies any inference at all, points against such a supposition, since it recognizes a great diversity both of inhabitants and of languages in the island, and designates Minôs as king specially of Knôssus : it refutes still more positively the idea that Minôs put down piracy, which the Homeric Krêtans as well as others continue to practise without scruple.

Herodotus, though he in some places speaks of Minôs as a person historically cognizable, yet in one passage severs him pointedly from the generation of man. The Samian despot " Polykratês (he tells us) was the first person who aspired to nautical dominion, excepting Minôs of Knôssus, and others before him (if any such there ever were) who may have ruled the sea; but Polykratês is the first of that which is called *the generation of man* who aspired with much chance of success to govern Iônia and the islands of the Ægæan."[1] Here we find it manifestly intimated that Minôs did not belong to the generation of man, and the tale given by the historian respecting the tremendous calamities which the wrath of the departed Minôs inflicted on Krête confirms the impression. The king of Knôssus is a god or a hero, but not a man; he belongs to legend, not to history. He is the son as well as the familiar companion of Zeus ; he marries the daughter of Hêlios, and Ariadnê is numbered among his offspring. To this superhuman person are ascribed the oldest and most revered institutions of the island, religious and political, together with a period of supposed ante-historical dominion. That there is much of Krêtan religious ideas and practice embodied in the fables concerning Minôs can hardly be doubted : nor is it improbable that the tale of the youths and maidens sent

---

[1] Herodot. iii. 122. Πολυκράτης γάρ ἐστι πρῶτος τῶν ἡμεῖς ἴδμεν Ἑλλήνων, ὃς θαλασσοκρατέειν ἐπενοήθη, παρὲξ Μίνωός τε τοῦ Κνωσσίου, καὶ εἰ δή τις ἄλλος πρότερος τούτου ἦρξε τῆς θαλάττης· *τῆς δὲ ἀνθρωπηίης λεγομένης γενέης* Πολυκράτης ἐστὶ πρῶτος ἐλπίδας πολλὰς ἔχων Ἰωνίης τε καὶ νήσων ἄρξειν.

The expression exactly corresponds to that of Pausan'as, ix. 5, 1, ἐπὶ τῶν καλουμένων Ἡρώων, for the age preceding the ἀνθρωπηίη γενέη ; also viii. 2. 1, ἐς τὰ ἀνωτέρω τοῦ ἀνθρώπων γένους.

from Athens may be based in some expiatory offerings rendered to a Krêtan divinity. The orgiastic worship of Zeus, solemnized by the armed priests with impassioned motions and violent excitement, was of ancient date in that island, as well as the connection with the worship of Apollo both at Delphi and at Dêlos. To analyze the fables and to elicit from them any trustworthy particular facts, appears to me a fruitless attempt. The religious recollections, the romantic invention, and the items of matter of fact, if any such there be, must forever remain indissolubly amalgamated as the poet originally blended them, for the amusement or edification of his auditors. Hoeckh, in his instructive and learned collection of facts respecting ancient Krête, construes the mythical genealogy of Minôs to denote a combination of the orgiastic worship of Zeus, indigenous among the Eteokrêtes, with the worship of the moon imported from Phœnicia, and signified by the names Europê, Pasiphaê, and Ariadnê.[1] This is specious as a conjecture, but I do not venture to speak of it in terms of greater confidence.

From the connection of religious worship and legendary tales between Krête and various parts of Asia Minor, — the Trôad, the coast of Milêtus and Lykia, especially between Mount Ida in Krête and Mount Ida in Æôlis, — it seems reasonable to infer an ethnographical kindred or relationship between the inhabitants anterior to the period of Hellenic occupation. The tales of Krêtan settlement at Minoa and Engyiôn on the south-western coast of Sicily, and in Iapygia on the Gulf of Tarentum, conduct us to a similar presumption, though the want of evidence forbids our tracing it farther. In the time of Herodotus, the Eteokrêtes, or aboriginal inhabitants of the island, were confined to Polichna and Præsus; but in earlier times, prior to the encroachments of the Hellênes, they had occupied the larger portion, if not the whole of the island. Minôs was originally their hero, subsequently adopted by the immigrant Hellênes, — at least Herodotus considers him as barbarian, not Hellenic.[2]

---

[1] Hoeckh, Kreta, vol. ii. pp. 56–67. K. O. Müller also (Dorier. ii. 2, 14) puts a religious interpretation upon these Kreto-Attic legends, but he explains them in a manner totally different from Hoeckh.

[2] Herodot. i. 173

CHAPTER XIII.

ARGONAUTIC EXPEDITION.

THE ship Argô was the theme of many songs during the oldest periods of the Grecian epic, even earlier than the Odyssey.

The king Æêtês, from whom she is departing, the hero Jasôn, who commands her, and the goddess Hêrê, who watches over him, enabling the Argô to traverse distances and to escape dangers which no ship had ever before encountered, are all circumstances briefly glanced at by Odysseus in his narrative to Alkinous. Moreover, Eunêus, the son of Jasôn and Hypsipylê, governs Lemnos during the siege of Troy by Agamemnôn, and carries on a friendly traffic with the Grecian camp, purchasing from them their Trojan prisoners.[1]

The legend of Halus in Achaia Phthiôtis, respecting the religious solemnities connected with the family of Athamas and Phryxus (related in a previous chapter), is also interwoven with the voyage of the Argonauts; and both the legend and the solemnities seem evidently of great antiquity. We know further, that the adventures of the Argô were narrated not only by Hesiod and in the Hesiodic poems, but also by Eumêlus and the author of the Naupactian verses — by the latter seemingly at considerable length.[2] But these poems are unfortunately lost, nor have we

---

[1] Odyss. xii. 69.—

Οἴη δὴ κείνη γε παρέπλει ποντόπορος νῆυς,
'Αργὼ πασιμέλουσα, παρ' Αἰήταο πλέουσα
Καί νύ κε τὴν ἐνθ' ὦκα βάλεν μεγάλας ποτὶ πέτρας.
'Αλλ' 'Ηρη παρέπεμψεν, ἐπεὶ φίλος ἦεν 'Ιήσων.

See also Iliad, vii. 470.

[2] See Hesiod, Fragm. Catalog. Fr. 6. p. 33, Düntz.; Eoiai, Frag. 36. p. 39; Frag. 72. p. 47. Compare Schol. ad Apollôn. Rhod. i. 45; ii. 178-297, 1125; iv. 254-284. Other poetical sources —

The old epic poem Ægimius, Frag. 5. p. 57, Düntz.

any means of determining what the original story was; for the narrative, as we have it, borrowed from later sources, is enlarged by local tales from the subsequent Greek colonies — Kyzikus, Herakleia, Sinopê, and others.

Jasôn, commanded by Pelias to depart in quest of the golden fleece belonging to the speaking ram which had carried away Phryxus and Hellê, was encouraged by the oracle to invite the noblest youth of Greece to his aid, and fifty of the most distin guished amongst them obeyed the call. Hêraklês, Thêseus, Telamôn and Pêleus, Kastôr and Pollux, Idas and Lynkeus — Zêtês and Kalaïs, the winged sons of Boreas — Meleager, Amphiaraus, Kêpheus, Laertês, Autolykus, Mencetius, Aktor, Erginus, Euphêmus, Ankæus, Pœas, Periklymenus, Augeas, Eurytus, Admêtus, Akastus, Kæneus, Euryalus, Pêneleôs and Lêitus, Askalaphus and Ialmenus, were among them. Argus the son of Phryxus, directed by the promptings of Athênê, built the ship, inserting in the prow a piece of timber from the celebrated oak of Dodona, which was endued with the faculty of speech:[1] Tiphys was the steersman, Idmôn the son of Apollo and Mopsus

---

Kincethôn in the *Herakleia* touched upon the death of Hylas near Kius in Mysia (Schol. Apollôn. Rhod. i. 1357).

The epic poem *Naupactia*, Frag. 1 to 6, Düntz. p. 61.

Eumêlus, Frag. 2, 3, 5, p. 65, Düntz.

Epimenidês, the Krêtan prophet and poet, composed a poem in 6500 lines, 'Ἀργοῦς ναυπηγίαν τε, καὶ 'Ιάσονος εἰς Κόλχους ἀποπλοῦν (Diogen. Laër. i. 10, 5), which is noticed more than once in the Scholia on Apollônius, on subjects connected with the poem (ii. 1125; iii. 42). See Mimnerm. Frag. 10, Schneidewin, p. 15.

Antimachus, in his poem *Lydê*, touched upon the Argonautic expedition, and has been partially copied by Apollônius Rhod. (Schol. Ap. Rh. i. 1290; ii. 296: iii. 410; iv. 1153).

The logographers Pherekydês and Hekatæus seem to have related the expedition at considerable length.

The Bibliothek der alten Literatur und Kunst (Göttingen, 1786, 2ᵗᵉ Stück, p. 61) contains an instructive Dissertation by Groddeck, Ueber die Argonautika, a summary of the various authorities respecting this expedition.

[1] Apollôn. Rhod. i. 525; iv. 580. Apollodôr. i. 9, 16. Valerius Flaccus (i. 300) softens down the speech of the ship Argô into a dream of Jasôn. Alexander Polyhistor explained what wood was used (Plin. H. N. xiii. 22).

accompanied them as prophets, while Orpheus came to amuse their weariness and reconcile their quarrels with his harp.[1] First they touched at the island of Lêmnos, in which at that time there were no men ; for the women, infuriated by jealousy and ill-treatment, had put to death their fathers, husbands and brothers. The Argonauts, after some difficulty, were received with friendship, and even admitted into the greatest intimacy. They staid some months, and the subsequent population of the island was

---

[1] Apollônius Rhodius, Apollodôrus, Valerius Flaccus, the Orphic Argonautica, and Hyginus, have all given Catalogues of the Argonautic heroes (there was one also in the lost tragedy called Λήμνιαι of Sophoklês, see Welcker, Gr. Trag. i. 327) : the discrepancies among them are numerous and irreconcilable. Burmann, in the Catalogus Argonautarum, prefixed to his edition of Valerius Flaccus, has discussed them copiously. I transcribe one or two of the remarks of this conscientious and laborious critic, out of many of a similar tenor, on the impracticability of a fabulous chronology. Immediately before the first article, *Acastus* — " Neque enim in ætatibus Argonautarum ullam rationem temporum constare, neque in stirpe et stemmate deducendâ ordinem ipsum naturæ congruere videbam. Nam et huic militiæ adscribi videbam Heroas, qui per naturæ leges et ordinem fati eo usque vitam extrahere non potuêre, ut aliis ab hac expeditione remotis Heroum militiis nomina dedisse narrari deberent a Poetis et Mythologis. In idem etiam tempus avos et Nepotes conjici, consanguineos ætate longe inferiores prioribus ut æquales adjungi, concoquere vix posse videtur." — Art. *Ancæus* : " Scio objici posse, si seriem illam majorem respiciamus, hunc Ancæum simul cum proavo suo Talao in eandem profectum fuisse expeditionem. Sed similia exempla in aliis occurrent, et in fabulis rationem temporum non semper accuratam licet deducere." — Art. *Jasôn* : " Herculi enim jam provectâ ætate ad hæsit Theseus juvenis, et in Amazoniâ expeditione socius fuit, interfuit hui•. expeditioni, venatui apri Calydonii, et rapuit Helenam, quæ circa Trojanum bellum maxime floruit : quæ omnia si Theseus tot temporum intervallis distincta egit, secula duo vel tria vixisse debuit. Certe Jason Hypsipylem neptem Ariadnes, nec videre, nec Lemni cognoscere potuit." — Art. *Meleager* : " Unum est quod alicui longum ordinem majorum recensenti scrupulum movere possit : nimis longum intervallum inter Æolum et Meleagrum intercedere, ut potuerit interfuisse huic expeditioni : cum nonus fere numeretur ab Æolo, et plurimi ut Jason, Argus, et alii tertiâ tantum ab Æolo generatione distent. Sed sæpe jam notavimus, frustra temporum concordiam in fabulis quæri."

Read also the articles *Castôr and Pollux, Nestôr Pêleus, Staphylus*, etc.

We may stand excused for keeping clear of a chronology which is fertile only in difficulties, and ends in nothing but illusions.

the fruit of their visit. Hypsipylê, the queen of the island, bore to Jasôn two sons.[1]

They then proceeded onward along the coast of Thrace, up the Hellespont, to the southern coast of the Propontis, inhabited by the Doliones and their king Kyzikus. Here they were kindly entertained, but after their departure were driven back to the same spot by a storm; and as they landed in the dark, the inhabitants did not know them. A battle took place, in which the chief, Kyzikus, was killed by Jasôn; whereby much grief was occasioned as soon as the real facts became known. After Kyzikus had been interred with every demonstration of mourning and solemnity, the Argonauts proceeded along the coast of Mysia.[2] In this part of the voyage they left Hêraklês behind. For Hylas, his favorite youthful companion, had been stolen away by the nymphs of a fountain, and Hêraklês, wandering about in search of him, neglected to return. At last he sorrowfully retired, exacting hostages from the inhabitants of the neighboring town of Kius that they would persist in the search.[3]

---

[1] Apollodôr. i. 9, 17; Apollôn. Rhod. i. 609–915; Herodot. iv. 145. Theocritus (Idyll. xiii. 29) omits all mention of Lêmnos, and represent the Argô as arriving on the third day from Iôlkos at the Hellespont. Diodôrus (iv 41) also leaves out Lêmnos.

[2] Apollôn. Rhod. 940–1020; Apollodôr. i. 9, 18

[3] Apollodôr. i. 9, 19. This was the religious legend, explanatory of a cere mony performed for many centuries by the people of Prusa: they ran round the lake Askanias shouting and clamoring for Hylas — "ut littus Hyla, Hyla :mne sonaret." (Virgil, Eclog.).......... "in cujus memoriam adhuc solemni cursatione lacum populus circuit et Hylam voce clamat." Solinus, c. 42.

There is endless discrepancy as to the concern of Hêraklês with the Argonautic expedition. A story is alluded to in Aristotle (Politic. iii. 9) that the ship Argô herself refused to take him on board, because he was so much superior in stature and power to all the other heroes — οὐ γὰρ ἐθέλειν αὐτὸν ἄγειν τὴν Ἀργὼ μετὰ τῶν ἄλλων, ὡς ὑπερβάλλοντα πολὺ τῶν πλωτήρων. This was the story of Pherekydês (Fr. 67, Didot) as well as of Antimachus (Schol. Apoll. Rhod. i. 1290): it is probably a very ancient portion of the legend, inasmuch as it ascribes to the ship sentient powers, in consonance with her other miraculous properties. The etymology of Aphetæ in Thessaly was connected with the tale of Hêraklês having there been put on shore from the Argô (Herodot. vii. 193): Ephorus said that he staid away voluntarily from fondness for Omphalê (Frag. 9, Didot). The old epic poet

They next stopped in the country of the Bebrykians, where the boxing contest took place between the king Amykus and the Argonaut Pollux:[1] they then proceeded onward to Bithynia, the residence of the blind prophet Phineus. His blindness had been inflicted by Poseidôn as a punishment for having communicated to Phryxus the way to Kolchis. The choice had been allowed to him between death and blindness, and he had preferrec the latter.[2] He was also tormented by the harpies, winged monsters who came down from the clouds whenever his table was set, snatched the food from his lips and imparted to it a foul and unapproachable odor. In the midst of this misery, he hailed the Argonauts as his deliverers—his prophetic powers having enabled him to foresee their coming. The meal being prepared for him, the harpies approached as usual, but Zêtês and Kalais, the winged sons of Boreas, drove them away and pursued them. They put forth all their speed, and prayed to Zeus to be enabled to overtake the monsters; when Hermês appeared and directed them to desist, the harpies being forbidden further to molest Phineus,[3] and retiring again to their native cavern in Krête.[4]

Phineus, grateful for the relief afforded to him by the Argonauts, forewarned them of the dangers of their voyage and of the precautions necessary for their safety; and through his suggestions they were enabled to pass through the terrific rocks called Symplêgadcs. These were two rocks which alternately opened and

Kinæthôn said that Hêraklês had placed the Kian hostages at Trachin, and that the Kians ever afterwards maintained a respectful correspondence with that place (Schol. Ap. Rh. i. 1357). This is the explanatory legend connected with some existing custom, which we are unable further to unravel.

[1] See above, chap. viii. p. 169.

[2] Such was the old narrative of the Hesiodic Catalogue and Eoiai. See Schol. Apollôn. Rhod. ii. 181-296.

[3] This again was the old Hesiodic story (Schol. Apoll. Rhod. ii. 296), —

Ἐνθ᾽ οἵγ᾽ εὔχοσθον Αἰνηΐῳ ὑψιμέδοντι.

Apollodôrus (i. 9, 21), Apollônius (178-300), and Valerius Flacc. (iv. 428-530) agree in most of the circumstances.

[4] Such was the fate of the harpies as given in the old Naupaktian Verses (See Fragm. Ep. Græc. Düntzer, Naupakt. Fr. 2. p. 61).

The adventure of the Argonauts with Phineus is given by Diodôrus in a manner totally different (Diodôr. iv. 44): he seems to follow Dionysius of Mitylênê (see Schol. Apollôn. Rhod. ii. 207).

shut, with a swift and violent collision, so that it was difficult even
for a bird to fly through during the short interval. When the
Argô arrived at the dangerous spot, Euphêmus let loose a dove,
which flew through and just escaped with the loss of a few feath-
ers of her tail. This was a signal to the Argonauts, according
to the prediction of Phineus, that they might attempt the passage with confidence. Accordingly they rowed with all their
might, and passed safely through: the closing rocks, held for
a moment asunder by the powerful arms of Athênê, just crushed
the ornaments at the stern of their vessel. It had been decreed
by the gods, that so soon as any ship once got through, the passage should forever afterwards be safe and easy to all. The rocks
became fixed in their separate places, and never again closed.[1]

After again halting on the coast of the Maryandinians, where
their steersman Tiphys died, as well as in the country of the
Amazons, and after picking up the sons of Phryxus, who had
been cast away by Poseidôn in their attempt to return from Kolchis to Greece, they arrived in safety at the river Phasis and the
residence of Æêtes. In passing by Mount Caucasus, they saw
the eagle which gnawed the liver of Promêtheus nailed to the
rock, and heard the groans of the sufferer himself. The sons of
Phryxus were cordially welcomed by their mother Chalciopê.[2]
Application was made to Æêtês, that he would grant to the Argonauts, heroes of divine parentage and sent forth by the man-
date of the gods, possession of the golden fleece: their aid in
return was proffered to him against any or all of his enemies.
But the king was wroth, and peremptorily refused, except upon
conditions which seemed impracticable.[3] Hêphæstos had given
him two ferocious and untamable bulls, with brazen feet, which
breathed fire from their nostrils: Jasôn was invited, as a proof
both of his illustrious descent and of the sanction of the gods to
his voyage, to harness these animals to the yoke, so as to plough
a large field and sow it with dragon's teeth.[4] Perilous as the
condition was, each one of the heroes volunteered to make the

[1] Apollodór. i. 9, 22.   Apollôn. Rhod. ii. 310–615.
[2] Apollodòr. i. 9, 23.   Apollôn. Rhod. ii. 850–1257.
[3] Apollôn. Rhod. iii. 320–385.
[4] Apollôn. Rhod. iii. 410   Apollodôr. i. 9, 23

attempt. Idmôn especially encouraged Jasôn to undertake it,[1] and the goddesses Hêrê and Aphroditê made straight the way for him.[2] Mêdea, the daughter of Æêtês and Eidyia, having seen the youthful hero in his interview with her father, had conceived towards him a passion which disposed her to employ every means for his salvation and success. She had received from Hekatê preëminent magical powers, and she prepared for Jasôn the powerful Prometheian unguent, extracted from an herb which had grown where the blood of Promêtheus dropped. The body of Jasôn having been thus pre-medicated, became invulnerable[3] either by fire or by warlike weapons. He undertook the enterprise, yoked the bulls without suffering injury, and ploughed the field: when he had sown the dragon's teeth, armed men sprung out of the furrows. But he had been forewarned by Mêdea to cast a vast rock into the midst of them, upon which they began to fight with each other, so that he was easily enabled to subdue them all.[4]

The task prescribed had thus been triumphantly performed. Yet Æêtês not only refused to hand over the golden fleece, but even took measures for secretly destroying the Argonauts and burning their vessel. He designed to murder them during the night after a festal banquet; but Aphroditê, watchful for the safety of Jasôn,[5] inspired the Kolchian king at the critical moment with an irresistible inclination for his nuptial bed. While he slept, the wise Idmôn counselled the Argonauts to make their escape, and Mêdea agreed to accompany them.[6] She lulled to sleep by a magic potion the dragon who guarded the golden fleece,

---

[1] This was the story of the Naupaktian Verses (Schol. Apollôn. Rhod. iii. 515–525): Apollônius and others altered it. Idmôn, according to them, died in the voyage before the arrival at Kolchis.

[2] Apollôn. Rhod. iii. 50–200. Valer. Flacc. vi. 440–480. Hygin. fab. 22.

[3] Apollôn. Rhod. iii. 835. Apollodôr. i. 9, 23. Valer. Flacc. vii. 356 Ovid, Epist. xii. 15.

" Isset anhelatos non præmedicatus in ignes
Immemor Æsonides, oraque adunca boum."

[4] Apollôn. Rhod. iii. 1230–1400.

[5] The Naupaktian Verses stated this (see the Fragm. 6, ed. Düntzer, p. 61), ap. Schol. Apollôn. Rhod. iv. 59–86).

[6] Such was the story of the Naupaktian Verses (See Fragm. 6. p. 61 Düntzer ap. Schol. Apollôn. Rhod. iv. 59, 86, 87).

placed that much-desired prize on board the vessel, and accom
panied Jasôn with his companions in their flight, carrying along
with her the young Apsyrtus, her brother.[1]

Æêtês, profoundly exasperated at the flight of the Argonauts
with his daughter, assembled his forces forthwith, and put to sea
in pursuit of them. So energetic were his efforts that he shortly
overtook the retreating vessel, when the Argonauts again owed
their safety to the stratagem of Mêdea. She killed her brother
Apsyrtus, cut his body in pieces and strewed the limbs round
about in the sea. Æêtês on reaching the spot found these sorrowful traces of his murdered son; but while he tarried to collect the
scattered fragments, and bestow upon the body an honorable in-
terment, the Argonauts escaped.[2] The spot on which the unfortunate Apsyrtus was cut up received the name of Tomi.[3] This
fratricide of Mêdea, however, so deeply provoked the indignation
of Zeus, that he condemned the Argô and her crew to a trying

---

[1] Apollodôr. i. 9, 23. Apollôn. Rhod. iv. 220.
Pherekydês said that Jasôn killed the dragon (Fr. 74, Did.).

[2] This is the story of Apollodôrus (i. 9, 24), who seems to follow Pherekydês (Fr. 73, Didot). Apollônius (iv. 225-480) and Valerius Flaccus (viii.
262 seq.) give totally different circumstances respecting the death of Apsyrtus; but the narrative of Pherekydês seems the oldest: so revolting a story
as that of the cutting up of the little boy cannot have been imagined in later
times.

Sophoklês composed two tragedies on the adventures of Jasôn and Mêdea,
both lost — the Κολχίδες and the Σκύθαι. In the former he represented the
murder of the child Apsyrtus as having taken place in the house of Æêtês:
in the latter he introduced the mitigating circumstance, that Apsyrtus was
the son of Æêtês by a different mother from Mêdea (Schol. Apollôn Rhod.
iv. 223).

[3] Apollodôr. i. 9, 24, τὸν τόπον προσηγόρευσε Τόμους. Ovid. Trist. iii. 9.
The story that Apsyrtus was cut in pieces, is the etymological legend explanatory of the name Tomi.

There was however a place called Apsarus, on the southern coast of the
Euxine, west of Trapezus, where the tomb of Apsyrtus was shown, and
where it was affirmed that he had been put to death. He was the eponymus
of the town, which was said to have been once called Apsyrtus, and only
corrupted by a barbarian pronunciation (Arrian. Periplus, Euxin. p. 6;
Geogr. Min. v. 1). Compare Procop. Bell. Goth. iv. 2.

Strabo connects the death of Apsyrtus with the Apsyrtides, islands off the
coast of Illyria, in the Adriatic (vii. p. 315).

voyage, full of hardship and privation, before she was permitted to reach home. The returning heroes traversed an immeasurable length both of sea and of river: first up the river Phasis into the ocean which flows round the earth — then following the course of that circumfluous stream until its junction with the Nile,[1] they came down the Nile into Egypt, from whence they carried the Argô on their shoulders by a fatiguing land-journey to the lake Tritônis in Libya. Here they were rescued from the extremity of want and exhaustion by the kindness of the local god Tritôn, who treated them hospitably, and even presented to Euphêmus a clod of earth, as a symbolical promise that his descendants should one day found a city on the Libyan shore. The promise was amply redeemed by the flourishing and powerful city of Kyrênê,[2] whose princes the Battiads boasted themselves as lineal descendants of Euphêmus.

Refreshed by the hospitality of Tritôn, the Argonauts found themselves again on the waters of the Mediterranean in their way homeward. But before they arrived at Iôlkos they visited Circê, at the island of Ææa, where Mêdea was purified for the murder of Apsyrtus: they also stopped at Korkyra, then called Drepanê, where Alkinous received and protected them. The cave in that island where the marriage of Mêdea with Jason was consummated, was still shown in the time of the historian Timæus, as well as the altars to Apollo which she had erected, and the rites

---

[1] The original narrative was, that the Argô returned by navigating the circumfluous ocean. This would be almost certain, even without positive testimony, from the early ideas entertained by the Greeks respecting geography; but we know further that it was the representation of the Hesiodic poems, as well as of Mimnermus, Hekatæus and Pindar, and even of Antimachus. Schol. Parisina Ap. Rhod. iv. 254. Ἑκαταῖος δὲ ὁ Μιλήσιος διὰ τοῦ Φάσιδος ἀνελθεῖν φησὶν αὐτοὺς εἰς τὸν Ὠκεανόν· διὰ δὲ τοῦ Ὠκεανοῦ κατελθεῖν εἰς τὸν Νεῖλον· ἐκ δὲ τοῦ Νείλου εἰς τὴν καθ' ἡμᾶς θάλασσαν. Ἡσίοδος δὲ καὶ Πίνδαρος ἐν Πυθιονίκαις καὶ Ἀντίμαχος ἐν Λυδῇ διὰ τοῦ Ὠκεανοῦ φασὶν ἐλθεῖν αὐτοὺς εἰς τὴν Λιβύην· εἶτα βαστάσαντας τὴν Ἀργὼ εἰς τὸ ἡμέτερον ἀφικέσθαι πέλαγος. Compare the Schol. Edit. ad iv. 259.

[2] See the fourth Pythian Ode of Pindar, and Apollôn. Rhod. iv. 1551-1756. The tripod of Jasôn was preserved by the Euesperitæ in Libya, Diod. iv 56: but the legend, connecting the Argonauts with the lake Tritônis in Libya is given with some considerable differences in Herodotus, iv. 179.

and sacrifices which she had first instituted.¹ After leaving
Korkyra, the Argô was overtaken by a perilous storm near the
island of Thêra. The heroes were saved from imminent peril by
the supernatural aid of Apollo, who, shooting from his golden bow
an arrow which pierced the waves like a track of light, caused a
new island suddenly to spring up in their track and present to
them a port of refuge. The island was called Anaphê; and the
grateful Argonauts established upon it an altar and sacrifices in
honor of Apollo Æglêtês, which were ever afterwards continued,
and traced back by the inhabitants to this originating adventure.²

On approaching the coast of Krête, the Argonauts were prevented from landing by Talôs, a man of brass, fabricated by
Hêphæstos, and presented by him to Minôs for the protection of
the island.³ This vigilant sentinel hurled against the approaching vessel fragments of rock, and menaced the heroes with destruction. But Mêdea deceived him by a stratagem and killed
him; detecting and assailing the one vulnerable point in his body.
The Argonauts were thus enabled to land and refresh themselves.
They next proceeded onward to Ægina, where however they
again experienced resistance before they could obtain water —
then along the coast of Eubœa and Locris back to Iôlkos in the
gulf of Pagasæ, the place from whence they had started. The
proceedings of Pelias during their absence, and the signal revenge
taken upon him by Mêdea after their return, have already been
narrated in a preceding section.⁴ The ship Argô herself, in
which the chosen heroes of Greece had performed so long a
voyage and braved so many dangers, was consecrated by Jasôn to
Poseidôn at the isthmus of Corinth. According to another

---

¹ Apollôn. Rhod. iv. 1153–1217. Timæus, Fr. 7–8, Didot. Τίμαιος ἐν
Κερκύρᾳ λέγων γενέοθαι τοὺς γάμους, καὶ περὶ τῆς θυσίας ἱστορεῖ, ἔτι καὶ νῦν
λέγων ἄγεσθαι αὐτὴν κατ᾿ ἐνιαυτὸν, Μηδείας πρῶτου θυσάσης ἐν τῷ τοῦ Ἀπόλλωνος ἱερῷ. Καὶ βωμοὺς δέ φησι μνημεῖα τῶν γάμων ἱδρύσασθαι συνεγγὺς
μὲν τῆς θαλάσσης, οὐ μακρὰν δὲ τῆς πόλεως. Ὀνομάζουσι δὲ τὸν μὲν, Νυμφῶν·
τὸν δὲ, Νηρηΐδων.

² Apollodôr. i. 9, 25. Apollôn. Rhod. iv. 1700–1725.

³ Some called Talôs a remnant of the brazen race of men (Schol. Apoll.
Rhod. iv. 1641).

⁴ Apollodôr. i. 9, 26. Apollôn. Rhod. iv. 1638.

account, she was translated to the stars by Athênê, and became a constellation.[1] Traces of the presence of the Argonauts were found not only in the regions which lay between Iôlkos and Kolchis, but also in the western portion of the Grecian world — distributed more or less over all the spots visited by Grecian mariners or settled by Grecian colonists, and scarcely less numerous than the wanderings of the dispersed Greeks and Trojans after the capture of Troy. The number of Jasonia, or temples for the heroic worship of Jasôn, was very great, from Abdêra in Thrace,[2] eastward along the coast of the Euxine, to Armenia and Medea. The Argonauts had left their anchoring-stone on the coast of Bebrykia, near Kyzikus, and there it was preserved during the historical ages in the temple of the Jasonian Athênê.[3] They had founded the great temple of the Idæan mother on the mountain Dindymon, near Kyzikus, and the Hieron of Zeus Urios on the Asiatic point at the mouth of the Euxine, near which was also the harbor of Phryxus.[4] Idmôn, the prophet of the expedition, who was believed to have died of a wound by a wild boar on the Maryandynian coast, was worshipped by the inhabitants of the Pontic Hêrakleia with great solemnity, as their Heros Poliuchus, and that too by the special direction of the Delphian god. Autolykus, another companion of Jasôn, was worshipped as Œkist by the inhabitants of Sinopê. Moreover, the historians of Hêrakleia pointed out a temple of Hekatê in the neighboring country of

---

[1] Diodôr. iv. 53. Eratosth. Catasterism. c. 35.

[2] Strabo, xi. p. 526-531.

[3] Apollôn. Rhod. i. 955-960, and the Scholia.

There was in Kyzikus a temple of Apollo under different ἐπικλήσεις; some called it the temple of the Jasonian Apollo.

Another anchor however was preserved in the temple of Rhea on the banks of the Phasis, which was affirmed to be the anchor of the ship Argô. Arrian saw it there, but seems to have doubted its authenticity (Periplus, Euxin. Pont. p. 9. Geogr. Min. v. 1).

[4] Neanthês ap. strabo. i. p. 45. Apollôn. Rhod. i. 1125, and Schol. Steph. Byz. v. Φρίξος.

Apollônius mentions the fountain called Jasoneæ, on the hill of Dindymon. Apollôn. Rhod. ii. 532, and the citations from Timosthenês and Herodôrus in the Scholia. See also Appian. Syriac. c. 63.

Paphlagonia, first erected by Mêdea;[1] and the important town of Pantikapæon, on the European side of the Cimmerian Bosporus, ascribed its first settlement to a son of Æêtês.[2] When the returning ten thousand Greeks sailed along the coast, called the Jasonian shore, from Sinopê to Hêrakleia, they were told that the grandson of Æêtês was reigning king of the territory at the mouth of the Phasis, and the anchoring-places where the Argô had stopped were specially pointed out to them.[3] In the lofty regions of the Moschi, near Kolchis, stood the temple of Leukothea, founded by Phryxus, which remained both rich and respected down to the times of the kings of Pontus, and where it was an inviolable rule not to offer up a ram.[4] The town of Dioskurias, north of the river Phasis, was believed to have been hallowed by the presence of Kastôr and Pollux in the Argô, and to have received from them its appellation.[5] Even the interior of Mêdea and Armenia was full of memorials of Jasôn and Mêdea and their son Mêdus, or of Armenus the son of Jasôn, from whom the Greeks deduced not only the name and foundation of the Medes and Armenians, but also the great operation of cutting a channel through the mountains for the efflux of the river Araxes, which they compared to that of the Peneius in Thessaly.[6] And the

---

[1] See the historians of Hêrakleia, Nymphis and Promathidas, Fragm. Orelli, pp. 99, 100–104. Schol. ad Apollôn. Rhod. iv. 247. Strabo, xii. p. 546. Autolykus, whom he calls companion of Jasôn, was, according to another legend, comrade of Hêraklês in his expedition against the Amazons.

[2] Stephan. Byz. v. Παντικαπαῖον, Eustath. ad Dionys. Perieget. 311.

[3] Xenophôn, Anabas. vi. 2, 1 ; v. 7, 37.   [4] Strabo, xi. p. 499.

[5] Appian, Mithridatic. c. 101.

[6] Strabo, xi. p. 499, 503, 526, 531; i. p. 45–48. Justin, xlii. 3, whose statements illustrate the way in which men found a present home and application for the old fables, — "Jason, primus humanorum post Herculem et Liberum, qui reges Orientis fuisse traduntur, eam cœli plagam domuisse dicitur. Cum Albanis fœdus percussit, qui Herculem ex Italiâ ab Albano monte, cum, Geryone extincto, armenta ejus per Italiam duceret, secuti dicuntur; quique, memores Italicæ originis, exercitum Cn. Pompeii bello Mithridatico fratres consalutavêre. Itaque Jasoni totus fere Oriens, ut conditori, divinos honores templaque constituit; quae Parmenico, dux Alexandri Magni, post multos annos dirui jussit, ne cujusquam nomen in Oriente vene rabilius quam Alexandri esset."

The Thessalian companions of Alexander the Great, placed by his victories in possession of rich acquisitions in these regions, pleased themselves by

Roman general Pompey, after having completed the conquest and
expulsion of Mithridatês, made long marches through Kolchis
into the regions of Caucasus, for the express purpose of contemplating the spots which had been ennobled by the exploits of the
Argonaüts, the Dioskuri and Hêraklês.[1]

In the west, memorials either of the Argonauts or of the pursuing Kolchians were pointed out in Korkyra, in Krête, in Epirus near the Akrokeraunian mountains, in the islands called Apsyrtides near the Illyrian coast, at the bay of Caieta as well as at
Poseidônia on the southern coast of Italy, in the island of Æthalia or Elba, and in Libya.[2]

Such is a brief outline of the Argonautic expedition, one of
the most celebrated and widely-diffused among the ancient tales
of Greece. Since so many able men have treated it as an undisputed reality, and even made it the pivot of systematic chronological calculations, I may here repeat the opinion long ago
expressed by Heyne, and even indicated by Burmann, that the
process of dissecting the story, in search of a basis of fact, is one
altogether fruitless.[3] Not only are we unable to assign the date

---

vivifying and multiplying all these old fables, proving an ancient kindred
between the Medes and Thessalians. See Strabo, xi. p. 530. The temples
of Jasôn were τιμώμενα σφόδρα ὑπὸ τῶν βαρβάρων (ib. p, 526).

The able and inquisitive geographer Eratosthenês was among those who
fully believed that Jasôn had left his ships in the Phasis, and had undertaken
a land expedition into the interior country, in which he had conquered Media
and Armenia (Strabo, i. p. 48).

[1] Appian, Mithridatic. 103 : τοὺς Κόλχους ἐπῄει, καθ' ἱστορίαν τῆς Ἀργο
ναυτῶν καὶ Διοσκούρων καὶ Ἡρακλέους ἐπιδημίας, καὶ μάλιστα τὸ πάθος ἰδεῖν
ἐθέλων, ὃ Προμηθεῖ φασὶ γενέσθαι περὶ τὸ Καύκασον ὄρος. The lofty crag
of Caucasus called Strobilus, to which Prometheus had been attached,
was pointed out to Arrian himself in his Periplus (p. 12. Geogr. Minor.
vol. i.).

[2] Strabo, i. pp. 21, 45, 46 ; v. 224–252. Pompon. Mel. ii 3. Diodôr. iv.
56. Apollôn. Rhod. iv. 656. Lycophron, 1273.—

Τύρσιν μακεδνὰς ἀμφὶ Κιρκαίου νάπας
Ἀργοῦς τε κλεινὸν ὅρμον Αἰήτην μέγαν.

[3] Heyne, Observ. ad Apollodôr. i. 9, 16. p. 72. " Mirum in modum fallitur
qui in his commentis certum fundum historicum vel geographicum aut ex-

or identify the crew, or decipher the log-book, of the Argô, but
we have no means of settling even the preliminary question,
whether the voyage be matter of fact badly reported, or legend
from the beginning. The widely-distant spots in which the monuments of the voyage were shown, no less than the incidents of
the voyage itself, suggests no other parentage than epical fancy.
The supernatural and the romantic not only constitute an inseparable portion of the narrative, but even embrace all the prominent and characteristic features; if they do not comprise the
whole, and if there be intermingled along with them any sprink-
ling of historical or geographical fact, — a question to us indeter-
minable, — there is at least no solvent by which it can be disengaged, and no test by which it can be recognized. Wherever
the Grecian mariner sailed, he carried his religious and patriotic
mythes along with him. His fancy and his faith were alike full
of the long wanderings of Jasôn, Odysseus, Perseus, Hêraklês,
Dionysus, Triptolemus or Iô; it was pleasing to him in success,
and consoling to him in difficulty, to believe that their journeys
had brought them over the ground which he was himself travers-
ing. There was no tale amidst the wide range of the Grecian
epic more calculated to be popular with the seaman, than the
history of the primæval ship Argô and her distinguished crew,
comprising heroes from all parts of Greece, and especially the

---

quirere studet, aut se reperisse, atque historicam vel geographicam aliquam
doctrinam, systema nos dicimus, inde procudi posse, putat," etc.

See also the observations interspersed in Burmann's Catalogus Argonautarum, prefixed to his edition of Valerius Flaccus.

The Persian antiquarians whom Herodotus cites at the beginning of his
history (i. 2–4 — it is much to be regretted that Herodotus did not inform us
who they were, and whether they were the same as those who said that Perseus was an Assyrian by birth and had become a Greek, vi. 54), joined
together the abductions of Iô and of Eurôpê, of Mêdea and of Helen, as
pairs of connected proceedings, the second injury being a retaliation for the
first, — they drew up a debtor and creditor account of abductions between
Asia and Europe. The Kolchian king (they said) had sent a herald to
Greece to ask for his satisfaction for the wrong done to him by Jasôn and to
re-demand his daughter Mêdea; but he was told in reply that the Greeks had
received no satisfaction for the previous rape of Iô.

There was some ingenuity in thus binding together the old fables, so as to
represent the invasions of Greece by Darius and Xerxês as retaliations for
the unexpiated destruction wrought by Agamemnôn.

Tyndarids Kastôr and Pollux, the heavenly protectors invoked during storm and peril. He localized the legend anew wherever he went, often with some fresh circumstances suggested either by his own adventures or by the scene before him. He took a sort of religious possession of the spot, connecting it by a bond of faith with his native land, and erecting in it a temple or an altar with appropriate commemorative solemnities. The Jasonium thus established, and indeed every visible object called after the name of the hero, not only served to keep alive the legend of the Argô in the minds of future comers or inhabitants, but was accepted as an obvious and satisfactory proof that this marvellous vessel had actually touched there in her voyage.

The epic poets, building both on the general love of fabulous incident and on the easy faith of the people, dealt with distant and unknown space in the same manner as with past and unrecorded time. They created a mythical geography for the former, and a mythical history for the latter. But there was this material difference between the two: that while the unrecorded time was beyond the reach of verification, the unknown space gradually became trodden and examined. In proportion as authentic local knowledge was enlarged, it became necessary to modify the geography, or shift the scene of action, of the old mythes; and this perplexing problem was undertaken by some of the ablest historians and geographers of antiquity, — for it was painful to them to abandon any portion of the old epic, as if it were destitute of an ascertainable basis of truth.

Many of these fabulous localities are to be found in Homer and Hesiod, and the other Greek poets and logographers, — Erytheia, the garden of the Hesperides, the garden of Phœbus,[1] to which Boreas transported the Attic maiden Orithyia, the delicious country of the Hyperboreans, the Elysian plain,[2] the fleeting island of Æolus, Thrinakia, the country of the Æthiopians, the

---

[1] Sophokl. ap. Strabo. vii. p. 295. —

Ὑπέρ τε πόντον πάντ' ἐπ' ἔσχατα χθονὸς,
Νυκτός τε πηγὰς οὐρανοῦ τ' ἀναπτυχὰς,
Φοίβου τε παλαιὸν κῆπον.

[2] Odyss. iv. 562. The Islands of the Blessed, in Hesiod, are near the ocean (Opp. Di. 169).

Læstrygones, the Kyklôpes, the Lotophagi, the Sirens, the Cim
merians and the Gorgons,[1] etc. These are places which (to use
the expression of Pindar respecting the Hyperboreans) you cannot approach either by sea or by land :[2] the wings of the poet
alone can carry you thither. They were not introduced into the
Greek mind by incorrect geographical reports, but, on the contrary, had their origin in the legend, and passed from thence into
the realities of geography,[3] which they contributed much to per-
vert and confuse. For the navigator or emigrant, starting with
an unsuspicious faith in their real existence, looked out for them
in his distant voyages, and constantly fancied that he had seen or
heard of them, so as to be able to identify their exact situation.
The most contradictory accounts indeed, as might be expected,
were often given respecting the latitude and longitude of such
fanciful spots, but this did not put an end to the general belief
in their real existence.

In the present advanced state of geographical knowledge, the
story of that man who after reading Gulliver's Travels went to

---

[1] Hesiod, Theogon. 275–290. Homer, Iliad, i. 423. Odyss. i. 23; ix.
86–206; x 4–83; xii. 135. Mimnerm. Fragm. 13, Schneidewin.

[2] Pindar, Pyth. x. 29.—

Ναυσὶ δ' οὔτε πεζὸς ἰὼν ἂν εὕροις
'Ες 'Υπερβορέων ἀγῶνα θαυματὰν ὁδόν.
Παρ' οἷς ποτε Περσεὺς ἐδαίσατο λαγετὰς, etc.

Hesiod, and the old epic poem called the Epigoni, both mentioned the Hypei
boreans (Herod. iv. 32–34).

[3] This idea is well stated and sustained by Völcker (Mythische Geographie
der Griechen und Römer, cap. i. p. 11), and by Nitzsch in his Comments on
the Odyssey — Introduct. Remarks to b. ix. p. xii.–xxxiii. The twelfth
and thirteenth chapters of the History of Orchomenos, by O. Müller, are
also full of good remarks on the geography of the Argonautic voyage (pp.
274–299).

The most striking evidence of this disposition of the Greeks is to be
found in the legendary discoveries of Alexander and his companions, when
they marched over the untrodden regions in the east of the Persian empire
(see Arrian, Hist. Al. v. 3: compare Lucian. Dialog. Mortuor. xiv. vol. i. p.
212. Tauch), because these ideas were first broached at a time when geographical science was sufficiently advanced to canvass and criticize them.
The early settlers in Italy, Sicily and the Euxine, indulged their fanciful
vision without the fear of any such monitor: there was no such thing as a
map before the days of Anaximander, the disciple of Thalês.

look in his map for Lilliput, appears an absurdity. But those who fixed the exact locality of the floating island of Æolus or the rocks of the Sirens did much the same;[1] and, with their ignorance of geography and imperfect appreciation of historical evidence, the error was hardly to be avoided. The ancient belief which fixed the Sirens on the islands of Sirenusæ off the coast of Naples — the Kyklôpes, Erytheia, and the Læstrygones in Sicily — the Lotophagi on the island of Mêninx[2] near the Lesser Syrtis — the Phæakians at Korkyra — and the goddess Circê at the promontory of Circeium — took its rise at a time when these regions were first Hellenized and comparatively little visited. Once embodied in the local legends, and attested by visible monuments and ceremonies, it continued for a long time unassailed ; and Thucydidês seems to adopt it, in reference to Korkyra and Sicily before the Hellenic colonization, as matter of fact generally unquestionable,[3] though little avouched as to details. But when geograpical knowledge became extended, and the criticism upon the ancient epic was more or less systematized by the literary men of Alexandria and Pergamus, it appeared to many of them impossible that Odysseus could have seen so many wonders, or undergone such monstrous dangers, within limits so narrow, and in the familiar track between the Nile and the Tiber. The scene of his weather-driven course was then shifted further westward. Many convincing evidences were discovered, especially by Asklepiadês of Myrlea, of his having visited various places in Iberia:[4] several critics imagined that he

---

[1] See Mr. Payne Knight, Prolegg. ad Homer. c. 49. Compare Spohn — "de extremâ Odysseæ parte" — p. 97.

[2] Strabo, xvii. p. 834. An altar of Odysseus was shown upon this island, as well as some other evidences (σύμβολα) of his visit to the place.

Apollônius Rhodius copies the Odyssey in speaking of the island of Thrinakia and the cattle of Helios (iv. 965, with Schol.). He conceives Sicily as Thrinakia, a name afterwards exchanged for Trinakria. The Scholiast ad Apoll. (1. c.) speaks of Trinax king of Sicily. Compare iv. 291 with the Scholia.

[3] Thucyd. i. 25-vi. 2. These local legends appear in the eyes of Strabo convincing evidence (i. p. 23-26), — the tomb of the siren Parthenopê at Naples, the stories at Cumæ and Dikæarchia about the νεκυομαντεῖον of Avernus, and the existence of places named after Baius and Misênus, the companions of Odysseus, etc.

[4] Strabo, iii. p. 150-157. Οὐ γὰρ μόνον οἱ κατὰ τὴν Ἰταλίαν καὶ Σικελίαν

had wandered about in the Atlantic Ocean outside of the Strait
of Gibraltar,[1] and they recognized a section of Lotophagi on the

τόποι καὶ ἄλλοι τινὲς τῶν τοιούτων σημεῖα ὑπογράφουσιν, ἀλλὰ καὶ ἐν τῇ
'Ιβηρίᾳ 'Οδύσσεια πόλις δείκνυται, καὶ 'Αθηνᾶς ἱερὸν, καὶ ἄλλα μύρια ἴχνη
τῆς ἐκείνου πλάνης, καὶ ἄλλων τῶν ἐκ τοῦ Τρωϊκοῦ πολέμου περιγενομένων
(I adopt Grosskurd's correction of the text from γενομένων to περιγενομένων,
in the note to his German translation of Strabo).

Asklepiadês (of Myrlea in Bithynia, about 170 B. C.) resided some time
in Turditania, the south-western region of Spain along the Guadalquivir,
as a teacher of Greek literature (παιδεύσας τὰ γραμματικὰ), and composed a periegesis of the Iberian tribes, which unfortunately has not been
preserved. He made various discoveries in archæology, and successfully
connected his old legends with several portions of the territory before him.
His discoveries were, — 1. In the temple of Athênê, at this Iberian town of
Odysseia, there were shields and beaks of ships affixed to the walls, monuments of the visit of Odysseus himself. 2. Among the Kallæki, in the
northern part of Portugal, several of the companions of Teukros had settled and left descendants: there were in that region two Grecian cities, one
called Hellenês, the other called Amphilochi; for Amphilochus also, the son
of Amphiaraus, had died in Iberia, and many of his soldiers had taken up
their permanent residence in the interior. 3. Many new inhabitants had
come into Iberia with the expedition of Hêraklês; some also after the conquest of Mesênê by the Lacedæmonians. 4. In Cantabria, on the north
coast of Spain, there was a town and region of Lacedæmonians colonists.
5. In the same portion of the country there was the town of Opsikella,
founded by Opsikellas, one of the companions of Antenor in his emigration
from Troy (Strabo, iii. p. 157).

This is a specimen of the manner in which the seeds of Grecian mythus
came to be distributed over so large a surface. To an ordinary Greek
reader, these legendary discoveries of Asklepiadês would probably be more
interesting than the positive facts which he communicated respecting the
Iberian tribes; and his Turditanian auditors would be delighted to hear —
while he was reciting and explaining to them the animated passage of the
Iliad, in which Agamemnôn extols the inestimable value of the bow of
Teukros (viii. 281) — that the heroic archer and his companions had actually
set foot in the Iberian peninsula.

¹ This was the opinion of Kratês of Mallus, one of the most distinguished
of the critics on Homer: it was the subject of an animated controversy between him and Aristarchus (Aulus Gellius, N. A. xiv. 6; Strabo, iii. p. 157).
See the instructive treatise of Lehrs, De Aristarchi Studiis, c. v. § 4. p. 251.
Much controversy also took place among the critics respecting the ground
which Menelaus went over in his wanderings (Odyss. iv.). Kratês affirmed
that he had circumnavigated the southern extremity of Africa and gone to

coast of Mauritania, over and above those who dwelt on the island of Mêninx.[1] On the other hand, Eratosthenês and Apollodôrus treated the places visited by Odysseus as altogether un real, for which scepticism they incurred much reproach.[2] The fabulous island of Erytheia, — the residence of the three headed Geryôn with his magnificent herd of oxen, under the custody of the two-headed dog Orthrus, and described by Hesiod, like the garden of the Hesperides, as extra-terrestrial, on the farther side of the circumfluous ocean;— this island was supposed by the interpreters of Stesichorus the poet to be named by him off the south-western region of Spain called Tartêssus, and in the immediate vicinity of Gadês. But the historian Hekatæus, in his anxiety to historicize the old fable, took upon himself to remove·Erytheia from Spain nearer home to Epirus. He thought it incredible that Hêraklês should have traversed Europe from east.to west, for the purpose of bringing the cattle of Geryôn to Eurystheus at Mykênæ, and he pronounced Geryôn to have been a king of Epirus, near the Gulf of Ambrakia. The oxen reared in that neighborhood were proverbially magnificent, and to get them even from thence and bring them to Mykênæ (he contended) was ·no inconsiderable task. Arrian, who cites this passage from Hekatæus, concurs in the same view,— an illustration of the license with which ancient authors fitted on their fabulous geographical names to the real earth, and brought down the ethereal matter of legend to the lower atmosphere of history.[3]

India: the critic Aristonikus, Strabo's contemporary, enumerated all the different opinions (Strabo, i. p. 38).

[1] Strabo, iii. p. 157.   [2] Strabo, i. p. 22–44; vii. p. 299
[3] Stesichori Fragm. ed. Kleine; Geryonis, Fr. 5. p. 60; ap. Strabo. iii. p. 148; Herodot. iv. 8. It seems very doubtful whether Stesichorus meant to indicate any neighboring island as Erytheia, if we compare Fragm. 10. p. 67 of the Geryonis, and the passages of Athenæus and Eustathius there ctied. He seems to have adhered to the old fable, placing Erytheia on the opposite side of the ocean-stream, for Hêraklês crosses the ocean to get to it.

Hekatæus, ap. Arrian. Histor. Alex. ii. 16. Skylax places Erytheia, " whither Geryôn is said to have come to feed his oxen," in the Kastid territory near the Greek city of Apollônia on the Ionic Gulf, northward of the Keraunian mountains. There were splendid cattle consecrated to Hélios

11*

Both the track and the terminus of the Argonautic voyage appear in the most ancient epic as little within the conditions of reality, as the speaking timbers or the semi-divine crew of the vessel. In the Odyssey, Æêtês and Circê (Hesiod names Mêdea also) are brother and sister, offspring of Hêlios. The Ææan island, adjoining the circumfluous ocean, " where the house and dancing-ground of Eôs are situated, and where Hêlios rises," is both the residence of Circê and of Æêtês, inasmuch as Odysseus, in returning from the former, follows the same course as the Argô had previously taken in returning from the latter.[1] Even in the conception of Mimnermus, about 600 B. C., Æa still retained its fabulous attributes in conjunction with the ocean and Hêlios, without having been yet identified with any known portion of the solid earth ;[2] and it was justly remarked by Dêmêtrius of Skêpsis in antiquity[3] (though

---

near Apollônia, watched by the citizens of the place with great care (Herodot. ix. 93; Skylax, c. 26).

About Erytheia, Cellerius observes (Geogr. Ant. ii. 1, 227), "Insula Erytheia, quam veteres adjungunt Gadibus, vel demersa est, vel in scopulis quærenda, vel pars est ipsarum Gadium, neque hodie ejus formæ aliqua, uti descripta est, fertur superesse." To make the disjunctive catalogue complete, he ought to have added, " or it never really existed," — not the least probable supposition of all.

[1] Hesiod, Theogon. 956–992; Homer, Odyss. xii. 3–69. —

$$\text{Νῆσον ἐς Αἰαίην, ὄθι τ' 'Ηοῦς ἠριγενείης}$$
$$\text{Οἴκια καὶ χόροι εἰσί, καὶ ἀντολαὶ ἠελίοιο.}$$

[2] Mimnerm. Fragm. 10–11, Schneidewin; Athenæ. vii. p. 277. —

$$\text{Οὐδέ κοτ' ἂν μέγα κῶας ἀνήγαγεν αὐτὸς 'Ιήσων}$$
$$\text{'Εξ Αἴης τελέσας ἀλγινόεσσαν ὁδόν,}$$
$$\text{'Υβρίστῃ Πελίῃ τελέων χαλεπῆρες ἄεθλον,}$$
$$\text{Οὐδ' ἂν ἐπ' 'Ωκεανοῦ καλὸν ἵκοντο ῥόον.}$$

* * * * *

$$\text{Αἰήταο πόλιν, τόθι τ' ὠκέος 'Ηελίοιο}$$
$$\text{'Ακτῖνες χρυσέῳ κείαται ἐν θαλάμῳ,}$$
$$\text{'Ωκεανοῦ παρὰ χείλεσ', ἵν' ᾤχετο θεῖος 'Ιήσων.}$$

[3] Strabo, i. p. 45–46. Δεμήτριος ὁ Σκήψιος ...... πρὸς Νεάνθη τὸν Κυζικηνὸν φιλοτιμοτέρως ἀντιλέγων, εἰπόντα, ὅτι οἱ 'Αργοναῦται πλέοντες εἰς Φᾶσιν τὸν ὑφ' 'Ομήρου καὶ τῶν ἄλλων ὁμολογούμενον πλοῦν, ἱδρύσαντο τὰ τῆς 'Ιδαίας μητρὸς ἱερὰ ἐπὶ Κύζικον ...... ἀρχήν φησὶ μηδ' εἰδέναι τὴν εἰς Φᾶσιν ἀποδημίαν τοῦ 'Ιάσονος 'Ομηρον. Again, p. 46, παραλαβὼν μάρτυρα Μίμνερμον, ὃς ἐν τῷ 'Ωκεανῷ ποιήσας οἴκησιν Αἰήτου, etc.

The adverb φιλοτιμοτέρως reveals to us the municipal rivalry and conten-

Strabo vainly tries to refute him), that neither Homer nor Mimnermus designates Kolchis either as the residence of Æêtês, or as the terminus of the Argonautic voyage. Hesiod carried the returning Argonauts through the river Phasis into the ocean. But some of the poems ascribed to Eumêlus were the first which mentioned Æêtês and Kolchis, and interwove both of them into the Corinthian mythical genealogy.[1] These poems seem to have been composed subsequent to the foundation of Sinopê, and to the commencement of Grecian settlement on the Borysthenês, between the years 600 and 500 B. C. The Greek mariners who explored and colonized the southern coast of the Euxine, found at the extremity of their voyage the river Phasis and its barbarous inhabitants: it was the easternmost point which Grecian navigation (previous to the time of Alexander the Great) ever attained, and it was within sight of the impassable barrier of Caucasus.[2] They believed, not unnaturally, that they had here found "the house of Eôs (the morning) and the rising place of the sun," and that the river Phasis, if they could follow it to its unknown beginning, would conduct them to the circumfluous ocean. They gave to the spot the name of Æa, and the fabulous and real title gradually became associated together into one compound appellation, — the Kolchian Æa, or Æa of Kolchis.[3] While Kolchis was thus entered on the map as a fit representative for the Homeric "house of the morning," the narrow strait of the Thracian Bosporus attracted to itself the poetical fancy of the Symplêgades, or colliding rocks, through which the heaven-protected Argo had been the first to pass. The powerful Greek cities of Kyzikus, Hêrakleia and Sinopê, each fertile in local legends, still farther contributed to give this direction to the voyage ; so that in the time of Hekatæus it had become the established belief that the Argô had started from Iôlkos and gone to Kolchis.

Æêtês thus received his home from the legendary faith and

tion between the small town Skêpsis and its powerful neighbor Kyzikus, respecting points of comparative archæology.

[1] Eumêlus, Fragm. Εὑρωπία 7, Κορινϑιακὰ 2–5. pp. 63–68, Düntzer.

[2] Arrian, Periplus Pont. Euxin. p. 12; ap. Geogr. Minor. vol. i. He saw the Caucasus from Dioskurias.

[3] Herodot i. 2; vii. 193–197. Eurip. Med. 2. Valer. Flacc. v. 51

fancy of the eastern Greek navigators: his sister Circê, originally his fellow-resident, was localized by the western. The
Hesiodic and other poems, giving expression to the imaginative
impulses of the inhabitants of Cumæ and other early Grecian
settlers in Italy and Sicily,¹ had referred the wanderings of
Odysseus to the western or Tyrrhenian sea, and had planted the
Cyclôpes, the Læstrygones, the floating island of Æolus, the
Lotophagi, the Phæacians, etc., about the coast of Sicily, Italy,
Libya, and Korkyra. In this way the Ææan island,— the resi
dence of Circê, and the extreme point of the wanderings of
Odysseus, from whence he passes only to the ocean and into
Hadês — came to be placed in the far west, while the Æa of
Æêtês was in the far east,— not unlike our East and West Indies. The Homeric brother and sister were separated and sent
to opposite extremities of the Grecian terrestrial horizon.²

The track from Iôlkos to Kolchis, however, though plausible
as far as it went, did not realize all the conditions of the genuine
fabulous voyage: it did not explain the evidences of the visit of
these maritime heroes which were to be found in Libya, in Krêtê

---

¹ Strabo, i. p. 23. Völcker (Ueber Homerische Geographie, v. 66) is instructive upon this point, as upon the geography of the Greek poets generally. He recognizes the purely mythical character of Æa in Homer and
Hesiod, but he tries to prove — unsuccessfully, in my judgment — that
Homer places Æêtês in the east, while Circê is in the west, and that Homer
refers the Argonautic voyage to the Euxine Sea.

² Strabo (or Polybius, whom he has just been citing) contends that Homer
knew the existence of Æêtês in Kolchis, and of Circê at Circeium, as historical persons, as well as the voyage of Jasôn to Æa as an historical fact.
Upon this he (Homer) built a superstructure of fiction (προσμύϑευμα): he
invented the brotherhood between them, and he placed both the one and the
other in the exterior ocean (συγγενείας τε ἔπλασε τῶν οὕτω διῳκισμένων, καὶ
ἐξωκεανισμὸν ἀμφοῖν, i. p. 20); perhaps also Jasôn might have wandered as
far as Italy, as evidences (σημεῖά τινα) are shown that he did (ib.).

But the idea that Homer conceived Æêtês in the extreme east and Circê
in the extreme west, is not reconcilable with the Odyssey. The supposition
of Strabo is alike violent and unsatisfactory.

Circê was worshipped as a goddess at Circeii (Cicero, Nat. Deor. iii. 19).
Hesiod, in the Theogony, represents the two sons of Circê by Odysseus as
reigning over all the warlike Tyrrhenians (Theog. 1012), an undefined
western sovereignty. The great Mamilian gens at Tusculum traced their
descent to Odysseus and Circê (Dionys. Hal. iv. 45).

in Anaphê, in Korkyra, in the Adriatic Gulf, in Italy and in
Æthalia. It became necessary to devise another route for them
in their return, and the Hesiodic narrative was (as I have before
observed), that they came back by the circumfluous ocean; first
going up the river Phasis into the circumfluous ocean; following that deep and gentle stream until they entered the Nile,
and came down its course to the coast of Libya. This seems
also to have been the belief of Hekatæus.[1] But presently several Greeks (and Herodotus among them) began to discard the
idea of a circumfluous ocean-stream, which had pervaded their
old geographical and astronomical fables, and which explained
the supposed easy communication between one extremity of the
earth and another. Another idea was then started for the returning voyage of the Argonauts. It was supposed that the river
Ister, or Danube, flowing from the Rhipæan mountains in the
north-west of Europe, divided itself into two branches, one of
which fell into the Euxine Sea, and the other into the Adriatic.

The Argonauts, fleeing from the pursuit of Æêtês, had been
obliged to abandon their regular course homeward, and had gone
from the Euxine Sea up the Ister; then passing down the other
branch of that river, they had entered into the Adriatic, the
Kolchian pursuers following them. Such is the story given by
Apollônius Rhodius from Timagêtus, and accepted even by so
able a geographer as Eratosthenês — who preceded him by one
generation, and who, though sceptical in regard to the localities
visited by Odysseus, seems to have been a firm believer in the
reality of the Argonautic voyage.[2] Other historians again, among

---

[1] See above, p. 239. There is an opinion cited from Hekatæus in Schol.
Apoll. Rhod. iv. 284. contrary to this, which is given by the same scholiast
on iv. 259. But, in spite of the remarks of Klausen (ad Fragment. Hekatæi, 187. p. 98), I think that the Schol. ad. iv. 284 has made a mistake in
citing Hekatæus; the more so as the scholiast, as printed from the Codex
Parisinus, cites the same opinion without mentioning Hekatæus. Accord
ing to the old Homeric idea, the ocean stream flowed all round the earth,
and was the source of all the principal rivers which flowed into the great internal sea, or Mediterranean (see Hekatæus, Fr. 349; Klausen, ap. Arrian.
ii. 16, where he speaks of the Mediterranean as the μεγάλη θάλασσα). Retaining this old idea of the ocean-stream, Hekatæus would naturally believe
that the Phasis joined it: nor can I agree with Klausen (ad Fr. 187) that
this implies a degree of ignorance too gross to impute to him.

[2] Apollôn. Rhod. iv. 287; Schol. ad iv. 284: Pindar. Pyth. iv. 447, with

whom was Timæus, though they considered the ocean as an outer sea, and no longer admitted the existence of the old Homeric ocean-stream, yet imagined a story for the return-voyage of the Argonauts somewhat resembling the old tale of Hesiod and Hekatæus. They alleged that the Argô, after entering into the Palus Mæotis, had followed the upward course of the river Tanais; that she had then been carried overland and launched in a river which had its mouth in the ocean or great outer sea. When in the ocean, she had coasted along the north and west of Europe until she reached Gadês and the Strait of Gibraltar, where she entered into the Mediterranean, and there visited the many places specified in the fable. Of this long voyage, in the outer sea to the north and west of Europe, many traces were affirmed to exist along the coast of the ocean.[1] There was again a third version, according to which the Argonauts came back as they went, through the Thracian Bosporus and the Hellespont. In this way geographical plausibility was indeed maintained, but a large portion of the fabulous matter was thrown overboard.[2]

Such were the various attempts made to reconcile the Argonautic legend with enlarged geographical knowledge and improved historical criticism. The problem remained unsolved, but the

---

Schol.; Strabo, i. p. 46–57; Aristot. Mirabil. Auscult. c. 105. Altars were shown in the Adriatic, which had been erected both by Jasôn and by Mêdea (*ib*).

Aristotle believed in the forked course of the Ister, with one embochure in the Euxine and another in the Adriatic: he notices certain fishes called τρι-χίαι, who entered the river (like the Argonauts) from the Euxine, went up it as far as the point of bifurcation and descended into the Adriatic (Histor. Animal. viii. 15). Compare Ukert, Geographie der Griech. und Römer, vol. iii. p. 145–147, about the supposed course of the Ister.

[1] Diodôr. iv. 56; Timæus, Fragm. 53. Göller. Skymnus the geographer also adopted this opinion (Schol. Apoll. Rhod. 284–287). The pseudo-Orpheus in the poem called Argonautica seems to give a jumble of all the different stories.

[2] Diodôr. iv. 49. This was the tale both of Sophoklês and of Kallimachus (Schol. Apoll. Rhod. iv. 2f4).

See the Dissertation of Ukert, Beylage iv. vol. i. part 2. p. 320 of his Geographie der Griechen und Römer, which treats of the Argonautic voyage at some length; also J. H. Voss, Alte Weltkunde über die Gestalt der Erde, published in the second volume of the Kritische Blätter, pp. 162, 314–326; and Forbiger, Handbuch der Alten Geographie-Einleitung, p. 8.

faith in the legend did not the less continue. It was a faith
originally generated at a time when the unassisted narrative of
the inspired poet sufficed for the conviction of his hearers; it
consecrated one among the capital exploits of that heroic and
superhuman race, whom the Greek was accustomed at once to
look back upon as his ancestors and to worship conjointly with
his gods: it lay too deep in his mind either to require historical
evidence for its support, or to be overthrown by geographical
difficulties as they were then appreciated. Supposed traces of
the past event, either preserved in the names of places, or embodied in standing religious customs with their explanatory comments, served as sufficient authentication in the eyes of the curious
inquirer. And even men trained in a more severe school of
criticism contented themselves with eliminating the palpable contradictions and softening down the supernatural and romantic
events, so as to produce an Argonautic expedition of their own
invention as the true and accredited history. Strabo, though he
can neither overlook nor explain the geographical impossibilities
of the narrative, supposes himself to have discovered the basis
of actual fact, which the original poets had embellished or exaggerated. The golden fleece was typical of the great wealth of
Kolchis, arising from gold-dust washed down by the rivers; and
the voyage of Jasôn was in reality an expedition at the head of
a considerable army, with which he plundered this wealthy country and made extensive conquests in the interior.[1] Strabo has
nowhere laid down what he supposes to have been the exact
measure and direction of Jasôn's march, but he must have regarded it as very long, since he classes Jasôn with Dionysus and
Hêraklês, and emphatically characterizes all the three as having

---

[1] Strabo, i. p. 45. He speaks here of the voyage of Phryxus, as well as
that of Jasôn, as having been a military undertaking (στρατεία): so again,
iii. p. 149, he speaks of the military expedition of Odysseus — ἡ τοῦ 'Οδυσ-
σέως στρατία, and ἡ 'Ηρακλέους στρατία (ib.). Again xi. p. 498. Οἱ μῦθοι,
αἰνιττόμενοι τὴν 'Ιάσονος στρατείαν προελθόντος μέχρι καὶ Μηδίας· ἔτι δὲ
πρότερον τὴν Φρίξου. Compare also Justin, xlii. 2-3; Tacit. Annal. vi. 34.

Strabo cannot speak of the old fables with literal fidelity: he unconsciously transforms them into quasi-historical incidents of his own imagination.
Diodôrus gives a narrative of the same kind, with decent substitutes for the
fabulous elements (iv. 40-47-56).

traversed wider spaces of ground than any moderns could equal.[1]
Such was the compromise which a mind like that of Strabo made
with the ancient legends. He shaped or cut them down to the
level of his own credence, and in this waste of historical criticism,
without any positive evidence, he took to himself the credit of
greater penetration than the literal believers, while he escaped
the necessity of breaking formally with the bygone heroic world

---

CHAPTER XIV.

LEGENDS OF THEBES.

The Bœôtians generally, throughout the historical age, though
well endowed with bodily strength and courage,[2] are represented
as proverbially deficient in intelligence, taste and fancy. But
the legendary population of Thêbes, the Kadmeians, are rich in
mythical antiquities, divine as well as heroic. Both Dionysus
and Hêraklês recognize Thêbes as their natal city. Moreover,
the two sieges of Thêbes by Adrastus, even taken apart from

---

[1] Strabo, i. p. 48. The far-extending expeditions undertaken in the eastern regions by Dionysus and Hêraklês were constantly present to the mind
of Alexander the Great as subjects of comparison with himself: he imposed
upon his followers perilous and trying marches, from anxiety to equal or
surpass the alleged exploits of Semiramis, Cyrus, Perseus, and Hêraklês.
(Arrian, v. 2, 3; vi. 24, 3; vii. 10, 12. Strabo, iii. p. 171; xv. p. 686; xvii.
p. 81).

[2] The eponym Bœôtus is son of Poseidôn and Arnê (Euphorion ap.
Eustath. ad Iliad. ii. 507). It was from Arnê in Thessaly that the Bœôtians
were said to have come, when they invaded and occupied Bœôtia. Euripidês made him son of Poseidôn and Melanippê. Another legend recited
Bœôtus and Hellên as sons of Poseidôn and Antiopê (Hygin. f. 157-186).

The Tanagræan poetess Korinna (the rival of Pindar, whose compositions
in the Bœôtian dialect are unfortunately lost) appears to have dwelt upon
this native Bœôtian genealogy: she derived the Ogygian gates of Thêbes
from Ogygus, son of Bœôtus (Schol. Apollôn. Rhod. iii. 1178), also the Frag
ments of Korinna in Schneidewin's edition, fr. 2. p. 432.

Kadmus, Antiopê, Amphiôn and Zethus, etc., are the most prominent and most characteristic exploits, next to the siege of Troy,
of that preëxisting race of heroes who lived in the imagination
of the historical Hellênes.

It is not Kadmus, but the brothers Amphiôn and Zethus, who
are given to us in the Odyssey as the first founders of Thêbes
and the first builders of its celebrated walls. They are the sons
of Zeus by Antiopê, daughter of Asôpus. The scholiasts who
desire to reconcile this tale with the more current account of the
foundation of Thêbes by Kadmus, tell us that after the death of
Amphiôn and Zethus, Eurymachus, the warlike king of the
Phlegyæ, invaded and ruined the newly-settled town, so that
Kadmus on arriving was obliged to re-found it.[1] But Apollodôrus, and seemingly the older logographers before him, placed
Kadmus at the top, and inserted the two brothers at a lower
point in the series. According to them, Bêlus and Agenôr were
the sons of Epaphus, son of the Argeian Iô, by Libya. Agenôr
went to Phœnicia and there became king: he had for his offspring Kadmus, Phœnix, Kilix, and a daughter Eurôpa; though
in the Iliad Eurôpa is called daughter of Phœnix.[2] Zeus fell in
love with Eurôpa, and assuming the shape of a bull, carried her
across the sea upon his back from Egpyt to Krête, where she
bore to him Minôs, Rhadamanthus and Sarpêdôn. Two out of
the three sons sent out by Agenôr in search of their lost sister,
wearied out by a long-protracted as well as fruitless voyage,
abandoned the idea of returning home: Kilix settled in Kilikia,
and Kadmus in Thrace.[3] Thasus, the brother or nephew of

---

[1] Homer, Odyss. xi. 262, and Eustath. ad loc. Compare Schol. ad Iliad.
xiii. 301.

[2] Iliad, xiv. 321. Iô is κερόεσσα προμάτωρ of the Thêbans. Eurip. Phœniss. 247–676.

[3] Apollodôr. ii. 1, 3; iii. 1, 8. In the Hesiodic poems (ap. Schol. Apoll.
Rhod. ii. 178), Phœnix was recognized as son of Agenôr. Pherekydês also
described both Phœnix and Kadmus as sons of Agenôr (Pherekyd. Fragm.
40, Didot). Compare Servius ad. Virgil. Æneid. 1. 338. Pherekydês expressly mentioned Kilix (Apollod. ib.). Besides the Εὐρώπεια of Stesichorus (see Stesichor. Fragm. xv. p. 73, ed. Kleine), there were several other
ancient poems on the adventures of Europa; one in particular by Eumêlus
(Schol. ad Iliad. vi. 138), which however can hardly be the same as the τὰ

Kadmus, who had accompanied them in the voyage, settled and gave name to the island of Phasus.

Both Herodotus and Euripidês represent Kadmus as an emigrant from Phœnicia, conducting a body of followers in quest of Eurôpa. The account of Apollodôrus describes him as having come originally from Libya or Egypt to Phœnicia: we may presume that this was also the statement of the earlier logographers Pherekydês and Hellanikus. Conôn, who historicizes and politicizes the whole legend, seems to have found two different accounts; one connecting Kadmus with Egypt, another bringing him from Phœnicia. He tries to melt down the two into one, by representing that the Phœnicians, who sent out Kadmus, had acquired great power in Egypt — that the seat of their kingdom was the Egyptian Thêbes — that Kadmus was despatched, under pretence indeed of finding his lost sister, but really on a project of conquest — and that the name Thêbes, which he gave to his new establishment in Bœôtia, was borrowed from Thêbes in Egypt, his ancestorial seat.[1]

Kadmus went from Thrace to Delphi to procure information respecting his sister Eurôpa, but the god directed him to take no further trouble about her; he was to follow the guidance of a cow, and to found a city on the spot where the animal should lie down. The condition was realized on the site of Thêbes. The neighboring fountain Areia was guarded by a fierce dragon, the offspring of Arês, who destroyed all the persons sent to fetch water. Kadmus killed the dragon, and at the suggestion of Athênê sowed his teeth in the earth:[2] there sprang up at once the armed men called the Sparti, among whom he flung stones,

---

ἔπη τὰ εἰς Εὐρώπην alluded to by Pausanias (ix. 5, 4). See Wüllner de Cyclo Epico, p. 57 (Münster 1825).

[1] Conôn, Narrat. 37. Perhaps the most remarkable thing of all is the tone of unbounded self-confidence with which Conôn winds up this tissue of uncertified suppositions — περὶ μὲν Κάδμου καὶ Θηβῶν οἰκίσεως οὗτος ὁ ἀληθῆς λόγος· τὸ δὲ ἄλλο μῦθος καὶ γοητεία ἀκοῆς.

[2] Stesichor. (Fragm. 16; Kleine) ap. Schol. Eurip. Phœniss. 680. The place where the heifer had lain down was still shown in the time of Pausanias (ix. 12, 1).

Lysimachus, a lost author who wrote Thebaïca, mentioned Eurôpa as having come with Kadmus to Thêbes, and told the story in many other respects very differently (Schol. Apoll. Rhod. iii. 1179).

and they immediately began to assault each other until all were slain except five. Arês, indignant at this slaughter, was about to kill Kadmus; but Zeus appeased him, condemning Kadmus to an expiatory servitude of eight years, after which he married Harmonia, the daughter of Arês and Aphroditê — presenting to her the splendid necklace fabricated by the hand of Hêphæstos, which had been given by Zeus to Eurôpa.[1] All the gods came to the Kadmeia, the citadel of Thêbes, to present congratulations and gifts at these nuptials, which seem to have been hardly less celebrated in the mythical world than those of Pêleus and Thetis. The issue of the marriage was one son, Polydôrus, and four daughters, Autonoê, Inô, Semelê and Agavê.[2]

From the five who alone survived of the warriors sprung from the dragon's teeth, arose five great families or gentes in Thêbes; the oldest and noblest of its inhabitants, coeval with the foundation of the town. They were called Sparti, and their name seems to have given rise, not only to the fable of the sowing of the teeth, but also to other etymological narratives.[3]

All the four daughters of Kadmus are illustrious in fabulous history. Inô, wife of Athamas, the son of Æolus, has already been included among the legends of the Æolids. Semelê became the mistress of Zeus, and inspired Hêrê with jealousy. Misguided by the malicious suggestions of that goddess, she solicited Zeus to visit her with all the solemnity and terrors which sur-

---

[1] Apollodôr. iii. 4, 1–3 Pherekydês gave this account of the necklace, which seems to imply that Kadmus must have found his sister Eurôpa. The narrative here given is from Hellanikus; that of Pherekydês differed from it in some respects: compare Hellanik. Fragm. 8 and 9, and Pherekyd. Frag. 44. The resemblance of this story with that of Jasôn and Æêtês (see above, chap. xiii. p. 237) will strike every one. It is curious to observe how the old logographer Pherekydês explained this analogy in his narrative; he said that Athênê had given half the dragon's teeth to Kadmus and half to Æêtês (see Schol. Pindar. Isthm. vi. 13).

[2] Hesiod, Theogon. 976. Leukothea, the sea-goddess, daughter of Kadmus, is mentioned in the Odyssey, v. 334; Diodôr. iv. 2.

[3] Eurip. Phœniss. 680, with the Scholia; Pherekydês, Fragm. 44; Andrôtion, ap. Schol. Pindar. Isthm. vi. 13. Dionysius (?) called the Sparti an ἔθνος Βοιωτίας (Schol. Phœniss. 1. c.).

Even in the days of Plutarch, there were persons living who traced their descent to the Sparti of Thêbes (Plutarch, Ser. Num. Vindict. p. 563).

rounded him when he approached Hêrê herself. The god unwillingly consented, and came in his chariot in the midst of
thunder and lightning, under which awful accompaniments the
mortal frame of Semelê perished. Zeus, taking from her the
child of which she was pregnant, sewed it into his own thigh:
after the proper interval the child was brought out and born, and
became the great god Dionysus or Bacchus. Hermês took him
to Inô and Athamas to receive their protection. Afterwards,
however, Zeus having transformed him into a kid to conceal him
from the persecution of Hêrê, the nymphs of the mountain Nysa
became his nurses.[1]

Autonoê, the third daughter of Kadmus, married the pastoral
hero or god Aristæas, and was mother of Aktæôn, a devoted
hunter and a favorite companion of the goddess Artemis. She
however became displeased with him — either because he looked
into a fountain while she was bathing and saw her naked — or
according to the legend set forth by the poet Stesichorus, because
he loved and courted Semelê — or according to Euripidês, because he presumptuously vaunted himself as her superior in the
chase. She transformed him into a stag, so that his own dogs
set upon and devoured him. The rock upon which Aktæôn used
to sleep when fatigued with the chase, and the spring whose
transparent waters had too clearly revealed the form of the goddess, were shown to Pausanias near Platæa, on the road to
Megara.[2]

---

[1] Apollodôr. iii. 4, 2–9 ; Diodôr. iv. 2.

[2] See Apollodôr. iii. 4, 3; Stesichor. Fragm. xvii. Kleine; Pausan. ix. 2,
3; Eurip. Bacch. 337; Diodôr. iv. 81. The old logographer Akusilaus
copied Stesichorus.

Upon this well-known story it is unnecessary to multiply references. I
shall however briefly notice the remarks made upon it by Diodôrus and by
Pausanias, as an illustration of the manner in which the literary Greeks of a
later day dealt with their old national legends.

Both of them appear implicitly to believe the fact, that Aktæôn was
devoured by his own dogs, but they differ materially in the explanation
of it.

Diodôrus accepts and vindicates the miraculous interposition of the displeased goddess to punish Aktæôn, who, according to one story, had boasted
of his superiority in the chase to Artemis, — according to another story, had
presumed to solicit the goddess in marriage, emboldened by the great numbers of the feet of animals slain in the chase which he had hung up as offer-

Agavê, the remaining daughter of Kadmus, married Echiôn, one of the Sparti. The issue of these nuptials was Pentheus, who, when Kadmus became old succeeded him as king of Thêbes. In his reign Dionysus appeared as a god, the author or discoverer of the vine with all its blessings. He had wandered over Asia, India and Thrace, at the head of an excited troop of female enthusiasts — communicating and inculcating everywhere the Bacchic ceremonies, and rousing in the minds of women that impassioned religious emotion which led them to ramble in solitary mountains at particular seasons, there to give vent to violent fanatical excitement, apart from the men, clothed in fawn-skins and armed with the thyrsus. The obtrusion of a male spectator upon these solemnities was esteemed sacrilegious. Though the rites had been rapidly disseminated and fervently welcomed in many parts of Thrace, yet there were some places in which they had been obstinately resisted and their votaries treated with rudeness ; especially by Lykurgus, king of the Edonian Thracians, upon whom a sharp and exemplary punishment was inflicted by Dionysus.

Thêbes was the first city of Greece to which Dionysus came,

---

ings in her temple. "It is not improbable (observes Diodôrus) that the goddess was angry on both these accounts. For whether Aktæôn abused these hunting presents so far as to make them the means of gratifying his own desires towards one unapproachable in wedlock, or whether he presumed to call himself an abler hunter than her with whom the gods themselves will not compete in this department, — in either case the wrath of the goddess against him was just and legitimate (ὁμολογουμένην καὶ δικαίαν ὀργὴν ἔσχε πρὸς αὐτὸν ἡ θεός). With perfect propriety therefore (Καθόλου δὲ πιθανῶς) was he transformed into an animal such as those he had hunted, and torn to pieces by the very dogs who had killed them." (Didot. iv. 80.)

Pausanias, a man of exemplary piety, and generally less inclined to scepticism than Diodôrus, thinks the occasion unsuitable for a miracle or special interference. Having alluded to the two causes assigned for the displeasure of Artemis (they are the two first-mentioned in my text, and distinct from the two noticed by Diodôrus), he proceeds to say, "But I believe that the dogs of Aktæôn went mad, without the interference of the goddess: in this state of madness they would have torn in pieces without distinction any one whom they met (Paus. ix. 2, 3. ἐγὼ δὲ καὶ ἄνευ θεοῦ πείθομαι νόσον λύσσαν ἐπιβαλεῖν τοῦ ᾿Ακταίωνος τοὺς κύνας)." He retains the truth of the final catastrophe, but rationalizes it, excluding the special intervention of Artemis.

at the head of his Asiatic troop of females, to obtain divine hon, ors and to establish his peculiar rites in his native city. The venerable Kadmus, together with his daughters and the prophet Teiresias, at once acknowledged the divinity of the new god, and began to offer their worship and praise to him along with the solemnities which he enjoined. But Pentheus vehemently opposed the new ceremonies, reproving and maltreating the god who introduced them: nor was his unbelief at all softened by the miracles which Dionysus wrought for his own protection and for that of his followers. His mother Agavê, with her sisters and a large body of other women from Thêbes, had gone out from Thêbes to Mount Kithærôn to celebrate their solemnities under the influence of the Bacchic frenzy. Thither Pentheus followed to watch them, and there the punishment due to his impiety overtook him. The avenging touch of the god having robbed him of his senses, he climbed a tall pine for the purpose of overlooking the feminine multitude, who detected him in this position, pulled down the tree, and tore him in pieces. Agavê, mad and bereft of consciousness, made herself the foremost in this assault, and carried back in triumph to Thêbes the head of her slaughtered son. The aged Kadmus, with his wife Harmonia, retired among the Illyrians, and at the end of their lives were changed into serpents, Zeus permitting them to be transferred to the Elysian fields.[1]

---

[1] Apollod. iii. 5, 3–4; Theocrit. Idyll. xxvi. Eurip. Bacch. *passim.* Such is the tragical plot of this memorable drama. It is a striking proof of the deep-seated reverence of the people of Athens for the sanctity of the Bacchic ceremonies, that they could have borne the spectacle of Agavê on the stage with her dead son's head, and the expressions of triumphant sympathy in her action on the part of the Chorus (1168), Μάκαιρ᾿ Ἀγαύη ! This drama, written near the close of the life of Euripidês, and exhibited by his son after his death (Schol. Aristoph. Ran. 67), contains passages strongly inculcating the necessity of implicit deference to ancestorial authority in matters of religion, and favorably contrasting the uninquiring faith of the vulgar with the dissenting and inquisitive tendencies of superior minds : see v. 196; compare vv. 389 and 422.—

Οὐδὲν σοφιζώμεσθα τοῖσι δαίμοσιν.
Πατρίους παραδοχὰς, ἃς θ᾿ ὁμήλικας χρόνῳ
Κεκτήμεθ᾿, οὐδεὶς αὐτὰ καταβαλεῖ λόγος,
Οὐδ᾿ ἢν δι᾿ ἄκρων τὸ σοφὸν εὕρηται φρένων.

Such reproofs " insanientis sapientiæ " certainly do not fall in with the plot

Polydôrus and Labdakus successively became kings of Thêbes: the latter at his death left an infant son, Laius, who was deprived of his throne by Lykus. And here we approach the legend of Antiopê, Zêthus and Amphiôn, whom the fabulists insert at this point of the Thêban series. Antiopê is here the daughter of Nykteus, the brother of Lykus. She is deflowered by Zeus, and then, while pregnant, flies to Epôpeus king of Sikyôn: Nykteus dying entreats his brother to avenge the injury, and Lykus accordingly invades Sikyôn, defeats and kills Epôpeus, and brings back Antiopê prisoner to Thêbes. In her way thither, in a cave near Eleutheræ, which was shown to Pausanias,[1] she is delivered of the twin sons of Zeus — Amphiôn and Zêthus — who, exposed to perish, are taken up and nourished by a shepherd, and pass their youth amidst herdsmen, ignorant of their lofty descent.

Antiopê is conveyed to Thêbes, where, after undergoing a long persecution from Lykus and his cruel wife Dirkê, she at length escapes, and takes refuge in the pastoral dwelling of her sons, now grown to manhood. Dirkê pursues and requires her to be delivered up; but the sons recognize and protect their mother, taking an ample revenge upon her persecutors. Lykus is slain, and Dirkê is dragged to death, tied to the horns of a bull.[2]

---

of the drama itself, in which Pentheus appears as a Conservative, resisting the introduction of the new religious rites. Taken in conjunction with the emphatic and submissive piety which reigns through the drama, they countenance the supposition of Tyrwhitt, that Euripidês was anxious to repel the imputations, so often made against him, of commerce with the philosophers and participation in sundry heretical opinions.

Pacuvius in his Pentheus seems to have closely copied Euripidês; see Servius ad Virg. Æneid. iv. 469.

The old Thespis had composed a tragedy on the subject of Pentheus: Suidas, Θέσπις; also Æschylus; compare his Eumenidês, 25.

According to Apollodôrus (iii. 5, 5), Labdakus also perished in a similar way to Pentheus, and from the like impiety, — ἐκείνῳ φρονῶν παραπλήσια.

[1] Pausan. i. 38, 9.

[2] For the adventures of Antiopê and her sons, see Apollodôr. iii. 5; Pausan. ii. 6, 2; ix. 5, 2.

The narrative given respecting Epôpeus in the ancient Cyprian verses seems to have been very different from this, as far as we can judge from the brief notice in Proclus's Argument, — ὡς Ἐπωπεὺς φθείρας τὴν Λυκούργου (Λύκου) γυναῖκα ἐξεπορθήθη: it approaches more nearly to the story given in the seventh fable of Hyginus, and followed by Propertius (iii. 15); the

Amphiôn and Zêthus, having banished Laius, become kings of Thêbes. The former, taught by Hermês, and possessing exquisite skill on the lyre, employs it in fortifying the city, the stones of the walls arranging themselves spontaneously in obedience to the rhythm of his song.[1]

Zêthus marries Aêdôn, who, in the dark and under a fatal mistake, kills her son Itylus: she is transformed into a nightingale, while Zêthus dies of grief.[2] Amphiôn becomes the husband of Niobê, daughter of Tantalus, and the father of a numerous offspring, the complete extinction of which by the hands of Apollo and Artemis has already been recounted in these pages.

Here ends the legend of the beautiful Antiopê and her twin sons — the rude and unpolished, but energetic, Zêthus — and the refined and amiable, but dreamy, Amphiôn. For so Euripidês, in the drama of Antiopê unfortunately lost, presented the two

---

eighth fable of Hyginus contains the tale of Antiopê as given by Euripidês and Ennius. The story of Pausanias differs from both.

The Scholiast ad Apollôn. Rhod. i. 735. says that there were two persons named Antiopê; one, daughter of Asôpus, the other, daughter of Nykteus. Pausanias is content with supposing one only, really the daughter of Nykteus, but there was a φήμη that she was daughter of Asôpus (ii. 6, 2). Asius made Antiopê daughter of Asôpus, and mother (both by Zeus and by Epôpeus: such a junction of divine and human paternity is of common occurrence in the Greek legends) of Zêthus and Amphiôn (ap. Paus. 1. c.).

The contradictory versions of the story are brought together, though not very perfectly, in Sterk's Essay De Labdacidarum Historiâ, p. 38–43 (Leyden, 1829).

[1] This story about the lyre of Amphiôn is not noticed in Homer, but it was narrated in the ancient ἔπη ἐς Εὐρώπην which Pausanias had read: the wild beasts as well as the stones were obedient to his strains (Paus. ix. 5, 4). Pherekydês also recounted it (Pherekyd. Fragm. 102, Didot). The tablet of inscription ('Αναγραφὴ) at Sikyôn recognized Amphiôn as the first composer of poetry and harp-music (Plutarch, de Musicâ, c. 3. p. 1132).

[2] The tale of the wife and son of Zêthus is as old as the Odyssey (xix. 525). Pausanias adds the statement that Zêthus died of grief (ix. 5, 5; Pherekydês, Fragm. 102, Did.). Pausanias, however, as well as Apollodôrus, tells us that Zêthus married Thêbê, from whom the name Thêbes was given to the city. To reconcile the conflicting pretensions of Zêthus and Amphiôn with those of Kadmus, as founders of Thêbes, Pausanias supposes that the latter was the original settler of the hill of the Kadmeia, while the two former extended the settlement to the lower city (ix. 5, 1–3).

brothers, in affectionate union as well as in striking contrast.[1] It is evident that the whole story stood originally quite apart from the Kadmeian family, and so the rudiments of it yet stand in the Odyssey; but the logographers, by their ordinary connecting artifices, have opened a vacant place for it in the descending series of Thêban mythes. And they have here proceeded in a manner not usual with them. For whereas they are generally fond of multiplying entities, and supposing different historical personages of the same name, in order to introduce an apparent smoothness in the chronology — they have here blended into one person Amphiôn the son of Antiopê and Amphiôn the father of Chlôris, who seem clearly distinguished from each other in the Odyssey. They have further assigned to the same person all the circumstances of the legend of Niobê, which seems to have been originally framed quite apart from the sons of Antiopê.

Amphiôn and Zêthus being removed, Laius became king of Thêbes. With him commences the ever-celebrated series of adventures of Œdipus and his family. Laius forewarned by the oracle that any son whom he might beget would kill him, caused Œdipus as soon as he was born to be exposed on Mount Kithærôn. Here the herdsmen of Polybus king of Corinth accidentally found him and conveyed him to their master, who brought him up as his own child. In spite of the kindest treatment, however, Œdipus when he grew up found himself exposed to taunts on the score of his unknown parentage, and went to Delphi to inquire of the god the name of his real father. He received for answer an admonition not to go back to his country; if he did so, it was his destiny to kill his father and become the husband of his mother. Knowing no other country but Corinth, he accordingly determined to keep away from that city, and quitted Delphi by the road towards Bœôtia and Phôkis. At the exact spot

---

[1] See Valckenaer. Diatribê in Eurip. Reliq. cap. 7, p. 58; Welcker, Griechisch. Tragöd. ii. p. 811. There is a striking resemblance between the Antiopê of Euripidês and the Tyrô of Sophoklês in many points.

Plato in his Gorgias has preserved a few fragments, and a tolerably clear general idea of the characters of Zêthus and Amphiôn (Gorg. 90–92); see also Horat. Epist. i. 18, 42.

Both Livius and Pacuvius had tragedies on the scheme of this of Euripi lês, the former seemirgly a translation.

where the roads leading to these two countries forked, he met
Laius in a chariot drawn by mules, when the insolence of one of
the attendants brought on an angry quarrel, in which Œdipus
killed Laius, not knowing him to be his father. The exact
place where this event happened, called the Divided Way[1], was
memorable in the eyes of all literary Greeks, and is specially
adverted to by Pausanias in his periegesis.

On the death of Laius, Kreôn, the brother of Jokasta, succeeded to the kingdom of Thêbes. At this time the country was
under the displeasure of the gods, and was vexed by a terrible
monster, with the face of a woman, the wings of a bird, and the
tail of a lion, called the Sphinx[2] — sent by the wrath of Hêrê,
and occupying the neighboring mountain of Phikium. The
Sphinx had learned from the Muses a riddle, which she proposed
to the Thêbans to resolve: on every occasion of failure she took
away one of the citizens and ate him up. Still no person could
solve the riddle; and so great was the suffering occasioned, that
Kreôn was obliged to offer both the crown and the nuptials of
his sister Jokasta to any one who could achieve the salvation of
the city. At this juncture Œdipus arrived and solved the riddle: upon which the Sphinx immediately threw herself from the
acropolis and disappeared. As a recompense for this service,
Œdipus was made king of Thêbes, and married Jokasta, not
aware that she was his mother.

These main tragical circumstances — that Œdipus had ignorantly killed his father and married his mother — belong to
the oldest form of the legend as it stands in the Odyssey. The
gods (it is added in that poem) quickly made the facts known to
mankind. Epikasta (so Jokasta is here called) in an agony of
sorrow hanged herself: Œdipus remained king of the Kadmeians, but underwent many and great miseries, such as the

---

[1] See the description of the locality in K. O. Müller (Orchomenos, c. i. p.
37).
The tombs of Laius and his attendant were still seen there in the days of
Pausanias (x. 5, 2).

[2] Apollodôr. iii. 5, 8. An author named Lykus, in his work entitled *Thê-
baïca*, ascribed this visitation to the anger of Dionysus (Schol. Hesiod,
Theogon. 326). The Sphinx (or *Phix*, from the Bœôtian Mount Phikium)
is as old as the Hesiodic Theogony, — Φῖκ' ὀλόην τέκε, Καδμείοισιν ὄλεθρον
(Theog. 326).

Erinnyes, who avenge an injured mother, inflict.[1] A passage in the Iliad implies that he died at Thêbes, since it mentions the funeral games which were celebrated there in honor of him. His misfortunes were recounted by Nestôr, in the old Cyprian verses, among the stories of aforetime.[2] A fatal curse hung both upon himself and upon his children, Eteoklês, Polynikês, Antigonê and Ismênê. According to that narrative which the Attic tragedians have rendered universally current, they were his children by Jokasta, the disclosure of her true relationship to him having been very long deferred. But the ancient epic called Œdipodia, treading more closely in the footsteps of Homer, represented him as having after her death married a second wife, Euryganeia, by whom the four children were born to him : and the painter Onatas adopted this story in preference to that of Sophoklês.[3]

---

[1] Odyss. xi. 270. Odysseus, describing what he saw in the under-world, says, —

Μητέρα τ' Οἰδιπόδαο ἴδον, καλὴν 'Επικάστην,
'Η μέγα ἔργον ἔρεξεν ἀιδρείησι νόοιο,
Γημαμένη ᾧ υἱεῖ· ὁ δ' ὃν πατέρ' ἐξεναρίξας
Γῆμεν· ἄφαρ δ' ἀνάπυστα θεοὶ θέσαν ἀνθρώποισι.
'Αλλ' ὁ μὲν ἐν Θήβῃ πολυηράτῳ ἄλγεα πάσχων,
Καδμείων ἤνασσε, θεῶν ὀλόας διὰ βουλάς·
'Η δ' ἔβη εἰς Αἰδάο πυλάρταο κρατεροῖο
'Αψαμένη βρόχον αἰπὺν ἀφ' ὑψήλοιο μελάθρου,
'Ω ἄχεϊ σχομένη· τῷ δ' ἄλγεα κάλλιπ' ὀπίσσω
Πολλὰ μάλ', ὅσσα τε μητρὸς 'Εριννύες ἐκτελέουσιν.

[2] Iliad, xxiii. 680, with the scholiast who cites Hesiod. Proclus, Argum ad Cypria, ap. Düntzer, Fragm. Epic. Græc. p. 10. Νέστωρ δὲ ἐν παρεκβάσει διηγεῖται...... καὶ τὰ περὶ Οἰδίπουν, etc.

[3] Pausan. ix. 5, 5. Compare the narrative from Peisander in Schol. ad Eurip. Phœniss. 1773; where, however, the blindness of Œdipus seems to be unconsciously interpolated out of the tragedians. In the old narrative of the Cyclic Thêbaïs, Œdipus does not seem to be represented as blind (Leutsch, Thebaidis Cyclici Reliquiæ, Götting. 1830, p. 42).

Pherekydês (ap. Schol. Eurip. Phœniss. 52) tells us that Œdipus had three children by Jokasta, who were all killed by Erginus and the Minyæ (this must refer to incidents in the old poems which we cannot now recover) ; then the four celebrated children by Euryganeia ; lastly, that he married a third wife, Astymedusa. Apollodôrus follows the narrative of the tragedians, but alludes to the different version about Euryganeia, — εἰσὶ δ' οἵ φασιν, etc. (iii. 5, 8).

Hellanikus (ap. Schol. Eur. Phœniss. 59) mentioned the self-inflicted blind

The disputes of Eteoklês and Polynikês for the throne of their father gave occasion not only to a series of tragical family incidents, but also to one of the great quasi-historical events of legendary Greece — the two sieges of Thêbes by Adrastus, king of Argos. The two ancient epic poems called the Thêbaïs and the Epigoni (if indeed both were not parts of one very comprehensive poem) detailed these events at great length, and as it appears, with distinguished poetical merit; for Pausanias pronounces the Cyclic Thêbaïs (so it was called by the subsequent critics to distinguish it from the more modern Thêbaïs of Antimachus) inferior only to the Iliad and Odyssey; and the ancient elegiac poet Kallinus treated it as an Homeric composition.[1] Of this once-valued poem we unfortunately possess nothing but a few scanty fragments. The leading points of the legend are briefly glanced at in the Iliad; but our knowledge of the details is chiefly derived from the Attic tragedians, who transformed the narratives of their predecessors at pleasure, and whose popularity constantly eclipsed and obliterated the ancient version. Antimachus of Kolophôn, contemporary with Euripidês, in his long epic, probably took no less liberties with the old narrative. His Thêbaïd never became generally popular, but it exhibited marks of study and elaboration which recommended it to the esteem of the Alexandrine critics, and probably contributed to discredit in their eyes the old cyclic poem.

The logographers, who gave a continuous history of this siege of Thêbes, had at least three preëxisting epic poems — the Thêbias, the Œdipodia, and the Alkmæônis, — from which they

---

ness of Œdipus; but it seems doubtful whether this circumstance was included in the narrative of Pherekydês.

[1] Pausan, ix. 9. 3. Ἐποιήθη δὲ ἐς τὸν πόλεμον τοῦτον καὶ ἔπη, Θηβαΐς τὰ δὲ ἔπη ταῦτα Καλλῖνος, ἀφικόμενος αὐτῶν ἐς μνήμην, ἔφησεν Ὅμηρον τὸν ποιήσαντα εἶναι. Καλλίνῳ δὲ πολλοί τε καὶ ἄξιοι λόγου κατὰ ταῦτα ἔγνωσαν · ἐγὼ δὲ τὴν ποίησιν ταύτην μετά γε Ἰλιάδα καὶ τὰ ἔπη τὰ ἐς Ὀδυσσέα ἐπαινῶ μάλιστα. The name in the text of Pausanias stands Καλαῖνος, an unknown person: most of the critics recognize the propriety of substituting Καλλῖνος, and Leutsch and Welcker have given very sufficient reasons for doing so.

The Ἀμφιάρεω ἐξελασία ἐς Θήβας, alluded to in the pseudo-Herodotean life of Homer, seems to be the description of a special passage in this Thêbaïs.

could borrow. The subject was also handled in some of the Hesiodic poems, but we do not know to what extent.[1] The Thêbaïs was composed more in honor of Argos than of Thêbes, as the first line of it, one of the few fragments still preserved, betokens.[2]

SIEGES OF THEBES.

The legend, about to recount fraternal dissension of the most implacable kind, comprehending in its results not only the immediate relations of the infuriated brothers, but many chosen companions of the heroic race along with them, takes its start from the paternal curse of Œdipus, which overhangs and determines all the gloomy sequel.

Œdipus, though king of Thêbes and father of four children by Euryganeia (according to the Œdipodia), has become the devoted victim of the Erinnyes, in consequence of the self-inflicted death of his mother, which he has unconsciously caused, as well as of his unintentional parricide. Though he had long forsworn the use of all the ornaments and luxuries which his father had inherited from his kingly progenitors, yet when through age he had come to be dependent upon his two sons, Polynikês one day broke through this interdict, and set before him the silver table and the splendid wine-cup of Kadmus, which Laius had always been accustomed to employ. The old king had no sooner seen these precious appendages of the regal life of his father, than his mind was overrun by a calamitous phrenzy, and he imprecated terrible curses on his sons, predicting that there would be bitter and endless warfare between them. The goddess Erinnys' heard and heeded him ; and he repeated the curse again on another occasion, when his sons, who had always been accustomed to send to him the shoulder of the victims sacrificed on the altar, caused the but-

---

[1] Hesiod, ap. Schol. Iliad. xxiii. 680, which passage does not seem to me so much at variance with the incidents stated in other poets as Leutsch imagines.

[2] Ἄργος ἄειδε, θεὰ, πολυδίψιον, ἔνθεν ἄνακτες (see Leutsch, ib. c. 4. p 29).

tock to be served to him in place of it.[1] He resented this as an
insult, and prayed the gods that they might perish each by the
hand of the other. Throughout the tragedians as well as in the
old epic, the paternal curse, springing immediately from the misguided Œdipus himself, but remotely from the parricide and
incest with which he has tainted his breed, is seen to domineer
over the course of events — the Erinnys who executes that curse
being the irresistible, though concealed, agent. Æschylus not
only preserves the fatal efficiency of the paternal curse, but even
briefly glances at the causes assigned for it in the Thêbaïs, without superadding any new motives. In the judgment of Sophoklês, or of his audience, the conception of a father cursing his
sons upon such apparently trifling grounds was odious ; and that
great poet introduced many aggravating circumstances, describing
the old blind father as having been barbarously turned out of
doors by his sons to wander abroad in exile and poverty. Though
by this change he rendered his poem more coherent and self-
justifying, yet he departed, from the spirit of the old legend,

----

[1] Fragm. of the Thêbaïs, ap. Athenæ. xii. p. 465, ὅτι αὐτῷ παρέθηκαν ἐκπώ-
ματα ἃ ἀπηγορεύκει, λέγων οὕτως.

> Αὐτὰρ ὁ διογένης ἥρως ξανθὸς Πολυνείκης
> Πρῶτα μὲν Οἰδίποδι καλὴν παρέθηκε τράπεζαν
> Ἀργυρέην Κάδμοιο θεόφρονος· αὐτὰρ ἔπειτα
> Χρύσεον ἔμπλησεν καλὸν δέπας ἡδέος οἴνου·
> Αὐτὰρ ὅγ' ὡς φράσθη παρακείμενα πατρὸς ἑοῖο
> Τιμήεντα γέρα, μέγα οἱ κακὸν ἔμπεσε θυμῷ.
> Αἶψα δὲ παισὶν ἑοῖσι μετ' ἀμφοτέροισιν ἐπαρὰς
> Ἀργαλέας ἠρᾶτο· θεὸν δ' οὐ λάνθαν' Ἐριννύν·
> Ὡς οὐ οἱ πατρῷα γ' ἐνὶ φιλότητι δάσαιντο,
> Εἶεν δ' ἀμφοτέροις αἰεὶ πόλεμοί τε μάχαί τε.

See Leutsch, Thebaid. Cycl. Reliq, p. 38.
The other fragment from the same Thêbaïs is cited by the Schol. ad Soph
Œdip. Colon. 1378.—

> Ἰσχίον ὡς ἐνόησε, χαμαὶ βάλεν, εἶπέ τε μῦθον·
> Ὦ μοι ἐγώ, παῖδές μοι ὀνειδείοντες ἔπεμψαν.
> Εὐκτο Διὶ βασιλῆϊ καὶ ἄλλοις ἀθανάτοισι,
> Χερσὶν ὑπ' ἀλλήλων καταβήμεναι Ἄϊδος εἴσω.

Τὰ δὲ παραπλήσια τῷ ἐποποιῷ καὶ Αἰσχύλος ἐν τοῖς Ἕπτα ἐπὶ Θήβας. In
spite of the protest of Schutz, in his note, I think that the scholiast has understood the words ἐπίκοτος τροφᾶς (Sept. ad Theb. 787) in their plain and
just meaning.

according to which Œdipus has contracted by his unconscious misdeeds an incurable taint destined to pass onward to his progeny. His mind is alienated, and he curses them, not because he has suffered seriously by their guilt, but because he is made the blind instrument of an avenging Erinnys for the ruin of the house of Laius.[1]

After the death of Œdipus and the celebration of his funeral games, at which amongst others, Argeia, daughter of Adrastus (afterwards the wife of Polynikês), was present,[2] his two sons soon quarrelled respecting the succession. The circumstances are differently related; but it appears that, according to the original narrative, the wrong and injustice was on the part of Polynikês, who, however, was obliged to leave Thêbes and to seek shelter with Adrastus, king of Argos. Here he met Tydeus, a fugitive, at the same time, from Ætôlia: it was dark when they arrived, and a broil ensued between the two exiles, but Adrastus came out and parted them. He had been enjoined by an oracle to give his two daughters in marriage to a lion and a boar, and he thought this occasion had now arrived, inasmuch as one of the combatants carried on his shield a lion, the other a boar. He accordingly gave Deipylê in marriage to Tydeus, and Argeia to Polynikês: moreover, he resolved to restore by armed resistance both his sons-in-law to their respective countries.[3]

---

[1] The curses of Œdipus are very frequently and emphatically dwelt upon both by Æschylus and Sophoklês (Sept. ad Theb. 70–586, 655–697, etc.; Œdip. Colon. 1293–1378). The former continues the same point of view as the Thêbaïs, when he mentions —

> .... Τὰς περιθύμους
> Κατάρας βλαψίφρονος Οἰδιπόδα (727) ;

or, λόγου τ' ἄνοια καὶ φρενῶν 'Ερινύς (Soph. Antig. 584).

The Scholiast on Sophoklês (Œd. Col. 1378) treats the cause assigned by the ancient Thêbaïs for the curse vented by Œdipus as trivial and ludicrous.

The Ægeids at Sparta, who traced their descent to Kadmus, suffered from terrible maladies which destroyed the lives of their children; an oracle directed them to appease the Erinnyes of Laius and Œdipus by erecting a temple, upon which the maladies speedily ceased (Herodot. iv.).

[2] Hesiod. ap. Schol. Iliad. xxiii. 680.

[3] Apollodôr. iii. 5, 9; Hygin. f. 69; Æschyl. Sept. ad Theb. 573. Hyginus says that Polynikês came clothed in the skin of a lion, and Tydeus in that of a boar; perhaps after Antimachus, who said that Tydeus had been brought

On proposing the expedition to the Argeian chiefs around him
he found most of them willing auxiliaries; but Amphiaräus —
formerly his bitter opponent, but now reconciled to him, and
husband of his sister Eriphylê — strongly opposed him.[1] He
denounced the enterprise as unjust and contrary to the will of
the gods. Again, being of a prophetic stock, descended from
Melampus, he foretold the certain death both of himself and of
the principal leaders, should they involve themselves as accom-
plices in the mad violence of Tydeus or the criminal ambition of
Polynikês. Amphiaräus, already distinguished both in the Kalydônian boar-hunt and in the funeral games of Pelias, was in the
Thêban war the most conspicuous of all the heroes, and absolutely
indispensable to its success. But his reluctance to engage in it
was invincible, nor was it possible to prevail upon him except
through the influence of his wife Eriphylê. Polynikês, having
brought with him from Thêbes the splendid robe and necklace
given by the gods to Harmonia on her marriage with Kadmus,
offered it as a bribe to Eriphylê, on condition that she would
influence the determination of Amphiaràus. The sordid wife,
seduced by so matchless a present, betrayed the lurking-place of
her husband, and involved him in the fatal expedition.[2] Amphiaräus, reluctantly dragged forth, and foreknowing the disastrous
issue of the expedition both to himself and to his associates,
addressed his last injunctions, at the moment of mounting his
chariot, to his sons Alkmæôn and Amphilochus, commanding
Alkmæôn to avenge his approaching death by killing the venal
Eriphylê, and by undertaking a second expedition against Thêbes.

The Attic dramatists describe this expedition as having been
conducted by seven chiefs, one to each of the seven celebrated
gates of Thêbes. But the Cyclic Thêbaïs gave to it a much

---

up by swineherds (Antimach. Fragm. 27, ed. Düntzer; ap. Schol. Iliad. iv.
400). Very probably, however, the old Thêbaïs compared Tydeus and Polynikês to a lion and a boar, on account of their courage and fierceness; a
simile quite in the Homeric character. Mnaseas gave the words of the oracle
(ap. Schol. Eurip. Phœniss. 411).

[1] See Pindar, Nem. ix. 30, with the instructive Scholium

[2] Apollodôr. iii. 6, 2. The treachery of "the hateful Eriphylê" is noticed
in the Odyssey, xi. 327: Odysseus sees her in the under-world along with
the many wives and daughters of the heroes.

more comprehensive character, mentioning auxiliaries from Arcadia, Messênê, and various parts of Peloponnêsus;[1] and the application of Tydeus and Polynikês at Mykênæ in the course of their circuit made to collect allies, is mentioned in the Iliad. They were well received at Mykênæ; but the warning signals given by the gods were so terrible that no Mykenæan could venture to accompany them.[2] The seven principal chiefs however were Adrastus, Amphiaräus, Kapaneus, Hippomedôn, Parthenopæus, Tydeus and Polynikês.[3] When the army had advanced as far as the river Asôpus, a halt was made for sacrifice and banquet; while Tydeus was sent to Thêbes as envoy to demand the restoration of Polynikês to his rights. His demand was refused; but finding the chief Kadmeians assembled at the banquet in the house of Eteoklês, he challenged them all to contend with him in boxing or wrestling. So efficacious was the aid of the goddess Athênê that he overcame them all; and the Kadmeians were so indignant at their defeat, that they placed an ambuscade of fifty men to intercept him in his way back to the army. All of them perished by the hand of this warrior, small in stature and of few words, but desperate and irresistible in the fight. One alone was spared, Mæon, in consequence of special signals from the gods.[4]

The Kadmeians, assisted by their allies the Phôkians and the Phlegyæ, marched out to resist the invaders, and fought a battle

---

[1] Pausan. ii. 20, 4; ix. 9, 1. His testimony to this, as he had read and admired the Cyclic Thêbaïs, seems quite sufficient, in spite of the opinion of Welcker to the contrary (Æschylische Trilogie. p. 375).

[2] Iliad, iv. 376.

[3] There are differences in respect to the names of the seven: Æschylus (Sept. ad Theb. 461) leaves out Adrastus as one of the seven, and includes Eteoklus instead of him; others left out Tydeus and Polynikês, and inserted Eteoklus and Mekisteus (Apollodôr. iii. 6, 3). Antimachus, in his poetical Thêbaïs, called Parthenopæus an Argeian, not an Arcadian (Schol. ad Æschyl. Sept. ad. Theb. 532).

[4] Iliad, iv. 381-400, with the Schol. The first celebration of the Nemean games is connected with this march of the army of Adrastus against Thêbes: they were celebrated in honor of Archemorus, the infant son of Lykurgus, who had been killed by a serpent while his nurse Hypsipylê went to show the fountain to the thirsty Argeian chiefs (Apollod. iii. 6, 4; Schol. ad Pindar. Nem. 1).

near the Ismênian hill, in which they were defeated and forced to
retire within the walls. The prophet Teiresias acquainted them
that if Menœkeus, son of Kreôn, would offer himself as a victim
to Arês, victory would be assured to Thêbes. The generous
youth, as soon as he learnt that his life was to be the price of
safety to his country, went and slew himself before the gates.
The heroes along with Adrastus now commenced a vigorous
attack upon the town, each of the seven selecting one of the gates
to assault. The contest was long and strenuously maintained;
but the devotion of Menœkeus had procured for the Thêbans the
protection of the gods. Parthenopæus was killed with a stone by
Periklymenus; and when the furious Kapaneus, having planted
a scaling-ladder, had mounted the walls, he was smitten by a
thunderbolt from Zeus and cast down dead upon the earth. This
event struck terror into the Argeians, and Adrastus called back
his troops from the attack. The Thêbans now sallied forth to
pursue them, when Eteoklês, arresting the battle, proposed to
decide the controversy by single combat with his brother. The
challenge, eagerly accepted by Polynikês, was agreed to by
Adrastus: a single combat ensued between the two brothers, in
which both were exasperated to fury and both ultimately slain by
each other's hand. This equal termination left the result of the
general contest still undetermined, and the bulk of the two armies
renewed the fight. In the sanguinary struggle which ensued the
sons of Astakus on the Thêban side displayed the most conspicuous and successful valor. One of them,[1] Melanippus, mortally
wounded Tydeus — while two others, Leades and Amphidikus,
killed Eteoklus and Hippomedôn. Amphiaräus avenged Tydeus
by killing Melanippus; but unable to arrest the rout of the army,

---

[1] The story recounted that the head of Melanippus was brought to Tydeus
as he was about to expire of his wound, and that he knawed it with his teeth,
a story touched upon by Sophoklês (apud Herodian. in Rhetor. Græc. t. viii.
p. 601, Walz.).

The lyric poet Bacchylidês (ap. Schol. Aristoph. Aves, 1535) seems to have
handled the story even earlier than Sophoklês.

We find the same allegation embodied in charges against real historical
men: the invective of Montanus against Aquilius Regulus, at the beginning
of the reign of Vespasian, affirmed, "datam interfectori Pisonis pecuniam a
Regulo, appetitumque morsu Pisonis caput" (Tacit. Hist. iv. 42).

he fled with the rest, closely pursued by Periklymenus. The latter was about to pierce him with his spear, when the beneficence of Zeus rescued him from this disgrace — miraculously opening the earth under him, so that Amphiaräus with his chariot and horses was received unscathed into her bosom.[1] The exact spot where this memorable incident happened was indicated by a sepulchral building, and shown by the Thêbans down to the days of Pausanias — its sanctity being attested by the fact, that no animal would consent to touch the herbage which grew within the sacred inclosure. Amphiaräus, rendered immortal by Zeus, was worshipped as a god at Argos, at Thêbes and at Orôpus — and for many centuries gave answers at his oracle to the questions of the pious applicant.[2]

---

[1] Apollodôr. iii. 6, 8. Pindar, Olymp. vi. 11; Nem. ix. 13-27. Pausan. ix. 8, 2; 18, 2-4.

Euripidês, in the Phœnissæ (1122 *seqq.*), describes the battle generally; see also Æsch. S. Th. 392. It appears by Pausanias that the Thêbans had poems or legends of their own, relative to this war : they dissented in various points from the Cyclic Thêbaïs (ix. 18, 4). The Thêbaïs said that Periklymenus had killed Parthenopæus; the Thêbans assigned this exploit to Asphodikus, a warrior not commemorated by any of the poets known to us.

The village of Harma, between Tanagra and Mykalêssus, was affirmed by some to have been the spot where Amphiaräus closed his life (Strabo, ix. p 404): Sophoklês placed the scene at the Amphiaræium near Orôpus (ap Strabon. ix. p. 399).

[2] Pindar, Olymp. vi. 16. Ἕπτα δ' ἔπειτα πυρᾶν νέκρων τελεσθέντων Ταλαϊονίδας Εἶπεν ἐν Θήβαισι τοιοῦτόν τι ἔπος· Ποθέω στρατιᾶς ὀφθαλμὸν ἐμᾶς Ἀμφότερον, μάντιν τ' ἀγαθὸν καὶ δουρὶ μάχεσθαι.

The scholiast affirms that these last expressions are borrowed by Pindar from the Cyclic Thêbaïs.

The temple of Amphiaräus (Pausan. ii. 23, 2), his oracle, seems to have been inferior in estimation only to that of Delphi (Herodot. i. 52; Pausan. i. 34; Cicero, Divin. i. 40). Crœsus sent a rich present to Amphiaräus, πυθόμενος αὐτοῦ τήν τε ἀρετὴν καὶ τὴν πάθην (Herod. l. c) ; a striking proof how these interesting legends were recounted and believed as genuine historical facts. Other adventures of Amphiaräus in the expedition against Thêbes were commemorated in the carvings on the Thronus at Amyklæ (Pausan. iii. 18, 4).

Æschylus (Sept. Theb. 611) seems to enter into the Thêban view, doubtless highly respectful towards Amphiaräus, when he places in the mouth of the Kadmeian king Eteoklês such high encomiums on Amphiaräus, and so marked a contrast with the other chiefs from Argos.

Adrastus, thus deprived of the prophet and warrior whom he
regarded as "the eye of his army," and having seen the other
chiefs killed in the disastrous fight, was forced to take flight singly, and was preserved by the matchless swiftness of his horse
Areiôn, the offspring of Poseidôn. He reached Argos on his
return, bringing with him nothing except "his garments of woe
and his black-maned steed."[1]

Kreôn, father of the heroic youth Menœkeus, succeeding to
the administration of Thêbes after the death of the two hostile
brothers and the repulse of Adrastus, caused Eteoklês to be
buried with distinguished honor, but cast out ignominiously the
body of Polynikês as a traitor to his country, forbidding every
one on pain of death to consign it to the tomb. He likewise
refused permission to Adrastus to inter the bodies of his fallen
comrades. This proceeding, so offensive to Grecian feeling, gave
rise to two further tales; one of them at least of the highest
pathos and interest. Antigonê, the sister of Polynikês, heard
with indignation the revolting edict consigning her brother's body
to the dogs and vultures, and depriving it of those rites which
were considered essential to the repose of the dead. Unmoved
by the dissuading counsel of an affectionate but timid sister, and
unable to procure assistance, she determined to brave the hazard
and to bury the body with her own hands. She was detected in
the act; and Kreôn, though forewarned by Teiresias of the consequences, gave orders that she should be buried alive, as having
deliberately set at naught the solemn edict of the city. His son
Hæmôn, to whom she was engaged to be married, in vain inter-
ceded for her life. In an agony of despair he slew himself in
the sepulchre to which the living Antigonê had been consigned;

---

[1] Pausan. viii. 25, 5, from the Cyclic Thêbaïs, Εἵματα λυγρὰ φέρων σὺν
'Αρείονι κυανοχαίτῃ; also Apollodôr. iii. 6, 8.

The celebrity of the horse Areiôn was extolled in the Iliad (xxiii. 346),
in the Cyclic Thêbaïs, and also in the Thêbaïs of Antimachus (Pausan. l.
c.): by the Arcadians of Thelpusia he was said to be the offspring of Dêmêtêr by Poseidôn, — he, and a daughter whose name Pausanias will not com-
municate to the uninitiated (ἧς τὸ ὄνομα ἐς ἀτελέστους λέγειν οὐ νομίζουσι,
l. c.). A different story is in the Schol. Iliad. xxiii. 346; and in Antimachus, who affirmed that "Gæa herself had produced him, as a wonder to mortal men" (see Antimach. Frag. 16. p. 102; Epic. Græc. Frag. ed. Düntzer).

and his mother Eurydikê, the wife of Kreôn, inconsolable for his death, perished by her own hand. And thus the new light which seemed to be springing up over the last remaining scion of the devoted family of Œdipus, is extinguished amidst gloom and horrors — which overshadowed also the house and dynasty of Kreôn.[1]

The other tale stands more apart from the original legend, and seems to have had its origin in the patriotic pride of the Athenians. Adrastus, unable to obtain permission from the Thêbans to inter the fallen chieftains, presented himself in suppliant guise, accompanied by their disconsolate mothers, to Thêseus at Eleusis. He implored the Athenian warrior to extort from the perverse Thêbans that last melancholy privilege which no decent or pious Greeks ever thought of withholding, and thus to stand forth as the champion of Grecian public morality in one of its most essential points, not less than of the rights of the subterranean gods. The Thêbans obstinately persisting in their refusal, Thêseus undertook an expedition against their city, vanquished them in the field, and compelled them by force of arms to permit the sepulture of their fallen enemies. This chivalrous interposition, celebrated in one of the preserved dramas of Euripidês, formed a subject of glorious recollection to the Athenians throughout the historical age: their orators dwelt upon it in terms of animated panegyric; and it seems to have been accepted as a real fact of the past time, with not less implicit conviction than the battle of Marathôn.[2] But the Thêbans, though equally persuaded of the truth of the main story, dissented from the Athenian version of it, maintaining that they had given up the bodies for sepulture voluntarily and of their own accord. The tomb of

---

[1] Sophokl. Antigon. 581. Νῦν γὰρ ἐσχάτας ὑπὲρ 'Ρίζας ἐτέτατο φάος ἐν Οἰδίπου δόμοις, etc.

The pathetic tale here briefly recounted forms the subject of this beautiful tragedy of Sophoklês, the argument of which is supposed by Boeckh to have been borrowed in its primary rudiments from the Cyclic Thêbaïs or the Œdipodia (Boeckh, Dissertation appended to his translation of the Antigonê, c. x. p. 146); see Apollodôr. iii. 7, 1.

Æschylus also touches upon the heroism of Antigonê (Sep. Theb. 984).

[2] Apollodôr. iii. 7, 1; Eurip. Supp. passim; Herodot. ix. 27; Plato, Menex en. c. 9; Lysias, Epitaph. c 4; Isokrat. Orat. Panegyr. p 196, Auger.

the chieftains was shown near Eleusis even in the days of Pausanias.[1]

A large proportion both of the interesting persons and of the exalted acts of legendary Greece belongs to the female sex. Nor can we on this occasion pass over the name of Evadnê, the devoted widow of Kapaneus, who cast herself on the funeral pile of her husband and perished.[2]

The defeat of the seven chiefs before Thêbes was amply avenged by their sons, again under the guidance of Adrastus:—Ægialeus son of Adrastus, Thersander son of Polynikês, Alkmæôn and Amphilochus, sons of Amphiaräus, Diomêdês son of Tydeus, Sthenelus son of Kapaneus, Promachus son of Parthenopæus, and Euryalus son of Mekistheus, joined in this expedition. Though all these youthful warriors, called the Epigoni, took part in the expedition, the grand and prominent place appears to have been occupied by Alkmæôn, son of Amphiaräus. Assistance was given to them from Corinth and Megara, as well as from Messênê and Arcadia; while Zeus manifested his favorable dispositions by signals not to be mistaken.[3] At the river Glisas the Epigoni were met by the Thêbans in arms, and a battle took place in which the latter were completely defeated. Laodamas, son of Eteoklês, killed Ægialeus, son of Adrastus; but he and his army were routed and driven within the walls by the valor and energy of Alkmæôn. The defeated Kadmeians consulted the prophet Teiresias, who informed them that the gods had declared for their enemies, and that there was no longer any hope of successful resistance. By his advice they sent a herald to the assailants offering to surrender the town, while they themselves conveyed away their wives and children, and fled under the com

---

[1] Pausan. i. 39, 2.

[2] Eurip. Supplic. 1004–1110.

[3] Homer, Iliad, iv. 406. Sthenelus, the companion of Diomêdês and one of the Epigoni, says to Agamemnôn,—

Ἡμεῖς τοι πατέρων μεγ' ἀμείνονες εὐχόμεθ' εἶναι·
Ἡμεῖς καὶ Θήβης ἕδος εἵλομεν ἑπταπύλοιο,
Παυρότερον λαὸν ἀγαγόνθ' ὑπὸ τεῖχος Ἄρειον,
Πειθόμενοι τερᾴεσσι θεῶν καὶ Ζηνὸς ἀρωγῇ·
Αὐτοὶ δὲ σφετέρῃσιν ἀτασθαλίῃσιν ὄλοντο.

mand of Laodamas to the Illyrians,[1] upon which the Epigoni entered Thêbes, and established Thersander, son of Polynikês, on the throne.

Adrastus, who in the former expedition had been the single survivor amongst so many fallen companions, now found himself the only exception to the general triumph and joy of the conquerors: he had lost his son Ægialeus, and the violent sorrow arising from the event prematurely cut short his life. His soft voice and persuasive eloquence were proverbial in the ancient epic.[2] He was worshipped as a hero both at Argos and at Sikyôn, but with especial solemnity in the last-mentioned place, where his Herôum stood in the public agora, and where his exploits as well as his sufferings were celebrated periodically in lyric tragedies. Melanippus, son of Astakus, the brave defender of Thêbes, who had slain both Tydeus and Mekistheus, was worshipped with no less solemnity by the Thêbans.[3] The enmity of these two heroes rendered it impossible for both of them to be worshipped close upon the same spot. Accordingly it came to pass during the historical period, about the time of the Solonian legislation at Athens, that Kleisthenês, despot of Sikyôn, wishing to banish the hero Adrastus and abolish the religious solemnities celebrated in honor of the latter by the Sikyonians, first applied to the Delphian oracle for permission to carry this banishment into effect directly and forcibly. That permission being refused, he next sent to Thêbes an intimation that he was anxious to introduce their hero Melanippus into Sikyôn. The Thêbans willingly consented, and he assigned to the new hero a consecrated spot in the strongest and most commanding portion of the Sikyonian prytaneium. He did this (says the historian) " knowing that Adrastus would forthwith go away of his own accord; since

---

[1] Apollodôr. iii. 7, 4. Herodot. v. 57–61. Pausan. ix. 5, 7; 9, 2. Diodôr. iv. 65–66.

Pindar represents Adrastus as concerned in the second expedition against Thêbes (Pyth. viii. 40–58).

[2] Γλῶσσαν τ᾽ Ἀδρήστου μειλιχόγηρυν ἔχοι (Tyrtæus, Eleg. 9, 7, Schneidewin); compare Plato, Phædr. c. 118. " Adrasti pallentis imago" meets the eye of Æneas in the under-world (Æneid, vi. 480).

[3] About Melanippus, see Pindar, Nem. x. 36. His sepulchre was shown near the Prœtid gates of Thêbes (Pausan. ix. 18, 1).

Melanippus was of all persons the most odious to him, as having slain both his son-in-law and his brother." Kleisthenês moreover diverted the festivals and sacrifices which had been offered to Adrastus, to the newly established hero Melanippus; and the lyric tragedies from the worship of Adrastus to that of Dionysus. But his dynasty did not long continue after his decease, and the Sikyonians then reëstablished their ancient solemnities.[1]

Near the Prœtid gate of Thêbes were seen the tombs of two combatants who had hated each other during life even more than Adrastus and Melanippus — the two brothers Eteoklês and Polynikês. Even as heroes and objects of worship, they still continued to manifest their inextinguishable hostility: those who offered sacrifices to them observed that the flame and the smoke from the two adjoining altars abhorred all communion, and flew off in directions exactly opposite. The Thêban exegetes assured Pausanias of this fact. And though he did not himself witness it, yet having seen with his own eyes a miracle not very dissimilar at Pioniæ in Mysia, he had no difficulty in crediting their assertion.[2]

Amphiaräus when forced into the first attack of Thêbes — against his own foreknowledge and against the warnings of the

---

[1] This very curious and illustrative story is contained in Herodot. v. 67. Ἐπεὶ δὲ ὁ θεὸς τοῦτο οὐ παρεδίδου, ἀπελθὼν ὀπίσω (Kleisthenês, returning from Delphi) ἐφρόντιζε μηχανὴν τῇ αὐτὸς ὁ Ἀδρήστος ἀπαλλάξεται. Ὡς δὲ οἱ ἐξευρῆσθαι ἐδόκεε, πέμψας ἐς Θήβας τὰς Βοιωτίας, ἔφη θέλειν ἐπαγαγέσθαι Μελάνιππον τὸν Ἀστακοῦ· οἱ δὲ Θηβαῖοι ἔδοσαν. Ἐπηγάγετο δὲ τὸν Μελάνιππον ὁ Κλεισθένης, καὶ γὰρ τοῦτο δεῖ ἀπηγήσασθαι, ὡς ἔχθιστον ἐόντα Ἀδρήστῳ· ὃς τόν τε ἀδέλφεον Μηκιστέα ἀπεκτόνεε, καὶ τὸν γαμβρὸν Τυδέα.

The Sikyonians (Herodotus says) τά τε δὴ ἄλλα ἐτίμων τὸν Ἄδρηστον, καὶ πρὸς τὰ πάθεα αὐτοῦ τραγικοῖσι χόροισι ἐγέραιρον· τὸν μὲν Διόνυσον οὐ τιμέωντες, τὸν δὲ Ἄδρηστον.

Adrastus was worshipped as a hero at Megara as well as at Sikyôn: the Megarians affirmed that he had died there on his way back from Thêbes (Pausan. i. 43, 1; Dieuchidas, ap. Schol. ad Pindar. Nem. ix. 31). His house at Argos was still shown when Pausanias visited the town (ii. 23, 2).

[2] Pausan. ix. 18, 3. Τὰ ἐπ᾽ αὐτοῖς δρώμενα οὐ θεασάμενος πιστὰ ὅμως ὑπείληφα εἶναι. Compare Hygin. f. 68.

"Et nova fraterno veniet concordia fumo,
Quem vetus accensâ separat ira pyrâ." (Ovid, Ibis, 35.)

The tale was copied by Ovid from Kallimachus (Trist. v. 5, 38.)

gods — had enjoined his sons Alkmæôn and Amphilochus not only to avenge his death upon the Thêbans, but also to punish the treachery of their mother, " Eriphylê, the destroyer of her husband."[1] In obedience to this command, and having obtained the sanction of the Delphian oracle, Alkmæôn slew his mother;[2] but the awful Erinnys, the avenger of matricide, inflicted on him a long and terrible punishment, depriving him of his reason, and chasing him about from place to place without the possibility of repose or peace of mind. He craved protection and cure from the god at Delphi, who required him to dedicate at the temple, as an offering, the precious necklace of Kadmus, that irresistible bribe which had originally corrupted Eriphylê.[3] He further intimated to the unhappy sufferer, that though the whole earth was tainted with his crime, and had become uninhabitable for him, yet there was a spot of ground which was not under the eye of the sun at the time when the matricide was committed, and where

---

[1] 'Ανδροδάμαντ' 'Εριφύλην (Pindar, Nem. ix. 16). A poem Eryphilê was included among the mythical compositions of Stesichorus : he mentioned in it that Asklêpius had restored Kapaneus to life, and that he was for that reason struck dead by thunder from Zeus (Stesichor. Fragm. Kleine, 18, p. 74). Two tragedies of Sophoklês once existed, Epigoni and Alkmæôn (Welcker, Griechisch. Tragöd. i. p. 269) : a few fragments also remain of the Latin Epigoni and Alphesibœa of Attius : Ennius and Attius both composed or translated from the Greek a Latin Alkmæôn (Poet. Scenic. Latin. ed. Both. pp. 33, 164, 198).

[2] Hyginus gives the fable briefly (f. 73 ; see also Asclepiadês, ap. Schol. Odyss. xi. 326). In like manner, in the case of the matricide of Orestês, Apollo not only sanctions, but enjoins the deed ; but his protection against the avenging Erinnyês is very tardy, not taking effect until after Orestês has been long persecuted and tormented by them (see Æschyl. Eumen. 76, 197, 462).

In the Alkmæôn of the later tragic writer Thodektês, a distinction was drawn : the gods had decreed that Eriphylê should die, but not that Alkmæôn should kill her (Aristot. Rhetoric. ii. 24). Astydamas altered the story still more in his tragedy, and introduced Alkmæôn as killing his mother ignorantly and without being aware who she was (Aristot. Poetic. c. 27). The murder of Eriphylê by her son was one of the παρειλημμένοι μῦθοι which could not be departed from ; but interpretations and qualifications were resorted to, in order to prevent it from shocking the softened feelings of the spectators : see the criticism of Aristotle on the Alkmæôn of Euripidês (Ethic. Nicom. iii. 1, 8).

[3] Ephorus ap. Athenæ. vi. p. 232.

therefore Alkmæôn yet might find a tranquil shelter. The promise was realized at the mouth of the river Achelôus, whose turbid stream was perpetually depositing new earth and forming additional islands. Upon one of these, near Œniadæ, Alkmæôn settled, permanently and in peace: he became the primitive hero of Akarnania, to which his son Akarnan gave name.[1] The necklace was found among the treasures of Delphi, together with that which had been given by Aphroditê to Helen, by the Phôkian plunderers who stripped the temple in the time of Philip of Macedôn. The Phôkian women quarrelled about these valuable ornaments: and we are told that the necklace of Eriphylê was allotted to a woman of gloomy and malignant disposition, who ended by putting her husband to death; that of Helen to a beautiful but volatile wife, who abandoned her husband from a preference for a young Epirot.[2]

There were several other legends respecting the distracted Alkmæôn, either appropriated or invented by the Attic tragedians. He went to Phêgeus, king of Psôphis in Arcadia, whose daughter Arsinoê he married, giving as a nuptial present the necklace of Eriphylê. Being however unable to remain there, in consequence of the unremitting persecutions of the maternal Erinnys, he sought shelter at the residence of king Achelôus, whose daughter Kallirhoê he made his wife, and on whose soil he obtained repose.[3] But Kallirhoê would not be satisfied without

---

[1] Thucyd. ii. 68–102.　　　　　　　[2] Athenæ. 1. c.

[3] Apollodôr. iii. 7, 5–6; Pausan. viii. 24, 4. These two authors have preserved the story of the Akarnanians and the old form of the legend, representing Alkmæôn as having found shelter at the abode of the person or king Achelôus, and married his daughter: Thucydidês omits the *personality* of Achelôus, and merely announces the wanderer as having settled on certain new islands deposited by the river.

I may remark that this is a singularly happy adaptation of a legend to an existing topographical fact. Generally speaking, before any such adaptation can be rendered plausible, the legend is of necessity much transformed; here it is taken exactly as it stands, and still fits on with great precision.

Ephorus recounted the whole sequence of events as so much political history, divesting it altogether of the legendary character. Alkmæôn and Diomêdês, after having taken Thêbes with the other Epigoni, jointly undertook an expedition into Ætôlia and Akarnania: they first punished the enemies of the old Œneus, grandfather of Diomêdês, and established the latter as king in Kalydôn; next they conquered Akarnania for Alkmæôn. Alkmæôn,

the possession of the necklace of Eriphylê, and Alkmæôn went back to Psôphis to fetch it, where Phêgeus and his sons slew him. He had left twin sons, infants, with Kallirhoê, who prayed fervently to Zeus that they might be preternaturally invested with immediate manhood, in order to revenge the murder of their father. Her prayer was granted, and her sons Amphoterus and Akarnan, having instantaneously sprung up to manhood, proceeded into Arcadia, slew the murderers of their father, and brought away the necklace of Eriphylê, which they carried to Delphi.[1]

Euripidês deviated still more widely from the ancient epic, by making Alkmæôn the husband of Mantô, daughter of Teiresias, and the father of Amphilochus. According to the Cyclic Thêbaïs, Mantô was consigned by the victorious Epigoni as a special offering to the Delphian god; and Amphilochus was son of Amphiaräus, not son of Alkmæôn.[2] He was the eponymous hero of the town called the Amphilochian Argos, in Akarnania, on the shore of the Gulf of Ambrakia. Thucydidês tells us that he went thither on his return from the Trojan war, being dissatisfied with the state of affairs which he found at the Peloponnêsian Argos.[3] The Akarnanians were remarkable for the numerous prophets which they supplied to the rest of Greece: their heroes

---

though invited by Agamemnôn to join in the Trojan war, would not consent to do so (Ephor. ap. Strabo. vii. p. 326; x. p. 462).

[1] Apollodôr. iii. 7, 7; Pausan. viii. 24, 3–4. His remarks upon the mischievous longing of Kallirhoê for the necklace are curious: he ushers them in by saying, that "many men, and still more women, are given to fall into absurd desires," etc. He recounts it with all the *bonne foi* which belongs to the most assured matter of fact.

A short allusion is in Ovid's Metamorphoses (ix. 412)

[2] Thêbaïd, Cy. Reliqu. p. 70, Leutsch; Schol. Apollôn. Rhod. i. 408. The following lines cited in Athenæus (vii. p. 317) are supposed by Boeckh, with probable reason, to be taken from the Cyclic Thêbaïs; a portion of the advice of Amphiaräus to his sons at the time of setting out on his last expedition, —

Πουλύποδός μοι, τέκνον, ἔχων νόον, Ἀμφίλοχ' ἥρως,
Τοῖσιν ἐφαρμόζου, τῶν ἂν κατὰ δῆμον ἵκηαι.

There were two tragedies composed by Euripidês, under the title of Ἀλκμαίων, ὁ διὰ Ψωφῖδος, and Ἀλκμαίων, ὁ διὰ Κορίνθου (Dindorf, Fragm. Eurip. p. 77).

[3] Apollodôr. iii. 7, 7; Thucyd. ii. 68.

were naturally drawn from the great prophetic race of the Melampodids.

Thus ends the legend of the two sieges of Thêbes; the greatest event, except the siege of Troy, in the ancient epic; the greatest enterprise of war, between Greeks and Greeks, during the time of those who are called the Heroes.

CHAPTER XV.

LEGEND OF TROY.

WE now arrive at the capital and culminating point of the Grecian epic, — the two sieges and capture of Troy, with the destinies of the dispersed heroes, Trojan as well as Grecian, after the second and most celebrated capture and destruction of the city.

It would require a large volume to convey any tolerable idea of the vast extent and expansion of this interesting fable, first handled by so many poets, epic, lyric and tragic, with their endless additions, transformations and contradictions, — then purged and recast by historical inquirers, who under color of setting aside the exaggerations of the poets, introduced a new vein of prosaic invention,— lastly, moralized and allegorized by philosophers. In the present brief outline of the general field of Grecian legend, or of that which the Greeks believed to be their antiquities, the Trojan war can be regarded as only one among a large number of incidents upon which Hekatæus and Herodotus looked back as constituting their fore-time. Taken as a special legendary event, it is indeed of wider and larger interest than any other, but it is a mistake to single it out from the rest as if it rested upon a different and more trustworthy basis. I must therefore confine myself to an abridged narrative of the current and leading facts; and amidst the numerous contradictory statements which are to be found respecting every one of them, I know no better ground of preference than comparative antiquity, though even the oldest tales which we possess — those contained in the Iliad — evidently presuppose others of prior date.

The primitive ancestor of the Trojan line of kings is Dardanus, son of Zeus, founder and eponymus of Dardania :[1] in the account of later authors, Dardanus was called the son of Zeus by Elektra, daughter of Atlas, and was further said to have come from Samothrace, or from Arcadia, or from Italy ;[2] but of this Homer mentions nothing. The first Dardanian town founded by him was in a lofty position on the descent of Mount Ida; for he was not yet strong enough to establish himself on the plain. But his son Erichthonius, by the favor of Zeus, became the wealthiest of mankind. His flocks and herds having multiplied, he had in his pastures three thousand mares, the offspring of some of whom, by Boreas, produced horses of preternatural swiftness. Trôs, the son of Erichthonius, and the eponym of the Trojans, had three sons — Ilus, Assaracus, and the beautiful Ganymêdês, whom Zeus stole away to become his cup-bearer in Olympus, giving to his father Trôs, as the price of the youth, a team of immortal horses.

From Ilus and Assaracus the Trojan and Dardanian lines diverge; the former passing from Ilus to Laomedôn, Priam and Hectôr; the latter from Assaracus to Capys, Anchisês and Æneas. Ilus founded in the plain of Troy the holy city of Ilium; Assaracus and his descendants remained sovereigns of Dardania.[4]

It was under the proud Laomedôn, son of Ilus, that Poseidôn and Apollo underwent, by command of Zeus, a temporary servitude; the former building the walls of the town, the latter tending the flocks and herds. When their task was completed and the penal period had expired, they claimed the stipulated reward; but Laomedôn angrily repudiated their demand, and even threatened to cut off their ears, to tie them hand and foot, and to sell them in some distant island as slaves.[5] He was punished for this

---

[1] Iliad, xx. 215.
[2] Hellanik. Fragm. 129, Didot; Dionys. Hal. i. 50–61; Apollodôr. iii. 12, 1; Schol. Iliad. xviii. 486; Varro, ap. Servium ad Virgil. Æneid. iii. 167; Kephalon. Gergithius ap. Steph. Byz. v. 'Αρίσβη.
[3] Iliad, v. 265; Hellanik. Fr. 146; Apollod. ii. 5, 9.
[4] Iliad, xx. 236.
[5] Iliad, vii. 451; xxi. 456. Hesiod. ap. Schol. Lycophr. 393

treachery by a sea-monster, whom Poseidôn sent to ravage his fields and to destroy his subjects. Laomedôn publicly offered the immortal horses given by Zeus to his father Trôs, as a reward to any one who would destroy the monster. But an oracle declared that a virgin of noble blood must be surrendered to him, and the lot fell upon Hesionê, daughter of Laomedôn himself. Hêraklês arriving at this critical moment, killed the monster by the aid of a fort built for him by Athênê and the Trojans,[1] so as to rescue both the exposed maiden and the people; but Laomedôn, by a second act of perfidy, gave him mortal horses in place of the matchless animals which had been promised. Thus defrauded of his due, Hêraklês equipped six ships, attacked and captured Troy and killed Laomedôn,[2] giving Hesionê to his friend and auxiliary Telamôn, to whom she bore the celebrated archer Teukros.[3] A painful sense of this expedition was preserved among the inhabitants of the historical town of Ilium, who offered no worship to Hêraklês.[4]

Among all the sons of Laomedôn, Priam[5] was the only one who had remonstrated against the refusal of the well-earned guerdon of Hêraklês; for which the hero recompensed him by placing him on the throne. Many and distinguished were his sons and daughters, as well by his wife Hekabê, daughter of Kisseus, as by other women.[6] Among the sons were Hectôr,[7] Paris, Dëipho-

---

[1] Iliad, xx. 145; Dionys. Hal. i. 52.

[2] Iliad, v. 640. Meneklês (ap. Schol. Venet. ad loc.) affirmed that this expedition of Hêraklês was a fiction; but Dikæarchus gave, besides, other exploits of the hero in the same neighborhood, at Thêbê Hypoplakiê (Schol. Iliad. vi. 396).

[3] Diodôr. iv. 32–49. Compare Venet. Schol. ad Iliad. viii. 284.

[4] Strabo, xiii. p. 596.

[5] As Dardanus, Trôs and Ilus are respectively eponyms of Dardania, Troy and Ilium, so Priam is eponym of the acropolis *Pergamum*. Πρίαμος is in the Æolic dialect Πέρραμος (Hesychius): upon which Ahrens remarks, " Cæterum ex hac Æolicâ nominis formâ apparet, Priamum non minus arcis Περγάμων eponymum esse, quam Ilum urbis, Troem populi: Πέργαμα enim a Περίαμα natum est, ι in γ mutato." (Ahrens, De Dialecto Æolicâ, 8, 7. p. 56: compare ibid. 28, 8. p. 150, περρ' ἀπύλω).

[6] Iliad, vi. 245; xxiv. 495.

[7] Hectôr was affirmed, both by Steisichorus and Ibykus, to be the son of Apollo (Stesichorus, ap. Schol. Ven. ad Iliad. xxiv. 259; Ibyki Fragm. xiv

bus, Helenus, Trôilus, Politês, Polydôrus; among the daughters
Laodikê, Kreüsa, Polyxena, and Kassandra.

The birth of Paris was preceded by formidable presages; for
Hekabê dreamt that she was delivered of a firebrand, and Priam,
on consulting the soothsayers, was informed that the son about
to be born would prove fatal to him. Accordingly he directed
the child to be exposed on Mount Ida; but the inauspicious kindness of the gods preserved him, and he grew up amidst the flocks
and herds, active and beautiful, fair of hair and symmetrical in
person, and the special favorite of Aphroditê.[1]

It was to this youth, in his solitary shepherd's walk on Mount
Ida, that the three goddesses Hêrê, Athênê, and Aphroditê were
conducted, in order that he might determine the dispute respecting their comparative beauty, which had arisen at the nuptials of
Pêleus and Thetis, — a dispute brought about in pursuance of the
arrangement, and in accomplishment of the deep-laid designs, of
Zeus. For Zeus, remarking with pain the immoderate numbers of
the then existing heroic race, pitied the earth for the overwhelming
burden which she was compelled to bear, and determined to
lighten it by exciting a destructive and long-continued war.[2]

---

ed. Schneidewin): both Euphoriôn (Fr. 125, Meineke) and Alexander Ætôlus-
follow the same idea. Stesichorus further stated, that after the siege Apollo
had carried Hekabê away into Lykia to rescue her from captivity (Pausanias, x. 27, 1): according to Euripidês, Apollo had promised that she should
die in Troy (Troad. 427).

By Sapphô, Hectôr was given as a surname of Zeus, Ζεὺς Ἕκτωρ (Hesychius, v. Ἕκτορες); a prince belonging to the regal family of Chios, anterior
to the Ionic settlement, as mentioned by the Chian poet Iôn (Pausan. vii. 3,
3), was so called.

[1] Iliad, iii. 45–55; Schol. Iliad. iii. 325; Hygin. fab. 91; Apollodôr. iii. 12, 5.
[2] This was the motive assigned to Zeus by the old epic poem, the Cyprian
Verses (Frag. 1. Düntz. p. 12; ap. Schol. ad Iliad. i. 4):—

Ἡ δὲ ἱστορία παρὰ Στασίνῳ τῷ τὰ Κύπρια πεποιηκότι εἰπόντ οὕτως·

Ἦν ὅτε μύρια φῦλα κατὰ χϑόνα πλαζόμενα......

.................βαρυστέρνου πλάτος αἴης.

Ζεὺς δὲ ἰδὼν ἐλέησε, καὶ ἐν πυκιναῖς πραπίδεσσι

Σύνϑετο κουφίσαι ἀνϑρώπων παμβώτορα γαῖαν,

Ῥιπίσας πολέμου μεγάλην ἔριν Ἰλιακοῖο,

Ὄφρα κενώσειεν ϑάνατῳ βάρος· οἱ δ' ἐνὶ Τροίῃ

Ἥρωες κτείνοντο, Διὸς δ' ἐτελείετο βουλή.

The same motive is touched upon by Eurip. Orest, 1635; Helen. 38; and

Paris awarded the palm of beauty to Aphroditê, who promised
him in recompense the possession of Helena, wife of the Spartan
Menelaus, — the daughter of Zeus and the fairest of living women.
At the instance of Aphroditê, ships were built for him, and he
embarked on the enterprise so fraught with eventual disaster
to his native city, in spite of the menacing prophecies of his
brother Helenus, and the always neglected warnings of Kassandra.[1]

Paris, on arriving at Sparta, was hospitably entertained by
Menelaus as well as by Kastôr and Pollux, and was enabled to
present the rich gifts which he had brought to Helen.[2] Menelaus
then departed to Krête, leaving Helen to entertain his Trojan
guest — a favorable moment which was employed by Aphroditê
to bring about the intrigue and the elopement. Paris carried
away with him both Helen and a large sum of money belonging
to Menelaus — made a prosperous voyage to Troy — and arrived
there safely with his prize on the third day.[3]

Menelaus, informed by Iris in Krête of the perfidious return
made by Paris for his hospitality, hastened home in grief and

---

seriously maintained, as it seems, by Chrysippus, ap. Plutarch. Stoic. Rep. p.
1049 : but the poets do not commonly go back farther than the passion of
Paris for Helen (Theognis, 1232 ; Simonid. Amorg. Fragm. 6, 118).

The judgment of Paris was one of the scenes represented on the ancient
chest of Kypselus at Olympia (Pausan. v. 19, 1).

[1] Argument of the Ἔπη Κύπρια (ap. Düntzer, p. 10). These warnings of
Kassandra form the subject of the obscure and affected poem of Lycophrôn.

[2] According to the Cyprian Verses, Helena was daughter of Zeus by Nemesis, who had in vain tried to evade the connection (Athenæ. viii. 334).
Hesiod (Schol. Pindar. Nem. x. 150) represented her as daughter of Oceanus
and Têthys, an oceanic nymph: Sapphô (Fragm. 17, Schneidewin), Pausanias (i. 33, 7), Apollodôrus (iii. 10, 7), and Isokratês (Encom. Helen. v. ii. p.
366, Auger) reconcile the pretensions of Lêda and Nemesis to a sort of joint
maternity (see Heinrichsen, De Carminibus Cypriis, p. 45–46).

[3] Herodot. ii. 117. He gives distinctly the assertion of the Cyprian Verses,
which contradicts the argument of the poem as it appears in Proclus (Fragm.
l. l.), according to which latter, Paris is driven out of his course by a storm
and captures the city of Sidôn. Homer (Iliad, vi. 293) seems however to
countenance the statement in the argument.

That Paris was guilty of robbery, as well as of the abduction of Helen, is
several times mentioned in the Iliad (iii. 144 ; vii. 350–363), also in the argument of the Cyprian Verses (see Æschyl. Agam. 534)

indignation to consult with his brother Agamemnôn, as well as with the venerable Nestôr, on the means of avenging the outrage. They made known the event to the Greek chiefs around them, among whom they found universal sympathy: Nestôr, Palamêdês and others went round to solicit aid in a contemplated attack of Troy, under the command of Agamemnôn, to whom each chief promised both obedience and unwearied exertion until Helen should be recovered.[1] Ten years were spent in equipping the expedition. The goddesses Hêrê and Athênê, incensed at the preference given by Paris to Aphroditê, and animated by steady attachment to Argos, Sparta and Mykênæ, took an active part in the cause; and the horses of Hêrê were fatigued with her repeated visits to the different parts of Greece.[2]

By such efforts a force was at length assembled at Aulis[3] in Bœôtia, consisting of 1186 ships and more than 100,000 men,— a force outnumbering by more than ten to one anything that the Trojans themselves could oppose, and superior to the defenders

---

[1] The ancient epic (Schol. ad Il. ii. 286–339) does not recognize the story of the numerous suitors of Helen, and the oath by which Tyndareus bound them all before he made the selection among them, that each should swear not only to acquiesce, but even to aid in maintaining undisturbed possession to the husband whom she should choose. This story seems to have been first told by Stesichorus (see Fragm, 20, ed. Kleine; Apollod. III. 10, 8). Yet it was evidently one of the prominent features of the current legend in the time of Thucydidês (i. 9; Euripid. Iphig. Aul. 51–80; Soph. Ajax, 1100). The exact spot in which Tyndareus exacted this oath from the suitors, near Sparta, was pointed out even in the time of Pausanias (iii. 20, 9).

[2] Iliad, iv. 27–55; xxiv. 765. Argument. Carm. Cypri. The point is emphatically touched upon by Dio Chrysostom (Orat. xi. p. 335–336) in his assault upon the old legend. Two years' preparation — in Dictys Cret. i. 16.

[3] The Spartan king Agesilaus, when about to start from Greece on his expedition into Asia Minor (396 B. C.) went to Aulis personally, in order that he too might sacrifice on the spot where Agamemnôn had sacrificed when he sailed for Troy (Xenoph. Hellen. iii. 4, 4).

Skylax (c. 60) notices the ἱερὸν at Aulis, and nothing else: it seems to have been like the adjoining Delium, a temple with a small village grown up around it.

Aulis is recognized as the port from which the expedition started, in the Hesiodic Works and Days (v. 650'

of Troy even with all her allies included.[1] It comprised heroes
with their followers from the extreme points of Greece — from
the north-western portions of Thessaly under Mount Olympus,
as well as the western islands of Dulichium and Ithaca, and the
eastern islands of Krête and Rhodes. Agamemnôn himself contributed 100 ships manned with the subjects of his kingdom of
Mykênæ, besides furnishing 60 ships to the Arcadians, who possessed none of their own. Menelaus brought with him 60 ships,
Nestôr from Pylus 90, Idomeneus from Krête and Diomêdês
from Argos 80 each. Forty ships were manned by the Eleians,
under four different chiefs; the like number under Megês from
Dulichium and the Echinades, and under Thoas from Kalydôn
and the other Ætôlian towns. Odysseus from Ithaca, and Ajax
from Salamis, brought 12 ships each. The Abantes from Eubœa, under Elephênôr, filled 40 vessels; the Bœôtians, under
Peneleôs and Lêitus, 50; the inhabitants of Orchomenus and
Aspledôn, 30; the light-armed Locrians, under Ajax son of Oileus,[2] 40; the Phôkians as many. The Athenians, under Menestheus, a chief distinguished for his skill in marshalling an army,
mustered 50 ships; the Myrmidons from Phthia and Hellas, under
Achilles, assembled in 50 ships; Protesilaus from Phylakê and
Pyrasus, and Eurypylus from Ormenium, each came with 40
ships; Machaôn and Podaleirius, from Trikka, with 30; Admêtus, from Pheræ and the lake Bœbêis, with 11; and Philoktêtês
from Melibœa with 7: the Lapithæ, under Polypœtes, son of
Peirithous, filled 40 vessels; the Ænianes and Perrhæbians,
under Guneus,[3] 22; and the Magnêtês under Prothous, 40; these
last two were from the northernmost parts of Thessaly, near the
mountains Pêlion and Olympus. From Rhodes, under Tlêpole-
mus, son of Hêraklês, appeared 9 ships; from Symê, under the
comely but effeminate Nireus, 3; from Kôs, Krapathus and the

---

[1] Iliad, ii. 128. Uschold (Geschichte des Trojanischen Kriegs, p. 9, Stutgart
1836) makes the total 135,000 men.

[2] The Hesiodic Catalogue notices Oileus, or Ileus, with a singular etymo
logy of his name (Fragm. 136, ed. Marktscheffel).

[3] Γουνεύς is the Heros Eponymus of the town of Gonnus in Thessaly; the
duplication of the consonant and shortening of the vowel belong to the
Æolic dialect (Ahrens, De Dialect. Æolic. 50, 4. p. 220).

neighboring islands, 30, under the orders of Pheidippus and Antiphus, sons of Thessalus and grandsons of Hêraklês.[1]
Among this band of heroes were included the distinguished warriors Ajax and Diomêdês, and the sagacious Nestôr; while Agamemnôn himself, scarcely inferior to either of them in prowess, brought with him a high reputation for prudence in command.

But the most marked and conspicuous of all were Achilles and Odysseus; the former a beautiful youth born of a divine mother, swift in the race, of fierce temper and irresistible might; the latter not less efficient as an ally from his eloquence, his untiring endurance, his inexhaustible resources under difficulty, and the mixture of daring courage with deep-laid cunning which never deserted him:[2] the blood of the arch-deceiver Sisyphus, through an illicit connection with his mother Antikleia, was said to flow in his veins,[3] and he was especially patronized and protected by the goddess Athênê. Odysseus, unwilling at first to take part in the expedition, had even simulated insanity; but Palamêdês, sent to Ithaca to invite him, tested the reality of his madness by placing in the furrow where Odysseus was ploughing, his infant son Telemachus. Thus detected, Odysseus could not refuse to join the Achæan host, but the prophet Halithersês predicted to him that twenty years would elapse before he revisited his native land.[4] To Achilles the gods had promised the full effulgence of

---

[1] See the Catalogue in the second book of the Iliad. There must probably have been a Catalogue of the Greeks also in the Cyprian Verses; for a Catalogue of the allies of Troy is specially noticed in the Argument of Proclus (p. 12. Düntzer).

Euripidês (Iphig. Aul. 165–300) devotes one of the songs of the Chorus to a partial Catalogue of the chief heroes.

According to Dictys Cretensis, all the principal heroes engaged in the expedition were kinsmen, all Pelopids (i. 14): they take an oath not to lay down their arms until Helen shall have been recovered, and they receive from Agamemnôn a large sum of gold.

[2] For the character of Odysseus, Iliad, iii. 202–220; x. 247. Odyss. xiii. 295.

The Philoktêtês of Sophoklês carries out very justly the character of the Homeric Odysseus (see v. 1035)—more exactly than the Ajax of the same poet depicts it.

[3] Sophokl. Philoktêt. 417, and Schol.—also Schol. ad Soph. Ajac. 190.

[4] Homer, Odyss. xxiv. 115; Æschyl. Agam. 841; Sophokl. Philoktêt. 1011.

heroic glory before the walls of Troy; nor could the place be
taken without both his coöperation and that of his son after him.
But they had forewarned him that this brilliant career would be
rapidly brought to a close; and that if he desired a long life, he
must remain tranquil and inglorious in his native land. In spite
of the reluctance of his mother Thetis, he preferred few years
with bright renown, and joined the Achæan host.[1] When Nestôr and Odysseus came to Phthia to invite him, both he and his
intimate friend Patroclus eagerly obeyed the call.[2]

Agamemnôn and his powerful host set sail from Aulis; but
being ignorant of the locality and the direction, they landed by
mistake in Teuthrania, a part of Mysia near the river Kaïkus,
and began to ravage the country under the persuasion that it
was the neighborhood of Troy. Telephus, the king of the country,[3] opposed and repelled them, but was ultimately defeated and
severely wounded by Achilles. The Greeks now, discovering
their mistake, retired; but their fleet was dispersed by a storm
and driven back to Greece. Achilles attacked and took Skyrus,
and there married Deidamia, the daughter of Lycomêdês.[4] Telephus, suffering from his wounds, was directed by the oracle to
come to Greece and present himself to Achilles to be healed, by
applying the scrapings of the spear with which the wound had
been given: thus restored, he became the guide of the Greeks
when they were prepared to renew their expedition.[5]

---

with the Schol. Argument of the Cypria in Heinrichsen, De Carmin. Cypr.
p. 23 (the sentence is left out in Düntzer, p. 11).

A lost tragedy of Sophoklês, 'Οδυσσεὺς Μαινόμενος, handled this subject.

Other Greek chiefs were not less reluctant than Odysseus to take part in
the expedition: see the tale of Pœmandrus, forming a part of the temple-
legend of the Achilleium at Tanagra in Bœôtia (Plutarch, Quæstion. Græc.
p. 299).

[1] Iliad, i. 352; ix. 411.   [2] Iliad, xi. 782.

[3] Telephus was the son of Augê, daughter of king Aleus of Tegea in
Arcadia, by Hêraklês: respecting her romantic adventures, see the previous
chapter on Arcadian legends — Strabo's faith in the story (xii. p. 572).

The spot called the Harbor of the Achæans, near Gryneium, was stated
to be the place where Agamemnôn and the chiefs took counsel whether they
should attack Telephus or not (Skylax, c. 97; compare Strabo, xiv. p. 622).

[4] Iliad, xi. 664; Argum. Cypr. p. 11, Düntzer; Diktys Cret. ii. 3· 4.

[5] Euripid. Telephus, Frag. 26, Dindorf; Hygin. f. 101; Diktys, ii. 10. Euripidês had treated the adventure of Telephus in this lost tragedy: he gave

The armament was again assembled at Aulis, but the goddess
Artemis, displeased with the boastful language of Agamemnôn,
prolonged the duration of adverse winds, and the offending chief
was compelled to appease her by the well-known sacrifice of his
daughter Iphigeneia.[1] They then proceeded to Tenedos, from
whence Odysseus and Menelaus were despatched as envoys to
Troy, to redemand Helen and the stolen property. In spite of
the prudent counsels of Antenôr, who received the two Grecian
chiefs with friendly hospitality, the Trojans rejected the demand,
and the attack was resolved upon. It was foredoomed by the
gods that the Greek who first landed should perish: Protesilaus was generous enough to put himself upon this forlorn hope,
and accordingly fell by the hand of Hectôr.

Meanwhile the Trojans had assembled a large body of allies
from various parts of Asia Minor and Thrace: Dardanians under
Æneas, Lykians under Sarpedôn, Mysians, Karians, Mæonians,
Alizonians,[2] Phrygians, Thracians, and Pæonians.[3] But vain

the miraculous cure with the dust of the spear, πριστοῖσι λογχῆς θέλγεται
ῥινήμασι. Diktys softens down the prodigy: " Achilles cum Machaone et
Podalirio adhibentes curam vulneri," etc. Pliny (xxxiv. 15) gives to the
rust of brass or iron a place in the list of genuine remedies.

" Longe omnino a Tiberi ad Caicum: quo in loco etiam Agamemnôn
errasset, nisi ducem Telephum invenisset" (Cicero, Pro L. Flacco, c. 29).
The portions of the Trojan legend treated in the lost epics and the tragedians, seem to have been just as familiar to Cicero as those noticed in the
Iliad.

Strabo pays comparatively little attention to any portion of the Trojan
war except what appears in Homer. He even goes so far as to give a reason
why the Amazons *did not* come to the aid of Priam: they were at enmity
with him, because Priam had aided the Phrygians agaist them (Iliad, iii
188: in Strabo, τοῖς Ἰῶσιν must be a mistake for τοῖς Φρυξίν). Strabo can
hardly have read, and never alludes to, Arktinus; in-whose poem the brave
and beautiful Penthesileia, at the head of her Amazons, forms a marked
epoch and incident of the war (Strabo, xii. 552).

[1] Nothing occurs in Homer respecting the sacrifice of Iphigeneia (see
Schol. Ven. ad Il. ix. 145).

[2] No portion of the Homeric Catalogue gave more trouble to Dêmêtrius
of Skêpsis and the other expositors than these Alizonians (Strabo, xii. p.
549; xiii. p. 603): a fictitious place called Alizonium, in the region of Ida,
was got up to meet the difficulty (εἶτ' Ἀλιζώνιον, τοῦτ' ἤδη πεπλασμέ-
νον πρὸς τὴν τῶν Ἀλιζώνων ὑπόθεσιν, etc., Strabo, l. c.).

[3] See the Catalogue of the Trojans (Iliad, ii. 815–877).

was the attempt to oppose the landing of the Greeks: the Trojans were routed, and even the invulnerable Cycnus,[1] son of
Poseidôn, one of the great bulwarks of the defence, was slain by
Achilles. Having driven the Trojans within their walls, Achilles
attacked and stormed Lyrnêssus, Pêdasus, Lesbos and other
places in the neighborhood, twelve towns on the sea-coast and
eleven in the interior; he drove off the oxen of Æneas and
pursued the hero himself, who narrowly escaped with his life:
he surprised and killed the youthful Trôilus, son of Priam, and
captured several of the other sons, whom he sold as prisoners
into the islands of the Ægean.[2] He acquired as his captive the
fair Brisêis, while Chrysêis was awarded to Agamemnôn: he
was moreover eager to see the divine Helen, the prize and stimulus of this memorable struggle; and Aphroditê and Thetis
contrived to bring about an interview between them.[3]

At this period of the war the Grecian army was deprived of
Palamêdês, one of its ablest chiefs. Odysseus had not forgiven
the artifice by which Palamêdês had detected his simulated insanity, nor was he without jealousy of a rival clever and cunning in a degree equal, if not superior, to himself; one who had
enriched the Greeks with the invention of letters, of dice for

---

[1] Cycnus was said by later writers to be king of Kolônæ in the Troad
(Strabo, xiii. p. 589–603; Aristotel. Rhetoric. ii. 23). Æschylus introduced
upon the Attic stage both Cycnus and Memnôn in terrific equipments (Aristophan. Ran. 957. Οὐδ' ἐξέπληττον αὐτοὺς Κύκνους ἄγων καὶ Μέμνονας κω-
δωνοφαλαροπώλους). Compare Welcker, Æschyl. Trilogie, p. 433.

[2] Iliad, xxiv. 752; Argument of the Cypria, pp. 11, 12, Düntzer. These
desultory exploits of Achilles furnished much interesting romance to the
later Greek poets (see Parthênius, Narrat. 21). See the neat summary of
the principal events of the war in Quintus Smyrn. xiv. 125–140; Dio Chrysost. Or. xi. p. 338–342.

Trôilus is only once named in the Iliad (xxiv. 253); he was mentioned
also in the Cypria; but his youth, beauty, and untimely end made him an
object of great interest with the subsequent poets. Sophoklês had a tragedy
called Trôilus (Welcker, Griechisch. Tragöd. i. p. 124); Τὸν ἀνδρόπαιδα δεσ-
πότην ἀπώλεσα, one of the Fragm. Even earlier than Sophoklês, his beauty was celebrated by the tragedian Phrynichus (Athenæ. xiii. p. 564; Virgil,
Æneid, i. 474; Lycophrôn, 307).

[3] Argument. Cypr. p. 11, Düntz. Καὶ μετὰ ταῦτα Ἀχιλλεὺς Ἑλένην ἐπι-
θυμεῖ θεάσασθαι, καὶ συνήγαγον αὐτοὺς εἰς τὸ αὐτὸ Ἀφροδίτη καὶ Θέτις. A
scene which would have been highly interesting in the hands of Homer.

cn.a.ement, of night-watches, as well as with other useful suggestions. According to the old Cyprian epic, Palamêdês was drowned while fishing, by the hands of Odysseus and Diomêdês.[1] Neither in the Iliad nor the Odyssey does the name of Palamêdês occur: the lofty position which Odysseus occupies in both those poems — noticed with some degree of displeasure even by Pindar, who described Palamêdês as the wiser man of the two — is sufficient to explain the omission.[2] But in the more advanced period of the Greek mind, when intellectual superiority came to acquire a higher place in the public esteem as compared with military prowess, the character of Palamêdês, combined with his unhappy fate, rendered him one of the most interesting personages in the Trojan legend. Æschylus, Sophoklês and Euripidês each consecrated to him a special tragedy; but the mode of his death as described in the old epic was not suitable to Athenian ideas, and accordingly he was represented as having been falsely accused of treason by Odysseus, who caused gold to be buried in his tent, and persuaded Agamemnôn and the Grecian chiefs that Palamêdês had received it from the Trojans.[3] He thus forfeited his life, a victim to the calumny of Odysseus and to the delusion

---

[1] Argum. Cypr. 1. 1.; Pausan. x. 31. The concluding portion of the Cypria seems to have passed under the title of Παλαμηδεία (see Fragm. 16 and 18. p. 15, Düntz.; Welcker, Der Episch. Cycl. p. 450; Eustath. ad Hom. Odyss. i. 107).

The allusion of Quintus Smyrnæus (v. 197) seems rather to point to the story in the Cypria, which Strabo (viii. p. 368) appears not to have read.

[2] Pindar, Nem. vii. 21; Aristidês, Orat. 46. p. 260.

[3] See the Fragments of the three tragedians, Παλαμήδης — Aristeidês, Or. xlvi. p. 260; Philostrat. Heroic. x.; Hygin. fab. 95-105. Discourses for and against Palamêdês, one by Alkidamas, and one under the name of Gorgias, are printed in Reiske's Orr. Græc. t. viii. pp. 64, 102; Virgil, Æneid, ii. 82, with the ample commentary of Servius — Polyæn. Procœ. p. 6.

Welcker (Griechisch. Tragöd. v. i. p. 130, vol. ii. p. 500) has evolved with ingenuity the remaining fragments of the lost tragedies.

According to Diktys, Odysseus and Diomêdês prevail upon Palamêdês to he let down into a deep well, and then cast stones upon him (ii. 15).

Xenophôn (De Venatione, c. 1) evidently recognizes the story in the Cypria, that Odysseus and Diomêdês caused the death of Palamêdês; but he cannot believe that two such exemplary men were really guilty of so iniquitous an act — κακοὶ δὲ ἐπραξαν τὸ ἔργον.

One of the eminences near Napoli still bears the name of Palamidhi.

of the leading Greeks. In the last speech made by the philosopher Socratês to his Athenian judges, he alludes with solemnity
and fellow-feeling to the unjust condemnation of Palamêdês, as
analogous to that which he himself was about to suffer, and his
companions seem to have dwelt with satisfaction on the comparison. Palamêdês passed for an instance of the slanderous enmity
and misfortune which so often wait upon superior genius.[1]

In these expeditions the Grecian army consumed nine years,
during which the subdued Trojans dared not give battle without
their walls for fear of Achilles. Ten years was the fixed epical
duration of the siege of Troy, just as five years was the duration
of the siege of Kamikus by the Krêtan armament which came
to avenge the death of Minôs :[2] ten years of preparation, ten
years of siege, and ten years of wandering for Odysseus, were
periods suited to the rough chronological dashes of the ancient
epic, and suggesting no doubts nor difficulties with the original
hearers. But it was otherwise when the same events came to be
contemplated by the historicizing Greeks, who could not be satisfied without either finding or inventing satisfactory bonds of coherence between the separate events. Thucydidês tells us that
the Greeks were less numerous than the poets have represented,
and that being moreover very poor, they were unable to procure
adequate and constant provisions : hence they were compelled to
disperse their army, and to employ a part of it in cultivating the
Chersonese, — a part in marauding expeditions over the neighborhood. Could the whole army have been employed against
Troy at once (he says), the siege would have been much more
speedily and easily concluded.[3] If the great historian could permit himself thus to amend the legend in so many points, we
might have imagined that the simpler course would have been to
include the duration of the siege among the list of poetical exaggerations, and to affirm that the real siege had lasted only one

---

[1] Plato, Apolog. Socr. c. 32; Xenoph. Apol. Socr. 26; Memor. iv. 2, 33;
Liban. pro Socr. p. 242, ed. Morell.; Lucian, Dial. Mort. 20.

[2] Herodot. vii. 170. Ten years is a proper mythical period for a great war
to last : the war between the Olympic gods and the Titan gods lasts ten
years (Hesiod, Theogon. 636). Compare δεκάτῳ ἐνιαυτῷ (Hom. Odyss.
xvi. 17).

[3] Thucyd. i. 11.

year instead of ten. But it seems that the ten years' duration was so capital a feature in the ancient tale, that nò critic ventured to meddle with it.

A period of comparative intermission however was now at hand for the Trojans. The gods brought about the memorable fit of anger of Achilles, under the influence of which he refused to put on his armor, and kept his Myrmidons in camp. According to the Cypria, this was the behest of Zeus, who had compassion on the Trojans: according to the Iliad, Apollo was the originating cause,[1] from anxiety to avenge the injury which his priest Chrysês had endured from Agamemnôn. For a considerable time, the combats of the Greeks against Troy were conducted without their best warrior, and severe indeed was the humiliation which they underwent in consequence. How the remaining Grecian chiefs vainly strove to make amends for his absence — how Hectôr and the Trojans defeated and drove them to their ships — how the actual blaze of the destroying flame, applied by Hectôr to the ship of Protesilaus, roused up the anxious and sympathizing Patroclus, and extorted a reluctant consent from Achilles, to allow his friend and his followers to go forth and avert the last extremity of ruin — how Achilles, when Patroclus had been killed by Hectôr, forgetting his anger in grief for the death of his friend, reëntered the fight, drove the Trojans within their walls with immense slaughter, and satiated his revenge both upon the living and the dead Hectôr — all these events have been chronicled, together with those divine dispensations on which most of them are made to depend, in the immortal verse of the Iliad.

Homer breaks off with the burial of Hectôr, whose body has just been ransomed by the disconsolate Priam; while the lost poem of Arktinus, entitled the Æthiopis, so far as we can judge from the argument still remaining of it, handled only the subsequent events of the siege. The poem of Quintus Smyrnæus, composed about the fourth century of the Christian æra, seems in its first books to coincide with the Æthiopis, in the subsequent books partly with the Ilias Minor of Leschês.[2]

[1] Homer, Iliad, i. 21.
[2] Tychsen, Commentat. de Quinto Smyrnæo, § iii. c. 5–7. The 'Ιλίου
13*

The Trojans, dismayed by the death of Hector, were again animated with hope by the appearance of the warlike and beautiful
queen of the Amazons, Penthesileia, daughter of Arês, hitherto
invincible in the field, who came to their assistance from Thrace
at the head of a band of her countrywomen. She again led the
besieged without the walls to encounter the Greeks in the open
field; and under her auspices the latter were at first driven back,
until she too was slain by the invincible arm of Achilles. The
victor, on taking off the helmet of his fair enemy as she lay on
the ground, was profoundly affected and captivated by her
charms, for which he was scornfully taunted by Thersitês: exasperated by this rash insult, he killed Thersitês on the spot with
a blow of his fist. A violent dispute among the Grecian chiefs
was the result, for Diomêdês, the kinsman of Thersitês, warmly
resented the proceeding; and Achilles was obliged to go to Les-
bus, where he was purified from the act of homicide by Odysseus.[1]

Next arrived Memnôn, son of Tithônus and Eôs, the most
stately of living men, with a powerful band of black Æthiopians,
to the assistance of Troy. Sallying forth against the Greeks, he
made great havoc among them: the brave and popular Antilochus perished by his hand, a victim to filial devotion in defence
of Nestôr.[2] Achilles at length attacked him, and for a long time
the combat was doubtful between them: the prowess of Achilles
and the supplication of Thetis with Zeus finally prevailed;

Πέρσις was treated both by Arktinus and by Leschês: with the latter it
formed a part of the Ilias Minor.

[1] Argument of the Æthiopis, p. 16, Düntzer; Quint. Smyrn. lib. i.; Diktys Cret. iv. 2–3.

In the Philoktêtês, of Sophoklês, Thersitês survives Achilles (Soph. Phil
358–445).

[2] Odyss. xi. 522. Κεῖνον δὴ κάλλιστον ἴδον, μετὰ Μέμνονα δῖον : see also
Odyss. iv. 187; Pindar, Pyth. vi. 31. Æschylus (ap. Strabo. xv. p. 728)
conceives Memnôn as a Persian starting from Susa.

Ktêsias gave in his history full details respecting the expedition of Memnôn, sent by the king of Assyria to the relief of his dependent, Priam of
Troy; all this was said to be recorded in the royal archives. The Egyptians affirmed that Memnôn had come from Egypt (Diodôr. ii. 22; compare
iv. 77): the two stories are blended together in Pausanias, x. 31, 2. The
Phrygians pointed out the road along which he had marched.

whilst Eôs obtained for her vanquished son the consoling gift of immortality. His tomb, however,[1] was shown near the Propontis, within a few miles of the mouth of the river Æsêpus, and was visited annually by the birds called Memnonides, who swept it and bedewed it with water from the stream. So the traveller Pausanias was told, even in the second century after the Christian æra, by the Hellespontine Greeks.

But the fate of Achilles himself was now at hand. After routing the Trojans and chasing them into the town, he was slain near the Skæan gate by an arrow from the quiver of Paris, directed under the unerring auspices of Apollo.[2] The greatest efforts were made by the Trojans to possess themselves of the body, which was however rescued and borne off to the Grecian camp by the valor of Ajax and Odysseus. Bitter was the grief of Thetis for the loss of her son: she came into the camp with the Muses and the Nêreids to mourn over him; and when a magnificent funeral-pile had been prepared by the Greeks to burn him with every mark of honor, she stole away the body and conveyed it to a renewed and immortal life in the island of Leukê in the Euxine Sea. According to some accounts he was there blest with the nuptials and company of Helen.[3]

---

[1] Argum. Æth. ut sup.; Quint. Smyrn. ii. 396–550; Pausan. x. 31, 1. Pindar, in praising Achilles, dwells much on his triumphs over Hectôr, Têlephus, Memnôn, and Cycnus, but never notices Penthesileia (Olymp. ii. 90 Nem. iii. 60; vi. 52. Isthm. v. 43).

Æschylus, in the Ψυχοστασία, introduced Thetis and Eôs, each in an attitude of supplication for her son, and Zeus weighing in his golden scales the souls of Achilles and Memnôn (Schol. Ven. ad Iliad. viii. 70: Pollux, iv. 130; Plutarch, De Audiend. Poet. p. 17). In the combat between Achilles and Memnôn, represented on the chest of Kypselus at Olympia, Thetis and Eôs were given each as aiding her son (Pausan. v. 19, 1).

[2] Iliad, xxii. 360; Sophokl. Philokt. 334; Virgil, Æneid, vi. 56.

[3] Argum. Æthiop. ut sup.; Quint. Smyrn. 151–583; Homer, Odyss. v. 310; Ovid, Metam. xiii. 284; Eurip. Androm. 1262; Pausan. iii. 19, 13. According to Diktys (iv. 11), Paris and Deiphobus entrap Achilles by the promise of an interview with Polyxena and kill him.

A minute and curious description of the island Leukê, or Ἀχιλλέως νῆσος, is given in Arriau (Periplus, Pont. Euxin. p. 21; ap. Geogr. Min. t. 1).

The heroic or divine empire of Achilles in Scythia was recognized by Alkæus the poet (Alkæi Fragm. Schneidew. Fr. 46), Ἀχίλλευ, ὃ γας Σκυ-

Thetis celebrated splendid funeral games in honor of her son,
and offered the unrivalled panoply, which Hêphæstos had forged
and wrought for him, as a prize to the most distinguished warrior
in the Grecian army. Odysseus and Ajax became rivals for the
distinction, when Athênê, together with some Trojan prisoners,
who were asked from which of the two their country had sustained
greatest injury, decided in favor of the former. The gallant Ajax
lost his senses with grief and humiliation: in a fit of phrenzy he
slew some sheep, mistaking them for the men who had wronged
him, and then fell upon his own sword.[1]

Odysseus now learnt from Helenus son of Priam, whom he had
captured in an ambuscade,[2] that Troy could not be taken unless
both Philoktêtês, and Neoptolemus, son of Achilles, could be prevailed upon to join the besiegers. The former, having been stung
in the foot by a serpent, and becoming insupportable to the
Greeks from the stench of his wound, had been left at Lemnus in

---

ϑικᾶς μέδεις. Eustathius (ad Dionys. Periêgêt. 307) gives the story of his
having followed Iphigeneia thither: compare Antonin. Liberal. 27.

Ibykus represented Achilles as having espoused Mêdea in the Elysian
Field (Idyk. Fragm. 18. Schneidewin). Simondês followed this story (ap-
Schol. Apoll. Rhod. iv. 815).

[1] Argument of Æthiopis and Ilias Minor, and Fragm. 2 of the latter, pp.
17, 18, Düntz.; Quint. Smyrn. v. 120–482; Hom. Odyss. xi. 550; Pindar,
Nem. vii. 26. The Ajax of Sophoklês, and the contending speeches between
Ajax and Ulysses in the beginning of the thirteenth book of Ovid's Metamorphoses, are too well known to need special reference.

The suicide of Ajax seems to have been described in detail in the Æthiopis : compare Pindar. Isthm. iii. 51, and the Scholia ad loc., which show the
attention paid by Pindar to the minute circumstances of the old epic.
See Fragm. 2 of the Ἰλίου Πέρσις of Arktinus, in Düntz. p. 22, which would
seem more properly to belong to the Æthiopis. Diktys relates the suicide
of Ajax, as a consequence of his unsuccessful competition with Odysseus,
not about the arms of Achilles, but about the Palladium, after the taking of
the city (v. 14).

There were, however, many different accounts of the manner in which
Ajax had died, some of which are enumerated in the argument to the drama
of Sophoklês. Ajax is never wounded in the Iliad: Æschylus made him
invulnerable except under the armpits (see Schol. ad Sophok. Ajac. 833);
the Trojans pelted him with mud — εἴ πως βαρηϑείη ὑπὸ τοῦ πήλου (Schol.
Iliad. xiv. 404).

[2] Soph. Philokt. 604.

the commencement of the expedition, and had spent ten years[1] in misery on that desolate island; but he still possessed the peerless bow and arrows of Hêraklês, which were said to be essential to the capture of Troy. Diomêdês fetched Philoktêtês from Lemnus to the Grecian camp, where he was healed by the skill of Machaôn,[2] and took an active part against the Trojans — engaging in single combat with Paris, and killing him with one of the Hêrakleian arrows. The Trojans were allowed to carry away for burial the body of this prince, the fatal cause of all their sufferings; but not until it had been mangled by the hand of Menelaus.[3] Odysseus went to the island of Skyrus to invite Neoptolemus to the army. The untried but impetuous youth gladly obeyed the call, and received from Odysseus his father's armor, while on the other hand, Eurypylus, son of Têlephus, came from Mysia as auxiliary to the Trojans and rendered to them valuable service — turning the tide of fortune for a time against the Greeks, and killing some of their bravest chiefs, amongst whom was numbered Peneleôs, and the unrivalled leech Machaôn.[4] The exploits of

---

[1] Soph. Philokt. 703. 'Ω μελέα ψυχὴ, 'Ος μηδ' οἰνοχύτου πόματος 'Ησθη δεκετῆ χρόνον, etc.

In the narrative of Diktys (ii. 47), Philoktêtês returns from Lemnus to Troy much earlier in the war before the death of Achilles, and without any assigned cause.

[2] According to Sophoklês, Hêraklês sends Asklêpius to Troy to heal Philok têtês (Soph. Philokt. 1415).

The subject of Philoktêtês formed the subject of a tragedy both by Æschylus and by Euripidês (both lost) as well as by Sophoklês.

[3] Argument. Iliad. Minor. Düntz. 1. c. Καὶ τὸν νεκρὸν ὑπὸ Μενελάου κατακισθέντα ἀνελόμενοι θάπτουσιν οἱ Τρῶες. See Quint. Smyrn, x. 240 : he differs here in many respects from the arguments of the old poems as given by Proclus, both as to the incidents and as to their order in time (Diktys, iv. 20). The wounded Paris flees to Œnônê, whom he had deserted in order to follow Helen, and entreats her to cure him by her skill in simples : she refuses, and permits him to die; she is afterwards stung with remorse, and hangs herself (Quint. Smyrn. x. 285-331 ; Apollodôr. iii. 12, 6; Conôn. Narrat. 23; see Bachet de Meziriac, Comment. sur les Epîtres d'Ovide, t. i. p. 456). The story of Œnônê is as old as Hellanikus and Kephalôn of Gergis (see Hellan. Fragm. 126, Didot).

[4] To mark the way in which these legendary events pervaded and became embodied in the local worship, I may mention the received practice in the great temple of Asklêpius (father of Machaôn) at Pergamus, even in the

Neoptolemus were numerous, worthy of the glory of his race and the renown of his father. He encountered and slew Eurypylus, together with numbers of the Mysian warriors : he routed the Trojans and drove them within their walls, from whence they never again emerged to give battle : nor was he less distinguished for his good sense and persuasive diction, than for forward energy in the field.[1]

Troy however was still impregnable so long as the Palladium, a statue given by Zeus himself to Dardanus, remained in the citadel; and great care had been taken by the Trojans not only to conceal this valuable present, but to construct other statues so like it as to mislead any intruding robber. Nevertheless the enterprising Odysseus, having disguised his person with miserable clothing and self-inflicted injuries, found means to penetrate into the city and to convey the Palladium by stealth away : Helen alone recognized him; but she was now anxious to return to Greece, and even assisted Odysseus in concerting means for the capture of the town.[2]

To accomplish this object, one final stratagem was resorted to. By the hands of Epeius of Panopeus, and at the suggestion of Athênê, a capacious hollow wooden horse was constructed, capable of containing one hundred men : the *élite* of the Grecian heroes, Neoptolemus, Odysseus, Menelaus and others, concealed themselves in the inside of it, and the entire Grecian army sailed away

---

time of Pausanias. Têlephus, father of Eurypylus, was the local hero and mythical king of Teuthrania, in which Pergamus was situated. In the hymns there sung, the proem and the invocation were addressed to Têlephus ; but nothing was said in them about Eurypylus, nor was it permitted even to mention his name in the temple, — " they knew him to be the slayer of Machaôn :" ἄρχονται μὲν ἀπὸ Τηλέφου τῶν ὕμνων, προσᾴδουσι δὲ οὐδὲν ἐς τὸν Εὐρύπυλον, οὐδὲ ἀρχὴν ἐν τῷ ναῷ θέλουσιν ὀνομάζειν αὐτὸν, οἷα ἐπιστάμενοι φονέα ὄντα Μαχάονος (Pausan. iii. 26, 7).

The combination of these qualities in other Homeric chiefs is noted in a subsequent chapter of his work, ch. xx. vol. ii.

[1] Argument. Iliad. Minor. p. 17, Düntzer. Homer, Odyss. xi. 510–520. Pausan. iii. 26, 7. Quint. Smyrn. vii. 553; viii. 201.

[2] Argument. Iliad. Minor. p. 18, Düntz.; *Arktinus* ap. Dionys. Hal. i. 69; Homer, Odyss. iv. 246; Quint. Smyrn. x. 354: Virgil, Æneid, ii. 164, and the 9th Excursus of Heyne on that book.

Compare with this legend about the Palladium, the Roman legend respecting the Ancylia (Ovid, Fasti, III. 381).

to Tenedos, burning their tents and pretending to have abandoned the siege. The Trojans, overjoyed to find themselves free, issued from the city and contemplated with astonishment the fabric which their enemies had left behind: they long doubted what should be done with it; and the anxious heroes from within heard the surrounding consultations, as well as the voice of Helen when she pronounced their names and counterfeited the accents of their wives.[1] Many of the Trojans were anxious to dedicate it to the gods in the city as a token of gratitude for their deliverance; but the more cautious spirits inculcated distrust of an enemy's legacy; and Laocoôn, the priest of Poseidôn, manifested his aversion by striking the side of the horse with his spear. The sound revealed that the horse was hollow, but the Trojans heeded not this warning of possible fraud; and the unfortunate Laocoôn, a victim to his own sagacity and patriotism, miserably perished before the eyes of his countrymen, together with one of his sons, — two serpents being sent expressly by the gods out of the sea to destroy him. By this terrific spectacle, together with the perfidious counsels of Sinon, a traitor whom the Greeks had left behind for the special purpose of giving false information, the Trojans were induced to make a breach in their own walls, and to drag the fatal fabric with triumph and exultation into their city.[2]

---

[1] Odyss. iv. 275; Virgil, Æneid, ii. 14; Heyne, Excurs. 3. ad Æneid. ii. Stesichorus, in his 'Ιλίου Πέρσις, gave the number of heroes in the wooden horse as one hundred (Stesichor. Fragm. 26, ed. Kleine; compare Athenæ· xlii. p. 610).

[2] Odyss. viii. 492; xi. 522. Argument of the 'Ιλίου Πέρσις of Arktinus, p. 21. Düntz. Hydin. f. 108–135. Bacchylidês and Euphorion ap. Servium ad Virgil. Æneid. ii. 201.

Both Sinon and Laocoôn came originally from the old epic poem of Arktinus, though Virgil may perhaps have immediately borrowed both them, and other matters in his second book, from a poem passing under the name of Pisander (see Macrob. Satur. v. 2; Heyne, Excurs. 1. ad Æn. ii.; Welcker, Der Episch. Kyklus, v. 97). We cannot give credit either to Arktinus or Pisander for the masterly specimen of oratory which is put into the mouth of Sinon in the Æneid.

In Quintus Smyrnæus (xii. 366), the Trojans torture and mutilate Sinon to extort from him the truth: his endurance, sustained by the inspiration of Hêrê, is proof against the extremity of suffering, and he adheres to his false tale. This is probably an incident of the old epic, though the delicate taste

The destruction of Troy, according to the decree of the gods, was now irrevocably sealed. While the Trojans indulged in a night of riotous festivity, Sinon kindled the fire-signal to the Greeks at Tenedos, loosening the bolts of the wooden horse, from out of which the enclosed heroes descended. The city, assailed both from within and from without, was thoroughly sacked and destroyed, with the slaughter or captivity of the larger portion of its heroes as well as its people. The venerable Priam perished by the hand of Neoptolemus, having in vain sought shelter at the domestic altar of Zeus Herkeios; but his son Deiphobus, who since the death of Paris had become the husband of Helen, defended his house desperately against Odysseus and Menelaus, and sold his life dearly. After he was slain, his body was fearfully mutilated by the latter.[1]

Thus was Troy utterly destroyed — the city, the altars and temples,[2] and the population. Æneas and Antenôr were permitted to escape, with their families, having been always more favorably regarded by the Greeks than the remaining Trojans. According to one version of the story, they had betrayed the

---

of Virgil, and his sympathy with the Trojans, has induced him to omit it. Euphorion ascribed the proceedings of Sinon to Odysseus: he also gave a different cause for the death of Laocoön (Fr. 35–36. p. 55, ed. Düntz., in tae Fragments of Epic Poets after Alexander the Great). Sinon is ἑταῖρος Ὀδυσσέως in Pausan. x. 27, 1.

[1] Odyss. viii. 515; Argument of Arktinas, *ut sup.;* Euripid. Hecub. 903, Virg. Æn. vi. 497; Quint. Smyrn. xiii. 35–229; Leschês ap. Pausan. x. 27, 2; Diktys, v. 12. Ibykus and Simonidês also represented Deiphobus as the ἀντεράστης ʿΕλένης (Schol. Hom. Iliad. xiii. 517).

The night-battle in the interior of Troy was described with all its fearful details both by Leschês and Arktinus: the ʾΙλίου Πέρσις of the latter seems to have been a separate poem, that of the former constituted a portion of the Ilias Minor (see Welcker, Der Epische Kyklus, p. 215): the ʾΙλίου Πέρσις by the lyric poets Sakadas and Stesichorus probably added many new incidents. Polygnôtus had painted a succession of the various calamitous scenes, drawn from the poem of Leschês, on the walls of the leschê at Delphi, with the name written over each figure (Pausan. x. 25-26).

Hellanikus fixed the precise day of the month on which the capture took place (Hellan. Fr. 143–144), the twelfth day of Thargeliôn.

[2] Æschyi. Agamemn. 527. —

Βωμοὶ δ' ἄϊστοι καὶ θεῶν ἱδρύματα,
Καὶ σπέρμα πάσης ἐξαπόλλυται χθονός.

city to the Greeks: a panther's skin had been hung over the door of Antenor's house as a signal for the victorious besiegers to spare it in the general plunder.[1] In the distribution of the principal captives, Astyanax, the infant son of Hectôr, was cast from the top of the wall and killed, by Odysseus or Neoptolemus: Polyxena, the daughter of Priam, was immolated on the tomb of Achilles, in compliance with a requisition made by the shade of the deceased hero to his countrymen;[2] while her sister Kassandra was presented as a prize to Agamemnôn. She had sought sanctuary at the altar of Athênê, where Ajax, the son of Oileus, making a guilty attempt to seize her, had drawn both upon himself and upon the army the serious wrath of the goddess, insomuch that the Greeks could hardly be restrained from stoning him to death.[3] Andromachê and Helenus were both given to Neoptolemus, who, according to the Ilias Minor, carried away also Æneas as his captive.[4]

Helen gladly resumed her union with Menelaus: she accompanied him back to Sparta, and lived with him there many years in comfort and dignity,[5] passing afterwards to a happy immortality

[1] This symbol of treachery also figured in the picture of Polygnôtus. A different story appears in Schol. Iliad. iii. 206.

[2] Euripid. Hecub. 38–114, and Troad. 716; Leschês ap. Pausan. x. 25, 9; Virgil, Æneid, iii. 322, and Servius ad loc. A romantic tale is found in Diktys respecting the passion of Achilles for Polyxena (iii. 2).

[3] Odyss. xi. 422. Arktinus, Argum. p. 21, Düntz. Theognis, 1232 Pausan. i. 15, 2; x. 26, 3; 81, 1. As an expiation of this sin of their national hero, the Lokrians sent to Ilium periodically some of their maidens, to do menial service in the temple of Athênê (Plutarch. Ser. Numin. Vindict. p. 557, with the citation from Euphorion or Kallimachus, Düntzer, Epicc. Vet. p. 118).

[4] Leschês, Fr. 7, Düntz.; ap. Schol. Lycophr. 1263. Compare Schol. ad. 1232, for the respectful recollection of Andromachê, among the traditions of the Molossian kings, as their heroic mother, and Strabo, xiii. p. 594.

[5] Such is the story of the old epic (see Odyss. iv. 260, and the fourth book generally; Argument of Ilias Minor, p. 20. Düntz.). Polygnôtus, in the paintings above alluded to, followed the same tale (Pausan. x. 25, 3). The anger of the Greeks against Helen, and the statement that Menelaus after the capture of Troy approached her with revengeful purposes, but was so mollified by her surpassing beauty as to cast away his uplifted sword, belongs to the age of the tragedians (Æschyl. Agamem. 685–1455 : Eurip

in the Elysian fields. She was worshipped as a goddess with her brothers the Dioskuri and her husband, having her temple, statue and altar at Therapnæ and elsewhere, and various examples of her miraculous interventions were cited among the Greeks.[1] The lyric poet Stesichorus had ventured to denounce her, conjointly with her sister Klytæmnêstra, in a tone of rude and plain-spoken severity, resembling that of Euripidês and Lycophrôn afterwards, but strikingly opposite to the delicacy and respect with which she is always handled by Homer, who never admits reproaches against her except from her own lips.[2] He was smitten with blindness,

---

Androm. 600–629; Helen. 75–120; Troad. 890–1057; compare also the fine lines in the Æneid, ii. 567–588).

[1] See the description in Herodot. vi. 61, of the prayers offered to her, and of the miracle which she wrought, to remove the repulsive ugliness of a little Spartan girl of high family. Compare also Pindar, Olymp. iii. 2, and the Scholia at the beginning of the ode; Eurip. Helen. 1662, and Orest. 1652–1706; Isokrat. Encom. Helen. ii. p. 368, Auger; Dio Chrysost. Or. xi. p. 311. θεὸς ἐνομίσθη παρὰ τοῖς Ἕλλησι; Theodectês ap. Aristot. Pol. i. 2, 19. Θείων ἀπ' ἀμφοῖν ἔκγονον ῥιζωμάτων.

[2] Euripid. Troad. 982 seq.; Lycophrôn ap. Steph. Byz. v. Αἰγύς; Stesichorus ap. Schol. Eurip. Orest. 239; Fragm. 9 and 10 of the 'Ιλίου Πέρσις, Schneidewin: —

Οὔνεκα Τυνδάρεως ῥέζων ἅπασι θεοῖς μιᾶς λαθετ' ἠπιοδώρου
Κύπριδος· κείνα δὲ Τυνδάρεω κούραισι χολωσαμένα
Διγάμους τριγάμους τίθησι
Καὶ λιπεσάνορας..........
Further ....'Ελένη ἑκοῦσ' ἄπηρε, etc.

He had probably contrasted her with other females carried away by force.

Stesichorus also affirmed that Iphigeneia was the daughter of Helen, by Thêseus, born at Argos before her marriage with Menelaus and made over to Klytæmnêstra: this tale was perpetuated by the temple of Eileithyia at Argos, which the Argeians affirmed to have been erected by Helen (Pausan. ii. 22, 7). The ages ascribed by Hellanikus and other logographers (Hellan. Fr. 74) to Thêseus and Helen — he fifty years of age and she a child of seven — when he carried her off to Aphidnæ, can never have been the original form of any poetical legend: these ages were probably imagined in order to make the mythical chronology run smoothly; for Thêseus belongs to the generation before the Trojan war. But we ought always to recollect that Helen never grows old (τὴν γὰρ φάτις ἔμμεν' ἀγήρω — Quint. Smyrn. x. 312), and that her chronology consists only with an immortal being. Servius observes (ad Æneid. ii. 601) — "Helenam immortalem fuisse indicat tempus. Nam constat fratres ejus cum Argonautis fuisse. Argonautarum filii cum Thebanis (Thebano Eteoclis et Polynicis bello) dimicaverunt. Item illorum filii

and made sensible of his impiety; but having repented and composed a special poem formally retracting the calumny, was permitted to recover his sight. In his poem of recantation (the
famous palinode now unfortunately lost) he pointedly contradicted
the Homeric narrative, affirming that Helen had never been to
Troy at all, and that the Trojans had carried thither nothing but
her image or *eidôlon*.[1] It is, probably, to the excited religiou
feelings of Stesichorus that we owe the first idea of this glaring
deviation from the old legend, which could never have been
recommended by any considerations of poetical interest.

Other versions were afterwards started, forming a sort of compromise between Homer and Stesichorus, admitting that Helen
had never really been at Troy, without altogether denying her
elopement. Such is the story of her having been detained in
Egypt during the whole term of the siege. Paris, on his departure from Sparta, had been driven thither by storms, and the
Egyptian king Prôteus, hearing of the grievous wrong which he

contra Trojam bella gesserunt. Ergo, si immortalis Helena non fuisset, tot
sine dubio seculis durare non posset." So Xenophon, after enumerating
many heroes of different ages, all pupils of Cheirôn, says that the life of
Cheirôn suffices for all, he being brother of Zeus (De Venatione, c. 1).

The daughters of Tyndareus are Klytæmnêstra, Helen, and Timandra, all
open to the charge advanced by Stesichorus: see about Timandra, wife of
the Tegeate Echemus, the new fragment of the Hesiodic Catalogue, recently
restored by Geel (Göttling, Pref. Hesiod. p. lxi.).

It is curious to read, in Bayle's article *Hélène*, his critical discussion of the
adventures ascribed to her — as if they were genuine matter of history, more
or less correctly reported.

[1] Plato, Republic. ix. p. 587. c. 10. ὥσπερ τὸ τῆς 'Ελένης εἴδωλον Στη-
σίχορός φησι περιμάχητον γένεσθαι ἐν Τροίῃ, ἀγνοίᾳ τοῦ ἀληθοῦς.
Isokrat. Encom. Helen. t. ii. p. 370, Auger; Plato, Phædr. c. 44. p. 243-
244; Max. Tyr. Diss. xi. p. 320, Davis; Conôn, Narr. 18; Dio Chrysost.
Or. xi. p. 323. Τὸν μὲν Στησίχορον ἐν τῇ ὑστερον ᾠδῇ λέγειν, ὡς τὸ παράπαν οὐδὲ πλεύσειεν ἡ 'Ελένη οὐδάμοσε. Horace, Od. i. 17;
Epod. xvii. 42.—

"Infamis Helenæ Castor offensus vice,
Fraterque magni Castoris, victi prece,
Adempta vati reddidere lumina."

Pausan. iii. 19, 5. Virgil, surveying the war from the point of view of the
Trojans, had no motive to look upon Helen with particular tenderness:
Deiphobus imputes to her the basest treachery (Æneid, vi. 511. "*scelus
exitiale Lacœnæ;*" compare ii. 567).

had committed towards Menelaus, had sen; him away from the country with severe menaces, detaining Helen until her lawful husband should come to seek her. When the Greeks reclaimed Helen from Troy, the Trojans assured them solemnly, that she neither was, nor ever had been, in the town; but the Greeks, treating this allegation as fraudulent, prosecuted the siege until their ultimate success confirmed the correctness of the statement, nor did Menelaus recover Helen until, on his return from Troy, he visited Egypt.[1] Such was the story told by the Egyptian priests to Herodotus, and it appeared satisfactory to his historicizing mind. "For if Helen had really been at Troy (he argues) she would certainly have been given up, even had she been mistress of Priam himself instead of Paris: the Trojan king, with all his family and all his subjects, would never knowingly have incurred utter and irretrievable destruction for the purpose of retaining her: their misfortune was, that while they did not possess, and therefore could not restore her, they yet found it impossible to convince the Greeks that such was the fact." Assuming the historical character of the war of Troy, the remark of Herodotus admits of no reply; nor can we greatly wonder that he acquiesced in the tale of Helen's Egyptian detention, as a substitute for the "incredible insanity" which the

---

[1] Herodot. ii. 120. οὐ γὰρ δὴ οὕτω γε φρενοβλαβὴς ἦν ὁ Πρίαμος, οὐδ' οἱ ἄλλοι προσήκοντες αὐτῷ, etc. The passage is too long to cite, but is highly curious: not the least remarkable part is the religious coloring which he gives to the new version of the story which he is adopting, — "the Trojans, though they had not got Helen, yet could not persuade the Greeks that this was the fact; for it was the divine will that they should be destroyed root and branch, in order to make it plain to mankind that upon great crimes the gods inflict great punishments."

Dio Chrysostom (Or. xi. p. 333) reasons in the same way as Herodotus against the credibility of the received narrative. On the other hand, Isokratês, in extolling Helen, dwells on the calamities of the Trojan war as a test of the peerless value of the prize (Encom. Hel. p. 360, Aug.): in the view of Pindar (Olymp. xiii. 56), as well as in that of Hesiod (Opp. Di. 165), Helen is the one prize contended for.

Euripidês, in his tragedy of Helen, recognizes the detention of Helen in Egypt and the presence of her εἴδωλον at Troy, but he follows Stesichorus in denying her elopement altogether, — Hermês had carried her to Egypt in a cloud (Helen. 35–45, 706): compare Von Hoff, De Mytho Helenæ Euripideæ, cap. 2. p. 35 (Leyden, 1843).

genuine legend imputes to Priam and the Trojans. Pausanias, upon the same ground and by the same mode of reasoning, pronounces that the Trojan horse must have been in point of fact a battering-engine, because to admit the literal narrative would be to impute utter childishness to the defenders of the city. And Mr. Payne Knight rejects Helen altogether as the real cause of the Trojan war, though she may have been the pretext of it; for he thinks that neither the Greeks nor the Trojans could have been so mad and silly as to endure calamities of such magnitude " for one little woman."[1] Mr. Knight suggests various political causes as substitutes; these might deserve consideration, either if any evidence could be produced to countenance them, or if the subject on which they are brought to bear could be shown to belong to the domain of history.

The return of the Grecian chiefs from Troy furnished matter to the ancient epic hardly less copious than the siege itself, and the more susceptible of indefinite diversity, inasmuch as those who had before acted in concert were now dispersed and isolated. Moreover the stormy voyages and compulsory wanderings of the heroes exactly fell in with the common aspirations after an heroic founder, and enabled even the most remote Hellenic settlers to connect the origin of their town with this prominent event of their ante-historical and semi-divine world. And an absence of ten years afforded room for the supposition of many domestic changes in their native abode, and many family misfortunes and misdeeds during the interval. One of these heroic " Returns," that of Odysseus, has been immortalized by the verse of Homer. The hero, after a series of long-protracted suffering and expatriation, inflicted on him by the anger of Poseidôn, at last reaches his native island, but finds his wife beset, his youthful son insulted, and his substance plundered, by a troop of insolent suitors; he is forced to appear as a wretched beggar, and to endure in his own person their scornful treatment; but finally, by the interference of Athênê coming in aid of his own courage

---

[1] Pausan. i. 23, 8; Payne Knight, Prolegg. ad Homer. c. 53. Euphorion construed the wooden horse into a Grecian ship called Ἵππος, " The Horse (Euphorion, Fragm. 34. ap. Düntzer, Fragm. Epicc. Græc. p. 55). See Thucyd. i. 12; vi. 2.

and stratagem, he is enabled to overwhelm his enemies, to resume
his family position, and to recover his property. The return of
several other Grecian chiefs was the subject of an epic poem by
Hagias, which is now lost, but of which a brief abstract or argument still remains: there were in antiquity various other poems
of similar title and analogous matter.[1]

As usual with the ancient epic, the multiplied sufferings of this
back-voyage are traced to divine wrath, justly provoked by the
sins of the Greeks; who, in the fierce exultation of a victory purchased by so many hardships, had neither respected nor even[2]
spared the altars of the gods in Troy; and Athênê, who had been
their most zealous ally during the siege, was so incensed by their
final recklessness, more especially by the outrage of Ajax, son
of Oïleus, that she actively harassed and embittered their return,
in spite of every effort to appease her. The chiefs began to
quarrel among themselves; their formal assembly became a
scene of drunkenness; even Agamemnôn and Menelaus lost
their fraternal harmony, and each man acted on his own separate
resolution.[3]   Nevertheless, according to the Odyssey, Nestôr,
Diomêdês, Neoptolemus, Idomeneus and Philoktêtês reached
home speedily and safely: Agamemnôn also arrived in Peloponnêsus, to perish by the hand of a treacherous wife; but Menelaus was condemned to long wanderings and to the severest pri-
vations in Egypt, Cyprus and elsewhere, before he could set foot
in his native land.   The Lokrian Ajax perished on the Gyræan
rock.[4]   Though exposed to a terrible storm, he had already
reached this place of safety, when he indulged in the rash boast
of having escaped in defiance of the gods: no sooner did Poseidôn hear this language, than he struck with his trident the

---

[1] Suidas, v. Νόστος. Wüllner, De Cyclo Epico, p. 93. Also a poem
'Ατρειδῶν κάθοδος (Athenæ. vii. p. 281).

[2] Upon this the turn of fortune in Grecian affairs depends (Æschyl. Agamemn. 338; Odyss. iii. 130; Eurip. Troad. 69–95).

[3] Odyss. iii. 130–161; Æschyl. Agamemn. 650–662.

[4] Odyss. iii. 188–196; iv. 5–87. The Egyptian city of Kanopus, at the
mouth of the Nile, was believed to have taken its name from the pilot of
Menelaus, who had died and was buried there (Strabo, xvii. p. 801; Tacit.
Ann. ii. 60). Μενελάϊος νόμος, so called after Menelaus (Dio Chrysost. xi
p. 361).

rock which Ajax was grasping and precipitated both into the sea.[1] Kalchas the soothsayer, together with Leonteus and Polypœtes, proceeded by land from Troy to Kolophôn.[2]

In respect however to these and other Grecian heroes, tales were told different from those in the Odyssey, assigning to them a long expatriation and a distant home. Nestôr went to Italy, where he founded Metapontum, Pisa and Hêrakleia:[3] Philoktêtês[4] also went to Italy, founded Petilia and Krimisa, and sent settlers to Egesta in Sicily. Neoptolemus, under the advice of Thetis, marched by land across Thrace, met with Odysseus, who had come by sea, at Maroneia, and then pursued his journey to Epirus, where he became king of the Molossians.[5] Idomeneus came to Italy, and founded Uria in the Salentine peninsula. Diomêdês, after wandering far and wide, went along the Italian coast into the innermost Adriatic gulf, and finally settled in Daunia, founding the cities of Argyrippa, Beneventum, Atria and Diomêdeia: by the favor of Athênê he became immortal, and was worshipped as a god in many different places.[6] The Lo-

---

[1] Odyss. iv. 500. The epic Νόστοι of Hagias placed this adventure of Ajax on the rocks of Kaphareus, a southern promontory of Eubœa (Argum. Νόστοι, p. 23, Düntzer). Deceptive lights were kindled on the dangerous rocks by Nauplius, the father of Palamêdês, in revenge for the death of his son (Sophoklês, Ναύπλιος Πυρκαεύς, a lost tragedy; Hygin. f. 116; Senec. Agamemn. 567).

[2] Argument. Νόστοι, ut sup. There were monuments of Kalchas near Sipontum in Italy also (Strabo, vi. p. 284), as well as at Selgê in Pisidia (Strabo, xii. p. 570).

[3] Strabo, v. p. 222; vi. p. 264. Vellei. Paterc. i. 1; Servius ad Æn. x. 179. He had built a temple to Athênê in the island of Keôs (Strabo, x. p. 487).

[4] Strabo, vi. pp. 254, 272; Virgil, Æn. iii. 401, and Servius ad loc.; Lycophrôn, 912.

Both the tomb of Philoktêtês and the arrows of Hêraklês which he had used against Troy, were for a long time shown at Thurium (Justin, xx. 1).

[5] Argument. Νόστοι, p. 23, Düntz.; Pindar, Nem. iv. 51. According to Pindar, however, Neoptolemus comes from Troy by sea, misses the island of Skyrus, and sails round to the Epeirotic Ephyra (Nem. vii. 37).

[6] Pindar, Nem. x. 7, with the Scholia. Strabo, iii. p. 150; v. p. 214–215; vi, p. 284. Stephan. Byz. Ἀργύριππα, Διομηδεία. Aristotle recognizes him as buried in the Diomedean islands in the Adriatic (Anthol. Gr. Brunck. i. p. 178).

The identical tripod which had been gained by Diomêdês, as victor in

krian followers of Ajax founded the Epizephyrian Lokri on the
southernmost corner of Italy,[1] besides another settlement in Libya.
I have spoken in another place of the compulsory exile of Teukros, who, besides founding the city of Salamis in Cyprus, is said
to have established some settlements in the Iberian peninsula.[2]
Menestheus the Athenian did the like, and also founded both Elæa
in Mysia and Skylletium in Italy.[3]   The Arcadian chief Agapenôr founded Paphus in Cyprus.[4]   Epeius, of Panopeus in
Phôkis, the constructor of the Trojan horse with the aid of the
goddess Athênê, settled at Lagaria near Sybaris on the coast of
Italy; and the very tools which he had employed in that remarkable fabric were shown down to a late date in the temple of
Athênê at Metapontum.[5]   Temples, altars and towns were also
pointed out in Asia Minor, in Samos and in Krête, the foundation
of Agamemnôn or of his followers.[6]   The inhabitants of the Grecian town of Skionê, in the Thracian peninsula called Pallênê or
Pellênê, accounted themselves the offspring of the Pellênians
from Achæa in Peloponnêsus, who had served under Agamemnôn before Troy, and who on their return from the siege had
been driven on the spot by a storm and there settled.[7]   The
Pamphylians, on the southern coast of Asia Minor, deduced their

---

the chariot-race at the funeral games of Patroclus, was shown at Delphi in
the time of Phanias, attested by an inscription, as well as the dagger which
had been worn by Helikaôn, son of Antenôr (Athenæ. vi. p. 232).

[1] Virgil, Æneid, iii. 399.; xi. 265; and Servius, *ibid.*   Ajax, the son of
Oïleus, was worshipped there as a hero (Conôn, Narr. 18).

[2] Strabo, iii. p. 257; Isokratês, Evagor. Encom. p. 192; Justin, xliv. 3.
Ajax, the son of Teukros, established a temple of Zeus, and an hereditary
priesthood always held by his descendants (who mostly bore the name of
Ajax or Teukros), at Olbê in Kilikia (Strabo, xiv. p. 672).   Teukros carried
with him his Trojan captives to Cyprus (Athenæ. vi. p. 256).

[3] Strabo, iii. p. 140–150; vi. p. 261; xiii. p. 622.   See the epitaphs on
Teukros and Agapenôr by Aristotle (Antholog. Gr. ed. Brunck. i. p. 179–180).

[4] Strabo, xiv. p. 683; Pausan. viii. 5, 2.

[5] Strabo, vi. p. 263; Justin, xx. 2; Aristot. Mirab. Ausc. c. 108. Also the
epigram of the Rhodian Simmias called Πελεκύς (Antholog. Gr. Brunck. i.
p. 210).

[6] Vellei. Patercul. i. 1. Stephan. Byz. v. Λάμπη.   Strabo, xiii. p. 605; xiv
p. 639.   Theopompus (Fragm. 111, Didot) recounted that Agamemnôn and
nis followers had possessed themselves of the larger portion of Cyprus

[7] Thucydid. iv. 120.

origin from the wanderings of Amphilochus and Kalchas after the siege of Troy : the inhabitants of the Amphilochian Argos on the Gulf of Ambrakia revered the same Amphilochus as their founder.[1] The Orchomenians under Ialmenus, on quitting the conquered city, wandered or were driven to the eastern extremity of the Euxine Sea; and the barbarous Achæans under Mount Caucasus were supposed to have derived their first establishment from this source.[2] Merionês with his Krêtan followers settled at Engyion in Sicily, along with the preceding Krêtans who had remained there after the invasion of Minôs. The Elyminians in Sicily also were composed of Trojans and Greeks separately driven to the spot, who, forgetting their previous differences, united in the joint settlements of Eryx and Egesta.[3] We hear of Podaleirius both in Italy and on the coast of Karia ;[4] of Akamas, son of Thêseus, at Amphipolis in Thrace, at Soli in Cyprus, and at Synnada in Phrygia ;[5] of Guneus, Prothous and Eurypylus, in Krête as well as in Libya.[6] The obscure poem of Lycophrôn enumerates many of these dispersed and expatriated heroes, whose conquest of Troy was indeed a Kadmeian victory (according to the proverbial phrase of the Greeks), wherein the sufferings of the victor were little inferior to those of the vanquished.[7] It was particularly among the Italian Greeks, where they were worshipped with very special solemnity, that their presence as wanderers from Troy was reported and believed.[8]

---

[1] Herodot. vii. 91; Thucyd. ii. 68. According to the old elegiac poet Kallinos, Kalchas himself had died at Klarus near Kolophôn after his march from Troy, but Mopsus, his rival in the prophetic function, had conducted his followers into Pamphylia and Kilikia (Strabo, xii. p. 570; xiv. p. 668). The oracle of Amphilochus at Mallus in Kilikia bore the highest character for exactness and truth-telling in the time of Pausanias, μαντεῖον ἀψευδέστατον τῶν ἐπ' ἐμοῦ (Paus. i. 34, 2). Another story recognized Leonteus and Polypætês as the founders of Aspendus in Kilikia (Eustath. ad Iliad. ii. 138).

[2] Strabo, ix. p. 416.　　　　　[3] Diodôr. iv. 79; Thucyd. vi. 2.

[4] Stephan, Byz. v. Σύρνα; Lycophrôn, 1047.

[5] Æschines, De Falsâ Legat. c. 14; Strabo, xiv. p. 683; Stephan. Byz. v. Σύνναδα.

[6] Lycophrôn, 877–902, with Scholia; Apollodôr. Fragm. p. 386, Heyne. There is also a long enumeration of these returning wanderers and founders of new settlements in Solinus (Polyhist. c. 2).

[7] Strabo, iii. p. 150.

[8] Aristot. Mirabil. Auscult. 79, 106, 107, 109, 111.

I pass over the numerous other tales which circulated among
the ancients, illustrating the ubiquity of the Grecian and Trojan
heroes as well as that of the Argonauts, — one of the most striking features in the Hellenic legendary world.[1] Amongst them
all, the most interesting, individually, is Odysseus, whose romantic adventures in fabulous places and among fabulous persons
have been made familiarly known by Homer. The goddesses
Kalypso and Circê; the semi-divine mariners of Phæacia, whose
ships are endowed with consciousness and obey without a steersman; the one-eyed Cyclôpes, the gigantic Læstrygones, and the
wind-ruler Æolus; the Sirens who ensnare by their song, as the
Lotophagi fascinate by their food — all these pictures formed in-
tegral and interesting portions of the old epic. Homer leaves
Odysseus reëstablished in his house and family; but so marked
a personage could never be permitted to remain in the tameness
of domestic life: the epic poem called the Telegonia ascribed to
him a subsequent series of adventures. After the suitors had
been buried by their relatives, he offered sacrifice to the Nymphs,
and then went to Elis to inspect his herds of cattle there pastur-
ing: the Eleian Polyxenus welcomed him hospitably, and made
him a present of a bowl: Odysseus then returned to Ithaka, and
fulfilled the rites and sacrifices prescribed to him by Teiresias in
his visit to the under-world. This obligation discharged, he went
to the country of the Thesprotians, and there married the queen
Kallidikê: he headed the Thesprotians in a war against the
Brygians, the latter being conducted by Arês himself, who fierce-
ly assailed Odysseus; but the goddess Athênê stood by him, and
he was enabled to make head against Arês until Apollo came

---

[1] Strabo, i. p. 48. After dwelling emphatically on the long voyages of
Dionysus, Hêraklês, Jasôn, Odysseus, and Menelaus, he says, Aἰνείαν δὲ καὶ
᾿Αντήνορα καὶ ῾Ενετοὺς, καὶ ἁπλῶς τοὺς ἐκ τοῦ Τρωϊκοῦ πολέμου πλανηθέντας
εἰς πᾶσαν τὴν οἰκουμένην, ἄξιον μὴ τῶν παλαιῶν ἀνθρώπων νομίσαι;
Συνέβη γὰρ δὴ τοῖς τότε ῞Ελλησιν, ὁμοίως καὶ τοῖς βαβάροις, διὰ τὸν τῆς στρα-
τείας χρόνον, ἀποβαλεῖν τά τε ἐν οἴκῳ καὶ τῇ στρατείᾳ πορισθέντα· ὥστε μετὰ
τὴν τοῦ ᾿Ιλίου καταστροφὴν τούς τε νικήσαντας ἐπὶ λῄστειαν τραπέσθαι διὰ
τὰς ἀπορίας, καὶ πολλῷ μᾶλλον τοὺς.ἡττηθέντας καὶ περιγενομένους ἐκ τοῦ
πολέμου. Καὶ δὴ καὶ πόλεις ὑπὸ τούτων κτισθῆναι λέγονται κατὰ
πᾶσαν τὴν ἔξω τῆς ῾Ελλάδος παραλίαν, ἔστι δ' ὅπου καὶ τὴν μεσό-
γαιαν.

and parted them. Odysseus then returned to Ithaka, leaving the Thesprotian kingdom to Polypœtês, his son by Kallidikê. Telegonus, his son by Circê, coming to Ithaka in search of his father, ravaged the island and killed Odysseus without knowing who he was. Bitter repentance overtook the son for his undesigned parricide: at his prayer and by the intervention of his mother Circê, both Penelopê and Têlemachus were made immortal: Telegonus married Penelopê, and Têlemachus married Circê.[1]

We see by this poem that Odysseus was represented as the mythical ancestor of the Thesprotian kings, just as Neoptolemus was of the Molossian.

It has already been mentioned that Antenôr and Æneas stand distinguished from the other Trojans by a dissatisfaction with Priam and a sympathy with the Greeks, which is by Sophoklês and others construed as treacherous collusion,[2] — a suspicion indirectly glanced, though emphatically repelled, by the Æneas of Virgil.[3] In the old epic of Arktinus, next in age to the Iliad and Odyssey, Æneas abandons Troy and retires to Mount Ida, in terror at the miraculous death of Laocoôn, before the entry of the Greeks into the town and the last night-battle: yet Leschês, in another of the ancient epic poems, represented him as having been carried away captive by Neoptolemus.[4] In a remarkable

---

[1] The Telegonia, composed by Eugammôn of Kyrênê, is lost, but the Argument of it has been preserved by Proclus (p. 25, Düntzer; Dictys, vi. 15).

Pausanias quotes a statement from the poem called *Thesprôtis*, respecting a son of Odysseus and Penelopê, called Ptoliporthus, born after his return from Troy (viii. 12, 3). Nitzsch (Hist. Homer. p. 97) as well as Lobeck seem to imagine that this is the same poem as the Telegonia, under another title.

Aristotle notices an oracle of Odysseus among the Eurytanes, a branch of the Ætolian nation: there were also places in Epirus which boasted of Odysseus as their founder (Schol. ad Lycophrôn. 800; Stephan. Byz. v. Βούνειμα; Etymolog. Mag. Ἀρκείσιος; Plutarch, Quæst. Gr. c. 14).

[2] Dionys. Hal. i. 46–48; Sophokl. ap. Strab. xiii. p. 608; Livy, i. 1; Xenophon, Venat. i. 15.

[3] Æn. ii. 433.

[4] Argument of Ἰλίου Πέρσις; Fragm. 7. of Leschês, in Düntzer's Collection, p. 19–21.

Hellanikus seems to have adopted this retirement of Æneas to the strong

passage of the Iliad, Poseidôn describes the family of Priam as
having incurred the hatred of Zeus, and predicts that Æneas
and his descendants shall reign over the Trojans: the race of
Dardanus, beloved by Zeus more than all his other sons, would
thus be preserved, since Æneas belonged to it. Accordingly,
when Æneas is in imminent peril from the hands of Achilles,
Poseidôn specially interferes to rescue him, and even the implacable miso-Trojan goddess Hêrê assents to the proceeding.[1] These
passages have been construed by various able critics to refer to a
family of philo-Hellenic or semi-Hellenic Æneadæ, known even
in the time of the early singers of the Iliad as masters of some
territory in or near the Troad, and professing to be descended
from, as well as worshipping, Æneas. In the town of Skêpsis,
situated in the mountainous range of Ida, about thirty miles eastward of Ilium, there existed two noble and priestly families who
professed to be descended, the one from Hectôr, the other from
Æneas. The Skêpsian critic Dêmêtrius (in whose time both these
families were still to be found) informs us that Skamandrius son
of Hectôr, and Ascanius son of Æneas, were the archegets or
heroic founders of his native city, which had been originally
situated on one of the highest ranges of Ida, and was subse-

est parts of Mount Ida, but to have reconciled it with the stories of the
migration of Æneas, by saying that he only remained in Ida a little time,
and then quitted the country altogether by virtue of a convention concluded
with the Greeks (Dionys. Hal. i. 47–48). Among the infinite variety of
stories respecting this hero, one was, that after having effected his settlement in Italy, he had returned to Troy and resumed the sceptre, bequeath-
ing it at his death to Ascanius (Dionys. Hal. i. 53): this was a comprehensive scheme for apparently reconciling all the legends.

   [1] Iliad, xx. 300. Poseidôn speaks, respecting Æneas —

   'Αλλ' ἄγεθ', ἡμεῖς πέρ μιν ὑπ' ἐκ θανάτου ἀγάγωμεν,
   Μήπως καὶ Κρονίδης κεχολώσεται, αἴκεν 'Αχιλλεὺς
   Τόνδε κατακτείνῃ· μόριμον δέ οἱ ἔστ' ἀλέασθαι,
   'Οφρα μὴ ἄσπερμος γενεὴ καὶ ἄφαντος ὄληται
   Δαρδάνου, ὃν Κρονίδης περὶ πάντων φίλατο παίδων,
   Οἱ ἔθεν ἐξεγένοντο, γυναικῶν τε θνητάων.
   Ἤδη γὰρ Πριάμου γενεὴν ἤχθηρε Κρονίων·
   Νῦν δὲ δὴ Αἰνείαο βίη Τρώεσσιν ἀνάξει,
   Καὶ παίδων παῖδες, τοί κεν μετόπισθε γένωνται.

Again, v. 339, Poseidôn tells Æneas that he has nothing to dread from any
other Greek than Achilles.

quently transferred by them to the less lofty spot on which it stood in his time.[1] In Arisbê and Gentinus there seem to have been families professing the same descent, since the same archegets were acknowledged.[2] In Ophrynium, Hectôr had his consecrated edifice, and in Ilium both he and Æneas were worshipped as gods;[3] and it was the remarkable statement of the Lesbian Menekratês, that Æneas, " having been wronged by Paris and stripped of the sacred privileges which belonged to him, avenged himself by betraying the city, and then became one of the Greeks."[4]

One tale thus among many respecting Æneas, and that too the most ancient of all, preserved among the natives of the Troad, who worshipped him as their heroic ancestor, was, that after the capture of Troy he continued in the country as king of the remaining Trojans, on friendly terms with the Greeks. But there were other tales respecting him, alike numerous and irreconcil-

---

[1] See O. Müller, on the causes of the mythe of Æneas and his voyage to Italy, in Classical Journal, vol. xxvi. p. 308; Klausen, Æneas und die Penteu, vol. i. p. 43–52.

Dêmêtrius Skêps. ab. Strab. xiii. p. 607; Nicolaus ap. Steph. Byz. v. Ἀσκανία. Dêmêtrius conjectured that Skêpsis had been the regal seat of Æneas : there was a village called Æneia near to it (Strabo, xiii. p. 603).

[2] Steph. Byz. v. Ἀρίσβη, Γεντῖνος. Ascanius is king of Ida after the departure of the Greeks (Conôn, Narr. 41; Mela, i. 18). Ascanius portus between Phokæ and Kymê.

[3] Strabo, xiii. p. 595; Lycophrôn, 1208, and Sch.; Athenagoras, Legat. 1. Inscription in Clarke's Travels, vol. ii. p. 86, Οἱ Ἰλιεῖς τὸν πάτριον θεὸν Αἰνείαν. Lucian, Deor. Concil. c. 12. i. 111. p. 534, Hemst.

[4] Menekrat. ap. Dionys. Hal. i. 48. Ἀχαιοὺς δὲ ἀνίη εἶχε (after the burial) καὶ ἐδόκεον τῆς στρατιῆς τὴν κεφαλὴν ὑπηράχθαι. Ὅμως δὲ τάφον αὐτῷ δαίσαντες, ἐπολέμεον γῇ πάσῃ, ἄχρις Ἴλιος ἑάλω, Αἰνείεω ἐνδόντος. Αἰνείης γὰρ ἄτιτος ἐὼν ὑπὸ Ἀλεξάνδρου, καὶ ἀπὸ γερέων ἱερῶν ἐξειργόμενος, ἀνέτρεψε Πρίαμον, ἐργασάμενος δὲ ταῦτα, εἰς Ἀχαιῶν ἐγεγόνει.

Abas, in his Troica, gave a narrative different from any other preserved : " Quidam ab Abante, qui Troica scripsit, relatum ferunt, post discessum a Trojà Græcorum Astyanacti ibi datum regnum, hunc ab Antenore expulsum sociatis sibi finitimis civitatibus, inter quas et Arisba fuit: Ænean hoc ægre tulisse, et pro Astyanacte arma cepisse ac prospere gestâ re Astyanact. restituisse regnum" (Servius ad Virg. Æneid. ix. 264). According to Diktys, Antenôr remains king and Æneas goes away (Dikt. v. 17): Antenôr brings the Palladium to the Greeks (Dikt. v. 8). Syncellus, on the contrary, tells us that the sons of Hectôr recovered Ilium by the suggestions of Helenus, expelling the Atenorids (Syncell. p. 322, ed. Bonn).

able: the hand of destiny marked him as a wanderer (*fato pro-fugus*), and his ubiquity is not exceeded even by that of Odysseus. We hear of him at Ænus in Thrace, in Pallênê, at Æneia in the Thermaic Gulf, in Delus, at Orchomenus and Mantineia in Arcadia, in the islands of Kythêra and Zakynthus, in Leukas and Ambrakia, at Buthrotum in Epirus, on the Salentine peninsula and various other places in the southern region of Italy; at Drepana and Segesta in Sicily, at Carthage, at Cape Palinurus, Cumæ, Misenum, Caieta, and finally in Latium, where he lays the first humble foundation of the mighty Rome and her empire.[1] And the reason why his wanderings were not continued still further was, that the oracles and the pronounced will of the gods directed him to settle in Latium.[2] In each of these numerous places his visit was commemorated and certified by local monuments or special legends, particularly by temples and permanent ceremonies in* honor of his mother Aphroditê, whose worship accompanied him everywhere: there were also many temples and many different tombs of Æneas himself.[3] The vast ascendency acquired by Rome, the ardor with which all the literary Romans espoused the idea of a Trojan origin, and the fact that the Julian family recognized Æneas as their gentile primary ancestor, — all contributed to give to the Roman version of his legend the preponderance over every other. The various other places in which monuments of Æneas were found came thus to be represented as places where he had halted for a time

---

[1] Dionys. Halic. A. R. i. 48–54; Heyne, Excurs. 1 ad Æncid. iii.; De Æneæ Erroribus, and Excurs. 1 ad Æn. v.; Conôn. Narr. 46; Livy, xl. 4; Stephan. Byz. Αἴνεια. The inhabitants of Æneia in the Thermaic Gulf worshipped him with great solemnity as their heroic founder (Pausan. iii. 22, 4; viii. 12, 4). The tomb of Anchisês was shown on the confines of the Arcadian Orchomenus and Mantincia (compare Steph. Byz. v. Κάφυαι), under the mountain called Anchisia, near a temple of Aphroditê: on the discrepancies respecting the death of Anchisês (Heyne. Excurs. 17 ad Æn. iii.): Segesta in Sicily founded by Æneas (Cicero, Verr. iv. 33).

[2] Τοῦ δὲ μηκέτι προσωτέρω τῆς Εὐρώπης πλεῦσαι τὸν Τρωϊκὸν στόλον, οἵ τε χρησμοὶ ἐγένοντο αἴτιοι, etc. (Dionys. Hal. i. 55).

[3] Dionys. Hal. i. 54. Among other places, his tomb was shown at Bere-cynthia, in Phrygia (Festus, v. *Romam*, p. 224, ed. Müller): a curious article, which contains an assemblage of the most contradictory statements respecting both Æneas and Latinus.

on his way from Troy to Latium. But though the legendary pretensions of these places were thus eclipsed in the eyes of those who constituted the literary public, the local belief was not extinguished : they claimed the hero as their permanent property, and his tomb was to them a proof that he had lived and died among them.

Antenôr, who shares with Æneas the favorable sympathy of the Greeks, is said by Pindar to have gone from Troy along with Menelaus and Helen into the region of Kyrênê in Libya.[1] But according to the more current narrative, he placed himself at the head of a body of Eneti or Veneti from Paphlagonia, who had come as allies of Troy, and went by sea into the inner part of the Adriatic Gulf, where he conquered the neighboring barbarians and founded the town of Patavium (the modern Padua); the Veneti in this region were said to owe their origin to his immigration.[2] We learn further from Strabo, that Opsikellas, one of the companions of Antenôr, had continued his wanderings even into Ibêria, and that he had there established a settlement bearing his name.[3]

Thus endeth the Trojan war; together with its sequel, the dispersion of the heroes, victors as well as vanquished. The account here given of it has been unavoidably brief and imperfect; for in a work intended to follow consecutively the real history of the Greeks, no greater space can be allotted even to the most splendid gem of their legendary period. Indeed, although it would be easy to fill a large volume with the separate incidents which have been introduced into the "Trojan cycle," the misfortune is that they are for the most part so contradictory as to exclude all possibility of weaving them into one connected narrative. We are compelled to select one out of the number, generally without any solid ground of preference, and then to note the variations of the rest. No one who has not studied the original documents

---

[1] Pindar, Pyth. v., and the citation from the Νόστοι of Lysimachus in the Scholia; given still more fully in the Scholia ad Lycophrôn. 875. There was a λόφος 'Αντηνοριδῶν at Kyrênê.

[2] Livy, i. 1. Servius ad Æneid. i. 242. Strabo, i. 48; v. 212. Ovid, Fasti, iv. 75.

[3] Strabo, iii. p. 157.

can imagine the extent to which this discrepancy proceeds; it covers almost every portion and fragment of the tale.[1]

But though much may have been thus omitted of what the reader might expect to find in an account of the Trojan war, its genuine character has been studiously preserved, without either exaggeration or abatement. The real Trojan war is that which was recounted by Homer and the old epic poets, and continued by all the lyric and tragic composers. For the latter, though they took great liberties with the particular incidents, and introduced to some extent a new moral tone, yet worked more or less faithfully on the Homeric scale: and even Euripides, who departed the most widely from the feeling of the old legend, never lowered down his matter to the analogy of contemporary life. They preserved its well-defined object, at once righteous and romantic, the recovery of the daughter of Zeus and sister of the Dioskuri — its mixed agencies, divine, heroic and human — the colossal force and deeds of its chief actors — its vast magnitude and long duration, as well as the toils which the conquerors underwent, and the Nemesis which followed upon their success. And these were the circumstances which, set forth in the full blaze of epic and tragic poetry, bestowed upon the legend its powerful and imperishable influence over the Hellenic mind. The enterprise was one comprehending all the members of the Hellenic body, of which each individually might be proud, and in which, nevertheless, those feelings of jealous and narrow patriotism, so lamentably prevalent in many of the towns, were as much as possible excluded. It supplied them with a grand and inexhaustible object of common sympathy, common faith, and common admiration; and when occasions arose for bringing together a Pan-Hellenic force against the barbarians, the precedent of the Homeric expedition was one upon which the elevated minds of Greece could dwell with the certainty of rousing an unanimous impulse, if not always of counterworking sinister by-

---

[1] These diversities are well set forth in the useful Dissertation of Fuchs De Varietate Fabularum Troicarum (Cologne, 1830).

Of the number of romantic statements put forth respecting Helen and Achilles especially, some idea may be formed from the fourth, fifth and sixth chapters of Ptolemy Hêphæstion (apud Westermann. Scriptt. Mythograph. p. 188, etc.).

motives, among their audience. And the incidents comprised in the Trojan cycle were familiarized, not only to the public mind but also to the public eye, by innumerable representations both of the sculptor and the painter, — those which were romantic and chivalrous being better adapted for this purpose, and therefore more constantly employed, than any other.

Of such events the genuine Trojan war of the old epic was for the most part composed. Though literally believed, reverentially cherished, and numbered among the gigantic phænomena of the past, by the Grecian public, it is in the eyes of modern inquiry essentially a legend and nothing more. If we are asked whether it be not a legend embodying portions of historical matter, and raised upon a basis of truth, — whether there may not really have occurred at the foot of the hill of Ilium a war purely human and political, without gods, without heroes, without Helen, without Amazons, without Ethiopians under the beautiful son of Eôs, without the wooden horse, without the characteristic and expressive features of the old epical war, — like the mutilated trunk of Deïphobus in the under-world; if we are asked whether there was not really some such historical Trojan war as this, our answer must be, that as the possibility of it cannot be denied, so neither can the reality of it be affirmed. We possess nothing but the ancient epic itself without any independent evidence: had it been an age of records indeed, the Homeric epic in its exquisite and unsuspecting simplicity would probably never have come into existence. Whoever therefore ventures to dissect Homer, Arktinus and Leschês, and to pick out certain portions as matters of fact, while he sets aside the rest as fiction, must do so in full reliance on his own powers of historical divination, without any means either of proving or verifying his conclusions. Among many attempts, ancient as well as modern, to identify real objects in this historical darkness, that of Dio Chrysostom deserves attention for its extraordinary boldness. In his oration addressed to the inhabitants of Ilium, and intended to demonstrate that the Trojans were not only blameless as to the origin of the war, but victorious in its issue — he overthrows all the leading points of the Homeric narrative, and re-writes nearly the whole from beginning to end: Paris is the lawful husband of Helen, Achilles is slain by Hectôr, and the Greeks retire without taking Troy, dis-

graced as well as baffled. Having shown without difficulty that
the Iliad, if it be looked at as a history, is full of gaps, incongrui-
ties and absurdities, he proceeds to compose a more plausible narrative of his own, which he tenders as so much authentic matter
of fact. The most important point, however, which his Oration
brings to view is, the literal and confiding belief with which the
Homeric narrative was regarded, as if it were actual history, not
only by the inhabitants of Ilium, but also by the general Grecian
public.[1]

The small town of Ilium, inhabited by Æolic Greeks,[2] and
raised into importance only by the legendary reverence attached
to it, stood upon an elevated ridge forming a spur from Mount
Ida, rather more than three miles from the town and promontory
of Sigeium, and about twelve stadia, or less than two miles, fron
the sea at its nearest point. From Sigeium and the neighboring
town of Achilleium (with its monument and temple of Achilles),
to the town of Rhœteium on a hill higher up the Hellespont
(with its monument and chapel of Ajax called the Aianteium[3]),
was a distance of sixty stadia, or seven miles and a half in the
straight course by sea: in the intermediate space was a bay and
an adjoining plain, comprehending the embouchure of the Sca-
mander, and extending to the base of the ridge on which Ilium
stood. This plain was the celebrated plain of Troy, in which
the great Homeric battles were believed to have taken place: the
portion of the bay near to Sigeium went by the name of the
Naustathmon of the Achæans (i. e. the spot where they dragged
their ships ashore), and was accounted to have been the camp of
Agamemnôn and his vast army.[4]

---

[1] Dio Chrysost. Or. xi. p. 310–322.

[2] Herodot. v. 122. Pausan. v. 8, 3: viii. 12, 4. Αἰολεὺς ἐκ πόλεως Τρῴα
δος, the title proclaimed at the Olympic games; like Αἰολεὺς ἀπὸ Μουρίνας,
from Myrina in the more southerly region of Æolis, as we find in the list
of visitors at the Charitêsia, at Orchomenos in Bœôtia (Corp. Inscrip.
Boeckh. No. 1583).

[3] See Pausanias, i. 35, 3, for the legends current at Ilium respecting the
vast size of the bones of Ajax in his tomb. The inhabitants affirmed that
after the shipwreck of Odysseus, the arms of Achilles, which he was carrying away with him, were washed up by the sea against the tomb of Ajax
Pliny gives the distance at thirty stadia: modern travellers make it some
thing more than Pliny, but considerably less than Strabo.

[4] Strabo, xiii. p. 596–598 Strabo distinguishes the 'Αχαιῶν Ναύσταϑμον,

Historical Ilium was founded, according to the questionable statement of Strabo, during the last dynasty of the Lydian kings,[1] that is, at some period later than 720 B. C. Until after the days of Alexander the Great — indeed until the period of Roman preponderance — it always remained a place of inconsiderable power and importance, as we learn not only from the assertion of the geographer, but also from the fact that Achilleium, Sigeium and Rhœteium were all independent of it.[2] But inconsiderable as it might be, it was the only place which ever bore the venerable name immortalized by Homer. Like the Homeric Ilium, it had its temple of Athênê,[3] wherein she was worshipped as the presiding goddess of the town : the inhabitants affirmed that Agamemnôn had not altogether destroyed the town, but that it had been reoccupied after his departure, and had never ceased to exist.[4] Their acropolis was called Pergamum, and in it was shown the house of Priam and the altar of Zeus Herkeius where that unhappy old man had been slain : moreover there were exhibited, in the temples, panoplies which had been worn by the Homeric heroes,[5] and doubtless many other relics appreciated by admirers of the Iliad.

which was near to Sigeium, from the Ἀχαιῶν λιμήν, which was more towards the middle of the bay between Sigeium and Rhœteium ; but we gather from his language that this distinction was not universally recognized. Alexander landed at the Ἀχαιῶν λιμήν (Arrian, i. 11).

[1] Strabo, xiii. p. 593.

[2] Herodot. v. 95 (his account of the war between the Athenians and Mitylenæans about Sigeium and Achilleium) ; Strabo, xiii. p. 593. Τὴν δὲ τῶν Ἰλιέων πόλιν τὴν νῦν τέως μὲν κωμόπολιν εἶναί φασι, τὸ ἱερὸν ἔχουσαν τῆς Ἀθηνᾶς μικρὸν καὶ εὐτελές. Ἀλεξάνδρου δὲ ἀναβάντα μετὰ τὴν ἐπὶ Γρανίκῳ νίκην, ἀναθήμασι τε κοσμῆσαι τὸ ἱερὸν καὶ προσαγορεῦσαι πόλιν, etc.

Again, Καὶ τὸ Ἴλιον, ὃ νῦν ἐστι, κωμόπολίς τις ἦν ὅτε πρῶτον Ῥωμαῖοι τῆς Ἀσίας ἐπέβησαν.

[3] Besides Athênê, the Inscriptions authenticate Ζεὺς Πολιεὺς at Ilium (Corp. Inscrip. Bœckh. No. 3599).

[4] Strabo, xiii. p. 600. Λέγουσι δ᾽ οἱ νῦν Ἰλιεῖς καὶ τοῦτο, ὡς οὐδὲ τέλεως συνέβαινεν ἠφανίσθαι τὴν πόλιν κατὰ τὴν ἅλωσιν ὑπὸ τῶν Ἀχαιῶν, οὐδ᾽ ἐξηλείφθη οὐδέποτε.

The situation of Ilium (or as it is commonly, but erroneously, termed, New Ilium) appears to be pretty well ascertained, about two miles from the sea (Rennell, On the Topography of Troy, p. 41-71; Dr. Clarke's Travels, vol. ii. p 102).

[5] Xerxês passing by Adramyttium, and leaving the range of Mount Ida on

These were testimonies which few persons in those ages were inclined to question, when combined with the identity of name and general locality; nor does it seem that any one did question them until the time of Dêmêtrius of Skêpsis. Hellanikus expressly described this Ilium as being the Ilium of Homer, for which assertion Strabo (or probably Dêmêtrius, from whom the narrative seems to be copied) imputes to him very gratuitously an undue partiality towards the inhabitants of the town.[1] Herodotus relates, that Xerxês in his march into Greece visited the place, went up to the Pergamum of Priam, inquired with much interest into the details of the Homeric siege, made libations to the fallen heroes, and offered to the Athênê of Ilium his magnificent sacrifice of a thousand oxen: he probably represented and believed himself to be attacking Greece as the avenger of the Priamid family. The Lacedæmonian admiral Mindarus, while his fleet lay at Abydus, went personally to Ilium to offer sacrifice to Athênê, and saw from that elevated spot the battle fought between the squadron of Dorieus and the Athenians, on the shore near Rhœteium.[2] During the interval between the

---

his left hand, *ἤïε ἐς τὴν Ἰλιάδα γῆν .... Ἀπικομένου δὲ τοῦ στρατοῦ ἐπὶ τὸν Σκάμανδρον .... ἐς τὸ Πριάμου Πέργαμον ἀνέβη, ἵμερον ἔχων θεήσασθαι. Θεησάμενος δὲ, καὶ π υ θ ό μ ε ν ο ς κ ε ί ν ω ν ἔ κ α σ τ α, τ ῇ Ἀθηναίῃ τῇ Ἰλιάδι ἔθυσε βοῦς χιλίας· χοὰς δὲ οἱ μάγοι τοῖσιν ἥρωσιν ἐχέαντο .... Ἅμα ἡμέρῃ δὲ ἐπορεύετο, ἐν ἀριστέρῃ μὲν ἀπέργων Ῥοιτεῖον πόλιν καὶ Ὀφρυνεῖον καὶ Δάρδανον, ἥπερ δὴ Ἀβύδῳ ὅμουρός ἐστιν· ἐν δεξίῃ δὲ, Γέργιθας Τευκρούς* (Herod. vii. 43).

Respecting Alexander (Arrian, i. 11), *Ἀνελθόντα δὲ ἐς Ἴλιον, τῇ Ἀθηνᾷ θῦσαι τῇ Ἰλιάδι, καὶ τὴν πανοπλίαν τὴν αὐτοῦ ἀναθεῖναι εἰς τὸν ναὸν, καὶ καθελεῖν ἀντὶ ταύτης τῶν ἱερῶν τινα ὅπλων ἔτι ἐκ τοῦ Τρωϊκοῦ ἔργου σωζόμενα· καὶ ταῦτα λέγουσιν ὅτι οἱ ὑπασπισταὶ ἔφερον πρὸ αὐτοῦ ἐς τὰς μάχας. Θῦσαι δὲ αὐτὸν ἐπὶ τοῦ βωμοῦ τοῦ Διὸς τοῦ Ἑρκείου λόγος κατέχει, μῆνιν Πριάμου παραιτούμενον τῷ Νεοπτολέμου γένει, ὃ δὴ ἐς αὐτὸν καθῆκε.*

The inhabitants of Ilium also showed the lyre which had belonged to Paris (Plutarch, Alexand. c. 15).

Chandler, in his History of Ilium, chap. xxii. p. 89, seems to think that the place called by Herodotus the Pergamum of Priam is different from the historical Ilium. But the mention of the Iliean Athênê identifies them as the same.

[1] Strabo, xiii. p. 602. *Ἑλλάνικος δὲ χαριζόμενος τοῖς Ἰλιεῦσιν, οἷος ὁ ἐκείνου μῦθος, συνηγορεῖ τῷ τὴν αὐτὴν εἶναι πόλιν τὴν νῦν τῇ τότε.* Hellanikus had written a work called Τρωϊκά.

[2] Xenoph. Hellen. i. 1, 10. Skylax places Ilium twenty-five stadia, or

Peloponnesian war and the Macedonian invasion of Persia, Ilium was always garrisoned as a strong position; but its domain was still narrow, and did not extend even to the sea which was so near to it.[1] Alexander, on crossing the Hellespont, sent his army from Sestus to Abydus, under Parmenio, and sailed personally from Elæeus in the Chersonese, after having solemnly sacrificed at the Elæuntian shrine of Prôtesilaus, to the harbor of the Achæans between Sigeium and Rhœteium. He then ascended to Ilium, sacrificed to the Iliean Athênê, and consecrated in her temple his own panoply, in exchange for which he took some of the sacred arms there suspended, which were said to have been preserved from the time of the Trojan war. These arms were carried before him when he went to battle by his armor-bearers. It is a fact still more curious, and illustrative of the strong working of the old legend on an impressible and eminently religious mind, that he also sacrificed to Priam himself, on the very altar of Zeus Herkeius from which the old king was believed to have been torn by Neoptolemus. As that fierce warrior was his heroic ancestor by the maternal side, he desired to avert from himself the anger of Priam against the Achilleid race.[2]

about three miles, from the sea (c. 94). But I do not understand how he can call Skêpsis and Kebrên πόλεις ἐπὶ θαλάσσῃ.

[1] See Xenoph. Hellen. iii. i. 16; and the description of the seizure of Ilium, along with Skêpsis and Kebrên, by the chief of mercenaries, Charidêmus, in Demosthen. cont. Aristocrat. c. 38. p. 671: compare Æneas Poliorcetic. c. 24, and Polyæn. iii. 14.

[2] Arrian, 1. c. Dikæarchus composed a separate work respecting this sacrifice of Alexander, περὶ τῆς ἐν Ἰλίῳ θυσίας (Athenæ. xiii. p. 603; Dikæarch. Fragm. p. 114, ed. Fuhr).

Theophrastus, in noticing old and venerable trees, mentions the φηγοὶ (Quercus æsculus) on the tomb of Ilus at Ilium, without any doubt of the authenticity of the place (De Plant. iv. 14); and his contemporary, the harper Stratonikos, intimates the same feeling, in his jest on the visit of a bad sophist to Ilium during the festival of the Ilieia (Athenæ. viii. p. 351). The same may be said respecting the author of the tenth epistle ascribed to the orator Æschinês (p. 737), in which his visit of curiosity to Ilium is described — as well as about Apollônius of Tyana, or the writer who describes his life and his visit to the Trôad; it is evident that he did not distrust the ἀρχαιολογία of the Ilieans, who affirmed their town to be the real Troy (Philostrat. Vit. Apollôn. Tyan. iv. 11).

The godless Athênê of Ilium was reported to have rendered valuable

Alexander made to the inhabitants of Ilium many munificent
promises, which he probably would have executed, had he not
been prevented by untimely death: for the Trojan war was
amongst all the Grecian legends the most thoroughly Pan-Hellenic, and the young king of Macedôn, besides his own sincere
legendary faith, was anxious to merge the local patriotism of the
separate Greek towns in one general Hellenic sentiment under
himself as chief. One of his successors, Antigonus,[1] founded the
city of Alexandreia in the Trôad, between Sigeium and the more
southerly promontory of Lektum; compressing into it the inhabitants of many of the neighboring Æolic towns in the region
of Ida, — Skêpsis, Kebrên, Hamaxitus, Kolônæ, and Neandria,
though the inhabitants of Skêpsis were subsequently permitted
by Lysimachus to resume their own city and autonomous government. Ilium however remained without any special mark of
favor until the arrival of the Romans in Asia and their triumph
over Antiochus (about 190 B. C.). Though it retained its walls
and its defensible position, Dêmêtrius of Skêpsis, who visited it
shortly before that event, described it as being then in a state of
neglect and poverty, many of the houses not even having tiled
roofs.[2] In this dilapidated condition, however, it was still mythi-

---

assistance to the inhabitants of Kyzikus, when they were besieged by
Mithridatês, commemorated by inscriptions set up in Ilium (Plutarch,
Lucull. 10).

[1] Strabo, xiii. p. 603-607.

[2] Livy, xxxv. 43; xxxvii. 9. Polyb. v. 78-111 (passages which prove that
Ilium was fortified and defensible about B. C. 218). Strabo, xiii. p. 594. Καὶ
τὸ Ἴλιον δ᾽, ὃ νῦν ἐστι, κωμόπολίς τις ἦν, ὅτε πρῶτον Ῥωμαῖοι τῆς Ἀσίας ἐπέβησαν καὶ ἐξέβαλον Ἀντίοχον τὸν μέγαν ἐκ τῆς ἐντὸς τοῦ Ταύρου. Φησὶ γοῦν
Δημήτριος ὁ Σκήψιος, μειράκιον ἐπιδήμησαν εἰς τὴν πόλιν κατ᾽ ἐκείνους τοὺς
καιρούς, οὕτως ὠλιγωρημένην ἰδεῖν τὴν κατοικίαν, ὥστε μηδὲ κεραμωτὰς ἔχειν
τὰς στέγας. Ἡγησιάναξ δὲ, τοὺς Γαλάτας περαιωθέντας ἐκ τῆς Εὐρώπης, ἀνα-
βῆναι μὲν εἰς τὴν πόλιν δεομένους ἐρύματος, παραχρῆμα δ᾽ ἐκλιπεῖν διὰ τὸ
ἀτείχιστον· ὕστερον δ᾽ ἐπανόρθωσιν ἔσχε πολλήν. Εἶτ᾽ ἐκάκωσαν αὐτὴν πάλιν οἱ μετὰ Φιμβρίου, etc.

This is a very clear and precise statement, attested by an eye-witness.
But it is thoroughly inconsistent with the statement made by Strabo in the
previous chapter, a dozen lines before, as the text now stands; for he there
informs us that Lysimachus, after the death of Alexander, paid great attention to Ilium, surrounded it with a wall of forty stadia in circumference,
erected a temple, and aggregated to Ilium the ancient cities around, which

cally recognized both by Antiochus and by the Roman consul Livius, who went up thither to sacrifice to the Iliean Athênê. The Romans, proud of their origin from Troy and Æneas, treated Ilium with signal munificence; not only granting to it immunity from tribute, but also adding to its domain the neighboring territories of Gergis, Rhœteium and Sigeium — and making the Ilieans masters of the whole coast[1] from the Perœa (or conti-

---

were in a state of decay. We know from Livy that the aggregation of Gergis and Rhœteium to Ilium was effected, not by Lysimachus, but by the Romans (Livy, xxxviii. 37); so that the *first* statement of Strabo is not only inconsistent with his second, but is contradicted by an independent authority.

I cannot but think that this contradiction arises from a confusion of the text in Strabo's *first* passage, and that in that passage Strabo really meant to speak only of the improvements brought about by Lysimachus in *Alexandreia Trôas;* that he never meant to ascribe to Lysimachus any improvements in *Ilium,* but, on the contrary, to assign the remarkable attention paid by Lysimachus to *Alexandreia Trôas,* as the reason why he had neglected to fulfil the promises held out by Alexander to *Ilium.* The series of facts runs thus: — 1. Ilium is nothing better than a κώμη at the landing of Alexander; 2. Alexander promises great additions, but never returns from Persia to accomplish them; 3. Lysimachus is absorbed in Alexandreia Trôas, into which he aggregates several of the adjoining old towns, and which flourishes under his hands; 4. Hence Ilium remained a κώμη when the Romans entered Asia, as it had been when Alexander entered.

This alteration in the text of Strabo might be effected by the simple transposition of the words as they now stand, and by omitting ὅτε καὶ, ἤδη ἐπεμελήθη, without introducing a single new or conjectural word, so that the passage would read thus: Μετὰ δὲ τὴν ἐκείνου (Alexander's) τελευτὴν Λυσίμαχος μάλιστα τῆς Ἀλεξανδρείας ἐπεμελήθη, συνῳκισμένης μὲν ἤδη ὑπ᾿ Ἀντιγόνου,καὶ προσηγορευομένης Ἀντιγόνιας, μεταβαλούσης δὲ τοὔνομα · (ἔδοξε γὰρ εὐσεβὲς εἶναι τοὺς Ἀλεξάνδρου διαδεξαμένους ἐκείνου πρότερον κτίζειν ἐπωνύμους πόλεις, εἶθ᾿ ἑαυτῶν) καὶ νέων κατεσκεύασε καὶ τεῖχος περιεβάλετο ὅσον 40 σταδίων · συνῴκισε δὲ εἰς αὐτὴν τὰς κύκλῳ πόλεις ἀρχαίας, ἤδη κεκακωμένας. Καὶ δὴ καὶ συνέμεινε . . . . . πόλεων. If this reading be adopted, the words beginning that which stands in Tzschucke's edition as sect. 27, and which immediately follow the last word πόλεων, will read quite suitably and coherently,— Καὶ τὸ Ἴλιον δ᾿, ὃ νῦν ἐστὶ, κωμόπολίς τις ἦν, ὅτε πρῶτον Ῥωμαῖοι τῆς Ἀσίας ἐπέβησαν, etc., whereas with the present reading of the passage they show a contradiction, and the whole passage is entirely confused.

[1] Livy, xxxviii. 39; Strabo, xiii. p. 600. Κατέσκαπται δὲ καὶ τὸ Σίγειον ὑπὸ τῶν Ἰλιέων διά τὴν ἀπείθειαν · ὑπ᾿ ἐκείνοις γὰρ ἦν ὕστερον ἡ παραλία πᾶσα ἡ μέχρι Δαρδάνου, καὶ νῦν ὑπ᾿ ἐκείνοις ἐστι.

nental possessions) of Tenedos (southward of Sigeium) to the
boundaries of Dardanus, which had its own title to legendary
reverence as the special sovereignty of Æneas. The inhabitants
of Sigeium could not peaceably acquiesce in this loss of their
autonomy, and their city was destroyed by the Ilieans.

The dignity and power of Ilium being thus prodigiously enhanced, we cannot doubt that the inhabitants assumed to themselves exaggerated importance as the recognized parents of all-
conquering Rome. Partly, we may naturally suppose, from the
jealousies thus aroused on the part of their neighbors at Skêpsis
and Alexandreia Trôas — partly from the pronounced tendency
of the age (in which Kratês at Pergamus and Aristarchus at
Alexandria divided between them the palm of literary celebrity)
towards criticism and illustration of the old poets — a blow was
now aimed at the mythical legitimacy of Ilium. Dêmêtrius of
Skêpsis, one of the most laborious of the Homeric critics, had
composed thirty books of comment upon the Catalogue in the
Iliad: Hestiæa, an authoress of Alexandreia Trôas, had written
on the same subject: both of them, well-acquainted with the
locality, remarked that the vast battles described in the Iliad
could not be packed into the narrow space between Ilium and
the Naustathmon of the Greeks; the more so, as that space, too
small even as it then stood, had been considerably enlarged since
the date of the Iliad by deposits at the mouth of the Skamander.[1] They found no difficulty in pointing out topographical in-
congruities and impossibilities as to the incidents in the Iliad,
which they professed to remove by the startling theory that the
Homeric Ilium had not occupied the site of the city so called.
There was a village, called the village of the Ilieans, situated

---

[1] Strabo, xiii. 599. Παρατίθησι δὲ ὁ Δημήτριος καὶ τὴν ᾿Αλεξανδρίνην ῾Εστί-
αιαν μάρτυρα, τὴν συγγράψασαν περὶ τῆς ῾Ομήρου ᾿Ιλιάδος, πυνθανομένην, εἰ
περὶ τὴν νῦν πόλιν ὁ πόλεμος συνέστη, καὶ τὸ Τρωϊκὸν πέδιον ποῦ ἐστιν, ὃ μέ-
ταξυ τῆς πόλεως καὶ τῆς θαλάσσης ὁ ποιητὴς φράζει· τὸ μὲν γὰρ πρὸ τῆς νῦν
πόλεως ὁρώμενον, πρόχωμα εἶναι τῶν ποταμῶν, ὕστερον γεγονός.

The words ποῦ ἐστιν are introduced conjecturally by Grosskurd, the excellent German translator of Strabo, but they seem to me necessary to make
the sense complete.

Hesitæa is cited more than once in the Homeric Scholia (Schol. Venet. ad
Iliad. iii. 64; Enstath. ad Iliad. ii. 538).

rather less than four miles from the city in the direction of Mount Ida, and further removed from the sea; here, they affirmed the "holy Troy" had stood.

No positive proof was produced to sustain the conclusion, for Strabo expressly states that not a vestige of the ancient city remained at the Village of the Ilieans:[1] but the fundamental supposition was backed by a second accessory supposition, to explain how it happened that all such vestiges had disappeared. Nevertheless Strabo adopts the unsupported hypothesis of Dêmêtrius as if it were an authenticated fact — distinguishing pointedly between Old and New Ilium, and even censuring Hellanikus for having maintained the received local faith. But I cannot find that Dêmêtrius and Hestiæa have been followed in this respect by any other writer of ancient times excepting Strabo. Ilium still continued to be talked of and treated by every one as the genuine Homeric Troy : the cruel jests of the Roman rebel Fimbria, when he sacked the town and massacred the inhabitants — the compensation made by Sylla, and the pronounced favor of Julius Cæsar and Augustus, — all prove this continued recognition of identity.[2] Arrian, though a native of Nicomedia, holding a high appointment in Asia Minor, and remarkable for the exactness of his topographical notices, describes the visit of Alexander to Ilium, without any suspicion that the place with all its relics was a mere counterfeit: Aristidês, Dio Chrysostom, Pausanias, Appian, and Plutarch hold the same language.[3] But modern writers seem for the most part to have taken up the

---

[1] Strabo, xiii. p. 599.   Οὐδὲν δ' ἴχνος σώζεται τῆς ἀρχαίας πόλεως — εἰκότως · ἅτε γὰρ ἐκπεπορθημένων τῶν κύκλῳ πόλεων, οὐ τελέως δὲ κατεσπασμένων, οἱ λίθοι πάντες εἰς τὴν ἐκείνων ἀνάληψιν μετηνέχθησαν.

[2] Appian, Mithridat. c. 53; Strabo, xiii. p. 594; Plutarch, Sertorius, c. 1; Velleius Paterc. ii. 23.

The inscriptions attest Panathenaic games celebrated at Ilium in honor of Athênê by the Ilieans conjointly with various other neighboring cities (see Corp. Inscr. Boeckh. No. 3601-3602, with Boeckh's observations). The valuable inscription No. 3595 attests the liberality of Antiochus Soter towards the Iliean Athênê as early as 278 B. C.

[3] Arrian, i. 11; Appian ut sup.; also Aristidês, Or. 43, Rhodiaca, p. 820 (Dindorf. p. 369). The curious Oratio xi. of Dio Chrysostom, in which he writes his new version of the Trojan war, is addressed to the inhabitants of Ilium.

supposition from Strabo as implicitly as he took it from Dêmê
trius.   They call Ilium by the disrespectful appellation of *New*
Ilium — while the traveller in the Trôad looks for *Old* Ilium as
if it were the unquestionable spot where Priam had lived and
moved ; the name is even formally enrolled on the best maps recently prepared of the ancient Trôad.[1]

---

[1] The controversy, now half a century old, respecting Troy and the
Trojan war — between Bryant and his various opponents, Morritt, Gilbert
Wakefield, the British Critic, etc., seems now nearly forgotten, and I cannot
think that the pamphlets on either side would be considered as displaying
much ability, if published at the present day.   The discussion was first
raised by the publication of Le Chevalier's account of the plain of Troy, in
which the author professed to have discovered the true site of Old Ilium
(the supposed Homeric Troy), about twelve miles from the sea near Bounarbashi.   Upon this account Bryant published some animadversions, followed
up by a second treatise, in which he denied the historical reality of the Trojan
war, and advanced the hypothesis that the tale was of Egyptian origin (Dissertation on the War of Troy, and the Expedition of the Grecians as de
scribed by Homer, showing that no such Expedition was ever undertaken,
and that no such city of Phrygia existed, by Jacob Bryant; seemingly 1797,
though there is no date in the title-page : Morritt's reply was published in
1798).   A reply from Mr. Bryant and a rejoinder from Mr. Morritt, as well
as a pamphlet from G. Wakefield, appeared in 1799 and 1800, besides an
Expostulation by the former addressed to the British Critic.

Bryant, having dwelt both on the incredibilities and the inconsistencies of
the Trojan war, as it is recounted in Grecian legend generally, nevertheless
admitted that Homer had a groundwork for his story, and maintained that
that groundwork was Egyptian.   Homer (he thinks) was an Ithacan, descended from a family originally emigrant from Egypt: the war of Troy
was originally an Egyptian war, which explains how Memnôn the Ethiopian
came to take part in it : "upon this history, which was originally Egyptian,
Homer founded the scheme of his two principal poems, adapting things to
Greece and Phrygia by an ingenious transposition:" he derived information
from priests of Memphis or Thêbes (Bryant, pp. 102, 108, 126).   The Ἥρως
Αἰγύπτιος, mentioned in the second book of the Odyssey (15), is the Egyptian hero, who affords, in his view, an evidence that the population of that
island was in part derived from Egypt.   No one since Mr. Bryant, I appre-
hend, has ever construed the passage in the same sense.

Bryant's Egyptian hypothesis is of no value ; but the negative portion of
his argument, summing up the particulars of the Trojan legend, and contending against its historical credibility, is not so easily put aside.   Few
persons will share in the zealous conviction by which Morritt tries to make it
appear that the 1100 ships, the ten years of war, the large confederacy of
princes from all parts of Greece, etc., have nothing but what is consonant with

Strabo has here converted into geographical matter of fact an
hypothesis purely gratuitous, with a view of saving the accuracy
of the Homeric topography ; though in all probability the locality of the pretended Old Ilium would have been found open to
difficulties not less serious than those which it was introduced to
obviate.[1] It may be true that Dêmêtrius and he were justified in

historical probability; difficulties being occasionally eliminated by the plea of
our ignorance of the time and of the subject (Morritt, p. 7-21). Gilbert Wakefield, who maintains the historical reality of the siege with the utmost inten-
sity, and even compares Bryant to Tom Paine (W. p. 17), is still more
displeased with those who propound doubts, and tells us that "grave dispu-
tation in the midst of such darkness and uncertainty is a conflict with chi-
mœras " (W. p. 14).

The most plausible line of argument taken by Morritt and Wakefield is,
where they enforce the positions taken by Strabo and so many other authors,
ancient as well as modern, that a superstructure of fiction is to be distin
guished from a basis of truth, and that the latter is to be amintained
while the former is rejected (Morritt, p. 5; Wake. p. 7-8). To this Bryant
replies, that " if we leave out every absurdity, we can make anything plausible ; that a fable may be made consistent, and we have many romances
that are very regular in the assortment of characters and circumstances : this
may be seen in plays, memoirs, and novels. But this regularity and correspondence alone will not ascertain the truth " (Expostulation, pp. 8, 12, 13)
" That there are a great many other fables besides that of Troy, regular and
consistent among themselves, believed and chronologized by the Greeks, and
even looked up to by them in a religious view (p. 13), which yet no one now
thinks of admitting as history."

Morritt, having urged the universal belief of antiquity as evidence that
the Trojan war was historically real, is met by Bryant, who reminds him
that the same persons believed in centaurs, satyrs, nymphs, augury, aruspicy ;
Homer maintaining that horses could speak, etc. To which Morritt replies,
" What has religious belief to do with historical facts ? Is not the evidence
on which our faith rests in matters of religion totally different in all its
parts from that on which we ground our belief in history?" (Addit. Remarks, p. 47).

The separation between the grounds of religious and historical belief is by
no means so complete as Mr. Morritt supposes, even in regard to modern
times; and when we apply his position to the ancient Greeks, it will be
found completely the reverse of the truth. The contemporaries of Herodotus and Thucydidês conceived their early history in the most intimate conjunction with their religion.

[1] For example, adopting his own line of argument (not to mention those
battles in which the pursuit and the flight reaches from the city to the ships
and back again), it might have been urged to him, that by supposing the

their negative argument, so as to show that the battles described
in the Iliad could not possibly have taken place if the city of
Priam had stood on the hill inhabited by the Ilieans.   But the
legendary faith subsisted before, and continued without abatement afterwards, notwithstanding such topographical impossibilities.   Hellanikus, Herodotus, Mindarus, the guides of Xerxês,
and Alexander, had not been shocked by them: the case of the
latter is the strongest of all, because he had received the best
education of his time under Aristotle — he was a passionate admirer and constant reader of the Iliad — he was moreover personally familiar with the movements of armies, and lived at a
time when maps, which began with Anaximander, the disciple of
Thalês, were at least known to all who sought instruction.   Now
if, notwithstanding such advantages, Alexander fully believed in
the identity of Ilium, unconscious of these many and glaring topographical difficulties, much less would Homer himself, or the
Homeric auditors, be likely to pay attention to them, at a period,
five centuries earlier, of comparative rudeness and ignorance,
when prose records as well as geographical maps were totally
unknown.[1]   The inspired poet might describe, and his hearers

Homeric Troy to be four miles farther off from the sea, he aggravated the
difficulty of rolling the Trojan horse into the town: it was already sufficiently
hard to propel this vast wooden animal full of heroes from the Greek Naustathmon to the town of Ilium.

The Trojan horse, with its accompaniments Sinon and Laocoôn, is one
of the capital and indispensable events in the epic : Homer, Arktinus, Leschês, Virgil, and Quintus Smyrnæus, all dwell upon it emphatically as the
proximate cause of the capture.

The difficulties and inconsistencies of the movements ascribed to Greeks
and Trojans in the Iliad, when applied to real topography, are well set forth
in Spohn, De Agro Trojano, Leipsic, 1814 ; and Mr. Maclaren has shown
(Dissertation on the Topography of the Trojan War, Edinburgh, 1822) that
these difficulties are nowise obviated by removing Ilium a few miles further
from the sea.

[1] Major Rennell argues differently from the visit of Alexander, employ-
ing it to confute the hypothesis of Chevalier, who had placed the Homeric
Troy at Bounarbashi, the site supposed to have been indicated by Dêmêtrius and Strabo : —

" Alexander is said to have been a passionate admirer of the Iliad, and
he had an opportunity of deciding on the spot how far the topography was
consistent with the narrative.   Had he been shown the site of Bounarbashi

would listen with delight to the tale, how Hectôr, pursued by Achilles, ran thrice round the city of Troy, while the trembling Trojans were all huddled into the city, not one daring to come out even at this last extremity of their beloved prince — and while the Grecian army looked on, restraining unwillingly their uplifted spears at the nod of Achilles, in order that Hectôr might perish by no other hand than his; nor were they, while absorbed by this impressive recital, disposed to measure distances or calculate topographical possibilities with reference to the site of the real Ilium.[1] The mistake consists in applying to Homer and to the Homeric siege of Troy, criticisms which would be perfectly just if brought to bear on the Athenian siege of Syracuse, as described by Thucydidês;[2] in the Peloponnesian war[3] — but which

for that of Troy, he would probably have questioned the fidelity either of the historical part of the poem or his guides. It is not within credibility, that a person of so correct a judgment as Alexander could have admired a poem, which contained a long history of military details, and other transactions that could not physically have had an existence. What pleasure could he receive, in contemplating as subjects of history, events which could not have happened? Yet he did admire the poem, and *therefore must have found the topography consistent*: that is, Bounarbashi, surely, was not shown to him for Troy   (Reynell, Observations on the Plain of Troy, p. 128).

Major Rennell here supposes in Alexander a spirit of topographical criticism quite foreign to his real character. We have no reason to believe that the site of Bounarbashi was shown to Alexander as the Homeric Troy, or that *any* site was shown to him *except Ilium*, or what Strabo calls New Ilium. Still less reason have we to believe that any scepticism crossed his mind, or that his deep-seated faith required to be confirmed by measurement of distances.

[1] Strabo, xiii. p. 599.   Οὐδ' ἡ τοῦ Ἕκτορος δὲ περιδρομὴ ἡ περὶ τὴν πόλιν ἔχει τι εὔλογον · οὐ γάρ ἐστι περίδρομος ἡ νῦν, διὰ τὴν συνεχῆ ῥάχιν · ἡ δὲ παλαιὰ ἔχει περιδρομήν.

[2] Mannert (Geographie der Griechen und Römer, th. 6. heft 3. b. 8. cap 8) is confused in his account of Old and New Ilium: he represents that Alexander raised up a new spot to the dignity of having been the Homeric Ilium, which is not the fact: Alexander adhered to the received local belief. Indeed, as far as our evidence goes, no one but Dêmêtrius, Hestiæa, and Strabo appears ever to have departed from it.

[3] There can hardly be a more singular example of this same confusion, than to find elaborate military criticisms from the Emperor Napoleon, upon the description of the taking of Troy in the second book of the Æneid. He shows that gross faults are committed in it, when looked at from the

are not more applicable to the epic narrative than they would be
to the exploits of Amadis or Orlando.

There is every reason for presuming that the Ilium visited by
Xerxês and Alexander was really the "holy Ilium" present to
the mind of Homer; and if so, it must have been inhabited, either
by Greeks or by some anterior population, at a period earlier than
that which Strabo assigns. History recognizes neither Troy the
city, nor Trojans, as actually existing; but the extensive region
called Trôas, or the Trôad (more properly Trôïas), is known
both to Herodotus and to Thucydidês: it seems to include the
territory westward of an imaginary line drawn from the north-
east corner of the Adramyttian gulf to the Propontis at Parium,
since both Antandrus, Kolônæ, and the district immediately
round Ilium, are regarded as belonging to the Trôad.[1] Herodotus further notices the Teukrians of Gergis[2] (a township conter-
minous with Ilium, and lying to the eastward of the road from
Ilium to Abydus), considering them as the remnant of a larger
Teukrian population which once resided in the country, and
which had in very early times undertaken a vast migration from
Asia into Europe.[3] To that Teukrian population he thinks that
the Homeric Trojans belonged :[4] and by later writers, especially
by Virgil and the other Romans, the names Teukrians and Trojans are employed as equivalents. As the name *Trojans* is not
mentioned in any contemporary historical monument, so the

point of view of a general (see an interesting article by Mr. G. C. Lewis, in the
Classical Museum, vol. i. p. 205, "Napoleon on the Capture of Troy").

Having cited this criticism from the highest authority on the art of war,
we may find a suitable parallel in the works of distinguished publicists. The
attack of Odysseus on the Ciconians (described in Homer, Odyss. ix. 39–61) is
cited both by Grotius (De Jure Bell. et Pac. iii. 3, 10) and by Vattel (Droit
des Gens, iii. 202) as a case in point in international law. Odysseus is con
sidered to have sinned against the rules of international law by attacking
them as allies of the Trojans, without a formal declaration of war.

[1] Compare Herodot. v. 24–122; Thucyd. i. 131. The Ἰλιὰς γῆ is a part
of the Trôad.

[2] Herodot. vii. 43.

[3] Herodot. v. 122. εἶλε μὲν Αἰολέας πάντας, ὅσοι τὴν Ἰλιάδα γῆν νέμονται,
εἶλε δὲ Γέργιθας, τοὺς ἀπολειφθέντας τῶν ἀρχαίων Τεύκρων.

For the migration of the Teukrians and Mysians into Europe, see Herodot
vii. 20; the Pæonians, on the Strymôn, called themselves their descendants.

[4] Herodot. ii. 118; v. 13.

name *Teukrians* never once occurs in the old epic. It appears to have been first noticed by the elegiac poet Kallinus, about 660 B. C., who connected it by an alleged immigration of Teukrians from Krête into the region round about Ida. Others again denied this, asserting that the primitive ancestor, Teukrus, had come into the country from Attica,[1] or that he was of indigenous origin, born from Skamander and the nymph Idæa — all various manifestations of that eager thirst after an eponymous hero which never deserted the Greeks. Gergithians occur in more than one spot in Æolis, even so far southward as the neighborhood of Kymê :[2] the name has no place in Homer, but he mentions Gorgythion and Kebriones as illegitimate sons of Priam, thus giving a sort of epical recognition both to Gergis and Kebrên. As Herodotus calls the old epical Trojans by the name Teukrians, so the Attic Tragedians call them Phrygians ; though the Homeric hymn to Aphroditê represents Phrygians and Trojans as completely distinct, specially noting the diversity of language ;[3] and in the Iliad the Phrygians are simply numbered among the allies of Troy from the far Ascania, without inlication of any more intimate relationship.[4] Nor do the tales which connect Dardanus with Samothrace and Arcadia find countenance in the Homeric poems, wherein Dardanus is the son of Zeus, having no root anywhere except in Dardania.[5] The mysterious solemnities of Samothrace, afterwards so highly venerated throughout the Grecian world, date from a period much later than Homer ; and the religious affinities of that island as well as of Krête with the territories of Phrygia and Æolis, were certain, according to the established tendency of the Grecian mind, to beget stories of a common genealogy.

To pass from this legendary world, — an aggregate of streams distinct and heterogeneous, which do not willingly come into con

---

[1] Strabo, xiii. p. 604 ; Apollodôr. iii. 12, 4.
Kephalôn of Gergis called Teukrus a Krêtan (Stephan. Byz. v. Ἀρίσβη).
[2] Clearchus ap. Athæne. vi. p. 256 ; Strabo, xiii. p. 589–616.
[3] Homer, Hymn. in Vener. 116.
[4] Iliad, ii. 863. Asius, the brother of Hecabê, lives in Phrygia on the banks of the Sangarius (Iliad, xvi. 717).
[5] See Hellanik. Fragm. 129, 130. ed. Didot : and Kephalôn Gergithius ap. Steph. Byz. v. Ἀρισβή.

fluence, and cannot be forced to intermix, — into the clearer vision afforded by Herodotus, we learn from him that in the year 500 B. C. the whole coast-region from Dardanus southward to the promontory of Lektum (including the town of Ilium), and from Lektum eastward to Adramyttium, had been Æolized, or was occupied by Æolic Greeks — likewise the inland towns of Skêpsis[1] and Krebên. So that if we draw a line northward from Adramyttium to Kyzikus on the Propontis, throughout the whole territory westward from that line, to the Hellespont and the Ægean Sea, all the considerable towns would be Hellenic, with the exception of Gergis and the Teukrian population around it, — all the towns worthy of note were either Ionic or Æolic. A century earlier, the Teukrian population would have embraced a wider range — perhaps Skêpsis and Krebên, the latter of which places was colonized by Greeks from Kyme :[2] a century afterwards, during the satrapy of Pharnabazus, it appears that Gergis had become Hellenized as well as the rest. The four towns, Ilium, Gergis, Kebrên and Skêpsis, all in lofty and strong positions, were distinguished each by a solemn worship and temple of Athênê, and by the recognition of that goddess as their special patroness.[3]

The author of the Iliad conceived the whole of this region as occupied by people not Greek, — Trojans, Dardanians, Lykians, Lelegians, Pelasgians, and Kilikians. He recognizes a temple and worship of Athênê in Ilium, though the goddess is bitterly

---

[1] Skêpsis received some colonists from the Ionic Miletus (Anaximenês apud Strabo, xiv. p. 635) ; but the coins of the place prove that its dialect was Æolic. See Klausen, Æneas und die Penaten, tom. i. note 180.

Arisbê also, near Abydus, seems to have been settled from Mitylênê (Eustath. ad Iliad. xii 97).

The extraordinary fertility and rich black mould of the plain around Ilium is noticed by modern travellers (see Franklin, Remarks and Observations on the Plain of Troy, London, 1800, p. 44) : it is also easily worked : "a couple of buffaloes or oxen were sufficient to draw the plough, whereas near Constantinople it takes twelve or fourteen.

[2] Ephôrus ap. Harpocrat. v. Κεβρῆνα.

[3] Xenoph. Hellen. i. 1, 10 ; iii. 1, 10–15.

One of the great motives of Dio in setting aside the Homeric narrative of the Trojan war, is to vindicate Athênê from the charge of having unjustly destroyed her own city of Ilium (Orat. xi. p. 310 : μάλιστα διὰ τὴν Ἀθηνᾶν ὅπως μὴ δοκῇ ἀδίκως διαφθεῖραι τὴν ἑαυτῆς πόλιν).

hostile to the Trojans : and Arktinus described the Palladium as the capital protection of the city. But perhaps the most remarkable feature of identity between the Homeric and the historical Æolis, is, the solemn and diffused worship of the Sminthian Apollo. Chrysê, Killa and Tenedos, and more than one place called Sminthium, maintain the surname and invoke the protection of that god during later times, just as they are emphatically described to do by Homer.[1]

When it is said that the Post-Homeric Greeks gradually Hellenized this entire region, we are not to understand that the whole previous population either retired or was destroyed. The Greeks settled in the leading and considerable towns, which enabled them both to protect one another and to gratify their predominant tastes. Partly by force — but greatly also by that superior activity, and power of assimilating foreign ways of thought to their own, which distinguished them from the beginning — they invested all the public features and management of the town with an Hellenic air, distributed all about it their gods, their heroes and their legends, and rendered their language the medium of public administration, religious songs and addresses to the gods, and generally for communications wherein any number of persons were concerned. But two remarks are here to be made : first, in doing this they could not avoid taking to themselves more or less of that which belonged

---

[1] Strabo, x. p. 473; xiii. p. 604–605. Polemon. Fragm. 31. p. 63, ed. Preller.

Polemon was a native of Ilium, and had written a periegesis of the place (about 200 B. C., therefore earlier than Dêmêtrius of Skêpsis) : he may have witnessed the improvement in its position effected by the Romans. He noticed the identical stone upon which Palamêdês had taught the Greeks to play at dice.

The Sminthian Apollo appears inscribed on the coins of Alexandreia Trôas; and the temple of the god was memorable even down to the time of the emperor Julian (Ammian. Marcellin. xxii. 8). Compare Menander (the Rhetor) περὶ Ἐπιδεικτικῶν, iv. 14; apud Walz. Collect. Rhetor. t. ix. p. 304; also περὶ Σμινθιακῶν, iv. 17.

Σμίνθος, both in the Krêtan and the Æolic dialect, meant a *field-mouse*: the region seems to have been greatly plagued by these little animals.

Polemo could not have accepted the theory of Dêmêtrius, that Ilium was not the genuine Troy: his Periegesis, describing the localities and relics of Ilium, implied the legitimacy of the place as a matter of course.

to the parties with whom they fraternized, so that the result was not pure Hellenism; next, that even this was done only in the towns, without being fully extended to the territorial domain around, or to those smaller townships which stood to the town in a dependent relation. The Æolic and Ionic Greeks borrowed from the Asiatics whom they had Hellenized, musical instruments and new laws of rhythm and melody, which they knew how to turn to account: they further adopted more or less of those violent and maddening religious rites, manifested occasionally in self-inflicted suffering and mutilation, which were indigenous in Asia Minor in the worship of the Great Mother. The religion of the Greeks in the region of Ida as well as at Kyzikus was more orgiastic than the native worship of Greece Proper, just as that of Lampsacus, Priapus and Parium was more licentious. From the Teukrian region of Gergis, and from the Gergithes near Kymê, sprang the original Sibylline prophecies, and the legendary Sibyll who plays so important a part in the tale of Æneas: the mythe of the Sibyll, whose prophecies are supposed to be heard in the hollow blast bursting out from obscure caverns and apertures in the rocks,[1] was indigenous among the Gergithian Teukrians, and passed from the Kymæans in Æolis, along with the other circumstances of the tale of Æneas, to their brethren the inhabitants of Cumæ in Italy. The date of the Gergithian Sibyll, or rather of the circulation of her supposed prophecies, is placed during the reign of Crœsus, a period when Gergis was thoroughly Teukrian. Her prophecies, though embodied in Greek verses, had their root in a Teukrian soil and feelings; and the promises of future empire which they so liberally make to the fugitive hero escaping from the flames of Troy into Italy, become interesting from the remarkable way in which they were realized by Rome.[2]

---

[1] Virgil, Æneid, vi. 42:—

Excisum Euboïcæ latus ingens rupis in antrum,
Quo lati ducunt aditus centum, ostia centum;
Unde ruunt totidem voces, responsa Sibyllæ.

[2] Pausanias, x. 12, 8; Lactantius, i. 6, 12; Steph. Byz. v. Μέρμησσος; Schol. Plat. Phædr. p. 315, Bekker.

The date of this Gergithian Sibyll, or of the prophecies passing under her

At what time Ilium and Dardanus became Æolized we have no information. We find the Mitylenæans in possession of Sigeium in the time of the poet Alkæus, about 600 B. C.; and the Athenians during the reign of Peisistratus, having wrested it from them and trying to maintain their possession, vindicate the proceeding by saying that they had as much right to it as the Mitylenæans, "for the latter had no more claim to it than any of the other Greeks who had aided Menelaus in avenging the abduction of Helen."[1] This is a very remarkable incident, as attesting the celebrity of the legend of Troy, and the value of a mythical title in international disputes — yet seemingly implying that the establishment of the Mitylenæans on that spot must have been sufficiently recent. The country near the junction of the Hellespont and the Propontis is represented as originally held[2] by Bebrykian Thracians, while Abydus was first occupied by Milesian colonists in the reign and by the permission of the Lydian king Gygês[3] — to whom the whole Trôad and the neighboring territory belonged, and upon whom therefore the Teukrians of Ida must have been dependent. This must have been about 700 B. C., a period

name, is stated by Hêrakleidês of Pontus, and there seems no reason for calling it in question.

Klausen (Æneas und die Penaten, book ii. p. 205) has worked out copiously the circulation and legendary import of the Sibylline prophecies.

[1] Herodot. v. 94. Σίγειον ...... τὸ εἷλε Πεισίστρατος αἰχμῇ παρὰ Μιτυληναίων. ..... Ἀθηναῖοι, ἀποδεικνύντες λόγῳ οὐδὲν μᾶλλον Αἰολεῦσι μετεὸν τῆς Ἰλιάδος χώρης, ἢ οὐ καί σφι καὶ τοῖσι ἄλλοισι, ὅσοι Ἑλλήνων συνεξεπρήξαντο Μενέλεῳ τὰς Ἑλένης ἁρπαγάς. In Æschylus (Eumenid. 402) the goddess Athênê claims the land about the Skamander, as having been presented to the sons of Thêseus by the general vote of the Grecian chiefs: —

Ἀπὸ Σκαμάνδρου γῆν καταφθατουμένη,
Ἥν δὴ τ' Ἀχαιῶν ἄκτορες τε καὶ πρόμοι
Τῶν αἰχμαλώτων χρημάτων λάχος μέγα,
Ἔνειμαν αὐτόπρεμνον εἰς τὸ πᾶν ἐμοὶ,
Ἐξαιρετὸν δώρημα Θησέως τόκοις.

In the days of Peisistratus, it seems Athens was not bold enough or powerful enough to advance this vast pretension.

[2] Charôn of Lampsacus ap. Schol. Apollôn. Rhod. ii. 2; Bernhardy ad Dionys. Periêgêt. 805. p. 747.

[3] Such at least is the statement of Strabo (xii. p. 590); though such an extent of Lydian rule at that time seems not easy to reconcile with the proceedings of the subsequent Lydian kings.

considerably earlier than the Mitylenæan occupation of Sigeium. Lampsacus and Pæsus, on the neighboring shores of the Propontis, were also Milesian colonies, though we do not know their date : Parium was jointly settled from Miletus, Erythræ and Parus.

CHAPTER XVI.

RECIAN MYTHES, AS UNDERSTOOD, FELT AND INTERPRETED BY THE GREEKS THEMSELVES.

THE preceding sections have been intended to exhibit a sketch of that narrative matter, so abundant, so characteristic and so interesting, out of which early Grecian history and chronology have been extracted. Raised originally by hands unseen and from data unassignable, it existed first in the shape of floating talk among the people, from whence a large portion of it passed into the song of the poets, who multiplied, transformed and adorned it in a thousand various ways.

These mythes or current stories, the spontaneous and earliest growth of the Grecian mind, constituted at the same time the entire intellectual stock of the age to which they belonged. They are the common root of all those different ramifications into which the mental activity of the Greeks subsequently diverged ; containing, as it were, the preface and germ of the positive history and philosophy, the dogmatic theology and the professed romance, which we shall hereafter trace each in its separate development. They furnished aliment to the curiosity, and solution to the vague doubts and aspirations of the age ; they explained the origin of those customs and standing peculiarities with which men were familiar ; they impressed moral lessons, awakened patriotic sympathies, and exhibited in detail the shadowy, but anxious presentiments of the vulgar as to the agency of the gods : moreover they satisfied that craving for adventure and appetite for the marvellous, which has in modern times become the province of fiction proper.

It is difficult, we may say impossible, for a man of mature age to carry back his mind to his conceptions such as they stood when he was a child, growing naturally out of his imagination and feelings, working upon a scanty stock of materials, and borrowing from authorities whom he blindly followed but imperfectly apprehended. A similar difficulty occurs when we attempt to place ourselves in the historical and quasi-philosophical point of view which the ancient mythes present to us. We can follow perfectly the imagination and feeling which dictated these tales, and we can admire and sympathize with them as animated, sublime, and affecting poetry; but we are too much accustomed to matter of fact and philosophy of a positive kind, to be able to conceive a time when these beautiful fancies were construed literally and accepted as serious reality.

Nevertheless it is obvious that Grecian mythes cannot be either understood or appreciated except with reference to the system of conceptions and belief of the ages in which they arose. We must suppose a public not reading and writing, but seeing, hearing and telling — destitute of all records, and careless as well as ignorant of positive history with its indispensable tests, yet at the same time curious and full of eagerness for new or impressive incidents — strangers even to the rudiments of positive philosophy and to the idea of invariable sequences of nature either in the physical or moral world, yet requiring some connecting theory to interpret and regularize the phænomena before them. Such a theory was supplied by the spontaneous inspirations of an early fancy, which supposed the habitual agency of beings intelligent and voluntary like themselves, but superior in extent of power, and different in peculiarity of attributes. In the geographical ideas of the Homeric period, the earth was flat and round, with the deep and gentle ocean-stream flowing around and returning into itself: chronology, or means of measuring past time, there existed none; but both unobserved regions might be described, the forgotten past unfolded, and the unknown future predicted — through particular men specially inspired by the gods, or endowed by them with that peculiar vision which detected and interpreted passing signs and omens.

If even the rudiments of scientific geography and physics, now
so universally diffused and so invaluable as a security against
error and delusion, were wanting in this early stage of society,
their place was abundantly supplied by vivacity of imagination
and by personifying sympathy. The unbounded tendency of the
Homeric Greeks to multiply fictitious persons, and to construe
the phænomena which interested them into manifestations of design, is above all things here to be noticed, because the form of
personal narrative, universal in their mythes, is one of its many
manifestations. Their polytheism (comprising some elements of
an original fetichism, in which particular objects had themselves
been supposed to be endued with life, volition, and design) recognized agencies of unseen beings identified and confounded with
the different localities and departments of the physical world.
Of such beings there were numerous varieties, and many gradations both in power and attributes ; there were differences of age,
sex and local residence, relations both conjugal and filial between
them, and tendencies sympathetic as well as repugnant. The
gods formed a sort of political community of their own, which
had its hierarchy, its distribution of ranks and duties, its conten-
tions for power and occasional revolutions, its public meetings in
the agora of Olympus, and its multitudinous banquets or festivals.[1] The great Olympic gods were in fact only the most exalted
amongst an aggregate of quasi-human or ultra-human personages,
— dæmons, heroes, nymphs, eponymous (or name-giving) genii,
identified with each river, mountain,[2] cape, town, village, or known

---

[1] Homer, Iliad, i. 603; xx. 7.   Hesiod. Theogon. 802.

[2] We read in the Iliad that Asteropæus was grandson of the beautiful
river Axius, and Achilles, after having slain him, admits the dignity of this
parentage, but boasts that his own descent from Zeus was much greater,
since even the great river Achelôus and Oceanus himself is inferior to Zeus
(xxi. 157–191). Skamander fights with Achilles, calling his brother Simoïs
to his aid (213–308). Tyrô, the daughter of Salmôneus, falls in love with
Enipeus, the most beautiful of rivers (Odyss. xi. 237). Achelôus appears
as a suitor of Deianira (Sophokl. Trach. 9).
There cannot be a better illustration of this feeling than what is told of
the New Zealanders at the present time. The chief Heu-Heu appeals to his
ancestor, the great mountain Tonga Riro : " I am the Heu-Heu, and rule
over you all, just as my ancestor Tonga Riro, the mountain of snow, stands
above all this land." (E. J. Wakefield, Adventures in New Zealand, vol. i.

circumscription of territory, — besides horses, bulls, and dogs, of immortal breed and peculiar attributes, and monsters of strange

ch. 17. p. 465). Heu-Heu refused permission to any one to ascend the mountain, on the ground that it was his *tipuna* or ancestor: " he constantly iden tified himself with the mountain and called it his sacred ancestor" (vol. ii. c. 4. p. 113). The mountains in New Zealand are accounted by the natives masculine and feminine: Tonga Riro, and Taranaki, two male mountains, quarrelled about the affections of a small volcanic female mountain in the neighborhood (*ibid.* ii. c. 4. p. 97).

The religious imagination of the Hindoos also (as described by Colonel Sleeman in his excellent work, Rambles and Recollections of an Indian Official), affords a remarkable parallel to that of the early Greeks. Colonel Sleeman says, —

" I asked some of the Hindoos about us why they called the river Mother Nerbudda, if she was really never married. Her Majesty (said they with great respect) would really never consent to be married after the indignity she suffered from her affianced bridegroom the Sohun: and we call her *mother* because she blesses us all, and we are anxious to accost her by the name which we consider to be the most respectful and endearing.

" Any Englishman can easily conceive a poet in his highest calenture of the brain, addressing the Ocean as a steed that knows his rider, and patting the crested billow as his flowing mane. But he must come to India to understand how every individual of a *whole community of many millions can address a fine river as a living being — a sovereign princess who hears and understands all they say, and exercises a kind of local superintendence over their affairs,* without a single temple in which her image is worshipped, or a single priest to profit by the delusion. As in the case of the Ganges, *it is the river itself to whom they address themselves, and not to any deity residing in it, or presiding over it* — the stream itself is the deity which fills their imaginations, and receives their homage" (Rambles and Recollections of an Indian Official, ch. iii. p. 20). Compare also the remarks in the same work on the sanctity of *Mother Nerbudda* (chapter xxvii. p. 261); also of the holy personality of the earth. " The land is considered as the MOTHER of the prince or chief who holds it, the great parent from whom he derives all that maintains him, his family, and his establishments. If well-treated, she yields this in abundance to her son; but if he presumes to look upon her with the eye of *desire,* she ceases to be fruitful; or the Deity sends down hail or blight to destroy all that she yields. The measuring the surface of the fields, and the frequently inspecting the crops by the chief himself or his immediate agents, were considered by the people in this light — either it should not be done at all, or the duty should be delegated to inferior agents, whose close inspection of the *great parent* could not be so displeasing to the Deity " (Ch. xxvii. p. 248).

See also about the gods who are believed to reside in trees — the Peepul-

lineaments and combinations, " Gorgons and Harpies and Chimæras dire." As there were in every *gens* or family special gentile deities and foregone ancestors who watched over its members, forming in each the characteristic symbol and recognized guarantee of their union, so there seem to have been in each guild or trade peculiar beings whose vocation it was to coöperate or to impede in various stages of the business.[1]

The extensive and multiform personifications, here faintly sketched, pervaded in every direction the mental system of the Greeks, and were identified intimately both with their conception and with their description of phænomena, present as well as past. That which to us is interesting as the mere creation of an exuberant fancy, was to the Greek genuine and venerated reality. Both the earth and the solid heaven (Gæa and Uranos) were both conceived and spoken of by him as endowed with appetite, feeling, sex, and most of the various attributes of humanity. Instead of a sun such as we now see, subject to astronomical laws, and forming the centre of a system the changes of which we can ascertain and foreknow, he saw the great god Hêlios, mounting his chariot in the morning in the east, reaching at mid-day the height of the solid heaven, and arriving in the evening at the western horizon, with horses fatigued and desirous of repose.

---

tree, the cotton-tree, etc. (ch. ix. p. 112), and the description of the annual marriage celebrated between the sacred pebble, or pebble-god, Saligram, and the sacred shrub Toolsea, celebrated at great expense and with a numerous procession (chap. xix. p. 158; xxiii. p. 185).

[1] See the song to the potters, in the Homeric Epigrams (14) : —

Εἰ μὲν δώσετε μίσθον, ἀείσω, ὦ κεραμῆες·
Δεῦρ' ἄγ' 'Αθηναίη, καὶ ὑπείρεχε χεῖρα καμίνου.
Εὖ δὲ μελανθεῖεν κότυλοι, καὶ πάντα κάναστρα
Φρυχθῆναί τε καλῶς, καὶ τιμῆς ὦνον ἀρέσθαι.
. . . . . . 'Ην δ' ἐπ' ἀναιδείην τρεφθέντες ψευδῆ ἄρησθε,
Συγκαλέω δὴ 'πειτα καμίνῳ δηλητῆρας·
Σύντριβ' ὅμως, Σμάραγόν τε, καὶ 'Ασβετον, ἠδὲ Σαβάκτην,
'Ωμόδαμόν θ', ὃς τῆδε τέχνῃ κακὰ πολλὰ πορίζει, etc.

A certain kindred between men and serpents (ουγγένειάν τινα πρὸς τοὺς ὄφεις) was recognized in the peculiar gens of the ὀφιογενεῖς near Parion, who possessed the gift of healing by their touches the bite of the serpent: the original hero of this gens was said to have been transformed from a serpent into a man (Strabo, xiii. p. 588).

Hêlios, having favorite spots wherein his beautiful cattle grazed, took pleasure in contemplating them during the course of his journey, and was sorely displeased if any man slew or injured them : he had moreover sons and daughters on earth, and as his all-seeing eye penetrated everywhere, he was sometimes in a situation to reveal secrets even to the gods themselves — while on other occasions he was constrained to turn aside in order to avoid contemplating scenes of abomination.[1] To us these now appear puerile, though pleasing fancies, but to an Homeric Greek

---

[1] Odyss. ii. 388; viii. 270; xii. 4, 128, 416; xxiii. 362. Iliad, xiv. 344.
The Homeric Hymn to Dêmêtêr expresses it neatly (63) —

'Ηέλιον δ' ἵκοντο, θεῶν σκόπον ἠδὲ καὶ ἀνδρῶν.

Also the remarkable story of Euênius of Apollônia, his neglect of the sacred cattle of Hêlios, and the awful consequences of it (Herodot. ix. 93 : compare Theocr. Idyll. xxv. 130).

I know no passage in which this conception of the heavenly bodies as Persons is more strikingly set forth than in the words of the German chief Boiocalus, pleading the cause of himself and his tribe the Ansibarii before the Roman legate Avitus. This tribe, expelled by other tribes from its native possessions, had sat down upon some of that wide extent of lands on the Lower Rhine which the Roman government reserved for the use of its soldiers, but which remained desert, because the soldiers had neither the means nor the inclination to occupy them. The old chief, pleading his cause before Avitus, who had issued an order to him to evacuate the lands, first dwelt upon his fidelity of fifty years to the Roman cause, and next touched upon the enormity of retaining so large an area in a state of waste (Tacit. Ann. xiii. 55):
" Quotam partem campi jacere, in quam pecora et armenta militum aliquando transmitterentur ? Servarent sane receptos gregibus, inter hominum famam : modo ne vastitatem et solitudinem mallent, quam amicos populos. Chamavorum quondam ea arva, mox Tubantum, et post Usipiorum fuisse. Sicuti cœlum Diis, ita terras generi mortalium datas: quæque vacuæ, eas publicas esse. *Solem* deinde respiciens, et *cætera sidera* vocans, *quasi coram* interrogabat — *vellentne contueri inane solum ? potius mare superfunderent adversus terrarum ereptores.* Commotus his Avitus," etc. The legate refused the request, but privately offered to Boiocalus lands for himself apart from the tribe, which that chief indignantly spurned. He tried to maintain himself in the lands, but was expelled by the Roman arms, and forced to seek a home among the other German tribes, all of whom refused it. After much wandering and privation, the whole tribe of the Ansibarii was annihilated: its warriors were all slain, its women and children sold as slaves.

I notice this afflicting sequel, in order to show that the brave old chief was pleading before Avitus a matter of life and death both to himself and his tribe, and that the occasion was one least of all suited for a mere rhetorical

they seemed perfectly natural and plausible. In his view, the description of the sun, as given in a modern astronomical treatise, would have appeared not merely absurd, but repulsive and impious. Even in later times, when the positive spirit of inquiry had made considerable progress, Anaxagoras and other astronomers incurred the charge of blasphemy for dispersonifying Hêlios, and trying to assign invariable laws to the solar phænomena.[1] Personifying fiction was in this way blended by the Homeric

---

prosopopœia. His appeal is one sincere and heartfelt to the personal feelings and sympathies of Hêlios.

Tacitus, in reporting the speech, accompanies it with the gloss "quasi coram," to mark that the speaker here passes into a different order of ideas from that to which himself or his readers were accustomed. If Boiocalus could have heard, and reported to his tribe, an astronomical lecture, he would have introduced some explanation, in order to facilitate to his tribe the comprehension of Hêlios under a point of view so new to them. While Tacitus finds it necessary to illustrate by a comment the *personification of the sun*, Boiocalus would have had some trouble to make his tribe comprehend the *re-ification of the god Hêlios*.

[1] Physical astronomy was both new and accounted impious in the time of the Peloponnesian war: see Plutarch, in his reference to that eclipse which proved so fatal to the Athenian army at Syracuse, in consequence of the religious feelings of Nikias : οὐ γὰρ ἠνείχοντο τοὺς φυσικοὺς καὶ μετεωρολέσχας τότε καλουμένους ὡς, εἰς αἰτίας ἀλόγους καὶ δυνάμεις ἀπρονοήτους καὶ κατηναγκασμένα πάθη διατρίβοντας τὸ θεῖον (Plutarch, Nikias, c. 23, and Periklês, c. 32 ; Diodôr. xii. 39 ; Dêmêtr. Phaler. ap. Diogen. Laërt, ix. 9, 1).

"You strange man, Melêtus," said Socratês, on his trial, to his accuser, "are you seriously affirming that I do not think Hêlios and Selênê to be gods, as the rest of mankind think?" "Certainly not, gentlemen of the Dikastery (*this is the reply of Melêtus*), Socrates says that the sun is a stone, and the moon earth." "Why, my dear Melêtus, you think you are preferring an accusation against Anaxagoras! You account these Dikasts so contemptibly ignorant, as not to know that the books of Anaxagoras are full of such doctrines! Is it from me that the youth acquire such teaching, when they may buy the books for a drachma in the theatre, and may thus laugh me to scorn if I pretended to announce such views as my own — *not to mention their extreme absurdity?*" (ἄλλως τε καὶ οὕτως ἄτοπα ὄντα, Plato, Apolog. Socrat. c. 14. p. 26).

The divinity of Hêlios and Selênê is emphatically set forth by Plato, Legg. x. p. 886-889. He permits physical astronomy only under great restrictions and to a limited extent. Compare Xenoph. Memor. iv. 7, 7; Diogen. Laërt. ii. 8; Plutarch, De Stoicor. Repugnant. c. 40. p. 1053; and Schaubach ad Anaxagoræ Fragmenta, p. 6.

Greeks with their conception of the physical phænomena pefore them, not simply in the way of poetical ornament, but as a genuine portion of their every-day belief.

It was in this early state of the Grecian mind, stimulating so forcibly the imagination and the feelings, and acting through them upon the belief, that the great body of the mythes grew up and obtained circulation. They were, from first to last, personal narratives and adventures; and the persons who predominated as subjects of them were the gods, the heroes, the nymphs, etc., whose names were known and reverenced, and in whom every one felt interested. To every god and every hero it was consistent with Grecian ideas to ascribe great diversity of human motive and attribute : each indeed has his own peculiar type of character, more or less strictly defined; but in all there was a wide foundation for animated narrative and for romantic incident. The gods and heroes of the land and the tribe belonged, in the conception of a Greek, alike to the present and to the past : he worshipped in their groves and at their festivals; he invoked their protection, and believed in their superintending guardianship, even in his own day : but their more special, intimate, and sympathizing agency was cast back into the unrecorded past.[1] To

---

[1] Hesiod, Catalog. Fragm. 76. p. 48, ed. Düntzer :—

Ξυναὶ γὰρ τότε δαῖτες ἔσαν ξυνοί τε θόωκοι,
'Αθανάτοις τε θεοῖσι καταθνήτοις τ' ἀνθρώποις.

Both the Theogonia and the Works and Days bear testimony to the same general feeling. Even the heroes of Homer suppose a preceding age, the inmates of which were in nearer contact with the gods than they themselves (Odyss. viii. 223; Iliad, v. 304; xii. 382). Compare Catullus, Carm. 64; Epithalam. Peleôs et Thetidos, v. 382–408.

Menander the Rhetor (following generally the steps of Dionys. Hal. Art Rhetor. cap. 1–8) suggests to his fellow-citizens at Alexandria Trôas, proper and complimentary forms to invite a great man to visit their festival of the Sminthia :—ὥσπερ γὰρ 'Απόλλωνα πολλάκις ἐδέχετο ἡ πόλις τοῖς Σμινθίοις, ἡνίκα ἐξῆν θεοὺς προφανῶς ἐπιδημεῖν τοῖς ἀνθρώποις, οὕτω καὶ σὲ ἡ πόλις νῦν προσδέχεται (περὶ 'Επιδεικτικ. s. iv. c. 14. ap. Walz. Coll. Rhetor. t. ix. p. 304). Menander seems to have been a native of Alexandria Trôas, though Suidas calls him a Laodicean (see Walz. Præf. ad t. ix. p. xv.-xx.; and περὶ Σμινθιακῶν, sect. iv. c. 17). The festival of the Sminthia lasted down to his time, embracing the whole duration of paganism from Homer downwards.

give suitable utterance to this general sentiment, — to furnis-
body and movement and detail to these divine and heroic pre-
existences, which were conceived only in shadowy outline, — to
lighten up the dreams of what the past must have been,[1] in the
minds of those who knew not what it really had been — such was
the spontaneous aim and inspiration of productive genius in the
community, and such were the purposes which the Grecian
mythes preëminently accomplished.

The love of antiquities, which Tacitus notices as so prevalent
among the Greeks of his day,[2] was one of the earliest, the most
durable, and the most widely diffused of the national propensities. But the antiquities of every state were divine and heroic,
reproducing the lineaments, but disregarding the measure and
limits, of ordinary humanity. The gods formed the starting-point,
beyond which no man thought of looking, though some gods were
more ancient than others : their progeny, the heroes, many of
them sprung from human mothers, constitute an intermediate link
between god and man. The ancient epic usually recognizes the
presence of a multitude of nameless men, but they are introduced chiefly for the purpose of filling the scene, and of executing
the orders, celebrating the valor, and bringing out the personality,
of a few divine or heroic characters.[3] It was the glory of bards
and storytellers to be able to satisfy those religious and patriotic
predispositions of the public, which caused the primary demand

---

[1] P. A. Müller observes justly, in his *Saga-Bibliothek*, in reference to the
Icelandic mythes, "In dem Mythischen wird das Leben der Vorzeit darges-
tellt, wie es wirklich dem kindlichen Verstande, der jugendlichen Einbildung-
skraft, und dem vollen Herzen, erscheint."

(Lange's Untersuchungen über die Nordische und Deutsche Heldensage,
translated from P. A. Müller, Introd. p. 1.)

[2] Titus visited the temple of the Paphian Venus in Cyprus, "spectatâ
opulentiâ donisque regum, quæque *alia lætum* antiquitatibus Græcorum
genus *incertæ vetustati adfingit*, de navigatione primum consuluit" (Tacit.
Hist. ii. 4-5).

[3] Aristotel. Problem. xix. 48. Οἱ δὲ ἡγεμόνες τῶν ἀρχαίων ᾿μόνοι ἦσαν
ἥρωες· οἱ δὲ λαοὶ ἄνθρωποι. Istros followed this opinion also: but the
more common view seems to have considered all who combated at Troy as
heroes (see Schol. Iliad. ii. 110 ; xv. 231), and so Hesiod treats them (Opp.
Di. 158).

In reference to the Trojan war, Aristotle says — καθάπερ ἐν τοῖς ᾿Η ρ ω ι̇-
κ ο ῖ ς περὶ Πριάμου μυθεύεται (Ethic. Nicom. i. 9 ; compare vii. 1).

for their tales, and which were of a nature eminently inviting and expansive. For Grecian religion was many-sided and many colored; it comprised a great multiplicity of persons, together with much diversity in the types of character; it divinized every vein and attribute of humanity, the lofty as well as the mean — the tender as well as the warlike — the self-devoting and adventurous as well as the laughter-loving and sensual. We shall hereafter reach a time when philosophers protested against such identification of the gods with the more vulgar ʹappetites and enjoyments, believing that nothing except the spiritual attributes of man could properly be transferred to superhuman beings, and drawing their predicates respecting the gods exclusively from what was awful, majestic and terror-striking in human affairs. Such restrictions on the religious fancy were continually on the increase, and the mystic and didactic stamp which marked the last century of paganism in the days of Julian and Libanius, contrasts forcibly with the concrete and vivacious forms, full of vigorous impulse and alive to all the capricious gusts of the human temperament, which people the Homeric Olympus.[1] At present, how-

---

[1] Generation by a god is treated in the old poems as an act entirely human and physical (ἐμίγη — παρελέξατο); and this was the common opinion in the days of Plato (Plato, Apolog. Socrat. c. 15. p. 15); the hero Astrabakus is father of the Lacedæmonian king Demaratus (Herod. vi. 66). [Herodotus does not believe the story told him at Babylon respecting Belus (i. 182)] Euripidês sometimes expresses disapprobation of the idea (Ion. 350), but Plato passed among a large portion of his admirers for the actual son of Apollo, and his reputed father Aristo on marrying was admonished in a dream to respect the person of his wife Periktionê, then pregnant by Apollo, until after the birth of the child Plato (Plutarch, Quæst. Sympos. p. 717. viii. 1; Diogen. Laërt. iii. 2; Origen, cont. Cels. i. p. 29). Plutarch (in Life of Numa, c. 4; compare Life of Thêseus, 2) discusses the subject, and is inclined to disallow everything beyond mental sympathy and tenderness in a god: Pausanias deals timidly with it, and is not always consistent with himself; while the later rhetors spiritualize it altogether. Meander, περὶ Ἐπιδεικτικῶν, (towards the end of the third century B. C.) prescribes rules for praising a king: you are to praise him for the gens to which he belongs: perhaps you may be able to make out that he really is the son of some god; for many who seem to be from men, are really *sent down by God* and are *emanations from the Supreme Potency* — πολλοὶ τὸ μὲν δοκεῖν ἐξ ἀνθρώπων εἰσὶ, τῇ δ' ἀληθείᾳ παρὰ τοῦ θεοῦ καταπέμποντα. καί εἰσιν ἀπόρροιαι ὄντως τοῦ κρείττονος · καὶ γὰρ Ἡρακλῆς ἐνομίζετο μὲν Ἀμφιτρύωνος, τῇ δὲ ἀληθείᾳ ἦν Διός. Οὕτω καὶ βασιλεὺς ὁ ἡμέ-ερος τὸ μὲν δοκεῖν ἐξ ἀνθρώπων, τῇ δὲ ἀλη

ever, we have only to consider the early, or Homeric and Hesiodic paganism, and its operation in the genesis of the mythical narratives. We cannot doubt that it supplied the most powerful stimulus, and the only one which the times admitted, to the creative faculty of the people; as well from the sociability, the gradations, and the mutual action and reaction of its gods and heroes, as from the amplitude, the variety, and the purely human cast, of its fundamental types.

θεία τὴν καταβολὴν οὐράνοθεν ἔχει, etc. (Menander ap. Walz. Collect. Rhetor. t. ix. c. i. p. 218). Again — περὶ Σμινθιακῶν Ζεὺς — γένεσιν παιδῶν δημιουργεῖν ἐνενόησε — Ἀπόλλων τὴν Ἀσκληπιοῦ γένεσιν ἐδημιούργησε, p.322–327; compare Hermogenês, about the story of Apollo and Daphnê, Progymnasm. c. 4; and Julian. Orat. vii. p. 220.

The contrast of the pagan phraseology of this age (Menander had himself composed a hymn of invocation to Apollo — περὶ Ἐγκωμίων, c. 3. t. ix. y. 136, Walz.) with that of Homer is very worthy of notice. In the Hesiodic Catalogue of Women much was said respecting the marriages and amours of the gods, so as to furnish many suggestions, like the love-songs of Sapphô, to the composers of Epithalamic Odes (Menand. ib. sect. iv. c. 6. p. 268).

Menander gives a specimen of a prose hymn fit to be addressed to the Sminthian Apollo (p. 320); the spiritual character of which hymn forms the most pointed contrast with the Homeric hymn to the same god.

We may remark an analogous case in which the Homeric hymn to Apollo is modified by Plutarch. To provide for the establishment of his temple at Delphi, Apollo was described as having himself, in the shape of a dolphin, swam before a Krêtan vessel and guided it to Krissa, where he directed the terrified crew to open the Delphian temple. But Plutarch says that this old statement was not correct: the god had not himself appeared in the shape of a dolphin — he had sent a dolphin expressly to guide the vessel (Plutarch. de Solertiâ Animal. p. 983). See also a contrast between the Homeric Zeus, and the genuine Zeus, (ἀληθινός) brought out in Plutarch, Defect Oracul. c. 30. p. 426.

Illicit amours seem in these later times to be ascribed to the δαίμονες : see the singular controversy started among the fictitious pleadings of the ancient rhetors — Νόμου ὄντος, παρθένους καὶ καθαρὰς εἶναι τὰς ἱερείας, ἱερεία τις εὑρέθη ἀτόκιον φέρουσα, καὶ κρίνεται........Ἀλλ' ἐρεῖ, φασὶ, διὰ τὰς τῶν δαιμόνων ἐπιφοιτήσεις καὶ ἐπιβουλὰς περιτεθεῖσθαι· Καὶ πῶς οὐκ ἀνόητον κομιδῇ τὸ τοιοῦτον ; ἔδει γὰρ πρὸς τὸ μὴ ἀφαιρεθῆναι τὴν παρθενίαν φορεῖν τι ἀποτρόπαιον, οὐ μὴν πρὸς τὸ τεκειν (Anonymi Scholia ad Hermogen. Στάσεις, ap. Walz. Coll. Rh. t. vii. p. 162).

Apsinês of Gadara, a sophist of the time of Diocletian, pretended to be a son of Pan (see Suidas, v. Ἀψίνης). The anecdote respecting the rivers Skamander and Mæander, in the tenth epistle ascribed to the orator Æschines (p. 737), is curious, but we do not know the date of that epistle.

Though we may thus explain the mythopœic fertility of the Greeks, I am far from pretending that we can render any sufficient account of the supreme beauty of their chief epic and artistical productions. There is something in the first-rate productions of individual genius which lies beyond the compass of philosophical theory: the special breath of the Muse (to speak the language of ancient Greece) must be present in order to give them being. Even among her votaries, many are called, but few are chosen; and the peculiarities of those few remain as yet her own secret.

We shall not however forget that Grecian language was also an indispensable requisite to the growth and beauty of Grecian mythes — its richness, its flexibility and capacity of new combinations, its vocalic abundance and metrical pronunciation: and many even among its proper names, by their analogy to words really significant, gave direct occasion to explanatory or illustrative stories. Etymological mythes are found in sensible proportion among the whole number.

To understand properly then the Grecian mythes, we must try to identify ourselves with the state of mind of the original mythopœic age; a process not very easy, since it requires us to adopt a string of poetical fancies not simply as realities, but as the governing realities of the mental system;[1] yet a process

---

[1] The mental analogy between the early stages of human civilization and the childhood of the individual is forcibly and frequently set forth in the works of Vico. That eminently original thinker dwells upon the poetical and religious susceptibilities as the first to develop themselves in the human mind, and as furnishing not merely connecting threads for the explanation of sensible phænomena, but also aliment for the hopes and fears, and means of socializing influence to men of genius, at a time when reason was yet asleep. He points out the *personifying instinct* ("istinto d' animazione") as the spontaneous philosophy of man, "to make himself the rule of the universe," and to suppose everywhere a quasi-human agency as the determining cause. He remarks that in an age of fancy and feeling, the conceptions and language of poetry coincide with those of reality and common life, instead of standing apart as a separate vein. These views are repeated frequently (and with some variations of opinion as he grew older) in his Latin work *De Uno Universi Juris Principio*, as well as in the two successive *rédactions* of his great Italian work, *Scienza Nuova* (it must be added that Vico as an expositor is prolix, and does not do justice to his own powers of original thought): I select the following from the second edition of the latter treatise,

which would only reproduce something analogous to our own childhood. The age was one destitute both of recorded history and of positive science, but full of imagination and sentiment and religious impressibility; from these sources sprung that multitude of supposed persons around whom all combinations of sensible

published by himself in 1744, *Della Metafisica Poetica* (see vol. v. p. 189 of Ferrari's edition of his Works, Milan, 1836): "Adunque la sapienza poetica, che fu la prima sapienza della Gentilità, dovette incominciare da una Metafisica, non *ragionata ed astratta*, qual è questa or degli addottrinati, ma *sentita ed immaginata*, quale dovett' essere di tai primi uomini, siccome quelli ch' erano di niun raziocinio, e tutti robusti sensi e vigorosissime fantasie, come è stato nelle degnità (the *Axioms*) stabilito. Questa fu la loro propria poesia, la qual in essi fu una facultà loro connaturale, perche erano di tali sensi e di si fatte fantasie naturalmente forniti, nata da *ignoranza di cagioni* — la qual fu loro madre di maraviglia di tutte le cose, che quelli ignoranti di tutte le cose fortemente ammiravano. Tal poesia incominciò in essi divina: perchè nello stesso tempo ch' essi immaginavano le cagioni delle cose, che sentivano ed ammiravano, essere Dei, come ora il confermiamo con gli Americani, i quali tutte le cose che superano la loro picciol capacità, dicono esser Dei..... nello stesso tempo, diciamo, alle cose ammirate davano l' essere di sostanze dalla propria lor idea: ch' è appunto la natura dei fanciulli, che osserviamo prendere tra mani cose inanimate, e transtullarsi e favellarvi, come fussero quelle persone vive. In cotal guisa i primi uomini delle nazioni gentili, come fanciulli del nascente gener umano, dalla lor idea creavan essi le cose...... per la loro robusta ignoranza, il facevano in forza d' una corpolentissima fantasia, e perch' era corpolentissima, il facevano con una maravigliosa sublimità, tal e tanta, che perturbava all' eccesso essi medesimi, che fingendo le si creavano...... Di questa natura di cose umane restò eterna proprietà spiegata con nobil espressione da Tacito, che vanamente gli uomini spaventati *fingunt simul creduntque*."

After describing the condition of rude men, terrified with thunder and other vast atmospheric phænomena, Vico proceeds (*ib.* p. 172) — "In tal caso la natura della mente umana porta ch' ella attribuisca all' effetto la sua natura: e la natura loro era in tale stato d' uomini tutti robuste forze di corpo, che urlando, brontolando, spiegavano le loro violentissime passioni, si finsero il cielo esser un gran corpo animato, che per tal aspetto chiamavano Giove, che col fischio dei fulmini e col fragore die tuoni volesse lor dire qualche cosa...... E sì fanno di tutta la natura un vasto corpo animato, che senta passioni ed affetti."

Now the contrast with modern habits of thought: —

"Ma siccome *ora* per la natura delle nostre umane menti troppo ritirata dai sensi nel medesimo volgo — con le tante astrazioni, di quante sono piene le lingue — con tanti vocaboli astratti — e di troppo assottigliata con l' arti dello scrivere, e quasi spiritualezzata con la practica dei numeri — *ci e natu-*

phænomena were grouped, and towards whom curiosity, sympathies, and reverence were earnestly directed. The adventures of such persons were the only aliment suited at once both to the appetites and to the comprehension of an early Greek; and the mythes which detailed them, while powerfully interesting his

ralmente niegato di poter formare la vasta imagine di cotal donna che dicono Natura simpatetica, che mentre con la bocca dicono, non hanno nulla in lor mente, perocchè la lor mente è dentro il falso, che è nulla; nè sono soccorsi dalla fantasia a poterne formare una falsa vastissima imagine. *Così ora ci è naturalmente niegato di poter entrare nella vasta immaginativa di quei primi uomini,* le menti dei quali di nulla erano assottigliate, di nulla astratte, di nulla spiritualezzate....... Onde dicemmo sopra ch' *ora appena intender si può, affatto immaginar non sì può,* come pensassero i primi uomini che fondarono la umanità gentilesca."

In this citation (already almost too long for a note) I have omitted several sentences not essential to the general meaning. It places these early divine fables and theological poets (so Vico calls them) in their true point of view, and assigns to them their proper place in the ascending movement of human society: it refers the mythes to an early religious and poetical age, in which feeling and fancy composed the whole fund of the human mind, over and above the powers of sense: the great mental change which has since taken place has robbed us of the power, not merely of believing them as they were originally believed, but even of conceiving completely that which their first inventors intended to express.

The views here given from this distinguished Italian (the precursor of F. A. Wolf in regard to the Homeric poems, as well as of Niebuhr in regard to the Roman history) appear to me no less correct than profound; and the obvious inference from them is, that attempts to *explain* (as it is commonly called) the mythes (*i. e.* to translate them into some physical, moral or historical statements, suitable to our order of thought) are, even as guesses, essentially unpromising. Nevertheless Vico, inconsistently with his own general view, bestows great labor and ingenuity in attempting to discover internal meaning symbolized under many of the mythes; and even lays down the position, " che i primi uomini della Gentilità essendo stati semplicissimi, quanto i fanciulli, i quali per natura son veritieri: le prime favole non poterono finger nulla di falso: per lo che dovettero necessariamente essere *vere narrazioni.*" (See vol. v. p. 194; compare also p. 99, Axiom xvi.) If this position be meant simply to exclude the idea of designed imposture, it may for the most part be admitted; but Vico evidently intends something more. He thinks that there lies hid under the fables a basis of matter of fact — not literal but symbolized — which he draws out and exhibits under the form of a civil history of the divine and heroic times: a confusion of doctrine the more remarkable, since he distinctly tells us (in perfect conformity with the long passage above transcribed from him) that the special matter of

emotions, furnished to him at the same time a quasi-history and
quasi-philosophy: they filled up the vacuum of the unrecorded
past, and explained many of the puzzling incognita of the present.[1] Nor need we wonder that the same plausibility which cap-

---

these early mythes is "impossibility accredited as truth,"—"che la di lei propria materia è l' impossibile credibile" (p. 176, and still more fully in the first
rédaction of the *Scienza Nuova*, b. iii. c. 4; vol. iv. p. 187 of his Works).

When we read the *Canones Mythologici* of Vico (De Constantia Philologiæ,
Pars Posterior, c. xxx.; vol. iii. p. 363), and his explanation of the legends
of the Olympic gods, Herculês, Thêseus, Kadmus, etc., we see clearly that
the meaning which he professes to bring out is one previously put in by
himself.

There are some just remarks to the same purpose in Karl Ritter's *Vor-
halle Europäischer Völker — Geschichten*, Abschn. ii. p. 150 *seq.* (Berlin, 1820)
He too points out how much the faith of the old world (der Glaube der Vor-
welt) has become foreign to our minds, since the recent advances of "Politik
und Kritik," and how impossible it is for us to elicit history from their conceptions by our analysis, in cases where they have not distinctly laid it out
for us. The great length of this note prevents me from citing the passage:
and he seems to me also (like Vico) to pursue his own particular investigations in forgetfulness of the principle laid down by himself.

[1] O. Muller, in his *Prolegomena zu einer wissenschaftlichen Mythologie* (cap.
iv. p. 108), has pointed out the mistake of supposing that there existed originally some nucleus of pure reality as the starting-point of the mythes, and
that upon this nucleus fiction was superinduced afterwards: he maintains
that the real and the ideal were blended together in the primitive conception
of the mythes. Respecting the general state of mind out of which the mythos
grew, see especially pages 78 and 110 of that work, which is everywhere full
of instruction on the subject of the Grecian mythes, and is eminently suggestive, even where the positions of the author are not completely made out.

The short *Heldensage der Griechen by* Nitzsch (Kiel, 1842, t. v.) contains more
of just and original thought on the subject of the Grecian mythes than any
work with which I am acquainted. I embrace completely the subjective
point of view in which he regards them; and although I have profited much
from reading his short tract, I may mention that before I ever saw it, I had
enforced the same reasonings on the subject in an article in the Westminster
Review, May 1843, on the *Heroen-Geschichten* of Niebuhr.

Jacob Grimm, in the preface to his *Deutsche Mythologie* p. 1, 1st edit. Gött.
1835), pointedly insists on the distinction between "*Sage*" and history, as
well as upon the fact that the former has its chief root in religious belief.
"Legend and history (he says) are powers each by itself, adjoining indeed
on the confines, but having each its own separate and exclusive ground;"
also p. xxvii. of the same introduction.

A view substantially similar is adopted by William Grimm, the other of
the two distinguished brothers whose labors have so much elucidated Teu-

tivated his imagination and his feelings was sufficient to engender spontaneous belief; or rather, that no question as to truth or falsehood of the narrative suggested itself to his mind. His faith is ready, literal and uninquiring, apart from all thought of discriminating fact from fiction, or of ·detecting hidden and symbolized meaning; it is enough that what he hears be intrinsically plausible and seductive, and that there be no special cause to provoke doubt. And if indeed there were, the poet overrules such doubts by the holy and all-sufficient authority of the Muse, whose omniscience is the warrant for his recital, as her inspiration is the cause of his success.

The state of mind, and the relation of speaker to hearers, thus depicted, stand clearly marked in the terms and tenor of the ancient epic, if we only put a plain meaning upon what we read. The poet — like the prophet, whom he so much resembles — sings under heavenly guidance, inspired by the goddess to whom he has prayed for her assisting impulse : she puts the word into his mouth and the incidents into his mind : he is a privileged man, chosen as her organ and speaking from her revelations.[1] As the

tonic philology and antiquities. He examines the extent to which either historical matter of fact or historical names can be traced in the *Deutsche Heldensage*; and he comes to the conclusion that the former is next to nothing, the latter not considerable. He draws particular attention to the fact, that the audience for whom these poems were intended had not learned to distinguish history from poetry (W. Grimm, *Deutsche Heldensage*, pp. 8, 337, 342 345, 399, Gött. 1829).

[1] Hesiod, Theogon. 32. —

.... ἐνέπνευσαν δέ (the Muses) μοι αὐδὴν,
Θείην, ὡς κλείοιμι τά τ' ἐσσόμενα, πρό τ' ἐόντα,
Καί με κέλονθ' ὑμνεῖν μακάρων γένος αἰὲν ἐόντων, etc.

Odyss. xxii. 347; viii. 63, 73, 481, 489. Δημόδοκ'......ἤ σέ γε Μοῦσ' ἐδίδαξε, Διὸς παῖς, ἤ σέγ' Ἀπόλλων : that is, Demodocus has either been inspired as a poet by the Muse, or as a prophet by Apollo : for the Homeric Apollo is not the god of song. Kalchas the prophet receives his inspiration from Apollo, who confers upon him the same knowledge both of past and future as the Muses give to Hesiod (Iliad, i. 69) : —

Κάλχας Θεστορίδης, οἰωνοπόλων ὄχ' ἄριστος
Ὅς ἤδη τά τ' ἐόντα, τά τ' ἐσσόμενα, πρό τ' ἐόντα
Ἤν διὰ μαντοσύνην, τὴν οἱ πόρε Φοῖβος Ἀπόλλων.

Also Iliad, ii. 485.

Both the μάντις and the ἀοιδὸς are standing, recognized professions (Odyss. xvii. 383), like the physician and the carpenter, δημιόεργοι.

Muse grants the gift of song to whom she will, so she sometimes in her anger snatches it away, and the most consummate human genius is then left silent and helpless.[1] It is true that these expressions, of the Muse inspiring and the poet singing a tale of past times, have passed from the ancient epic to compositions produced under very different circumstances, and have now degenerated into unmeaning forms of speech; but they gained currency originally in their genuine and literal acceptation. If poets had from the beginning written or recited, the predicate of singing would never have been ascribed to them; nor would it have ever become customary to employ the name of the Muse as a die to be stamped on licensed fiction, unless the practice had begun when her agency was invoked and hailed in perfect good faith. Belief, the fruit of deliberate inquiry and a rational scrutiny of evidence, is in such an age unknown: the simple faith of the time slides in unconsciously, when the imagination and feeling are exalted; and inspired authority is at once understood, easily admitted, and implicitly confided in.

The word mythe ($\mu\tilde{\upsilon}\vartheta o\varsigma$, fabula, story), in its original meaning, signified simply a statement or current narrative, without any connotative implication either of truth or falsehood. Subsequently the meaning of the word (in Latin and English as well as in Greek) changed, and came to carry with it the idea of an old personal narrative, always uncertified, sometimes untrue or avowedly fictitious.[2] And this change was the result of a silent alteration in the mental state of the society, — of a transition on the

---

[1] Iliad, ii. 599.

[2] In this later sense it stands pointedly opposed to $\iota\sigma\tau o\rho\iota\alpha$, history, which seems originally to have designated matter of fact, present and seen by the describer, or the result of his personal inquiries (see Herodot. i. 1; Verrius Flacc. ap. Aul. Gell. v. 18; Eusebius, Hist. Eccles. iii. 12; and the observations of Dr. Jortin, Remarks on Ecclesiastical History, vol. i. p. 59).

The original use of the word $\lambda o\gamma o\varsigma$ was the same as that of $\mu\tilde{\upsilon}\vartheta o\varsigma$ — a current tale, true or false, as the case might be; and the term designating a person much conversant with the old legends ($\lambda o\gamma\iota o\varsigma$) is derived from it (Herod. i. 1; ii. 3). Hekatæus and Herodotus both use $\lambda o\gamma o\varsigma$ in this sense. Herodotus calls both Æsop and Hekatæus $\lambda o\gamma o\pi o\iota o\iota$ (ii. 134–143).

Aristotle (Metaphys. i. p. 8, ed. Brandis) seems to use $\mu\tilde{\upsilon}\vartheta o\varsigma$ in this sense, where he says — $\delta\iota o\ \kappa\alpha\iota\ \phi\iota\lambda o\mu\upsilon\vartheta o\varsigma\ o\ \phi\iota\lambda o\sigma o\phi o\varsigma\ \pi\omega\varsigma\ \epsilon\sigma\tau\iota\nu\cdot\ o\ \gamma\grave{\alpha}\rho\ \mu\tilde{\upsilon}\vartheta o\varsigma\ \sigma\upsilon\gamma\kappa\epsilon\iota\tau\alpha\iota\ \epsilon\kappa\ \vartheta\alpha\upsilon\mu\alpha\sigma\iota\omega\nu$, etc. In the same treatise (xi. p. 254), he uses it to signify fabulous amplification and transformation of a doctrine true in the main.

part of the superior minds (and more or less on the part of all) to a stricter and more elevated canon of credibility, in conse quence of familiarity with recorded history, and its essential tests affirmative as well as negative. Among the original hearers of the mythes, all such tests were unknown; they had not yet learn ed the lesson of critical disbelief; the mythe passed unquestioned from the mere fact of its currency, and from its harmony with existing sentiments and preconceptions. The very circumstances which contributed to rob it of literal belief in after-time, strength ened its hold upon the mind of the Homeric man. He looked for wonders and unusual combinations in the past; he expected to hear of gods, heroes and men, moving and operating together upon earth; he pictured to himself the fore-time as a theatre in which the gods interfered directly, obviously and frequently, for the protection of their favorites and the punishment of their foes. The rational conception, then only dawning in his mind, of a sys tematic course of nature was absorbed by this fervent and lively faith. And if he could have been supplied with as perfect and philosophical a history of his own real past time, as we are now enabled to furnish with regard to the last century of England or France, faithfully recording all the successive events, and ac counting for them by known positive laws, but introducing no special interventions of Zeus and Apollo — such a history would have appeared to him not merely unholy and unimpressive, but destitute of all plausibility or title to credence. It would have provoked in him the same feeling of incredulous aversion as a description of the sun (to repeat the previous illustration) in a modern book on scientific astronomy.

To us these mythes are interesting fictions; to the Homeric and Hesiodic audience they were "rerum divinarum et huma narum scientia," — an aggregate of religious, physical and his torical revelations, rendered more captivating, but not less true and real, by the bright coloring and fantastic shapes in which they were presented. Throughout the whole of "mythe-bearing Hel las"[1] they formed the staple of the uninstructed Greek mind,

---

[1] M. Ampère, in his *Histoire Littéraire de la France* (ch. viii. v. i. p. 310) distinguishes the Saga (which corresponds as nearly as possible with the Greek μῦθος, λόγος, ἐπιχώριος λόγος), as a special product of the intellect.

upon which history and philosophy were by so slow degrees superinduced; and they continued to be the aliment of ordinary thought and conversation, even after history and philosophy had partially supplanted the mythical faith among the leading men, and disturbed it more or less in the ideas of all. The men, the women, and the children of the remote dêmes and villages of Greece, to whom Thucydidês, Hippocratês, Aristotle, or Hipparchus were unknown, still continued to dwell upon the local fables which formed their religious and patriotic antiquity. And Pausanias, even in his time, heard everywhere divine or heroic legends yet alive, precisely of the type of the old epic; he found the conceptions of religious and mythical faith, coëxistent with those of positive science, and contending against them at more or less of odds, according to the temper of the individual. Now it is the remarkable characteristic of the Homeric age, that no such coëxistence or contention had yet begun. The religious and mythical point of view covers, for the most part, all the phænomena of nature; while the conception of invariable sequence exists only in the background, itself personified under the name of the Mœræ, or Fates, and produced generally as an exception to the omnipotence of Zeus for all ordinary purposes.

---

not capable of being correctly designated either as history, or as fiction, or as philosophy: —

"Il est un pays, la Scandinavie, où la tradition racontée s'est développée plus complètement qu'ailleurs, où ses produits ont été plus soigneusement recueillis et mieux conservés: dans ce pays, lis ont reçu un nom particulier, dont l'équivalent exact ne se trouve pas hors des langues Germaniques: c'est le mot *Saga, Sage*, ce *qu'on dit, ce qu'on raconte*, — la tradition orale. Si l'on prend ce mot non dans une acception restreinte, mais dans le sens général où le prenait Niebuhr quand il l'appliquoit, par exemple, aux traditions populaires qui ont pu fournir à Tite Live une portion de son histoire, la Saga doit être comptée parmi les produits spontanés de l'imagination humaine. La Saga a son existence propre comme la poësie, comme l'histoire, comme le roman. Elle n'est pas la poësie, parcequ'elle n'est pas chantée, mais parlée: elle n'est pas l'histoire, parcequ'elle est denuée de critique; elle n'est pas le roman, parcequ'elle est sincère, parcequ'elle a foi à ce qu'elle raconte. Elle n'invente pas, mais répète: elle peut se tromper, mais elle ne ment jamais. Ce récit souvent merveilleux, que personne ne fabrique sciemment, et que tout le monde altère et falsifie sans le vouloir, qui se perpétue à la manière des chants primitifs et populaires, — ce récit, quand il se rapporte non à un héros, mais à un saint, s'appelle une légende."

Voluntary agents, visible and invisible, impel and govern everything. Moreover this point of view is universal throughout the
community, — adopted with equal fervor, and carried out with
equal consistency, by the loftiest minds and by the lowest. The
great man of that day is he who, penetrated like others with the
general faith, and never once imagining any other system of nature than the agency of these voluntary Beings, can clothe them
in suitable circumstances and details, and exhibit in living body
and action those types which his hearers dimly prefigure. Such
men were the authors of the Iliad and the Odyssey; embodying
in themselves the whole measure of intellectual excellence which
their age was capable of feeling: to us, the first of poets — but
to their own public, religious teachers, historians, and philosophers besides — inasmuch as all that then represented history
and philosophy was derived from those epical effusions and from
others homogeneous with them. Herodotus recognizes Homer
and Hesiod as the main authors of Grecian belief respecting the
names and generations, the attributes and agency, the forms and
the worship of the gods.[1]

History, philosophy, etc., properly so called and conforming to
our ideas (of which the subsequent Greeks were the first crea-
tors), never belonged to more than a comparatively small number of thinking men, though their influence indirectly affected
more or less the whole national mind. But when positive science
and criticism, and the idea of an invariable sequence of events,
came to supplant in the more vigorous intellects the old mythical
creed of omnipresent personification, an inevitable scission was
produced between the instructed few and the remaining community. The opposition between the scientific and the religious
point of view was not slow in manifesting itself: in general language, indeed, both might seem to stand together, but in every
particular case the admission of one involved the rejection of the
other. According to the theory which then became predominant, the course of nature was held to move invariably on, by
powers and attributes of its own, unless the gods chose to interfere and reverse it; but they had the power of interfering as
often and to as great an extent as they thought fit. Here the

---

[1] Herodot. ii. 53.

question was at once opened, respecting a great variety of particular phænomena, whether they were to be regarded as natural
or miraculous. No constant or discernible test could be suggested to discriminate the two : every man was called upon to settle
the doubt for himself, and each settled it according to the extent
of his knowledge, the force of his logic, the state of his health,
his hopes, his fears, and many other considerations affecting his
separate conclusion. In a question thus perpetually arising, and
full of practical consequences, instructed minds, like Periklês,
Thucydidês, and Euripidês, tended more and more to the scientific point of view,[1] in cases where the general public were constantly gravitating towards the religious.

---

[1] See Plutarch, Perikl. capp. 5, 32, 38; Cicero, De Republ. i. 15–16, ed.
Maii.

The phytologist Theophrastus, in his valuable collection of facts respecting vegetable organization, is often under the necessity of opposing his scientific interpretation of curious incidents in tne vegetable world to the
religious interpretation of them which he found current. Anomalous phænomena in the growth or decay of trees were construed as signs from the
gods, and submitted to a prophet for explanation (see Histor. Plantar. ii. 3 ,
iv. 16 ; v. 3).

We may remark, however, that the old faith had still a certain hold over
his mind. In commenting on the story of the willow-tree at Philippi, and
the venerable old plane-tree at Antandros (more than sixty feet high, and
requiring four men to grasp it round in the girth), having been blown down
by a high wind, and afterwards spontaneously resuming their erect posture,
he offers some explanations how such a phænomenon might have happened,
but he admits, at the end, that there *may* be something extra-natural in the
case, Ἀλλὰ ταῦτα μὲν ἴσως ἔξω φυσικῆς αἰτίας ἐστιν, etc. (De Caus. Plant. v.
4) : see a similar miracle in reference to the cedar-tree of Vespasian (Tacit.
Hist. ii. 78).

Euripidês, in his lost tragedy called Μελανίππη Σοφή, placed in the mouth
of Melanippê a formal discussion and confutation of the whole doctrine of
τέρατα, or supernatural indications (Dionys. Halicar. Ars Rhetoric. p. 300–
356, Reisk). Compare the Fables of Phædrus, iii. 3 ; Plutarch, Sept. Sap.
Conviv. ch. 3. p. 149; and the curious philosophical explanation by which
the learned men of Alexandria tranquillized the alarms of the vulgar, on
occasion of the serpent said to have been seen entwined round the head of
the crucified Kleomenês (Plutarch, Kleomen. c. 39).

It is one part of the duty of an able physician, according to the Hippo-
cratic treatise called Prognosticon (c. 1. t. ii. p. 112, ed. Littré), when he
visits his patient, to examine whether there is anything divine in the malady,
ἅμα δὲ καὶ εἴ τι θεῖον ἔνεστιν ἐν τῇσι νούσοισι : this, however, does not agree

The age immediately prior to this unsettled condition of thought is the really mythopœic age; in which the creative faculties of the society know no other employment, and the mass of the society no other mental demand. The perfect expression of such a period, in its full peculiarity and grandeur, is to be found in the Iliad and Odyssey, — poems of which we cannot determine the exact date, but which seem both to have existed prior to the first Olympiad, 776 B. C., our earliest trustworthy mark of Grecian time. For some time after that event, the mythopœic tendencies continued in vigor (Arktinus, Leschês, Eumêlus, and seemingly most of the Hesiodic poems, fall within or shortly after the first century of recorded Olympiads) ; but from and after this first century, we may trace the operation of causes which gradually enfeebled and narrowed them, altering the point of view from which the mythes were looked at. What these causes were, it will be necessary briefly to intimate.

with the memorable doctrine laid down in the treatise, De Aëre, Locis et Aquis (c. 22. p. 78, ed. Littré), and cited hereafter, in this chapter. Nor does Galen seem to have regarded it as harmonizing with the general views of Hippocratês. In the excellent Prolegomena of Mr. Littré to his edition of Hippocratês (t. i. p. 76) will be found an inedited scholium, wherein the opinion of Baccheius and other physicians is given, that the affections of the plague were to be looked upon as divine, inasmuch as the disease came from God ; and also the opinion of Xenophôn, the friend of Praxagoras, that the "genus of days of crisis" in fever was divine; "For (said Xenophôn) just as the Dioskuri, being gods, appear to the mariner in the storm and bring him salvation, so also do the days of crisis, when they arrive, in fever." Galen, in commenting upon this doctrine of Xenophôn, says that the author "has expressed his own individual feeling, but has no way set forth the opinion of Hippocratês:" Ὁ δὲ τῶν κρισίμων γένος ἡμερῶν εἰπὼν εἶναι θεῖον, ἑαυτοῦ τι πάθος ὡμολόγησεν· οὐ μὴν Ἱπποκράτους γε τὴν γνώμην ἔδειξεν (Galen, Opp. t. v. p. 120, ed. Basil).

The comparison of the Dioskuri appealed to by Xenophôn is a precise reproduction of their function as described in the Homeric Hymn (Hymn xxxiii. 10) : his personification of the "days of crisis" introduces the old religious agency to fill up a gap in his medical science.

I annex an illustration from the Hindoo vein of thought:—"It is a rule with the Hindoos to bury, and not to burn, the bodies of those who die of the small-pox : for (say they) the small pox is not only caused by the goddess Davey, but is, in fact, *Davey herself;* and to burn the body of a person affected with this disease, is, in reality, neither more nor less than *to burn the goddess.*" (Sleeman, Rambles and Recollections, etc., vol. i. ch. xxv. p. 221.)

The foremost and most general of all is, the expansive force of Grecian intellect itself, — a quality in which this remarkable people stand distinguished from all their neighbors and contemporaries. Most, if not all nations have had mythes, but no nation except the Greeks have imparted to them immortal charm and universal interest ; and the same mental capacities, which raised the great men of the poetic age to this exalted level, also pushed forward their successors to outgrow the early faith in which the mythes had been generated and accredited.

One great mark, as well as means, of such intellectual expansion, was the habit of attending to, recording, and combining, positive and present facts, both domestic and foreign. In the genuine Grecian epic, the theme was an unknown and aoristic past ; but even as early as the Works and Days of Hesiod, the present begins to figure : the man who tills the earth appears in his own solitary nakedness, apart from gods and heroes — bound indeed by serious obligations to the gods, but contending against many difficulties which are not to be removed by simple reliance on their help. The poet denounces his age in the strongest terms as miserable, degraded and profligate, and looks back with reverential envy to the extinct heroic races who fought at Troy and Thêbes. Yet bad as the present time is, the Muse condescends to look at it along with him, and to prescribe rules for human life— with the assurance that if a man be industrious, frugal, provident, just and friendly in his dealings, the gods will recompense him with affluence and security. Nor does the Muse disdain, while holding out such promise, to cast herself into the most homely details of present existence and to give advice thoroughly practical and calculating. Men whose minds were full of the heroes of Homer, called Hesiod in contempt the poet of the Helots ; and the contrast between the two is certainly a remarkable proof of the tendency of Greek poetry towards the present and the positive.

Other manifestations of the same tendency become visible in the age of Archilochus (B. C. 680–660). In an age when metrical composition and the living voice are the only means whereby the productive minds of a community make themselves felt, the invention of a new metre, new forms of song and recitation, or diversified accompaniments, constitute an epoch. The iambic, elegiac, choric, and lyric poetry, from Archilochus downwards, all indicate purposes in the poet, and impressibilities of the hearers, very different from those of the ancient epic. In all of them the personal feeling of the poet and the specialties of present time and place, are brought prominently forward, while in the Homeric hexameter the poet is a mere nameless organ of the historical Muse — the hearers are content to learn, believe, and feel, the incidents of a foregone world, and the tale is hardly less suitable to one time and place than to another. The iambic metre (we are told) was first suggested to Archilochus by the bitterness of his own private antipathies; and the mortal wounds inflicted by his lampoons, upon the individuals against whom they were directed, still remain attested, though the verses themselves have perished. It was the metre (according to the well-known judgment of Aristotle) most nearly approaching to common speech, and well suited both to the coarse vein of sentiment, and to the smart and emphatic diction of its inventor.[1] Simonidês of Amorgus, the younger contemporary of Archilochus, employed the same metre, with less bitterness, but with an anti-heroic tendency not less decided. His remaining fragments present a mixture of teaching and sarcasm, having a distinct bearing upon actual life,[2] and carrying out the spirit which partially appears in the Hesiodic Works and Days. Of Alkæus and Sapphô, though unfortunately we are compelled to speak of them upon hearsay only, we know enough to satisfy us that their own personal sentiments and sufferings, their relations private or public

---

[1] Horat. de Art. Poet. 79 : —

" Archilochum proprio rabies armavit Iambo," etc.

Compare Epist. i. 19, 23, and Epod. vi. 12 ; Aristot. Rhetor. iii. 8, 7, and Poetic. c. 4 — also Synesius de Somniis — ὥσπερ Ἀλκαῖος καὶ Ἀρχίλοχος, οἱ δεδαπανήκασι τὴν εὐστομίαν εἰς τὸν οἰκεῖον βίον ἑκάτερος (Alcæi Fragment. Halle, 1810, p. 205). Quintilian speaks in striking language of the power of expression manifested by Archilochus (x. 1, 60).

[2] Simonidês of Amorgus touches briefly, but in a tone of contempt upon the Trojan war — γυναικὸς οὕνεκ' ἀμφιδηριωμένους (Simonid. Fragm. 8. p. 36. v. 118); he seems to think it absurd that so destructive a struggle should have taken place "pro unâ mulierculâ," to use the phrase of Mr. Payne Knight.

with the contemporary world, constituted the soul of those short
effusions which gave them so much celebrity :[1] and in the few remains of the elegiac poets preserved to us — Kallinus, Mimner
mus, Tyrtæus — the impulse of some present motive or circum
stance is no less conspicuous. The same may also be said of So
lôn, Theognis and Phokylidês, who preach, encourage, censure, or
complain, but do not recount — and in whom a profound ethical
sensibility, unknown to the Homeric poems, manifests itself: the
form of poetry (to use the words of Solôn himself) is made the
substitute for the public speaking of the agora.[2]

Doubtless all these poets made abundant use of the ancient
mythes, but it was by turning them to present account, in the
way of illustration, or flattery, or contrast, — a tendency which
we may usually detect even in the compositions of Pindar, in
spite of the lofty and heroic strain which they breathe throughout. That narrative or legendary poetry still continued to be
composed during the seventh and sixth centuries before the Christian æra is not to be questioned; but it exhibited the old epical

---

[1] See Quintilian, x. 1, 63. Horat. Od. i. 32; ii. 13. Aristot. Polit. iii. 10,
4. Dionys. Halic. observes (Vett. Scriptt. Censur. v. p. 421) respecting
Alkæus — πολλαχοῦ γοῦν τὸ μέτρον εἴ τις περιέλοι, ῥητορικὴν ἂν εὕροι
πολιτείαν; and Strabo (xiii. p. 617), τὰ στασιωτικὰ καλούμενα τοῦ 'Αλκαίου
ποιήματα.

There was a large dash of sarcasm and homely banter aimed at neighbors
and contemporaries in the poetry of Sapphô, apart from her impassioned
love-songs — ἄλλως σκώπτει τὸν ἄγροικον νύμφιον καὶ τὸν θυρωρὸν τὸν ἐν
τοῖς γάμοις, εὐτελέστατα καὶ ἐν πέζοις ὀνόμασι μᾶλλον ἢ ἐν ποιητικοῖς. ῞Ωστε
αὐτῆς μᾶλλόν ἐστι τὰ ποιήματα ταῦτα διαλέγ:σθαι ἢ ἄδειν · οὐδ' ἂν ἅρμοσαι
πρὸς τὸν χόρον ἢ πρὸς τὴν λύραν, εἰ μή τις εἴη χόρος διαλεκτικός (Dêmêtr.
Phaler, De Interpret. c. 167).

Compare also Herodot. ii. 135, who mentions the satirical talent of Sapphô, employed against her brother for an extravagance about the courtezan
Rhodôpis.

[2] Solôn, Fragm. iv. 1, ed. Schneidewin : —

Αὐτὸς κήρυξ ἦλθον ἀφ' ἱμερτῆς Σαλαμῖνος
Κόσμον ἐπέων ᾠδὴν ἀντ' ἀγορῆς θέμενος, etc.

See *Brandis*, Handbuch der Griechischen Philosophie, sect. xxiv.–xxv.
Plato states that Solôn, in his old age, engaged in the composition of an
epic poem, which he left unfinished, on the subject of the supposed island
of Atlantis and Attica (Plato, Timæus, p. 21, and Kritias, p. 113). Plutarch, Solôn, c. 31.

character without the old epical genius; both the inspiration of
the composer and the sympathies of the audience had become
more deeply enlisted in the world before them, and disposed to
fasten on incidents of their own actual experience. From Solôn
and Theognis we pass to the abandonment of all metrical restrictions and to the introduction of prose writing, — a fact, the importance of which it is needless to dwell upon, — marking as well
the increased familiarity with written records, as the commencement of a separate branch of literature for the intellect, apart
from the imagination and emotions wherein the old legends had
their exclusive root.

Egypt was first unreservedly opened to the Greeks during
the reign of Psammetichus, about B. C. 660; gradually it became
much frequented by them for military or commercial purposes,
or for simple curiosity, and enlarged the range of their thoughts
and observations, while it also imparted to them that vein of
mysticism, which overgrew the primitive simplicity of the Homeric religion, and of which I have spoken in a former chapter
They found in it a long-established civilization, colossal wonders
of architecture, and a certain knowledge of astronomy and geo-
metry, elementary indeed, but in advance of their own. Moreover
it was a portion of their present world, and it contributed to form
in them an interest for noting and describing the actual realities
before them. A sensible progress is made in the Greek mind
during the two centuries from B. C. 700 to B. C. 500, in the record and arrangement of historical facts: an *historical sense* arises
in the superior intellects, and some idea of evidence as a discriminating test between fact and fiction. And this progressive tendency was further stimulated by increased communication and
by more settled and peaceful social relations between the various
members of the Hellenic world, to which may be added material
improvements, purchased at the expense of a period of turbu-
lence and revolution, in the internal administration of each separate state. The Olympic, Pythian, Nemean, and Isthmian games
became frequented by visitors from the most distant parts of
Greece : the great periodical festival in the island of Dêlos brought
together the citizens of every Ionic community, with their wives
and children, and an ample display of wealth and ornaments.[1]

---

[1] Homer, Hymn. ad Apollin. 155; Thucydid. iii. 104.

Numerous and flourishing colonies were founded in Sicily, the
south of Italy, the coasts of Epirus and of the Euxine Sea: the
Phokæans explored the whole of the Adriatic, established Mas-
salia, and penetrated even as far as the south of Ibêria, with
which they carried on a lucrative commerce.[1] The geographical
ideas of the Greeks were thus both expanded and rectified : the
first preparation of a map, by Anaximander the disciple of Thalês,
is an epoch in the history of science. We may note the ridicule
bestowed by Herodotus both upon the supposed people called
Hyperboreans and upon the idea of a circumfluous ocean-stream,
as demonstrating the progress of the age in this department of
inquiry.[2] And even earlier than Herodotus, Xanthus had noticed the occurrence of fossil marine productions in the interior
of Asia Minor, which led him to reflections on the changes of the
earth's surface with respect to land and water.[3]

If then we look down the three centuries and a half which
elapsed between the commencement of the Olympic æra and the
age of Herodotus and Thucydidês, we shall discern a striking
advance in the Greeks, — ethical, social and intellectual. Positive history and chronology has not only been created, but in the
case of Thucydidês, the qualities necessary to the historiographer,
in their application to recent events, have been developed with
a degree of perfection never since surpassed. Men's minds have
assumed a gentler as well as a juster cast ; and acts come to be
criticized with reference to their bearing on the internal happiness of a well-regulated community, as well as upon the stand-

---

[1] Herodot. i. 163.
[2] Herodot. iv. 36. γελῶ δὲ ὁρέων Γῆς περιόδους γράψαντας πολλοὺς ἤδη,
καὶ οὐδένα νόον ἔχοντας ἐξηγησάμενον· οἱ Ὠκέανόν τε ῥέοντα γράφουσι πέριξ
τὴν γῆν, ἐοῦσαν κυκλοτερέα ὡς ἀπὸ τόρνου, etc., a remark probably directed
against Hekatæus.
    Respecting the map of Anaximander, Strabo, i. p. 7; Diogen. Laërt. ii.
1; Agathemer ap. Geograph. Minor. i. 1. πρῶτος ἐτόλμησε τὴν οἰκουμένην
ἐν πίνακι γράψαι.
    Aristagoras of Milêtus, who visited Sparta to solicit aid for the revolted
Ionians against Darius, brought with him a brazen tablet or map, by means
of which he exhibited the relative position of places in the Persian empire
(Herodot. v. 49).
[3] Xanthus ap. Strabo. i. p. 50; xii. p. 579. Compare Creuzer, Fragmenta
Xanthi, p. 162.

ing harmony of fraternal states. While Thucydidês treats the habitual and licensed piracy, so coolly alluded to in the Homeric poems, as an obsolete enormity, many of the acts described in the old heroic and Theogonic legends were found not less repugnant to this improved tone of feeling. The battles of the gods with the Giants and Titans, — the castration of Uranus by his son Kronus, — the cruelty, deceit and licentiousness, often supposed both in the gods and heroes, provoked strong disapprobation. And the language of the philosopher Xenophanês, who composed both elegiac and iambic poems for the express purpose of denouncing such tales, is as vehement and unsparing as that of the Christian writers, who, eight centuries afterwards, attacked the whole scheme of paganism.[1]

Nor was it alone as an ethical and social critic that Xenophanês stood distinguished. He was one of a great and eminent triad — Thalês and Pythagoras being the others — who, in the sixth century before the Christian æra, first opened up those veins of speculative philosophy which occupied afterwards so large a portion of Grecian intellectual energy. Of the material differences between the three I do not here speak ; I regard them only in reference to the Homeric and Hesiodic philosophy which preceded them, and from which all three deviated by a step, perhaps the most remarkable in all the history of philosophy. In the scheme of ideas common to Homer and to the Hesiodic Theogony (as has been already stated), we find nature distributed into a variety of personal agencies, administered according to the free-will of different Beings more or less analogous to man — each of these Beings having his own character, attributes and powers, his own sources of pain and pleasure, and his own especial sympathies or antipathies with human individuals ; each being determined to act or forbear, to grant favor or inflict injury in his own department of phænomena, according as men, or perhaps other Beings analogous to himself, might conciliate or offend him. The Gods, properly so called, (those who bore a proper name and received some public or family worship,) were the most commanding and capital members amidst this vast network of agents

---

[1] Xenophan. ap. Sext. Empiric. adv. Mathemat. ix. 193. Fragm. 1. Poet. Græc. ed. Schneidewin. Diogen. Laërt. ix. 18.

visible and invisible, spread over the universe.[1] The whole view
of nature was purely religious and subjective, the spontaneous
suggestion of the early mind. It proceeded from the instinctive
tendencies of the feelings and imagination to transport, to the
world without, the familiar type of free-will and conscious personal action : above all, it took deep hold of the emotions, from
the widely extended sympathy which it so perpetually called
forth between man and nature.[2]

The first attempt to disenthral the philosophic intellect from
this all-personifying religious faith, and to constitute a method of
interpreting nature distinct from the spontaneous inspirations of
untaught minds, is to be found in Thalês, Xenophanês and Pythagoras, in the sixth century before the Christian æra. It is in
them that we first find the idea of Person tacitly set aside or
limited, and an impersonal Nature conceived as the object of
study. The divine husband and wife, Oceanus and Têthys,
parents of many gods and of the Oceanic nymphs, together with
the avenging goddess Styx, are translated into the material substance *water*, or, as we ought rather to say, the Fluid : and
Thalês set himself to prove that water was the primitive element,
out of which all the different natural substances had been formed.[3]
He, as well as Xenophanês and Pythagoras, started the problem
of physical philosophy, with its objective character and invariable
laws, to be discoverable by a proper and methodical application
of the human intellect. The Greek word Φύσις, denoting *nature*,
and its derivatives *physics* and *physiology*, unknown in that large
sense to Homer or Hesiod, as well as the word *Kosmos*, to denote
the mundane system, first appears with these philosophers.[4] The

---

[1] Hesiod, Opp. Di. 122; Homer, Hymn. ad Vener. 260.

[2] A defence of the primitive faith, on this ground, is found in Plutarch,
Quæstion. Sympos. vii. 4, 4, p. 703.

[3] Aristotel. Metaphys. i. 3.

[4] Plutarch, Placit. Philos. ii. 1; also Stobæus, Eclog. Physic. i. 22, where
the difference between the Homeric expressions and those of the subsequent
philosophers is seen. Damm, Lexic. Homeric. v. Φύσις; Alexander von
Humboldt, *Kosmos*, p. 76, the note 9 on page 62 of that admirable work.

The title of the treatises of the early philosophers (Melissus, Dêmokritus,
Parmenidês, Empedoclês, Alkmæôn, etc.) was frequently Περὶ Φύσεως (Galen.
Opp. tom. i. p. 56, ed. Basil).

elemental analysis of Thalês — the one unchangeable cosmic substance, varying only in appearance, but not in reality, as suggested by Xenophanês, — and the geometrical and arithmetical combinations of Pythagoras, — all these were different ways of approaching the explanation of physical phænomena, and each gave rise to a distinct school or succession of philosophers. But they all agreed in departing from the primitive method, and in recognizing determinate properties, invariable sequences, and objective truth, in nature — either independent of willing or designing agents, or serving to these latter at once as an indispensable subject-matter and as a limiting condition. Xenophanês disclaimed openly all knowledge respecting the gods, and pronounced that no man could have any means of ascertaining when he was right, and when he was wrong, in affirmations respecting them :[1] while Pythagoras represents in part the scientific tendencies of his age, in part also the spirit of mysticism and of special fraternities for religious and ascetic observance, which became diffused throughout Greece in the sixth century before the Christian æra. This was another point which placed him in antipathy with the simple, unconscious and demonstrative faith of the old poets, as well as with the current legends.

If these distinguished men, when they ceased to follow the primitive instinct of tracing the phænomena of nature to personal and designing agents, passed over, not at once to induction and observation, but to a misemployment of abstract words, substituting metaphysical *eideóla* in the place of polytheism, and to an exaggerated application of certain narrow physical theories — we must remember that nothing else could be expected from the scanty stock of facts then accessible, and that the most profound study of the human mind points out such transition as an inevitable law of intellectual progress.[2] At present, we have to compare

---

[1] Xenophan. ap. Sext. Empiric. vii. 50 ; viii. 326. —

Καὶ τὸ μὲν οὖν σαφὲς οὔτις ἀνὴρ ἴδεν, οὔτε τίς ἐστιν
Εἰδὼς ἀμφὶ θεῶν τε καὶ ἅσσα λέγω περὶ πάντων·
Εἰ γὰρ καὶ τὰ μάλιστα τύχοι τετελεσμένον εἰπὼν,
Αὐτὸς ὅμως οὐκ οἶδε, δόκος δ' ἐπὶ πᾶσι τέτυκται.

Compare Aristotel. De Xenophane, Zenone, et Georgiâ, capp. 1-2.

[2] See the treatise of M. Auguste Comte (*Cours de Philosophie Positive*), and

them only with that state of the Greek mind[1] which they partially
superseded, and with which they were in decided opposition. The
rudiments of physical science were conceived and developed
among superior men; but the religious feeling of the mass was
averse to them; and the aversion, though gradually mitigated,
never wholly died away. Some of the philosophers were not
backward in charging others with irreligion, while the multitude
seems to have felt the same sentiment more or less towards all —
or towards that postulate of constant sequences, with determinate
conditions of occurrence, which scientific study implies, and which
they could not reconcile with their belief in the agency of the
gods, to whom they were constantly praying for special succor
and blessings.

The discrepancy between the scientific and the religious point
of view was dealt with differently by different philosophers. Thus
Socratês openly admitted it, and assigned to each a distinct and
independent province. He distributed phænomena into two classes: one, wherein the connection of antecedent and consequent was
invariable and ascertainable by human study, and therefore future results accessible to a well-instructed foresight; the other,
and those, too, the most comprehensive and important, which the
gods had reserved for themselves and their own unconditional
agency, wherein there was no invariable or ascertainable sequence, and where the result could only be foreknown by some
omen, prophecy, or other special inspired communication from
themselves. Each of these classes was essentially distinct, and
required to be looked at and dealt with in a manner radically in-
compatible with the other. Socratês held it wrong to apply the
scientific interpretation to the latter, or the theological interpretation to the former. Physics and astronomy, in his opinion,

---

his doctrine of the three successive stages of the human mind in reference to
scientific study — the theological, the metaphysical, and the positive; — a
doctrine laid down generally in his first lecture (vol. i. p. 4–12), and largely
applied and illustrated throughout his instructive work. It is also re-stated
and elucidated by Mr. John Stuart Mill, in his System of Logic, Ratiocinative
and Inductive, vol. ii. p. 610.

[1] "Human wisdom (ἀνθρωπίνη σοφία), as contrasted with the primitive
theology (οἱ ἀρχαῖοι καὶ διατρίβοντες περὶ τὰς θεολογίας)," to take the words
of Aristotle (Meteorolog. ii. 1. pp. 41–42, ed. Tauchnitz).

belonged to the divine class of phænomena, in which human research was insane, fruitless, and impious.[1]

On the other hand, Hippocratês, the contemporary of Socratês, denied the discrepancy, and merged into one those two classes of phænomena, — the divine and the scientifically determinable, — which the latter had put asunder. Hippocratês treated all phænomena as at once both divine and scientifically determinable. In discussing certain peculiar bodily disorders found among the Scythians, he observes, "The Scythians themselves ascribe the cause of this to God, and reverence and bow down to such sufferers, each man fearing that he may suffer the like; and I myself think too that these affections, as well as all others, are divine : no one among them is either more divine or more human than another, but all are on the same footing, and all divine; nevertheless each of them has its own physical conditions, and not one occurs without such physical conditions."[2]

---

[1] Xenoph. Memor. i. 1, 6–9. Τὰ μὲν ἀναγκαῖα (Σωκράτης) συνεβούλευε καὶ πράττειν, ὡς ἐνόμιζεν ἄριστ᾽ ἂν πραχθῆναι· περὶ δὲ τῶν ἀδήλων ὅπως ἀποβήσοιτο, μαντευσομένους ἔπεμπεν, εἰ ποιητέα. Καὶ τοὺς μέλλοντας οἴκους τε καὶ πόλεις καλῶς οἰκήσειν μαντικῆς ἔφη προσδεῖσθαι· τεκτονικὸν μὲν γὰρ ἢ χαλκευτικὸν ἢ γεωργικὸν ἢ ἀνθρώπων ἀρχικὸν, ἢ τῶν τοιούτων ἔργων ἐξεταστικὸν, ἢ λογιστικὸν, ἢ οἰκονομικὸν, ἢ στρατηγικὸν γενέσθαι, πάντα τὰ τοιαῦτα, μαθήματα καὶ ἀνθρώπου γνώμῃ αἱρετέα, ἐνόμιζεν εἶναι· τὰ δὲ μέγιστα τῶν ἐν τούτοις ἔφη τοὺς θεοὺς ἑαυτοῖς καταλείπεσθαι, ὧν οὐδὲν δῆλον εἶναι τοῖς ἀνθρώποις.........Τοὺς δὲ μηδὲν τῶν τοιούτων οἰομένους εἶναι δαιμόνιον, ἀλλὰ πάντα τῆς ἀνθρωπίνης γνώμης, δαιμονᾷν ἔφη· δαιμονᾷν δὲ καὶ τοὺς μαντευομένους ἃ τοῖς ἀνθρώποις ἔδωκαν οἱ θεοὶ μαθοῦσι διακρίνειν. ....Ἔφη δὲ δεῖν, ἃ μὲν μαθόντας ποιεῖν ἔδωκαν οἱ θεοί, μανθάνειν · ἃ δὲ μὴ δῆλα τοῖς ἀνθρώποις ἐστι, πειρᾶσθαι διὰ μαντικῆς παρὰ τῶν θεῶν πυνθάνεσθαι· τοὺς θεοὺς γὰρ, οἷς ἂν ὦσιν ἵλεω, σημαίνειν. Compare also Memorab. iv. 7. 7; and Cyropæd. i. 6, 3, 23–46.

Physical and astronomical phænomena are classified by Socratês among the divine class, interdicted to human study (Memor. i. 1, 13): τὰ θεῖα or δαιμόνια as supposed to τἀνθρώπεια. Plato (Phileb. c. 16; Legg. x. p. 886–889 ; xii. p. 967) held the sun and stars to be gods, each animated with its special soul : he allowed astronomical investigation to the extent necessary for avoiding blasphemy respecting these beings — μέχρι τοῦ μὴ βλασφημεῖν περὶ αὐτά (vii. 821).

[2] Hippocratês, De Aëre, Locis et Aquis, c. 22 (p. 78, ed. Littré, sect. 106, ed. Petersen): Ἔτι τε πρὸς τουτέοισι εὐνούχιαι γίγνονται οἱ πλεῖστοι ἐν Σκύθῃσι, καὶ γυνακήια ἐργάζονται καὶ ὡς αἱ γυναῖκες διαλέγονταί τε ὁμοίως· καλεῦνταί τε οἱ τοιοῦτοι ἀνανδιεῖς. Οἱ μὲν οὖν ἐπιχώριοι τὴν αἰτίην προσ-

A third distinguished philosopher of the same day, Anaxagoras, allegorizing Zeus and the other personal gods, proclaimed the doctrine of one common pervading Mind, as having first established order and system in the mundane aggregate, which had once been in a state of chaos — and as still manifesting its uninterrupted agency for wise and good purposes. This general doctrine obtained much admiration from Plato and Aristotle; but they at the same time remarked with surprise, that Anaxagoras never made any use at all of his own general doctrine for the explanation of the phænomena of nature, — that he looked for nothing but physical causes and connecting laws,[1] — so that in fact the spirit of his particular researches was not materially different from those of Demokritus or Leukippus, whatever might be the difference in their general theories. His investigations in meteorology and astronomy, treating the heavenly bodies as subjects for calculation, have been already noticed as offensive, not only to the general public of Greece, but even to Socratês himself among them: he was tried at Athens, and seems to have escaped con demnation only by voluntary exile.[2]

τιθέασι θεῷ καὶ σέβονται τουτέους τοὺς ἀνθρώπους καὶ προσκυνέουσι, δεδοι κότες περὶ ἑωϋτέων ἕκαστοι. Ἐμοὶ δὲ καὶ αὐτέῳ δοκέει ταῦτα τὰ πάθεα θεῖε εἶναι, καὶ τἄλλα πάντα, καὶ οὐδὲν ἕτερον ἑτέρου θειότερον οὐδὲ ἀνθρωπινώ τερον, ἀλλὰ πάντα θεῖα· ἕκαστον δὲ ἔχει φύσιν τῶν τοιουτέων, καὶ οὐδὲν ἄνευ φύσιος γίγνεται. Καὶ τουτυ τὸ πάθος, ὡς μοὶ δοκέει γίγνεσθαι, φράσω, etc.

Again, sect. 112. Ἀλλὰ γὰρ, ὥσπερ καὶ πρότερον ἔλεξα, θεῖα μὲν καὶ ταῦτά ἐστι ὁμοίως τοῖσι ἄλλοισι, γίγνεται δὲ κατὰ φύσιν ἕκαστα.

Compare the remarkable treatise of Hippocratês, De Morbo Sacro, capp 1 and 18, vol. vi. p. 352–394, ed. Littré. See this opinion of Hippocratês illustrated by the doctrines of some physical philosophers stated in Aristotle, Physic. ii. 8. ὥσπερ ὕει ὁ Ζεὺς, οὐχ ὅπως τὸν σῖτον αὐξήσῃ, ἀλλ᾽ ἐξ ἀνάγκης, etc. Some valuable observations on the method of Hippocratês are also found in Plato, Phædr. p. 270.

[1] See the graphic picture in Plato, Phædon. p. 97–98 (cap. 46–47): compare Plato, Legg. xii. p. 967; Aristotel. Metaphysic. i. p. 13–14 (ed. Brandis); Plutarch, Defect. Oracul. p. 435.

Simplicius, Commentar. in Aristotel. Physic. p. 38. καὶ ὅπερ δὲ ὁ ἐν Φαίδωνι Σωκράτης ἐγαλεῖ τῷ Ἀναξαγόρᾳ, τὸ ἐν ταῖς τῶν κατὰ μέρος αἰτιολογίαις μὴ τῷ νῷ κεχρῆσθαι, ἀλλὰ ταῖς ὑλικαῖς ὑποδόσεσιν, οἰκεῖον ἦν τῇ φυσιολογίᾳ. Anaxagoras thought that the superior intelligence of men, as compared with other animals, arose from his possession of hands (Aristot. de Part. Animal. iv. 10. p. 687, ed. Bekk.).

[2] Xenophôn, Memorab. iv. 7. Socratês said, καὶ παραφρονῆσαι τὸν ταῦτα

The three eminent men just named, all essentially different from each other, may be taken as illustrations of the philosophical mind of Greece during the last half of the fifth century B. C. Scientific pursuits had acquired a powerful hold, and adjusted themselves in various ways with the prevalent religious feelings of the age. Both Hippocratês and Anaxagoras modified their ideas of the divine agency so as to suit their thirst for scientific research. According to the former, the gods were the really efficient agents in the production of all phænomena, — the mean and indifferent not less than the terrific or tutelary. Being thus alike connected with all phænomena, they were specially associated with none — and the proper task of the inquirer was, to find out those rules and conditions by which (he assumed) their agency was always determined, and according to which it might be foretold. And this led naturally to the proceeding which Plato and Aristotle remark in Anaxagoras, — that the all-governing and Infinite Mind, having been announced in sublime language at the beginning of his treatise, was afterward left out of sight, and never applied to the explanation of particular phænomena, being as much consistent with one modification of nature as with

---

μεριμνῶντα οὐδὲν ἧττον ἢ 'Αναξαγόρας παρεφρόνησεν, ὁ μέγιστον φρονήσας ἐπὶ τῷ τὰς τῶν θεῶν μηχανὰς ἐξηγεῖσθαι, etc. Compare Schaubach, Anaxagoræ Fragment. p. 50–141 ; Plutarch, Nikias, 23, and Periklês, 6–32 ; Dio gen. Laërt. ii. 10–14.

The Ionic philosophy, from which Anaxagoras receded more in language than in spirit, seems to have been the least popular of all the schools, though some of the commentators treat it as conformable to vulgar opinion, because it confined itself for the most part to phænomenal explanations, and did not recognize the *noumena* of Plato, or the τὸ ἓν νοητὸν of Parmenidês, — "qualis fuit Ionicorum, quæ tum dominabatur, ratio, vulgari opinione et communi sensu comprobata" (Karsten, Parmenidis Fragment., De Parmenidis Philosophiâ, p. 154). This is a mistake: the Ionic philosophers, who constantly searched for and insisted upon physical laws, came more directly into conflict with the sentiment of the multitude than the Eleatic school.

The larger atmospheric phænomena were connected in the most intimate manner with Grecian religious feeling and uneasiness (see Demokritus ap. Sect. Empiric. ix. sect. 19–24. p. 552–554, Fabric.): the attempts of Anaxagoras and Demokritus to explain them were more displeasing to the public than the Platonic speculations (Demokritus ap. Aristot. Meteorol. ii 7: Stobæus, Eclog. Physic. p. 594: compare Mullach, Democriti Fragmenta, lib. iv. p. 394).

another. Now such a view of the divine agency could never be
reconciled with the religious feelings of the ordinary Grecian
believer, even as they stood in the time of Anaxagoras ; still
less could it have been reconciled with those of the Homeric
man, more than three centuries earlier. By him Zeus and
Athênê were conceived as definite Persons, objects of special
reverence, hopes, and fears, and animated with peculiar feelings,
sometimes of favor, sometimes of wrath, towards himself or his
family or country. They were propitiated by his prayers, and
prevailed upon to lend him succor in danger — but offended and
disposed to bring evil upon him if he omitted to render thanks
or sacrifice. This sense of individual communion with, and de-
pendence upon them was the essence of his faith ; and with that
faith, the all-pervading Mind proclaimed by Anaxagoras —
which had no more concern with one man or one phænomenon
than with another, — could never be brought into harmony. Nor
could the believer, while he prayed with sincerity for special
blessings or protection from the gods, acquiesce in the doctrine
of Hippocratês, that their agency was governed by constant laws
and physical conditions.

That radical discord between the mental impulses of science
and religion, which manifests itself so decisively during the
most cultivated ages of Greece, and which harassed more or
less so many of the philosophers, produced its most afflicting result in the condemnation of Socratês by the Athenians. According to the remarkable passage recently cited from Xenophôn, it
will appear that Socratês agreed with his countrymen in denouncing physical speculations as impious, — that he recognized the religious process of discovery as a peculiar branch, coördinate with
the scientific, — and that he laid down a theory, of which the basis was, the confessed divergence of these two processes from the
beginning — thereby seemingly satisfying the exigencies of religious hopes and fears on the one hand, and those of reason, in
her ardor for ascertaining the invariable laws of phænomena, on
the other. We may remark that the theory of this religious and
extra-scientific process of discovery was at that time sufficiently
complete ; for Socratês could point out, that those anomalous phænomena which the gods had reserved for themselves, and into

which science was forbidden to pry, were yet accessible to the seekings of the pious man, through oracles, omens, and other exceptional means of communication which divine benevolence vouchsafed to keep open. Considering thus to how great an extent Socratês was identified in feeling with the religious public of Athens, and considering moreover that his performance of open religious duties was assiduous — we might wonder, as Xenophôn does wonder,[1] how it could have happened that the Athenian dikasts mistook him at the end of his life for an irreligious man. But we see, by the defence which Xenophôn as well as Plato gives for him, that the Athenian public really considered him, in spite of his own disclaimer, as homogeneous with Anaxagoras and the other physical inquirers, because he had applied similar scientific reasonings to moral and social phænomena. They looked upon him with the same displeasure as he himself felt towards the physical philosophers, and we cannot but admit that in this respect they were more unfortunately consistent than he was. It is true that the mode of defence adopted by Socratês contributed much to the verdict found against him, and that he was further weighed down by private offence given to powerful individuals and professions; but all these separate antipathies found their best account in swelling the cry against him as an over-curious sceptic, and an impious innovator.

Now the scission thus produced between the superior minds and the multitude, in consequence of the development of science and the scientific point of view, is a fact of great moment in the history of Greek progress, and forms an important contrast between the age of Homer and Hesiod and that of Thucydidês; though in point of fact even the multitude, during this later age, were partially modified by those very scientific views which they regarded with disfavor. And we must keep in view the primitive religious faith, once universal and unobstructed, but subsequently disturbed by the intrusions of science; we must follow the great change, as well in respect to enlarged intelligence as to refinement of social and ethical feeling, among the Greeks, from the Hesiodic times downward, in order to render some account of the altered manner in which the ancient mythes came

---

[1] Xenophôn, Memorab. i. 1.

to be dealt with.   These mythes, the spontaneous growth of a
creative and personifying interpretation of nature, had struck
root in Grecian associations at a time when the national faith
required no support from what we call evidence.   They were
now submitted, not simply to a feeling, imagining, and believing
public, but also to special classes of instructed men, —philosophers, historians, ethical teachers, and critics, — and to a public
partially modified by their ideas[1] as well as improved by a wider
practical experience.   They were not intended for such an audience ; they had ceased to be in complete harmony even with the
lower strata of intellect and sentiment, — much more so with the
higher.   But they were the cherished inheritance of a past time ;
they were interwoven in a thousand ways with the religious faith,
the patriotic retrospect, and the national worship, of every Grecian community ; the general type of the mythe was the ancient,
familiar, and universal form of Grecian thought, which even the
most cultivated men had imbibed in their childhood from the
poets,[2] and by which they were to a certain degree unconsciously

---

[1] It is curious to see that some of the most recondite doctrines of the Py
thagorean philosophy were actually brought before the general Syracusan
public in the comedies of Epicharmus : " In comœdiis suis personas sæpe ita
colloqui fecit, ut sententias Pythagoricas et in universum sublimia vitæ præ-
cepta immisceret" (Grysar, De Doriensium Comœdiâ, p. 111, Col. 1828).
The fragments preserved in Diogen. Laërt. (iii. 9–17) present both criticisms
upon the Hesiodic doctrine of a primæval chaos, and an exposition of the
archetypal and immutable ideas (as opposed to the fluctuating phænomena
of sense) which Plato afterwards adopted and systematized.

Epicharmus seems to have combined with this abstruse philosophy a
strong vein of comic shrewdness and some turn to scepticism (Cicero, Epistol. ad Attic. i. 19) : " ut crebro mihi vafer ille Siculus Epicharmus insusurret
cantilenam suam." Clemens Alex. Strom. v. p. 258. Νᾶφε καὶ μέμνασ᾽ ἀπι-
στεῖν· ἄρϑρα ταῦτα τῶν φρενῶν. Ζῶμεν ἀριϑμῷ καὶ λογισμῷ· ταῦτα γὰρ σώζει
βροτούς. Also his contemptuous ridicule of the prophetesses of his time
who cheated foolish women out of their money, pretending to universal
knowledge, καὶ πάντα γιγνώσκοντι τῷ τηνᾶν λόγῳ (ap Polluc. ix. 81).   See,
about Epicharmus, O. Müller, Dorians, iv. 7, 4.

These dramas seem to have been exhibited at Syracuse between 480–460
B. C., anterior even to Chionides and Magnês at Athens (Aristot. Poet. c. 3):
he says π ο λ λ ῷ πρότερος, which can hardly be literally exact.   The critics of
the Horatian age looked upon Epicharmus as the prototype of Plautus (Hor
Epistol. ii. 1. 58).

[2] The third book of the republic of Plato is particularly striking in refer-

enslaved. Taken as a whole the mythes had acquired prescriptive and ineffaceable possession: to attack, call in question, or repudiate them, was a task painful even to undertake, and far beyond the power of any one to accomplish.

For these reasons the anti-mythic vein of criticism was of no effect as a destroying force, but nevertheless its dissolving decomposing and transforming influence was very considerable. To accommodate the ancient mythes to an improved tone of sentiment and a newly created canon of credibility, was a function which even the wisest Greeks did not disdain, and which occupied no small proportion of the whole intellectual activity of the nation.

The mythes were looked at from a point of view completely foreign to the reverential curiosity and literal imaginative faith of the Homeric man; they were broken up and recast in order to force them into new moulds such as their authors had never conceived. We may distinguish four distinct classes of minds, in the literary age now under examination, as having taken them in hand — the poets, the logographers, the philosophers, and the historians.

With the poets and logographers, the mythical persons are real predecessors, and the mythical world an antecedent fact; but it is divine and heroic reality, not human; the present is only half-brother of the past (to borrow[1] an illustration from Pindar in his allusion to gods and men), remotely and generically, but not closely and specifically, analogous to it. As a general habit, the old feelings and the old unconscious faith, apart from all proof or evidence, still remain in their minds; but recent feelings have grown up which compel them to omit, to alter, sometimes even to reject and condemn, particular narratives.

Pindar repudiates some stories and transforms others, because they are inconsistent with his conceptions of the gods. Thus he formally protests against the tale that Pelops had been killed and served up at table by his father, for the immortal gods to eat; he shrinks from the idea of imputing to them so horrid an appe-

---

ence to the use of the poets in education: see also his treatise De Legg. vii. p. 810–811. Some teachers made their pupils learn whole poets by heart (ὅλους ποιητὰς ἐκμανθάνων), others preferred extracts and selections.

[1] Pindar, Nem. vi. 1. Compare Simonidês, Fragm. 1 (Gaisford).

tite; he pronounces the tale to have been originally fabricated by a slanderous neighbor. Nor can he bring himself to recount the quarrels between different gods.[1] The amours of Zeus and Apollo are no way displeasing to him; but he occasionally suppresses some of the simple details of the old mythe, as deficient in dignity: thus, according to the Hesiodic narrative, Apollo was informed by a raven of the infidelity of the nymph Korônis: but the mention of the raven did not appear to Pindar consistent with the majesty of the god, and he therefore wraps up the mode of detection in vague and mysterious language.[2] He feels considerable repugnance to the character of Odysseus, and intimates more than once that Homer has unduly exalted him, by force of poetical artifice. With the character of the Æakid Ajax, on the other hand, he has the deepest sympathy, as well as with his untimely and inglorious death, occasioned by the undeserved preference of a less worthy rival.[3] He appeals for his authority usually to the Muse, but sometimes to "ancient sayings of men," accompanied with a general allusion to story-tellers and bards,—admitting, however, that these stories present great discrepancy, and sometimes that they are false.[4] Yet the marvellous and the supernatural afford no ground whatever for rejecting a story: Pindar makes an express declaration to this effect in reference to the romantic adventures of Perseus and the Gorgon's head.[5] He treats even those mythical characters, which conflict the most palpably with positive experience, as connected by a real genealogical thread with the world before him. Not merely the heroes of Troy and Thêbes, and the demigod seamen of Jasôn and the ship Argô, but also the Centaur Cheirôn, the hundred-headed Typhôs, the giant Alkyoneus, Antæus, Bellero-

---

[1] Pindar, Olymp. i. 30–55; ix. 32–45.

[2] Pyth. iii. 25. See the allusions to Semclê, Alkmêna, and Danaê, Pyth. iii. 98; Nem. x. 10. Compare also *supra*, chap. ix. p. 245.

[3] Pindar. Nem. vii. 20–30; viii. 23–31. Isthm. iii. 50–60.

It seems to be sympathy for Ajax, in odes addressed to noble Æginetan victors, which induces him thus to depreciate Odysseus; for he eulogizes Sisyphus, specially on account of his cunning and resources (Olymp. xiii. 50). in the ode addressed to Xenophôn the Corinthian.

[4] Olymp. i. 28; Nem. viii. 20; Pyth. i. 93; Olymp. vii. 55; Nem. vi. 43 πάντι δ' ἀνθρώπων παλαιαὶ ῥήσιες, etc.

[5] Pyth. x. 49. Compare Pyth. xii. 11–22.

phôn and Pegasus, the Chimæra, the Amazons and the Hyperboreans — all appear painted on the same canvas, and touched with the same colors, as the men of the recent and recorded past, Phalaris and Krœsus ; only they are thrown back to a greater distance in the perspective.[1] The heroic ancestors of those great Æginetan, Thessalian, Thêban, Argean, etc. families, whose present members the poet celebrates for their agonistic victories, sympathize with the exploits and second the efforts of their descendants: the inestimable value of a privileged breed and of the stamp of nature is powerfully contrasted with the impotence of unassisted teaching and practice.[2] The power and skill of the Argeian Theræus and his relatives as wrestlers, are ascribed partly to the fact that their ancestors Pamphaês in aforetime had hospitably entertained the Tyndarids Kastôr and Pollux.[3] Perhaps however the strongest proof of the sincerity of Pindar's mythical faith is afforded when he notices a guilty incident with shame and repugnance, but with an unwilling confession of its truth, as in the case of the fratricide committed on Phokus by his brothers Pêleus and Telamôn.[4]

Æschylus and Sophoklês exhibit the same spontaneous and uninquiring faith as Pindar in the legendary antiquities of Greece, taken as a whole ; but they allow themselves greater license as to the details. It was indispensable to the success of their compositions that they should recast and group anew the legendary events, preserving the names and general understood relation of those characters whom they introduced. The demand for novelty of combination increased with the multiplication of tragic spectacles at Athens: moreover the feelings of the Athenians, ethical as well as political, had become too critical to tolerate the literal reproduction of many among the ancient stories.

Both of them exalted rather than lowered the dignity of the mythical world, as something divine and heroic rather than human.

---

[1] Pyth. i. 17; iii. 4–7; iv. 12; viii. 16. Nem. iv. 27–32 ; v. 89. Isthm. v. 31; vi. 44–48. Olymp. iii. 17; viii. 63; xiii. 61–87.

[2] Nem. iii. 39; v. 40. συγγενὴς εὐδοξία — πότμος συγγενής; v. 8. Olymp. ix. 103. Pindar seems to introduce φύᾳ in cases where Homer would have mentioned the divine assistance.

[3] Nem. x. 37–51. Compare the family legend of the Athenian Dêmocrates, in Plato, Lysis, p. 295.   [4] Nem. v. 12–16.

The Promêtheus of Æschylus is a far more exalted conception than his keen-witted namesake in Hesiod, and the more homely details of the ancient Thêbaïs and Œdipodia were in like manner modified by Sophoklês.[1] The religious agencies of the old epic are constantly kept prominent, and the paternal curse, — the wrath of deceased persons against those from whom they have sustained wrong, — the judgments of the Erinnys against guilty or foredoomed persons, sometimes inflicted directly, sometimes brought about through dementation of the sufferer himself (like the Homeric Atê), — are frequent in their tragedies.[2]

---

[1] See above, chap. xiv. p. 368. on the Legend of the Siege of Thêbes.

[2] The curse of Œdipus is the determining force in the Sept. ad Thêb., 'Αρά τ', 'Ερινννὺς πατρὸς ἡ μεγασθενής (v. 70); it reappears several times in the course of the drama, with particular solemnity in the mouth of Eteoklês (695–709, 725, 785, etc.); he yields to it as an irresistible force, as carrying the family to ruin: —

'Επεὶ τὸ πρᾶγμα κάρτ' ἐπισπέρχει θεός,
'Ιτω κατ' οὖρον, κῦμα Κωκυτοῦ λαχὸν,
Φοίβῳ στυγηθὲν πᾶν τὸ Λαΐου γένος.

* * * *

Φίλου γὰρ ἐχθρά μοι πατρὸς τέλει' ἄρα
Ξηροῖς ἀκλαύστοις ὄμμασιν προσιζάνει, etc.

So again at the opening of the Agamemnôn, the μνάμων μῆνις τεκνόποινος (v. 155) and the sacrifice of Iphigeneia are dwelt upon as leaving behind them an avenging doom upon Agamemnôn, though he took precautions for gagging her mouth during the sacrifice and thus preventing her from giving utterance to imprecations—Φθόγγον ἀραῖον οἴκοις Βίᾳ χαλινῶν τ' ἀναύδῳ μένει (κατασχεῖν), v. 346. The Erinnys awaits Agamemnôn even at the moment of his victorious consummation at Troy (467; compare 762–990, 1336–1433): she is most to be dreaded after great good fortune: she enforces the curse which ancestral crimes have brought upon the house of Atreus— πρώταρχος ἄτη — παλαιαὶ ἀμαρτίαι δόμων (1185–1197, Choëph. 692) — the curse imprecated by the outraged Thyestês (1601). In the Choëphorœ, Apollo menaces Orestês with the wrath of his deceased father, and all the direful visitations of the Erinnyes, unless he undertakes to revenge the murder (271–296). Αἶσα and 'Ερινννὺς bring on blood for blood (647). But the moment that Orestês, placed between these conflicting obligations (925), has achieved it, he becomes himself the victim of the Erinnyes, who drive him mad even at the end of the Choëphoræ (ἕως δ' ἔτ' ἔμφρων εἰμί, 1026), and who make their appearance bodily, and pursue him throughout the third drama of this fearful trilogy. The Eidôlon of Klytæmnêstra impels them to vengeance (Eumenid. 96) and even spurs them on when they appear to relax.

Æschylus in two of his remaining pieces brings forward the gods as the chief personages, and far from sharing the objection of Pindar to dwell upon dissensions of the gods, he introduces Promêtheus and Zeus in the one, Apollo and the Eumenidês in the other, in marked opposition. The dialogue, first superinduced by him upon the primitive Chorus, gradually became the most important portion of the drama, and is more elaborated in Sophoklês than in Æschylus. Even in Sophoklês, however, it still generally retains its ideal majesty as contrasted with the rhetorical and forensic tone which afterwards crept in; it grows out of the piece, and addresses itself to the emotions more than to the reason of the audience. Nevertheless, the effect of Athenian political discussion and democratical feeling is visible in both these dramatists. The idea of rights and legitimate privileges as opposed to usurping force, is applied by Æschylus even to the society of the gods: the Eumenidês accuse Apollo of having, with the insolence of youthful ambition, "ridden down" their old preroga-

---

Apollo conveys Orestês to Athens, whither the Erinnyes pursue him, and prosecute him before the judgment-seat of the goddess Athênê, to whom they submit the award; Apollo appearing as his defender. The debate between "the daughters of Night" and the god, accusing and defending, is eminently curious (576–730): the Erinnyes are deeply mortified at the humiliation put upon them when Orestês is acquitted, but Athênê at length reconciles them, and a covenant is made whereby they become protectresses of Attica, accepting of a permanent abode and solemn worship (1006): Orestês returns to Argos, and promises that even in his tomb he will watch that none of his descendants shall ever injure the land of Attica (770). The solemn trial and acquittal of Orestês formed the consecrating legend of the Hill and Judicature of Areiopagus.

This is the only complete triology of Æschylus which we possess, and the avenging Erinnyes (416) are the movers throughout the whole — unseen in the first two dramas, visible and appalling in the third. And the appearance of Cassandra under the actual prophetic fever in the first, contributes still farther to impart to it a coloring different from common humanity.

The general view of the movement of the Oresteia given in Welcker (Æschyl. Trilogie, p. 445) appears to me more conformable to Hellenic ideas than that of Klausen (Theologumena Æschyli, pp. 157–169), whose valuable collection and comparison of passages is too much affected, both here and elsewhere, by the desire to bring the agencies of the Greek mythical world into harmony with what a religious mind of the present day would approve. Moreover, he sinks the personality of Athênê too much in the supreme authority of Zeus (p. 158–168).

tives[1] — while the Titan Promêtheus, the champion of suffering
humanity against the unfriendly dispositions of Zeus, ventures to
depict the latter as a recent usurper reigning only by his superior
strength, exalted by one successful revolution, and destined at
some future time to be overthrown by another, — a fate which
cannot be averted except through warnings communicable only
by Promêtheus himself.[2]

It is commonly understood that Æschylus disapproved of the
march of democracy at Athens during his later years, and that
the Eumenidês is intended as an indirect manifestation in favor
of the senate of Areiopagus. Without inquiring at present whether
such a special purpose can be distinctly made out, we may plainly see that the poet introduces, into the relations of the gods with
each other, a feeling of political justice, arising out of the times
in which he lived and the debates of which he was a witness.
But though Æschylus incurred reproaches of impiety from Plato,
and seemingly also from the Athenian public, for particular speeches and incidents in his tragedies,[3] and though he does not adhere

---

[1] Eumenidês, 150. —

    Ἰὼ παῖ Διὸς, ἐπίκλοπος πέλει,
    Νέος δὲ γραίας δαίμονας καθιππάσω, etc.

The same metaphor again, v. 731. Æschylus seems to delight in contrasting the young and the old gods: compare 70-162, 882.

The Erinnyes tell Apollo that he assumes functions which do not belong
to him, and will thus desecrate those which do belong to him (715-754): —

    Ἀλλ᾽ αἱματηρὰ πράγματ᾽, οὐ λαχὼν, σέβεις,
    Μαντεῖα δ᾽ οὐκ ἔθ᾽ ἀγνὰ μαντεύσει μένων.

The refusal of the king Pelasgos, in the Supplices, to undertake what he
feels to be the sacred duty of protecting the suppliant Danaïdes, without first
submitting the matter to his people and obtaining their expressed consent, and
the fear which he expresses of their blame (κατ᾽ ἀρχὰς γὰρ φιλαίτιος λέως), are
more forcibly set forth than an old epic poet would probably have thought necessary (see Supplices, 369, 397, 485, 519). The solemn wish to exclude both
anarchy and despotism from Athens bears still more the mark of political
feeling of the time — μήτ᾽ ἄναρχον μήτε δεσποτουμένον (Eumenid. 527-696)

[2] Promêtheus, 35, 151, 170, 309, 524, 910, 940, 956.

[3] Plato, Republ. ii. 381-383; compare Æschyl. Fragment. 159, ed. Dindorf. He was charged also with having divulged in some of his plays secret
matters of the mysteries of Dêmêtêr, but is said to have excused himself by
alleging ignorance: he was not aware that what he had said was comprised

to the received vein of religious tradition with the same strictness as Sophoklês — yet the ascendency and interference of the gods is never out of sight, and the solemnity with which they are represented, set off by a bold, figurative, and elliptical style of

in the mysteries (Aristot. Ethic. Nicom. iii. 2; Clemens Alex. Strom. ii. p. 387); the story is different again in Ælian, V. H. v. 19.

How little can be made out distinctly respecting this last accusation may be seen in Lobeck, Aglaopham. p. 81.

Cicero (Tusc. Dis. ii. 10) calls Æschylus " almost a Pythagorean :" upon what the epithet is founded we do not know.

There is no evidence to prove to us that the Promêtheus Vinctus was considered as impious by the public before whom it was represented; but its obvious meaning has been so regarded by modern critics, who resort to many different explanations of it, in order to prove that when properly construed it is not impious. But if we wish to ascertain what Æschylus really meant, we ought not to consult the religious ideas of modern times; we have no tast except what we know of the poet's own time and that which had preceded him. The explanations given by the ablest critics seem generally to exhibit a predetermination to bring out Zeus as a just, wise, merciful, and all-powerful Being; and all, in one way or another, distort the figures, alter the perspective, and give far-fetched interpretations of the meaning, of this striking drama, which conveys an impression directly contrary (see Welcker, Trilogie, Æsch. p. 90-117, with the explanation of Dissen there given; Klausen, Theologum. Æsch. p. 140-154; Schömann, in his recent translation of the play, and the criticism on that translation in the Wiener Jahrbucher, vol. cix. 1845, p. 245, by F. Ritter). On the other hand, Schutz (Excurs. ad Prom. Vinct. p. 149) thinks that Æschylus wished by means of this drama to enforce upon his countrymen the hatred of a despot. Though I do not agree in this interpretation, it appears to me less wide of the truth than the forcible methods employed by others to bring the poet into harmony with their own religious ideas.

Without presuming to determine whether Æschylus proposed to himself any special purpose, if we look at the Æschylean Promêtheus in reference only to ancient ideas, it will be found to borrow both its characters and all its main circumstances from the legend in the Hesiodic Theogony. Zeus acquires his supremacy only by overthrowing Kronos and the Titans the Titan god Promêtheus is the pronounced champion of helpless man, and negotiates with Zeus on their behalf: Zeus wishes to withhold from them the most essential blessings, which Promêtheus employs deceit and theft to procure for them, and ultimately with success; undergoing, however, severe punishment for so doing from the superior force of Zeus. These are the main features of the Æschylean Promêtheus, and they are all derived from the legend as it stands in the Theogony. As for the human race, they are depicted as abject and helpless in an extreme degree, in Æschylus even

expression (often but imperfectly intelligible to modern readers), reaches its maximum in his tragedies. As he throws round the

---

more than in Hesiod: they appear as a race of aboriginal savages, having the god Promêtheus for their protector.

Æschylus has worked up the old legend, homely and unimpressive as we read it in Hesiod, into a sublime ideal. We are not to forget that Promêtheus is not a man, but a god, — the equal of Zeus in race, though his inferior in power, and belonging to a family of gods who were once superior to Zeus: he has moreover deserted his own kindred, and lent all his aid and superior sagacity to Zeus, whereby chiefly the latter was able to acquire supremacy (this *last* circumstance is an addition by Æschylus himself to the Hesiodic legend). In spite of such essential service, Zeus had doomed him to cruel punishment, for no other reason than because he conferred upon helpless man the prime means of continuance and improvement, thus thwarting the intention of Zeus to extinguish the race.

Now Zeus, though superior to all the other gods and exercising general control, was never considered, either in Grecian legend or in Grecian religious belief, to be superior in so immeasurable a degree as to supersede all free action and sentiment on the part of gods less powerful. There were many old legends of dissension among the gods, and several of disobedience against Zeus: when a poet chose to dramatize one of these, he might so turn his composition as to sympathize either with Zeus or with the inferior god, without in either case shocking the general religious feeling of the country. And if there ever was an instance in which preference of the inferior god would be admissible, it is that of Promêtheus, whose proceedings are such as to call forth the maximum of human sympathy, — superior intelligence pitted against superior force, and resolutely encountering foreknown suffering, for the sole purpose of rendering inestimable and gratuitous service to mortals.

Of the Promêtheus Solutus, which formed a sequel to the Promêtheus Vinctus (the entire trilogy is not certainly known), the fragments preserved are very scanty, and the guesses of critics as to its plot have little base to proceed upon. They contend that, in one way or other, the apparent objections which the Prometh. Vinctus presents against the justice of Zeus were in the Prometh. Solutus removed. Hermann, in his *Dissertatio de Æschyli Prometheo Soluto* (Opuscula, vol. iv. p. 256), calls this position in question: I transcribe from his Dissertation one passage, because it contains an important remark in reference to the manner in which the Greek poets handled their religious legends: " while they recounted and believed many enormities respecting individual gods, they always described the Godhead in the abstract as holy and faultless."………

" Immo illud admirari oportet, quod quum de singulis Diis indignissima quæque crederent, tamen ubi sine certo nomine Deum dicebant, immunem ab omni vitio, summâque sanctitate præditum intelligebant. Illam igitur Jovis sævitiam ut excusent defensores Trilogiæ, et jure punitum volunt Pro-

gods a kind of airy grandeur, so neither do his men or heroes appear like tenants of the common earth: the mythical world from which he borrows his characters is peopled only with " the immediate seed of the gods, in close contact with Zeus, in whom the divine blood has not yet had time to degenerate:"[1] his individuals are taken, not from the iron race whom Hesiod acknowledges with shame as his contemporaries, but from the extinct heroic race which had fought at Troy and Thêbes. It is to them that his conceptions aspire, and he is even chargeable with frequent straining, beyond the limits of poetical taste, to realize his picture. If he does not consistently succeed in it, the reason is because consistency in such a matter is unattainable, since, after all, the analogies of common humanity, the only materials which the most creative imagination has to work upon, obtrude themselves involuntarily, and the lineaments of the man are thus seen even under a dress which promises superhuman proportions.

Sophoklês, the most illustrious ornament of Grecian tragedy, dwells upon the same heroic characters, and maintains their grandeur, on the whole, with little abatement, combining with it a far better dramatic structure, and a wider appeal to human sympathies. Even in Sophoklês, however, we find indications that an altered ethical feeling and a more predominant sense of artistic perfection are allowed to modify the harsher religious agencies of the old epic; occasional misplaced effusions[2] of rhetoric, as well

---

metheum — et in sequente fabulâ reconciliato Jove, restitutam arbitrantur divinam justitiam. Quo invento, vereor ne non optime dignitati consuluerint supremi Deorum, quem decuerat potius non sævire omnino, quam placari eâ lege, ut alius Promethei vice lueret."

[1] Æschyl. Fragment. 146, Dindorf; ap. Plato. Repub. iii. p. 391; compare Strabo, xii. p. 580. —

$$\text{.................. } οἱ \ \vartheta εῶν \ ἀγχίσποροι$$
$$Οἱ \ Ζηνὸς \ ἐγγὺς, \ οἷς \ ἐν \ ᾿Ιδαίῳ \ πάγῳ$$
$$Διὸς \ πατρῴου \ βωμός \ ἐστ᾿ \ ἐν \ αἰθέρι,$$
$$Κούπω \ σφιν \ ἐξίτηλον \ αἷμα \ δαιμόνων.$$

There is one real exception to this statement — the Persæ — which is founded upon an event of recent occurrence; and one apparent exception — the Promêtheus Vinctus. But in that drama no individual mortal is made to appear; we can hardly consider Iô as an ἐφήμερος (253).

[2] For the characteristics of Æschylus see Aristophan. Ran. 755, ad fin. passim. The competition between Æschylus and Euripidês turns upon γνω-

as of didactic prolixity, may also be detected.   It is Æschylus,
not Sophoklês, who forms the marked antithesis to Euripidês; it
is Æschylus, not Sophoklês, to whom Aristophanês awards the
prize of tragedy, as the poet who assigns most perfectly to the
heroes of the past those weighty words, imposing equipments,
simplicity of great deeds with little talk, and masculine energy
superior to the corruptions of Aphroditê, which beseem the comrades of Agamemnôn and Adrastus.[1]

How deeply this feeling, of the heroic character of the mythical world, possessed the Athenian mind, may be judged by the
bitter criticisms made on Euripidês, whose compositions were
pervaded, partly by ideas of physical philosophy learnt under
Anaxagoras, partly by the altered tone of education and the wide
diffusion of practical eloquence, forensic as well as political, at

---

μαι ἀγαθαὶ, 1497; the weight and majesty of the words, 1362; πρῶτος τῶν
'Ελλήνων πυργώσας ῥήματα σεμνά, 1001, 921, 930 ("sublimis et gravis et
grandiloquus sæpe usque ad vitium," Quintil. x. 1); the imposing appearance
of his heroes, such as Memnôn and Cycnus, 961; their reserve in speech,
908; his dramas "full of Arês" and his lion-hearted chiefs, inspiring the
auditors with fearless spirit in defence of their country, — 1014, 1013, 1040;
his contempt of feminine tenderness, 1042. —

ÆSCH.   Οὐδ' οἶδ' οὐδεὶς ἥντιν' ἐρῶσαν πώποτ' ἐποίησα γυναῖκα.

EURIP.   Μὰ Δί', οὐδὲ γὰρ ἦν τῆς 'Αφροδίτης οὐδέν σοι.

ÆSCH.   μηδέ γ' ὀπείη·

'Αλλ' ἐπὶ σοί τοι καὶ τοῖς σοῖσιν πολλὴ πολλοῦ 'πικάθοιτο.

To the same general purpose Nubes (1347–1356), composed so many years
earlier. The weight and majesty of the Æschylean heroes (βάρος, τὸ μεγαλο-
πρεπὲς) is dwelt upon in the life of Æschylus, and Sophoklês is said to have
derided it — 'Ωσπερ γὰρ ὁ Σοφοκλῆς ἔλεγε, τὸν Αἰσχύλου διαπεπαιχὼς
ὄγκον, etc. (Plutarch, De Profect. in Virt. Sent. c. 7), unless we are to understand this as a mistake of Plutarch quoting Sophoklês instead of Euripidês, as he speaks in the Frogs of Aristophanês, which is the opinion both
of Lessing in his Life of Sophoklês and of Welcker (Æschyl. Trilogie, p.
525).

[1] See above, Chapters xiv. and xv.

Æschylus seems to have been a greater innovator as to the matter of the
mythes than either Sophoklês or Euripidês (Dionys. Halic. Judic. de Vett.
Script. p. 422, Reisk.). For the close adherence of Sophoklês to the Homeric
epic, see Athenæ. vii. p. 277; Diogen. Laërt. iv. 20; Suidas, v. Πολέμων.
Æschylus puts into the mouth of the Eumenidês a serious argument derived
from the behavior of Zeus in chaining his father Kronos (Eumen. 640.)

Athens.[1] While Aristophanês assails Euripidês as the representative of this "young Athens," with the utmost keenness of sarcasm, — other critics also concur in designating him as having vulgarized the mythical heroes, and transformed them into mere characters of common life, — loquacious, subtle, and savoring of the market-place.[2] In some of his plays, sceptical expressions and sentiments were introduced, derived from his philosophical studies, sometimes confounding two or three distinct gods into one, sometimes translating the personal Zeus into a substantial Æther with determinate attributes. He put into the mouths of some of his unprincipled dramatic characters, apologetic speeches which were denounced as ostentatious sophistry, and as setting out a triumphant case for the criminal.[3] His thoughts, his words, and the rhythm of his choric songs, were all accused of being deficient in dignity and elevation. The mean attire and miserable attitude

---

[1] See Valckenaer, Diatribe in Euripid. Fragm. capp. 5 and 6.

The fourth and fifth lectures among the *Dramatische Vorlesungen* of August Wilhelm Schlegel depict both justly and eloquently the difference between Æschylus, Sophoklês and Euripidês, especially on this point of the gradual sinking of the mythical colossus into an ordinary man; about Euripidês especially in lecture 5, vol. i. p. 206, ed. Heidelberg 1809.

[2] Aristot. Poetic, c. 46. Οἷον καὶ Σοφοκλῆς ἔφη, αὐτὸς μὲν οἵους δεῖ ποιεῖν Εὐριπίδης δὲ, οἷοί εἰσι.

The Ranæ and Acharneis of Aristophanês exhibit fully the reproaches urged against Euripidês: the language put into the mouth of Euripidês in the former play (vv. 935–977) illustrates specially the point here laid down. Plutarch (De Gloriâ Atheniens. c. 5) contrasts ἡ Εὐριπίδου σοφία καὶ ἡ Σοφοκλεοῦς λογιότης. Sophoklês either adhered to the old mythes or introduced alterations into them in a spirit comformable to their original character, while Euripidês refined upon them. The comment of Dêmêtrius Phalereus connects τὸ λόγιον expressly with the maintenance of the dignity of the tales. Αρξομαι δὲ ἀπὸ τοῦ μεγαλοπρεποῦς, ὅπερ νῦν λ ό γ ι ο ν ὀνομάζουσιν (c. 38).

[3] Aristophan. Ran. 770, 887, 1066.

Euripidês says to Æschylus, in regard to the language employed by both of them, —

Ἦν οὖν σὺ λέγῃς Λυκαβήττους
Καὶ Παρνάσσων ἡμῖν μεγέθη, τοῦτ᾽ ἐστὶ τὸ χρηστὰ διδάσκειν,
Ὃν χρὴ φράζειν ἀνθρωπείως;

Æschylus replies, —

Ἀλλ᾽, ὦ κακόδαιμον, ἀνάγκη
Μεγάλων γνωμῶν καὶ διανοιῶν ἴσα καὶ τὰ ῥήματα τίκτειν.
Κάλλως εἰκὸς τοὺς ἡ μ ι θ έ ο υ ς τοῖς ῥήμασι μείζοσι χρῆσθαι·

in which he exhibited Œneus, Têlephus, Thyestês, Inô, and
other heroic characters, were unmercifully derided,[1] though it
seems that their position and circumstances had always been
painfully melancholy; but the effeminate pathos which Euripidês
brought so nakedly into the foreground, was accounted unworthy
of the majesty of a legendary hero. And he incurred still greater obloquy on another point, on which he is allowed even by his
enemies to have only reproduced in substance the preëxisting
tales, — the illicit and fatal passion depicted in several of his
female characters, such as Phædra and Sthenobœa. His opponents admitted that these stories were true, but contended that
they ought to be kept back and not produced upon the stage, —
a proof both of the continued mythical faith and of the more
sensitive ethical criticism of his age.[2] The marriage of the six

---

Καὶ γὰρ τοῖς ἱματίοις ἡμῶν χρῶνται πολὺ σεμνοτέροισι.
᾽Α ᾽μοῦ χρηστῶς καταδείξαντος διελυμήνω σύ.
                                        EURIP. Τί δράσας,
ÆSCH. Πρῶτον μὲν τοὺς βασιλεύοντας ῥάκι᾽ ἀμπίσχων, ἵν᾽ ἐλεινοὶ
Τοῖς ἀνθρώποις φαίνοιντ᾽ εἶναι.

For the character of the language and measures of Euripidês, as represented by Æschylus, see also v. 1297, and Pac. 527. Philosophical discussion
was introduced by Euripidês (Dionys. Hal. Ars Rhetor. viii. 10–ix. 11) about
the Melanippê, where the doctrine of prodigies (τέρας) appears to have been
argued. Quintilian (x. 1) remarks that to young beginners in judicial pleading, the study of Euripidês was much more specially profitable than that of
Sophoklês : compare Dio Chrysostom, Orat. xviii. vol. i. p. 477, Reisk.

In Euripidês the heroes themselves sometimes delivered moralizing dis
courses : — εἰσάγων τὸν Βελλεροφόντην γνωμολογοῦντα (Welcker, Griechisch.
Tragöd. Eurip. Stheneb. p. 782). Compare the fragments of his Bellerophôn (15–25, Matthiæ), and of his Chrysippus (7, ib.). A striking story is
found in Seneca, Epistol. 115 ; and Plutarch, de Audiend. Poetis, c. 4. t. i. p.
70, Wytt.

[1] Aristophan. Ran. 840. —
                ὦ στωμυλιοσυλλεκτάδη
Καὶ πτωχοποιὲ καὶ ῥακιοσυρραπτάδη ·

See also Aristophan. Acharn. 385–422. For an unfavorable criticism upon
such proceeding, see Aristotat. Poet. 27.

[2] Aristophan. Ran. 1050.
EURIP. Πότερον δ᾽ οὐκ ὄντα λόγον τοῦτον περὶ τῆς Φαίδρας ξυνέθηκα ;
ÆSCH. Μὰ Δί᾽, ἀλλ᾽ ὄντ᾽· ἀλλ᾽ ἀποκρύπτειν χρὴ τὸ πονηρὸν τόν γε ποιητήν,
Καὶ μὴ παράγειν μηδὲ διδάσκειν.

In the Hercules Furens, Euripidês puts in relief and even exaggerates the

daughters to the six sons of Æolus is of Homeric origin, and
stands now, though briefly stated, in the Odyssey: but the incestuous passion of Macareus and Canacê, embodied by Euripidês[1]
in the lost tragedy called *Æolus*, drew upon him severe censure.
Moreover, he often disconnected the horrors of the old legends
with those religious agencies by which they had been originally
forced on, prefacing them by motives of a more refined character,
which carried no sense of awful compulsion: thus the considerations by which the Euripidean Alkmæôn was reduced to the necessity of killing his mother appeared to Aristotle ridiculous.[2]
After the time of this great poet, his successors seem to have
followed him in breathing into their characters the spirit of common life, but the names and plot were still borrowed from the
stricken mythical families of Tantalus, Kadmus, etc.: and the
heroic exaltation of all the individual personages introduced, as
contrasted with the purely human character of the Chorus, is

worst elements of the ancient mythes: the implacable hatred of Hêrê towards
Hêraklês is pushed so far as to deprive him of his reason (by sending down
Iris and the unwilling Λύσσα), and thus intentionally to drive him to slay his
wife and children with his own hands.

[1] Aristoph. Ran. 849, 1041, 1080; Thesmophor. 547; Nubes, 1354. Grauert
De Mediâ Græcorum Comœdiâ in Rheinisch. Museum, 2nd Jahrs. 1 Heft, p.
51. It suited the plan of the drama of Æolus, as composed by Euripidês, to
place in the mouth of Macareus a formal recommendation of incestuous
marriages: probably this contributed much to offend the Athenian public.
See Dionys. Hal. Rhetor. ix. p. 355.

About the liberty of intermarriage among relatives, indicated in Homer,
parents and children being alone excepted, see Terpstra, Antiquitas Homerica,
cap. xiii. p. 104.

Ovid, whose poetical tendencies led him chiefly to copy Euripidês, observes
(Trist. ii. 1, 380) —

" Omne genus scripti gravitate Tragœdia vincit,
   Hæc quoque materiam semper amoris habet.
Nam quid in Hippolyto nisi cæcæ flamma novercæ ?
   Nobilis est Canace fratris amore sui."

This is the reverse of the truth in regard to Æschylus and Sophoklês, and
only very partially true in respect to Euripidês.

[2] Aristot. Ethic. Nicom. iii. 1, 8. καὶ γὰρ τὸν Εὐριπίδου ᾿Αλκμαίωνα γελοῖα
φαίνεται τὰ ἀναγκάσαντα μητροκτονῆσαι   (In the lost tragedy called ᾿Αλκμα-
ίων ὁ διὰ Ψωφῖδος).

still numbered by Aristotle among the essential points of the theory of tragedy.[1] The tendency then of Athenian tragedy — powerfully manifested in Æschylus, and never wholly lost — was to uphold an unquestioning faith and a reverential estimate of the general mythical world and its personages, but to treat the particular narratives rather as matter for the emotions than as recitals of actual fact. The logographers worked along with them to the first of these two ends, but not to the second. Their grand object was, to cast the mythes into a continuous readable series, and they were in consequence compelled to make selection between inconsistent or contradictory narratives; to reject some narratives as false, and to receive others as true. But their preference was determined more by their sentiments as to what was appropriate, than by any pretended historical test. Pherekydês, Akusilaus and Hellanikus[2] did not seek to banish miraculous or fantastic incidents from the mythical world; they regarded it as peopled with loftier beings, and expected to find in it phænomena not paralleled in their own degenerate days. They reproduced the fables as they found them in the poets, rejecting little except the discrepancies, and producing ultimately what they believed to be not only a continuous but an exact and trustworthy history of the past — wherein they carry indeed their precision to such a length, that Hellanicus gives the year, and even the day of the capture of Troy.[3]

Hekatæus of Milêtus (500 B. C.), anterior to Pherekydês and Hellanikus, is the earliest writer in whom we can detect any disposition to disallow the prerogative and specialty of the mythes, and to soften down their characteristic prodigies, some of which

---

[1] Aristot. Poetic. 26-27. And in his Problemata also, in giving the reason why the Hypo-Dorian and Hypo-Phrygian musical modes were never assigned to the Chorus, he says —

Ταῦτα δὲ ἀμφω χόρῳ μὲν ἀναρμοστὰ, τοῖς δὲ ἀπὸ σκηνῆς οἰκειότερα. Ἐκεῖνοι μὲν γὰρ ἡρώων μίμηται· οἱ δὲ ἡγεμόνες τῶν ἀρχαίων μόνοι ἦσαν ἥρωες, οἱ δὲ λαοὶ ἄνθρωποι, ὧν ἐστὶν ὁ χόρος. Διὸ καὶ ἁρμόζει αὐτῷ τὸ γοερὸν καὶ ἡσύχιον ἦθος καὶ μέλος· ἀνθρωπικὰ γάρ.

[2] See Müller, Prolegom. zu einer wissenschaftlichen Mythologie, c. iii. p 93.

[3] Hellanic. Fragment. 143, ed. Didot.

however still find favor in his eyes, as in the case of the speaking ram who carried Phryxus over the Hellespont. He pronounced the Grecian fables to be "many and ridiculous;" whether from their discrepancies or from their intrinsic improbabilities we do not know: and we owe to him the first attempt to force them within the limits of historical credibility; as where he transforms the three-headed Cerberus, the dog of Hadês, into a serpent inhabiting a cavern on Cape Tænarus — and Geryôn of Erytheia into a king of Epirus rich in herds of oxen.[1] Hekatæus traced the genealogy of himself and the gens to which he belonged through a line of fifteen progenitors up to an initial god,[2] — the clearest proof both of his profound faith in the reality of the mythical world, and of his religious attachment to it as the point of junction between the human and the divine personality.

We have next to consider the historians, especially Herodotus and Thucydidês. Like Hekatæus, Thucydidês belonged to a gens which traced its descent from Ajax, and through Ajax to Æakus and Zeus.[3] Herodotus modestly implies that he himself had no such privilege to boast of.[4] Their curiosity respecting the

---

[1] Hekatæi Fragm. ed. Didot. 332, 346, 349; Schol. Apollôn. Rhod. l. 256; Athenæ. ii. p. 133; Skylax, c. 26.

Perhaps Hekatæus was induced to look for Erytheia in Epirus by the brick-red color of the earth there in many places, noticed by Pouqueville and other travellers (Voyage dans la Grèce, vol. ii. 248: see Klausen, Æneas und die Penaten, vol. i. p. 222). Ἑκαταῖος ὁ Μιλήσιος — λόγον εὗρεν εἰκότα, Pausan. iii. 25, 4. He seems to have written expressly concerning the fabulous Hyperboreans, and to have upheld the common faith against doubts which had begun to rise in his time: the derisory notice of Hyperboreans in Herodotus is probably directed against Hekatæus, iv. 36; Schol. Apollôn. Rhod. ii. 675; Diodôr. ii. 47.

It is maintained by Mr. Clinton (Fast. Hell. ii. p. 480) and others (see not. ad Fragment. Hecatæi, p. 30, ed. Didot), that the work on the Hyperboreans was written by Hekatæus of Abdera, a literary Greek of the age of Ptolemy Philadelphus — not by Hekatæus of Milêtus. I do not concur in this opinion. I think it much more probable that the earlier Hekatæus was the author spoken of.

The distinguished position held by Hekatæus at Milêtus is marked not only by the notice which Herodotus takes of his opinions on public matters, but also by his negotiation with the Persian satrap Artaphernes on behalf of his countrymen (Diodôr. Excerpt. xlvii. p. 41, ed. Dindorf).

[2] Herodot. ii. 143.   [3] Marcellin. Vit. Thucyd. init
[4] Herodot. ii. 143.

past had no other materials to work upon except the mythes;
but these they found already cast by the logographers into a continuous series, and presented as an aggregate of antecedent history, chronologically deduced from the times of the gods.   In
common with the body of the Greeks, both Herodotus and Thucydidês had imbibed that complete and unsuspecting belief in the
general reality of mythical antiquity, which was interwoven with
the religion and the patriotism, and all the public demonstrations
of the Hellenic world. To acquaint themselves with the genuine
details of this foretime, was an inquiry highly interesting to them:
but the increased positive tendencies of their age, as well as their
own habits of personal investigation, had created in them an *historical sense* in regard to the past as well as to the present. Hav
ing acquired a habit of appreciating the intrinsic tests of historical credibility and probability, they found the particular narratives of the poets and logographers, inadmissible as a whole even
in the eyes of Hekatæus, still more at variance with their stricter
canons of criticism.   And we thus observe in them the constant
struggle, as well as the resulting compromise, between these two
opposite tendencies; on one hand a firm belief in the reality of
the mythical world, on the other hand an inability to accept the
details which their only witnesses, the poets and logographers,
told them respecting it.

Each of them however performed the process in his own way
Herodotus is a man of deep and anxious religious feeling; he
often recognizes the special judgments of the gods as determining
historical events: his piety is also partly tinged with that mystical
vein which the last two centuries had gradually infused into the
religion of the Greeks — for he is apprehensive of giving offence
to the gods by reciting publicly what he has heard respecting
them; he frequently stops short in his narrative and intimates
that there *is* a sacred legend, but that he will not tell it: in othei
cases, where he feels compelled to speak out, he entreats forgiveness for doing so from the gods and heroes.   Sometimes he will
not even mention the name of a god, though he generally thinks
himself authorized to do so, the names being matter of public
notoriety.[1]   Such pious reserve, which the open-hearted Herodo-

---

[1] Herodot. ii. 3, 51, 61, 65, 170. He alludes briefly (c. 51) to an ἱρὸς λόγος
which was communicated in the Samothracian mysteries, but he does not

ius avowedly proclaims as chaining up his tongue, affords a striking contrast with the plain-spoken and unsuspecting tone of the
ancient epic, as well as of the popular legends, wherein the gods
and their proceedings were the familiar and interesting subjects
of common talk as well as of common sympathy, without ceasing
to inspire both fear and reverence.

Herodotus expressly distinguishes, in the comparison of Polykratês with Minôs, the human race to which the former belonged,
from the divine or heroic race which comprised the latter.[1] But
he has a firm belief in the authentic personality and parentage of
all the names in the mythes, divine, heroic and human, as well
as in the trustworthiness of their chronology computed by generations. He counts back 1600 years from his own day to that of
Semelê, mother of Dionysus; 900 years to Hêraklês, and 800
years to Penelopê, the Trojan war being a little earlier in date.[2]
Indeed even the longest of these periods must have seemed to him
comparatively short, seeing that he apparently accepts the prodigious series of years which the Egyptians professed to draw from
a recorded chronology — 17,000 years from their god Hêraklês,
and 15,000 years from their god Osiris or Dionysus, down to
their king Amasis[3] (550 B. C.)   So much was his imagination
familiarized with these long chronological computations barren of
events, that he treats Homer and Hesiod as "men of yesterday,"
though separated from his own age by an interval which he reck-
ons as four hundred years.[4]

---

mention what it was: also about the Thesmophoria, or τελετὴ of Dêmêtêr
(c. 171).

Καὶ περὶ μὲν τούτων τοσαῦτα ἡμῖν εἰπούσι, καὶ παρὰ τῶν θεῶν καὶ ἡρώων
εὐμένεια εἴε (c. 45).

Compare similar scruples on the part of Pausanias (viii. 25 and 37).

The passage of Herodotus (ii. 3) is equivocal, and has been understood in
more ways than one (see Lobeck, Aglaopham. p. 1287).

The aversion of Dionysius of Halikarnassus to reveal the divine secrets is
not less powerful (see A. R. i. 67, 68), and Pausanias passim.

[1] Herod. iii. 122.   [2] Herod. ii. 145.
[3] Herodot. ii. 43–145.   Καὶ ταῦτα Αἰγύπτιοι ἀτρεκέως φασὶ ἐπίστασθαι,
ἀεί τε λογιζόμενοι καὶ ἀεὶ ἀπογραφόμενοι τὰ ἔτεα.
[4] Herodot, ii. 53. μέχρι οὗ πρώην τε καὶ χθὲς, ὡς εἰπεῖν λόγῳ. Ἡσίοδον
γὰρ καὶ Ὅμηρον ἡλικίην τετρακοσίοισι ἔτεσι δοκέω μευ πρεσβυτέρους γενέ
·θαι, καὶ οὐ πλέοσι.

17*

Herodotus had been profoundly impressed with what he saw
and heard in Egypt. The wonderful monuments, the eviden
antiquity, and the peculiar civilization of that country, acquired
such preponderance in his mind over his own native legends, that
he is disposed to trace even the oldest religious names or institutions of Greece to Egyptian or Phœnician original, setting aside
in favor of this hypothesis the Grecian legends of Dionysus and
Pan.[1] The oldest Grecian mythical genealogies are thus made
ultimately to lose themselves in Egyptian or Phœnician antiquity,
and in the full extent of these genealogies Herodotus firmly believes. It does not seem that any doubt had ever crossed his
mind as to the real personality of those who were named or described in the popular mythes: all of them have once had reality,
either as men, as heroes, or as gods. The eponyms of cities,
dêmês and tribes, are all comprehended in this affirmative category; the supposition of fictitious personages being apparently
never entertained. Deukaliôn, Hellên, Dorus,[2] — Iôn, with his
four sons, the eponyms of the old Athenian tribes,[3] — the autochthonous Titakus and Dekelus,[4] — Danaus, Lynkeus, Perseus,
Amphitryôn, Alkmêna, and Hêraklês,[5] — Talthybius, the heroic
progenitor of the privileged heraldic gens at Sparta, — the Tyndarids and Helena,[6] — Agamemnôn, Menelaus, and Orestes,[7] —
Nestôr and his son Peisistratus, — Asôpus, Thêbê, and Ægina,
— Inachus and Iô, Æêtês and Mêdea,[8] — Melanippus, Adrastus,
and Amphiaräus, as well as Jasôn and the Argô,[9] — all these are
occupants of the real past time, and predecessors of himself and
his contemporaries. In the veins of the Lacedæmonian kings
flowed the blood both of Kadmus and of Danaus, their splendid
pedigree being traceable to both of these great mythical names:
Herodotus carries the lineage up through Hêraklês first to Perseus and Danaê, then through Danaê to Akrisius and the Egyptian Danaus; but he drops the paternal lineage when he comes

---

[1] Herodot. ii. 146.   [2] Herod. i. 56.
[3] Herod. v. 66.   [4] Herod. ix. 73.
[5] Herod. ii, 43–44, 91-98, 171-182 (the Egyptians admitted the truth of
the Greek legend, that Perseus had come to Libya to fetch the Gorgon's
head).
[6] Herod. ii. 113–120; iv. 145; vii. 134.   [7] Herod. i. 67–68; ii. 113. vii. 159
[8] Herod. i. 1, 2, 4; v 81, 65.   [9] Herod. i. 52; iv. 145; v. 67; vii. 193.

to Perseus (inasmuch as Perseus is the son of Zeus by Danaê, without any reputed human father, such as Amphitryôn was to Hêraklês), and then follow the higher members of the series through Danaê alone.[1] He also pursues the same regal genealogy, through the mother of Eurysthenês and Proclês, up to Polynikês, Œdipus, Laius, Labdakus, Polydôrus and Kadmus; and he assigns various ancient inscriptions which he saw in the templé of the Ismenian Apollo at Thêbes, to the ages of Laius and Œdipus.[2] Moreover, the sieges of Thêbes and Troy, — the Argonautic expedition, — the invasion of Attica by the Amazons, — the protection of the Herakleids, and the defeat and death of Eurystheus, by the Athenians,[3] — the death of Mêkisteus and Tydeus before Thêbes by the hands of Melanippus, and the touching calamities of Adrastus and Amphiaräus connected with the same enterprise, — the sailing of Kastôr and Pollux in the Argô,[4] — the abductions of Iô, Eurôpa, Mêdea and Helena, — the emigration of Kadmus in quest of Eurôpa, and his coming to Bœôtia, as well as the attack of the Greeks upon Troy to recover Helen,[5] — all these events seem to him portions of past history, not less unquestionably certain, though more clouded over by distance and misrepresentation, than the battles of Salamis and Mykalê.

But though Herodotus is thus easy of faith in regard both to the persons and to the general facts of Grecian mythes, yet when he comes to discuss particular facts taken separately, we find him applying to them stricter tests of historical credibility, and often disposed to reject as well the miraculous as the extravagant. Thus even with respect to Hêraklês, he censures the levity of the Greeks in ascribing to him absurd and incredible exploits; he tries their assertion by the philosophical standard of nature, or of determinate powers and conditions governing the course of events. " How is it consonant to nature (he asks), that Hêraklês, being, as he was, according to the statement of the Greeks, *a man*, should kill many thousand persons? I pray that indulgence may be shown to me both by gods and heroes for saying so much

---

[1] Herod. vi. 52–53.   [2] Herod. iv. 147; v. 59–61.
[3] Herod v. 61; ix. 27–28.   [4] Herod. i. 52; iv. 145; v. 67,
[5] Herod. i. 1–4; ii. 49, 113: iv. 147; v. 94.

as this." The religious feelings of Herodotus here told him that
he was trenching upon the utmost limits of admissible scepticism.[1]

Another striking instance of the disposition of Herodotus to
rationalize the miraculous narratives of the current mythes, is to
be found in his account of the oracle of Dôdôna and its alleged
Egyptian origin. Here, if in any case, a miracle was not only
in full keeping, but apparently indispensable to satisfy the exigences of the religious sentiment; anything less than a miracle
would have appeared tame and unimpressive to the visitors of so
revered a spot, much more to the residents themselves. Accordingly, Herodotus heard, both from the three priestesses and from
the Dodonæans generally, that two black doves had started at
the same time from Thêbes in Egypt: one of them went to Libya,
where it directed the Libyans to establish the oracle of Zeus
Ammon; the other came to the grove of Dôdôna, and perched
on one of the venerable oaks, proclaiming with a human voice
that an oracle of Zeus must be founded on that very spot. The
injunction of the speaking dove was respectfully obeyed.[2]

Such was the tale related and believed at Dôdôna. But Herodotus had also heard, from the priests at Thêbes in Egypt, a
different tale, ascribing the origin of all the prophetic establishments, in Greece as well as in Libya, to two sacerdotal women,
who had been carried away from Thêbes by some Phœnician

[1] Herod. ii. 45. Λέγουσι δὲ πολλὰ καὶ ἄλλα ἀνεπισκέπτως οἱ Ἕλληνες·
εὐήθης δὲ αὐτέων καὶ ὅδε ὁ μῦθός ἐστι, τὸν περὶ τοῦ Ἡρακλέος λέγουσι ....
... Ἔτι δὲ ἕνα ἐόντα τὸν Ἡρακλέα, καὶ ἔτι ἄνθρωπον ὡς δή φασι, κῶς φύσιν
ἔχει πολλὰς μυριάδας φονεῦσαι; Καὶ περὶ μὲν τούτων τοσαῦτα ἡμῖν εἰπούσι,
καὶ παρὰ τῶν θεῶν καὶ παρὰ τῶν ἡρώων εὐμένεια εἴη.

We may also notice the manner in which the historian criticizes the strat
agem whereby Peisistratus established himself as despot at Athens — by
dressing up the stately Athenian woman Phyê in the costume of the goddess
Athênê, and passing off her injunctions as the commands of the goddess:
the Athenians accepted her with unsuspecting faith, and received Peisistratus
at her command. Herodotus treats the whole affair as a piece of extravagant silliness, πρᾶγμα εὐηθέστατον μακρῷ (i. 60).

[2] Herod. ii. 55. Δωδωναίων δὲ αἱ ἱρῆιαι ...... ἔλεγον ταῦτα, συνωμολόγεον
δέ σφι καὶ οἱ ἄλλοι Δωδωναῖοι οἱ περὶ τὸ ἱρόν.

The miracle sometimes takes another form; the oak at Dôdôna was itself
once endued with speech (Dionys. Hal. Ars. Rhetoric. i. 6; Strabo).

merchants and sold, the one in Greece, the other in Libya. The Theban priests boldly assured Herodotus that much pains had been taken to discover what had become of these women so exported, and that the fact of their having been taken to Greece and Libya had been accordingly verified.[1]

The historian of Halicarnassus cannot for a moment think of admitting the miracle which harmonized so well with the feelings of the priestesses and the Dodonæans.[2] " How (he asks) could a dove speak with human voice?" But the narrative of the priests at Thêbes, though its prodigious improbability hardly requires to be stated, yet involved no positive departure from the laws of nature and possibility, and therefore Herodotus makes no difficulty in accepting it. The curious circumstance is, that he turns the native Dodonæan legend into a figurative representation, or rather a misrepresentation, of the supposed true story told by the Theban priests. According to his interpretation, the woman who came from Thêbes to Dôdôna was called a dove, and affirmed to utter sounds like a bird, because she was non-Hellenic and spoke a foreign tongue: when she learned to speak the language of the country, it was then said that the dove spoke with a human voice. And the dove was moreover called black, because of the woman's Egyptian color.

That Herodotus should thus bluntly reject a miracle, recounted to him by the prophetic women themselves as the prime circumstance in the *origines* of this holy place, is a proof of the hold which habits of dealing with historical evidence had acquired over his mind; and the awkwardness of his explanatory mediation between the dove and the woman, marks not less his anxiety, while discarding the legend, to let it softly down into a story quasi-historical and not intrinsically incredible.

We may observe another example of the unconscious tendency

---

[1] Herod. ii. 54.

[2] Herod. ii. 57. 'Επεὶ τέῳ τρόπῳ ἂν πελειάς γε ἀνθρωπηίῃ φωνῇ φθέγξαιτο;
According to one statement, the word Πελειὰς in the Thessalian dialect meant both a dove and a prophetess (Scriptor. Rer. Mythicarum, ed. Bode, i. 96). Had there been any truth in this, Herodotus could hardly have failed to notice it, inasmuch as it would exactly have helped him out of the difficulty which he felt

of Herodotus to eliminate from the mythes the idea of special aid from the gods, in his remarks upon Melampus. He designates Melampus " as a clever man, who had acquired for himself the art of prophecy ;" and had procured through Kadmus much information about the religious rites and customs of Egypt, many of which he introduced into Greece[1] — especially the name, the sacrifices, and the phallic processions of Dionysus : he adds, " that Melampus himself did not accurately comprehend or bring out the whole doctrine, but wise men who came after him made the necessary additions."[2] Though the name of Melampus is here maintained, the character described[3] is something in the vein of Pythagoras — totally different from the great seer and leech of the old epic mythes — the founder of the gifted family of the Amythaonids, and the grandfather of Amphiaräus.[4] But that which is most of all at variance with the genuine legendary spirit, is the opinion expressed by Herodotus (and delivered with some emphasis as *his own*), that Melampus " was a clever man, who had acquired for himself prophetic powers." Such a supposition would have appeared inadmissible to Homer or Hesiod, or indeed to Solôn, in the preceding century, in whose view even inferior arts come from the gods, while Zeus or Apollo bestows the power

---

[1] Herod. ii. 49. 'Εγὼ μὲν νύν φημι Μελάμποδα γενόμενον ἄνδρα σοφὸν, μαντικήν τε ἑωυτῷ συστῆσαι, καὶ πυθόμενον ἀπ' Αἰγύπτου, ἄλλα τε πολλὰ ἐσηγήσασθαι Ἕλλησι, καὶ τὰ περὶ τὸν Διόνυσον, ὀλίγα αὐτῶν παραλλάξαντα.

[2] Herod. ii. 49. 'Ατρεκέως μὲν οὐ πάντα συλλαβὼν τὸν λόγον ἔφηνε · (Melampus) ἀλλ' οἱ ἐπιγνόμενοι τούτῳ σοφισταὶ μεζόνως ἐξέφηναν.

[3] Compare Herod. iv. 95; ii. 81. Ἑλλήνων οὐ τῷ ἀσθενεστάτῳ σοφιστῇ Πυθαγόρᾳ.

[4] Homer, Odyss. xi. 290; xv. 225. Apollodôr. i. 9, 11–12. Hesiod, Eoiai, Fragm. 55, ed. Düntzer (p. 43) —

Ἀλκὴν μὲν γὰρ ἔδωκεν 'Ολύμπιος Αἰακίδῃαι,
Νοῦν δ' Ἀμυθαονίδαις, πλοῦτον δ' ἔπορ' 'Ατρείδῃσι.

also Frag. 34 (p. 38), and Frag. 65 (p. 45); Schol. Apoll. Rhod. i. 118.

Herodotus notices the celebrated mythical narrative of Melampus healing the deranged Argive women (ix. 34); according to the original legend, the daughters of Prœtus. In the Hesiodic Eoiai (Fr. 16, Düntz.; Apollod. ii. 2) the distemper of the Prœtid females was ascribed to their having repudiated the rites and worship of Dionysus (Akusilaus, indeed, assigned a different cause), which shows that the old fable recognized a connection between Melampus and these rites of prophesying.[1] The intimation of such an opinion by Herodotus, himself a thoroughly pious man, marks the sensibly diminished omnipresence of the gods, and the increasing tendency to look for the explanation of phænomena among more visible and determinate agencies.

We may make a similar remark on the dictum of the historian respecting the narrow defile of Tempê, forming the embouchure of the Pêneus and the efflux of all the waters from the Thessalian basin. The Thessalians alleged that this whole basin of Thessaly had once been a lake, but that Poseidôn had split the chain of mountains and opened the efflux;[2] upon which primi-

---

[1] Homer, Iliad, i. 72–87; xv. 412. Odyss. xv. 245–252; iv. 233. Some times the gods inspired prophecy for the special occasion, without conferring upon the party the permanent gift and *status* of a prophet (compare Odyss. i. 202; xvii. 383). Solôn, Fragm. xi. 48–53, Schneidewin:—

> Ἄλλον μάντιν ἔθηκεν ἄναξ ἑκάεργος Ἀπόλλων,
> Ἔγνω δ' ἀνδρὶ κακὸν τήλοθεν ἐρχόμενον,
> Ὦι συνομαρτήσωσι θεοί........

Herodotus himself reproduces the old belief in the special gift of prophetic power by Zeus and Apollo, in the story of Euenius of Apollônia (ix. 94).

See the fine ode of Pindar, describing the birth and inspiration of Jamus, eponymous father of the great prophetic family in Elis called the Jamids (Herodot. ix. 33), Pindar, Olymp. vi. 40–75. About Teiresias, Sophoc. Œd. Tyr. 283–410. Neither Nestôr nor Odysseus possesses the gift of prophecy.

[2] More than one tale is found elsewhere, similar to this, about the defile of Tempê:—

"A tradition exists that this part of the country was once a lake, and that Solomon commanded two deeves, or genii, named Ard and Beel, to turn off the water into the Caspian, which they effected by cutting a passage through the mountains; and a city, erected in the newly-formed plain, was named after them Ard-u-beel." (Sketches on the Shores of the Caspian, by W. R. Holmes.)

Also about the plain of Santa Fe di Bogota, in South America, that it was once under water, until Bochica cleft the mountains and opened a channel of egress (Humboldt, Vues des Cordillères, p. 87–88); and about the plateau of Kashmir (Humboldt, Asie Centrale, vol. i. p 102), drained in a like miraculous manner by the saint Kásyapa. The manner in which conjectures, derived from local configuration or peculiarities, are often made to assume the form of *traditions*, is well remarked by the same illustrious traveller: "Ce qui se présente comme une tradition, n'est souvent que le reflet de l'impression que laisse l'aspect des lieux. Des bancs de coquilles à demi-fossiles, répandues dans les isthmes ou sut des plateaux, font naître

tive belief, thoroughly conformable to the genius of Homer and
Hesiod, Herodotus comments as follows: "The Thessalian statement is reasonable. For whoever thinks that Poseidôn shakes
the earth, and that the rifts of an earthquake are the work of
that god, will, on seeing the defile in question, say that Poseidôn
has caused it. For the rift of the mountains is, as appeared to
me (when I saw it), the work of an earthquake." Herodotus
admits the reference to Poseidôn, when pointed out to him, but
it stands only in the background : what is present to his mind is
the phænomenon of the earthquake, not as a special act, but as
part of a system of habitual operations.[1]

---

même chez les hommes les moins avancés dans la culture intellectuelle,
l'idée de grandes inondations, d'anciennes communications entre des bassins
limitrophes. Des opinions, que l'on pourroit appeler systématiques, se trouvent dans les forêts de l'Orénoque comme dans les îles de la Mer du Sud
Dans l'une et dans l'autre de ces contrées, elles ont pris la forme des tradi
tions." (A. von Humboldt, Asie Centrale, vol. ii. p. 147.) Compare a
similar remark in the same work and volume, p. 286–294.

[1] Herodot. vii. 129. (Poseidôn was worshipped as Πετραῖος in Thessaly.
in commemoration of this geological interference : Schol. Pindar. Pyth. iv.
245.) Τὸ δὲ παλαιὸν λέγεται, οὐκ ἐόντος κω τοῦ αὐλῶνος καὶ διεκρόου τούτου,
τοὺς ποτίμους τούτους.........ῥέοντας ποιεῖν τὴν Θεσσαλίην πᾶσαν πέλαγος.
Αὐτοὶ μέν νυν Θεσσαλοὶ λέγουσι Ποσειδέωνα ποιῆσαι τὸν αὐλῶνα, δι' οὖ ῥέει
ὁ Πηνειὸς, οἰκότα λέγοντες. Ὅστις γὰρ νομίζει Ποσειδέωνα τὴν γῆν σείειν,
καὶ τὰ διεστεῶτα ὑπὸ σεισμοῦ τοῦ θεοῦ τούτου ἔργα εἶναι, καὶ ἂν ἐκεῖνο ἰδὼν
φαίη Ποσειδέωνα ποιῆσαι. Ἐστὶ γὰρ σεισμοῦ ἔργον, ὡς ἐμοὶ ἐφαίνετο εἶναι,
ἡ διάστασις τῶν οὐρέων. In another case (viii. 129), Herodotus believes that
Poseidôn produced a preternaturally high tide, in order to punish the Persians, who had insulted his temple near Potidæa : here was a special motive
for the god to exert his power.

This remark of Herodotus illustrates the hostile ridicule cast by Aristophanês (in the Nubes) upon Socratês, on the score of alleged impiety, because he belonged to a school of philosophers (though in point of fact he
discountenanced that line of study) who introduced physical laws and forces
in place of the personal agency of the gods. The old man Strepsiades in
quires from Socratês, *Who rains?* *Who thunders?* To which Socratês re
plies, "*Not Zeus,* but the Nephelæ, *i. e. the clouds :* you never saw rain without clouds." Strepsiades then proceeds to inquire —" But who is it that
compels the clouds to move onward ? is it not Zeus ?" Socratês —" Not
at all ; it is æthereal rotation." Strepsiades —" Rotation ? that had escaped
me : Zeus then no longer exists, and Rotation reigns in his place."

STREPS.   Ὁ δ' ἀναγκάζων ἐστὶ τίς αὐτὰς (Νεφέλας), οὐχ ὁ Ζεὺς, ὥστε φέρεσ-
      θαι;

Herodotus adopts the Egyptian version of the legend of Troy, founded on that capital variation which seems to have originated with Stesichorus, and according to which Helen never left Sparta at all — her *eidólon* had been taken to Troy in her place. Upon this basis a new story had been framed, midway between Homer and Stesichorus, representing Paris to have really carried off Helen from Sparta, but to have been driven by storms to Egypt,

SOCRAT.   Ἥκιστ᾽, ἀλλ᾽ αἰθέριος δῖνος.
STREPS.   Δῖνος; τουτί μ᾽ ἐλελήθει —
          Ὁ Ζεὺς οὐκ ὤν, ἀλλ᾽ ἀντ᾽ αὐτοῦ Δῖνος νυνὶ βασιλεύων.

To the same effect v. 1454, Δῖνος βασιλεύει τὸν Δί᾽ ἐξεληλακώς — " Rotation has driven out Zeus, and reigns in his place."

If Aristophanês had had as strong a wish to turn the public antipathies against Herodotus as against Socratês and Euripidês, the explanation here given would have afforded him a plausible show of truth for doing so; and it is highly probable that the Thessalians would have been sufficiently displeased with the view of Herodotus to sympathize in the poet's attack upon him.   The point would have been made (waiving metrical considerations) —

          Σεισμὸς βασιλεύει, τὸν Ποσειδῶν᾽ ἐξεληλακώς.

The comment of Herodotus upon the Thessalian view seems almost as if it were intended to guard against this very inference.

Other accounts ascribed the cutting of the defile of Tempê to Hêraklês (Diodôr. iv. 18).

Respecting the ancient Grecian faith, which recognized the displeasure of Poseidôn as the cause of earthquakes, see Xenoph. Hellen. iii. 3, 2; Thucydid. i. 127; Strabo, xii. p. 579; Diodôr. xv. 48–49. It ceased to give universal satisfaction even so early as the time of Thalês and Anaximenês (see Aristot. Meteorolog. ii. 7–8; Plutarch, Placit. Philos. iii. 15; Seneca, Natural. Quæst. vi. 6–23); and that philosopher, as well as Anaxagoras, Democritus and others, suggested different physical explanations of the fact. Notwithstanding a dissentient minority, however, the old doctrine still continued to be generally received: and Diodôrus, in describing the terrible earthquake in 373 B. C, by which Helikê and Bura were destroyed, while he notices those philosophers (probably Kallisthenês, Senec. Nat. Quæst. vi. 23) who substituted physical causes and laws in place of the divine agency, rejects their views, and ranks himself with the religious public, who traced this formidable phænomenon to the wrath of Poseidôn (xv. 48–49).

The Romans recognized many different gods as producers of earthquakes; an unfortunate creed, since it exposed them to the danger of addressing their prayers to the wrong god: " Unde in ritualibus et pontificiis observatur, obtemperantibus sacerdotiis caute, ne alio Deo pro alio nominato, cum quis eorum terram concutiat, piacula committantur." (Ammian. Marcell. xvii. 7.)

where she remained during the whole siege of Troy, having been
detained by Prôteus, the king of the country, until Menelaus
came to reclaim her after his triumph. The Egyptian priests,
with their usual boldness of assertion, professed to have heard
the whole story from Menelaus himself — the Greeks had be-
seiged Troy, in the full persuasion that Helen and the stolen
treasures were within the walls, nor would they ever believe the
repeated denials of the Trojans as to the fact of her presence. In
intimating his preference for the Egyptian narrative, Herodotus
betrays at once his perfect and unsuspecting confidence that he is
dealing with genuine matter of history, and his entire distrust of
the epic poets, even including Homer, upon whose authority that
supposed history rested. His reason for rejecting the Homeric
version is that it teems with historical improbabilities. If Helen
had been really in Troy (he says), Priam and the Trojans would
never have been so insane as to retain her to their own utter
ruin: but it was the divine judgment which drove them into the
miserable alternative of neither being able to surrender Helen,
nor to satisfy the Greeks of the real fact that they had never
had possession of her — in order that mankind might plainly
read, in the utter destruction of Troy, the great punishments with
which the gods visit great misdeeds. Homer (Herodotus thinks)
had heard this story, but designedly departed from it, because
it was not so suitable a subject for epic poetry.[1]

Enough has been said to show how wide is the difference between Herodotus and the logographers with their literal tran-
script of the ancient legends. Though he agrees with them in
admitting the full series of persons and generations, he tries the
circumstances narrated by a new standard. Scruples have arisen
in his mind respecting violations of the laws of nature: the poets

---

[1] Herod. ii. 116. δοκέει δέ μοι καὶ Ὅμηρος τὸν λόγον τοῦτον πυθέσθαι· ἀλλ᾽
οὐ γὰρ ὁμοίως εὐπρεπὴς ἦν ἐς τὴν ἐποποιΐην ἥν τῷ ἑτέρῳ τῷ περ ἐχρήσατο·
ἐς ὃ μετῆκε αὐτὸν, δηλώσας ὡς καὶ τοῦτον ἐπισταῖτο τὸν λόγον.

Herodotus then produces a passage from the Iliad, with a view to prove
that Homer knew of the voyage of Paris and Helen to Egypt; but the
passage proves nothing at all to the point.

Again (c. 120), his slender confidence in the epic poets breaks out—εἰ χρή
τι τοῖσι ἐποποιοῖσι χρεώμενον λέγειν.

It is remarkable that Herodotus is disposed to identify Helen with the
ξείνη Ἀφροδίτη whose temple he saw at Memphis (c. 112).

are unworthy of trust, and their narratives must be brought into conformity with historical and ethical conditions, before they can be admitted as truth. To accomplish this conformity, Herodotus is willing to mutilate the old legend in one of its most vital points: he sacrifices the personal presence of Helena in Troy, which ran through every one of the ancient epic poems belonging to the Trojan cycle, and is indeed, under the gods, the great and present moving force throughout.

Thucydidês places himself generally in the same point of view as Herodotus with regard to mythical antiquity, yet with some considerable differences. Though manifesting no belief in present miracles or prodigies,[1] he seems to accept without reserve the preexistent reality of all the persons mentioned in the mythes, and of the long series of generations extending back through so many supposed centuries: in this category, too, are included the eponymous personages, Hellen, Kekrops, Eumolpus, Pandiôn, Amphilochus the son of Amphiaräus, and Akarnan. But on the other hand, we find no trace of that distinction between a human and an heroic ante-human race, which Herodotus still admitted, — nor any respect for Egyptian legends. Thucydidês, regarding the personages of the mythes as men of the same breed and stature with his own contemporaries, not only tests the acts imputed to them by the same limits of credibility, but presumes in them the same political views and feelings as he was accustomed to trace in the proceedings of Peisistratus or Periklês. He treats the Trojan war as a great political enterprise, undertaken by all Greece ; brought into combination through the imposing power of

---

[1] " Ut conquirere fabulosa (says Tacitus, Hist. ii. 50, a worthy parallel of Thucydidês) et fictis oblectare legentium animos, procul gravitate cœpti operis crediderim, ita vulgatis traditisque demere fidem non ausim. Die, quo Bebriaci certabatur, avem inusitatâ specie, apud Regium Lepidum celebri vico consedisse, incolæ memorant; nec deinde cœtu hominum aut circumvolitantium alitum, territam pulsamque, donec Otho se ipse interficeret: tum ablatam ex oculis : et tempora reputantibus, initium finemque miraculi cum Othonis exitu competisse." Suetonius (Vesp. 5) recounts a different miracle, in which three eagles appear.

This passage of Tacitus occurs immediately after his magnificent description of the suicide of the emperor Otho, a deed which he contemplates with the most fervent admiration. His feelings were evidently so wrought up that he was content to relax the canons of historical credibility.

Agamemnôn, not (according to the legendary narrative) through
the influence of the oath exacted by Tyndareus. Then he explains how the predecessors of Agamemnôn arrived at so vast a
dominion — beginning with Pelops, who came over (as he says)
from Asia with great wealth among the poor Peloponnêsians,
and by means of this wealth so aggrandized himself, though a
foreigner, as to become the eponym of the peninsula. Next followed his son Atreus, who acquired after the death of Eurystheus
the dominion of Mykênæ, which had before been possessed by
the descendants of Perseus: here the old legendary tale, which
described Atreus as having been banished by his father Pelops
in consequence of the murder of his elder brother Chrysippus, is
invested with a political bearing, as explaining the reason why
Atreus retired to Mykênæ. Another legendary tale — the defeat
and death of Eurystheus by the fugitive Herakleids in Attica, so
celebrated in Attic tragedy as having given occasion to the generous protecting intervention of Athens — is also introduced as
furnishing the cause why Atreus succeeded to the deceased Eurystheus: "for Atreus, the maternal uncle of Eurystheus, had been
entrusted by the latter with his government during the expedition
into Attica, and had effectually courted the people, who were
moreover in great fear of being attacked by the Herakleids."
Thus the Pelopids acquired the supremacy in Peloponnêsus, and
Agamemnôn was enabled to get together his 1200 ships and
100,000 men for the expedition against Troy. Considering that
contingents were furnished from every portion of Greece, Thucydidês regards this as a small number, treating the Homeric catalogue as an authentic muster-roll, perhaps rather exaggerated
than otherwise. He then proceeds to tell us why the armament
was not larger: many more men could have been furnished, but
there was not sufficient money to purchase provisions for their
subsistence; hence they were compelled, after landing and gaining
a victory, to fortify their camp, to divide their army, and to send
away one portion for the purpose of cultivating the Chersonese,
and another portion to sack the adjacent towns. This was the
grand reason why the siege lasted so long as ten years. For if
it had been possible to keep the whole army together, and to act

with an undivided force, Troy would have been taken both earlier and at smaller cost.[1]

Such is the general sketch of the war of Troy, as given by Thucydidês. So different is it from the genuine epical narrative, that we seem hardly to be reading a description of the same event; still less should we imagine that the event was known, to him as well as to us, only through the epic poets themselves. The men, the numbers, and the duration of the siege, do indeed remain the same; but the cast and juncture of events, the determining forces, and the characteristic features, are altogether heterogeneous. But, like Herodotus, and still more than Herodotus, Thucydidês was under the pressure of two conflicting impulses — he shared the general faith in the mythical antiquity, but at the same time he could not believe in any facts which contradicted the laws of historical credibility or probability. He was thus under the necessity of torturing the matter of the old mythes into conformity with the subjective exigencies of his own mind: he left out, altered, recombined, and supplied new connecting principles and supposed purposes, until the story became such as no one could have any positive reason for calling in question: though it lost the impressive mixture of religion, romance, and individual adventure, which constituted its original charm, it acquired a smoothness and plausibility, and a poetical *ensemble*, which the critics were satisfied to accept as historical truth. And historical truth it would doubtless have been, if any independent evidence could have been found to sustain it. Had Thucydidês been able to produce such new testimony, we should have been pleased to satisfy ourselves that the war of Troy, as he recounted it, was the real event; of which the war of Troy, as sung by the epic poets, was a misreported, exaggerated, and ornamented recital. But in this case the poets are the only real witnesses, and the narrative of Thucydidês is a mere extract and distillation from their incredibilities.

A few other instances may be mentioned to illustrate the views of Thucydidês respecting various mythical incidents. 1. He treats the residence of the Homeric Phæakians at Corkyra as an undisputed fact, and employs it partly to explain the efficiency of

the Korkyrean navy in times preceding the Peloponnesian war.[1]
2. He notices, with equal confidence, the story of Têreus and
Proknê, daughter of Pandiôn, and the murder of the child Itys
by Proknê his mother, and Philomêla; and he produces this
ancient mythe with especial reference to the alliance between the
Athenians and Têrês, king of the Odrysian Thracians, during the
time of the Peloponnesian war, intimating that the Odrysian
Têrês was neither of the same family nor of the same country as
Têreus the husband of Proknê.[2] The conduct of Pandiôn, in
giving his daughter Proknê in marriage to Têreus, is in his view
dictated by political motives and interests. 3. He mentions the
Strait of Messina as the place through which Odysseus is said to
have sailed.[3] 4. The Cyclôpes and the Læstrygones (he says)
were the most ancient reported inhabitants of Sicily; but he cannot tell to what race they belonged, nor whence they came.[4] 5.
Italy derived its name from Italus, king of the Sikels. 6. Eryx
and Egesto in Sicily were founded by fugitive Trojans after the
capture of Troy; also Skionê, in the Thracian peninsula of Pal
lênê, by Greeks from the Achæan town of Pellênê, stopping
thither in their return from the siege of Troy: the Amphilochian
Argos in the Gulf of Ambrakia was in like manner founded by

---

[1] Thucyd. i. 25.

[2] Thucyd. ii. 29. Καὶ τὸ ἔργον τὸ περὶ τὸν Ἴτυν αἱ γυναῖκες ἐν τῇ γῇ ταύτῃ
ἔπραξαν· πολλοῖς δὲ καὶ τῶν ποιητῶν ἐν ἀηδόνος μνήμῃ Δαυλιὰς ἡ ὄρνις
ἐπωνόμασται. Εἰκὸς δὲ καὶ τὸ κῆδος Πανδίονα ξυνάψασθαι τῆς θυγατρὸς διὰ
τοσούτου, ἐπ᾽ ὠφελείᾳ τῇ πρὸς ἀλλήλους, μᾶλλον ἢ διὰ πολλῶν ἡμερῶν ἐς
Ὀδρύσας ὁδοῦ. The first of these sentences would lead us to infer, if it came
from any other pen than that of Thucydidês, that the writer believed the
metamorphosis of Philomêla into a nightingale: see above, ch. xi. p. 270.

The observation respecting the convenience of neighborhood for the marriage is remarkable, and shows how completely Thucydidês regarded the
event as historical. What would he have said respecting the marriage of
Oreithyia, daughter of Erechtheus, with Boreas, and the prodigious distance
which she is reported to have been carried by her husband? Ὑπέρ τε πόντον
πάντ᾽, ἐπ᾽ ἔσχατα χθονός, etc. (Sophoklês ap. Strabo. vii. p. 295.)

From the way in which Thucydidês introduces the mention of this event,
we see that he intended to correct the misapprehension of his countrymen,
who having just made an alliance with the Odrysian Têrês, were led by that
circumstance to think of the old mythical Têreus, and to regard him as the
ancestor of Têrês.

[3] Thucyd. iv. 24.   [4] Thucyd. vi. 2.

Amphilochus son of Amphiaráus, in his return from the same
enterprise. The remorse and mental derangement of the matri-
cidal Alkmæôn, son of Amphiaräus, is also mentioned by Thucydidês,[1] as well as the settlement of his son Akarnan in the country
called after him Akarnania.[2]

Such are the special allusions made by this illustrious author
in the course of his history to mythical events. From the tenor
of his language we may see that he accounted all that could be
known about them to be uncertain and unsatisfactory; but he has
it much at heart to show, that even the greatest were inferior in

---

[1] Thucyd. ii. 68–102; iv. 120; vi. 2.   Antiochus of Syracuse, the contem
porary of Thucydidês, also mentioned Italus as the eponymous king of Italy.
he farther named Sikelus, who came to Morgos, son of Italus, after having
been banished from Rome.   He talks about Italus, just as Thucydidês talks
about Thêseus, as a wise and powerful king, who first acquired a great
dominion (Dionys. H. A. R. i. 12, 35, 73).   Aristotle also mentioned Italus
in the same general terms (Polit. vii. 9, 2).

[2] We may here notice some particulars respecting Isokratês.   He mani
fests entire confidence in the authenticity of the mythical genealogies and
chronology; but while he treats the mythical personages as historically real,
he regards them at the same time not as human, but as half-gods, superior
to humanity.   About Helena, Thêseus, Sarpêdôn, Cycnus, Memnôn, Achilles, etc., see Encom. Helen. Or. x. pp. 282, 292, 295. Bek.   Helena was worshipped in his time as a goddess at Therapnæ (*ib.* p. 295).   He recites the
settlements of Danaus, Kadmus, and Pelops in Greece, as undoubted historical facts (p. 297).   In his discourse called *Busiris*, he accuses Polykratês, the
sophist, of a gross anachronism, in having placed Busiris subsequent in point
of date to Orpheus and Æolus (Or. xi. p. 301, Bek.), and he adds that the
tale of Busiris having been slain by Hêraklês was chronologically impossible
(p. 309).   Of the long Athenian genealogy from Kekrops to Thêseus, he
speaks with perfect historical confidence (Panathenaic. p. 349, Bek.); not
less so of the adventures of Hêraklês and his mythical contemporaries, which
he places in the mouth of Archidamus as a justification of the Spartan title
to Messenia (Or. vi. *Archidamus*, p. 156, Bek.; compare Or. v. *Philippus*, pp.
114, 138), φάσιν, οἷς περὶ τῶν παλαιῶν πιστεύομεν, etc.   He condemns the
poets in strong language for the wicked and dissolute tales which they circulated respecting the gods : many of them (he says) had been punished for
such blasphemies by blindness, poverty, exile, and other misfortunes (Or. xi.
p. 309, Bek.).

In general, it may be said that Isokratês applies no principles of historical
criticism to the mythes; he rejects such as appear to him discreditable or
unworthy, and believes the rest.

magnituae and importance to the Peloponnesian war.[1] In this
respect his opinion seems to have been at variance with that
which was popular among his contemporaries.

---

[1] Thucyd. i. 21–22.

The first two volumes of this history have been noticed in an able article
of the Quarterly Review, for October, 1846 ; as well as in the Heidelberger
Jahrbücher der Literatur (1846. No. 41. pp. 641–655), by Professor Kortüm.
While expressing, on several points, approbation of my work, by which I
feel much flattered — both my English and my German critic take partial
objection to the views respecting Grecian legend.   While the Quarterly Reviewer contends that the mythopœic faculty of the human mind, though
essentially loose and untrustworthy, is never creative, but requires some basis
of fact to work upon — Kortüm thinks that I have not done justice to Thucydidês, as regards his way of dealing with legend ; that I do not allow sufficient weight to the authority of an historian so circumspect and so cold-
blooded (den kalt-blüthigsten und besonnensten Historiker des Alterthums,
p. 653) as a satisfactory voucher for the early facts of Grecian history in his
preface (Herr G. Fehlt also, wenn er das anerkannt kritische Pro-œmium als
Gewährsmann verschmäht, p. 654).

No man feels more powerfully than I do the merits of Thucydidês as an
historian, or the value of the example which he set in multiplying critical inquiries respecting matters recent and verifiable.   But the ablest judge or
advocate, in investigating specific facts, can proceed no further than he finds
witnesses having the means of knowledge, and willing more or less to tell
truth.   In reference to facts prior to 776 B. C., Thucydidês had nothing before
him except the legendary poets, whose credibility is not at all enhanced by
the circumstance that he accepted them as witnesses, applying himself only
to cut down and modify their allegations.   His credibility in regard to the
specific facts of these early times depends altogether upon theirs.   Now we
in our day are in a better position for appreciating their credibility than he
was in his, since the foundations of historical evidence are so much more fully
understood, and good or bad materials for history are open to comparison in
such large extent and variety.   Instead of wondering that he shared the
general faith in such delusive guides — we ought rather to give him credit
for the reserve with which he qualified that faith, and for the sound idea of
historical possibility to which he held fast as the limit of his confidence.
But it is impossible to consider Thucydidês as a *satisfactory guarantee*
(Gewährsmann) for matters of fact which he derives only from such sources.

Professor Kortüm considers that I am inconsistent with myself in refusing
to discriminate particular matters of historical fact among the legends —
and yet in accepting these legends (in my chap. xx.) as giving a faithful mirror of the general state of early Grecian society (p. 653).   It appears to me
that this is no inconsistency, but a real and important distinction.   Whether
Hêraklês, Agamemnôn, Odysseus, etc. were real persons, and performed all,

To touch a little upon the later historians by whom these mythes were handled, we find that Anaximenês of Lampsacus composed a consecutive history of events, beginning from the Theogony down to the battle of Mantineia.[1] But Ephorus professed to omit all the mythical narratives which are referred to times anterior to the return of the Herakleids, (such restriction would of course have banished the siege of Troy,) and even reproved those who introduced mythes into historical writing; adding, that everywhere truth was the object to be aimed at.[2] Yet in practice he seems often to have departed from his own rule.[3] Theopompus, on the other hand, openly proclaimed that

---

or a part, of the possible actions ascribed to them — I profess myself unable to determine But even assuming both the persons and their exploits to be fictions, these very fictions will have been conceived and put together in conformity to the general social phænomena among which the describer and his hearers lived — and will thus serve as illustrations of the manners then prevalent. In fact, the real value of the Preface of Thucydidês, upon which Professor Kortüm bestows such just praise, consists, not in the particular facts which he brings out by altering the legends, but in the rational general views which he sets forth respecting early Grecian society, and respecting the steps as well as the causes whereby it attained its actual position as he saw it.

Professor Kortüm also affirms that the mythes contain "real matter of fact along with mere conceptions:" which affirmation is the same as that of the Quarterly Reviewer, when he says that the mythopœic faculty is not creative. Taking the mythes in the mass, I doubt not that this is true, nor have I anywhere denied it. Taking them one by one, I neither affirm nor deny it. My position is, that, whether there be matter of fact or not, we have no test whereby it can be singled out, identified, and severed from the accompanying fiction. And it lies upon those, who proclaim the practicability of such severance, to exhibit some means of verification better than any which has been yet pointed out. If Thucydidês has failed in doing this, it is certain that none of the many authors who have made the same attempt after him have been more successful.

It cannot surely be denied that the mythopœic faculty is *creative*, when we have before us so many divine legends, not merely in Greece, but in other countries also. To suppose that these religious legends are mere exaggerations, etc. of some basis of actual fact — that the gods of polytheism were merely divinized men, with qualities distorted or feigned — would be to embrace in substance the theory of Euêmerus.

[1] Diodôr. xv. 89. He was a contemporary of Alexander the Great.

[2] Diodôr. iv. 1. Strabo, ix. p. 422, ἐπιτιμήσας τοῖς φιλομυθοῦσιν ἐν τῇ τῆς ἱστωρίας γραφῇ.

[3] Ephorus recounted the principal adventures of Hêraklês (Fragm. 8. 9

he could narrate fables in his history better than Herodotus, or Ktesias, or Hellanicus.[1] The fragments which remain to us, exhibit some proof that this promise was performed as to quantity;[2] though as to his style of narration, the judgment of Dionysius is unfavorable. Xenophôn ennobled his favorite amusement of the chase by numerous examples chosen from the heroic world, tracing their portraits with all the simplicity of an undiminished faith. Kallisthenês, like Ephorus, professed to omit all mythes which referred to a time anterior to the return of the Herakleids; yet we know that he devoted a separate book or portion of his history to the Trojan war.[3] Philistus introduced some mythes in the earlier portions of his Sicilian history; but Timæus was distinguished above all others for the copious and indiscriminate way in which he collected and repeated such legends.[4] Some of these

ed. Marx.), the tales of Kadmus and Harmonia (Fragm. 12), the banishment of Ætôlus from Elis (Fragm. 15; Strabo, viii. p. 357); he drew inferences from the chronology of the Trojan and Theban wars (Fragm. 28); he related the coming of Dædalus to the Sikan king Kokalus, and the expedition of the Amazons (Fragm. 99–103).

He was particularly copious in his information about κτίσεις, ἀποικίαι and συγγενείαι (Polyb. ix. 1).

[1] Strabo, i. p. 74.

[2] Dionys. Halic. De Vett. Scriptt. Judic. p. 428, Reisk; Ælian, V. H. iii. 18, Θεόπομπος . . . . . . δεινὸς μυθόλογος.

Theopompus affirmed, that the bodies of those who went into the forbidden precinct (τὸ ἄβατον) of Zeus, in Arcadia, gave no shadow (Polyb. xvi. 12). He recounted the story of Midas and Silênus (Fragm. 74, 75, 76, ed. Wichers); he said a good deal about the heroes of Troy; and he seems to have assigned the misfortunes of the Νόστοι to an historical cause—the rottenness of the Grecian ships, from the length of the siege, while the genuine epic ascribes it to the anger of Athênê (Fragm. 112, 113, 114; Schol. Homer. Iliad. ii. 135); he narrated an alleged expulsion of Kinyras from Cyprus by Agamemnôn (Fragm. 111); he gave the genealogy of the Macedonian queen Olympias up to Achilles and Æakus (Fragm. 232).

[3] Cicero, Epist. ad Familiar. v. 12; Xenophôn de Venation. c. 1.

[4] Philistus, Fragm. 1 (Göller), Dædalus, and Kokalus; about Liber and Juno (Fragm. 57); about the migration of the Sikels into Sicily, eighty years after the Trojan war (ap. Dionys. Hal. i. 3).

Timæus Fragm. 50, 51, 52, 53, Göller) related many fables respecting Jasôn, Mêdea, and the Argonauts generally. The miscarriage of the Athenian armament under Nikias, before Syracuse, is imputed to the anger of Hêraklês against the Athenians because they came to assist the Egestæns

writers employed their ingenuity in transforming the mythical circumstances into plausible matter of history : Ephorus, in particular, converted the serpent Pythô, slain by Apollo, into a tyrannical king.[1]

But the author who pushed this transmutation of legend into history to the greatest length, was the Messenian Euêmerus, contemporary of Kassander of Macedôn. He melted down in this way the divine persons and legends, as well as the heroic — representing both gods and heroes as having been mere earthborn men, though superior to the ordinary level in respect of force and capacity, and deified or heroified after death as a recompense for services or striking exploits. In the course of a voyage into the Indian sea, undertaken by command of Kassander, Euêmerus professed to have discovered a fabulous country called Panchaia, in which was a temple of the Triphylian Zeus : he there described a golden column, with an inscription purporting to have been put up by Zeus himself, and detailing his exploits while on earth.[2] Some eminent men, among whom may be numbered Polybius, followed the views of Euêmerus, and the Roman poet Ennius[3] translated his Historia Sacra ; but on the whole he never acquired favor, and the unblushing inventions which he put into circulation were of themselves sufficient to disgrace both the author and his opinions. The doctrine that all the gods had once existed as mere men offended the religious pagans, and drew upon Euêmerus the imputation of atheism ; but, on the other hand, it came to be warmly espoused by several of the Christian assailants of paganism, — by Minucius Felix, Lactantius, and St. Augustin, who found the ground ready prepared for them in their efforts to strip Zeus and the other pagan gods of the attributes of deity. They believed not only in the main theory, but also in the copious details of Euêmerus ; and the same man whom Strabo casts aside as almost a proverb for mendacity, was ex-

---

descendants of Troy (Plutarch, Nikias, 1), — a naked reproduction of genuine epical agencies by an historian; also about Diomêdês and the Daunians; Phaëthôn and the river Eridanus ; the combats of the Gigantes in the Phlegræan plains (Fragm. 97, 99, 102).

[1] Strabo, ix. p. 422.

[2] Compare Diodôr. v. 44–46 ; and Lactantius, De Falsâ Relig. i. 11.

[3] Cicero, De Naturâ Deor. i. 42 ; Varro, De Re Rust. i. 48.

tolled by them as an excellent specimen of careful historical inquiry.[1]

But though the pagan world repudiated that "lowering tone of explanation," which effaced the superhuman personality of Zeus and the great gods of Olympus, the mythical persons and narratives generally came to be surveyed more and more from the point of view of history, and subjected to such alterations as might make them look more like plausible matter of fact. Polybius, Strabo, Diodôrus, and Pausanias, cast the mythes into historical statements — with more or less of transformation, as the case may require, assuming always that there is a basis of truth, which may be discovered by removing poetical exaggerations and allowing for mistakes. Strabo, in particular, lays down that principle broadly and unequivocally in his remarks upon Homer. To give pure fiction, without any foundation of fact, was in his judgment utterly unworthy of so great a genius ; and he comments with considerable acrimony on the geographer Eratosthenês, who maintains the opposite opinion. Again, Polybius tells us that the Homeric Æolus, the dispenser of the winds by

---

[1] Strabo, ii. p. 102. Οὐ πολὺ οὖν λείπεται ταῦτα τῶν Πύθεω καὶ Εὐημέρου καὶ 'Αντιφάνους ψευσμάτων ; compare also i. p. 47, and ii. p. 104.

St. Augustin, on the contrary, tells us (Civitat. Dei, vi. 7), " Quid de ipso Jove senserunt, qui nutricem ejus in Capitolio posuerunt ? Nonne attestati sunt omnes Euemero, qui non fabulosâ garrulitate, sed historicâ diligentiâ, homines fuisse mortalesque conscripsit ? " And Minucius Felix (Octav. 20–21), " Euemerus exequitur Deorum natales : patrias, sepulcra dinumerat, et per provincias monstrat, Dictæi Jovis, et Apollinis Delphici, et Phariæ Isidis, et Cereris Eleusiniæ." Compare Augustin, Civit. Dei, xviii. 8–14 ; and Clemens Alexand. Cohort. ad Gent. pp. 15-18, Sylb.

Lactantius (De Falsâ Relig. c. 13, 14, 16) gives copious citations from Ennius's translation of the Historia Sacra of Euêmerus.

Εὐήμερος, ὁ ἐπικληθεὶς ἄθεος, Sextus Empiricus, adv. Physicos, ix. § 17–51. Compare Cicero, De Nat. Deor. i. 42 ; Plutarch, De Iside et Osiride, c. 23. tom. ii. p. 475, ed. Wytt.

Nitzsch assumes (Helden Sage der Griechen, sect. 7. p. 84) that the voyage of Euêmerus to Panchaia was intended only as an amusing romance, and that Strabo, Polybius, Eratosthenês and Plutarch were mistaken in construing it as a serious recital. Böttiger, in his Kunst-Mythologie der Griechen (Absch. ii. s. 6. p. 190), takes the same view. But not the least reason is given for adopting this opinion, and it seems to me far-fetched and improbable ; Lobeck (Aglaopham. p. 989), though Nitzsch alludes to him as holding it, manifests no such tendency, as far as I can observe.

appointment from Zeus, was in reality a man eminently skilled
in navigation, and exact in predicting the weather; that the Cy-
clòpes and Læstrygones were wild and savage real men in Sicily ;
and that Scylla and Charybdis were a figurative representation
of dangers arising from pirates in the Strait of Messina. Strabo
speaks of the amazing expeditions of Dionysus and Hêraklês,
and of the long wanderings of Jasôn, Menelaus, and Odysseus,
in the same category with the extended commercial range of the
Phœnician merchant-ships: he explains the report of Thêseus
and Peirithöus having descended to Hadês, by their dangerous
earthly pilgrimages, — and the invocation of the Dioskuri as the
protectors of the imperiled mariner, by the celebrity which they
had acquired as real men and navigators.

Diodôrus gave at considerable length versions of the current
fables respecting the most illustrious names in the Grecian mythical world, compiled confusedly out of distinct and incongruous
authors. Sometimes the mythe is reproduced in its primitive
simplicity, but for the most part it is partially, and sometimes
wholly, historicized. Amidst this jumble of dissentient authorities we can trace little of a systematic view, except the general
conviction that there was at the bottom of the mythes a real
chronological sequence of persons, and real matter of fact, historical or ultra-historical. Nevertheless, there are some few
occasions on which Diodôrus brings us back a step nearer to the
point of view of the old logographers. For, in reference to
Hêraklês, he protests against the scheme of cutting down the
mythes to the level of present reality, and contends that a special
standard of ultra-historical credibility ought to be constituted, so
as to include the mythe in its native dimensions, and do fitting
honor to the grand, beneficent, and superhuman personality of
Hêraklês and other heroes or demi-gods. To apply to such persons the common measure of humanity (he says), and to cavil at
the glorious picture which grateful man has drawn of them, is at
once ungracious and irrational. All nice criticism into the truth
of the legendary narratives is out of place: we show our reverence to the god by acquiescing in the incredibilities of his history, and we must be content with the best guesses which we can
make, amidst the inextricable confusion and numberless discrep-

ancies which they present.¹ Yet though Diodôrus here exhibits
a preponderance of the religious sentiment over the purely historical point of view, and thus reminds us of a period earlier
than Thucydidês — he in another place inserts a series of stories
which seem to be derived from Euêmerus, and in which Uranus,
Kronus, and Zeus appear reduced to the character of human
kings celebrated for their exploits and benefactions.² Many of
the authors, whom Diodôrus copies, have so entangled together
Grecian, Asiatic, Egyptian, and Libyan fables, that it becomes
impossible to ascertain how much of this heterogeneous mass can
be considered as at all connected with the genuine Hellenic
mind.

Pausanias is far more strictly Hellenic in his view of the Grecian mythes than Diodôrus : his sincere piety makes him inclined
to faith generally with regard to the mythical narratives, but
subject nevertheless to the frequent necessity of historicizing or
allegorizing them.   His belief in the general reality of the mythical history and chronology is complete, in spite of the many

¹ Diodôr. iv. 1–8. Ἔνιοι γὰρ τῶν ἀναγινωσκόντων, οὐ δικαίᾳ χρώμενοι κρίσει,
τἀκριβὲς ἐπιζητοῦσιν ἐν ταῖς ἀρχαίαις μυθολογίαις, ἐπίσης τοῖς πραττομένοις
ἐν τῷ καθ' ἡμᾶς χρόνῳ, καὶ τὰ δισταζόμενα τῶν ἔργων διὰ τὸ μέγεθος, ἐκ τοῦ
καθ' αὑτοὺς βίου τεκμαιρόμενοι, τὴν Ἡρακλέους δύναμιν ἐκ τῆς ἀσθενείας τῶν
νῦν ἀνθρώπων θεωροῦσιν, ὥστε διὰ τὴν ὑπερβολὴν τοῦ μεγέθους τῶν ἔργων
ἀπιστεῖσθαι τὴν γραφήν.   Καθόλου γὰρ ἐν ταῖς ἀρχαίαις μυθολογίαις οὐκ ἐκ
παντὸς τρόπου π ι κ ρ ῶ ς τ ὴ ν ἀ λ ή θ ε ι α ν ἐ ξ ε τ α σ τ έ ο ν.   Καὶ γὰρ ἐν
τοῖς θεάτροις π ε π ε ι σ μ έ ν ο ι μ ή τ ε Κ ε ν τ α ύ ρ ο υ ς διφυεῖς ἐξ ἑτερογε-
νῶν σωμάτων ὑπάρξαι, μήτε Γηρυόνην τρισώματον, ὅ μ ω ς π ρ ο σ δ ε χ ό μ ε θ α
τ ὰ ς τ ο ι α ύ τ α ς μ υ θ ο λ ο γ ί α ς, καὶ τ α ῖ ς ἐ π ι σ η μ α σ ί α ι ς σ υ ν α ύ ξ-
ο μ ε ν τ ὴ ν τ ο ῦ θ ε ο ῦ τ ι μ ή ν.   Καὶ γὰρ ἄτοπον, Ἡρακλέα μὲν ἔτι κατ'
ἀνθρώπους ὄντα τοῖς ἰδίοις πόνοις ἐξημερῶσαι τὴν οἰκουμένην, τοὺς δ' ἀνθρώπους, ἐπιλαθομένους τῆς κοινῆς εὐεργεσίας, σ υ κ ο φ α ν τ ε ῖ ν τὸν ἐπὶ τοῖς
καλλίστοις ἔργοις ἔπαινον, etc.
    This is a remarkable passage : first, inasmuch as it sets forth the total inap-
plicability of analogies drawn from the historical past as narratives about
Hêraklês ; next, inasmuch as it suspends the employment of critical and
scientific tests, and invokes an acquiescence interwoven and identified with
the feelings, as the proper mode of evincing pious reverence for the god
Hêraklês.   It aims at reproducing exactly that state of mind to which the
mythes were addressed, and with which alone they could ever be in thorough
harmony.
² Diodôr. iii 45–60 ; v. 44–46.

discrepancies which he finds in it, and which he is unable to reconcile.

Another author who seems to have conceived clearly, and applied consistently, the semi-historical theory of the Grecian mythes, is Palæphatus, of whose work what appears to be a short abstract has been preserved.[1] In the short preface of this treatise " concerning Incredible Tales," he remarks, that some men, from want of instruction, believe all the current narratives ; while others, more searching and cautious, disbelieve them altogether. Each of these extremes he is anxious to avoid. On the one hand, he thinks that no narrative could ever have acquired credence unless it had been founded in truth; on the other, it is impossible for him to accept so much of the existing narratives as conflicts with the analogies of present natural phænomena. If such things ever had been, they would still continue to be — but they never have so occurred; and the extra-analogical features of the stories are to be ascribed to the license of the poets. Palæphatus wishes to adopt a middle course, neither accepting all nor rejecting all : accordingly, he had taken great pains to separate the true from the false in many of the narratives ; he had visited the localities wherein they had taken place, and mad. careful inquiries from old men and others.[2] The results of his

---

[1] The work of Palæphatus, probably this original, is alluded to in the *Ciris* of Virgil (88): —

" Docta Palæphatiâ testatur voce papyrus."

The date of Palæphatus is unknown — indeed this passage of the *Ciris* seems the only ground that there is for inference respecting it. That which we now possess is probably an extract from a larger work — made by another person at some later time: see Vossius de Historicis Græcis, p. 478, ed. Westermann.

[2] Palæphat. init. ap. Script. Mythogr. ed. Westermann, p. 268. Τῶν ἀνθρώπων οἱ μὲν πείθονται πᾶσι τοῖς λεγομένοις, ὡς ἀνομίλητοι σοφίας καὶ ἐπιστήμης — οἱ δὲ πυκνότεροι τὴν φύσιν καὶ πολυπράγμονες ἀπιστοῦσι τὸ παράπαν μηδὲν γενέσθαι τούτων. Ἐμοὶ δὲ δοκεῖ γενέσθαι πάντα τὰ λεγόμενα· ...... γενόμενα δέ τινα οἱ ποιηταὶ καὶ λογόγραφοι παρέτρεψαν εἰς τὸ ἀπιστότερον καὶ θαυμασιώτερον τοῦ θαυμάζειν ἕνεκα τοὺς ἀνθρώπους. Ἐγὼ δὲ γινώσκω, ὅτι οὐ δύναται τὰ τοιαῦτα εἶναι οἷα καὶ λέγεται· τοῦτο δὲ καὶ ʼιείληφα, ὅτι εἰ μὴ ἐγένετο, οὐκ ἂν ἐλέγετο.

The main assumption of the semi-historical theory is here shortly and learly stated.

One of the early Christian writers, Minucius Felix, is astonished at the asy belief of his pagan forefathers in miracles If ever such things had

researches are presented in a new version of fifty legends, among the most celebrated and the most fabulous, comprising the Centaurs, Pasiphaê, Aktæôn, Kadmus and the Sparti, the Sphinx, Cycnus, Dædalus, the Trojan horse, Æolus, Scylla, Geryôn, Bellerophôn, etc.

It must be confessed that Palæphatus has performed his promise of transforming the "incredibilia" into narratives in themselves plausible and unobjectionable, and that in doing so he always follows some thread of analogy, real or verbal. The Centaurs (he tells us) were a body of young men from the village of Nephelê in Thessaly, who first trained and mounted horses for the purpose of repelling a herd of bulls belonging to Ixiôn king of the Lapithæ, which had run wild and done great damage: they pursued these wild bulls on horseback, and pierced them with their spears, thus acquiring both the name of *Prickers* (κέντορες) and the imputed attribute of joint body with the horse. Aktæôn was an Arcadian, who neglected the cultivation of his land for the pleasures of hunting, and was thus eaten up by the expense of his hounds. The dragon whom Kadmus killed at Thêbes, was in reality Drako, king of Thêbes; and the dragon's teeth which he was said to have sown, and from whence sprung a crop of armed men, were in point of fact elephants' teeth, which Kadmus as a rich Phœnician had brought over with him: the sons of Drako sold these elephants' teeth and employed the proceeds to levy troops against Kadmus. Dædalus, instead of flying across the sea on wings, had escaped from Krête in a swift sailing-boat under a violent storm: Kottus, Briareus, and Gygês were not persons with one hundred hands, but inhabitants of the village of Hekatoncheiria in Upper Macedonia, who warred with the inhabitants of Mount Olympus against the Titans: Scylla, whom Odysseus so narrowly escaped, was a fast-

---

been done in former times (he affirms), they would continue to be done now; as they cannot be done now, we may be sure that they never were *really* done formerly (Minucius Felix, Octav. c. 20): "Majoribus enim nostris tam facilis in mendaciis fides fuit, ut temerè crediderint etiam alia monstruosa mira miracula, Scyllam multiplicem, Chimæram multiformem, Hydram, et Centauros. Quid illas aniles fabulas — de hominibus aves, et feras homines, et de hominibus arbores atque flores? *Quæ, si essent facta, fierent; quia fieri non possunt, ideo nec facta sunt.*"

sailing piratical vessel, as was also Pegasus, the alleged winged
horse of Bellerophôn.[1]
By such ingenious conjectures, Palæphatus eliminates all the
incredible circumstances, and leaves to us a string of tales perfectly credible and commonplace, which we should readily believe,
provided a very moderate amount of testimony could be produced in their favor. If his treatment not only disenchants the
original mythes, but even effaces their generic and essential character, we ought to remember that this is not more than what is
done by Thucydidês in his sketch of the Trojan war. Palæphatus handles the mythes consistently, according to the semi-historical theory, and his results exhibit the maximum which that
theory can ever present. By aid of conjecture, we get out of the
impossible, and arrive at matters intrinsically plausible, but to-

[1] Palæphat. Narrat. 1, 3, 6, 13, 20, 21, 29. Two short treatises on the same
subject as this of Palæphatus, are printed along with it, both in the collection
of Gale and of Westermann; the one, *Heracliti de Incredibilibus*, the other
Anonymi de Incredibilibus. They both profess to interpret some of the extraordinary or miraculous mythes, and proceed in a track not unlike that of
Palæphatus. Scylla was a beautiful courtezan, surrounded with abominable
parasites: she ensnared and ruined the companions of Odysseus, though he
himself was prudent enough to escape her (Heraclit. c. 2. p. 313, West.).
Atlas was a great astronomer: Pasiphaê fell in lóve with a youth named
Taurus; the monster called the Chimæra was in reality a ferocious queen,
who had two brothers called Leo and Drako; the ram which carried Phryxus
and Hellê across the Ægean was a boatman named Krias (Heraclit. c. 2, 6.
15, 24).
A great number of similar explanations are scattered throughout the
Scholia on Homer and the Commentary of Eustathius, without specification
of their authors.
Theôn considers such resolution of fable into plausible history as a proof
of surpassing ingenuity (Progymnasmata, cap. 6, ap. Walz. Coll. Rhett.
Grœc. i. p. 219).   Others among the Rhetors, too, exercised their talents
sometimes in vindicating, sometimes in controverting, the probability of the
ancient mythes. See the Progymnasmata of Nicolaus—Κατασκευὴ ὅτι
εἰκότα τὰ κατὰ Νιόβην 'Ανασκευὴ ὅτι οὐκ εἰκότα τὰ κατὰ Νιόβην (ap. Walz.
Coll. Rhetor. i. p. 284–318), where there are many specimens of this fanciful
mode of handling.
Plutarch, however, in one of his treatises, accepts Minotaurs, Sphinxes,
Centaurs, etc. as realities; he treats them as products of the monstrous,
incestuous, and ungovernable lusts of man, which he contrasts with the
simple and moderate passions of animals (Plutarch, Gryllus, p. 990).

tally uncertified; beyond this point we cannot penetrate, without
the light of extrinsic evidence, since there is no intrinsic mark to
distinguish truth from plausible fiction.[1]

It remains that we should notice the manner in which the ancient mythes were received and dealt with by the philosophers.
The earliest expression which we hear, on the part of philosophy,
is the severe censure bestowed upon them on ethical grounds by
Xenophanês of Kolophôn, and seemingly by some others of his
contemporaries.[2] It was apparently in reply to such charges,
which did not admit of being directly rebutted, that Theagenês
of Rhêgium (about 520 B. C.) first started the idea of a double
meaning in the Homeric and Hesiodic narratives, — an interior
sense, different from that which the words in their obvious meaning bore, yet to a certain extent analogous, and discoverable by
sagacious divination. Upon this principle, he allegorized especially the battle of the gods in the Iliad.[2] In the succeeding cen-

---

[1] The learned Mr. Jacob Bryant regards the explanations of Palæphatus as
if they were founded upon real fact. He admits, for example, the city Ne-
phelé alleged by that author in his exposition of the fable of the Centaurs.
Moreover, he speaks with much commendation of Palæphatus generally:
" He (Palæphatus) wrote early, and seems to have been a serious and sensible person ; one who saw the absurdity of the fables upon which the
theology of his country was founded." (Ancient Mythology, vol. i. p. 411–
435.)

So also Sir Thomas Brown (Enquiry into Vulgar Errors, Book I. chap.
vi. p. 221, ed. 1835) alludes to Palæphatus as having incontestably pointed
out the real basis of the fables. "And surely the fabulous inclination of
those days was greater than any since ; which swarmed so with fables, and
from such slender grounds took hints for fictions, poisoning the world ever
after : wherein how far they succeeded, may be exemplified from Palæphatus, in his Book of Fabulous Narrations."

[2] Xenophan. ap. Sext. Empir. adv. Mathemat. ix. 193. He also disapproved of the rites, accompanied by mourning and wailing, with which the
Eleatês worshipped Leukothea: he told them, εἰ μὲν θεὸν ὑπολαμβάνουσι,
μὴ θρηνεῖν · εἰ δὲ ἄνθρωπον, μὴ θύειν (Aristotel. Rhet. ii. 23).

Xenophanês pronounced the battles of the Titans, Gigantes, and Centaurs
to be " fictions of our predecessors," πλάσματα τῶν προτέρων (Xenophan.
Fragm. 1. p. 42, ed. Schneidewin).

See a curious comparison of the Grecian and Roman theology in Dicnys,
Halicarn. Ant. Rom. ii. 20.

[2] Schol. Iliad. xx. 67: Tatian. adv. Græc. c. 48. Hêrakleitus indignantly
repelled the impudent atheists who found fault with the divine mythes of the

tury, Anaxagoras and Metrodôrus carried out the allegorical ex
planation more comprehensively and systematically; the formei
representing the mythical personages as mere mental conceptions,
invested with name and gender, and illustrative of ethical precepts, — the latter connecting them with physical principles and
phænomena. Metrodôrus resolved not only the persons of Zeus,
Hêrê, and Athênê, but also those of Agamemnôn, Achilles, and Hectôr, into various elemental combinations and physical agencies, and
treated the adventures ascribed to them as natural facts concealed
under the veil of allegory.[1] Empedoklês, Prodikus, Antisthenês,
Parmenidês, Hêrakleidês of Pontus, and in a later age, Chrysippus, and the Stoic philosophers generally,[2] followed more or less

Iliad, ignorant of their true allegorical meaning: ἡ τῶν ἐπιφυομένων τῷ
'Ομήρῳ τόλμα τοὺς 'Ηρας δεσμοὺς αἰτιᾶται, καὶ νομίζουσιν ὕλην τινα δαψιλῆ
τῆς ἀθέου πρὸς 'Ομηρον ἔχειν μανίας ταῦτα — 'Η οὐ μέμνη ὅτι τ' ἐκρέμω
ὑψοθεν, etc. λέληθε δ' αὑτοὺς ὅτι τούτοις τοῖς ἔπεσιν ἐκτεθεολόγηται ἡ τοῦ
παντὸς γένεσις, καὶ τὰ συνεχῶς φθόμενα τέσσαρα στοιχεῖα τούτων τῶν στίχων
ἐστὶ τάξις (Schol. ad Hom. Iliad. xv. 18).

[1] Diogen. Laërt. ii. 11; Tatian. adv. Græc. c. 37; Hesychius, v. 'Αγαμέμ-
νονα. See the ethical turn given to the stories of Circê, the Sirens, and
Scylla, in Xenoph. Memorab. i. 3, 7; ii. 6, 11–31. Syncellus, Chronic. p.
149. 'Ερμηνεύουσι δὲ οἱ 'Αναξαγόρειοι τοὺς μυθώδεις θεοὺς, νοῦν μὲν τὸν Δία,
τὴν δὲ 'Αθηνᾶν τέχνην, etc.

Uschold and other modern German authors seem to have adopted in its
full extent the principle of interpretation proposed by Metrodorus — treating Odysseus and Penelopê as personifications of the Sun and Moon, etc.
See Helbig, Die Sittlichen Zustände des Griechischen Helden Alters, Einlei
tung, p. xxix. (Leipzig, 1839.)

Corrections of the Homeric text were also resorted to, in order to escape
the necessity of imputing falsehood to Zeus (Aristotel. De Sophist. Elench.
c. 4).

[2] Sextus Empiric. ix. 18; Diogen. viii. 76; Plutarch, De Placit. Philo-
soph. i. 3–6; De Poesi Homericâ, 92–126; De Stoicor. Repugn. p. 1050;
Menander, De Encomiis, c. 5.

Cicero, De Nat. Deor. i. 14, 15, 16, 41; ii. 24–25. "Physica ratio non
inelegans inclusa in impias fabulas."

In the Bacchæ of Euripidês, Pentheus is made to deride the tale of the
motherless infant Dionysus having been sewn into the thigh of Zeus. Teiresias, while reproving him for his impiety, explains the story away in a sort
of allegory: the μηρὸς Διὸς (he says) was a mistaken statement in place of
the αἰθὴρ χθόνα ἐγκυκλούμενος (Bacch. 235–290).

Lucretius (iii. 995–1036) allegorizes the conspicuous sufferers in Hadês, —
Tantalus, Sisyphus, Tityus, and the Danaïds, as well as the ministers of

the same principle of treating the popular gods as allegorical personages; while the expositors of Homer (such as Stesimbrotus, Glaukôn, and others, even down to the Alexandrine age), though none of them proceeded to the same extreme length as Metrodôrus, employed allegory amongst other media of explanation for the purpose of solving difficulties, or eluding reproaches against the poet.

In the days of Plato and Zenophôn, this allegorizing interpretation was one of the received methods of softening down the obnoxious mythes — though Plato himself treated it as an insufficient defence, seeing that the bulk of youthful hearers could not see through the allegory, but embraced the story literally as it was set forth.[1] Pausanias tells us, that when he first began to write his work, he treated many of the Greek legends as silly and undeserving of serious attention; but as he proceeded, he gradually arrived at the full conviction, that the ancient sages had designedly spoken in enigmatical language, and that there was valuable truth wrapped up in their narratives : it was the duty of a pious man, therefore, to study and interpret, but not to reject,

---

penal infliction, Cerberus and the Furies. The first four are emblematic descriptions of various defective or vicious characters in human nature, — the deisidæmonic, the ambitious, the amorous, or the insatiate and querulous man; the last two represent the mental terrors of the wicked.

[1] Οἱ νῦν περὶ Ὅμηρον δεινοί — so Plato calls these interpreters (Kratylus, p. 407); see also Xenoph. Sympos. iii. 6 ; Plato, Ion. p. 530; Plutarch, De Audiend. Poet. p. 19. ὑπόνοια was the original ·word, afterwards succeeded by ἀλληγορία.

Ἥρας δὲ δεσμοὺς καὶ Ἡφαίστου ῥίψεις ὑπὸ πατρὸς, μέλλοντος τῇ μητρὶ τυπτομένῃ ἀμυνεῖν, καὶ θεομαχίας ὅσας Ὅμερος πεποίηκεν, οὐ παραδεκτέον εἰς τὴν πόλιν, οὔτ' ἐν ὑπονοίαις πεποιημένας, οὔτ' ἄνευ ὑπονοιῶν. Ὁ γὰρ νέος οὐχ' οἷός τε κρίνειν ὅ,τι τε ὑπόνοια καὶ ὃ μὴ, ἀλλ' ἃ ἂν τηλικοῦτος ὢν λάβῃ ἐν ταῖς δόξαις, δυσέκνιπτά τε καὶ ἀμετάστατα φιλεῖ γίγνεσθαι (Plato, Republ. ii. 17. p. 378).

The idea of an interior sense and concealed purpose in the ancient poets occurs several times in Plato (Theætet. c. 93. p. 180) : παρὰ μὲν τῶν ἀρχαίων, μετὰ ποιήσεως ἐπικρυπτομένων τοὺς πολλοὺς, etc.; also Protagor. c. 20. p. 316.

"Modo Stoicum Homerum faciunt, — modo Epicureum, —modo Peripateticum, —modo Academicum.   Apparat nihil horum esse in illo, quia omnia sunt." (Seneca, Ep. 88.)   Compare Plutarch, De Defectu Oracul. c. 11-12. t. ii. p. 702, Wytt., and Julian, Orat. vii. p. 216.

stories current and accredited respecting the gods.[1] And others,
— arguing from the analogy of the religious mysteries, which could
not be divulged without impiety to any except such as had been
specially admitted and initiated, — maintained that it would be a
profanation to reveal directly to the vulgar, the genuine scheme
of nature and the divine administration : the ancient poets and
philosophers had taken the only proper course, of talking to the
many in types and parables, and reserving the naked truth for
privileged and qualified intelligences.[2] The allegorical mode of
explaining the ancient fables[3] became more and more popular in

---

[1] Pausan. viii. 8, 2. To the same purpose (Strabo, x. p. 474), allegory is
admitted to a certain extent in the fables by Dionys. Halic. Ant. Rom. ii. 20.
The fragment of the lost treatise of Plutarch, on the Platæan festival of the
Dædala, is very instructive respecting Grecian allegory (Fragm. ix. t. 5. p.
754–763, ed. Wyt. ; ap. Euseb. Præpar. Evang. iii. 1).

[2] This doctrine is set forth in Macrobius (i. 2). He distinguishes between
fabula and *fabulosa narratio :* the former is fiction pure, intended either to
amuse or to instruct — the latter is founded upon truth, either respecting
human or respecting divine agency. The gods did not like to be publicly
talked of (according to his view) except under the respectful veil of a fable
(the same feeling as that of Herodotus, which led him to refrain from inserting the ἱεροὶ λόγοι in his history). The supreme god, the τἀγαθὸν, the
πρῶτον αἴτιον, could not be talked of in fables : but the other gods, the aëria.
or æthereal powers and the soul, might be, and ought to be, talked of in that
manner alone. Only superior intellects ought to be admitted to a knowledge
of the secret reality. "De Diis cæteris, et de animâ, non frustra se, nec ut
oblectent, ad fabulosa convertunt; sed quia sciunt *inimicam esse naturæ aper-
tam nudamque expositionem sui :* quæ sicut vulgaribus sensibus hominum
intellectum sui, vario rerum tegmine operimentoque, subtraxit; ita à pru-
dentibus arcana sua voluit per fabulosa tractari ...... Adeo semper ita se et
sciri et coli numina maluerunt, qualiter in vulgus antiquitus fabulata est.
...... Secundum hæc Pythagoras ipse atque Empedocles, Parmenides quoque et Heraclides, de Diis fabulati sunt: nec secus Timæus." Compare also
Maximus Tyrius, Dissert. x. and xxxii. Arnobius exposes the allegorical
interpretation as mere evasion, and holds the Pagans to literal historical fact
(Adv. Gentes, v. p. 185, ed. Elm.).

Respecting the allegorical interpretation applied to the Greek fables,
Böttiger (Die Kunst — Mythologie der Griechen, Abschn. ii. p. 176) ·
Nitzsch (Heldensage der Griech. sect. 6. p. 78) ; Lobeck (Aglaopham. p.
133–155).

[3] According to the anonymous writer ap. Westermann (Script. Myth. p.
328), every personal or denominated god may be construed in three different
ways : either πραγματικῶς (historically, as having been a king or a man) —

the third and fourth centuries after the Christian æra, especially among the new Platonic philosophers; being both congenial to

or ψυχικῶς, in which theory Hêrê signifies the *soul;* Athênê, *prudence;* Aphroditê, *desire;* Zeus, *mind,* etc. — or στοιχειακῶς, in which system Apollo signifies the *sun;* Poseidôn, the *sea;* Hêrê, the upper stratum of the air, or *æther;* Athênê, the lower or denser stratum; Zeus, the upper hemisphere; Kronus, the lower, etc. This writer thinks that all the three principles of construction may be resorted to, each on its proper occasion, and that neither of them excludes the others. It will be seen that the first is pure Euemerism; the two latter are modes of allegory.

The allegorical construction of the gods and of the divine mythes is copiously applied in the treatises, both of Phurnutus and Sallustius, in Gale's collection of mythological writers. Sallustius treats the mythes as of divine origin, and the chief poets as inspired (θεόληπτοι): the gods were propitious to those who recounted worthy and creditable mythes respecting them, and Sallustius prays that they will accept with favor his own remarks (cap. 3 and 4. pp. 245–251, Gale). He distributes mythes into five classes; theological, physical, spiritual, material, and mixed. He defends the practice of speaking of the gods under the veil of allegory, much in the same way as Macrobius (in the preceding note): he finds, moreover, a good excuse even for those mythes which imputed to the gods theft, adultery, outrages towards a father, and other enormities: such tales (he says) were eminently suitable, since the mind *must at once see* that the facts as told are *not* to be taken as being themselves the real truth, but simply as a veil, disguising some interior truth (p. 247).

Besides the Life of Homer ascribed to Plutarch (see Gale, p. 325–332). Hêraclidês (*not* Hêraclidês of Pontus) carries out the process of allegorizing the Homeric mythes most earnestly and most systematically. The application of the allegorizing theory is, in his view, the only way of rescuing Homer from the charge of scandalous impiety — πάντη γὰρ ἠσέβησεν, εἰ μηδὲν ἠλληγόρησεν (Hêrac. *in init.* p. 407, Gale). He proves at length, that the destructive arrows of Apollo, in the first book of the Iliad, mean nothing at the bottom except a contagious plague, caused by the heat of the summer sun in marshy ground (pp. 416–424). Athênê, who darts down from Olympus at the moment when Achilles is about to draw his sword on Agamemnôn, and seizes him by the hair, is a personification of repentant prudence (p. 435). The conspiracy against Zeus, which Homer (Iliad, i. 400) relates to have been formed by the Olympic gods, and defeated by the timely aid of Thetis and Briareus — the chains and suspension imposed upon Hêrê — the casting of Hêphæstos by Zeus out of Olympus, and his fall in Lêmnus — the destruction of the Grecian wall by Poseidôn, after the departure of the Greeks — the amorous scene between Zeus and Hêrê on Mount Gargarus — the distribution of the universe between Zeus, Poseidôn, and Hadês — all these he resolves into peculiar manifestations and conflicts of the elemental substances in nature. To the much-decried battle of the gods, he gives a

their orientalized turn of thought, and useful as a shield against the attacks of the Christians.

It was from the same strong necessity, of accommodating the old mythes to a new standard both of belief and of appreciation, that both the historical and the allegorical schemes of transforming them arose; the literal narrative being decomposed for the purpose of arriving at a base either of particular matter of fact,

---

turn partly physical, partly ethical (p. 481). In like manner, he transforms and vindicates the adventures of the gods in the Odyssey: the wanderings of Odysseus, together with the Lotophagi, the Cyclôps, Circê, the Sirens, Æolus, Scylla, etc., he resolves into a series of temptations, imposed as a trial upon a man of wisdom and virtue, and emblematic of human life (p. 496). The story of Arês, Aphroditê, and Hêphæstos, in the eighth book of the Odyssey, seems to perplex him more than any other: he offers two explanations, neither of which seems satisfactory even to himself (p. 494).

An anonymous writer in the collection of Westermann (pp. 329–344) has discussed the wanderings of Odysseus upon the same ethical scheme of interpretation as Hêraclidês: he entitles his treatise "A short essay on the Wanderings of Odysseus in Homer, worked out in conjunction with ethical reflections, and rectifying what is rotten in the story, as well as may be, for the benefit of readers." (τὸ μύθου σαθρὸν θεραπεύουσα.) The author resolves the adventures of Odysseus into narratives emblematic of different situations and trials of human life. Scylla and Charybdis, for example (c. 8. p. 338), represent, the one, the infirmities and temptations arising out of the body, the other, those springing from the mind, between which man is called upon to steer. The adventure of Odysseus with Æolus, shows how little good a virtuous man does himself by seeking, in case of distress, aid from conjurors and evil enchanters; the assistance of such allies, however it may at first promise well, ultimately deceives the person who accepts it, and renders him worse off than he was before (c. 3. p. 332). By such illustrations does the author sustain his general position, that there is a great body of valuable ethical teaching wrapped up in the poetry of Homer.

Proclus is full of similar allegorization, both of Homer and Hesiod: the third Excursus of Heyne ad Iliad. xxiii. (vol. viii. p. 563), De Allegoriâ Homericâ, contains a valuable summary of the general subject.

The treatise De Astrologiâ, printed among the works of Lucian, contains specimens of astrological explanations applied to many of the Grecian μῦθοι, which the author as a pious man cannot accept in their literal meaning. "How does it consist with holiness (he asks) to believe that Æneas was son of Aphroditê, Minôs of Zeus, or Askalaphus of Mars? No; these were men born under the favorable influences of the planets Venus, Jupiter, and Mars." He considers the principle of astrological explanation peculiarly fit to be applied to the mythes of Homer and Hesiod (Lucian, De Astrologiâ, c. 21–22).

or of general physical or moral truth. Instructed men **were**
commonly disposed to historicize only the heroic legends, and to
allegorize more or less of the divine legends: the attempt of
Euêmerus to historicize the latter was for the most part denounced
as irreligious, while that of Metrodôrus to allegorize the former
met with no success. In allegorizing, moreover, even the divine
legends, it was usual to apply the scheme of allegory only to the
inferior gods, though some of the great Stoic philosophers carried it farther, and allegorized all the separate personal gods,
leaving only an all-pervading cosmic Mind,[1] essential as a co-
efficient along with Matter, yet not separable from Matter. But
many pious pagans seem to have perceived that allegory pushed
to this extent was fatal to all living religious faith,[2] inasmuch as
it divested the gods of their character of Persons, sympathizing
with mankind and modifiable in their dispositions according to
the conduct and prayers of the believer: and hence they permitted themselves to employ allegorical interpretation only to
some of the obnoxious legends connected with the superior gods,
leaving the personality of the latter unimpeached.

One novelty, however, introduced seemingly by the philosopher
Empedoklês and afterwards expanded by others, deserves notice,
inasmuch as it modified considerably the old religious creed by
drawing a pointed contrast between gods and dæmons, — a distinction hardly at all manifested in Homer, but recognized in the
Works and Days of Hesiod.[3] Empedoklês widened the gap between the two, and founded upon it important consequences. The
gods were good, immortal, and powerful agents, having freewill

---

[1] See Ritter, Geschichte der Philosophie, 2nd edit. part 3. book 11. chap. 4.
p. 592; Varro ap. Augustin. Civitat. Dei, vi. 5, ix. 6 ; Cicero, Nat. Deor. ii.
24–28.

Chrysippus admitted the most important distinction between Zeus and the
other gods (Plutarch. de Stoicor. Repugnant. p. 1052.)

[2] Plutarch. de Isid. et Osirid. c. 66. p. 377 ; c. 70. p. 379. Compare on
this subject O. Müller, Prolegom. Mythol. p. 59 *seq.*, and Eckermann, Lehrbuch der Religions Geschichte, vol. i. sect. ii. p. 46.

[3] Hesiod, Opp. et Di. 122: to the same effect Pythagoras and Thalês
(Diogen. Laër. viii. 32 ; and Plutarch, Placit. Philos. i. 8).

The Hesiodic dæmons are all good : Athenagoras (Legat. Chr. p. 8.) says
that Thalês admitted a distinction between good and bad dæmors. wnich
seems very doubtful.

and intelligence, but without appetite, passion, or infirmity: the dæmons were of a mixed nature between gods and men, ministers and interpreters from the former to the latter, but invested also with an agency and dispositions of their own. They were very long-lived, but not immortal, and subject to the passions and propensities of men, so that there were among them beneficent and maleficent dæmons with every shade of intermediate difference.[1]

---

[1] The distinction between Θεοί and Δαίμονες is especially set forth in the treatise of Plutarch, De Defectu Oraculorum, capp. 10, 12, 13, 15, etc. He seems to suppose it traceable to the doctrine of Zoroaster or the Orphic mysteries, and he represents it as relieving the philosopher from great perplexities : for it was difficult to know where to draw the line in admitting or rejecting divine Providence : errors were committed sometimes in affirming God to be the cause of everything, at other times in supposing him to be the cause of nothing. Ἐπεὶ τὸ διορίσαι πῶς χρηστέον καὶ μέχρι τινων τῇ προνοίᾳ, χαλεπὸν, οἱ μὲν οὐδενὸς ἁπλῶς τὸν θεὸν, οἱ δὲ ὁμοῦ τι πάντων αἴτιον ποιοῦντες, ἀστοχοῦσι τοῦ μετρίου καὶ πρέποντος. Εὖ μὲν οὖν λέγουσιν οἱ λέγοντες, ὅτι Πλάτων τὸ ταῖς γεννωμέναις ποιότησιν ὑποκείμενον στοιχεῖον ἐξευρὼν, ὃ νῦν ὕλην καὶ φύσιν καλοῦσιν, πολλῶν ἀπήλλαξε καὶ μεγάλων ἀποριῶν τοὺς φιλοσόφους· ἐμοὶ δὲ δοκοῦσι πλείονας λῦσαι καὶ μείζονας ἀπορίας οἱ τὸ τῶν δαιμόνων γένος ἐν μέσῳ θεῶν καὶ ἀνθρώπων, καὶ τρόπον τινα τὴν κοινωνίαν ἡμῶν σύναγον εἰς ταὐτὸ καὶ σύναπτον, ἐξευρόντες (c. 10). Ἡ δαιμόνων φύσις ἔχουσα καὶ πάθος θνητοῦ καὶ θεοῦ δύναμιν (c. 13). Εἰσὶ γὰρ, ὡς ἐν ἀνθρώποις, καὶ δαίμοσιν ἀρετῆς διάφοραι, καὶ τοῦ παθητικοῦ καὶ ἀλόγου τοῖς μὲν ἀσθενὲς καὶ ἀμαυρὸν ἔτι λείψανον, ὥσπερ περίττωμα, τοῖς δὲ πολὺ καὶ δυσκατάσβεστον ἔνεστιν, ὧν ἴχνη καὶ σύμβολα πολλαχοῦ θυσίαι καὶ τελεταὶ καὶ μυθολογίαι σώζουσι καὶ διαφυλάττουσιν ἐνδιεσπαρμένα (ib.) : compare Plutarch. de Isid. et Osir. 25. p. 360.

Καὶ μὴν ὅσας ἔν τε μύθοις καὶ ὕμνοις λέγουσι καὶ ᾄδουσι, τοῦτο μὲν ἁρπαγὰς, τοῦτο δὲ πλάνας θεῶν, κρύψεις τε καὶ φυγὰς καὶ λατρείας, οὐ θεῶν εἰσίν ἀλλὰ δαιμόνων παθήματα, etc. (c. 15) : also c. 23 ; also De Isid. et Osir. c. 25. p. 366.

Human sacrifices and other objectionable rites are excused, as necessary for the purpose of averting the anger of bad dæmons (c. 14–15).

Empedoklês is represented as the first author of the doctrine which imputed vicious and abominable dispositions to many of the dæmons (c. 15, 16, 17, 20), τοὺς εἰσαγομένους ὑπὸ Ἐμπεδοκλέους δαίμονας; expelled from heaven by the gods, θεήλατοι καὶ οὐρανοπετεῖς (Plutarch, De Vitand. Aër. Alien. p. 830) ; followed by Plato, Xenokratês, and Chrysippus, c. 17 : compare Plato (Apolog. Socrat. p. 27 ; Politic. p. 271 ; Symposion, c. 28. p. 203), though he seems to treat the δαίμονες as defective and mutable beings, rather than actively maleficent. Xenokratês represents some of them both as wicked and powerful in a high degree :— Ξενοκράτης καὶ τῶν ἡμερῶν τὰς ἀπο-

It had been the mistake (according to these philosophers) of the old mythes to ascribe to the gods proceedings really belonging to the dæmons, who were always the immediate communicants with mortal nature, inspiring prophetic power to the priestesses of the oracles, sending dreams and omens, and perpetually interfering either for good or for evil. The wicked and violent dæmons, having committed many enormities, had thus sometimes incurred punishment from the gods: besides which, their bad dispositions had imposed upon men the necessity of appeasing them by religious ceremonies of a kind acceptable to such beings: hence, the human sacrifices, the violent, cruel, and obscene exhibitions, the wailings and fastings, the tearing and eating of raw flesh, which it had become customary to practise on various consecrated occasions, and especially in the Dionysiac solemnities. Moreover, the discreditable actions imputed to the gods, — the terrific combats, the Typhonic and Titanic convulsions, the rapes, abductions, flight, servitude, and concealment, — all these were really the doings and sufferings of bad dæmons, placed far below the sovereign agency — equable, undisturbed, and unpolluted — of the immortal gods. The action of such dæmons upon mankind was fitful and intermittent: they sometimes perished or changed their local abode, so that oracles which had once been inspired became after a time forsaken and disfranchized.[1]

This distinction between gods and dæmons appeared to save in a great degree both the truth of the old legends and the dig-

φρύδας, καὶ τῶν ἑορτῶν ὅσαι πληγύς τινας ἢ κοπετοὺς, ἢ νηστείας, ἢ δυσφημίας, ἢ αἰσχρολογίαν ἔχουσιν, οὔτε θεῶν τιμαῖς οὔτε δαιμόνων οἴεται προσήκειν χρηστῶν, ἀλλ᾽ εἶναι φύσεις ἐν τῷ περιέχοντι μεγάλας μὲν καὶ ἰσχυρὰς, δυστρόπους δὲ καὶ σκυθρωπὰς, αἱ χ α ί ρ ο υ σ ι τ ο ῖ ς τ ο ι ο ύ τ ο ι ς, καὶ τ υ γ χ ά ν ο υ σ α ι π ρ ὸ ς ο ὐ θ ὲ ν ἄ λ λ ο χ ε ῖ ρ ο ν τ ρ έ π ο ν τ α ι (Plutarch, De Isid. ut Osir. c. 26. p. 361; Quæstion. Rom. p. 283): compare Stobæus, Eclog. Phys. i. p. 62.

[1] Plutarch, De Defect. Orac. c. 15. p. 418. Chrysippus admitted, among the various conceivable causes to account for the existence of evil, the supposition of some negligent and reckless dæmons, δαιμόνια φαῦλα ἐν οἷς τῷ ὄντι γίνονται καὶ ἐγκλητέαι ἀμέλειαι (Plutarch, De Stoicor. Repugnant. p. 1051). A distinction, which I do not fully understand, between θεοὶ and δαίμονες, was also adopted among the Locrians at Opus: δαίμων with them seems to have been equivalent to ἥρως (Plutarch, Quæstion. Græc. c. 6. p. 292): see the note above. pp. 350–351.

nity of the gods: it obviated the necessity of pronouncing either that the gods were unworthy, or the legends untrue. Yet although devised for the purpose of satisfying a more scrupulous religious sensibility, it was found inconvenient afterwards, when assailants arose against paganism generally. For while it abandoned as indefensible a large portion of what had once been genuine faith, it still retained the same word dæmons with an entirely altered signification. The Christian writers in their controversies found ample warrant among the earlier pagan authors[1] for treating all the gods as dæmons — and not less ample warrant among the later pagans for denouncing the dæmons generally as evil beings.[2]

Such were the different modes in which the ancient mythes were treated, during the literary life of Greece, by the four classes above named — poets, logographers, historians, and philosophers.

Literal acceptance, and unconscious, uninquiring faith, such as they had obtained from the original auditors to whom they were addressed, they now found only among the multitude — alike retentive of traditional feeling[3] and fearful of criticizing the pro-

---

[1] Tatian. adv. Græcos, c. 20; Clemens Alexandrin. Admonit. ad Gentes, pp. 26-29, Sylb.; Minuc. Felix, Octav. c. 26. "Isti igitur impuri spiritus, ut ostensum a Magis, a philosophis, a Platone, sub statuis et imaginibus conse-ˉrati delitescunt, et afflatu suo quasi auctoritatem præsentis numinis conse-quuntur," etc. This, like so many other of the aggressive arguments of the Christians against paganism, was taken from the pagan philosophers them selves.

Lactantius, De Verá Philosophiá, iv. 28. "Ergo iidem sunt Dæmones, ios fatentur execrandos esse: iidem Dii, quibus supplicant. Si nobis cre-dˉndum esse non putant, credant Homero; qui summum illum Jovem Dæ-monibus aggregavit," etc.

[2] See above, Chapter II. p. 70, the remarks on the Hesiodic Theogony.

[3] A destructive inundation took place at Pheneus in Arcadia, seemingly in the time of Plutarch: the subterranean outlet (βάραθρον) of the river had become blocked up, and the inhabitants ascribed the stoppage to the anger of Apollo, who had been provoked by the stealing of the Pythian tripod by Héraklês: the latter had carried the tripod to Pheneus and de-posited it there. 'Αρ' οὖν οὐκ ἀτοπώτερος τούτων ὁ 'Απόλλων, εἰ Φενεάτας ἀπόλλυσι τοὺς νῦν, ἐμφράξας τὸ βάραθρον, καὶ κατακλύσας τὴν χώραν ἅπασαν αὐτῶν, ὅτι πρὸ χιλίων ἐτῶν, ὡς φασιν, ὁ 'Ηρακλῆς ἀνασπάσας τὸν τρίποδα τον μαντικὸν εἰς Φενεὸν ἀπήνεγκε; (Plutarch. de Serà Numin. Vindictà, p. 577; compare Pausan. viii. 14, 1.) The expression of Plutarch, that the abstraction of the tripod by Héraklês had taken place 1000 years

ceedings of the gods.[1] But with instructed men they became
rather subjects of respectful and curious analysis — all agreeing
that the Word as tendered to them was inadmissible, yet all equally
convinced that it contained important meaning, though hidden
yet not undiscoverable. A very large proportion of the force
of Grecian intellect was engaged in searching after this unknown
base, by guesses, in which sometimes the principle of semi-his
torical interpretation was assumed, sometimes that of allegori
cal, without any collateral evidence in either case, and without
possibility of verification. Out of the one assumption grew a
string of allegorized phænomenal truths, out of the other a long
series of seeming historical events and chronological persons, —
both elicited from the transformed mythes and from nothing
else.[2]

---

before, is that of the critic, who thinks it needful to historicize and chronol-
ogize the genuine legend; which, to an inhabitant of Pheneus, at the time of
the inundation, was doubtless as little questioned as if the theft of Hêraklês
had been laid in the preceding generation.

Agathoclês of Syracuse committed depredations on the coasts of Ithaca
and Korkyra: the excuse which he offered was, that Odysseus had come to
Sicily and blinded Polyphêmus, and that on his return he had been kindly
received by the Phæakians (Plutarch, *ib.*).

This is doubtless a jest, either made by Agathoclês, or more probably invented for him; but it is founded upon a popular belief.

[1] " Sanctiusque et reverentius visum, de actis Deorum credere quam scire."
(Tacit. German. c. 34.)

Aristidês, however, represents the Homeric theology (whether he would
have included the Hesiodic we do not know) as believed quite literally among
the multitude in his time, the second century after Christianity (Aristid. Orat.
iii. p. 25). Ἀπορῶ, ὅπη πότε χρή με διαθέσθαι μεθ' ὑμῶν, πότερα ὡς τοῖς
πολλοῖς δοκεῖ καὶ Ὁμήρῳ δὲ συνδοκεῖ, θεῶν παθήματα συμπεισθῆναι καὶ ἡμᾶς,
οἶον Ἄρεος δέσμα καὶ Ἀπόλλωνος θητείας καὶ Ἡφαίστου ῥίψεις εἰς θάλασσαν,
οὕτω δὲ καὶ Ἰνοῦς ἄχη καὶ φυγάς τινας. Compare Lucian, Ζεὺς Τραγῷδος,
c. 20, and De Luctu, c. 2 ; Dionys. Halicar. A. R. ii. p. 90, Sylb.

Kallimachus (Hymn. ad Jov. 9) distinctly denied the statement of the
Kretans that they possessed in Krête the tomb of Zeus, and treated it as an
instance of Kretan mendacity; while Celsus did not deny it, but explained
it in some figurative manner — αἰνιττόμενος τροπικὰς ὑπονοίας (Origen. cont
Celsum, iii. p. 137).

[2] There is here a change as compared with my first edition; I had inserted
here some remarks on the allegorical theory of interpretation, as compared
with the semi-historical. An able article on my work (in the Edinburgh

The utmost which we accomplish by means of the semi-historical theory, even in its most successful applications, is, that after leaving out from the mythical narrative all that is miraculous or high-colored or extravagant, we arrive at a series of credible incidents — incidents which *may*, *perhaps*, have really occurred, and against which no intrinsic presumption can be raised. This is exactly the character of a well-written modern novel (as, for example, several among the compositions of Defoe), the whole story of which is such as may well have occurred in real life: it is plausible fiction, and nothing beyond. To raise plausible fiction up to the superior dignity of truth, some positive testimony or positive ground of inference must be shown ; even the highest measure of intrinsic probability is not alone sufficient. A man who tells us that, on the day of the battle of Platæa, rain fell on the spot of ground where the city of New York now stands, will neither deserve nor obtain credit, because he can have had no means of positive knowledge ; though the statement is not in the slightest degree improbable. On the other hand, statements in themselves very improbable may well deserve belief, provided they be supported by sufficient positive evidence ; thus the canal dug by order of Xerxês across the promontory of Mount Athos, and the sailing of the Persian fleet through it, is a fact which I believe, because it is well-attested — notwithstanding its remarkable improbability, which so far misled Juvenal as to induce him to single out the narrative as a glaring example of Grecian mendacity.[1] Again, many critics have observed that the general tale of the Trojan war (apart from the superhuman agencies) is not more improbable than that of the Crusades, which every one admits to be an historical fact. But (even if we grant this position, which is only true to a small extent), it is not sufficient to show an analogy between the two cases in respect to negative presumptions alone ; the analogy ought to be shown to hold between them

---

Review, October 1846), pointed out that those remarks required modification, and that the idea of allegory in reference to the construction of the mythes was altogether inadmissible.

[1] Juvenal, Sat. x. 174 : —

> " Creditur olim
> Velificatus Athos, et quantum Græcia mendax
> Audet in historiâ," etc.

in respect to positive certificate also. The Crusades are a curious
phænomenon in history, but we accept them, nevertheless, as an
unquestionable fact, because the antecedent improbability is sur-
mounted by adequate contemporary testimony. When the like
testimony, both in amount and kind, is produced to establish the
historical reality of a Trojan war, we shall not hesitate to deal
with the two events on the same footing.

In applying the semi-historical theory to Grecian mythical narrative, it has been often forgotten that a certain strength of testimony, or positive ground of belief, must first be tendered, before
we can be called upon to discuss the antecedent probability or
improbability of the incidents alleged. The belief of the Greeks
themselves, without the smallest aid of special or contemporary
witnesses, has been tacitly assumed as sufficient to support the
case, provided only sufficient deduction be made from the mythical narratives to remove all antecedent improbabilities. It has
been taken for granted that the faith of the people must have
rested originally upon some particular historical event, involving
the identical persons, things, and places which the original mythes
exhibit, or at least the most prominent among them. But when
we examine the pyschagogic influences predominant in the society among whom this belief originally grew up, we shall see
that their belief is of little or no evidentiary value, and that the
growth and diffusion of it may be satisfactorily explained without
supposing any special basis of matters of fact. The popular
faith, so far as it counts for anything, testifies in favor of the entire and literal mythes, which are now universally rejected as
incredible.[1] We have thus the very minimum of positive proof,

---

[1] Colonel Sleeman observes, respecting the Hindoo historical mind —
" History to this people is all a fairy tale." (Rambles and Recollections of
an Indian Official, vol. i. ch. ix. p. 70.) And again, " The popular poem of
the Ramaen describes the abduction of the heroine by the monster king of
Ceylon, Rawun ; and her recovery by means of the monkey general, Hun-
nooman. Every word of this poem, the people assured me was written, if
not by the hand of the Deity himself, at least by his inspiration, which was
the same thing — and it must consequently be true. Ninety-nine out of a
hundred, among the Hindoos, implicitly believe, not only every word of the
poem, but every word of every poem that has ever been written in Sanscrit.
If you ask a man whether he really believes any very egregious absurdity
quoted from these books, he replies, with the greatest naïveté in the world, Is

and the maximum of negative presumption: we may diminish
the latter by conjectural omissions and interpolations, but we cannot by any artifice increase the former: the narrative ceases to
be incredible, but it still remains uncertified, — a mere common-
place possibility. Nor is fiction always, or essentially, extravagant and incredible. It is often not only plausible and coherent,
but even more like truth (if a paradoxical phrase may be allowed) than truth itself. Nor can we, in the absence of any extrinsic test, reckon upon any intrinsic mark to discriminate the one
from the other.[1]

---

it not written in the book; and how should it be there written, if not true?
The Hindoo religion reposes upon an entire prostration of mind, — that
continual and habitual surrender of the reasoning faculties, which we are
accustomed to make occasionally, while engaged at the theatre, or in the
perusal of works of fiction. We allow the scenes, characters, and incidents,
to pass before our mind's eye, and move our feelings — without stopping a
moment to ask whether they are real or true. There is only this difference
— that with people of education among us, even in such short intervals of
illusion or *abandon*, any extravagance in the acting, or flagrant improbability
in the fiction, destroys the charm, breaks the spell by which we have been so
mysteriously bound, and restores us to reason and the realities of ordinary
life. With the Hindoos, on the contrary, the greater the improbability, the
more monstrous and preposterous the fiction — the greater is the charm it
has over their minds; and the greater their learning in the Sanscrit, the
more are they under the influence of this charm. Believing all to be written
by the Deity, or under his inspirations, and the men and things of former
days to have been very different from men and things of the present day,
and the heroes of these fables to have been demigods, or people endowed
with powers far superior to those of the ordinary men of their own day —
the analogies of nature are never for a moment considered; nor do questions
of probability, or possibility, according to those analogies, ever obtrude to
dispel the charm with which they are so pleasingly bound. They go on
through life reading and talking of these monstrous fictions, which shock
the taste and understanding of other nations, without ever questioning the
truth of one single incident, or hearing it questioned. There was a time,
and that not far distant, when it was the same in England, and in every
other European nation; and there are, I am afraid, some parts of Europe
where it is so still. But the Hindoo faith, so far as religious questions are
concerned, is not more capacious or absurd than that of the Greeks or Romans in the days of Socrates or Cicero: the only difference is, that among
the Hindoos a greater number of the questions which interest mankind are
brought under the head of religion." (Sleeman, Rambles, etc., vol. i. ch.
xxvi. p. 227: compare vol. ii. ch. v. p. 51; viii. p. 97.)

[1] Lord Lyttleton, in commenting on the tales of the Irish bards, in his

In the semi-historical theory respecting Grecian mythical narrative, the critic unconsciously transports into the Homeric age those habits of classification and distinction, and that standard of acceptance or rejection, which he finds current in his own. Amongst us, the distinction between historical fact and fiction is highly valued as well as familiarly understood: we have a long history of the past, deduced from a study of contemporary evidences; and we have a body of fictitious literature, stamped with its own mark and interesting in its own way. Speaking generally, no man could now hope to succeed permanently in transferring any striking incident from the latter category into the former, nor could any man deliberately attempt it without incurring well-merited obloquy. But this *historical sense*, now so deeply rooted in the modern mind that we find a difficulty in conceiving any people to be without it, is the fruit of records and inquiries, first applied to the present, and then preserved and studied by subsequent generations; while in a society which has not yet formed the habit of recording its present, the real facts of the past can never be known; the difference between attested

---

History of Henry II., has the following just remarks (book iv. vol. iii. p. 13, quarto) : " One may reasonably suppose that in MSS. written since the Irish received the Roman letters from St. Patrick, *some* traditional truths recorded before by the bards in their unwritten poems may have been preserved to our times. Yet these cannot be so separated from many fabulous stories derived from the same sources, as to obtain a firm credit; it not being sufficient to establish the authority of *suspected* traditions, that they can be shown not to be so improbable or absurd as others with which they are mixed — *since there may be specious as well as senseless fictions.* Nor can a poet or bard, who lived in the sixth or seventh century after Christ, if his poem is still extant, be any voucher for facts supposed to have happened before the in carnation; though his evidence (allowing for poetical license) may be received on such matters as come within his own time, or the remembrance of old men with whom he conversed. The most judicious historians pay no regard to the Welsh or British traditions delivered by Geoffrey of Monmouth, though it is not impossible but that some of these may be true."

One definition of a mythe given by Plutarch coincides exactly with a *specious fiction:* Ὁ μῦθος εἶναι βούλεται λόγος ψευδὴς ἐοικὼς ἀληθινῷ (Plutarch, Bellone an pace clariores fuerunt Athenienses, p. 348).

"Der Grund-Trieb des Mythus (Creuzer justly expresses it) das Gedachte in ein Geschehenes umzusetzen." (Symbolik der Alten Welt, sect. 43. p. 99.)

matter of fact and plausible fiction — between truth and that which is like truth — can neither be discerned nor sought for. Yet it is precisely upon the supposition that this distinction is present to men's habitual thoughts, that the semi-historical theory of the mythes is grounded.

It is perfectly true, as has often been stated, that the Grecian epic contains what are called traditions respecting the past — the larger portion of it, indeed, consists of nothing else. But what are these traditions? They are the matter of those songs and stories which have acquired hold on the public mind; they are the creations of the poets and storytellers themselves, each of whom finds some preëxisting, and adds others of his own, new and previously untold, under the impulse and authority of the inspiring Muse. Homer doubtless found many songs and stories current with respect to the siege of Troy; he received and transmitted some of these traditions, recast and transformed others, and enlarged the whole mass by new creations of his own. To the subsequent poets, such as Arktinus and Leschês, these Homeric creations formed portions of preëxisting tradition, with which they dealt in the same manner; so that the whole mass of traditions constituting the tale of Troy became larger and larger with each successive contributor. To assume a generic difference between the older and the newer strata of tradition — to treat the former as morsels of history, and the latter as appendages of fiction — is an hypothesis gratuitous at the least, not to say inadmissible. For the further we travel back into the past, the more do we recede from the clear day of positive history, and the deeper do we plunge into the unsteady twilight and gorgeous clouds of fancy and feeling. It was one of the agreeable dreams of the Grecian epic, that the man who travelled far enough northward beyond the Rhipæan mountains, would in time reach the delicious country and genial climate of the virtuous Hyperboreans — the votaries and favorites of Apollo, who dwelt in the extreme north beyond the chilling blasts of Boreas. Now the hope that we may, by carrying our researches up the stream of time, exhaust the limits of fiction, and land ultimately upon some points of solid truth, appears to me no less illusory than his northward journey in quest of the Hyperborean elysium.

The general disposition to adopt the semi-historical theory as
to the genesis of Grecian mythes, arises in part from reluctance
in critics to impute to the mythopœic ages extreme credulity or
fraud; together with the usual presumption, that where much is
believed some portion of it must be true. There would be some
weight in these grounds of reasoning, if the ages under discussion had been supplied with records and accustomed to critical
inquiry. But amongst a people unprovided with the former and
strangers to the latter, credulity is naturally at its maximum, as
well in the narrator himself as in his hearers: the idea of deliberate fraud is moreover inapplicable,[1] for if the hearers are disposed to accept what is related to them as a revelation from the
Muse, the *œstrus* of composition is quite sufficient to impart a
similar persuasion to the poet whose mind is penetrated with it.
The belief of that day can hardly be said to stand apart by itself
as an act of reason. It becomes confounded with vivacious imagination and earnest emotion; and in every case where these
mental excitabilities are powerfully acted upon, faith ensues unconsciously and as a matter of course. How active and prominent such tendencies were among the early Greeks, the extraordinary beauty and originality of their epic poetry may teach us.

It is, besides, a presumption far too largely and indiscriminately
applied, even in our own advanced age, that where much is believed, something must necessarily be true — that accredited
fiction is always traceable to some basis of historical truth.[2] The

---

[1] In reference to the loose statements of the Highlanders, Dr. Johnson observes, "He that goes into the Highlands with a mind naturally acquies-
cent, and a credulity eager for wonders, may perhaps come back with an
opinion very different from mine; for the inhabitants, knowing the ignorance
of all strangers in their language and antiquities, are perhaps not very scrupulous adherents to truth; yet I do not say that they deliberately speak studied falsehood, or have a settled purpose to deceive. They have acquired and
considered little, and do not always feel their own ignorance. They are not
much accustomed to be interrogated by others, and seem never to have thought
of interrogating themselves; *so that if they do not know what they tell to be true,
they likewise do not distinctly perceive it to be false.* Mr. Boswell was very dili-
gent in his inquiries, and the result of his investigations was, that the answer
to the second question was commonly such as nullified the answer to the
first." (Journey to the Western Islands, p. 272, 1st edit., 1775).

[2] I considered this position more at large in an article in the "Westminster

influence of imagination and feeling is not confined simply to the process of retouching, transforming, or magnifying narratives originally founded on fact ; it will often create new narratives of its own, without any such preliminary basis. Where there is any general body of sentiment pervading men living in society, whether it be religious or political — love, admiration, or antipathy — all incidents tending to illustrate that sentiment are eagerly welcomed, rapidly circulated and (as a general rule) easily accredited. If real incidents are not at hand, impressive fictions will be provided to satisfy the demand. The perfect harmony of such fictions with the prevalent feeling stands in the place of certifying testimony, and causes men to hear them not merely with credence, but even with delight: to call them in question and require proof, is a task which cannot be undertaken without incurring obloquy. Of such tendencies in the human mind, abundant evidence is furnished by the innumerable religious legends which have acquired currency in various parts of the world, and of which no country was more fertile than Greece — legends which derived their origin, not from special facts misreported and exaggerated, but from pious feelings pervading the society, and translated into narrative by forward and imaginative minds — legends, in which not merely the incidents, but often even the personages are unreal, yet in which the generating sentiment is conspicuously discernible, providing its own matter as well as its own form. Other sentiments also, as well as the religious, provided they be fervent and widely diffused, will find expression in current narrative, and become portions of the general public belief — every celebrated and notorious character is the source of a thousand fictions exemplifying his peculiarities. And if it be true, as I think present observation may show us, that such creative agencies are even now visible and effective, when the materials of genuine history are copious and critically studied — much more are we warranted in concluding that, in ages destitute of records, strangers to historical testimony, and full of belief in divine inspiration both as to the future and as to the past, narratives purely fictitious will acquire ready and uninquiring credence,

---

Review " for May, 1843, on Niebuhr's Greek Legends, with which article much in the present chapter will be found to coincide.

provided only they be plausible and in harmony with the preconceptions of the auditors.

The allegorical interpretation of the mythes has been by several learned investigators, especially by Creuzer, connected with
the hypothesis of an ancient and highly instructed body of priests,
having their origin either in Egypt or in the East, and communicating to the rude and barbarous Greeks religious, physical, and
historical knowledge under the veil of symbols. At a time (we
are told) when language was yet in its infancy, visible symbols
were the most vivid means of acting upon the minds of ignorant
hearers: the next step was to pass to symbolical language and
expressions — for a plain and literal exposition, even if understood
at all, would at least have been listened to with indifference, as
not corresponding with any mental demand. In such allegoriz
ing way, then, the early priests set forth their doctrines respecting God, nature, and humanity — a refined monotheism and a
theological philosophy — and to this purpose the earliest mythes
were turned. But another class of mythes, more popular and
more captivating, grew up under the hands of the poets — mythes
purely epical, and descriptive of real or supposed past events.
The allegorical mythes, being taken up by the poets, insensibly
became confounded in the same category with the purely narrative mythes — the matter symbolized was no longer thought of,
while the symbolizing words came to be construed in their own
literal meaning — and the basis of the early allegory, thus lost
among the general public, was only preserved as a secret among
various religious fraternities, composed of members allied together
by initiation in certain mystical ceremonies, and administered by
hereditary families of presiding priests. In the Orphic and Bacchic sects, in the Eleusinian and Samothracian mysteries, was
thus treasured up the secret doctrine of the old theological and
philosophical mythes, which had once constituted the primitive
legendary stock of Greece, in the hands of the original priesthood and in ages anterior to Homer. Persons who had gone
through the preliminary ceremonies of initiation, were permitted
at length to hear, though under strict obligation of secrecy, this
ancient religious and cosmogonic doctrine, revealing the destina-
tion of man and the certainty of posthumous rewards and punish-

ments — all disengaged from the corruptions of poets, as well as from the symbols and allegories under which they still remained buried in the eyes of the vulgar. The mysteries of Greece were thus traced up to the earliest ages, and represented as the only faithful depository channels of that purer theology and physics which had originally been communicated, though under the unavoidable inconvenience of a symbolical expression, by an enlightened priesthood coming from abroad to the then rude barbarians of the country.[1]

---

[1] For this general character of the Grecian mysteries, with their concealed treasure of doctrine, see *Warburton*, Divine Legation of Moses, book ii. sect. 4.

Payne Knight, On the Symbolical Language of ancient Art and Mythology, sect. 6, 10, 11, 40, etc.

Saint Croix, Recherches sur les Mystères du Paganisme, sect. 3, p. 106; sect 4, p. 404, etc.

Creuzer, Symbolik und Mythologie der Alten Völker, sect. 2, 3, 23, 39, 42, etc. Meiners and Heeren adopt generally the same view, though there are many divergences of opinion between these different authors, on a subject essentially obscure. Warburton maintained that the interior doctrine communicated in the mysteries was the existence of one Supreme Divinity, combined with the Euemeristic creed, that the pagan gods had been mere men.

See Clemens Alex. Strom. v. p. 582, Sylb.

The view taken by Hermann of the ancient Greek mythology is in many points similar to that of Creuzer, though with some considerable difference. He thinks that it is an aggregate of doctrine — philosophical, theological, physical, and moral — expressed under a scheme of systematic personifications, each person being called by a name significant of the function personified: this doctrine was imported from the East into Greece, where the poets, retaining or translating the names, but forgetting their meaning and connection, distorted the primitive stories, the sense of which came to be retained only in the ancient mysteries. That true sense, however, (he thinks,) may be recovered by a careful analysis of the significant names: and his two dissertations (De Mythologiâ Græcorum Antiquissimâ, in the Opuscula, vol. ii.) exhibit a specimen of this systematic expansion of etymology into narrative. The dissent from Creuzer is set forth in their published correspondence, especially in his concluding " Brief an Creuzer über das Wesen und die Behandlung der Mythologie," Leipzig, 1819. The following citation from his Latin dissertation sets forth his general doctrine: —

Hermann, De Mythologiâ Græcorum Antiquissimâ, p. 4 (Opuscula, vol. ii. p. 171): " Videmus rerum divinarum humanarumque scientiam ex Asiâ per Lyciam migrantem in Europam : videmus fabulosos poëtas peregrinam doctrinam, monstruoso tumore orientis sive exutam, sive nondum

But this theory, though advocated by several learned men, has been shown to be unsupported and erroneous. It implies a mistaken view both of the antiquity and the purport of the mysteries, which cannot be safely carried up even to the age of Hesiod, and which, though imposing and venerable as religious ceremonies, included no recondite or esoteric teaching.[1]

indutam, quasi de integro Græcà specie procreantes; videmus poëtas, illos, quorum omnium vera nomina nominibus — ab arte, quâ clarebant, petitis — obliterata sunt, diu in Thraciâ hærentes, raroque tandem etiam cum aliis Græciæ partibus commercio junctos: qualis Pamphus, non ipse Atheniensis, Atheniensibus hymnos Deorum fecit. Videmus denique retrusam paulatim in mysteriorum secretam illam sapientum doctrinam, vitiatam religionum perturbatione, corruptam inscitià interpretum, obscuratam levitate amœniora sectantium — adeo ut eam ne illi quidem intelligerent, qui hæreditariam a prioribus poësin colentes, quum ingenii præstantiâ omnes præstinguerent, tantà illos oblivione merserunt, ut ipsi sint primi auctores omnis eruditionis habiti."

Hermann thinks, however, that by pursuing the suggestions of etymology, vestiges may still be discovered, and something like a history compiled, of Grecian belief as it stood anterior to Homer and Hesiod: "Est autem in hac omni ratione judicio maxime opus, quia non testibus res agitur, sed ad interpretandi solertiam omnia revocanda sunt" (p. 172). To the same general purpose the French work of M. Eméric David, Recherches sur le Dieu Jupiter — reviewed by O. Müller: see the Kleine Schriften of the latter, vol. ii. p. 82.

Mr. Bryant has also employed a profusion of learning, and numerous etymological conjectures, to resolve the Greek mythes into mistakes, perversions, and mutilations, of the exploits and doctrines of oriental tribes long-lost and by-gone, — Amonians, Cuthites, Arkites, etc. "It was Noah (he thinks) who was represented under the different names of Thoth, Hermês, Menês, Osiris, Zeuth, Atlas, Phorôneus, Prométheus, to which list a farther number of great extent might be added: the Νοῦς of Anaxagoras was in reality the patriarch Noah" (Ant. Mythol. vol. ii. pp. 253, 272). "The Cuthites or Amonians, descendants of Noah, settled in Greece from the east, celebrated for their skill in building and the arts" (ib. i. p. 502; ii. p. 187). The greatest part of the Grecian theology arose from misconception and blunders, the stories concerning their gods and heroes were founded on terms misinterpreted or abused" (ib. i. p. 452). "The number of different actions ascribed to the various Grecian gods or heroes all relate to one people or family, and are at bottom one and the same history" (ib. ii. p. 57). "The fables of Prométheus and Tityus were taken from ancient Amonian temples, from hieroglyphics misunderstood and badly explained" (i. p. 426): see especially vol. ii. p. 160.

[1] The Anti-Symbolik of Voss, and still more the Aglaophamus of Lobeck.

The doctrine, supposed to have been originally symbolized and subsequently overclouded, in the Greek mythes, was in reality first intruded into them by the unconscious fancies of later interpreters. It was one of the various roads which instructed men took to escape from the literal admission of the ancient mythes, and to arrive at some new form of belief, more consonant with their ideas of what the attributes and character of the gods ought to be. It was one of the ways of constituting, by help of the mysteries, a philosophical religion apart from the general public, and of connecting that distinction with the earliest periods of Grecian society. Such a distinction was both avowed and justified among the superior men of the later pagan world. Varro and Scævola distributed theology into three distinct departments, — the mythical or fabulous, the civil, and the physical. The first had its place in the theatre, and was left without any interference to the poets; the second belonged to the city of political community as such, — it comprised the regulation of all the public worship and religious rites, and was consigned altogether to the direction of the magistrate; the third was the privilege of philosophers, but was reserved altogether for private discussion in the schools, apart from the general public.[1] As a member of the

are full of instruction on the subject of this supposed interior doctrine, and on the ancient mysteries in general: the latter treatise, especially, is not less distinguished for its judicious and circumspect criticism than for its copious learning.

Mr. Halhed (Preface to the Gentoo Code of Laws, pp. xiii.–xiv.) has good observations on the vanity of all attempts to allegorize the Hindu mythology: he observes, with perfect truth, " The vulgar and illiterate have always understood the mythology of their country in its literal sense; and there was a time to every nation, when the highest rank in it was equally vulgar and illiterate with the lowest.......... A Hindu esteems the astonishing miracles attributed to a Brima, or a Kishen, as facts of the most indubitable authenticity, and the relation of them as most strictly historical."

Compare also Gibbon's remarks on the allegorizing tendencies of the later Platonists (Hist. Decl. and Fall, vol. iv. p. 71).

[1] Varro, ap. Augustin. De Civ. Dei, iv. 27; vi. 5-6. " Dicis fabulosos Deos accommodatos esse ad theatrum, naturales ad mundum, civiles ad urbem." " Varro, de religionibus loquens, multa esse vera dixit, quæ non modo vulgo scire non sit utile, sed etiam tametsi falsa sint, aliter existimare populum expediat: et ideo Græcos teletas et mysteria taciturnitate parietibusque clausisse" (ibid. iv. 31). See Villoison, De Triplici Theologià Com

city, the philosopher sympathized with the audience in the theatre, and took a devout share in the established ceremonies, nor was he justified in trying what he heard in the one or saw in the other by his own ethical standard. But in the private assemblies of instructed or inquisitive men, he enjoyed the fullest liberty of canvassing every received tenet, and of broaching his own theories unreservedly, respecting the existence and nature of the gods. By these discussions, the activity of the philosophical mind was maintained and truth elicited; but it was such truth as the body of the people ought not to hear, lest their faith in their own established religious worship should be overthrown. In thus distinguishing the civil theology from the fabulous, Varro was enabled to cast upon the poets all the blame of the objectionable points in the popular theology, and to avoid the necessity of pronouncing censure on the magistrates, who (he contended) had made as good a compromise with the settled prejudices of the public as the case permitted.

The same conflicting sentiments which led the philosophers to decompose the divine mythes into allegory, impelled the historians to melt down the heroic mythes into something like continuous political history, with a long series of chronology calculated upon the heroic pedigrees. The one process as well as the other was interpretative guesswork, proceeding upon unauthorized assumptions, and without any verifying test or evidence: while it frittered away the characteristic beauty of the mythe into something essentially anti-mythical, it sought to arrive both at history and philosophy by impracticable roads. That the superior men of antiquity should have striven hard to save the dignity of legends which constituted the charm of their literature as well as the substance of the popular religion, we cannot be at all surprised; but

mentatio, p. 8; and Lactantius, De Origin. Error. ii. 3. The doctrine of the Stoic Chrysippus, ap. Etymologicon Magn. v. Τελεταί—Χρύσιππος δέ φησι, τοὺς περὶ τῶν θείων λόγους εἰκότως καλεῖσθαι τελετὰς, χρῆναι γὰρ τούτους τελευταίους καὶ ἐπὶ πᾶσι διδάσκεσθαι, τῆς ψυχῆς ἐχούσης ἕρμα καὶ κεκρατημένης, καὶ πρὸς τοὺς ἀμυήτους σιωπᾶν δυναμένης· μέγα γὰρ εἶναι τὸ ἆθλον ὑπὲρ θεῶν ἀκοῦσαί τε ὀρθὰ, καὶ ἐγκρατεῖς γενέσθαι αὐτῶν.

The triple division of Varro is reproduced in Plutarch, Amatorius, p. 763. τὰ μὲν μύθῳ, τὰ δὲ νόμῳ, τὰ δὲ λόγῳ, πίστιν ἐξ ἀρχῆς ἔσχηκε· τῆς δ' οὖν περὶ θεῶν δόξης καὶ παντάπασιν ἡγεμόνες καὶ διδάσκαλοι γεγόνασιν ἡμῖν οἵ τε ποιηταὶ, καὶ οἱ νομοθέται, καὶ τρίτον, οἱ φιλόσοφοι

it is gratifying to find Plato discussing the subject in a more philosophical spirit. The Platonic Socratês, being asked whether he believed the current Attic fable respecting the abduction of Oreithyia (daughter of Erechtheus) by Boreas, replies, in substance, — "It would not be strange if I disbelieved it, as the clever men do; I might then show my cleverness by saying that a gust of Boreas blew her down from the rocks above while she was at play, and that, having been killed in this manner, she was reported to have been carried off by Boreas. Such speculations are amusing enough, but they belong to men ingenious and busy-minded overmuch, and not greatly to be envied, if it be only for this reason, *that, after having set right one fable, they are under the necessity of applying the same process to a host of others* — Hippocentaurs, Chimæras, Gorgons, Pegasus, and numberless other monsters and incredibilities. A man, who, disbelieving these stories, shall try to find a probable basis for each of them, will display an ill-placed acuteness and take upon himself an endless burden, for which I at least have no leisure: accordingly, I forego such researches, and believe in the current version of the stories."[1]

These remarks of Plato are valuable, not simply because they point out the uselessness of digging for a supposed basis of truth in the mythes, but because they at the same time suggest the true reason for mistrusting all such tentatives. The mythes form

---

[1] Plato, Phædr. c. 7. p. 229: —

PHÆDRUS. Εἰπέ μοι, ὦ Σώκρατες, σὺ τοῦτο τὸ μυθολόγημα πείθει ἀληθὲς εἶναι;

SOCRATES. Ἀλλ᾿ εἰ ἀπιστοίην, ὥσπερ οἱ σοφοί, οὐκ ἂν ἄτοπος εἴην, εἶτα σοφιζόμενος φαίην αὐτὴν πνεῦμα Βορέου κατὰ τῶν πλήσιον πετρῶν σὺν φαρμακείᾳ παίζουσαν ὦσαι, καὶ οὕτω δὴ τελευτήσασαν λεχθῆναι ὑπὸ τοῦ Βορέου ἀναρπαστὸν γεγονέναι . . . .᾿Εγὼ δὲ, ὦ Φαῖδρε, ἄλλως μὲν τὰ τοιαῦτα χαρίεντα ἡγοῦμαι, λίαν δὲ δεινοῦ καὶ ἐπιπόνου καὶ οὐ πάνυ εὐτυχοῦς ἀνδρὸς, κατ᾿ ἄλλο μὲν οὐδὲν, ὅτι δ᾿ αὐτῷ ἀνάγκη μετὰ τοῦτο τὸ τῶν Ἱπποκενταύρων εἶδος ἐπανορθοῦσθαι, καὶ αὖθις τὸ τῆς Χιμαίρας. Καὶ ἐπιρρεῖ δὲ ὄχλος τοιούτων Γοργόνων καὶ Πηγάσων, καὶ ἄλλων ἀμηχάνων πλήθη τε καὶ ἀτόπιαι τερα-τολόγων τινῶν φύσεων· αἷς εἴ τις ἀπιστῶν προσβιβᾷ κατὰ τὸ εἰκὸς ἕκαστον, ἅτε ἀγροίκῳ τινι σοφίᾳ χρώμενος, πολλῆς αὐτῷ σχολῆς δεήσει. ᾿Εμοὶ δὲ πρὸς ταῦτα οὐδαμῶς ἐστι σχολή . . . .῞Οθεν δὴ χαίρειν ἐάσας ταῦτα, πειθόμενος δὲ τῷ νομιζομένῳ περὶ αὐτῶν, ὃ νῦν δὴ ἔλεγον, σκοπῶ οὐ ταῦτα ἀλλ᾿ ἐμαυτὸν, etc.

a class apart, abundant as well as peculiar : to remove any individual mythe from its own class into that of history or philosophy,
by simple conjecture, and without any collateral evidence, is of no
advantage, unless you can perform a similar process on the remainder. If the process be trustworthy, it ought to be applied to
all ; and e converso, if it be not applicable to all, it is not trustworthy as applied to any one specially ; always assuming no
special evidence to be accessible. To detach any individual
mythe from the class to which it belongs, is to present it in an
erroneous point of view ; we have no choice except to admit them
as they stand, by putting ourselves approximatively into the
frame of mind of those for whom they were destined and to whom
they appeared worthy of credit.

If Plato thus discountenances all attempts to transform the
mythes by interpretation into history or philosophy, indirectly
recognizing the generic difference between them — we find substantially the same view pervading the elaborate precepts in his
treatise on the Republic. He there regards the mythes, not as
embodying either matter-of-fact or philosophical principle, but as
portions of religious and patriotic faith, and instruments of ethical
tuition. Instead of allowing the poets to frame them according
to the impulses of their own genius, and with a view to immediate popularity, he directs the legislator to provide types of his
own for the characters of the gods and heroes, and to suppress all
such divine and heroic legends as are not in harmony with these
preëstablished canons. In the Platonic system, the mythes are
not to be matters of history, nor yet of spontaneous or casual fiction, but of prescribed faith : he supposes that the people will
believe, as a thing of course, what the poets circulate, and he
therefore directs that the latter shall circulate nothing which does
not tend to ennoble and improve the feelings. He conceives the
mythes as stories composed to illustrate the general sentiments
of the poets and the community, respecting the character and
attributes of the gods and heroes, or respecting the social relations,
and ethical duties as well as motives of mankind : hence the obligation upon the legislator to prescribe beforehand the types of
character which shall be illustrated, and to restrain the poets from
following out any opposing fancies. " Let us neither believe ourselves (he exclaims), nor permit any one to circulate, that The-

seus son of Poseidôn and Peirithöus son of Zeus, or any other hero or son of a god, could ever have brought themselves to commit abductions or other enormities such as are now falsely ascribed to them. We must compel the poets to say, either that such persons were not the sons of gods, or that they were not the perpetrators of such misdeeds."[1]

Most of the mythes which the youth hear and repeat (according to Plato) are false, but some of them are true: the great and prominent mythes which appear in Homer and Hesiod are no less fictions than the rest. But fiction constitutes one of the indispensable instruments of mental training as well as truth; only the legislator must take care that the fiction so employed shall be beneficent and not mischievous.[2] As the mischievous fictions (he says) take their rise from wrong preconceptions respecting the character of the gods and heroes, so the way to correct them is to enforce, by authorized compositions, the adoption of a more correct standard.[3]

---

[1] Plato, Rcpub. iii. 5. p. 391. The perfect ignorance of all men respecting the gods, rendered the task of fiction easy (Plato, Kritias, p. 107).

[2] Plato, Repub. ii. 16. p. 377. Λόγων δὲ διττὸν εἶδος, τὸ μὲν ἀληθὲς, ψεῦδος δ' ἕτερον; Ναί. Παιδευτέον δ' ἐν ἀμφοτέροις, πρότερον δ' ἐν τοῖς ψεύδεσιν· ...... Οὐ μανθάνεις, ὅτι πρῶτον τοῖς παιδίοις μύθους λέγομεν· τοῦτο δέ που ὡς τὸ ὅλον εἰπεῖν ψεῦδος, ἔνι δὲ καὶ ἀληθῆ........Πρῶτον ἡμῖν ἐπιστατητέον τοῖς μυθοποιοῖς, καὶ ὃν μὲν ἂν καλὸν μῦθον ποιήσωσιν, ἐγκριτέον, ὃν δ' ἂν μὴ, ἀποκριτέον......ὧν δὲ νῦν λέγουσι, τοὺς πολλοὺς ἐκβλητέον ......οὓς Ἡσίοδος καὶ Ὅμηρος ἡμῖν ἐλεγέτην, καὶ οἱ ἄλλοι ποιηταί. Οὗτοι γάρ που μύθους τοῖς ἀνθρώποις ψευδεῖς συντιθέντες ἔλεγόν τε καὶ λέγουσι. Ποίους δὴ, ἦ δ' ὃς, καὶ τί αὐτῶν μεμφόμενος λέγεις; Ὅπερ, ἦν δ' ἐγὼ, χρὴ καὶ πρῶτον καὶ μάλιστα μέμφεσθαι, ἄλλως τε καὶ ἐάν τις μὴ καλῶς ψεύδηται. Τί τοῦτο; Ὅταν τις εἰκάζῃ κακῶς τῷ λόγῳ περὶ θεῶν τε καὶ ἡρώων, οἷοι εἰσιν, ὥσπερ γραφεὺς μηδὲν ἐοικότα γράφων οἷς ἂν ὅμοια βούληται γράψαι.

The same train of thought, and the precepts founded upon it, are followed up through chaps. 17, 18, and 19; compare De Legg. xii. p. 941.

Instead of recognizing the popular or dramatic theology as something distinct from the civil (as Varro did), Plato suppresses the former as a separate department and merges it in the latter.

[3] Plato, Repub. ii. c. 21. p. 382. Τὸ ἐν τοῖς λόγοις ψεῦδος πότε καὶ τί χρήσιμον, ὥστε μὴ ἄξιον εἶναι μίσους; Ἀρ' οὐ πρός τε τοὺς πολεμίους καὶ τῶν καλουμένων φίλων, ὅταν διὰ μανίαν ἤ τινα ἄνοιαν κακόν τι ἐπιχειρῶσι πράττειν, τότε ἀποτροπῆς ἕνεκα ὡς φάρμακον χρήσιμον γίγνεται; Καὶ ἐν αἷς νῦν δὴ ἐλέγομεν ταῖς μυθολογίαις, διὰ τὸ μὴ εἰδέναι ὅπη τἀληθὲς ἔχει περὶ τῶν παλαιῶν, ἀφομοιοῦντες τῷ ἀληθεῖ τὸ ψεῦδος, ὅτι μάλιστα, οὕτω χρήσιμον ποιοῦμεν·

The comments which Plato has delivered with so much force in his Republic, and the enactments which he deduces from them, are in the main an expansion of that sentiment of condemnation, which he shared with so many other philosophers, towards a large portion of the Homeric and Hesiodic stories.[1] But the manner in which he has set forth this opinion, unfolds to us more clearly the real character of the mythical narratives. They are creations of the productive minds in the community, deduced from the supposed attributes of the gods and heroes : so Plato views them, and in such character he proposes to amend them. The legislator would cause to be prepared a better and truer picture of the foretime, because he would start from truer (that is to say, more creditable) conceptions of the gods and heroes. For Plato rejects the mythes respecting Zeus and Hêrê, or Thêseus and Peirithöus, not from any want of evidence, but because they are unworthy of gods and heroes : he proposes to call forth new mythes, which, though he admits them at the outset to be fiction, he knows will soon be received as true, and supply more valuable lessons of conduct.

We may consider, then, that Plato disapproves of the attempt to identify the old mythes either with exaggerated history or with disguised philosophy. He shares in the current faith, without any suspicion or criticism, as to Orpheus, Palamêdês, Dædalus, Amphiôn, Thêseus, Achilles, Cheirôn, and other mythical personages ;[2] but what chiefly fills his mind is, the inherited sentiment of deep reverence for these superhuman characters and for the age to which they belonged, — a sentiment sufficiently strong to render him not only an unbeliever in such legends as conflict with it, but also a deliberate creator of new legends for the purpose of expanding and gratifying it. The more we examine this sentiment, both in the mind of Plato as well as in

---

[1] The censure which Xenophanês pronounced upon the Homeric legends has already been noticed : Herakleitus (Diogen. Laërt. ix. 1) and Metrodôrus, the companion and follower of Epicurus, were not less profuse in their invectives, ἐν γράμμασι τοσούτοις τῷ ποιητῇ λελοιδόρηται (Plutarch, Non posse suaviter vivi secundum Epicurum, p. 1086). He even advised persons not to be ashamed to confess their utter ignorance of Homer, to the extent of not knowing whether Hectôr was a Greek or a Trojan (Plut. ib. p. 1094).

[2] Plato, Republic. iii. 4–5. p. 391 ; De Legg. iii. 1. p. 677.

that of the Greeks generally, the more shall we be convinced that it formed essentially and inseparably a portion of Hellenic religious faith. The mythe both presupposes, and springs out of, a settled basis, and a strong expansive force of religious, social, and patriotic feeling, operating upon a past which is little better than a blank as to positive knowledge. It resembles history, in so far as its form is narrative ; it resembles philosophy, in so far as it is occasionally illustrative ; but in its essence and substance, in the mental tendencies by which it is created as well as in those by which it is judged and upheld, it is a popularized expression of the divine and heroic faith of the people.

Grecian antiquity cannot be at all understood except in connection with Grecian religion. It begins with gods and it ends with historical men, the former being recognized not simply as gods, but as primitive ancestors, and connected with the latter by a long mythical genealogy, partly heroic and partly human. Now the whole value of such genealogies arises from their being taken entire ; the god or hero at the top is in point of fact the most important member of the whole ;[1] for the length and continuity of the series arises from anxiety on the part of historical men to join themselves by a thread of descent with the being whom they worshipped in their gentile sacrifices. Without the ancestorial god, the whole pedigree would have become not only acephalous, but worthless and uninteresting. The pride of the Herakleids, Asklepiads, Æakids, Neleids, Dædalids, etc. was attached to the primitive eponymous hero and to the god from whom they sprung, not to the line of names, generally long and barren, through which the divine or heroic dignity gradually dwindled down into common manhood. Indeed, the length of the genealogy (as I have before remarked) was an evidence of the humility of the historical man, which led him to place himself at a respectful distance from the gods or heroes ; for Hekatæus of Milêtus, who ranked himself as the fifteenth descendant of a god, might per-

---

[1] For a description of similar tendencies in the Asiatic religions, see Mövers, Die Phönizier, ch. v. p. 153 (Bonn, 1841): he points out the same phænomena as in the Greek, — coalescence between the ideas of ancestry and worship, — confusion between gods and men in the past, — increasing tendency to Euemerize (pp. 156-157).

haps have accounted it an overweening impiety in any living man
to claim a god for his immediate father.

The whole chronology of Greece, anterior to 776 B. C., consists
of calculations founded upon these mythical genealogies, especially upon that of the Spartan kings and their descent from
Hêraklês, — thirty years being commonly taken as the equivalent of a generation, or about three generations to a century.
This process of computation was altogether illusory, as applying
historical and chronological conditions to a case on which they
had no bearing. Though the domain of history was seemingly
enlarged, the religious element was tacitly set aside : when the
heroes and gods were chronologized, they became insensibly approximated to the limits of humanity, and the process indirectly
gave encouragement to the theory of Euêmerus. Personages
originally legendary and poetical were erected into definite land-
marks for measuring the duration of the foretime, thus gaining in
respect to historical distinctness, but not without loss on the score
of religious association. Both Euêmerus and the subsequent
Christian writers, who denied the original and inherent divinity
of the pagan gods, had a great advantage in carrying their chronological researches strictly and consistently upwards — for all
chronology fails as soon as we suppose a race superior to common
humanity.

Moreover, it is to be remarked that the pedigree of the Spartan
kings, which Apollodôrus and Eratosthenês selected as the basis
of their estimate of time, is nowise superior in credibility and
trustworthiness to the thousand other gentile and family pedigrees
with which Greece abounded ; it is rather indeed to be numbered
among the most incredible of all, seeing that Hêraklês as a progenitor is placed at the head of perhaps more pedigrees than any
other Grecian god or hero.[1] The descent of the Spartan king
Leonidas from Hêraklês rests upon no better evidence than that
of Aristotle or Hippocratês from Asklêpius,[2] — of Evagoras or

---

[1] According to that which Aristotle seems to recognize (Histor. Animal.
vii. 6), Hêraklês was father of seventy-two sons, but of only one daughter —
he was essentially ἀρρενόγονος, illustrating one of the physical peculiarities
noticed by Aristotle. Euripidês, however, mentions daughters of Hêraklês in
the plural number (Euripid. Herakleid. 45).

[2] Hippocratês was twentieth in descent from Hêraklês, and nineteenth

Thucydidês from Æakus, — of Socratês from Dædalus, — of the
Spartan heraldic family from Talthybius, — of the prophetic
Iamid family in Elis from Iamus, — of the root-gatherers in
Pêlion from Cheirôn, — and of Hekatæus and his gens from
some god in the sixteenth ascending line of the series. There
is little exaggeration in saying, indeed, that no permanent combination of men in Greece, religious, social, or professional, was
without a similar pedigree; all arising out of the same exigences
of the feelings and imagination, to personify as well as to sanctify
the bond of union among the members. Every one of these
gentes began with a religious and ended with an historical person.
At some point or other in the upward series, entities of history
were exchanged for entities of religion; but where that point is
to be found we are unable to say, nor had the wisest of the ancient Greeks any means of determining. Thus much, however,
we know, that the series taken as a whole, though dear and precious to the believing Greek, possesses no value as chronological
evidence to the historian.

When Hekatæus visited Thêbes in Egypt, he mentioned to the
Egyptian priests, doubtless with a feeling of satisfaction and
pride, the imposing pedigree of the gens to which he belonged, —
with fifteen ancestors in ascending line, and a god as the initial
progenitor. But he found himself immeasurably overdone by the
priests " who genealogized against him."[1] They showed to him
three hundred and forty-one wooden colossal statues, representing
the succession of chief priests in the temple in uninterrupted
series from father to son, through a space of 11,300 years. Prior
to the commencement of this long period (they said), the gods
dwelling along with men, had exercised sway in Egypt; but they

from Asklêpius (Vita Hippocr. by Soranus, ap. Westermann, Scriptor.
Biographic. viii. 1); about Aristotle, see Diogen. Laërt. v. 1. Xenophôn, the
physician of the emperor Claudius, was also an Asklepiad (Tacit. Ann. xii.
61).

In Rhodes, the neighboring island to Kôs, was the gens Ἀλιάδαι, or sons
of Hêlios, specially distinguished from the Ἀλιασταὶ of mere associated
worshippers of Hêlios, τὸ κοινὸν τῶν Ἀλιαδῶν καὶ τῶν Ἀλιαστῶν (see the
Inscription in Boeckh's Collection, No. 2525, with Boeckh's comment).

[1] Herodot. ii. 144. Ἑκαταίῳ δὲ γενεηλογήσαντι ἑωυτὸν, καὶ ἀναδήσαντι
ἐς ἑκκαιδέκατον θεὸν, ἀντεγενεηλόγησαν ἐπὶ τῇ ἀριθμήσει, οὐ δεκόμενοι παρ'
αὐτοῦ, ἀπὸ θεοῦ γένεσθαι ἄνθρωπον· ἀντεγενεηλόγησαν δὲ ὧδε, etc

repudiated altogether the idea of men begotten by gods or of heroes.[1]

But these counter-genealogies, are, in respect to trustworthiness and evidence, on the same footing. Each represents partly the religious faith, partly the retrospective imagination, of the persons from whom it emanated; in each, the lower members of the series (to what extent we cannot tell) are real, the upper members fabulous; but in each also the series derived all its interest and all its imposing effect from being conceived unbroken and entire. Herodotus is much perplexed by the capital discrepancy between the Grecian and Egyptian chronologies, and vainly employs his ingenuity in reconciling them. There is no standard of objective evidence by which either the one or the other of them can be tried: each has its own subjective value, in conjunction with the faith and feelings of Egyptians and Greeks, and each presupposes in the believer certain mental prepossessions which are not to be found beyond its own local limits. Nor is the greater or less extent of duration at all important, when we once pass the limits of evidence and verifiable reality. One century of recorded time, adequately studded with authentic and orderly events, presents a greater mass and a greater difficulty of transition to the imagination than a hundred centuries of barren genealogy. Herodotus, in discussing the age of Homer and Hesiod, treats an anterior point of 400 years as if it were only yesterday; the reign of Henry VI. is separated from us by an equal interval, and the reader will not require to be reminded how long that interval now appears.

The mythical age was peopled with a mingled aggregate of gods, heroes, and men, so confounded together that it was often impossible to distinguish to which class any individual name belonged. In regard to the Thracian god Zalmoxis, the Hellespontic Greeks interpreted his character and attributes according to the scheme of Euêmerism. They affirmed that he had been a man, the slave of the philosopher Pythagoras at Samos, and that he had by abilities and artifice established a religious ascendency over the minds of the Thracians, and obtained from them

---

[1] Herod. ii. 143–145. Καὶ ταῦτα Αἰγύπτιοι ἀτρεκέως φασὶν ἐπίστασθαι, αἰεὶ τε λογιζόμενοι καὶ αἰεὶ ἀπογραφόμενοι τὰ ἔτεα.

divine honors. Herodotus cannot bring himself to believe this story, but he frankly avows his inability to determine whether Zalmoxis was a god or a man,[1] nor can he extricate himself from a similar embarrassment in respect to Dionysus and Pan. Amidst the confusion of the Homeric fight, the goddess Athênê confers upon Diomêdês the miraculous favor of dispelling the mist from his eyes, so as to enable him to discriminate gods from men ; and nothing less than a similar miracle could enable a critical reader of the mythical narratives to draw an ascertained boundary-line between the two.[2] But the original hearers of the mythes felt neither surprise nor displeasure from this confusion of the divine with the human individual. They looked at the past with a film

---

[1] Herod. iv. 94–96. After having related the Euemeristic version given by the Hellespontic Greeks, he concludes with his characteristic frankness and simplicity — Ἐγὼ δὲ, περὶ μὲν τούτου καὶ τοῦ καταγαίου οἰκήματος, οὔτε ἀπιστέω, οὔτε ὦν πιστεύω τι λίην. δοκέω δὲ πολλοῖσι ἔτεσι πρότερον τὸν Ζάλμοξιν τοῦτον γενέσθαι Πυθαγόρεω. Εἴτε δὲ ἐγένετό τις Ζάλμοξις ἄνθρωπος, εἴτ᾽ ἐστὶ δαίμων τις Γέτησι οὗτος ἐπιχώριος, χαιρέτω. So Plutarch (Numa, c. 19) will not undertake to determine whether Janus was a god or a king εἴτε δαίμων, εἴτε βασιλεὺς γενόμενος, etc.

Herakleitus the philosopher said that men were θεοὶ θνητοί, and the gods were ἄνθρωποι ἀθάνατοι (Lucian, Vitar. Auctio. c. 13. vol. i. p. 303, Tauch. compare the same author, Dialog. Mortuor. iii. vol. i. p. 182, ed. Tauchn).

[2] Iliad, v. 127 : —

Ἀχλὺν δ᾽ αὖ τοι ἀπ᾽ ὀφθαλμῶν ἕλον, ἣ πρὶν ἐπῆεν,
Ὄφρ᾽ εὖ γιγνώσκῃς ἠμὲν θεὸν, ἠδὲ καὶ ἄνδρα.

Of this undistinguishable confusion between gods and men, striking illustrations are to be found both in the third book of Cicero de Naturâ Deorum (16–21), and in the long disquisition of Strabo (x. pp. 467–474) respecting the Kabeiri, the Korybantes, the Dactyls of Ida ; the more so, as he cites the statements of Pherekydês, Akusilaus, Dêmêtrius of Skêpsis, and others. Under the Roman empire, the lands in Greece belonging to the immortal gods were exempted from tribute. The Roman tax-collectors refused to recognize as immortal gods any persons who had once been men ; but this rule could not be clearly applied (Cicero, Nat. Deor. iii. 20). See the remarks of Pausanias (ii. 26, 7) about Asklêpius : Galen, too, is doubtful about Asklêpius and Dionysus — Ἀσκληπιός γέ τοι καὶ Διόνυσος, εἴτ᾽ ἄνθρωποι πρότερον ἤστην, εἴτε καὶ ἀρχῆθεν θεοί (Galen in Protreptic. 9. tom. i. p. 22, ed. Kühn). Xenophôn (De Venat. c. i) considers Cheirôn as the brother of Zeus.

The ridicule of Lucian (Deorum Concilium, t. iii. p. 527–538, Hems.) brings out still more forcibly the confusion here indicated.

of faith over their eyes — neither knowing the value, nor desiring the attainment, of an unclouded vision. The intimate companionship, and the occasional mistake of identity between gods and men, were in full harmony with their reverential restrospect. And we, accordingly, see the poet Ovid in his Fasti, when he undertakes the task of unfolding the legendary antiquities of early Rome, reacquiring, by the inspiration of Juno, the power of seeing gods and men in immediate vicinity and conjunct action, such as it existed before the development of the critical and historical sense.[1]

To resume, in brief, what has been laid down in this and the preceding chapters respecting the Grecian mythes: —

1. They are a special product of the imagination and feelings, radically distinct both from history and philosophy: they cannot be broken down and decomposed into the one, nor allegorized into the other. There are indeed some particular and even assignable mythes, which raise intrinsic presumption of an allegorizing tendency; and there are doubtless some others, though not specially assignable, which contain portions of matter of fact, or names of real persons, embodied in them. But such matter of fact cannot be verified by any intrinsic mark, nor we are entitled to presume its existence in any given case unless some collateral evidence can be produced.

2. We are not warranted in applying to the mythical world the rules either of historical credibility or chronological sequence. Its personages are gods, heroes, and men, in constant juxtaposition and reciprocal sympathy; men, too, of whom we know a large proportion to be fictitious, and of whom we can never ascertain how many may have been real. No series of such personages can serve as materials for chronological calculation.

---

[1] Ovid, Fasti, vi. 6–20 : —

> "Fas mihi præcipue vultus vidisse Deorum,
> Vel quia sum vates, vel quia sacra cano ......
> ... Ecce Deas vidi ....
> Horrueram, tacitoque animum pallore fatebar:
> Cum Dea, quos fecit, sustulit ipsa metus.
> Namque ait — O vates, Romani conditor anni,
> Ause per exiguos magna referre modos;
> Jus tibi fecisti numen cœleste videndi,
> Cum placuit numeris condere festa tuis."

3. The mythes were originally produced in an age which had no records, no philosophy, no criticism, no canon of belief, and scarcely any tincture either of astronomy or geography — but which, on the other hand, was full of religious faith, distinguished for quick and susceptible imagination, seeing personal agents where we look only for objects and connecting laws; — an age, moreover, eager for new narrative, accepting with the unconscious impressibility of children (the question of truth or falsehood being never formally raised) all which ran in harmony with its preexisting feelings, and penetrable by inspired prophets and poets in the same proportion that it was indifferent to positive evidence. To such hearers did the primitive poet or story-teller address himself: it was the glory of his productive genius to provide suitable narrative expression for the faith and emotions which he shared in common with them, and the rich stock of Grecian mythes attests how admirably he performed his task. As the gods and the heroes formed the conspicuous object of national reverence, so the mythes were partly divine, partly heroic, partly both in one.[1] The adventures of Achilles, Helen, and Diomêdês, of Œdipus and Adrastus, of Meleager and Athæa, of Jasôn and the Argô, were recounted by the same tongues, and accepted with the same unsuspecting confidence, as those of Apollo and Artemis, of Arês and Aphroditê, of Poseidôn and Hêraklês.

4. The time however came, when this plausibility ceased to be complete. The Grecian mind made an important advance, socially, ethically, and intellectually. Philosophy and history were constituted, prose writing and chronological records became familiar; a canon of belief more or less critical came to be tacitly recognized. Moreover, superior men profited more largely by the stimulus, and contracted habits of judging different from the

---

[1] The fourth Eclogue of Virgil, under the form of a prophecy, gives a faithful picture of the heroic and divine past, to which the legends of Troy and the Argonauts belonged: —

"Ille Deûm vitam accipiet, Divisque videbit
Permixtos heroas," etc.

"Alter erit tum Tiphys et altera quæ vehat Argo
Delectos heroas : erunt etiam altera bella,
Atque iterum ad Trojam magnus mittetur Achilles."

vulgar: the god Elenchus[1] (to use a personification of Menander),
the giver and prover of truth, descended into their minds. Into
the new intellectual medium, thus altered in its elements, and no
longer uniform in its quality, the mythes descended by inheritance; but they were found, to a certain extent, out of harmony
even with the feelings of the people, and altogether dissonant
with those of instructed men. But the most superior Greek was
still a Greek, and cherished the common reverential sentiment
towards the foretime of his country. Though he could neither
believe nor respect the mythes as they stood, he was under an
imperious mental necessity to transform them into a state worthy
of his belief and respect. Whilst the literal mythe still continued
to float among the poets and the people, critical men interpreted,
altered, decomposed, and added, until they found something which
satisfied their minds as a supposed real basis. They manufactured some dogmas of supposed original philosophy, and a long
series of fancied history and chronology, retaining the mythical
names and generations even when they were obliged to discard
or recast the mythical events. The interpreted mythe was thus
promoted into a reality, while the literal mythe was degraded into
a fiction.[2]

---

[1] Lucian, Pseudol. c. 4. Παρακλητέος ἡμῖν τῶν Μενάνδρου προλόγων εἷς, ὁ
Ἔλεγχος, φίλος ἀληθείᾳ καὶ παρρησίᾳ θεὸς, οὐχ ὁ ἀσημότατος τῶν ἐπὶ τὴν
σκήνην ἀναβαινόντων. (See Meineke ad Menandr. p. 284.)

[2] The following passage from Dr. Ferguson's Essay on Civil Society (part
ii. sect. i. p. 126) bears well on the subject before us:—

"If conjectures and opinions formed at a distance have not a sufficient
authority in the history of mankind, the domestic antiquities of every nation
must for this very reason be received with caution. They are, for the most
part, the mere conjectures or the fictions of subsequent ages; and even where
at first they contained some resemblance of truth, they still vary with the
imagination of those by whom they were transmitted, and in every generation receive a different form. They are made to bear the stamp of the times
through which they have passed in the form of tradition, not of the ages to
which their pretended descriptions relate. . . . . When traditionary
fables are rehearsed by the vulgar, they bear the marks of a national character, and though mixed with absurdities, often raise the imagination and more
the heart: when made the materials of poetry, and adorned by the skill and
the eloquence of an ardent and superior mind, they instruct the understanding as well as engage the passions. It is only in the management of mere
antiquaries, or stript of the ornaments which the laws of history forbid them

The habit of distinguishing the interpreted from the literal mythe has passed from the literary men of antiquity to those of the modern world, who have for the most part construed the divine mythes as allegorized philosophy, and the heroic mythes as exaggerated, adorned, and over-colored history. The early ages of Greece have thus been peopled with quasi-historical persons and quasi-historical events, all extracted from the mythes after making certain allowances for poetical ornament. But we must not treat this extracted product as if it were the original substance; we cannot properly understand it except by viewing it in connection with the literal mythes out of which it was obtained, in their primitive age and appropriate medium, before the superior minds had yet outgrown the common faith in an all-personified Nature, and learned to restrict the divine free-agency by the supposition of invariable physical laws. It is in this point of view that the mythes are important for any one who would correctly appreciate the general tone of Grecian thought and feeling; for they were the universal mental stock of the Hellenic world — common to men and women, rich and poor, instructed and ignorant; they were in every one's memory and in every one's mouth,[1] while science and history were confined to com-

---

to wear, that *they become unfit even to amuse the fancy or to serve any purpose whatever.*

"It were absurd to quote the fable of the Iliad or the Odyssey, the legend of Hercules, Theseus, and Œdipus, as authorities in matters of fact relating to the history of mankind ; but they may, with great justice, be cited to ascertain what were the conceptions and sentiments of the age in which they were composed, or to characterize the genius of that people with whose imaginations they were blended, and by whom they were fondly rehearsed and admired. In this manner, fiction may be admitted to vouch for the genius of nations, while history has nothing to offer worthy of credit."

To the same purpose, M. Paulin Paris (in his Lettre à M. H. de Monmerqué, prefixed to the Roman de Berte aux Grans Piés, Paris, 1836), respecting the "romans" of the Middle Ages: "Pour bien connaître l'histoire du moyen âge, non pas celle des faits, mais celle des mœurs qui rendent les faits vraisemblables, il faut l'avoir étudiée dans les romans, et voilà pourquoi l'Histoire de France n'est pas encore faite." (p. xxi.)

[1] A curious evidence of the undiminished popularity of the Grecian mythes to the exclusion even of recent history, is preserved by Vopiscus at the beginning of his Life of Aurelian.

The præfect of the city of Rome, Junius Tiberianus, took Vopiscus into

paratively few. We know from Thucydidês how erroneously
and carelessly the Athenian public of his day retained the history of Peisistratus, only one century past;[1] but the adventures
of the gods and heroes, the numberless explanatory legends attached to visible objects and periodical ceremonies, were the
theme of general talk, and any man unacquainted with them
would have found himself partially excluded from the sympathy
of his neighbors. The theatrical representations, exhibited to the
entire city population, and listened to with enthusiastic interest,
both presupposed and perpetuated acquaintance with the great
lines of heroic fable: indeed, in later times even the pantomimic
dancers embraced in their representations the whole field of mythical incident, and their immense success proves at once how
popular and how well known such subjects were. The names
and attributes of the heroes were incessantly alluded to in the
way of illustration, to point out a consoling, admonitory, or re-
pressive moral: the simple mention of any of them sufficed to
call up in every one's mind the principal events of his life, and
the poet or rhapsode could thus calculate on touching chords not
less familiar than susceptible.[2]

---

his carriage on the festival-day of the Hilaria; he was connected by the ties
of relationship with Aurelian, who had died about a generation before — and
as the carriage passed by the splendid Temple of the Sun, which Aurelian
had consecrated, he asked Vopiscus, what author had written the life of that
emperor ? To which Vopiscus replied, that he had read some Greek works
which touched upon Aurelian, but nothing in Latin. Whereat the venerable
præfect was profoundly grieved : " Dolorem gemitûs sui vir sanctus per hæc
verba profudit : Ergo *Thersitem, Sinonem, cæteraque illa prodigia vetustatis,
et nos bene scimus, et posteri frequentabunt:* divum Aurelianum, clarissimum
principem, severissimum Imperatorem, per quem totus Romano nomini orbis
est restitutus, posteri nescient ? Deus avertat hanc amentiam ! Et tamen,
si bene memini, ephemeridas illius viri scriptas habemus," etc. (Historiæ
August. Scriptt. p. 209, ed. Salmas.)

This impressive remonstrance produced the Life of Aurelian by Vopiscus
The materials seem to have been ample and authentic ; it is to be regretted
that they did not fall into the hands of an author qualified to turn them to
better account.

[1] Thucyd. vi. 56.

[2] Pausan. i. 3, 3. Λέγεται μὲν δὴ καὶ ἄλλα οὐκ ἀληθῆ παρὰ τοῖς πολλοῖς,
οἷα ἱστορίας ἀνηκόοις οὖσι, καὶ ὅποσα ἤκουον εὐθὺς ἐκ παίδων ἔν τε χόροις καὶ
τραγῳδίαις πιστὰ ἡγουμένοις, etc. The treatise of Lucian, De Saltatione, is

POPULARITY OF GRECIAN MYTHES.   455

A similar effect was produced by the multiplied religious festivals and processions, as well as by the oracles and prophecies

a curious proof how much these mythes were in every one's memory, and how large the range of knowledge of them was which a good dancer possessed (see particularly c. 76–79. t. ii. p. 308–310, Hemst). Antiphanês ap. Athenæ. vi. p. 223 :—

Μακάριόν ἐστιν ἡ τραγῳδία
ποίημα κατὰ πάντ', εἴ γε πρῶτον οἱ λόγοι
ὑπὸ τῶν θεατῶν εἰσιν ἐγνωρίσμενοι
πρὶν καί τιν' εἰπεῖν· ὡς ὑπομνῆσαι μόνον
δεῖ τὸν ποιητήν. Οἰδίπουν γὰρ ἄν γε φῶ,
τὰ δ' ἄλλα παντ' ἴσασιν· ὁ πατὴρ Λαΐος.
μήτηρ Ἰοκάστη, θυγατέρες, παῖδες τίνες·
τί πείσεθ' οὗτος, τι πεποίηκεν. Ἀν πάλιν
εἴπη τις Ἀλκμαίωνα, καὶ τὰ παιδία
πάντ' εὐθὺς εἴρηχ', ὅτι μανεὶς ἀπέκτονε
τὴν μήτερ'· ἀγανακτῶν δ' Ἀδραστος εὐθέως
ἥξει, πάλιν δ' ἄπεισιν, etc.

The first pages of the eleventh Oration of Din Chrysostom contain some striking passages both as to the universal acquaintance with the mythes, and as to their extreme popularity (Or. xi. p. 307–312, Reisk). See also the commencement of Heraklidês, De Allegoriâ Homericâ (ap. Scriptt. Myth. ed. Gale, p. 408), about the familiarity with Homer.

The Lydê of the poet Antimachus was composed for his own consolation under sorrow, by enumerating the ἡρωΐκὰς συμφοράς (Plutarch, Consolat. ad Apollôn. c. 9. p. 106: compare Æschines cont. Ktesiph. c. 48) : a sepulchral inscription in Thêra, on the untimely death of Admêtus, a youth of the heroic gens Ægidæ, makes a touching allusion to his ancestors Pêleus and Pherês (Boeckh, C. I. t. ii. p. 1087).

A curious passage of Aristotle is preserved by Dêmêtrius Phalereus (Περὶ Ἐρμηνείας, c. 144), — 'Οσῳ γὰρ αὐτίτης καὶ μονώτης εἰμὶ, φιλομυθότερος γέγονα (compare the passage in the Nikomachean Ethics, i. 9, μονώτης καὶ ἄτεκνος). Stahr refers this to a letter of Aristotle written in his old age, the mythes being the consolation of his solitude (Aristotelia, i. p. 201).

For the employment of the mythical names and incidents as topics of pleasing and familiar comparison, see Menander, Περὶ Ἐπιδεικτἴκ. § iv. capp. 9 and 11, ap. Walz. Coll. Rhett. t. ix. pp. 283–294. The degree in which they passed into the ordinary songs of women is illustrated by a touching epigram contained among the Chian Inscriptions published in Boeckh's Collection (No. 2236):—

Βιττὼ καὶ Φαινὶς, φίλη ἡμέρη (?), αἱ συνέριθοι,
Αἱ πενιχραὶ, γραῖαι, τῇδ' ἐκλίθημεν ὁμοῦ.
Ἀμφότεραι Κῶαι, πρῶται γένος — ὢ γλυκὺς ὄρθρος,
Πρὸς λύχνον ᾧ μύθους ᾔδομεν ἡμιθέων.

These two poor women were not afraid to boast of their family descent

which circulated in every city. The annual departure of the
Theôric ship from Athens to the sacred island of Dêlos, kept
alive, in the minds of Athenians generally, the legend of Thêseus
and his adventurous enterprise in Krete;[1] and in like manner
most of the other public rites and ceremonies were of a commemorative character, deduced from some mythical person or
incident familiarly known to natives, and forming to strangers a
portion of the curiosities of the place.[2] During the period of
Grecian subjection under the Romans, these curiosities, together
with their works of art and their legends, were especially clung
to as a set-off against present degradation. The Thêban citizen
who found himself restrained from the liberty enjoyed by all
other Greeks, of consulting Amphiaräus as a prophet, though
the sanctuary and chapel of the hero stood in his own city —

---

they probably belonged to some noble gens which traced its origin to a god
or a hero. About the songs of women, see also Agathias, i. 7. p. 29, ed.
Bonn.

In the family of the wealthy Athenian Dêmocratês was a legend, that his
primitive ancestor (son of Zeus by the daughter of the Archêgetês of the
dême Aixôneis, to which he belonged) had received Heraklês at his table:
this legend was so rife that the old women sung it, — ἅπερ αἱ γραῖαι ᾄδουσι
(Plato, Lysis, p. 205). Compare also a legend of the dême Ἀναγυροῦς,
mentioned in Suidas ad voc.

"Who is this virgin?" asks Orestês from Pyladês in the Iphigeneia in
Tauris of Euripidês (662), respecting his sister Iphigeneia, whom he does
not know as priestess of Artemis in a foreign land: —

> Τίς ἐστιν ἡ νεᾶνις; ὡς Ἑλληνικῶς
> Ἀνήρεθ' ἡμᾶς τούς τ' ἐν Ἰλίῳ πόνους
> Νόστον τ' Ἀχαιῶν, τόν τ' ἐν οἰωνοῖς σοφὸν
> Κάλχαντ', Ἀχιλλέως τ' οὔνομ', etc.
> .... ἐστὶν ἡ ξένη γένος
> Ἐκεῖθεν. Ἀργεία τις, etc.

[1] Plato, Phædo, c. 2.

[2] The Philopseudes of Lucian (t. iii. p. 31, Hemst. cap. 2, 3, 4) shows not
only the pride which the general public of Athens and Thêbes took in their
old mythes (Triptolemus, Boreas, and Oreithyia, the Sparti, etc.), but the
way in which they treated every man who called the stories in question as a
fool or as an atheist. He remarks, that if the guides who showed the antiquities had been restrained to tell nothing but what was true, they would
have died of hunger; for the visiting strangers would not care to hear plain
truth, even if they could have got it for nothing (μηδὲ ἀμισθὶ τῶν ξένων
ἀληθὲς ἀκούειν ἐθελησάντων).

bould not be satisfied without a knowledge of the story which explained the origin of such prohibition,[1] and which conducted him back to the originally hostile relations between Amphiaräus and Thêbes. Nor can we suppose among the citizens of Sikyôn anything less than a perfect and reverential conception of the legend of Thêbes, when we read the account given by Herodotus of the conduct of the despot Kleisthenês in regard to Adrastus and Melanippus.[2] The Trœzenian youths and maidens,[3] who universally, when on the eve of marriage, consecrated an offering of their hair at the Herôon of Hippolytus, maintained a lively recollection of the legend of that unhappy recusant whom Aphroditê had so cruelly punished. Abundant relics preserved in many Grecian cities and temples, served both as mementos and attestations of other legendary events; and the tombs of the heroes counted among the most powerful stimulants of mythical reminiscence. The sceptre of Pelops and Agamemnôn, still preserved in the days of Pausanias at Chæroneia in Bœôtia, was the work of the god Hêphæstos. While many other alleged productions of the same divine hand were preserved in different cities of Greece, this is the only one which Pausanias himself believed to be genuine: it had been carried by Elektra, daughter of Agamemnôn to Phôkis, and received divine honors from the citizens of Chæroneia.[4] The spears of Mêriônes and Odysseus were treasured up at Engyium in Sicily, that of Achilles at Phasêlis; the sword of Memnôn adorned the temple of Asklêpius at Nicomêdia; and Pausanias, with unsuspecting confidence, adduces the two latter as proofs that the arms of the heroes were made of brass.[5] The hide of the Kalydônian boar was guarded and shown by the Tegeates as a precious possession; the shield of Euphorbus was in like manner suspended in the temple of Branchidæ near Milêtus, as well as in the temple of Hêrê in Argos. Visible

---

[1] Herodot. viii. 134.   [2] Herodot. v. 67.

[3] Euripid. Hippolyt. 1424; Pausan. ii. 32, 1; Lucian, De Deâ Syriâ, c. 60. vol. iv. p. 287, Tauch.

It is curious to see in the account of Pausanias how all the petty peculiarities of the objects around became connected with explanatory details growing out of this affecting legend. Compare Pausan. i. 22, 2.

[4] Pausan. ix. 40, 6.

[5] Plutarch, Marcell. c. 20; Pausan. iii. 3, 6.

relics of Epeius and Philoktêtês were not wanting, while Strabo
raises his voice with indignation against the numerous Palladia
which were shown in different cities, each pretending to be the
genuine image from Troy.[1] It would be impossible to specify
the number of chapels, sanctuaries, solemnities, foundations of
one sort or another, said to have been first commenced by heroic
or mythical personages, — by Hêraklês, Jasôn, Mêdea, Alkmæôn,
Diomêdês, Odysseus, Danaus, and his daughters,[2] etc. Perhaps
in some of these cases particular critics might raise objections, but
the great bulk of the people entertained a firm and undoubted
belief in the current legend.

If we analyze the intellectual acquisitions of a common Grecian townsman, from the rude communities of Arcadia or Phôkis
even up to the enlightened Athens, we shall find that, over and
above the rules of art or capacities requisite for his daily wants,
it consisted chiefly of the various mythes connected with his gens,
his city, his religious festivals, and the mysteries in which he
might have chosen to initiate himself, as well as with the works of
art and the more striking natural objects which he might see
around him, — the whole set off and decorated by some knowledge of the epic and dramatic poets. Such was the intellectual
and imaginative reach of an ordinary Greek, considered apart
from the instructed few: it was an aggregate of religion, of social and patriotic retrospect, and of romantic fancy, blended into
one indivisible faith. And thus the subjective value of the
mythes, looking at them purely as elements of Grecian thought
and feeling, will appear indisputably great, however little there
may be of objective reality, either historical or philosophical,
discoverable under them.

Nor must we omit the incalculable importance of the mythes
as stimulants to the imagination of the Grecian artist in sculp-
ture, in painting, in carving, and in architecture. From the
divine and heroic legends and personages were borrowed those

---

[1] Pausan. viii. 46, 1; Diogen. Laër. viii. 5; Strabo, vi. p. 263; Appian,
Bell. Mithridat. c. 77; Æschyl. Eumen. 380.

Wachsmuth has collected the numerous citations out of Pausanias on this
subject (Hellenische Alterthumskunde, part ii. sect. 115. p. 111).

[2] Herodot. ii. 182; Plutarch, Pyrrh. c. 32; Schol. Apoll. Rhod. iv. 1217;
Diodôr. iv. 56.

paintings, statues, and reliefs, which rendered the temples, por-
ticos, and public buildings, at Athens and elsewhere, objects of
surpassing admiration ; and such visible reproduction contributed
again to fix the types of the gods and heroes familiarly and in-
delibly on the public mind.[1] The figures delineated on cups and
vases, as well as on the walls of private houses, were chiefly
drawn from the same source — the mythes being the great store-
house of artistic scenes and composition.

To enlarge on the characteristic excellence of Grecian art
would here be out of place : I regard it only in so far as, having
originally drawn its materials from the mythes, it reacted upon
the mythical faith and imagination — the reaction imparting
strength to the former as well as distinctness to the latter. To
one who saw constantly before him representations of the battles
of the Centaurs or the Amazons,[2] of the exploits performed by
Perseus and Bellerophôn, of the incidents composing the Trojan
war or the Kalydônian boar-hunt — the process of belief, even
in the more fantastic of these conceptions, became easy in proportion as the conception was familiarized. And if any person
had been slow to believe in the efficacy of the prayers of Æakus, whereby that devout hero once obtained special relief from
Zeus, at a moment when Greece was perishing with long-continued sterility, his doubts would probably vanish when, on visiting the Æakeium at Ægina, there were exhibited to him the
statues of the very envoys who had come on the behalf of the
distressed Greeks to solicit that Æakus would pray for them.[3] A
Grecian temple[4] was not simply a place of worship, but the
actual dwelling-place of a god, who was believed to be introduced
by the solemn dedicatory ceremony, and whom the imagination
of the people identified in the most intimate manner with his

---

[1] Ἡμιθέων ἀρεταῖς, the subjects of the works of Polygnotus at Athens
(Melanthius ap. Plutarch. Cimôn. c. 4) : compare Theocrit. xv. 138.

[2] The Centauromachia and the Amazonomachia are constantly associated
together in the ancient Grecian reliefs (see the Expedition Scientifique de
Morée, t. ii. p. 16, in the explanation of the temple of Apollo Epikureius at
Phigaleia).

[3] Pausan. ii. 29, 6.

[4] Ernst Curtius, Die Akropolis von Athen, Berlin, 1844, p. 18. Arnobius
adv. Gentes, vi. p. 203, ed. Elmenhorst.

statue. The presence or removal of the statue was conceived as identical with that of the being represented, — and while the statue was solemnly washed, dressed, and tended with all the respectful solicitude which would have been bestowed upon a real person,[1] miraculous tales were often rife respecting the manifestation of real internal feeling in the wood and the marble. At perilous or critical moments, the statue was affirmed to have sweated, to have wept, to have closed its eyes, or brandished the spear in its hands, in token of sympathy or indignation.[2] Such legends, springing up usually in times of suffering and danger, and finding few men bold enough openly to contradict them, ran in complete harmony with the general mythical faith, and tended

---

[1] See the case of the Æginetans lending the Æakids for a time to the Thebans (Herodot. v. 80), who soon, however, returned them: likewise sending the Æakids to the battle of Salamis (viii. 64-80). The Spartans, when they decreed that only one of their two kings should be out on military service, decreed at the same time that only one of the Tyndarids should go out with them (v. 75): they once lent the Tyndarids as aids to the envoys of Epizephyrian Locri, who prepared for them a couch on board their ship (Diodôr. Excerpt. xvi. p. 15, Dindorf). The Thebans grant their hero Melanippus to Kleisthenês of Sikyôn (v. 68). What was sent, must probably have been a consecrated copy of the genuine statue.

Respecting the solemnities practised towards the statues, see Plutarch, Alkibiad. 34; Kallimach. Hymn. ad Lavacr. Palladis, init. with the note of Spanheim; K. O. Müller, Archæologie der Kunst, § 69; compare Plutarch, Quæstion. Romaic. § 61. p. 279; and Tacit. Mor. Germ. c. 40; Diodor. xvii. 49.

The manner in which the real presence of a hero was identified with his statue (τὸν δίκαιον δεῖ θεὸν οἴκοι μένειν σώζοντα τοὺς ἱδρυμένους. — Menander, Fragm. Ἡνίοχος, p. 71, Meineke), consecrated ground, and oracle, is nowhere more powerfully attested than in the Heroïca of Philostratus (capp. 2-20. pp. 674-692; also De Vit. Apollôn. Tyan. iv. 11), respecting Prôtesilaus at Elæus, Ajax at the Aianteium, and Hectôr at Ilium: Prôtesilaus appeared exactly in the equipment of his statue, — χλαμύδα ἐνῆπται, ξένε, τὸν Θετταλικὸν τρόπον, ὥσπερ καὶ τὸ ἄγαλμα τοῦτο (p. 674). The presence and sympathy of the hero Lykus is essential to the satisfaction of the Athenian dikasts (Aristophan. Vesp. 389-820): the fragment of Lucilius, quoted by Lactantius, De Falsâ Religione (i. 22), is curious. — Τοῖς ἥρωσι τοῖς κατὰ τὴν πόλιν καὶ τὴν χώραν ἱδρυμένοις (Lycurgus cont. Leocrat. c. 1).

[2] Plutarch, Timoleon, c. 12; Strabo, vi. p. 264. Theophrastus treats the perspiration as a natural phænomenon in the statues made of cedar-wood (Histor. Plant. v. 10). Plutarch discusses the credibility of this sort of miracles in his Life of Coriolanus, c. 37-38.

to strengthen it in all its various ramifications. The renewed activity of the god or hero both brought to mind and accredited the preëxisting mythes connected with his name. When Boreas, during the invasion of Greece by Xerxês, and in compliance with the fervent prayers of the Athenians, had sent forth a providential storm, to the irreparable damage of the Persian armada,[1] the sceptical minority (alluded to by Plato), who doubted the mythe of Boreas and Oreithyia, and his close connection thus acquired with Erechtheus, and the Erechtheids generally, must for the time have been reduced to absolute silence.

CHAPTER XVII.

THE GRECIAN MYTHICAL VEIN COMPARED WITH THAT OF MODERN EUROPE.

I HAVE already remarked that the existence of that popular narrative talk, which the Germans express by the significant word *Sage* or *Volks-Sage*, in a greater or less degree of perfection or development, is a phænomenon common to almost all stages of society and to almost all quarters of the globe. It is the natural effusion of the unlettered, imaginative, and believing man, and its maximum of influence belongs to an early state of the human mind; for the multiplication of recorded facts, the diffusion of positive science, and the formation of a critical standard of belief, tend to discredit its dignity and to repress its easy and

---

[1] Herodot. vii. 189. Compare the gratitude of the Megalopolitans to Boreas for having preserved them from the attack of the Lacedæmonian king Agis (Pausan. viii. 27, 4. — viii. 36, 4). When the Ten Thousand Greeks were on their retreat through the cold mountains of Armenia, Boreas blew in their faces, "parching and freezing intolerably." One of the prophets recommended that a sacrifice should be offered to him, which was done, "and the painful effect of the wind appeared to every one forthwith to cease in a marked manner;" (καὶ πᾶσι δὴ περιφανῶς ἔδοξε λῆξαι τὸ χαλεπὸν τοῦ πνεύματος. — Xenoph. Anab. iv. 5, 3.)

abundant flow.   It supplies to the poet both materials to recom-
bine and adorn, and a basis as well as a stimulus for further inventions of his own ; and this at a time when the poet is religious
teacher, historian, and philosopher, all in one, — not, as he becomes at a more advanced period, the mere purveyor of avowed,
though interesting, fiction.

Such popular stories, and such historical songs (meaning by
historical, simply that which is accepted as history) are found in
most quarters of the globe, and especially among the Teutonic
and Celtic populations of early Europe.   The old Gothic songs
were cast into a continuous history by the historian Ablavius ;[1]
and the poems of the Germans respecting Tuisto the earth-born
god, his son Mannus, and his descendants the eponyms of the various German tribes,[2] as they are briefly described by Tacitus,
remind us of Hesiod, or Eumêlus, or the Homeric Hymns.
Jacob Grimm, in his learned and valuable Deutsche Mythologie,
has exhibited copious evidence of the great fundamental analogy,
along with many special differences, between the German, Scandinavian, and Grecian mythical world ; and the Dissertation of
Mr. Price (prefixed to his edition of Warton's History of English Poetry) sustains and illustrates Grimm's view.   The same
personifying imagination — the same ever-present conception of
the will, sympathies, and antipathies of the gods as the producing
causes of phænomena, and as distinguished from a course of nature with its invariable sequence — the same relations between
gods, heroes, and men, with the like difficulty of discriminating
the one from the other in many individual names — a similar
wholesale transfer of human attributes to the gods, with the absence of human limits and liabilities — a like belief in Nymphs,
Giants, and other beings, neither gods nor men — the same coalescence of the religious with the patriotic feeling and faith
— these are positive features common to the early Greeks with
the early Germans : and the negative conditions of the two

---

[1] Jornandes, De Reb. Geticis, capp. 4–6.

[2] Tacit. Mor. German. c. 2.   " Celebrant carminibus antiquis, quod unum
apud eos memoriæ et annalium genus est, Tuistonem Deum terrâ editum, et
filium Mannum, originem gentis conditoresque.   Quidam licentiâ vetustatis,
plures Deo ortos, pluresque gentis appellationes, Marsos, Gambrivios, Sue-
vos, Vandaliosque affirmant : eaque vera et antiqua nomina."

are not less analogous — the absence of prose writing, positive records, and scientific culture. The preliminary basis and encouragements for the mythopœic faculty were thus extremely similar.

But though the prolific forces were the same in kind, the results were very different in degree, and the developing circumstances were more different still.

First, the abundance, the beauty, and the long continuance of early Grecian poetry, in the purely poetical age, is a phænomenon which has no parallel elsewhere.

Secondly, the transition of the Greek mind from its poetical to its comparatively positive state was self-operated, accomplished by its own inherent and expansive force — aided indeed, but by no means either impressed or provoked, from without. From the poetry of Homer, to the history of Thucydidês and the philosophy of Plato and Aristotle, was a prodigious step, but it was the native growth of the Hellenic youth into an Hellenic man; and what is of still greater moment, it was brought about without breaking the thread either of religious or patriotic tradition — without any coercive innovation or violent change in the mental feelings. The legendary world, though the ethical judgments and rational criticisms of superior men had outgrown it, still retained its hold upon their feelings as an object of affectionate and reverential retrospect.

Far different from this was the development of the early Germans. We know little about their early poetry, but we shall run no risk of error in affirming that they had nothing to compare with either Iliad or Odyssey. Whether, if left to themselves, they would have possessed sufficient progressive power to make a step similar to that of the Greeks, is a question which we cannot answer. Their condition, mental as well as political, was violently changed by a foreign action from without. The influence of the Roman empire introduced artificially among them new institutions, new opinions, habits, and luxuries, and, above all, a new religion; the Romanized Germans becoming themselves successively the instruments of this revolution with regard to such of their brethren as still remained heathen. It was a revolution often brought about by penal and coercive means: the old gods Thor and Woden were formally deposed and renounced, their images were crumbled into dust, and the sacred oaks of worship and prophecy hewn down. But even where conversion was the fruit of preaching and persuasion, it did not the less break up all the associations of a German with respect to that mythical world which he called his past, and of which the ancient gods constituted both the charm and the sanctity: he had now only the alternative of treating them either as men or as dæmons.[1] That mixed religious and patriotic retrospect, formed by the coalescence of piety with ancestral feeling, which constituted the appropriate sentiment both of Greeks and of Germans towards their unrecorded antiquity, was among the latter banished by Christianity: and while the root of the old mythes was thus cankered, the commemorative ceremonies and customs with which they were connected, either lost their consecrated character or disappeared altogether. Moreover, new influences of great importance were at the same time brought to bear. The Latin language, together with some tinge of Latin literature — the habit of writing and of recording present events — the idea of a systematic law and pacific adjudication of disputes, — all these formed a part of the general working of Roman civilization, even after the decline of the Roman empire, upon the Teutonic and Celtic

---

[1] On the hostile influence exercised by the change of religion on the old Scandinavian poetry, see an interesting article of Jacob Grimm in the Göttingen Gelehrte Anzeigen, Feb. 1830, pp. 268–273 ; a review of Olaf Tryggvson's Saga. The article *Helden*, in his Deutsche Mythologie, is also full of instruction on the same subject: see also the Einleitung to the book, p. 11, 2nd edition.

A similar observation has been made with respect to the old mythes of the pagan Russians by Eichhoff: " L'établissement du Christianisme, ce gage du bonheur des nations, fut vivement apprécié par les Russes, qui dans leur juste reconnaissance, le personnifièrent dans un héros. Vladimir le Grand, ami des arts, protecteur de la religion qu'il protégea, et dont les fruits firent oublier les fautes, devint l'Arthus et le Charlemagne de la Russie, et ses hauts faits furent un mythe national qui domina tous ceux du paganisme. Autour de lui se groupèrent ces guerriers aux formes athlétiques, au cœur généreux, dont la poésie aime à entourer le berceau mystérieux des peuples : et les exploits du vaillant Dobrinia, de Rogdai, d'Ilia, de Curilo, animèrent les ballades nationales, et vivent encore dans de naïfs récits." (Eichhoff, Histoire de la Langue et Littérature des Slaves, Paris, 1839, part iii. ch. 2. p. 190.)

tribes. A class of specially-educated men was formed, upon a
Latin basis and upon Christian principles, consisting too almost
entirely of priests, who were opposed, as well by motives of rivalry as by religious feeling, to the ancient bards and storytellers of
the community : the " lettered men"¹ were constituted apart from
" the men of story," and Latin literature contributed along with
religion to sink the mythes of untaught heathenism. Charlemagne, indeed, at the same time that he employed aggressive and
violent proceedings to introduce Christianity among the Saxons,
also took special care to commit to writing and preserve the old
heathen songs. But there can be little doubt that this step was
the suggestion of a large and enlightened understanding peculiar
to himself. The disposition general among lettered Christians
of that age is more accurately represented by his son Louis le
Debonnaire, who, having learned these songs as a boy, came to
abhor them when he arrived at mature years, and could never
be induced either to repeat or tolerate them.²

According to the old heathen faith, the pedigree of the Saxon,
Anglian, Danish, Norwegian, and Swedish kings, — probably also
those of the German and Scandinavian kings generally, — was
traced to Odin, or to some of his immediate companions or heroic
sons.³ I have already observed that the value of these genealo-

---

¹ This distinction is curiously brought to view by Saxo Grammaticus,
where he says of an Englishman named Lucas, that he was " literis quidem
tenuiter instructus, sed historiarum scientiâ apprime eruditus" (p. 330, apud
Dahlmann's Historische Forschungen, vol. i. p. 176).

² " Barbara et antiquissima carmina (says Eginhart, in his Life of Charlemagne), quibus veterum regum actus et bella canebantur, conscripsit."
Theganus says of Louis le Debonnaire, " Poetica carmina gentilia, quæ
in juventute didicerat, respuit, nec legere, nec audire, nec docere, voluit
(De Gestis Ludovici Imperatoris ap. Pithœum, p. 304, c. xix.)

³ See Grimm's Deutsche Mythologie, art. *Helden*, p. 356, 2nd edit. Hen.
gist and Horsa were fourth in descent from Odin (Venerable Bede, Hist. i.
15). Thiodolff, the Scald of Harold Haarfager king of Norway, traced the
pedigree of his sovereign through thirty generations to Yngarfrey, the son
of Niord, companion of Odin at Upsal; the kings of Upsal were called Yng-
linger, and the song of Thiodolff, Ynglingatal (Dahlmann, Histor. Forschung,
i. p. 379). Eyvind, another Scald, a century afterwards, deduced the pedigree of Jarl Hacon from Saming, son of Yngwifrey (p. 381). Are Frode,
the Icelandic historian, carried up his own genealogy through thirty-six
generations to Yngwe; a genealogy which Torfœus accepts as trustworthy,

gies consisted not so much in their length, as in the reverence
attached to the name serving as primitive source. After the
worship attached to Odin had been extinguished, the genealogical line was lengthened up to Japhet or Noah, — and Odin, no
longer accounted worthy to stand at the top, was degraded into
one of the simple human members of it.[1] And we find this
alteration of the original mythical genealogies to have taken
place even among the Scandinavians, although the introduction
of Christianity was in those parts both longer deferred, so as to

---

opposing it to the line of kings given by Saxo Grammaticus (p. 352). Tor-
fæus makes Harold Haarfager a descendant from Odin through twenty-seven
generations; Alfred of England through twenty-three generations; Offa of
Mercia through fifteen (p. 362). See also the translation by Lange of P. A.
Müller's Saga Bibliothek, Introd. p. xxviii. and the genealogical tables prefixed to Snorro Sturleson's Edda.

Mr. Sharon Turner conceives the human existence of Odin to be distinctly proved, seemingly upon the same evidence as Euêmerus believed in the
human existence of Zeus (History of the Anglo-Saxons, Appendix to b. ii.
ch. 3. p. 219, 5th edit).

[1] Dahlmann, Histor. Forschung. t. i. p. 390. There is a valuable article
on this subject in the Zeitschrift für Geschichts Wissenschaft (Berlin, vol. i.
pp. 237–282) by Stuhr, "Uber einige Hauptfragen des Nördischen Alterthums,"
wherein the writer illustrates both the strong motive and the effective tendency, on the part of the Christian clergy who had to deal with these newly-
converted Teutonic pagans, to Euêmerize the old gods, and to represent a
genealogy, which they were unable to efface from men's minds, as if it con
sisted only of mere men.

Mr. John Kemble (Uber die Stammtafel der Westsachsen, ap. Stuhr, p.
254) remarks, that "nobilitas," among that people, consisted in descent from
Odin and the other gods.

Colonel Sleeman also deals in the same manner with the religious legends
of the Hindoos, — so natural is the proceeding of Euêmerus, towards any
religion in which a critic does not believe: —

" They (the Hindoos) of course think that the incarnation of their three
great divinities were beings infinitely superior to prophets, being in all their
attributes and prerogatives equal to the divinities themselves. *But we are
disposed to think that these incarnations were nothing more than great men whom
their flatterers and poets have exalted into gods, — this was the way in which men
made their gods in ancient Greece and Egypt.* — All that the poets have sung
of the actions of these men is now received as revelation from heaven:
though nothing can be more monstrous than the actions ascribed to the best
incarnation, Krishna, of the best of the gods, Vishnoo." (Sleeman, Rambles
and Recollections of an Indian Official, vol. i. ch. viii. 61.)

leave time for a more ample development of the heathen poetical vein — and seems to have created a less decided feeling of anti pathy (especially in Iceland) towards the extinct faith.[1] The poems and tales composing the Edda, though first committed to writing after the period of Christianity, do not present the ancient gods in a point of view intentionally odious or degrading.

The transposition above alluded to, of the genealogical root from Odin to Noah, is the more worthy of notice, as it illustrates the genuine character of these genealogies, and shows that they sprung, not from any erroneous historical data, but from the turn of the religious feeling; also that their true value is derived from their being taken entire, as connecting the existing race of men with a divine original. If we could imagine that Grecian paganism had been superseded by Christianity in the year 500 B.C., the great and venerated gentile genealogies of Greece would have undergone the like modification; the Herakleids, Pelopids, Æakids, Asklepiads, &c., would have been merged in some larger aggregate branching out from the archæology of the Old Testament. The old heroic legends connected with these ancestral names would either have been forgotten, or so transformed as to suit the new vein of thought; for the altered worship, ceremonies, and customs would have been altogether at variance with them, and the mythical feeling would have ceased to dwell upon those to whom prayers were no longer offered. If the oak of Dôdôna had been cut down, or the Theôric ship had ceased to be sent from Athens to Dêlos, the mythes of Theseus and of the two black doves would have lost their pertinence, and died away. As it was, the change from Homer to Thucydidês and Aristotle took place internally, gradually, and imperceptibly. Philosophy and history were superinduced in the minds of the superior few, but the feelings of the general public continued unshaken — the sacred objects remained the same both to the eye and to the heart

---

[1] See P. E. Müller, Uber den Ursprung und Verfall der Isländischen Historiographie, p. 63.

In the Leitfaden zur Nördischen Alterthumskunde, pp. 4-5 (Copenhagen, 1837), is an instructive summary of the different schemes of interpretation applied to the northern mythes: 1, the historical; 2, the geographical; 3, the astronomical; 4, the physical· 5, the allegorical.

— and the worship of the ancient gods was even adorned by new architects and sculptors who greatly strengthened its imposing effect.

While then in Greece the mythopœic stream continued in the same course, only with abated current and influence, in modern Europe its ancient bed was blocked up, and it was turned into new and divided channels. The old religion — though as an ascendent faith, unanimously and publicly manifested, it became extinct — still continued in detached scraps and fragments, and under various alterations of name and form. The heathen gods and goddesses, deprived as they were of divinity, did not pass out of the recollection and fears of their former worshippers, but were sometimes represented (on principles like those of Euêmerus) as having been eminent and glorious men — sometimes degraded into dæmons, magicians, elfs, fairies, and other supernatural agents, of an inferior grade and generally mischievous cast. Christian writers, such as Saxo Grammaticus and Snorro Sturleson, committed to writing the ancient oral songs of the Scandivian Scalds, and digested the events contained in them into continuous narrative — performing in this respect a task similar to that of the Grecian logographers Pherekydês and Hellanikus, in reference to Hesiod and the Cyclic poets. But while Pherekydês and Hellanikus compiled under the influence of feelings substantially the same as those of the poets on whom they bestowed their care, the Christian logographers felt it their duty to point out the Odin and Thor of the old Scalds as evil dæmons, or cunning enchanters, who had fascinated the minds of men into a false belief in their divinity.[1]   In some cases, the heathen recitals and ideas

---

[1] Interea tamen homines Christiani in numina non credant ethnica, nec aliter fidem narrationibus hisce adstruere vel adhibere debent, quam in libri hujus procemio monitum est de causis et occasionibus cur et quomodo genus humanum a verâ fide aberraverit." (Extract from the Prose Edda, p. 75, in the Lexicon Mythologicum ad calcem Eddæ Sæmund. vol. iii. p. 357, Copenhag. edit.)

A similar warning is to be found in another passage cited by P. E. Müller Uber den Ursprung und Verfall der Isländischen Historiographie, p. 138 Copenhagen, 1813 ; compare the Prologue to the Prose Edda, p. 6, and Mallet, Introduction à l'Histoire de Dannemarc, ch. vii. pp. 114-132.

Saxo Grammaticus represents Odin sometimes as a magician, sometimes as an evil dæmon, sometimes as a high priest or pontiff of heathenism, who

were modified so as to suit Christian feeling. But when preserved without such a change, they exhibited themselves palpably, and were designated by their compilers, as at variance with the religious belief of the people, and as associated either with imposture or with evil spirits.

A new vein of sentiment had arisen in Europe, unsuitable indeed to the old mythes, yet leaving still in force the demand for mythical narrative generally. And this demand was satisfied, speaking generally, by two classes of narratives,—the legends of the Catholic Saints and the Romances of Chivalry, corresponding to two types of character, both perfectly accommodated to the feelings of the time,—the saintly ideal and the chivalrous ideal.

Both these two classes of narrative correspond, in character as well as in general purpose, to the Grecian mythes—being stories accepted as realities, from their full conformity with the predispositions and deep-seated faith of an uncritical audience, and prepared beforehand by their authors, not with any reference to

---

imposed so powerfully upon the people around him as to receive divine honors. Thor also is treated as having been an evil dæmon. (See Lexicon Mythologic. ut supra, pp. 567, 915.)

Respecting the function of Snorro as logographer, see Præfat. ad Eddam, ut supra, p. xi. He is much more faithful, and less unfriendly to the old religion, than the other logographers of the ancient Scandinavian Sagas (Leit-faden der Nördischen Altorthümer, p. 14, by the Antiquarian Society of Copenhagen, 1837.)

By a singular transformation, dependent upon the same tone of mind, the authors of the French Chansons de Geste, in the twelfth century, turned Apollo into an evil dæmon, patron of the Mussulmans (see the Roman of Garin le Loherain, par M. Paulin Paris, 1833, p. 31): " Car mieux vaut Diex que ne fait Apollis." M. Paris observes, " Cet ancien Dieu des beaux arts est l'un des démons le plus souvent désignés dans nos poëmes, comme patron des Musulmans."

The prophet Mahomet, too, anathematized the old Persian epic anterior to his religion. " C'est à l'occasion de Naser Ibn al-Hareth, qui avait apporté de Perse l'Histoire de Rustem et d'Isfendiar, et la faisait réciter par des chanteuses dans les assemblées des Koreischites, que Mahomet prononça le vers suivant (of the Koran): Il y a des hommes qui achètent des contes frivoles, pour détourner par-là les hommes de la voie de Dieu, d'une manière insensée, et pour la livrer à la risée : mais leur punition les couvrira de honte.' (Mohl, Préface au Livre des Rois de Ferdousi, p. xiii.)

the conditions of historical proof, but for the purpose of calling forth sympathy, emotion, or reverence. The type of the saintly character belongs to Christianity, being the history of Jesus Christ as described in the gospels, and that of the prophets in the Old Testament; whilst the lives of holy men, who acquired a religious reputation from the fourth to the fourteenth century of the Christian æra, were invested with attributes, and illustrated with ample details, tending to assimilate them to this revered model. The numerous miracles, the cure of diseases, the expulsion of dæmons, the temptations and sufferings, the teachings and commands, with which the biography of Catholic saints abounds, grew chiefly out of this pious feeling, common to the writer and to his readers. Many of the other incidents, recounted in the same performances, take their rise from misinterpreted allegories, from ceremonies and customs of which it was pleasing to find a consecrated origin, or from the disposition to convert the etymology of a name into matter of history : many have also been suggested by local peculiarities, and by the desire of stimulating or justifying the devotional emotions of pilgrims who visited some consecrated chapel or image. The dove was connected, in the faith of the age, with the Holy Ghost, the serpent with Satan; lions, wolves, stags, unicorns, etc. were the subjects of other emblematic associations; and such modes of belief found expression for themselves in many narratives which brought the saints into conflict or conjoint action with these various animals. Legends of this kind, so indefinitely multiplied and so preëminently popular and affecting, in the Middle Ages, are not exaggerations of particular matters of fact, but emanations in detail of some current faith or feeling, which they served to satisfy, and by which they were in turn amply sustained and accredited.[1]

---

[1] The legends of the Saints have been touched upon by M. Guizot (Cours d'Histoire Moderne, leçon xvii.) and by M. Ampère (Histoire Littéraire de la France, t. ii. cap. 14, 15, 16); but a far more copious and elaborate account of them, coupled with much just criticism, is to be found in the valuable Essai sur les Légendes Pieuses du Moyen Age, par L. F. Alfred Maury, Paris, 1843.

M. Guizot scarcely adverts at all to the more or less of matter of fact contained in these biographies : he regards them altogether as they grew out of and answered to the predominant emotions and mental exigences of the age :
* Au milieu d'un déluge de fables absurdes, la morale éclate avec un grand

Every reader of Pausanias will recognize the great general analogy between the stories recounted to him at the temples which he visited, and these legends of the Middle Ages. Though the type of character which the latter illustrate is indeed materially different, yet the source as well as the circulation, the generating as well as the sustaining forces, were in both cases the same. Such legends were the natural growth of a religious faith,

---

empire " (p. 159, ed. 1829). " Les légendes ont été pour les Chrétiens de ce temps (qu'on me permette cette comparaison purement littéraire) ce que sont pour les Orientaux ces longs récits, ces histoires si brillantes et si variées, dont les Mille et une Nuits nous donnent un échantillon. C'était là que l'imagination populaire errait librement dans un monde inconnu, merveilleux, plein de mouvement et de poésie" (p. 175, *ibid*).

M. Guizot takes his comparison with the tales of the Arabian Nights, as heard by an Oriental with uninquiring and unsuspicious credence. Viewed with reference to an instructed European, who reads these narratives as pleasing but recognized fiction, the comparison would not be just; for no one in that age dreamed of questioning the truth of the biographies. All the remarks of M. Guizot assume this implicit faith in them as literal histories : perhaps, in estimating the feelings to which they owed their extraordinary popularity, he allows too little predominance to the religious feeling, and too much influence to other mental exigences which then went along with it; more especially as he remarks, in the preceding lecture (p. 116), "Le caractère général de l'epoque est la concentration du développement intellectuel dans la sphère religieuse."

How this absorbing religious sentiment operated in generating and accrediting new matter of narrative, is shown with great fulness of detail in the work of M. Maury : "Tous les écrits du moyen âge nous apportent la preuve de cette préoccupation exclusive des esprits vers l'Histoire Sainte et les prodiges qui avaient signalé l'avènement du Christianisme. Tous nous montrent la pensée de Dieu et du Ciel, dominant les moindres œuvres de cette époque de naïve et de crédule simplicité. D'ailleurs, n'étaite-ce pas le moine, le clerc, qui constituaient alors les seuls écrivains ? Qu'y a-t-il d'étonnant que le sujet habituel de leurs méditations, de leurs études, se refiétât sans cesse dans leurs ouvrages ? Partout reparaissait à l'imagination Jésus et ses Saints : cette image, l'esprit l'accueillait avec soumission et obéissance : il n'osait pas encore envisager ces célestes pensées avec l'œil de la critique, armé de défiance et de doute ; au contraire, l'intelligence les acceptait toutes indistinctement et s'en nourrissait avec avidité. Ainsi s'accréditaient tous les jours de nouvelles fables. *Une foi vive veut sans cesse de nouveaux faits qu'elle puisse croire*, comme la charité veut de nouveaux bienfaits pours s'exercer" (p. 43). The remarks on the History of St. Christopher, whose personality was allegorized by Luther and Melancthon, are curious (p. 57).

earnest, unexamining, and interwoven with the feelings at a time
when the reason does not need to be cheated. The lives of the
Saints bring us even back to the simple and ever-operative theo
logy of the Homeric age; so constantly is the hand of God ex
hibited even in the minutest details, for the succor of a favored
individual, — so completely is the scientific point of view, respecting the phænomena of nature, absorbed into the religious.[1]
During the intellectual vigor of Greece and Rome, a sense of the
invariable course of nature and of the scientific explanation of
phænomena had been created among the superior minds, and
through them indirectly among the remaining community; thus
limiting to a certain extent the ground open to be occupied by a
religious legend. With the decline of the pagan literature and
philosophy, before the sixth century of the Christian æra, this
scientific conception gradually passed out of sight, and left the
mind free to a religious interpretation of nature not less simple
and *naïf* than that which had prevailed under the Homeric paganism.[2] The great religious movement of the Reformation, and

---

[1] " Dans les prodiges que l'on admettait avoir dû nécessairement s'opérer
au tombeau du saint nouvellement canonisé, l'expression, ' Cæci visum,
claudi gressum, muti loquelam, surdi auditum, paralytici debitum membro-
rum officium, recuperabant,' était devenue plûtot une formule d'usage que la
rélation littérale du fait." (Maury, Essai sur les Légendes Pieuses du
Moyen Age, p. 5.)

To the same purpose M. Ampère, ch. 14. p. 361: " Il y a un certain nombre de faits que l'agiographie reproduit constamment, quelque soit son héros :
ordinairement ce personnage a eu dans sa jeunesse une vision qui lui a
révélé son avenir: ou bien, une prophétie lui a annoncé ce qu'il serait un
jour. Plus tard, il opère un certain nombre de miracles, toujours les
mêmes; il exorcise des possédés, ressuscite des morts, il est averti de sa fin
par un songe. Puis sur son tombeau s'accomplissent d'autres merveilles
à-peu-près semblables."

[2] A few words from M. Ampère to illustrate this: " C'est donc au sixième
siècle que la légende se constitue: c'est alors qu'elle prend complètement le
caractère naïf qui lui appartient: qu'elle est elle-même, qu'elle se sépare de
toute influence étrangère. En même temps, l'ignorance devient de plus en
plus grossière, et par suite la crédulité s'accroit : les calamités du temps sont
plus lourdes, et l'on a un plus grand besoin de remède et de consolation.
.... Les récits miraculeux se substituent aux argumens de la théologie.
Les miracles sont devenus la meilleure démonstration du Christianisme :
c'est la seule que puissent comprendre les esprits grossiers des barbares " (c.
15. p. 373).

Again, c. 17. p. 401: " Un des caractères de la légende est de mêler con-

the gradual formation of critical and philosophical habits in the modern mind, have caused these legends of the Saints,— once

stamment le puéril au grand : il faut l'avouer, elle défigure parfois un peu ces hommes d'une trempe si forte, en mettant sur leur compte des anecdotes dont le caractère n'est pas toujours sérieux ; elle en a usé ainsi pour St. Columban, dont nous verrons tout à l'heure le rôle vis-à-vis de Brunehaut et des chefs Mérovingiens. La légende auroit pu se dispenser de nous apprendre, comment un jour, il se fît rapporter par un corbeau les gants qu'il avait perdus : comment, un autre jour, il empêcha la bière de couler d'un tonneau percé, et diverses merveilles, certainement indignes de sa mémoire."

The miracle by which St. Columban employed the raven to fetch back his lost gloves, is exactly in the character of the Homeric and Hesiodic age : the earnest faith, as well as the reverential sympathy, between the Homeric man and Zeus or Athênê, is indicated by the invocation of their aid for his own sufferings of detail, and in his own need and danger. The criticism of M. Ampère, on the other hand, is analogous to that of the later pagans, after the conception of a course of nature had become established in men's minds, so far as that exceptional interference by the gods was understood to be, comparatively speaking, rare, and only supposable upon what were called great emergencies.

In the old Hesiodic legend (see above, ch. ix. p. 245), Apollo is apprized by a raven of the infidelity of the nymph Korônis to him — τῷ μὲν ἄρ' ἄγγελος ἦλθε κόραξ, etc. (the raven appears elsewhere as companion of Apollo, Plutarch. de Isid. et Os. p. 379, Herod. iv. 15.) Pindar, in his version of the legend, eliminated the raven, without specifying how Apollo got his knowledge of the circumstance. The Scholiasts praise Pindar much for having rejected the puerile version of the story — Ἐπαινεῖ τὸν Πίνδαρον ὁ Ἀρτέμων ὅτι ...καμπρονσ.μενος τὴν περὶ τὸν κόρακα ἱστορίαν, αὐτὸν δι' ἑαυτοῦ ἐγνωκέναι φησὶ τὸν Ἀπόλλω .... χαίρειν οὖν ἐάσας τῷ τοιούτῳ μύθῳ τ ἐ λ ε ω ς ὄ ν τ ι λ η ρ ώ δ ε ι, etc. — compare also the criticisms of the Schol. ad Soph. Œdip. Kol. 1378, on the old epic Thebaïs ; and the remarks of Arrian (Exp. Al. iii. 4) on the divine interference by which Alexander and his army were enabled to find their way across the sand of the desert to the temple of Ammon.

In the eyes of M. Ampère, the recital of the biographer of St. Columban appears puerile (οὔπω ἴδον ὧδε θεοὺς ἀνάφανδα φιλεῦντας, Odyss. iii. 221) ; in the eyes of that biographer, the criticism of M. Ampère would have appeared impious. When it is once conceded that phænomena are distributable under two denominations, the natural and the miraculous, it must be left to the feelings of each individual to determine what is and what is not, a suitable occasion for a miracle. Diodôrus and Pausanias differed in opinion (as stated in a previous chapter) about the death of Actæôn by his own hounds, — the former maintaining that the case was one fit for the special intervention of the goddess Artemis: the latter, that it was not so. The

the charm and cherished creed of a numerous public,[1] to pass altogether out of credit, without even being regarded, among Protestants at least, as worthy of a formal scrutiny into the evidence, — a proof of the transitory value of public belief, however sincere and fervent, as a certificate of historical truth, if it be blended with religious predispositions.

question is one determinable only by the religious feelings and conscience of the two dissentients : no common standard of judgment can be imposed upon them ; for no reasonings derived from science or philosophy are available, inasmuch as in this case the very point in dispute is, whether the scientific point of view be admissible. Those who are disposed to adopt the supernatural belief, will find in every case the language open to them wherewith Dionysius of Halicarnassus (in recounting a miracle wrought by Vesta, in the early times of Roman history, for the purpose of rescuing an unjustly accused virgin) reproves the sceptics of his time : "It is well worth while (he observes) to recount the special manifestation (ἐπιφάνειαν) which the goddess showed to these unjustly accused virgins. For these circumstances, extraordinary as they are, have been held worthy of belief by the Romans, and historians have talked much about them. Those persons, indeed, who adopt the atheistical schemes of philosophy (if, indeed, we must call them *philosophy*), pulling in pieces as they do *all* the special manifestions (ἁπάσας διασύροντες τὰς ἐπιφανείας τῶν θεῶν) of the gods which have taken place among Greeks or barbarians, will of course turn *these* stories also into ridicule, ascribing them to the vain talk of men, as if none of the gods cared at all for mankind. But those who, having pushed their researches farther, believe the gods not to be indifferent to human affairs, but favorable to good men and hostile to bad — will not treat *these* special manifestations as *more* incredible than others." (Dionys. Halic. ii. 68–69.) Plutarch, after noticing the great number of miraculous statements in circulation, expresses his anxiety to draw a line between the true and the false, but cannot find where : "excess, both of credulity and of incredulity (he tells us) in such matters is dangerous ; caution, and nothing too much, is the best course." (Camillus, c. 6.) Polybius is for granting permission to historians to recount a sufficient number of miracles to keep up a feeling of piety in the multi tude, but not more : to measure out the proper quantity (he observes) is difficult, but not impossible (δυσπαράγραφός ἐστιν ἡ ποσότης, οὐ μὴν ὑπαράγραφός γε, xvi. 12).

[1] The great Bollandist collection of the Lives of the Saints, intended to comprise the whole year, did not extend beyond the nine months from January to October, which occupy fifty-three large volumes. The month of April fills three of those volumes, and exhibits the lives of 1472 saints. Had the collection run over the entire year, the total number of such biographies could hardly have been less than 25,000, and might have been even greater (see Guizot, Cours d'Histoire Moderne, leçon xvii. p. 157)

The same mythopœic vein, and the same susceptibility and facility of belief, which had created both supply and demand for the legends of the Saints, also provided the abundant stock of romantic narrative poetry, in amplification and illustration of the chivalrous ideal. What the legends of Troy, of Thêbes, of the Kalydônian boar, of Œdipus, Thêseus, etc. were to an early Greek, the tales of Arthur, of Charlemagne, of the Niebelungen, were to an Englishman, or Frenchman, or German, of the twelfth or thirteenth century. They were neither recognized fiction nor authenticated history: they were history, as it is felt and welcomed by minds unaccustomed to investigate evidence, and unconscious of the necessity of doing so. That the Chronicle of Turpin, a mere compilation of poetical legends respecting Charlemagne, was accepted as genuine history, and even pronounced to be such by papal authority, is well known; and the authors of the Romances announce themselves, not less than those of the old Grecian epic, as being about to recount real matter of fact.[1] It is certain that Charlemagne is a great historical name, and it

---

[1] See Warton's History of English Poetry, vol. i. dissert. i. p. xvii. Again, in sect. iii. p. 140: "Vincent de Beauvais, who lived under Louis IX. of France (about 1260), and who, on account of his extraordinary erudition, was appointed preceptor to that king's sons, very gravely classes Archbishop Turpin's Charlemagne among the real histories, and places it on a level with Suetonius and Cæsar. He was himself an historian, and has left a large history of the world, fraught with a variety of reading, and of high repute in the Middle Ages; but edifying and entertaining as this work might have been to his contemporaries, at present it serves only to record their prejudices and to characterize their credulity." About the full belief in Arthur and the Tales of the Round Table during the fourteenth century, and about the strange historical mistakes of the poet Gower in the fifteenth, see the same work, sect. 7. vol. ii. p. 33; sect. 19. vol. ii. p. 239.

"L'auteur de la Chronique de Turpin (says M. Sismondi, Littérature du Midi, vol. i. ch. 7. p. 289) n'avait point l'intention de briller aux yeux du public par une invention heureuse, ni d'amuser les oisifs par des contes merveilleux qu'ils reconnoitroient pour tels : il présentait aux Français tous ces faits étranges comme de l'histoire, et la lecture des légendes fabuleuses avait accoutumé à croire à de plus grandes merveilles encore; aussi plusieurs de ces fables furent elles reproduites dans la Chronique de St. Denis."

Again, ib. p. 290: " Souvent les anciens romanciers, lorsqu'ils entreprennent un récit de la cour de Charlemagne, prennent un ton plus élevé: ce ne sont point des fables qu'ils vont coûter, c'est de l'histoire nationale, — c'est la

is possible, though not certain, that the name of Arthur may be
historical also.   But the Charlemagne of history, and the Charlemagne of romance, have little except the name in common; nor
could we ever determine, except by independent evidence (which
in this case we happen to possess), whether Charlemagne was
a real or a fictitious person.[1]   That illustrious name, as well as
the more problematical Arthur, is taken up by the romancers, not
with a view to celebrate realities previously verified, but for the
purpose of setting forth or amplifying an ideal of their own, in
such manner as both to rouse the feelings and captivate the faith
of their hearers.

To inquire which of the personages of the Carlovingian epic
were real and which were fictitious, — to examine whether the
expedition ascribed to Charlemagne against Jerusalem had ever
taken place or not, — to separate truth from exaggeration in the
exploits of the Knights of the Round Table, — these were prob-

gloire de leurs ancêtres qu'ils veulent célébrer, et ils ont droit alors à deman-
der qu'on les écoute avec respect."

The Chronicle of Turpin was inserted, even so late as the year 1566, in
the collection printed by Scardius at Frankfort of early German historians
(Ginguené, Histoire Littéraire d'Italie, vol. iv. part ii. ch. 3. p. 157).

To the same point — that these romances were listened to as real stories
— see Sir Walter Scott's Preface to Sir Tristram, p. lxvii.   The authors of
the Legends of the Saints are not less explicit in their assertions that everything which they recount is true and well-attested (Ampère, c. 14. p. 358).

[1] The series of articles by M. Fauriel, published in the Revue des Deux
Mondes, vol. xiii. are full of instruction respecting the origin, tenor, and
influence of the Romances of Chivalry.   Though the name of Charlemagne
appears, the romancers are really unable to distinguish him from Charles
Martel or from Charles the Bald (pp. 537-539).   They ascribe to him an
expedition to the Holy Land, in which he conquered Jerusalem from the
Saracens, obtained possession of the relics of the passion of Christ, the
crown of thorns, etc.   These precious relics he carried to Rome, from
whence they were taken to Spain by a Saracen emir, named Balan, at the
head of an army.   The expedition of Charlemagne against the Saracens in
Spain was undertaken for the purpose of recovering the relics: " Ces
divers romans peuvent être regardés comme la suite, comme le développe
ment, de la fiction de la conquête de Jérusalem par Charlemagne."

Respecting the Romance of Rinaldo of Montauban (describing the strug
gles of a feudal lord against the emperor) M. Fauriel observes, " Il n'y a, je
crois, aucun fondement historique : c'est selon toute apparence, la pure ex
pression poétique du fait général, etc. (p. 542.)

tems which an audience of that day had neither disposition to undertake nor means to resolve. They accepted the narrative as they heard it, without suspicion or reserve; the incidents related, as well as the connecting links between them, were in full harmony with their feelings, and gratifying as well to their sympathies as to their curiosity: nor was anything farther wanting to induce them to believe it, though the historical basis might be ever so slight or even non-existent.[1]

---

[1] Among the "formules consacrées" (observes M. Fauriel) of the romancers of the Carlovingian epic, are asseverations of their own veracity, and of the accuracy of what they are about to relate—specification of witnesses whom they have consulted—appeals to pretended chronicles : "Que ces citations, ces indications, soient parfois sérieuses et sincères, cela peut être; mais c'est une exception et une exception rare. De telles allégations de la part des romanciers, sont en général un pur et simple mensonge, mais non toutefois un mensonge gratuit. C'est un mensonge qui a sa raison et sa convenance: il tient au désir et au besoin de satisfaire une opinion accoutumée à supposer et à chercher du vrai dans les fictions du genre de celles où l'on allègue ces prétendues autorités. La manière dont les auteurs de ces fictions les qualifient souvent eux-mêmes, est une conséquence naturelle de leur prétention d'y avoir suivi des documens vénérables. Ils les qualifient de chansons de *vieille histoire*, de *haute histoire*, de *bonne geste*, de *grande baronnie:* et ce n'est pas pour se vanter qu'ils parlent ainsi: la vanité d'auteur n'est rien chez eux, en comparaison du besoin qu'ils ont d'être crus, de passer pour de simples traducteurs, de simples répétiteurs de légendes ou d'histoire consacrée. Ces protestations de véracité, qui, plus ou moins expresses, sont de rigueur dans les romans Carlovingiens, y sont aussi fréquemment accompagnées de protestations accessoires contre les romanciers, qui, ayant déjà traité un sujet donné, sont accusés d'y avoir faussé la vérité." (Fauriel, Orig. d l'Epopée Chevaleresque, in the Revue des Deux Mondes, vol. xiii. p. 554.)

About the Cycle of the Round Table, see the same series of articles (Rev. D. M. t. xiv. pp. 170–184). The Chevaliers of the Saint Graal were a sort of *idéal* of the Knights Templars: "Une race de princes héroïques, originaires de l'Asie, fut prédestinée par le ciel même à la garde du Saint Graal. Perille fut le premier de cette race, qui s'étant converti au Christianisme, passa en Europe sous l'Empereur Vespasien," etc.; then follows a string of fabulous incidents : the epical agency is similar to that of Homer — Διὸς δ' ἐτελείετο βουλή.

M. Paulin Paris, in his Prefaces to the Romans des Douze Pairs de France, has controverted many of the positions of M. Fauriel, and with success, so far as regards the Provençal origin of the Chansons de Geste, asserted by the latter. In regard to the Romances of the Round Table, he

The romances of chivalry represented, to those who heard
them, real deeds of the foretime — "glories of the foregone men,"
to use the Hesiodic expression[1] — at the same time that they embodied and filled up the details of an heroic ideal, such as that
age could conceive and admire — a fervent piety, combined with
strength, bravery, and the love of adventurous aggression, directed
sometimes against infidels, sometimes against enchanters or monsters, sometimes in defence of the fair sex. Such characteristics
were naturally popular, in a century of feudal struggles and uni-

agrees substantially with M. Fauriel; but he tries to assign a greater historical value to the poems of the Carlovingian epic, — very unsuccessfully, in
my opinion. But his own analysis of the old poem of Garin de Loherain
bears out the very opinion which he is confuting: "Nous sommes au règne
de Charles Martel, et nous reconnaissons sous d'autres noms les détails
exacts de la fameuse défaite d'Attila dans les champs Catalauniques. Saint
Loup et Saint Nicaise, glorieux prélats du quatrième siècle, reviennent
figurer autour du père de Pépin le Bref: enfin pour compléter la confusion,
Charles Martel meurt sur le champ de bataille, à la place du roi des Visi-
goths, Théodoric...... *Toutes les parties de la narration sont vraies:* seule-
ment *toutes s'y trouvent déplacées.* En général, les peuples n'entendent rien à
la chronologie: les évènemens restent: les individus, les lieux et les époques,
ne laissent aucune trace: c'est pour ainsi dire, une décoration scénique que
l'on applique indifféremment à des récits souvent contraires." (Preface to
the Roman de Garin le Loherain, pp. xvi.–xx.: Paris, 1833.) Compare also
his Lettre à M. Monmerqué, prefixed to the Roman de Berthe aux Grans
Piés, Paris, 1836.

To say that *all* the parts of the narrative are true, is contrary to M. Paris's
own showing: *some* parts may be true, separately taken, but these fragments
of truth are melted down with a large mass of fiction, and cannot be dis-
criminated unless we possess some independent test. The poet who picks
out one incident from the fourth century, another from the fifth, and a few
more from the eighth, and then blends them all into a continuous tale along
with many additions of his own, shows that he takes the items of fact because
they suit the purposes of his narrative, not because they happen to be attested
by historical evidence. His hearers are not critical: they desire to have
their imaginations and feelings affected, and they are content to accept without question whatever accomplishes this end.

[1] Hesiod, Theogon. 100 — κλέα προτέρων ἀνθρώπων. Puttenham talks of
the remnant of bards existing in his time (1589): "Blind Harpers, or such
like Taverne Minstrels, whose matters are for the most part *stories of old
time,* as the Tale of Sir Topaze, the Reportes of Bevis of Southampton, Adam
Bell, Clymme of the Clough, and such other old Romances or *Historical
Rhymes.*" (Arte of English Poesie, book ii. cap. 9.)

versal insecurity, when the grand subjects of common respect and
interest were the Church and the Crusades, and when the latter
especially were embraced with an enthusiasm truly astonishing.
The long German poem of the Niebelungen Lied, as well as
the Volsunga Saga and a portion of the songs of the Edda, relate
to a common fund of mythical, superhuman personages, and of
fabulous adventure, identified with the earliest antiquity of the
Teutonic and Scandinavian race, and representing their primitive
sentiment towards ancestors of divine origin. Sigurd, Brynhilde,
Gudrun, and Atle, are mythical characters celebrated as well by
the Scandinavian Scalds as by the German epic poets, but with
many varieties and separate additions to distinguish the one from
the other. The German epic, later and more elaborated, includes
various persons not known to the songs in the Edda, in particular the prominent name of Dieterich of Bern — presenting, moreover, the principal characters and circumstances as Christian, while
in the Edda there is no trace of anything but heathenism. There
is, indeed, in this the old and heathen version, a remarkable analogy with many points of Grecian mythical narrative. As in the
case of the short life of Achilles, and of the miserable Labdakids
of Thêbes — so in the family of the Volsungs, though sprung from
and protected by the gods — a curse of destiny hangs upon them
and brings on their ruin, in spite of preëminent personal qualities.[1] The more thoroughly this old Teutonic story has been
traced and compared, in its various transformations and accompaniments, the less can any well-established connection be made
out for it with authentic historical names or events. We must
acquiesce in its personages as distinct in original conception from
common humanity, and as belonging to the subjective mythical
world of the race by whom they were sung.

Such were the compositions which not only interested the

---

[1] Respecting the Volsunga Saga and the Niebelungen Lied, the work of
Lange — Untersuchungen über die Geschichte und das Verhältniss der
Nordischen und Deutschen Heldensage — is a valuable translation from the
Danish Saga-Bibliothek of P. E. Müller.

P. E. Müller maintains, indeed, the historical basis of the tales respecting
the Volsungs (see pp. 102–107) — upon arguments very unsatisfactory;
though the genuine Scandinavian origin of the tale is perfectly made out.
The chapter added by Lange himself, at the close (see p. 432, etc.), contains

emotions, but also satisfied the undistinguishing historical curiosity, of the ordinary public in the middle ages. The exploits of many of these romantic heroes resemble in several points those of the Grecian: the adventures of Perseus, Achilles, Odysseus, Atalanta, Bellerophôn, Jasôn, and the Trojan war, or Argonautic expedition generally, would have fitted in perfectly to the Carlovingian or other epics of the period.[1] That of the middle ages,

---

juster views as to the character of the primitive mythology, though he too advances some positions respecting a something "reinsymbolisches" in the background, which I find it difficult to follow (see p. 477, etc). — There are very ancient epical ballads still sung by the people in the Faro Islands, many of them relating to Sigurd and his adventures (p. 412).

Jacob Grimm, in his Deutsche Mythologie, maintains the purely mythical character, as opposed to the historical, of Siegfried and Dieterich (Art. *Helden*, pp. 344–346).

So, too, in the great Persian epic of Ferdousi, the principal characters are religious and mythical. M. Mohl observes, — " Les caractères des personnages principaux de l'ancienne histoire de Perse se retrouvent dans le livre des Rois (de Ferdousi) tels que les indiquent les parties des livres de Zoroaster que nous possédons encore. Kaioumors, Djemschid, Feridoun, Gushtasp, Isfendiar, etc. jouent dans le poème épique le même rôle que dans les Livres sacrées : à celà près, que dans les derniers ils nous apparaissent à travers une atmosphère mythologique qui grandit tous leurs traits : mais cette différence est précisement celle qu'on devait s'attendre à trouver entre la tradition religieuse et la tradition épique." (Mohl, Livre des Rois par Ferdousi, Préface, p. 1.)

The Persian historians subsequent to Ferdousi have all taken his poem as the basis of their histories, and have even copied him faithfully and literally (Mohl, p. 53). Many of his heroes became the subjects of long epical biographies, written and recited without any art or grace, often by writers whose names are unknown (*ib.* pp. 54–70). Mr. Morier tells us that "the Shah Nameh is still believed by the present Persians to contain their ancient history" (Adventures of Hadgi Baba, c. 32). As the Christian romancers transformed Apollo into the patron of Mussulmans, so Ferdousi makes Alexander the Great a Christian : "La critique historique (observes M. Mohl) était du temps de Ferdousi chose presqu' inconnue." (*ib.* p. xlviii.) About the absence not only of all historiography, but also of all idea of it, or taste for it, among the early Indians, Persians, Arabians, etc., see the learned book of Nork, *Die Götter Syriens*, Preface, p. viii. *seqq.* (Stuttgart, 1842.)

[1] Several of the heroes of the ancient world were indeed themselves popular subjects with the romancers of the middle ages, Thêseus, Jasôn, etc.; Alexander the Great, more so than any of them.

Dr. Warton observes, respecting the Argonautic expedition, " Few stories

like the Grecian, was eminently expansive in its nature: new stories were successively attached to the names and companions of Charlemagne and Arthur, just as the legend of Troy was enlarged by Arktinus, Leschês, and Stesichorus, — that of Thêbes, by fresh miseries entailed on the fated head of Œdipus, — and that of the Kalydônian boar, by the addition of Atalanta. Altogether, the state of mind of the hearers seems in both cases to have been much the same, — eager for emotion and sympathy, and receiving any narrative attuned to their feelings, not merely with hearty welcome, but also with unsuspecting belief.

Nevertheless, there were distinctions deserving of notice, which render the foregoing proposition more absolutely exact with regard to Greece than with regard to the middle ages. The tales of the epic, and the mythes in their most popular and extended signification, were the only intellectual nourishment with which the Grecian public was supplied, until the sixth century before the Christian æra: there was no prose writing, no history, no philosophy. But such was not exactly the case at the time when the epic of the middle ages appeared. At that time, a portion of society possessed the Latin language, the habit of writing, and some tinge both of history and philosophy: there were a series of chronicles, scanty, indeed, and imperfect, but referring to con-

---

of antiquity have more the cast of one of the old romances than this of Jasôn. An expedition of a new kind is made into a strange and distant country, attended with infinite dangers and difficulties. The king's daughter of the new country is an enchantress; she falls in love with the young prince, who is the chief adventurer. The prize which he seeks is guarded by brazen-footed bulls, who breathe fire, and by a hideous dragon, who never sleeps. The princess lends him the assistance of her charms and incantations to conquer these obstacles; she gives him possession of the prize, leaves her father's court, and follows him into his native country." (Warton, Observations on Spenser, vol. i. p. 178.)

To the same purpose M. Ginguené: " Le premier modèle des Fées' n'est-il pas dans Circé, dans Calypso, dans Médée? Celui des géans, dans Polyphème, dans Cacus, et dans les géans, ou les Titans, cette race ennemie de Jupiter? Les serpens et les dragons des romans ne sont-ils pas des successeurs du dragon des Hesperides et de celui de la Toison d'or? Les Magiciens! la Thessalie en étoit pleine. Les armes enchantées impénétrables! elles sont de la même trempe, et l'on peut les croire forgées au même fourneau que celles d'Achille et d'Enée." (Ginguené, Histoire Littéraire d'Italie, vol. iv. part ii. ch. 3, p. 151.)

temporary events and preventing the real history of the past
from passing into oblivion: there were even individual scholars,
in the twelfth century, whose acquaintance with Latin literature
was sufficiently considerable to enlarge their minds and to improve their judgments. Moreover, the epic of the middle ages,
though deeply imbued with religious ideas, was not directly amalgamated with the religion of the people, and did not always find
favor with the clergy; while the heroes of the Grecian epic
were not only linked in a thousand ways with existing worship,
practices, and sacred localities, but Homer and Hesiod pass with
Herodotus for the constructors of Grecian theology. We thus
see that the ancient epic was both exempt from certain distract-
ing influences by which that of the middle ages was surrounded,
and more closely identified with the veins of thought and feeling
prevalent in the Grecian public. Yet these counteracting influences did not prevent Pope Calixtus II. from declaring the
Chronicle of Turpin to be a genuine history.

If we take the history of our own country as it was conceived
and written from the twelfth to the seventeenth century by Hard-
yng, Fabyan, Grafton, Hollinshed, and others, we shall find that
it was supposed to begin with Brute the Trojan, and was carried
down from thence, for many ages and through a long succession
of kings, to the times of Julius Cæsar. A similar belief of descent from Troy, arising seemingly from a reverential imitation
of the Romans and of their Trojan origin, was cherished in the
fancy of other European nations. With regard to the English,
the chief circulator of it was Geoffrey of Monmouth, and it passed with little resistance or dispute into the national faith — the
kings from Brute downward being enrolled in regular chronological series with their respective dates annexed. In a dispute
which took place during the reign of Edward I. (A. D. 1301)
between England and Scotland, the descent of the kings of England from Brute the Trojan was solemnly embodied in a docu-
ment put forth to sustain the rights of the crown of England, as
an argument bearing on the case then in discussion: and it passed without attack from the opposing party,[1] — an incident which

---

[1] See Warton's History of English Poetry, sect. iii. p. 131, note. "No
man before the sixteenth century presumed to doubt that the Francs derived

reminds us of the appeal made by Æschinês, in the contention between the Athenians and Philip of Macedôn, respecting Amphipolis, to the primitive dotal rights of Akamas son of Thêseus — and also of the defence urged by the Athenians to sustain their conquest of Sigeium, against the reclamations of the Mityleneans, wherein the former alleged that they had as much right to the place as any of the other Greeks who had formed part of the victorious armament of Agamemnôn.[1]

The tenacity with which this early series of British kings was defended, is no less remarkable than the facility with which it was admitted. The chroniclers at the beginning of the seventeenth century warmly protested against the intrusive scepticism which would cashier so many venerable sovereigns and efface so many noble deeds. They appealed to the patriotic feelings of their hearers, represented the enormity of thus setting up a presumptuous criticism against the belief of ages, and insisted on the danger of the precedent as regarded history generally.[2] How this controversy stood, at the time and in the view of the illus-

---

their origin from Francus son of Hector; that the Spaniards were descended from Japhet, the Britons from Brutus, and the Scotch from Fergus." (*Ibid.* p. 140.)

According to the Prologue of the prose Edda, Odin was the supreme king of Troy in Asia, " in eâ terrâ quam nos Turciam appellamus..... Hinc omnes Borealis plagæ magnates vel primores genealogias suas referunt, atque principes illius urbis inter numina locant: sed in primis ipsum Priamum pro Odeno ponunt," etc. They also identified *Tros* with *Thor.* (See Lexicon Mythologicum ad calcem Eddæ Sæmund, p. 552. vol. iii.)

[1] See above, ch. xv. p. 458; also Æschinês, De Falsâ Legatione, c. 14; Herodot. v. 94. The Herakleids pretended a right to the territory in Sicily near Mount Eryx, in consequence of the victory gained by their progenitor Hêraklês over Eryx, the eponymous hero of the place. (Herodot. v. 43.)

[2] The remarks in Speed's Chronicle (book v. c. 3. sect. 11–12), and the preface to Howes's Continuation of Stow's Chronicle, published in 1631, are curious as illustrating this earnest feeling. The Chancellor Fortescue, in impressing upon his royal pupil, the son of Henry VI., the limited character of English monarchy, deduces it from Brute the Trojan: " Concerning the different powers which kings claim over their subjects, I am firmly of opinion that it arises solely from the different nature of their original institution. So the kingdom of England had its original from Brute and the Trojans, who attended him from Italy and Greece, and became a mixed kind of government, compounded of the regal and the political." (Hallam, Hist. Mid. Ages, ch. viii. P. 3, page 230.)

trious author of Paradise Lost, I shall give in his own words, as they appear in the second page of his History of England. After having briefly touched upon the stories of Samothes son of Japhet, Albion son of Neptune, etc., he proceeds : —

"But now of Brutus and his line, with the whole progeny of kings to the entrance of Julius Cæsar, we cannot so easily be discharged: descents of ancestry long continued, laws and exploits not plainly seeming to be borrowed or devised, which on the common belief have wrought no small impression: *defended by many, denied utterly by few*. For what though Brutus and the whole Trojan pretence were yielded up, seeing they, who first devised to bring us some noble ancestor, were content at first with Brutus the Consul, till better invention, though not willing to forego the name, taught them to remove it higher into a more fabulous age, and by the same remove lighting on the Trojan tales, in affectation to make the Briton of one original with the Roman, pitched there : *Yet those old and inborn kings, never any to have been real persons, or done in their lives at least some part of what so long hath been remembered, cannot be thought without too strict incredulity*. For these, and those causes above mentioned, that which hath received approbation from so many, I have chosen not to omit. Certain or uncertain, be that upon the credit of those whom I must follow: *so far as keeps aloof from impossible or absurd*, attested by ancient writers from books more ancient, I refuse not, as the due and proper subject of story."[1]

Yet in spite of the general belief of so many centuries — in spite of the concurrent persuasion of historians and poets — in spite of the declaration of Milton, extorted from his feelings rather than from his reason, that this long line of quasi-historical kings and exploits could not be *all* unworthy of belief — in spite of so large a body of authority and precedent, the historians of the nineteenth century begin the history of England with Julius Cæsar. They do not attempt either to settle the date of king Bladud's accession, or to determine what may be the basis of truth in the affecting narrative of Lear.[2] The standard of his-

---

[1] "Antiquitas enim recepit fabulas fictas etiam nonnunquam incondite: hæc ætas autem jam exculta, præsertim eludens omne quod fieri non potest, respuit," etc. (Cicero, De Republicâ, ii. 10, p. 147, ed. Maii.)

[2] Dr. Zachary Grey has the following observations in his Notes on Shaks-

torical credibility, especially with regard to modern events, has indeed been greatly and sensibly raised within the last hundred years.

But in regard to ancient Grecian history, the rules of evidence still continue relaxed. The dictum of Milton, regarding the ante-Cæsarian history of England, still represents pretty exactly the feeling now prevalent respecting the mythical history of Greece "Yet those old and inborn kings (Agamemnôn, Achilles, Odysseus, Jasôn, Adrastus, Amphiaräus, Meleager, etc.), never any to have been real persons, or done in their lives at least some part of what so long hath been remembered, cannot be thought without too strict incredulity." Amidst much fiction (we are still told), there must be some truth : but how is such truth to be singled out ? Milton does not even attempt to make the severance : he contents himself with " keeping aloof from the impossible and the absurd," and ends in a narrative which has indeed the merit of being sober-colored, but which he never for a moment thinks of recommending to his readers as true. So in regard to the legends of Greece, — Troy, Thêbes, the Argonauts, the Boar of Kalydôn, Hêraklês, Thêseus, Œdipus, — the conviction still holds in men's minds, that there must be something true at the bottom ; and many readers of this work may be displeased, I fear, not to see conjured up before them the Eidôlon of an authentic history, even though the vital spark of evidence be altogether wanting.[1]

---

peare (London, 1754, vol. 1. p. 112). In commenting on the passage in King Lear, *Nero is an angler in the lake of darkness*, he says, "This is one of Shakspeare's most remarkable *anachronisms*. King Lear succeeded his father Bladud anno mundi 3105 ; and Nero, anno mundi 4017, was sixteen years old, when he married Octavia, Cæsar's daughter. See Funcii Chronologia, p. 94."

Such a supposed chronological discrepancy would hardly be pointed out in any commentary now written.

The introduction prefixed by Mr. Giles, to his recent translation of Geoffrey of Monmouth (1842), gives a just view both of the use which our old poets made of his tales, and of the general credence so long and so unsuspectingly accorded to them. The list of old British kings given by Mr. Giles also deserves attention, as a parallel to the Grecian genealogies anterior to the Olympiads.

[1] The following passage, from the Preface of Mr. Price to Warton's History of English Poetry, is alike just and forcibly characterized ; the whole

I presume to think that our great poet has proceeded upon
mistaken views with respect to the old British fables, not less in

---

Preface is, indeed, full of philosophical reflection on popular fables generally. Mr. Price observes (p. 79) : —

"The great evil with which this long-contested question appears to be
threatened at the present day, is an extreme equally dangerous with the
incredulity of Mr. Ritson, — a disposition to receive as authentic history,
under a slightly fabulous coloring, every incident recorded in the British
Chronicle. An allegorical interpretation is now inflicted upon all the marvellous circumstances ; a forced construction imposed upon the less glaring
deviations from probability ; and the usual subterfuge of baffled research, —
erroneous readings and etymological sophistry, — is made to reduce every
stubborn and intractable text to something like the consistency required. It
might have been expected that the notorious failures of Dionysius and Plutarch, in Roman history, would have prevented the repetition of an error,
which neither learning nor ingenuity can render palatable ; and that the
havoc and deadly ruin effected by these ancient writers (in other respects so
valuable) in one of the most beautiful and interesting monuments of traditional story, would have acted as sufficient corrective on all future aspirants.
The favorers of this system might at least have been instructed by the philosophic example of Livy, — if it be lawful to ascribe to philosophy a line
of conduct which perhaps was prompted by a powerful sense of poetic
beauty, — that traditional record can only gain in the hands of the future
historian by one attractive aid, — the grandeur and lofty graces of that in-
comparable style in which the first decade is written ; and that the best duty
towards antiquity, and the most agreeable one towards posterity, is to trans-
mit the narrative received as an unsophisticated tradition, in all the plenitude
of its marvels and the awful dignity of its supernatural agency. For, however largely we may concede that real events have supplied the substance of
any traditive story, yet the amount of absolute facts, and the manner of those
facts, the period of their occurrence, the names of the agents, and the locality given to the scene, are all combined upon principles so wholly beyond
our knowledge, that it becomes impossible to fix with certainty upon any
single point better authenticated than its fellow. Probability in such decis-
ions will often prove the most fallacious guide we can follow ; for, independ-
ently of the acknowledged historical axiom, that ' le vrai n'est pas toujours
le vraisemblable,' innumerable instances might be adduced, where tradition
has had recourse to this very probability to confer a plausible sanction upon
her most fictitious and romantic incidents. It will be a much more useful
labor, wherever it can be effected, to trace the progress of this traditional
story in the country where it has become located, by a reference to those
natural or artificial monuments which are the unvarying sources of fictitious
events ; and, by a strict comparison of its details with the analogous memorials of other nations, to separate those elements which are obviously of a
native growth, from the occurrences bearing the impress of a foreign origin

that which he leaves out than in that which he retains. To omit the miraculous and the fantastic, (it is that which he really means by " the impossible and the absurd,") is to suck the lifeblood out of these once popular narratives, — to divest them at once both of their genuine distinguishing mark, and the charm by which they acted on the feelings of believers. Still less ought we to consent to break up and disenchant in a similar manner the mythes of ancient Greece, — partly because they possess the mythical beauties and characteristics in far higher perfection, partly because they sank deeper into the mind of a Greek, and pervaded both the public and private sentiment of the country to a much greater degree than the British fables in England.

Two courses, and two only, are open ; either to pass over the mythes altogether, which is the way in which modern historians treat the old British fables, or else to give an account of them as mythes ; to recognize and respect their specific nature, and to abstain from confounding them with ordinary and certifiable history. There are good reasons for pursuing this second method in reference to the Grecian mythes ; and when so considered, they constitute an important chapter in the history of the Grecian mind, and indeed in that of the human race generally. The historical faith of the Greeks, as well as that of other people, in reference to early and unrecorded times, is as much subjective and peculiar to themselves as their religious faith : among the Greeks, especially, the two are confounded with an intimacy which nothing less than great violence can disjoin. Gods, heroes, and men — religion and patriotism — matters divine, heroic, and human — were all woven together by the Greeks into one indivisible web, in which the threads of truth and reality, whatever they might originally have been, were neither intended to be,

---

We shall gain little, perhaps, by such a course for the history of human events ; but it will be an important accession to our stock of knowledge on the history of the human mind. It will infallibly display, as in the analysis of every similar record, the operations of that refining principle which is ever obliterating the monotonous deeds of violence that fill the chronicle of a nation's early career, and exhibit the brightest attribute in the catalogue of man's intellectual endowments, — a glowing and vigorous imagination, — bestowing upon all the impulses of the mind a splendor and virtuous dignity, which, however fallacious historically considered, are never without a powerfully redeeming good, the ethical tendency of all their lessons "

nor were actually, distinguishable. Composed of such materials, and animated by the electric spark of genius, the mythical antiquities of Greece formed a whole at once trustworthy and captivating to the faith and feelings of the people; but neither trustworthy nor captivating, when we sever it from these subjective conditions, and expose its naked elements to the scrutiny of an objective criticism. Moreover, the separate portions of Grecian mythical foretime ought to be considered with reference to that aggregate of which they form a part: to detach the divine from the heroic legends, or some one of the heroic legends from the remainder, as if there were an essential and generic difference between them, is to present the whole under an erroneous point of view. The mythes of Troy and Thêbes are no more to be handled objectively, with a view to detect an historical base, than those of Zeus in Krête, of Apollo and Artemis in Dêlos, of Hermês, or of Promêtheus. To single out the Siege of Troy from the other mythes, as if it were entitled to preëminence as an ascertained historical and chronological event, is a proceeding which destroys the true character and coherence of the mythical world: we only transfer the story (as has been remarked in the preceding chapter) from a class with which it is connected by every tie both of common origin and fraternal affinity, to another with which it has no relationship, except such as violent and gratuitous criticism may enforce.

By drawing this marked distinction between the mythical and the historical world, — between matter appropriate only for subjective history, and matter in which objective evidence is attainable, — we shall only carry out to its proper length the just and well-known position long ago laid down by Varro. That learned man recognized three distinguishable periods in the time preceding his own age; "First, the time from the beginning of mankind down to the first deluge; a time wholly unknown. Secondly, the period from the first deluge down to the first Olympiad, which is called *the mythical period*, because many fabulous things are recounted in it. Thirdly, the time from the first Olympiad down to ourselves, which is called *the historical period*, because the things done in it are comprised in true histories."[1]

· Varro ap. Censorin. de Die Natali; Varronis Fragm. p. 219, ed. Scaliger, 1623. " Varro tria discrimina temporum esse tradit. Primum ab hom-

Taking the commencement of true or objective history at the point indicated by Varro, I still consider the mythical and historical periods to be separated by a wider gap than he would have admitted. To select any one year as an absolute point of commencement, is of course not to be understood literally: but in point of fact, this is of very little importance in reference to the present question, seeing that the great mythical events — the sieges of Thêbes and Troy, the Argonautic expedition, the Kalydônian boar-hunt, the Return of the Hêrakleids, etc. — are all placed long anterior to the first Olympiad, by those who have applied chronological boundaries to the mythical narratives. The period immediately preceding the first Olympiad is one exceedingly barren of events ; the received chronology recognizes four hundred years, and Herodotus admitted five hundred years, from that date back to the Trojan war.

---

inum principio usque ad cataclysmum priorem, quod propter ignorantiam vocatur *ἄδηλον*. Secundum, a cataclysmo priore ad Olympiadem primam, quod quia in eo multa fabulosa referuntur, *Mythicon* nominatur. Tertium a primâ Olympiade ad nos; quod dicitur *Historicon*, quia res in eo gestæ veris historiis continentur."

To the same purpose Africanus, ap. Eusebium, Præp. Ev. xx. p. 487: Μέχρι μὲν 'Ολυμπιάδων, οὐδὲν ἀκριβὲς ἱστόρηται τοῖς Ἕλλησι, πάντων συγκεχυμένων, καί κατὰ μηδὲν αὐτοῖς τῶν πρὸ τοῦ συμφωνούντων, etc.

3313817

Made in the USA